Tolley's
Effective Credit Control
and
Debt Recovery Handbook

Third Edition

LexisNexis™ UK

Members of the LexisNexis Group worldwide

United Kingdom	LexisNexis UK, a Division of Reed Elsevier (UK) Ltd, 2 Addiscombe Road, Croydon CR9 5AF
Argentina	LexisNexis Argentina, Buenos Aires
Australia	LexisNexis Butterworths, Chatswood, New South Wales
Austria	LexisNexis Verlag ARD Orac GmbH & Co KG, Vienna
Canada	LexisNexis Butterworths, Markham, Ontario
Chile	LexisNexis Chile Ltda, Santiago de Chile
Czech Republic	Nakladatelství Orac sro, Prague
France	Editions du Juris-Classeur SA, Paris
Germany	LexisNexis Deutschland GmbH, Frankfurt, Munster
Hong Kong	LexisNexis Butterworths, Hong Kong
Hungary	HVG-Orac, Budapest
India	LexisNexis Butterworths, New Delhi
Ireland	LexisNexis, Dublin
Italy	Giuffrè Editore, Milan
Malaysia	Malayan Law Journal Sdn Bhd, Kuala Lumpur
New Zealand	LexisNexis Butterworths, Wellington
Poland	Wydawnictwo Prawnicze LexisNexis, Warsaw
Singapore	LexisNexis Butterworths, Singapore
South Africa	LexisNexis Butterworths, Durban
Switzerland	Stämpfli Verlag AG, Berne
USA	LexisNexis, Dayton, Ohio

© Reed Elsevier (UK) Ltd 2004
Published by LexisNexis UK

A CIP Catalogue record for this book is available from the British Library.

ISBN 0 7545 2610 0

Typeset by Typeset by Kerrypress Ltd, Luton, Beds (www.kerrypress.co.uk)

Printed and bound in Great Britian by Hobbs the Printers Ltd, Totton, Hampshire

Visit LexisNexis UK at www.lexisnexis.co.uk

Contributors

Robert Addlestone,
LLB, MICM, Solicitor, Partner of CW Harwood & Co., Solicitors.

Glen Bullivant,
FICM, independent credit management consultant and Immediate Past Chairman of the Institute of Credit Management.

Stephen Cowan,
LLB, FICM, Notary Public, Solicitor to the Supreme Court, Tutor, Universities of Glasgow and Strathclyde, Glasgow Graduate School of Law; Managing Partner, Yuill & Kyle, Debt Recovery Lawyers, Scotland; Managing Director of CreditInterchange.

Stephen Hill,
ACA, MIPA, MABRP, Manager, Grant Thornton, Chartered Accountants.

Martin Posner,
FICM, MIEx, MCIJ, Writer and Researcher on commercial and industrial credit and the export trade

T Glyndwr Powell,
FICM, MIEx, Director of Quantum Trade Finance Ltd.

Barry Stamp,
BA, MICM, ACIB, joint Managing Director of Credit Reporting Agency.

Nick Wood,
Licensed insolvency practitioner, FIPA, MABRP, LLB, Partner, Grant Thornton, Chartered Accountants.

Contents

Contents

A6 Organisation of the Sales Ledger

Glen Bullivant

A7 Staff Training and Staff Recruitment
Glen Bullivant

A8 Computer Accounting Systems and Monitoring of the Sales Ledger
Glen Bullivant

Contents

A13 Collecting Outstanding Accounts

Glen Bullivant

Contents

Appendix A13

A14 Company and Consumer Legislation and Codes of Practice
Barry Stamp

Contents

B Debt Recovery

B1 Debt Recovery through the Courts

Robert Addlestone

Appendix B7

B8 Costs
Robert Addlestone

B9 Enforcement of a Judgment
Robert Addlestone

Appendix B9

B11 Scottish Legal Debt Recovery Procedure
Stephen Cowan

Contents

Introduction

Due to the many changes that are taking place in the world of trade and commerce, this new edition has been published to update credit personnel on current developments that affect credit policy, assessment of customers, management of the sales ledger, financial analysis, debt recovery, and cash flow management.

The basic principles of credit management have not changed. However, what has changed in the last three years since this title was first published is the speed that customers demand delivery of goods or services throughout the world. Far speedier methods of assessing new business and the monitoring of existing accounts have been developed since the last edition of this book.

In November 2001, I mentioned that the 11 September terrorist attack had completely changed the world's commercial and financial trading patterns.

Since then we have seen a general downturn of trade throughout the world. Between 2001 and 2002 the major accounting scandals in the USA reduced the public's and business's confidence when reviewing a corporate set of accounts. In late 2003 the Parmalat Group's collapse again showed how essential it is to have independent auditors. Share prices throughout the world have gradually risen. However for a number of major corporations their pensions black hole could give them serious financial problems for many years to come.

The Presidential elections in the USA and a number of recent changes of government in European countries may change their economic policy in the latter part of 2004.

The new candidate countries that joined the European Union in May 2004 may require the original EU countries to reduce their production costs, as labour and other costs are constantly being targeted by all businesses in the manufacturing and service industries.

Another factor that must be considered by all credit personnel is the risk of terrorism affecting trade in any part of the world. Also everyone still seems to want longer credit terms, interest rates are being kept low to stimulate growth, while profit margins are gradually being squeezed due to competition.

There are always opportunities for companies to sell overseas, but it should be remembered that some 80 countries have had to reschedule their sovereign debts. There is still constant pressure on the World Bank and the IMF to bail out ailing countries.

In the UK, although the manufacturing sectors have been declining and some firms have decided to move abroad to save labour costs, several high-street retailers are still increasing their sales, but their profit margins are down. Some IT companies are still doing well, but there are now strong indications that these types of high-flyer businesses can equally collapse with sudden speed. UK base rates are beginning to rise and there is now an enormous increase in lending to homeowners on the value of their housing stock which has increased by 15% annually; however, wage rates have increased by about 3%. If interest rates continue to rise, higher repayments could cause the retail economy to slow down. Reports by the Bank of England's Monetary Policy Committee should be closely watched. It is reported that household indebtedness is now over 100% of disposable income. For credit personnel who are normally advancing credit without security, there are a number of additional factors that they must consider. After four years of declining profits, in some sectors margins are beginning to rise; however, a rise in fuel costs in the Autumn of 2004, plus insurance and extra security and compliance costs, will put extra pressure on all businesses in the UK.

New legislation which will affect all credit personnel from 2004 are the *Money Laundering Regulations 2003 (SI 2003/3075)* which as of 1 March force more sectors of business to report suspected money laundering. I would also highlight the *Enterprise Act 2002* as I am certain that there will be a huge increase in bankruptcies. The Insolvency Service's *Guide to Bankruptcy* makes it sound so easy. Finally the timetable for the *Basel II* capital accord ratio preparation period is getting nearer. All the major credit bureaux are now working on analysis systems to reflect the new capital requirements.

This book is still designed to help businesses not only to increase their sales, but also enable them to control those sales by having a recognised credit policy. By assessing the risks first, the anxiety of not knowing when the payment may arrive is greatly reduced. Regrettably, there are always trade risks, but invoicing should not be a gamble!

Businesses must now monitor their major accounts on a far more regular basis. This can now be carried out in seconds as the biggest change I have noted since April 2002 is the speed at which credit information can be transmitted to credit personnel.

Summary

In concluding the review for this edition, I would like to thank all the authors for the many hours of research they carried out to rewrite their chapters.

I would particularly like to thank Burt Edwards, as he has now retired, for his original contributions. Glen Bullivant has now revised some of Burt's chapters. My thanks to Glyndwr Powell for rewriting Burt's chapter on Security for Commercial Credit.

All the contributors to this new edition have reviewed the changes that have taken place or may be taking place in legislation within their speciality. Glen Bullivent has carefully rewritten a number of introductions to show how the administration of a sales ledger should be tackled by professionals. He has significantly revised the application form to open a credit account and has revised the details of the 2003 consultation on the White Paper 'Modernising Company Law'.

In the section on Gaining Information to Support Credit Decisions there are three totally new interviews with Equifax, ICC Credit and Creditsafe.com and new credit information bureaux have been added (the Credit Bureaux) to show how the industry is reacting to customer demands and compliance requirements of the *Data Protection Act 1998*.

Glyndwr Powell has extensively revised the chapter on credit insurance (insurance of debts). He has shown the different strengths of the insurers and has considerably added to the information on Coface and other markets.

In the chapter on exporting, the section on UK Trade and Investment has been completely rewritten and the changes in the pattern of world trade have again been revised.

Barry Stamp has carefully updated a mass of company and consumer legislation as a number of changes have taken place since June 2002.

Robert Addlestone has made a number of revisions including the provisions of the *High Court Enforcement Officers Regulations 2004 (SI 2004/400)*.

Stephen Hill, the insolvency specialist, has revised the section on reforms under the *Enterprise Act 2002* on the new administration procedures.

Stephen Cowan has updated his chapter on Scottish Legal Debt Recovery Procedure to reflect changes in the law on Arrestment and has added a small section on Arrestment of Earnings and debt arrangement schemes.

Finally, I do hope that the examples of good practice in this edition will assist all readers to reduce their worry about not getting paid and help them to increase their cashflow, which is the lifeblood of every business.

Note

We have referred to 'he' and 'his' throughout this book, but of course this refers to 'she' and 'her' as well.

Martin Posner

Credit Control

A1

Credit Policy

Introduction A1.1

Most aspects of modern life involve organisation or structure of some kind. Society moulds itself into groups, social and economic, and survives and prospers under a code of conduct, enforced or voluntary. Rules can appear harsh to some individuals, but are recognised as being both necessary and beneficial to the whole. As such, it is in the interest of all to observe the conventions. The 21st Century motorist may be forgiven for imagining that chaos currently reigns, but the perceived chaos would be as nothing compared to that if driving was a complete free for all – no traffic lights, no roundabouts, no northbound or southbound, no left or right.

The airline passenger pays for a ticket, checks in at the airport, boards the plane and is jetted off to the destination. Behind that process is a support organisation of immense proportions, from aircraft design through air traffic control to the provision of cups of coffee at 33,000 feet. The passenger need not have detailed knowledge of every aspect, but only the understanding that all participants are performing their allotted roles according to organised principles. The end result is completing the journey safely, and the anticipation of future journeys maintaining the same standard and record.

The car driver and the airline passenger would not appreciate the prospect of either journey being a gamble, a role of the dice or a cut of the cards. A risk is involved, certainly, but that risk is calculated and the existence of rules, guidelines, codes of conduct and best practice minimises the risk to the level of acceptability. The same criteria apply to the granting of credit. It is not a gamble, but a calculation based upon known factors that enable confidence to be established in the activity. The likely outcome is known, the cost foreseen and the benefits appreciated. Credit without rules would be chaos – credit without a policy for control is a recipe for seriously bad business health.

Credit – an investment of resources, with cost and risk A1.2

Credit is a composite word meaning a sum of money, a period of time, or both. For example, a customer may be allowed £10,000 of credit (a sum of money), or 30 days credit (a period of time), or £10,000 on 30 days credit (both).

Credit has been described as the lubricating oil of commerce because it allows business to proceed without having to wait for actual cash payment from buyers. The proliferation of credit has produced the 'buy now and pay later' mentality, which gives rise to the possibility that some people may buy now but not be able to pay later. In other words, the concept of risk is introduced – it is risky for the seller to allow time to pay instead of demanding cash. If a seller's terms were 'cash only' however, he would not sell very much, especially if his competitors were offering credit terms.

While credit trust is a powerful selling aid, its very attractiveness to customers equates to an unattractive risk to sellers. The old adage that 'time is money' applies perfectly to credit because sellers incur an interest cost on the borrowings they need while waiting for payment. Thus, credit has a risk – that of being paid late or not at all, and a cost – the interest expense from the date of sale to the receipt of funds.

Debtors are usually funded by borrowings, so a seller is investing borrowed capital in credit, at a cost equal to its cost of borrowing. The return on that investment is the net profit, after interest, on the sales being so funded. This simple concept applies to all the sellers in an industry, to all the business in a nation's economy and to world trade. Restricted credit depresses sales volume and deflates an economy, while excessive credit boosts sales and is inflationary. For sellers and for national economies to achieve the right balance requires specific management of credit.

The modern demand for credit requires:

• a sound operating procedure to cope with continuous sales volumes;

• capital to fund the waiting time (between sale and cash receipt) with a worthwhile return on the investment; and

• regulation and enforcement, informally or by law, of credit agreements.

The evolution of credit management

Consumer credit   A1.3

The growth of consumer credit throughout the last century, and in particular the boom in consumer consumption following the decades after the Second World War, well illustrates the need for a reliable credit management structure. Before credit became the norm and not the exception, consumers had to find the cash to pay for what they wanted, or go without. A variety of credit arrangements came into existence, provided by sellers who were funded by banks, the purpose being to encourage larger and earlier purchases. These stimulated more trade, providing more employment, which in turn provided more scope for buying.

Nowadays consumer credit is well formalised. The repayment of principal, interest and administration expense by customers is set out in carefully worded agreements, regulated by the *Consumer Credit Act 1974*. Credit cards have taken the financing of much of the consumer credit away from the sellers and back to the banks – the advantage of credit cards to the seller lies in bringing the 'finance' of the sale closer to the selling task. The credit card is now an extremely powerful selling tool, connecting seller, buyer and money at the point where the buying decision is made.

Trade credit   A1.4

There is no real equivalent to the credit card in trade credit, where banks still lend money to sellers. The resulting credit to buyers is often quite chaotic due to sellers' misplaced tolerance and their lack of enforcement of agreed terms.

Trade credit has always been unstructured, with sellers allowing all sorts of credit without any interest charges or written agreements. The last decade of the 20th Century saw attempts being made to bring some structure to the process (see **A5.9** below) and survey results from the Credit Management Research Centre at the Leeds University Business School indicated a sharp rise in the number of companies with written credit policies between 1996 and 2002. Since the earliest days of trade credit, however, the trust that payment would be forthcoming was based on personal knowledge of the buyer, the banks being primarily interested in large loans to companies. Bank overdrafts were originally meant to carry firms over a temporary cash shortfall, but the funding became continuous as firms granted credit in increasing amounts to their customers. In the competitive environment of the market place today, volume growth has made it impossible for sellers to have personal knowledge of customers to justify simple 'trust'.

International credit   A1.5

From the earliest days of civilisation, trade between areas and communities developed into what we would now recognise as international trade. Centres of trade and finance were established in various areas, dominance moving as economies grew and weakened. The 'Old World' countries of Europe developed wealth and strength over several centuries, with the rise to economic dominance of the 'New World' of North America during the last 120 years. The 20th Century, and the appetite for oil which accompanied technological growth, witnessed the emergence of the powerful oil rich Middle East, while the term 'Pacific Rim' has come to mean the small group of highly industrialised countries of the Far East.

The list of 'relatively rich' countries exceeds 50, with the rest of the world lagging behind to greater or lesser degrees. The majority of the poor, undeveloped countries (usually referred to as 'Third World' countries) invariably import more than they export so would be regarded by most to be insolvent, at least in the technical sense. The major concern of sellers in the rich countries is whether buyers in poor countries can obtain the hard currency to pay for imports. The world's macro credit risk has taught banks who lend to 'sovereign risks' and the credit insurers of every OECD (Organisation for Economic Co-operation and

Development) country, to check the debt service ratio of a borrowing nation before getting involved in loans. There is no doubt that international credit continues to be riskier and costlier. (See **A11 EXPORTING** for more information.)

The future of credit management   A1.6

For individual companies, banks and governments the challenge remains to lend prudently. This involves applying the right resources for assessing the degree of risk and bringing back the funds on the agreed terms. The basic credit tasks remain as ever to:

- know a customer's ability to pay;

- assess how much credit to lend;

- process orders quickly to satisfy customers; and

- collect funds at agreed due dates.

Performance of these basic tasks continues to evolve, and the process of change will continue. Credit management is moving away from that of basic 'bean counters' though skills in balance sheet analysis and interpretation will always remain a requirement, together with similar cash related attributes. The credit profession is becoming more devoted to people contact, involving negotiation and understanding, as well as embracing market place knowledge and product awareness. Credit managers are going to need more skill in:

- integrating with sales colleagues;

- cultivating and meeting customers;

- automated risk assessment and order processing;

- collection actions by fax, videophone and e-mail;

- arranging electronic transfer of funds;

- how external services work, particularly:

    ○   credit reports,

    ○   insolvency warnings,

    ○   credit insurance,

    ○   factoring, and

    ○   collection agents;

- downsizing staff and outsourcing; and

- international trade, using electronic documents and banking.

The credit manager will also increasingly be aware of European as well as United Kingdom legislation in respect of credit and collection activities, with particular emphasis on:

- the rights to interest;

- rules in respect of competition and cartels; and

- human rights.

The Euro, an expanding European Union, the single market, the internet and many other developments will always impact upon the credit manager and the skills required to manage constant change.

New technology   A1.7

The 'Information Superhighway' introduced the use of a PC, modem and phone to access worldwide information through satellite links. The phone and fax remain prime communication tools, but increasingly credit managers are utilising e-mail and Electronic Data Interchange (EDI) as ever more important methods of contacting customers at home and overseas.

Trade debtors, or receivables, usually represent the largest balance sheet asset in a trading company and therefore the largest single consumer of borrowed capital. It is a high risk investment on which the return is profit – only earned when sales are actually paid. Any company's credit procedures should be regularly reviewed, at least every five years because, as with all investments, debtors are affected by economic changes. Rapid changes in technology require computer resources to be reviewed even more frequently.

Why is a credit policy needed?   A1.8

A company allows customers time to pay in order to boost sales volumes and, ideally, net profits in the same proportion. This sales support facility creates the debtors asset (accounts receivable or receivables – all common descriptions) which is normally the largest balance sheet asset and is simply comprised of unpaid sales. Until customers pay, that asset has to be funded. This involves financing the debtors ledger by way of bank borrowings, just to keep things going, and with an interest cost attached. When customers pay later than they should, the interest expense can wipe out the fragile net profit margin. If some customers do not pay at all, the bad debt write off can seriously erode, or even eradicate the total net profit margin. In other words, allowing credit to customers, though desirable as a boost to sales volume, is both risky and costly. If for no other reasons, these facts alone justify the need for sales credit to be carefully managed and not left to market forces.

Almost every function of a business plays a part in the life of a sale and therefore the debtors asset. It is created when a customer is prospected for business or when products or services are advertised, since expense begins then and has to be recouped by a sale which, by definition, must be fully paid on time. Anything less reduces the intended margin. Thus:

- the selling operation;

- the order processing system;

- the manufacturing or procurement action;

- the costing and pricing basis;

- the conditions of sale; and

- the customer service efficiency,

all play their part in conjunction with the company's credit control, sales ledger and cash collection departments.

Some might regard the word 'policy' as indicative of stuffiness, or bureaucracy, or both and may think that it has no place in a modern dynamic company. On the contrary, it is necessary to simply show the company's intended way of doing things and avoids the free for all or the right hand/left hand confused approach. Everybody in an organisation can readily recognise the need for company policies in respect of, say, health and safety, or can understand the company car policy, so why not a policy in respect of credit? Over the years, successful companies have set down their preferred operational approaches for several reasons, including the need to:

- involve all relevant functional heads in shaping the business for the future;

- clarify 'best practice' and iron out inconsistencies in procedures;

- define job responsibilities and objectives;

- avoid internecine disputes and save valuable management time;

- plug any 'profit leaks' caused by chaotic attitudes and procedures;

- ensure that all operations comply with the corporate focus on net profit; and

- ensure that all operations comply with the law of the land.

Newer companies can benefit from the experience of well-established firms by taking a strict look at how they do things and developing their own operating policies.

Instigating a credit policy A1.9

A credit policy should start at the highest level, be agreed at all levels, and be inclusive of all those areas of the business operation which leads to satisfying customer requirements. Everybody in the business should know:

- what the credit terms are;

- how and why they have been arrived at; and

- how, why and when they are implemented.

Starting at the top, the board delegates a director or senior manager to produce a brief document of collective policies and procedures to enable the debtor's asset to be managed efficiently. Producing or updating the policy document forces functional heads in sales, production and customer service, etc. to involve all staff and delegate responsibility. It invariably clarifies areas where staff have been unclear about authority, responsibility and seniority in certain situations. When a credit policy has been decided, it should signed by the board and issued to all departments to show its importance to the cash flow and profitability of the company.

The production and implementation of a credit policy document is an excellent opportunity for sales and credit staff to get together to decide responsibility for solving customer problems. The credit manager should bring sales staff together and explain key points such as:

- credit approval of new customers;

- observance of credit ratings and credit terms;

- joint visits to major customers; and

- action to recover seriously at risk debts, etc.

Considerations when developing a credit policy   A1.10

No credit policy (or any other policy) can be produced in isolation, without any reference to outside influences or circumstances. Several aspects of business need consideration in developing a credit policy, in particular these include:

- the seller's strength in the market;

- the capital needed to finance one seller's sales;

- the credit terms which the seller gets from his own suppliers;

- the range of customers (types and sizes);

- available net profit margins;

- any special arrangements, including longer terms and/or instalments;

- competitive pressures – i.e. 'what the others are doing';

- the type and nature of the goods supplied for example, the shorter the life of the goods, the shorter the credit period should be (a buyer may lose interest in paying if the goods or services are long gone);

- the customer's creditworthiness;

- the buyer's own cash cycle – if a buyer is retailing for cash, a seller's terms can be short but if his business process lasts for a long time, credit may be much longer;

- seasonal sales may be greater at specific times of the year;

- incentives to boost sales may include extra credit facilities; and

- the existence of any security for the credit exposure.

Much of this should be obvious – a supplier of lettuces to the greengrocery trade is clearly not in the same credit cycle as the supplier of steel girders to the bridge builder. Equally, it would be financial absurdity to give all customers 120 days, when all suppliers have to be paid on 30 days.

Modern technology brings techniques using electronic agreements and means of settlement, and such processes are increasingly commonplace. The fact will always remain, however, that sellers are not banks and credit continues to be very costly in relation to net margins. It is unlikely that 'nano-second' transfers of funds between banks, customers and suppliers will change the fundamental need for human enforcement of agreed terms. After all, the actual funds transfer only takes place after agreement to pay has been made – obtaining that agreement is the whole objective in the first place! As ever, the effectiveness of credit arrangements will continue to have its direct impact on the bottom line, i.e. net profit.

Contents of a credit policy   A1.11

Credit policy documents range from one-page memorandums to bulky volumes in a bound set of corporate guidelines. It should *always* be issued by top management and show a date for review with interim updates as circumstances dictate. Whatever the style, some useful contents would be:

- a simple statement of the company's business aims;

- a list of the company's types of customers, and their business sectors;

- the full conditions of sale, as issued to customers;

- the conditions of sale which affect credit management, for example:

  ○ the range of payment terms,

  ○ cash discount rules,

  ○ scope for special terms, prepayments, instalments, extensions, etc,

  ○ penalty interest, and

  ○ reservation of title;

- bad debt levels and method of reserves or provisions;

- DSO (days sales outstanding) calculation and uses (see **A9.10–A9.19** below for a more detailed look at DSO);

- methods of assessing customers, explaining credit ratings and risk codes;

- order referrals and stop list, actions and circulation;

- follow-up methods for various kinds of accounts;

- legal action and use of other third parties to collect;

- use of external services, e.g. credit data sources and credit insurance;

- staff responsibilities; and

- interaction with other departments and their responsibilities to achieve objectives.

Where the company is engaged in international business, there should be a separate part of the policy document devoted to export processes and policies.

Practical stages in operating a credit policy   A1.12

The elements of a well structured approach to credit management include:

- the credit policy;

- objectives;

- procedures; and

- an organisation chart which clearly indicates authority and responsibility levels.

It also lays out the financial measurement process from the initial budget to monthly reports of actual results compared to that budget, as follows:

- a credit policy statement including:

  o the part that credit plays in overall sales and financial objectives, and

  o the responsibilities of various job-holders;

- annual and monthly credit objectives showing:

  o criteria (e.g. DSO, overdues, bad debts etc.), and

  o ratios and percentages;

- annual budgets for monthly debtors and credit department costs;

- organisation chart to show credit jobs and their connections to other functions;

- procedures for credit assessment and collections; and

- credit manager's monthly report showing:

  o debtors results and variance from budget, with reasons, and

  o credit department costs and explanation of variances from budget.

APPENDIX A1 gives an extract from an actual company's credit and collections procedures section of its credit policy document.

Credit terms for different customers   A1.13

The credit policy is only set in stone to the extent that 'guidelines" are set in stone. That is to say that the policy itself has to be adaptable to changes in circumstances, perhaps both internal as well as external, and as already stated (see **A1.7** above) subject to regular review and update. The policy must take into account the fundamental principle that credit facilities enable a company to make sales which otherwise would not be possible. They also help create a continuing supply relationship and to obtain and/or improve customer loyalty. The credit terms are the hub of the contract between seller and buyer and establish, in a few concise words, the moment in time when the transaction will be completed. This may well, therefore, encompass variations from the norm from time to time.

All well conducted business is done on the *seller's* conditions of sale, and the payment terms must be integral to those conditions. As one of the legally binding sales conditions, credit terms, once established, must not be regarded by the buyer as flexible. The buyer would soon object if the type or price of goods or services were changed by the seller without prior agreement after the contract had been entered into. It is vital, therefore, to the success of a business that the credit terms are clearly stated at the order taking stage and subsequently enforced, just as other contract details are. This contractually based legal right should give the seller confidence whenever a buyer argues that he will pay according to his own conditions of purchase or whenever it suits him. This does not mean that standard terms need to be inviolate at all times, but simply that agreed terms are part of the negotiated and enforceable contract.

Trade credit terms are invariably expressed in days rather than months, e.g. 'net 30 days' or '60 days from invoice date'. Apart from the number of days credit, the seller has to decide how much money it is prudent to allow each customer to owe him. In accepting that maximum profitable sales remain the priority of most sellers, it makes sense to control the exposure to loss or delay, customer by customer. For all the reasons of cost and profit impact given earlier (see **A1.2** and **A1.8** above), the credit base must be kept as short as possible. When pushing for volume sales, it is well to remember that customers vary in their ability to generate cash. On the one hand, a giant corporation can find the money to pay almost any invoice any time, but on the other hand a small business might struggle to pay, for example, £10,000 within 30 days. That same small business, however, may well be able to pay on time if the credit terms were 90 days. The fact remains that 'the longer the credit, the greater the risk' and a seller would therefore need good evidence for risking large amounts of company funds for longer than its standard credit terms.

Credit manager's monthly report of results compared to plans   A1.14

The working effectiveness of the credit policy can be illustrated every month end by a standard one page report by the credit manager on the status of the debtors asset. The report should be issued primarily to his superior for a review of performance and a discussion of upcoming priorities. It is also sensible to copy it upwards to the board of directors and sideways to other relevant managers, especially in the sales area. Credit staff should review the month's results before proceeding to the next month's work. In this way, a pattern develops of 'plan it – do it – review it', month after month.

It is useful for the report to compare actual results with the budget and also with the previous month, segregating debtors between the different types. As well as monetary values, the report should deal with ratios and proportions to achieve consistency in comparisons. It should always incorporate the four key elements of:

- days sales outstanding (DSO);
- overdues as a percentage of total debtors;
- age of overdues within the total overdue; and
- disputed debts.

The more concise the report, the better – page after page of figures and statistics is guaranteed to switch off the reader, when the purpose and intention is in reality intended to inform and engage. It concentrates the mind of readers of the report if it is confined to one page. Extra details can be provided for others separately if considered necessary but should not be allowed to obscure the main picture. Subject to space, it can be very productive to add a few lines about the six largest problem accounts, showing clearly that action is already in hand to resolve them. That way, everyone is forewarned of problems from 'favourite' customers and become aware that the credit manager has a good grip on the asset. Figure 1.00 gives an example of a standard monthly report.

Figure 1.00 – Example of a monthly debtors report by credit manager

Credit manager's monthly report on debtors						
Item	*Actual*		*Last Month*		*Budget*	
		£000		£000		£000
Total debtors	64DSO	4351	65DSO	4612	60DSO	4000
Total overdue	11.2%	487	12.3%	567	10.0%	400
Age of overdues (in days)						
1–30	73%	356	69%	391	75%	300
31–60	18%	88	19%	108	20%	80
						(cont'd)

Credit manager's monthly report on debtors						
Item	**Actual**		**Last Month**		**Budget**	
Age of overdues (in days)						
61–90	6%	29	7%	40	4%	16
91+	3%	15	5%	28	1%	4
Totals	100%	487	100%	567	100%	400
Disputes	0.6DSO	39 ytd	1.2DSO	85 ytd	0.5DSO	33 ytd
Bad debts	0	14	0	14	2	20
Debtors by type						
Home trade	66DSO	2895	67DSO	3302	62DSO	2600
Ministry	41DSO	936	41DSO	888	40DSO	900
Inter-national	98DSO	520	98DSO	421	95DSO	500

Notes

DSO improvement on last month but still over budget. Oldest overdues and disputes reduced. Overbudget in home trade due to terms problem with Imperial Widgets and Extra Nerve Plc. Serious overdues problem with Italia Pronto and Nigerian Golf Products.

Action arranged

Visiting Imperial Widgets and Extra Nerve Plc with sales manager; set red flag targets for DSO and overdues percentage. New incentivised targets are set to clear overdues beyond 60 days.

Appendix A1

Appendix A1 – Example of a company's credit and collection procedures in its policy

Our objective is profit – not sales volume alone, but the highest achievable level of *profitable* sales. Do what it takes to get the customers' cash into our bank account – fast! With effective collaboration between our sales and credit staff, we expect to:

- get close to our customers;

- make our credit terms very clear;

- open new accounts properly;

- issue effective invoices rapidly;

- have a clear sales ledger display at all times;

- achieve full collection coverage;

- set targets and priorities;

- use third parties early rather than too late; and

- measure collection results and act immediately on variances.

Get close to our customers

Apply the 80/20 ratio – identify the few major customers who make up 80% of our business – these pay us the most.

Major accounts

Get good agency reports to indicate the right level of credit. Get to know customers' payment staff. Visit them at intervals. Cultivate them to get priority treatment – as we would buyers. Give them priority attention on queries and service.

Non-major accounts

Get an individual's name for letters and phone calls, perhaps from credit application forms or routine correspondence.

Make our credit terms very clear

In sales negotiations

It is professional, not anti-selling, to say 'we can allow 30 days to pay – does that give you any problems?'. Discuss the issue, do not duck it.

On order acknowledgements

Stress payment terms as a condition of sale to supersede any buyer's terms. Send the acknowledgement to a named person.

On credit application forms

Get the buyer to sign, agreeing to comply with our stated payment terms.

On invoices and statements

Show our payment terms boldly on the front. On invoices, also show the due date, e.g. 'Payment Terms: 30 days from invoice date – payment to reach us by 14 March'. On statements, repeat the terms and indicate debts which are past due dates.

Open new accounts properly

Attitude

Treat this as the best chance to get payments properly arranged. Our customer should expect to be checked out. Do not deliver until we are happy to allow credit. Allocating the account number will be the control point.

Actions

- Credit application form – ensure correct name, payment address, person for payments, telephone number, fax number and e-mail details. Also make sure that our terms are accepted.

- Seek credit references (or not), according to our policy. Decide maximum credit limit.

- Allocate account number and set up correct account details.

- Send 'welcome letter' to make contact with payments person, stating how and where we wish to receive payment.

- Now we are ready to sell to the customer on a credit basis.

- Use the special ledger category for three months, with telephone contact, to get the customer into good payment habits.

Issue effective invoices rapidly

We specially designed an attention-grabbing invoice that is better than any we see coming into our own company. It is brief and clear. We have got rid of 'clutter' such as advertising and technical detail – the invoice is for accounts staff to use.

Invoice within 24 hours of a chargeable event. Remember nothing happens until our bill gets into the customer's payment process.

We must always include:

- payment terms;
- due date;
- date;
- delivery date and method;
- description;
- price and total payable; and
- the customer order number or payment authorisation – these are essentials!

Send our invoice to a named individual. Use first class post to beat customer closing deadlines. Use a courier for values above £5,000.

Clearly we cannot expect customers to pay against incorrect invoices – make sure ours are accurate.

Always have a clear sales ledger display

- The aged debt analysis is the essential working tool for collectors and the best control document for senior management to spot problem accounts. It must be available online at any time.
- List accounts in order of size – largest debt first.
- Computer screens show an open-item version of the statement sent to each account showing all unpaid items, both current and overdue – with disputed billings segregated for action.

Achieve full collection coverage

We know that some customers pay on time, others only when we chase, and some only when we threaten. As well as collecting the actual debts due, we have to work to change these patterns for the better. Methods available to do this include:

- visit;
- e-mail;
- telephone;
- fax; and
- letter.

Visit the top major accounts to resolve problems and build relationships while collecting large cheques. Sales staff should assist in gaining access.

Telephone major accounts in advance of due dates to ensure payments are in process, in time to clear objections before our deadline. Telephone all other accounts, working down the list by size of debt, according to time available. Make sure of all large debts before phoning small ones. Working in alphabetical or account number order is dangerous.

Send letters to any accounts too small to telephone. Two standard letters are enough after an overdue message on the statement. A polite reminder letter should be enough for customers who 'pay when chased'. For those who only 'pay when threatened', a second and final demand is needed. The intervals between the letters may be varied, with a maximum of 14 days. If the final demand does not work, the threats made in it must be carried out. Bluffs are soon seen as weakness.

Faxes and e-mails convey urgency and often beat defensive barriers when letters are being ignored or phone calls diverted. We should send them to senior people and mention third-party action as a possibility.

Our stop-list can also be effective when late payers need products in short supply.

Set targets and priorities

Account queries

These are not low-level clerical chores. They are complaints from unhappy customers whom we have let down. They justify non-payment and should be resolved within seven days as prime customer service priorities.

Targets

The rate of cash inflow should always be in line with sales made. Work to a monthly cash target to achieve a specific DSO ratio which measures total debtors against total sales made. We constantly strive to reduce DSO. Secondary targets should be set to reduce certain grades of debt, e.g. those overdue 60 days and above £500.

Resources

As cash intake is highly competitive, we do not skimp on the resources needed but we must use them efficiently. A trained collector can control about 600 accounts, making about 20 calls per day, amongst other work. Inadequate staffing is a false economy because we suffer interest expense while waiting for slow payments. We prefer to separate collection from ledger input work – the skills used are different.

Timetable

We have a timetable which we revise at intervals, in light of experience, for following up accounts too small to telephone economically. It shows what to do if the previous action has failed. Currently, for invoices dated 28 June, the timetable is as follows.

	Action date	Days overdue
Invoice	28 June	0
Statement (debt not yet due)	3 July	0
Due date	28 July	0
Statement (overdue reminder)	3 August	6
Polite reminder letter/fax	10 August	13
Stoplist	15 August	18
Final reminder letter/fax	24 August	27
Collection agency	3 September	37
Cash received	10 September	44
Total time for revenue = 30 + 44 = 74 days		

Note: this example may be seen as too tough by some and too lenient by others. What matters is that sellers have a timetable that works for them.

Involve senior people as needed, aim requests for payment further up the hierarchy if normal contacts fail. Notify sales staff when stopping supplies – they may be able to get the payment. The financial director should sign final demands. The managing director should be kept informed of problem customers. He will not over-ride procedures unless he has a better idea and he may even be able to collect the debt.

Use third parties sooner rather than too late

If customers ignore reminders, it could be because they are waiting for a significant threat, using a third party for this can have a stirring effect.

Collection agents

Such agents work on a 'no collection – no fee' basis and charge us 5% of amounts collected. They collect about 80% in the first month because of their third-party effect and full-time effort. Send all undisputed debts below £500 to the agency after two months. This expense releases our own resources to collect larger amounts from active accounts.

Solicitors

Solicitors use powerful letters in a short space of time, charging a pre-agreed fee. We currently prefer collection agents but if we move to solicitors, it will be a firm specialising in debt collection, not just any solicitor.

Statutory demands

We can send these, or ask our collection agent or solicitors to do so. It promises an application to court for the formal winding-up of the customer's business if payment is not made within 21 days. Alternatively, we can obtain a court order for the debt.

Legal action

Our solicitors have to be used for High Court actions but we process our own County Court actions. Before suing, check there is no known dispute, no other useful steps are possible and the customer has the means to pay.

Measure collection results

Collection results can be measured by:

- DSO;
- cash collected in the month versus the cash target; and
- an aged debt analysis, looking at the largest accounts first.

Send a one page debtors summary at month-end, comparing actual results with the previous month and with any budgets made, to all managers and directors for action on major problems and trends. This is a good prompt for talking to key customers about their payment dates.

Finally: Compete for cash – profit depends on it.

A2

Credit Risk Analysis

Introduction A2.1

Statistics and anecdotes abound. Those involved in credit management have long held the view that time and effort spent at the 'front end' of a potential transaction saves time, effort and money at the 'back end'. Put another way, if the perceived risk is calculated, the manner in which the subsequent account is handled reduces the possibility of slow or non-payment. Credit managers have always believed this to be true, and output from the Credit Management Research Centre at the Leeds University Business School in its Quarterly Reviews confirms this again and again. As one former Chairman of the Institute of Credit Management succinctly put it some years ago, 'we always thought that we were right, but now we know it must be true, because an academic says so'!

It must be a fundamental principle in any business transaction based upon the concept of granting credit, that the seller knows as much as it is possible to know about the potential buyer. If the seller is to have confidence in the buyer's ability (and intention) to meet his obligations under the terms of the contract, then the seller requires to have knowledge of the buyer. Is the buyer a sole trader, partnership, limited liability partnership, private limited company, public limited company, government department, local government, quasi non-governmental organisation (quango), club, charity ......? The list is a long one. How long have they been established? What do they do? Are they financially sound? Do they pay their bills on time? Will business with them be profitable?

We can be talking different legal entities here, such as sole trader or limited company. All too often, sellers make assumptions, when the simplest of checks would have revealed basic truths that could have had a major impact on the outcome of the transaction. The salesman may well be tickled pink with the order he has just brought in from Smiths on the High Street, but there is a world of difference between Smiths, Jack Smith and Jack Smith & Co (High Street) Ltd. Establishing that difference is just the beginning, of course, because equally important will be the financial standing of that business and its reputation for meeting obligations.

The amount of time, effort and money spent by the seller in piecing together the jigsaw of trust will depend upon the relative size of potential exposure and what the risk impact will be. There is a direct financial risk of slow or non-payment, which is fairly obvious, but less well understood are the implications of tying up production or delivery processes for little or no reward. The full financial effects can therefore be even more serious than at first sight. All the more reason to know the customer.

The benefits of knowing customer worth   A2.2

Every few minutes of every working day, a business closes down somewhere in the UK, leaving suppliers, employees and other creditors unpaid. More often than not, closure is due to impending or actual insolvency, i.e. businesses find that they are unable to meet debts as they fall due. Quite frequently, such closures come as a shock to suppliers – they did not think that any of their customers would go bust. On the other hand, the more well organised suppliers have seen the 'end' approaching and, depending on the speed of the decline, have reduced their supply and collected any debts before the doors clamped shut. They had been able to see the end coming by keeping in regular contact with the bigger customers and by using credit data of various kinds.

The customer is always right?   A2.3

Most people would recognise the caution to be exercised if approached by a complete stranger in the street and asked 'lend me £500 till the end of the month'. Why, then, do so many firms put their financial well being at risk by allowing credit, regardless of the customer's ability to pay? The simple and most common answer is the need for sales volume. In addition, there is often a belief that 'the customer is always right' and a habit of always trying to please customers. However, the simple fact is that customers are not always right. They must always be regarded as important, but are not always automatically worthy of credit trust. Despite the keenness to sell, the astute seller should always be pushing for net profit, i.e. the tiny percentage of sale value left when customers have paid. Until a payment is collected, a sale is simply a collection of costs.

It follows, therefore, that though customers are vital for sales, sellers need cash. Unpaid sales are always costly and risky. More than that, they are dangerous in that net losses can bring down the rest of the business.

Knowledge based credit assessment   A2.4

Any decision to grant credit should be based upon knowledge of the customer. The three credit questions to be answered by knowledge based assessment are as follows.

- Is the customer about to go bust? (The solvency risk.)

- Can the customer pay our value by due date? (The liquidity risk.)

- Is the customer growing or declining? (The volume risk.)

If a company knew that a customer was going bust next week, surely they would not deliver goods today, payable in a month's time? However, often sellers do not know the customer's payment ability. Neither do they know whether the customer is growing or on the slippery downwards slope towards failure. If a company could have a total display of the financial state of every customer, they would see instantly how they range from high risk to low risk, or perhaps present no risk at all.

Credit is a calculated risk, not a gamble and credit trust should be based on knowledge, not blind faith. It does not take too much effort to operate a policy of obtaining inexpensive data on those customers who, for example, account for 80% of sales, processing that data into categories of risk levels and codifying the resulting opinions into the order processing system. Such a system enables orders and deliveries to speed through without the need for human intervention, the criteria having been established for granting credit and the customer meeting those criteria. It follows that for an order to be rejected or held up by the system is itself an indication that something is wrong, and sales staff are immediately aware.

When companies progress from low level credit control to good management of the debtors asset, several credit myths are exploded, whether consciously or not. For example:

● not all customers are worthy of credit;

● tomorrow's sales volume may not take care of today's bad debts;

● a badly overdue customer may not pay in the end; and

● the customer is not always right.

What is certain, however, is that, except for tactical blustering, customers always respect suppliers who are well organised and are correct and polite in their credit granting and collection procedures. They know that those companies are more likely to be there for future supplies.

Organisational responsibility for credit risk analysis
A2.5

It is wrong to relegate the credit function to mere operation of the sales ledger, and leave it there to carry out the credit check processes long after the sales lead has been established. The credit management process is an integral part of the business front end operation, working with sales and marketing to establish the fullest possible customer relationship. Collection and protection of the debtors asset begins when the risk is first entered into, and establishing that credit relationship with the customer is fundamental to collection success all through the process. Indeed, the credit manager should be seen as the commercial person in the finance area, and not the sweeper up of left over bits after the event. Risk control means looking for secure ways of saying 'yes' to risky orders. If resources allow it is highly beneficial for the credit manager to have a credit risk analyst on the staff.

Marketing and risk analysis   A2.6

Marketing is the commercial activity prior to selling, i.e. identifying markets, finding substantial customers, advertising, and checking on the competition. Selling is persuading customers to buy products and taking and servicing orders.

In successful companies, marketing people look for customers who are growing, solvent and liquid. Those marketing experts know that good credit control does not lose profitable sales – it directly increases profits by avoiding unplanned costs and it increases sales opportunities by directing sales efforts towards the better customers and away from the poor ones. Good risk assessment also reduces the need for excessive bad debt provisions – the higher such provisions, the lower the profitability. It follows that good risk assessment makes sense.

Early on, companies may assess prospective customers to judge the optimum sales to be made to them within workable periods. For example, planned sales of £10,000 per month to a customer on 30 days terms will mean a possible debt of £20,000 with perhaps a further 20% or £4,000 for overdue payments and disputes, totalling £24,000. The credit assessment must accommodate that amount. If the maximum credit rating of a customer is thought to be £50,000, with a credit term no longer than 30 days, then salesperson, customer and credit staff all know that an order must be broken down into deliveries of not more than £25,000 per month, unless a security can be arranged. If the credit rating was correct and deliveries exceed this, payments will probably be late and costly.

Clearly, therefore, it pays to check in advance that prospect customers are solvent and liquid enough to buy the planned values without financial strain. There are three opportunities to do this:

- prior to the sale, the names of prospects are passed by sales or marketing staff to the credit manager to assess credit – the company is better equipped for strong sales efforts when it knows the good, average and poor risk customers;

- at a sales planning meeting that is attended by the credit manager, since he may already know prospective customers or can quickly check them; or

- during a visit to a prospective customer by the credit manager and sales person, which gives a good opportunity of assessing a customer's character and premises – this adds depth to credit reports and gives the chance to establish personal contacts.

It is of great advantage to the company for a customer to see the sales and credit departments as a money-conscious team working together. The wrong kind of customer can easily play one function off against the other if he sees disunity or even competition. The customer may, for example, be able to say to the sales person, 'I would buy more from you if only your credit manager would ease up a little'. Alternatively, the customer may say to the credit manager, 'your salesman told me I could take another month's credit if I gave my next order to him and not to your competitors'.

Sequence of actions in credit risk analysis   A2.7

Credit risk analysis calls for an organised sequence of events at the outset of the business relationship. The following would be regarded as normal in credit-conscious companies.

- Credit application form – this equates to a request to borrow money. As such the seller is attempting to find out something about the borrower by use of this form, just as would be the case in borrowing cash from the bank (see **A2.8–A2.19** below and Figure 1.00).

- Credit check – thorough or brief, according to the value of the purchase.

- Credit rating (or limit) and/or risk category – this codifies the credit opinion so that it can be used for automated order processing and shown on relevant documents.

- Credit terms – these are standard or special terms, according to the buyer's status.

- Allocation of account number – no deliveries should be made until this key decision point.

- 'Welcome letter' to the customer's payments person – this should be issued as the important first contact in a relationship with the person responsible for payments.

- Special ledger section for three months – during a customer's time in this section, extra contact should be made with them to help the customer avoid getting into bad payment habits.

These stages are discussed in greater detail at **A2.8** onwards.

Opening new accounts   A2.8

New customers should complete an 'application for credit' form. Apart from giving the kind of information and background details the credit manager is looking for to assess risk, the customer:

- is reminded of the payment terms;

- signs an agreement and commitment to them; and

- provides the name of a payment contact.

Figure 1.00 gives an example of an application form to open a new credit account.

Figure 1.00 – Application to open a credit account

Application for credit account

Name and address of applicant
State FULL trading style, if any

State FULL name of proprietors/partners
and home addresses

_____

_____

_____

_____

_____

_____

Address for invoices/statements
if different from above

Limited company registration No. _____
Registered office address:

_____

_____

_____

_____

_____

_____

How long business established _____

Name and job title of payment contact _____

Telephone number and extension_____

Fax No. _____   E-mail address._____

Please also attach a copy of your letter heading.

References:

1. Bank name_____   Sort code _____

Address: _____

2. *Trade ref name:_____

Address: _____

3. *Trade ref name:_____

Address: _____

4. *Trade ref name: _____

Address: _____

* Not to be completed by customer – names to be supplied by salesperson.

[Seller company name] will make a search with a credit reference agency, which will keep a record of that search and will share information with other businesses. In some instances [seller company name] may also make a search on the personal credit file of principal directors. Should it become necessary to review the account, then again a credit reference may be sought and a record kept. [Seller company name] will monitor and record information relating to your trade performance, and such records will be made available to credit reference agencies who will share that information with other businesses when assessing applications for credit, and fraud prevention.

I/we agree that this information may be used to support a request for credit facilities with [seller company name] and associated companies (a list is available upon request) in accordance with their credit vetting procedures.

Customer signature _____   Position _____

Estimated purchase £ _____per month   Credit required £ _____
(i.e. 2 x monthly purchase)

We note your Standard Conditions of Sale and agree to all clauses and will pay for any goods/services supplied by you on the stated terms, i.e. ALL invoices are payable 30 days from invoice date. In addition our attention has been drawn to the clause relating to Retention of Title, which has been duly noted.

Customer signature _____   Position _____

In a quick delivery business, the first order can be made up to an amount that would not hurt the seller if lost.

The credit approval of the account should be communicated with enthusiasm to the new customer as a good opportunity to build the relationship and re-state the payment terms. Only the credit manager should be allowed to allocate new account numbers, without which deliveries cannot be made.

Newly opened accounts should be in a special ledger section, so that customers are telephoned specifically for three months, to let them see that the credit rules mean what they say.

It is extremely useful to make immediate contact with the customer's payments person by sending a new account letter (see Figure 2.00 for an example), which should be signed and personalised. Some companies add a small photograph of the collector. A follow up telephone call after a few days may indicate what kind of account behaviour can be expected.

Guidance notes to the credit application form A2.9

The following is a guide to the application form shown in Figure 1.00.

Name of applicant   A2.10

This shows the type of customer – individual, sole trader, partnership, limited liability partnership, limited company, plc, club, society, charity, etc. This information is essential to decide the risk and collection method.

Address for invoices and statements   A2.11

This may well be different from that for deliveries. Invoices sent to the delivery address may be delayed before being passed to the payment office. A letter heading request is a useful check on the name, address, etc. given in this section.

Full name(s) of proprietor or partner(s) and home address   A2.12

It is important to include the proprietor's address for two principal reasons.

- It reminds the customer in effect that as an individual or sole trader/partner, non-limited liability means that owners and/or partners are personally liable for debts incurred by the business.

- The home premises/property may represent wealth for future recovery if the need were to arise, and the lifestyle of the owner/partner may well have a bearing on the credit decisions going forward. The home address is a useful contact address if there has been no satisfaction at the place of business when trying to collect sums due.

It is worth remembering that partnerships, unless limited by deed between the partners or are formed as limited liability partnerships, have joint and several (i.e. separate) liability on all partners.

Limited company registered number and office A2.13

The number of the limited company and the address of the registered office is needed for legal action where writs and summonses have to be served on the registered address. Unique registered numbers are also useful when requesting credit reports and company searches – this prevents reports or searches being delivered on different companies with a similar name.

Length of time established   A2.14

Firms that are less than two years old have a high failure rate. It is wise to restrict credit until a relationship has blossomed, or obtain third party guarantees for higher credit (see **A12.22** below for further information on third party guarantees). Long established firms have track records that can be checked.

Name of payments contact   A2.15

It may not be obvious at an early stage of customer contact between salesman and buyer, but for credit control and collections, the name of a payments contact is essential. It is always good practice to address to an individual in any event, and relationships form a vital part of effective credit management.

Credit references   A2.16

Bank details are useful, but trade references supplied by the customer can be questionable. If trade references are required, it is better to insist that the sales person discreetly finds out the names of other suppliers.

It is a matter of conformity with data protection issues that it is made clear to the prospective customer that enquiries will be made with third parties, and that information will be shared where appropriate.

Estimated purchases and credit
rating requested   A2.17

An estimate of the purchases to be made should be the customer's, not the salesperson's. The credit rating should be a multiple of two or three times monthly sales, since the second month will be delivered before the first month is paid.

Acceptance section   A2.18

It is important for the customer to see the conditions of sales, which can be printed on the reverse of the form, and to sign agreement to those conditions. It is equally important for the customer to sign acceptance of credit terms.

The customer should be made aware quite clearly of both the credit terms to be agreed, the standard conditions of sale, and any particular clause in those conditions that will be routinely enforced. This avoids any confusion or dispute at a later date.

Receipt of the form   A2.19

On receipt of the completed credit application form, the credit manager should check for omissions, and organise the appropriate credit checks. On the basis of all data and credit checks proving acceptable, the account number can then be allocated.

Figure 2.00 – Example of a new account letter

Mr or Mrs _____ (name of payment contact given on credit application form)

XYZ Ltd

[ADDRESS LINE]

[ADDRESS LINE]

New Account number: _____

Dear Mr or Mrs _____

I am pleased to tell you that we have opened a credit account for your company with the above account number which will be shown on all invoices, statements and accounts correspondence.

Your account has been allocated a credit limit of £ _____ which should be ample for the purchases proposed on your credit application form. If you believe this should be increased, please contact me and I will be happy to discuss it with you.

Our credit terms are '30 days from invoice date'. This was agreed by your authorised person on the credit application form. I look forward to your prompt payments to these terms so that we can avoid any difficulties in supplies.

We do strive for accuracy in our invoices and statements. Please let me know of any errors or queries immediately. As the person looking after your account, I undertake to give you my prompt attention.

I shall telephone you in a few days to make sure you are quite happy with the credit arrangements and I look forward to talking to you.

Yours sincerely,_____(name)

Credit Controller (Extension _____)

Sources of information on customers   A2.20

There are many ways in which a seller can obtain information on the credit rating of a customer.

A visit by the company sales force   **A2.21**

An aware sales team should know industry developments, and as they visit customers and potential customers, they should be alert to what is going on around them. They hear information which is useful to the credit department, both in terms of ongoing credit appraisal and in terms of background to current collection problems. Customers who say 'we are going through a difficult phase', or 'we have a bit of a cash flow problem' or 'we have to cut back on orders' etc. are telling the supplier that something out of the norm is going on. It is important that feedback from the sales team is organised, and their input is not ignored. In essence, there are six important areas for credit and sales staff to consider when gathering information on customers.

- Outward impressions – bad impressions can be a warning sign, therefore it is important to assess whether the customer:

  o   is good to deal with;

  o   is well organised;

  o   replies promptly to phone calls/letters; and

  o   keeps their premises and plant in good order.

- The customer's product – the customer's fortunes depend largely on their product range. Therefore, it should be noted whether the product is attractive, of good quality and uses the latest technology.

- Demand for the customer's product – is the market expanding or contracting? Is it seasonal? These factors show how easily the customer can earn his money.

- Market competition – competition and resulting demand are prime factors in survival, therefore how is the customer placed versus his competitors?

- End customers – product for best companies or budget quality for riskiest ones? A customer's cash flow is strongly dependent upon the inflow of cash into his business.

- Management competence – good companies have balanced management skills and ensure that commitments are met. Therefore both credit and sales staff should consider whether the customer's management:

  o   is experienced;

  o   is of good repute;

  o   has balanced skills or an autocrat in charge;

  o   needs board approval for large payments; and

  o   has tight expense controls.

Account experience (existing customers)   A2.22

The seller's own sales ledger is a valuable source of information, revealing as it does actual experience with the buyer. Sales volumes, payment performance and disputes show trends which can indicate current and future risk. For example, slower payments as billings increase may mean stretched resources, or constant queries or disputes could point to delaying tactics.

Industry credit circles   A2.23

Credit circles can be useful grapevines, often being sections of trade associations. They are meetings of like-minded professionals, engaged in the same work in the same industry, the benefits to accrue very much dependent upon the accuracy of the customer data. Credit circles are not illegal, providing of course that there is no collaboration to restrict trade, but it has to be said that data protection and competition legislation has given rise to concern with some companies. As a result, industry credit circles may not be as popular or familiar as in the past. They do perform a useful role, and participation in credit circles, properly constituted and professionally organised, should be actively encouraged.

Press reports   A2.24

Reports in the media are an important source of information, both financial and general. Companies report their results, including interim results and market reaction, issue profit forecasts and/or profit warnings and again these are subjected to market interpretation and comment. Media reports can give early news on proposed mergers, buy outs, plant closures and 'downsizing'. The press should be scanned for news of actual and potential customers. In many instances, the 'local' press can report in greater detail regarding happenings at 'local' companies, especially if major changes are likely to impact on the local economy or employment situation.

Visits to customers   A2.25

It is often the case that visits to customers by credit control staff take place after problems with the account have been encountered, but it is far more beneficial to visit all large accounts on a planned basis. On-site is an excellent place to evaluate creditworthiness. Ask to sort out payment matters as a good way-in, then lead on to financial results. It is a good idea to visit first with the salesperson to ease introductions.

Credit agency reports   A2.26

Credit agency reports give the most comprehensive data and can be obtained by phone, fax or on-line. Reports range from a brief summary of main items to a full financial analysis of the customer and/or industry. Cost depends upon content, and the level of data is dictated by the amount of actual or intended credit risk exposure. Typical agency reports include the following.

- Full name and address – to capture the correct legal entity, as trading styles can be misleading. For example, a customer is generally known as 'Fantasy Fitness Clubs', but that is the trading style of Fantasy Holdings plc, or perhaps Ann Winters, trading as 'Fantasy Fitness Clubs'. Sellers must establish precisely who is legally liable for the debts.

- Legal status of the business – in the event of bankruptcy, proprietors or partners are personally liable to pay creditors, yet do not have to lodge accounts for public scrutiny. It is almost impossible to assess the personal worth of individuals. A private limited company, the commonest form of limited liability company, is owned by its shareholders, whose personal liability is their shareholding, so unsecured creditors have no claim on them as individuals. Accounts have to be regularly lodged at Companies House, usually within ten months of the company's financial year end, but the nature of the accounts varies according to size of the company. 'Small' companies only need to register 'modified' accounts (see **A2.38** below). A Public Limited Company ('plc') makes its shares available to the public and is thus subject to stricter regulation, e.g. it has to lodge fuller accounts with Companies House within seven months. (See **A2.29–A2.53** below for more information on accounts.)

- Owners of the business – shareholders' names and holdings may be of interest. Companies are subsidiaries when over 50% of their shares are owned by a parent company. A parent company is not responsible for a subsidiary's debts and few give guarantees. There may be a connection via a group overdraft with a cross-guarantee from all group companies.

- Time in business – there is a very high failure rate for companies less than two years old, yet there is little financial data available until then. A year in the title, such as ABC (2000) Ltd, may indicate a previously failed business, often with the same owners or directors.

- Activities and industrial sector – credit risk may well differ according to activity, such as manufacture, distribution (wholesale or retail), services or a mixture of these. Companies in some sectors have many competitors, e.g. engineering, others have new and small organisations, e.g. electronics, or high failure rates, e.g. construction. It also helps to know whether the customer exports to risky markets.

- Financial information – this usually comprises the latest three years of balance sheet and profit and loss information showing trends and comparisons with industry norms. (See **A2.29** below.)

- Background information – numbers of employees, size of premises, trade marks, product names, associated companies and names of directors may be useful.

- Legal action information – County Court judgments show that other suppliers have had to sue to get paid. There may also be data on other court action, e.g. for product liability or compensation claims.

- Payment experience – agency reports give the payment times experienced by other suppliers. Many credit reporting agencies also have their own debt collection divisions, and can relate their own experience in collection activity for other clients.

Bank references or banker's opinions   A2.27

References by a bank (see **A5.14–A5.17** below for additional information on bank references) are useful when used with other data, but should not be used alone for major credit decisions. The seller asks his own bank to ask specific questions of the customer's bank. It is possible to apply directly to the customer's bank if he gives prior approval, but in any event the customer MUST give approval to his own bank before any information is given out, and his own bank will inform the customer in writing of the contents of the intended reply. Request should be about the customer's ability to pay £x in y days.

The bank's brief and cryptic reply is due to its loyalty to its client, not the enquirer. It wishes to help its customer obtain credit but says as little as possible and never directly admits to a bad account situation. Its coded shades of 'OK' can be translated as follows:

- 'Undoubted' – the best reference but probably the least common. The debtor is considered an excellent risk.

- 'Good for your figures and purpose' – means 'probably good' for the credit limit suggested.

- 'Would not enter into a commitment they could not see their way to fulfil' – this is a euphemistic way of implying that the amount of credit is worryingly high.

- 'Unable to speak for your figure' – this means that the figure is too high and is a clear warning.

- 'Resources appear fully committed' – this is the worst possible reference, meaning an inability to meet existing obligations. The bank would not lend any more.

- 'There is a charge/debenture registered' – this is an extra comment to show that the bank have a first claim on assets, as registered at Companies House.

For information on how to obtain a banker's opinion see **A5.15–A5.17** below, which gives a detailed look at the requirements of the clearing banks.

Trade references   A2.28

Trade references (see **A5.18** below) are subjective, of limited use and are not recommended if provided by the customer. A customer is unlikely to provide the names of dissatisfied creditors. Trade references can be more useful if they have been obtained independently by the supplier – the salesperson can often be aware of other suppliers to the customer.

Time can be saved if the seller gives the referee a standard form to complete with boxes to tick, and of course a reply paid envelope. Many credit managers are willing to offer information over the phone, and a phone enquiry may produce more confidential information. See Figure 3.00.

Figure 3.00 – Credit reference enquiry form

Enquiry for a trade credit reference

Please tick appropriate boxes and return to us in the prepaid envelope.

Subject of enquiry

How long known?	Only recently	☐
	Less than one year	☐
	Several years	☐

| What credit terms? | 30 days | ☐ |
| | Longer (details?) | ☐ |

How much sold per month	Up to £1,000	☐
	£1,000–£5,000	☐
	More than £5,000	☐

Payment experience	Prompt	☐
	Up to 60 days late	☐
	More than 60 days late	☐

Name of collection contact:

Other useful information:

WE THANK YOU FOR YOUR HELP. PLEASE ASK US TO RECIPROCATE AT ANY TIME.

Financial statements   A2.29

Financial statements are often called 'balance sheets' and can be obtained from:

- Companies House;

- credit agencies; or

- the customer direct.

The set of financial statements gives an interesting look inside a company and aids the calculation of credit levels by ratios.

The more cynical credit analysts point out that balance sheets are always by definition out-of-date, and quite often may well have been set out to mislead. If 'qualified' by the auditors, there is a defect of some kind. The majority of company filed accounts are straightforward, however, and analysts learn to spot inconsistencies anyway. Except when the actual page called 'the balance sheet' is being discussed, the term 'balance sheet' covers the set of financial statements, as required by the *Companies Act 1985*. Some companies can be extremely late in filing their accounts at Companies House, often because they wish to delay public knowledge of a deterioration. As a result, late filing can itself be a credit warning and is worthy of further investigation.

The balance sheet itself is a statement of all the assets (items owned) and liabilities (items owed) at a given date. Total assets must always equal total liabilities, hence the balance. This apparently obvious point is not always so in some other countries where reserves and provisions are accepted as causing an imbalance. The liabilities indicate funds made available to the business and not repaid at the date shown, e.g. bank overdraft and trade creditors. The assets show how the business has used those funds, e.g. in debtors and stocks.

The statutory set of documents is lodged in a variety of styles, from glossy folders with photographs from large corporations wishing to impress, down to minimal typed pages from accountants representing small firms. Regardless of gloss, they all contain the key documents listed below. For example, the balance sheet itself is contained on a single A4 page for both Marks and Spencer plc and for Fred Inashed Ltd. The short layout is possible because the detail is explained in the notes to the accounts, which can be as extensive as the company wishes.

The key documents in a set of financial statements are:

- cover page (showing the name of the company and the date of balance sheet);

- list of directors, registered office, auditors and bankers;

- report of the directors to the shareholders;

- auditor's report to the shareholders;

- balance sheet, as at the date shown;

- profit and loss account, for the year up to the balance sheet date;

- source and application of funds statement (usually, 'funds flow' statement); and
- notes to the accounts.

Useful points in the set of financial statements when assessing credit

The report of the directors   A2.30

This report reminds the reader that it is the directors, who are employed by the shareholders to run the company within the rules of the *Companies Act 1985*, who are presenting the accounts to the owners, the shareholders. The report:

- shows the company's principal activities;
- reviews the year, usually just by referring to the later accounts;
- states any export content of the turnover;
- says whether dividends are being paid or not;
- shows directors' interests as shareholders and in any holding company;
- shows arrivals or departures of directors;
- gives a table of fixed assets, or refers to it being recorded in the notes; and
- names the auditors and whether they are to be re-appointed or not.

Credit managers derive a good deal from the tone of the report. Dividends should be paid but not if large losses have occurred, or if the company is less than about three years old, when profits are better retained to strengthen the new business. The resignation of directors may be significant as they may have advance knowledge of bad news which only becomes public at a later date. The departure of 'key' or founding directors may also have great significance. Auditors normally continue so not re-appointing them may indicate a serious disagreement over the true results, or simply over audit fees. Directors' connections with other companies may also be interesting.

The auditor's report   A2.31

The auditor's report should simply state that the figures add up and are legal, officially stated as 'giving a true and fair view' and 'comply with the Companies Act 1985'. There can be a qualification, where it is apparent that the auditors are not satisfied, e.g. 'where complete figures were not available to us, we have accepted the assurances of the directors', or 'the company has not complied with the Companies Act 1985, section xxx'. If they say that the 'going concern basis depends on continuing finance from XYZ Bank', or 'new finance is being sought', this is a distinct warning of credit risk.

The notes to the accounts   A2.32

This refers to numbered items in the balance sheet and profit and loss account. Items of interest to credit managers are details of:

- loans by directors;
- liabilities to the parent company; and
- 'contingent liabilities'.

The latter are usually cross-guarantees which may bring down the subject company if the bank calls on all subsidiaries to repay a loan to one of the group's companies in trouble.

The profit and loss account   A2.33

The profit and loss account shows details of the basic formula, 'sales minus costs equals profit', for the year's trading up to the financial year end. Four different stages of profit are shown.

- Gross profit is the difference between total sales and the costs of producing the sales, i.e. sales minus cost of sales equals gross profit.

- Operating profit is what is left from gross profit after operational expenses, such as office costs and sales commissions are deducted, i.e. gross profit minus operating expense equals operating profit.

- Net profit before tax adds or deducts items after the operating profit, e.g. interest paid on loans or received on deposits, and non-standard profits/losses such as sale of investments or fixed assets, i.e. operating profit less non-operating expenses equals net profit before tax (NPBT). The NBPT is the famous 'bottom-line'.

- The 'interest paid' is a major item for risk analysis. It should never be a significant proportion of the NPBT figure.

Tax on final profits reduces the amount available for dividends or to be retained in the business (net profit before tax less income tax equals net profit after tax).

The profit and loss account then shows the retained profits from previous years plus the new net amount to be added or deducted, forming the retained profit figure on the balance sheet, as shareholders' funds in the net worth.

Group accounts   A2.34

Group accounts are produced by a company owning more than one half the share capital of other companies, i.e. subsidiaries. Thus, a consolidated profit and loss account and balance sheet shows the position for the whole group. Associated companies are those with less than 50% of their share capital owned by a parent company and so do not file consolidated accounts.

Liabilities   **A2.35**

These are in three groups (fixed, current and shareholders funds (or equity)).

- Fixed liabilities are long-term obligations, normally with interest costs.

- Current liabilities are short-term obligations, repayable within twelve months, e.g:

  ○ bank overdrafts,

  ○ short term loans and accounts payable, or

  ○ trade creditors.

- Shareholders funds (equity) – when formed, a limited company is author-ised to issue a stated amount of share capital, called 'authorised' capital. Shareholders subscribe only as much as is needed, since other funds are usually available. Thus, many companies are formed with £100 authorised capital and operate from then on with only £2 issued capital. The shareholders also own the retained profits not yet paid out in dividends. So, the company owes shareholders the capital subscribed, this is only repayable when a company is wound-up (if there are sufficient funds when all other debts have been paid) and the retained profits, these are known together as shareholders funds, or equity. As shareholders own the business, their funds are listed separately from 'outsiders', such as banks and creditors.

Profits kept in the business are called retained earnings, or earned surplus. Increased value from revaluing assets is capital surplus. Both earned and capital surplus on the balance sheet are cumulative totals, built up over the years to the balance sheet date.

Net worth of a business is its current and fixed assets minus all external liabilities, short-term and long-term, equalling the shareholders funds. In a break-up situation, such as insolvency or acquisition, assets are rarely found to be worth their balance sheet figure – on the other hand, liabilities always are!

Working capital   **A2.36**

Working capital is most easily defined as current assets minus current liabilities, i.e. the short-term money available at any one time.

The funds flow statement   **A2.37**

This statement compares the current balance sheet with the previous one and uses data from the profit and loss account to show the changes in the funds available to the business and how they were used, i.e. where new money (sources) has come from and where it has gone (uses). As the sources must equal the uses, funds not used produce changes to working capital. Not many credit analysts use the funds flow statement as the most useful ratios are calculated from the balance sheet and the profit and loss account.

Exemptions permitted in filing of accounts under Companies Act requirements A2.38

The biggest problem for risk analysis in these provisions is the absence of a profit and loss account for a small company (see Figure 4.00 for exemptions in filing accounts). If an assessment is important enough, it is worth approaching the customer directly for the missing data, in order to decide on the credit level.

For many credit managers, the dilemma is quite simply that the level of credit for a particular supplier may be the same, or even greater, to a small company than to a medium-sized or large company – the factor being the product or market place, rather than size. The official definitions are liable to be misleading, therefore, and the danger for small companies is that lack of specific information could well hinder their ability to obtain the required credit support. Any review of the definition of the criteria upwards by the Government will only add to the problem – the Institute of Credit Management has been consistent in its opposition to such upwards proposals.

Figure 4.00 – Exemptions in filing accounts for small and medium-sized companies

	Small Company	Medium-sized Company
Balance sheet	Abbreviated content	No concession
Profit and loss account	Not required	Can start with gross profit
Notes to accounts	Very limited requirement	No need to show turnover/profit by activities or markets
Directors' report	Not required	No concession
Qualification for exemption (any 2 of the 3 factors)		
Turnover not exceeding	£5.6m	£22.8m
Balance sheet total not exceeding	£2.8m	£11.4m
Average employees not exceeding	50	250

In 2003 the Government consulted interested parties under its White Paper 'Modernising Company Law' as to the desirability of increasing the audit threshold for small companies, originally £350,000 and later £1m. The intention was to bring the UK into line with EU proposals. The result of the consultation, best described as 'mixed', indicated 97 responses with 3 respondents requesting that their responses remain confidential; 55 respondents were in favour of raising the audit threshold to the EU maximum of £5.6m, with 35 respondents opposed. It was proposed in the same White Paper that the threshold defining medium-sized companies be increased to £22.8m, and responses here totalled 36, with 29 in favour, and 4 opposed; 3 respondents commented, but did not express an opinion on the proposal.

Those 'in favour', principally the accountancy firms, argued cost savings for business, while those 'against', principally credit-related professional bodies and credit-related companies, argued that limiting disclosure actually limits the availability of credit. On 30 January 2004, the Government raised the audit threshold for small and medium-sized companies to £5.6m and £22.8m respectively. The Institute of Credit Management remains adamant in its contention, quite correctly, that a turnover of £5.6m and a balance sheet total of £2.8m is hardly 'small' by any commonsense definition, and restricting information on businesses of that size will be damaging for all business in the long term. There is much support for this contention from other areas.

Where can accounts be obtained? A2.39

For a limited company (private or public), accounts are filed annually at Companies House and are available for public inspection. Extreme lateness in filing is a warning that a deterioration will be seen when the accounts do eventually appear. Instead of waiting, a seller can ask a customer directly. For a sole trader or partnership, a seller can only ask the customer who may refuse. A good credit agency will provide selected balance sheet data as part of their report on all types of firm.

Dealing with the out-of-date aspect of accounts A2.40

As accounts are published some months after their year end, and in any event relate to the previous twelve months' trading, it is useful to look at figures for three consecutive years. Although some items will go up and down, the general pattern usually gets gradually better or gradually worse over three years. A rapid dive in vital indicators is a distinct warning of trouble. Companies in difficulty can survive for years when creditors and banks are too tolerant. That can change suddenly if a creditor or bank demands rapid repayment and threatens closure.

The use of ratios in interpreting accounts

Which customers need scrutiny? A2.41

All accounts need to be controlled, and the lesson of the boom/bust of the 1990s is that all customers need to be subject to some levels of scrutiny. In practical terms, however, the supplier should decide a 'pain level' of an account which would really hurt if it were lost. Organise an ongoing watch on all debtors, in particular all those debtors above that decided figure, by analysis of key balance sheet items. As a minimum, check the solvency and liquidity ratios (see **A2.42** and **A2.43** below).

Solvency   A2.42

Solvency, expressed either as a percentage or a number of 'times', indicates the proportion of shareholders funds in the total liabilities and is sometimes referred to as the creditors' protection ratio. The higher the proportion of shareholders funds, compared to external debts, the more ability there is to pay creditors. For credit risk analysis, it is better to show how assets are financed by free shareholders funds compared to interest-bearing borrowed funds. A high solvency ratio, i.e. a high proportion of shareholders represents low gearing, low risk and capacity for borrowing more external finance, or credit. A low solvency ratio indicates high gearing, high risk and less scope in the event of credit difficulties.

Liquidity   A2.43

Liquidity can be expressed in terms of:

- current ratio, which equals current assets divided by current liabilities; and
- quick ratio, which equals current assets minus stock divided by current liabilities.

There should be enough current assets to turn into cash to settle current debts. A current ratio below 1 indicates a credit risk because of insufficient cash-producing assets. A very high ratio, say over 3, although comfortable for creditors, does illustrate inefficient use of assets. A ratio of 1.5 to 2 is good. The quick ratio, also known as the 'acid test', ignores stocks, which may not be fast moving, to measure the more immediate liquidity to meet current liabilities. A quick ratio of 1 or above is good, although in today's economic climate many companies survive with a quick ratio of about 0.8.

Sales comparison   A2.44

Current year's sales can be compared to previous year's sales. A reduction leads a credit manager to see how other ratios have been managed in a sales decline.

Profit comparison   A2.45

Current year's NPBT compared to previous year's. The percentage should equal or better the percentage sales growth or decline. Lower growth in profits than sales indicates lack of management control and further checks will be needed.

Sales compared to working capital (i.e. net current assets) A2.46

Comparing sales to working capital shows the efficiency in the use of working capital to produce sales. An excessively high ratio, or sudden increase, may indicate overtrading, where profits are not retained in the business. Where sales race ahead of liquidity, the company may have to delay payments to suppliers.

Net profit before tax as a percentage of sales A2.47

This shows the overall efficiency and control of costs. It is difficult when sales decline to reduce costs in the same proportion and serious trouble can follow.

Sales compared to stocks A2.48

This ratio shows how long stocks take to be sold. A ratio of three times, means that sales value is held in stocks for four months. A higher than average ratio for the particular industry indicates competitive success. Slow moving stocks can be a major reason for slow payments.

Stocks compared to working capital (net current assets) A2.49

This ratio is used to illustrate how much of the working capital is tied up by raw materials, work in progress and finished goods. It should be steady in relation to sales growth, subject to seasonal trade. An increasing level may indicate obsolete stocks or weak stock control.

Sales compared to trade debtors A2.50

This ratio shows the average time taken to collect debts from customers. A ratio of 3:1 shows that one third of a year's sales are unpaid. This equates to debts being unpaid for an average of 120 days, excessive if terms are 30 days. This indicates a lack of credit control and a shortage of liquidity to pay creditors.

A recommended set of ratios for risk analysis A2.51

The following ratios can be used in risk analysis.

- Current ratio – current assets divided by current liabilities.

- Acid test – current assets minus stocks divided by current liabilities.

- Stock turnover – stocks x 360 days, divided by annual sales.

- DSO (days sales outstanding or collection period) – debtors x 360, divided by sales.

- External debt/net worth – either all debt (current and long-term), divided by net assets, or just the current liabilities.

- Interest burden – interest paid as a proportion of profit before tax and interest.

- Profit on sales – net profit before tax ('the bottom line') as a percentage of total sales.

Trends in ratios A2.52

Ratios alone can be misleading, so it is always better to compare a ratio with a previous year or, better still, two years. Three successive years of financial ratios are a reliable indicator of the progress of a company. It is worth devising a standard worksheet to record a customer's ratios and trends (see **A2.53** and Figure 5.00 below). It can be on screen or in hard copy and is then available at a glance, instead of having to search for reasons for previous decisions.

Key ratios for a simple credit analysis worksheet A2.53

The following ratios can be used in a credit analysis worksheet:

Liquidity

(a) Current ratio (times)
$$= \frac{\text{current assets}}{\text{current liabilities}}$$

(b) Quick ratio (or acid test) (times)
$$= \frac{\text{current assets less stocks}}{\text{current liabilities}}$$

(c) Stock turnover (days)
$$= \frac{\text{stock} \times 365}{\text{sales}}$$

Debt

(a) Collection period (DSO) (days)
$$= \frac{\text{debtors} \times 365}{\text{sales}}$$

(b) Creditor protection ratio (%)
$$= \frac{\text{net worth} \times 100}{\text{current liabilities}}$$

(c) Interest burden ratio (%)
$$= \frac{\text{interest expense} \times 100}{\text{profit before tax} + \text{interest}}$$

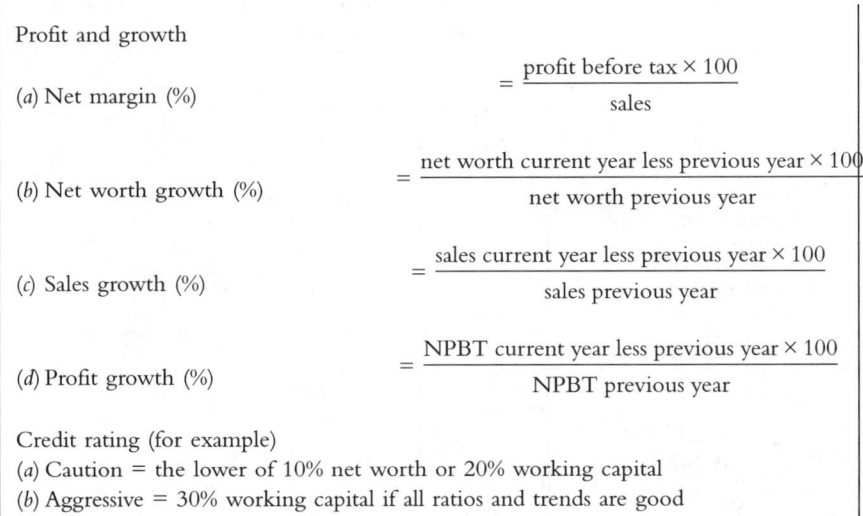

Profit and growth

(*a*) Net margin (%) $\qquad = \dfrac{\text{profit before tax} \times 100}{\text{sales}}$

(*b*) Net worth growth (%) $\qquad = \dfrac{\text{net worth current year less previous year} \times 100}{\text{net worth previous year}}$

(*c*) Sales growth (%) $\qquad = \dfrac{\text{sales current year less previous year} \times 100}{\text{sales previous year}}$

(*d*) Profit growth (%) $\qquad = \dfrac{\text{NPBT current year less previous year} \times 100}{\text{NPBT previous year}}$

Credit rating (for example)
(*a*) Caution = the lower of 10% net worth or 20% working capital
(*b*) Aggressive = 30% working capital if all ratios and trends are good

A blank worksheet with these ratios is given in Figure 5.00 below. Worksheets should be held on file or disk for all major accounts and updated annually and/or when a significant event occurs.

Any credit manager can devise appropriate scores for risk analysis, by reference to performance ratios for the various industries of his customers. The basis is to take a number of companies, say 100, who were trading three years earlier and divide them between those still trading and those which failed. A comparison of their key ratios, as set out above, will show the dividing lines between success and failure. Scores can then be allocated in a range from good to poor and a decision taken to allow credit to customers who achieve a 'survival' score. This can be flexed to suit prudent or high risk strategies.

Figure 5.00 – Blank worksheet for risk assessment

Ratio analysis – worksheet				
Customer:	Date:			
	Latest Year	Previous Year	Year Before	Comments
Liquidity				
1. Current ratio (times)				
2. Quick ratio (times)				
3. Stock ratio (days)				
4. Collection period (days)				*(cont'd)*

49

Ratio analysis – worksheet				
Customer:	Date:			
	Latest Year	Previous Year	Year Before	Comments
Debt				
5. Creditor protection ratio (%)				
6. Interest burden ratio (%)				
Profit and growth				
7. Net margin (%)				
8. Net worth growth (%)				
9. Sales growth (%)				
10. Profit growth (%)				
Overall opinion (including credit rating and score if needed)				
Note: Accounts show latest and previous year. Previous accounts needed for third year.				

Software programs for risk analysis   A2.54

There are a number of computer assisted methods commercially available for risk assessment, broadly divided into three main types, as detailed below.

- Self-designed spreadsheet programs, using balance sheet data loaded by the user to produce ratios as decided by the credit manager. In some cases, these automatically calculate credit ratings and even risk codes, according to scores achieved by ratios and year-on-year trends.

- Proprietary PC programs, specifying data to be loaded by the user, some giving scope for weighting according to the seller's preferred ratios. These produce scores for the user to apply to decide credit ratings.

- Solvency model programs, using disks provided by software companies, enabling the user to load specific data and compare the resulting ratios to industry performance, with predictive indicators of insolvency risk, based on scores for past failures. These are for solvency prediction rather than credit ratings. They are usually based on variations of the long established Z-score approach, widely used in the USA and by UK banks, companies, investors and Government departments.

Export credit risk analysis   A2.55

The four key questions for managing export credit risks are as follows.

- Will the customer go bust before we are paid?
- Can he pay our value on our terms?
- If he can pay – can his country find the hard currency?
- Are he and his country worth marketing for the future?

Credit insurance companies have had to amplify these risks into the list that follows. With or without credit insurance cover, exporters should check their customers and markets to avoid the following loss events.

The buyer may:

- become insolvent;
- not have paid six months after the due date; or
- refuse to take up the goods.

The buyer's Government may:

- cancel an existing import licence;
- impose a new import licence;
- have a non-transferable hard currency;
- have a moratorium on external debts;
- have a law preventing contract performance;
- have war or civil disorder;
- not ratify contracts;
- expropriate or damage plant or property; or
- unfairly call bonds.

The exporter's Government may:

- cancel or impose an export licence; or
- prevent contract performance.

Any other Government may:

- take action preventing contract performance.

Information on country (political) risks

Commercial agencies   **A2.56**

Various agencies sell topical information on country risks. The most concise and easily read is D&B's *International Risk and Payment Review*, which shows the usual payment terms of other exporters for over 120 markets, the length of transfer delays, if any, and the availability of credit insurance cover. (See also **A3.16–A3.26** and **A11.10** below.)

Bank reviews   A2.57

Bank reviews can be obtained, usually free of charge, from the major UK banks and show if any significant delays are being met in collections for exporters. Major UK banks also issue information on the indebtedness of countries, indicating their ability to pay for future imports.

Credit insurance companies   A2.58

The Export Credits Guarantee Department (ECGD), which only covers medium-term credit for capital goods, publishes the OECD consensus list of countries in three categories of wealth, this being a fair indication of political risk. NCM, as the main short-term insurer, issues policy holders a list of any restrictions on country cover. By using a specialist broker, an exporter has access to a wide range of country risk information. (See **A12.2–A12.21** below.)

Agents   A2.59

In overseas markets, agents (see **A12.2–A12.21** below) should be required to send data to the exporter on import restrictions and local bank priorities for foreign currency allocations.

Credit groups   A2.60

In many industries, credit groups meet regularly to compare views on terms, delays and risks for countries their companies sell to.

Finance and Credit in International Business (FCIB) A2.61

The FCIB is the European arm of NACM of the USA. It is a major information body for credit and treasury professionals which organises round-tables in European centres. Members discuss topical questions on country risks and export credit techniques.

A suggested plan for controlling political risks   A2.62

The following is a suggested course of action for controlling political risks.

- List the countries to which a company sell, or plans to sell.
- Collect economic data on each country in a file.
- Allocate a risk grade to each country as follows.

○   Grade I – the hard currency countries, which are obvious, and present a negligible risk.

○   Grade II – all other countries which do not fall into Grades I or III, which present an average risk.

○   Grade III – these include countries which:

    ■   have difficulty funding imports;

    ■   are oil-dependent with small export earnings;

    ■   are single-crop exporters;

    ■   are dependent on Western aid;

    ■   have a military government; or

    ■   have rapid changes of administration.

    These present a high risk.

●   Use the categories as follows:

○   for Grade I – agree any sensible terms, this is good for market development;

○   for Grade II – keep terms as short as possible as this is good for short-term marketing; and

○   for Grade III – only accept a CILC or guaranteed payment, no marketing expense but take any contracts with pre-arranged funding, e.g. from the World Bank or the European Union.

●   Amend the categories when data justifies it.

●   Review the categories at intervals.

Information on customer risks

Credit agencies   A2.63

These offer a worldwide service for reports similar to the UK except that data is only as good as that available in the market, e.g. very extensive for the USA but only estimates are available for some Gulf States.

Foreign bank reports   A2.64

These are generally more informative than UK bank reports but are still unlikely to relate bad news. European banks have been less forthcoming with information in recent years, with a move towards less and less disclosure in spite of the adverse effect on their customers seeking credit.

Agents   A2.65

Where agents have been appointed in local territories, they should be expected to supply topical data on customers and prospects, with the reporting method formalised in the agency agreement.

Sales visit reports   A2.66

Reports should be made by travelling staff on a special form to record the latest basic financial data on customers and prospects. This helps sales staff to develop financial awareness and makes business forecasts more reliable.

Financial accounts   A2.67

For the few customers who provide 80% of business, financial accounts should be routinely requested, with refusal taken as a warning sign. Customer attitude to giving suppliers sight of company figures varies from country to country, but accounts can be obtained from the local equivalent of Companies House in developed countries.

Embassies and Consulates   A2.68

Credit value opinions will not be provided by Embassies and Consulates, but these institutions are very valuable sources of information on local reputations of companies and businesses. They are also useful for introductions to other sources of help, particularly business clubs and chambers of commerce.

NCM and other credit insurance companies   A2.69

Policyholders get credit decisions when applying for credit limits (together with recommended terms) and indications for possible future needs. NCM have a vast databank and there is a good chance that a new buyer is already known to other policyholders. (See **A12.6–A12.21** below.)

Credit groups   A2.70

As explained earlier (see **A2.60** above), for country information, trade groups and organisations such as FCIB, provide excellent forums for exchanging topical credit opinions on buyers, as well as credit terms and experience of payment problems.

Evaluating customer risks   A2.71

The choice is to accept ready-made credit ratings or to make assessments using the financial data available on customers. If an exporter uses several sources, he could find, for example:

- that a D&B report might recommend £10,000 credit on 60 days terms;

- a sales visit report and local agent might suggest £100,000 on maximum terms; and

- a trade group might agree that debts are paid promptly below £15,000 but late for larger amounts.

This illustrates that the sales input is optimistic – the customer could well place larger orders but cannot generate the funds promptly.

The exporter needs to keep close to major customers, especially where credit exposure is higher than recommended by others. It is not worth 'hiding' behind credit insurance cover, because the exporter still needs to know the ongoing status of the bigger outlets. There is no exact science in calculating credit ratings in export, but typical approaches would be:

(*a*)   any amount, as long as there are no serious overpayments;

(*b*)   20% of working capital; or

(*c*)   10% of net worth.

The method described in (*a*) is obviously dangerous. Even if the amount is low, e.g. £10,000, when the customer is able to pay £10 million, it requires extra work to increase it at intervals, when it could have been set higher in the first place. It is even more dangerous when the amount is beyond a buyer's capability if he no longer regards the exporter as a key supplier.

The methods described in (*b*) and (*c*) allow an exposure well within the customer's declared financial strength. For example, where an order would give a regular exposure of £150,000, analysis might show that the customer is solvent, liquid, not overstretched on interest-bearing debt and has capital and reserves (net worth) of £1 million. Taking 10% of this, a credit rating of £100,000 might be set, with orders put into manufacture up to three times that figure, i.e. £300,000, because of a long lead time. Deliveries and terms can be adjusted to the satisfaction of both sides.

Figures and ratios in foreign balance sheets may require some knowledge of local accounting treatment, e.g. generous reserves for stocks and debtors, which may be provided by local agents or international auditors.

Codifying information   A2.72

Credit data can either be filed for when needed or, preferably, coded into credit ratings and risk categories. It makes sense for credit opinions to be visible to all staff who may commit the company to a credit risk, especially in sales.

Customer risk categories A2.73

These show the degree of security and care needed with payment terms, e.g:

- Category A represents no discernible risk and should be given any reasonable terms and reviewed annually.

- Category B represents an average risk, some care to be taken with the terms, which should be reviewed quarterly.

- Category C represents a high risk and should be granted on secure terms only.

Country risk categories A2.74

These indicate the availability of hard currency and the scope for marketing.

- I = Strong market, any sensible terms should be granted – good for marketing expense.

- II = Average market, care should be taken with terms – short-term marketing only.

- III = Weak market, secure terms only should be granted – no marketing.

Displaying credit ratings and risk categories A2.75

Printouts and computer screens typically show codings alongside customer names and account numbers, making little need to refer to hard copy data. For example:

	Country Risk Category	Customer Risk Category	Amount of Credit	Number of Days Credit
Customer X	I	B	£10,000	60 days draft
Customer Y	III	A	£0	Confirmed Irrevocable Letter of Credit (CILC)

Note: customer X is an average risk in an average country. Although customer Y is 'no-risk', he is in a 'high risk, secure terms only' country, so CILC (Confirmed Irrevocable Letter of Credit) has to apply.

Using credit ratings and risk categories A2.76

Having allocated codes to all accounts, the exporter can systemise them for everyday use, e.g. incoming orders and outgoing shipments, by allowing the computer to check that the value, when added to existing debts, does not exceed the stated limit. If it does, the order need not be refused, nor a shipment cancelled, but it needs urgent action by a credit person to secure payment. Top management can therefore relax in the knowledge that all business is within agreed guidelines of exposure – or at the very least that an expert is dealing with specific excesses.

Information supplied to travelling sales staff   A2.77

The risk codes and ratings should be built into sales order points which communicate with travelling staff, for assessing the worth of sales and marketing efforts. Figure 6.00 shows a useful credit checking system for exports.

Figure 6.00 – Typical credit checking system for exports

Action		*Checks*
Enquiry Quotation Sales visit prospects		Early warning for credit check
Order from	New customer	Assess credit rating Assess risk category Decide payment terms
Order from	Approved customer	Check ledger for overdues Check stop/referral list Compare to 3× credit rating less balance
Shipment to	Approved Customer	Check ledger for overdues Check stop/referral list Compare to credit rating less balance

A3

Gaining Information to Support Credit Decisions

Introduction A3.1

In the UK we are fortunate to have a wealth of information sources that will enable credit controllers or managers and sales managers to make a decision on whether to supply on credit or use different payment terms.

Many credit scoring systems are now highly sophisticated and are able to assess what is a reasonable amount of credit to advance. A number of credit information companies are in competition with each other to improve the commercial information and speed of access for their customers.

Since this chapter was updated in May 2002 there have been many advances in technology which means that most of the services which major credit bureaux offer can be delivered via the Internet. This has lead to major improvements in delivery speed and cost competition.

In an interview Andy Coney, a Consultant with APC Services Limited, confirmed that the credit manager and his staff now have many choices of information from the different product ranges that are being offered. There has also been a shift towards more sophisticated decision managing systems that allow larger credit departments to set their own credit scoring criteria using in-house information combined with data provided from credit bureaux. He emphasised that in 2002 there has never been a better time to buy cost effective credit information in the UK. In a further interview, he said that ultimately as the price of information becomes less, the credit bureaux seek to make more added value products and services that compliment the core data services. Such examples are where trade specific data services are coming back into fashion. Trade groups such as electronics, fuels, construction, transport and metals all have added value services provided in unique ways to credit managers in those industries.

Blending a mix of public data (such as that from Companies House) and value added services that are industry specific, would appear to be a more profitable route for both the credit information supplier and the risk manager. Overall, the price of publicly available data will continue to slide whilst new services that add value will provide new and more appropriate data on which credit managers can base their decisions. Credit bureaux that are able to provide the type of real added value services that will be required in the future will outpace the information providers who are not able to make this point of competitive difference.

Other sources of information such as credit circles, industry groups, customer visits and intelligence from trade journals and local, provincial and national newspapers make this fascinating job of assessing customers to protect profits far easier.

Information from credit bureaux A3.2

Supplying goods or services on credit with little or no knowledge of your customer's background is taking a risk at a time when short-term trade cycles can create boom and bust conditions. In the period from the year 2000 we have seen some decline in the manufacturing, telecommunication and technology sectors in the UK. Businesses can and do fail remarkably quickly.

With the excitement of gaining a new customer or repeat orders, the last thought managers in a business have is that they will not get paid. Often the only thought is, can they achieve the sales for the month end and have enough funds in the bank to pay staff wages?

The risk of a delayed or non-payment, or even the forewarning of a business failure, can often be anticipated by using one of the major credit bureaux or specialist sector bureaux which operate in the UK. It is still estimated in the UK that only 20% of businesses take out credit reports on their customers. Therefore for many businesses the unexpected bad debt is bound to occur when pre-assessment of their customers is not carried out. There are two significant changes that have taken place between 2003 and the first quarter of 2004. The first is that credit bureaux are reporting that more credit reports are being requested. This is due to far more transactions being carried out via the Internet where there may be no physical contact between the buyer and the seller.

Secondly, at the end of March 2004 the statutory audit threshold was increased for small-sized companies from a turnover of £1 million to £5.6 million, and medium-sized companies to £22.8 million respectively. These changes will affect 890,000 small companies who are now exempt from the requirement of an outside independent audit.

Therefore credit bureau information, such as payment performance history, is now even more vital to ascertain the business strength of a limited company.

With budget and staff cuts the cry, 'I cannot afford to pay for a credit report, our profit margins are too small', is often heard. In reply the author of this chapter would like to say that it takes the profit of many extra sales to cover the losses of one bad debt. Credit reports are now less expensive than they were ten years ago due to massive investment in computerised data storage. A fifteen-page analytical credit report, which in the past would have taken two to three weeks to produce, may now be online, or can be e-mailed, faxed or obtained via a CD-ROM in a matter of seconds.

Why are these services required to be delivered so quickly? Businesses are now under intense pressure to agree to a transaction within hours. This is due to severe competition at a time when there is often over-supply of goods and services and consequently price cutting has increased to gain orders. This is why it is critically important to obtain up-to-date commercial and financial information on the payment habits of customers so that a profit can be made on everything that is sold. There is always a commercial risk in selling on credit – even a cash sale transaction where a cheque is presented can be hazardous, as regrettably cheques can sometimes bounce.

Major bureaux   A3.3

In order to give readers an outline of the range of services available in the UK, I have again interviewed the five major credit information bureaux which still generate a large proportion of all credit reports. They are:

- Experian;
- D&B;
- Equifax;
- ICC Credit;
- Graydon; and
- Company Watch.

All the major credit bureaux I have interviewed are constantly developing systems that will give their clients immediate credit assessment information.

These on-line services are vital, as competition to gain orders has intensified since July 2003.

New on-line bureaux   A3.4

As a number of new on-line credit information and specialist bureaux have been established, I have researched the following companies:

- Creditsafe.com;
- Checkit; and
- ACS.

Experian   A3.5

Experian is a global leader in providing information solutions to organisations and consumers. It helps organisations find, develop and manage profitable customer relationships by providing information, decision-making solutions and processing services. It empowers consumers to understand, manage and protect their personal information and assets. Experian works with more than 40,000 clients across diverse industries, including financial services, telecommunications, health-care, insurance, retail and catalogue, automotive, manufacturing, leisure, utilities, property, e-commerce and government. Experian is a subsidiary of GUS plc and has headquarters in Nottingham, UK, and Costa Mesa, California. Its 13,000 staff support clients in more than 60 countries. Annual sales exceed £1.2 billion.

For more information, visit the company's website on www.experian.com.

Interview with Experian   A3.6

In an interview with Phil Cotter, the Managing Director of Experian's Business Information division, he confirmed that one of the biggest changes he has seen in recent years is the desire among lenders for automated systems which not only improve credit management, but also their productivity, operational efficiency and customer service. There has also been a rapid movement towards delivery over the Internet through Experian's e-series business website at www.uk.experian.com/bi which provides online access to the firm's full range of business information reports and services including non-limited and limited company reports, directors database, limited company monitoring, international reports, pre-screened marketing information and payment performance information.

The growth in the use of automated systems for commercial decisioning reflects the way in which commercial credit scoring has followed the consumer lending market that some 20 years ago saw vast improvements by using technology to automate many of the manual processes involved in credit granting. As consumers, we are now all used to applying for credit and expect immediate decisions as to whether our application has been accepted. Experian has been at the forefront of this development, with its systems being used to process tens of millions of credit applications every year. Utilising this experience, Experian is bringing the benefits of automation to the commercial lending environment.

Experian has developed a number of products that deliver speed, consistency and accuracy of decision-making in a commercial lending environment. These include the Commercial Autoscore system, the UK's first fully automated commercial credit application processing system to deliver instant credit decisioning to trade and commercial lending departments. Commercial Delphi, Experian's highly predictive risk index is an integral part of the system, providing risk scores for even newly established companies that have yet to file their first set of accounts. Independent research has declared that the Commercial Delphi scoring system, which is able to forecast the likelihood of limited company failure, is the most predictive scorecard on the market.

The Commercial Autoscore system provides credit decisions within seconds. Its flexible decisioning engine enables customers to access over 200 policy rules in order to define credit policies to mirror their own internal credit evaluation policies and procedures. This ensures that consistent decisions are employed on all credit decisions. Commercial Autoscore also frees up resources so that expertise can be focused on more complex cases, eliminating the need to waste valuable staff resources on manually processing simple, low-risk decisions and administration tasks.

Credit limits A3.7

When Experian assigns a credit limit to a company, it reviews the financial factors that are available alongside payment performance information, which is a good indicator on how the company pays its bills, and compares this with the trends in the company's sector. Both consumer and business information is also assessed – the information behind the people who run companies, including their track records and business interests provides a much more valuable insight into a company's financial stability and creditworthiness.

Modern credit checks can be done easily and instant reports are available over the Internet, making it easy to access statistically reliable recommended credit limits and credit ratings to help reach decisions on whether or not to grant credit to a customer, how much and under what terms.

Phil Cotter confirmed that, in his many discussions with credit managers from many companies, especially where they have a relatively low volume of business, many still rely on manual decision-making but have an almost infinite variety of ways of deciding how much credit their customers should be granted. Despite this, he also confirmed that more and more companies are now embracing automated credit scoring and enabling their credit managers to make more accurate and profitable lending decisions.

Consistency A3.8

With UK profit margins under increasing pressure, companies are reassessing their credit policies. Experian systems are designed to be consistent across all departments and office locations. This ensures that, as individuals, credit managers are not relying solely on their own personal experience and views to make a decision. Another benefit is that the credit manager can start taking greater control of his or her credit management policy.

Phil Cotter emphasised that credit ratings are not just based on filed financial data. Experian uses a wide range of information sources, including payment performance data. Uniquely, the firm is also able to combine its consumer and business information to provide a valuable insight into the business interests and track records of people who run companies. For smaller and newly formed companies, where financial data is scarce, this combined data is often the best indicator of a business's creditworthiness and provides the best picture of a company's customer base and who they should be extending credit terms to.

All this information is taken into account in the Commercial Delphi scorecard. Recent independent analysis suggests that this is the most predictive score for limited companies on the market.

From a risk manager's point of view, what they really want to know is 'which of my current portfolio is most likely to start running into financial difficulties in the next three to six months?' Commercial Delphi provides highly accurate and predictive risk scores to help companies reduce bad debt costs and save money.

Other new products   A3.9

The move away from simply providing information to more value-added solutions extends right across Experian's business information product range. The company is committed to innovative product development and continual invest-ment in its services, products and people and recent innovations include the launch of a new International Service and Commercial Delphi (see **A3.6** and **A3.8** above) for non-limited companies.

Within its B2B Marketing division, Experian has introduced Commercial MOSAIC, a unique B2B segmentation and targeting system which allows existing and prospective customers to be segmented according to a range of characteristics, enabling businesses to identify, understand and thereby target their best prospects cost effectively and, ultimately, increase profits.

Commercial MOSAIC illustrates how credit and marketing departments can work together. By segmenting their customer base using credit scoring informa-tion, for example, companies are able to screen out potential customers that are not creditworthy, reduce mailing wastage and reduce costs.

In addition, Experian has also re-launched its National Business Database (NBD). The NBD is the most comprehensive and accurate business database in the UK, holding more quality information on more businesses with greater coverage for both data solutions and list buying purposes. The new database is made up of a unique combination of data sources including Thomson, Companies House and Yell, following Experian's acquisition of the Yell Data business in 2003. The enhanced NBD contains over 400,000 more business records than ever before and provides an even stronger foundation for Experian's innovative product develop-ment. The combination of the NBD's superior data, coupled with the expertise of Experian's expanding team of data specialists, is enabling the company to offer an even wider range of B2B marketing products with new and advanced data enrichment, hygiene and analytic capabilities.

Conclusion   A3.10

Phil Cotter's philosophy is that he wants to be able to support his clients throughout their whole customer life cycle. He wants to help companies find those prospects that will be most likely to be profitable and help them to manage the subsequent relationships with those customers. This is where Experian's solutions are so valuable – helping clients to target new business more efficiently. It enables them to check the financial strengths of their prospects, to reduce rejection rates and increase the profitability of new customers, right up to the use of automated decisioning. It enables the client to make the right credit decision, not just at the outset of the relationship but throughout the relationship, leading to greater customer loyalty, lower bad debt rates and greater account profitability.

Limited company databases   A3.11

Experian's limited company database has details on over 7 million UK director-ships and company secretaries online, of which 2.5 million are current directors. The personal financial track record of those directors can be included in these reports using the Directors Database. Some adverse information, especially if the background of some directors shows that they have been involved in failed companies or financial mismanagement, is especially useful.

Often a credit enquiry does not reveal that the application is from a newly formed company, or from a limited company where they have just appointed a new director.

On another database is a list of 7,750 directors who have been disqualified for periods of between 2 and 15 years.

Non-limited business   A3.12

Experian has created its information on over 2.2 million small businesses, which include sole traders and partnerships, from a number of different sources.

Information is gathered from sales ledgers, consumer records, telephone directories, trade and professional directories and public records. A unique feature of the Experian non-limited business report is that on entering details about the proprietor or partner of the business, subscribers will get information that considers both the business and the individuals that run it.

It should be remembered that as non-limited businesses have no legal requirement to publish any financial details, so every extra piece of information is vital in assessing the risk. These businesses are heavily dependent on the management skills of their proprietors. Often a business may even cease to trade without notifying anyone. Some unethical individuals also set up businesses and then fold one business after another. However, some sole traders and partnerships can be far stronger financially than a two pound private limited company.

Experian produces five basic reports on non-limited companies, which can include the business address, principal activities, number of employees, CCJs, CCLs (consumer credit licenses), bankruptcies, previous searches, credit rating, risk score, payment performance and consumer/directorship information on proprietors.

Payment performance   A3.13

Experian's payment performance data sheds light on how businesses are actually paying their accounts. These reports are built from an independent supply of sales ledgers that show whether accounts are settled on time or the degree of lateness in making payment. A further advantage of these reports is that the average payment term for the industry or sector is noted.

Government legislation has reduced the amount of information smaller businesses need to submit to Companies House. The new audit threshold, which came into force in January 2004, has raised the audit threshold to £5.6m, resulting in a further 69,000 companies being exempted from the requirement to have their accounts audited. Payment performance is now even more vital to assess the strengths and weaknesses of a business and is an integral part of commercial credit referencing today. In the past, commercial credit scoring did rely more on historical financial information but, with the gradual erosion of the thresholds for audits and filing requirements, this is simply not the case now and scoring systems are no longer solely reliant on years of detailed financial accounts. For example, with the introduction of commercial scoring systems such as Experian's Commercial Delphi, additional information sources are used to generate highly accurate and predictive risk scores that are capable of assessing creditworthiness of companies of all different types and size, including newly formed companies, companies without accounts and small companies.

These reports are available for limited and non-limited businesses and information can also include:

- the number and value of accounts placed for collection;
- number of accounts that remain unpaid; and
- a warning if further adverse information is available.

Overseas reports   A3.14

In 2004, Experian launched its new international service – providing financial and credit checking information on over 220 countries worldwide. In total, information on over 35 million companies globally is available online with an enhanced manual credit report service also available.

The new International Credit Report Service is designed to provide a fast and efficient service. All reports come in a standard format, regardless of origin, and have a consistent look and feel in keeping with Experian's UK credit report service. This ensures that information is easy to use and read without any prior knowledge of overseas accounting practices. All international reports can be accessed using Experian's e-series business website at www.uk.experian.com/bi with European company reports and US company reports available online. These countries account for 65% of exports by British companies. Reports for all other countries can be ordered online through Experian's manual report service.

Changing trends   A3.15

Jo Howard, Marketing Director for Experian's Business Information division, in explaining Experian's speed in delivering credit reports, said: 'In the mid 1980s the credit world started to change. Customers were prepared to wait weeks for a report, then it became days, then hours and now information is required straight away.'

For further information on the above services, contact:

Central Sales Manager, Experian, Riverleen House, Lower East Ground, Electric Avenue, Nottingham NG80 1RH. Tel: 0115 941 0888 or visit www.experian.co.uk or www.uk.experian.com/bi to access Experian's e-series business website.

D&B   A3.16

D&B, formerly called Dun & Bradstreet, are leading providers of business to business credit, marketing and supplier information. The firm's history goes back many years: the original development of the business took place in New York, USA, when in 1841, Lewis Tappan realised that he could no longer extend credit to country debtors without independent credit information. The company expanded into Europe and specifically the UK in 1859 when they opened the first mercantile agency in London.

D&B maintain data on over 80 million companies from around the world that is available instantly via the Internet. The rapid technological advances through the Internet and the increasing demands on credit managers to support their business with instantaneous decisions has meant that D&B now serves almost all its customers over the Internet through their service D&B Access for the Internet (DBAI), or through bespoke solutions that integrate D&B data within credit function processes.

A completely new group of decision tools has been developed in the last two years enabling the credit manager to add even greater value to his organisation. The control of risk is advanced and the identification of profitable additional business opportunities makes the credit manager a key executive.

Data collection, verification and quality assurance   A3.17

D&B have calculated that in any '60 working minutes' in the UK:

- 89 business failures will take place;
- 96 new businesses will start up;
- 35 corporate entities will change their name;
- 7 businesses will move address; and
- 3 directors will resign, or be appointed.

In a year, 7% of businesses move, 1% change chief executive and even 3% change their telephone number! Hence maintaining an up-to-date quality database of over 80 million businesses requires significant resources.

Consequently D&B invests over a quarter of a billion dollars in its data collection, verification and quality assurance each year. In order to ensure their customers can make decisions on their data in total confidence, D&B has introduced a process for collecting and enhancing data quality called the DUNSRight™ process, which consists of quality assurance plus 5 quality drivers:

- Global Data collection;

- company Entity Matching;

- the unique D&B D-U-N-S Number™;

- Corporate Family Linkages; and

- Predictive Risk Indicators.

The D&B D-U-N-S Number   A3.18

The D-U-N-S Number is a unique nine-digit sequence identifying a single business entity. This 'birth certificate' is applied as soon as a new business entity becomes verified by D&B and will remain unaltered throughout and beyond the existence of the business. It is the only global identifier and is used as a standard by organisations such as the United Nations, European Commission and US Federal Government.

Through this unique identifier D&B links all company families by parents, subsidiaries, headquarters and branches, providing data on more than 1.6 million corporate families including over 7.6 million company entities.

The D-U-N-S Number means that D&B are able to expose credit risk that might occur through a financially weak group of companies in the same country or overseas. The recent collapses of companies such as Parmalat had repercussions for its subsidiaries that without family linkage would not have been detected. D&B's credit risk indicators react to severe changes in the financial status of parent and subsidiary companies providing an early warning of heightened risk.

Online credit reports and portfolio
risk management   A3.19

For accounts of high value or where high risk is expected and a full synopsis of a business is required, the D&B Comprehensive Report is recommended. This report contains all the information and analysis available from D&B on the concern. It includes the latest publicly filed data; annual accounts, annual return and changes of ownership as well as the D&B Rating and Score which identify the potential risk of business failure.

D&B also collects over 49 million trade references each year and these are aggregated to create the D&B Payment and Delinquency score indicating the likelihood of default on credit. With all their reports there is a recommended maximum credit amount to provide guidance on the amount to be extended on credit on normal terms. This is calculated according to the business's risk assessment, line and size of business.

The D&B Report is for use with ongoing credit customers, containing the same credit indicators for failure and delinquency but without the industry and trend analysis contained in the Comprehensive Report.

The Compact Report is for use with lower value transactions and is a summary of the risk indicators typically providing an overview of the company.

For the sole trader or family business, there is a specific Non Corporate Report that provides risk assessment and insight relative to the organisational and legal structure.

Managing the risk on every account   A3.20

D&B have introduced a new concept for risk management and tracking credit exposure in a single system. Called e-Portfolio, this new service enables the credit manager to see the level of risk across all his accounts in a single view, live and up to date every single day – without having to buy additional reports.

It is recognised that 80% of bad debts come from established customers and not new accounts; being constantly aware of changes in the entire customer base is critical to avoid bad debt. Credit reports taken from D&B can be placed in the e-Portfolio service and the latest information on that company can then be reviewed as often as required for the next 12 months without additional charge, thus removing the need to purchase additional reports. Should any changes occur, subscribers will be notified by email (optional). The service also provides multiple views to track increasing or decreasing risk across all the companies.

New features were introduced in Summer 2004 to add greater flexibility, with new search and risk tools included as part of the service.

Another new service from D&B is Portfolio Manager. This is an online analysis tool which merges customer receivables data with D&B's databases to provide a unique insight into the customer portfolios. It enables better targeting of credit management resources and a clearer, more informed view of which credit policies are most appropriate for a business's circumstances. It helps answer questions such as:

- 'What is the distribution of risk across the portfolio?'

- 'Who are the riskiest, and best, customers?'

- 'What is the aggregated exposure across corporate groups?'

- 'How much loss is likely through commercial risk over the next 12 months?'

County court and High Court judgments A3.21

D&B still publish *Stubbs Gazette*. This is a weekly online publication which prints all judgments that have been issued by the county courts in England and Wales. All this judgment information is automatically included in any D&B report when registered details of a business are supplied. There are separate sections for Scotland and Northern Ireland.

The risk of trading overseas – Country Risk Evaluation A3.22

D&B's Country Risk Services monitors changes in the risk environment of individual countries and forecasts countrywide developments which may have effects in the short to medium term. The suite of products analyses topics such as a country's overall political, economic and commercial performance and answer questions such as:

- 'How can I manage or reduce payment risk?'

- 'What is the financial and overall risk of doing business in a country?'

- 'Am I going to get paid, and if so, when?'

- 'What are the prospects for a country's economy?'

Two different types of country reports are available:

- Country RiskLine Report – this seven-page report provides a concise analysis on the risks of doing business abroad. Data includes a Country Risk Indicator, a guide to payment terms and delays, key economic indicators with forecasts and an overview of the latest developments.

- Country Report – provides critical information and analysis on the trade environment of an individual country. This report offers approximately 60 pages of in-depth political, economic, and commercial data and analysis for evaluating risks and opportunities worldwide.

Consumer information A3.23

D&B provides consumer information products and services through its partner, CallCredit (owned by Skipton Building Society) via the Internet, giving instant access to high-quality data 24 hours a day.

When buying business information from D&B, it is possible to run a credit check against a director's, sole trader's or partner's details. In this case consent must be obtained first from the individual concerned.

Consumer information can be accessed via D&B's DBAI system as part of a normal D&B contract. The products available are:

- CallReport – including the address and postcode, CCJs, details of the number and nature of searches against an individual in the past 12 months, bankruptcies, administration orders and insolvencies, demographic profiling information and CallScore, a Fair Issac® score that ranks consumers according to their relative risk of credit default.

- ShareReport – available to the members of the SHARE closed user group, a forum for people who want to maximise their ability to manage risk by sharing industry experiences. Negative Shared Data reports give public data (as above) plus seriously delinquent account information. Full Shared Data reports provide public data (as above) plus seriously delinquent and positive account information such as balances and payment history.

Corporate Linkages – eWOW   A3.24

Identifying which company is associated with another is becoming more critical as the global economy develops and the impact of corporate failure ripples across continents. D&B is the only company that provides global corporate family trees – also called corporate linkages.

The eWOW product (web product which replaced the old Who Owns Whom book, hence the name) enables you to view the family tree visually and understand the structure of the corporate group being researched. It is possible to evaluate risk across groups, conduct due diligence and know the customers as legislated through *Basel II*, identify new sales opportunities for cross selling within groups and reduce supply costs through improved negotiating when dealing with more than one company in a group.

Cheque fraud   A3.25

D&B also provides information on fighting cheque fraud. Organisations believing they may have been affected by cheque fraud can email fraudinfo@dnb.com or call the Fraud Hotline number on 01494 424000.

Overseas reports   A3.26

Credit reports on individual businesses overseas can be obtained through D&B's worldwide network. They now cover more than 230 countries with information on the financial background of an enterprise and a credit rating. Where it is possible, a maximum credit rating, average days beyond terms and a D&B rating are included. Marketing information is also available.

D&B produce country reports on more than 160 countries which normally cover a four year time span. Their 54 page report on France gives an executive summary on political risk, macroeconomic and external risk, and the commercial risk. It then goes into far more detail to include short and long-term outlooks, technical progress, and investment. The trade overview is particularly useful as it covers EU/USA trade relations, and tariff and non-tariff barriers. The sections highlighting private consumption, unemployment, and population changes, plus the main import/export markets and sectors, give a clear guide on how their economy has changed over the last two years.

The section on commercial risk covers the statistics for quarterly business failures up to the last quarter of 2001, and there is a payment performance commentary and chart which includes 'days beyond terms' and a late payment trend up to the second quarter of 2002. The section on corruption makes interesting reading.

Finally the commercial risk outlook would help any credit personnel new to exporting or to the French market to be able to consider the risk of selling and the terms of sale.

I would still recommend these reports as they give a good independent overview on which credit personnel can easily judge the risk when entering many of the new markets that may open up to UK traders in 2003.

Since their monthly *International Risk and Payment Review* was last reviewed in May 2002, D&B's editors have greatly increased the amount of economic, political and commercial commentaries relating to activities on the 136 countries which are updated monthly and are now available on the web. Their risk pointers on page one give immediate notice of any positive or negative information on a country, for example, 'Venezuela downgraded to DB6a'.

The review covers:

- local currency swings;
- import cover in months;
- FX/bank delays;
- local payment delays;
- usual payment terms; and
- minimum payment terms.

This is available online, in hard copy or on CD-ROM. (See **A11.10** below.)

For further information on any of the above services contact D&B, Holmers Farm Way, High Wycombe, Bucks HP12 4UL; tel: 01494 422000.

Equifax A3.27

Equifax is a major supplier of consumer and commercial credit information. Equifax was founded in the USA in 1899 and purchased the UK credit agencies Infolink and Infocheck in 1994 and 1995 respectively. In the UK Equifax holds 44.5 million consumer credit profiles, full reports on over 2 million limited companies and information on over 2.4 million non-limited companies.

Utilising this extensive data resource, Equifax can offer the following range of products and services to assist businesses reduce risk when granting credit, avoid fraud and enable them to trade profitably.

The following interview with Neil Munroe, Director of External Affairs illustrates how Equifax's systems help their clients.

Commercial credit information   A3.28

Essentially, Equifax is a provider of consumer and business information for the complete customer life cycle. This has always been its primary focus in delivering solutions to its customers. Whether its customer's relationship is with a consumer or with a business, what they look to do is to provide information which allows them (its customers) to identify the people or businesses with whom they wish to do business. Equifax will then assist its customers to assess the risk of doing that business and help manage the relationship once they have taken the customer on board.

Detection of fraud   A3.29

Whilst they maintain and develop all their credit risk management products, one of Equifax's initiatives is the development of fraud risk products for both the consumer and trade credit markets. A large investment has enabled them to develop anti-fraud systems that cover basic fraud, ID theft and money laundering. Equifax are utilising the data and skills that they have developed in credit risk for the assessment, detection and prevention of fraud. These products help protect the lender from dealing with or lending money to people or businesses who are undertaking fraudulent activities, as well as protecting those organisations once they have those relationships. Not only does Equifax provide tools that will stop fraud at the point of application, they also offer fraud prevention monitoring tools and services. An example of a successful monitoring service for the commercial sector is the Equifax Portfolio Monitoring service, which provides a sophisticated and timely monitoring tool for credit risk assessment, as well as fraud detection.

Knowing your customer   A3.30

Companies have a firm obligation to undertake 'reasonable steps' to Know Your Customer (KYC). The latest version of the Joint Money Laundering Steering Group Regulations acknowledges the role that electronic checks now play in this important battle against crime and terrorism. Equifax has a range of generic services, which include generic report services such as FraudScan, IDplus, eIDverifier and Company Essentials along with monitoring tools such as Portfolio Monitor and the Global Regulatory Information Database (GRID) to assist companies. In addition, Equifax has pioneered its Re-verification Service for those companies regulated by the Financial Services Authority (FSA) having to undertake a retrospective exercise to KYC and others wishing to adopt best practice.

A risk manager's responsibility   **A3.31**

The role of the risk manager has changed quite significantly over recent years and will now include a broader range of responsibilities such as data protection compliance. Compliance is a growth area which many organisations treat as a chore, but others treat as an opportunity. The issues of data protection and third party compliance require all lenders and all UK bureaux to work on third party data compliance by 2004.

Third party data   **A3.32**

Under the *Data Protection Act 1998*, data on individuals is supplied to lenders where the data is held on the credit reference agency's database in the same surname as the applicant, or where there is a proven financial association between another individual with a different surname to the applicant. The *Data Protection Act 1998* (*DPA 1998*), which came into force on 24 October 2001 only allows data to be returned where the applicant has the same forename and surname. The changes in *DPA 1998* require significant changes to lending and credit reference agency systems.

Due to the extent of the changes, the Office of the Information Commissioner has accepted that it will take some time for lenders and credit reference agencies to make the necessary amendments and as such has not sought to enforce *DPA 1998* even though it is now in force. It is anticipated that all lenders and credit reference agencies will be compliant with *DPA 1998* by the end of 2004.

The tighter matching requirements that *DPA 1998* requires will reduce the amount of information that the credit reference agencies can supply to lenders and will necessitate the re-calibration of scoring systems as a result.

Statistics on consumers and businesses   **A3.33**

Equifax holds the following records:

- 44 million people;
- 260 million consumer payment records;
- 27 million addresses;
- 11 million CCJs;
- 2 million limited companies; and
- 2.4 million non-limited companies.

65 million searches per annum are undertaken by Equifax's client.

Fraud   A3.34

In today's ever-changing world where regulations and legislation are demanding greater control on both the recruitment of customers and the on-going controls surrounding the relationship, electronic solutions are now leading the way forward for organisations to meet these obligations. Anti-Money Laundering Regulations and the growing threat of sophisticated fraud means that the most alert organisations take the necessary steps to avoid exposure to this type of activity. Equifax offers a range of solutions to help businesses in the fight against fraud, whether it be by an individual or a company.

Use of the web and new developments   A3.35

The development of the web as a service delivery channel has been a key focus of Equifax's product development strategy for some time. Several of their products and services can now be accessed via the web and they continue to add to and enhance this quick and efficient access method.

Quality of data and technical delivery   A3.36

The quality of Equifax's data and the delivery of it to its customers is at an exceptionally advanced level. Their systems are available 99.9% of a 24 hour day. With the new monitoring services it is critical that all the data is passed as quickly as possible to Equifax's clients. A risk manager must be able to check updated information at any time as new data is being added minute by minute 365 days a year. The changing needs of customers allow them to continuously monitor repeat orders so that the risks of 'long firm fraud' are greatly reduced.

Types of products   A3.37

Equifax's products and services include the following.

- Consumer Information Services.

    o   Risk Navigator – a generic score designed to assess the level of risk associated with granting credit. It harnesses the power of Equifax's credit reference database containing over half a billion records to deliver accurate and predictive credit scores.

    o   Decision Navigator – a leading application processing and decisioning system, enabling the processing of immense volumes of data within seconds.

    o   Equifax Explorer – a web-based service that gives instant access to the most comprehensive and up-to-date consumer information to enable immediate lending decisions.

    ○   FraudScan – an online application fraud detection tool that automates the checking of key data provided on credit applications through access to Equifax's extensive consumer information database.

    ○   eIDverifer – pioneering technology that uses 'shared secret' information known only by the consumer and Equifax to provide an accurate online real-time consumer identity authentication service.

●   Commercial Information Services.

    ○   Full Report – provides comprehensive data on companies, including company identification, up to four years of accounting data, directors' details and Gazette and CCJ data.

    ○   Company Essentials – provides the information necessary to establish the legal identity of a subject company, thereby helping businesses towards compliance with money laundering regulations.

    ○   Connections – allows the tracing of connected directors of a subject company, listing the connected companies and highlighting any adverse director records. This helps organisations protect themselves from trading with high-risk individuals and their connected companies.

    ○   Protect – provides a fraud risk score based on researched characteristics on every UK limited company.

    ○   Non-limited Company Reports – Equifax can provide comprehensive data on non-limited companies, including name and business address, trading style, CCJ and Gazette data, employee bands, plus an automated credit limit, grade and score.

    ○   Portfolio Monitoring Service – a powerful and flexible credit monitoring tool, that enables a business to monitor changes to their business customers' financial standing, enabling them to spot the indications of potential business failure before it happens.

International company reports are available via the Internet through Equifax's Global Online (www.globalonline.equifax.com) Their online databases contain more than 10 million commercial credit reports and a global network of offices and locally based affiliates.

Equifax Global Online can quickly provide detailed commercial reports on businesses in more than 200 countries.

Guide to Commercial Risk Management   A3.38

The Equifax *Guide to Commercial Risk Management* is not only a guide on how to read their commercial reports, but it would also particularly help students who are studying for the Institute of Credit Management examinations as there are useful notes on balance sheet analysis and credit limits.

New developments at Equifax A3.39

In a further interview with Neil Munroe in February 2004 I asked what changes were taking place in the commercial and consumer credit reporting fields. He confirmed that major work was being carried out on the capital adequacy ratios under the *Basel II Regulations*, and this will have a substantial impact on many of Equifax's services used by their clients in accessing commercial risk. When these banking assessment rules come into force in 2006 it will mean that sets of accounts will only be analysed in a certain way to reflect the *Basel II* accounting convention. Equifax is at present working on a solution to reflect the new ratios for lending purposes.

Many people in the business community do not yet realise the way in which the accounting information they use to access their customers will change. You will only be able to review data in a certain way. Neil was confident that by the time the *Basel II* guidelines come into force, his company would have new products to offer its clients. He emphasised that *Basel II* will affect the major lending organisations; however, if companies are borrowing, it will equally affect them.

Another change that is taking place is that the credit industry is increasingly moving to online and anti money-laundering services, and Equifax are presently developing a new service which reduces much of the manual processing. This online service will be launched in September 2004.

On the consumer side a new service is being developed to help combat indebtedness. New data will be included called 'Balance and Limits', being a monthly snapshot of the state of that account.

What has been discussed through various government Working Parties is a requirement of not only a snapshot, but a history of an account for lending purposes. For example, is someone continuously spending up to their limit on a credit card, or for various reasons is it in that month when they reached their limit? This information will actually show how indebted a person is. Are they at a particular ceiling or are they using the card as a cash-flow vehicle? A balance of limits is seen as quite a major part of the indebtedness of a consumer. Basically, it is a response to the Government's desire to make sure that not only are you assessing somebody's risks, but also assessing their indebtedness at the time. The balance of limits allows you to see how much of that available credit those people are using.

The outcome of these developments in 'risks and indebtedness' is that Equifax launched a commercial application platform in summer 2004 called Decision, and this technology will be moving to the commercial field where a large number of applications for a small value order are constantly received by a supplier.

Many of Equifax's services have been extended as a response to retail establishments staying open for longer hours.

There is now an instant online access to your personal credit file information. This helps stop fraudulent stealing of your identity.

Findout is a new pay-as-you-go system for accessing commercial data (in many competitor companies, information is obtained via a yearly subscription).

Findout is primarily for the SMEs who previously may not have purchased data, but now find it essential to check their major accounts and new business. If the business just wants to purchase a £10 report, this system is ideal for them as all they require is a credit or debit card to gain information.

Around this data is a considerable amount of information on how to interpret the data for the newcomer to credit assessment.

Overview   A3.40

In reviewing consumer indebtedness, although there have been many features in the national press which report huge indebtedness, Equifax has not seen any larger percentage of defaults.

On the commercial side there is a growth in the amount of monitoring that Equifax customers are carrying out on their sales ledgers.

Clients of Equifax are more aware that consumer and commercial data is now available.

Businesses are also becoming more remote due to the use of e-mail and the Internet for buying and selling. Companies do not now have day-to-day personal contact with their customers.

For further information on Equifax's services on Commercial Credit Information, Tel: 0845 603 3000. Consumer Credit Information – Tel: 0845 600 1772.

ICC Credit Ltd   A3.41

ICC Information Ltd was formed in 1969 and provides business information with corporate financial and credit reports and original document images. ICC has continued to develop a number of sophisticated products so that an objective view on how much credit can be safely granted can be given. ICC is the largest UK subsidiary of the Swedish publishing group Bonnier Business Information Abof Sweden.

ICC's credit reports can be accessed via www.icc-credit.co.uk. ICC splits the market into small, general and specialist.

The ICC Credit Portal is an online system set up to enable the two-way exchange of information within the credit environment. For example, credit news, survey information and online discussion forums allow users to interact.

In an interview in March 2004 Darren Spratt, the Managing Director of ICC Credit, said that what ICC basically did a number of years ago was to create a generic product that served both the credit and general business information marketplaces.

What ICC have done over the last few years is to develop two distinct products for these markets:

- Aquila was launched in February 2003. This completely replaces the Juniper range of reports. Aquila is a unique Internet information system that has been developed specifically with the credit manager in mind, so the layout and prioritisation of information would be of immediate use to credit personnel.

- Delphinus is a very simple Internet-based, budget-priced credit report service. It is ideal for SMEs and budget-conscious customers.

Because of price pressure in the credit information world, ICC has developed top-quality data in an affordable format for companies who are starting to use credit reports for the first time.

Aquila – a closer review   A3.42

Before reviewing ICC's four types of report, I particularly liked their initial 'free of charge' identity information on a company which can include:

- date of incorporation;

- date of last filed accounts, if given;

- name of holding company and its credit score; and

- outstanding mortgages and charges.

This new system gives instant critical information at a glance before the subscriber decides which of the four levels of information they require.

Research has shown that 90% of customers' credit decisions will be made by using one of the four levels of report which contain different degrees of information.

Darren Spratt confirmed that what most ICC clients want first is a credit opinion. When they download the report the first thing they see is the credit limit and score – looking at the score immediately helps inexperienced credit personnel to understand the financial strengths and weaknesses of a company.

One of the developments in the Decision Report is that a headline and comment section is included which gives non-credit professionals a commentary on the activities of the business being searched. Another development is that not only county court judgments, but also High Court writs (now called High Court Claims) are highlighted.

Detailed information   A3.43

In an Aquila report up to ten years of key business ratios can now be shown and within the four types of online report it is possible to obtain details on mortgages and charges. In the section on county court judgments information, these records are available for up to six years.

The Aggregate Risk Report is available on all companies who have subsidiaries. These reports include detailed information on each company within the group including the essential risk score and shareholder and accounts details. The target company and its subsidiaries are listed to show all the credit limits and scores.

The Overview Report is particularly useful as it is approved by Euler Hermes, insurers of debt.

The following notes give just a few of the principal key data items that appear in the Decision Reports. I would emphasise that they are all exceptionally well designed and clear to read.

Decision One Report   A3.44

This report gives the latest risk score and the previous score (provided that the business has been established long enough). Where profits and turnover can be shown (within the modified accounts legislation – please refer to the Credit Risk Analysis chapter under **A2.38**) these profits plus a financial commentary, gearing changes and shareholder funds are highlighted.

Decision Two Report   A3.45

This report gives three years of credit limits, risk scores and county court judgments. Under Company Identification the registered office, previous registered office, issued capital, date of incorporation and (vitally important) trading address are noted. The telephone//fax numbers, bankers, auditors and audit qualification statements, principal activities and SIC codes are included. Under Key Financial Data, three years of turnover (where available), pre-tax profits, current assets and liabilities, cash flow, net worth and working capital are set out. Under Directors Information, the names of the company secretary and all the company directors are listed, and included is a summary of existing directorships and a list of resigned directorships of solvent and insolvent companies including any companies which have winding-up petitions. Cash flow is shown over a four-year period. Under Ratios, a list of the main liquidity, performance, employee and gearing ratios and also comparisons in the sector with the subject company, are shown. There is a separate section covering the ability to pay, with a payment profile which includes DSO's, performance, turnover, gearing and employee ratios.

Decision Three Report A3.46

The Decision Three Report includes the above, plus:

- up to four years of credit score and risk score plus a credit limit and contract limit;
- key financial changes with a commentary;
- county court judgments, plus the total amount of county court judgments outstanding;
- the holding and ultimate holding company details.

Under the Profit and Loss and Balance Sheet section, there are details for up to four years.

Decision Four Report A3.47

The Decision Four Report includes all the above, plus:

- a greatly enhanced section on county court judgments;
- mortgages, plus a summary of any satisfied or partially satisfied mortgages and charges;
- under Profit and Loss and Balance Sheet, five years of data;
- accounting notes including such items as exports, bank overdrafts, and funds due to the directors and the group;
- the Directors section is enhanced by giving previous addresses, total directorships including the current risk score, and a full list of the previous directors of the company.

Within all these services Companies House Documents can be obtained through the ICC Image Bank. New documents are added to this database from Companies House each day.

A new service A3.48

ICC can now deliver a freshly commissioned report within one hour on all limited or non-limited companies in the UK (see also **A3.53** and **A3.54** below).

In the small business market this service allows access to two key reports which include the ICC credit score and a credit limit.

A new service is the Base monitoring system which allows the monitoring of companies against a number of criteria with online alerting of changes. Premium monitoring allows the grouping of customers by users. Both these systems allow users to react more quickly to adverse events and monitor high-risk companies very closely.

Risk scoring model   **A3.49**

ICC's new risk scoring model takes into account the strongest criteria influencing company performance. In building the model, large samples of historic data were extracted from their database to analyse two types of companies:

- those which had become involuntarily insolvent; and

- those which continued to trade.

Some 400 distinct characteristics based on over ten years of financial data were modelled to identify patterns and trends. ICC's research shows that smaller companies (those with a turnover of less than £1 million, and especially those filing modified accounts) exhibited different performance characteristics from larger companies. Ratios were also compared across and within industry sectors and the impact of both county court judgments and audit qualifications assessed.

To show degrees of risk, ICC have developed a scoring system, with 1 being the poorest risk and 100 the least risk. The average risk score of a company is between 47 and 50. Any companies falling below this level will be more likely to go into insolvency within 12 months. As the score drops further towards 1 that risk increases. Conversely, those with a score of 51 or over are less likely to fail and as the score moves towards 100 the risk declines further.

ICC's risk score has been approved by Euler Hermes, who insure commercial debts, and by a number of other trade credit insurers, subject to their individual policy terms.

European reports   **A3.50**

Through their International Report Service, ICC can provide online predictive financial analysis on over 22 million businesses in the following countries:

- Australia;

- Belgium;

- Denmark;

- France;

- Germany;

- Italy;

- the Netherlands;

- Portugal; and

- Spain.

Overseas reports   A3.51

ICC's overseas correspondents are hand picked to provide and compile reliable commercial reports on companies located in over 200 countries and tax havens around the world. Their analysts confirm that as every individual country has different filing requirements, they try to obtain the maximum information that is available. They are also sometimes able to obtain information on unincorporated businesses.

Publications from the ICC Group

Key Note Ltd   A3.52

Part of the ICC Group, Key Note has been providing commercially relevant market intelligence services for over 25 years. They publish 680 reports covering 27 market sectors. Key Note reports are recognised by the Chartered Institute of Marketing.

There are 4 ranges of reports and they cost between £380 and £799 per copy. These reports are being constantly updated and the full range can be viewed on www.keynote.co.uk.

Further information can be obtained from: ICC Group Ltd, Field House, 72 Oldfield Road, Hampton, Middlesex TW12 2HQ. Tel: 020 8481 8800 (020 8481 8750 for Key Notes).

ACS Credit Services Plc   A3.53

ACS has been established since 1978. Its historic business was the provision of credit information to its construction client base. ACS was the first Internet-based commercial credit reference agency, building up a bespoke service for some of its major clients from 1997. In addition, ACS has built an immense database covering both historic credit ratings on limited companies and sole traders operating within the construction industry in the UK. In recent years it has developed a considerable information database on the business characteristics of the building community. This includes such items as which merchants businesses use, what they buy, what their typical expenditure is and what sort of work they undertake. This information has been gained through an extensive use of the ACS traditional database and telemarketing, and the information is proprietary to ACS.

ACS is well established within the community of builders' merchants and has forged a trading relationship with four of the top five merchants in the UK. Collectively these represent some £3.5 billion of turnover which equates to 40% of market share.

Today, ACS leads its market with business details held on over 700,000 trading entities (300,000 corporate, 400,000 non-corporate). This is without doubt the largest database of its kind for the construction sector within the UK.

Background to the market   A3.54

Credit vetting in the construction industry is extremely difficult because of the huge number of sole traders and partnerships that do not need to produce statutory information. Even for those construction businesses that are incorporated, the majority are so small that they are not required to file full accounts at Companies House and with changes to audit requirements, it is likely that they will no longer need to have their accounts audited.

During the 1990s the need to credit vet these businesses grew quickly as the nature of the construction industry changed. This change involved the major construction companies moving away from a position of employing tradesmen to making extensive use of self-employed subcontractors in an effort to reduce fixed costs and improve overall flexibility. This then had the knock-on effect of taking the purchasing of materials away from these larger companies to the much smaller subcontractors. As a result the builders' merchants were suddenly faced with a rapidly growing number of customers, many of whom were making substantial purchases and represented a significant credit risk.

The systems of the major credit vetting agencies were not designed for this market and they found it difficult to gather and accumulate data on subcontractors in order to give them a credit rating. ACS developed methodologies designed specifically for the market and thus became the credit checking agency of choice for the builders' merchants, who themselves were undergoing round after round of acquisitions, mergers and consolidations.

Today, the market seems set to undergo further change in the relationship between subcontractors, main contractors, builders' merchants and even building material manufacturers. Additionally, the impact of e-business can no longer be ignored. The Internet is likely to reshape the way business is done, and credit transactions via the Internet need to be sanctioned instantaneously if the e-commerce opportunity is to be maximised.

ACS is perfectly placed to assist with the provision of specialist in-depth credit marketing and business intelligence extracted from the UK's largest construction database.

ACS Credit Services provides Credit Status Reports specialising in the construction industry and all non-limited companies. Their information is sourced from the largest database of its type in the UK, containing details on over two million sole traders and partnerships, with all requested reports freshly investigated.

The ACS website has just been updated.

ACS Credit Services Plc, ACS House, 191 Chaddock Lane, Boothstown, Worsley, Manchester M28 1DW; www.acs–cs.co.uk.

Check It (UK) Ltd   A3.55

Dr David Kyte, Michael Kyte and Ian Southworth set up Checkit (UK) Ltd in 1994. While they were running other businesses, the idea for Check It grew out of their own needs for fast, inexpensive credit check information. At the time they found that this was difficult, slow or expensive to obtain. They wanted to be able to pick up the phone, order a report and receive it instantly.

Dr Kyte then set about designing the sophisticated software needed to make this possible, and Check It's automated credit check system emerged. The first reports were delivered so fast that callers using a combined phone/fax machine didn't even have time to put the phone down before the system tried to deliver their report.

From that point Check It has not looked back and now has a website capable of delivering a wide variety of reports and services.

Businesses with enquiries for low value but high volume will find this a most useful service with very competitive prices.

Check It has detailed information on thousands of businesses that can be accessed in a variety of ways, including on the web. For businesses that require just a single report there is a pay-as-you-go service, and a snapshot report costs £4.95.

Check It (UK) Ltd., 3rd Floor, Bridge House, Station Road, Westbury, Wiltshire BA13 4HR. Tel: 08701 525 455; 08701 525 456; sales@checkit.co.uk; www.checkit.co.uk.

Scorex (UK) Ltd   A3.56

Scorex will develop and build credit scoring systems for companies who have exceptionally large sales ledgers. Their strategic performance indicators provide information for marketing, credit and risk management staff to highlight delinquency rates and many other performance indicators. These specialist systems can easily take four to five months to build. For organisations with a large turnover, Scorex systems can help profitability.

In their training seminars they cover the impact of the new Basel II Accord on credit scorecards and new third-party data regulations.

Further information can be obtained from: Scorex (UK) Ltd, Scorex House, 1 Commercial Street, Foster Square, Bradford BD1 4AS. Tel: 01438 744 300.

Graydon UK Ltd   A3.57

Graydon's name was established in 1940 when they started to develop specialist reports for credit insurers. They are still building bespoke credit assessment systems for a number of multinational companies who have special needs. The Graydon Group has a different background from the other information providers as they are owned by three major credit insurance companies, Coface, Atradius (formerly Gerling NCM) and Euler Hermes. In addition to the aforementioned, their reports are approved by many other major credit insurers worldwide.

Four levels of report   A3.58

Graydon produce four levels of credit reports. Level One includes basic information on the limited company including:

- date of incorporation;

- the date when annual accounts were filed at Companies House; and

- the all important risk category.

In a Level Two report, the amount of credit is analysed and if there is a 'yes' decision, a credit rating and monthly credit guide is added. A guide to Graydon's credit ratings is available through their website at www.graydon.co.uk.

A Level Three report contains:

- Graydon credit rating and monthly credit guide;

- the history of the company;

- details of the most recent documents filed;

- full details of directors and their addresses and details of other directorships and associate directorships;

- any County Court judgment data; and

- accounting analysis covering four years' trading and ratios.

What is different, however, is that Graydon does not rely solely on officially registered data, and now collects debt placement data from debt collection agencies plus trade payment data from donors, revealing how companies are paying trade suppliers. Also included in the final section of the report is a financial summary, which highlights any changes in:

- turnover;

- operating profit;

- pre-tax profit;

- net worth;

- working capital;
- fixed assets; and
- long-term liabilities.

This summary would save any credit controller or manager much valuable time.

In a Level Four report, Graydon offer the facility of a fresh investigation, incorporating an interview with the subject company. Their investigated report is delivered to match the speed of service required.

Directors report   A3.59

Since the author of this chapter reviewed Graydon's credit reports in May 2002 they have now introduced a Directors Report. This database covers up-to-date information on over 5.3 million director/company officer appointments within UK registered companies.

Every report provides the Graydon Credit Risk category, it details what level of risk is associated with each active company and the risk score of associated companies where the director or company secretary is currently appointed can be highlighted.

The total number of resignations that have occurred in the directors/company officers past is also available.

Since December 2003 the Directors Report also includes information on disqualified directors.

This Directors Report is particularly useful for credit personnel when a company record cannot provide a track record of the subject company (for instance when a company has been recently established).

Other services   A3.60

Graydon have developed a management portfolio tool called Creditscan Analysis, which analyses a business's complete sales ledgers with a report which identifies, at a glance, areas of risk and opportunities for selling. Under each scanned name on any limited company a summary is produced covering:

- credit ratings;
- monthly credit guide;
- net worth;
- accounts date; and
- registration number.

Creditscan has now been surpassed by the more dynamic ePatrol, its Internet version. Credit data which includes the latest credit ratings is passed back to the end user via an Internet connection to a bespoke database fully maintained by Graydon. Through this system a customer can instantly access this database containing both Graydon credit data and its own sales ledger records daily in order to determine the up-to-date risk which any account poses. The reports can be delivered online or on CD-ROM.

Graydon's CreditWatch risk monitoring service alerts credit controllers and accounts staff to any critical events that could affect a business. For example, new accounts filed at Companies House, county court judgments, Receiver appointed or resignation of a director.

In 2001, Graydon UK launched a scoring product aimed at the finance, insurance and utility sector, in partnership with Fair Isaac (the credit scoring specialist). The product suite is marketed under the name Augur. The scoring system saves time for commercial credit granters and insurers as the effort of compiling and assessing data from multiple sources is no longer required. The Augur monitoring service system uses changes in the score as the main parameter to enable credit personnel to get a more balanced view of the impact of events on the risk profile of the organisation that is being assessed.

These reports and Augur scores include a commentary and provide the probability of default odds in every company report.

Graydon also runs closed user groups for the telecommunications, computer and petroleum distribution sectors. Graydon's subsidiary, Status Credit Reports Ltd in Cardiff, also uses Graydon technology and expertise to run closed user groups for the timber and steel sectors. A number of credit circles also meet on a regular basis, and membership is by agreement within the groups.

Xsellence is a new auto-decisioning software solution that provides businesses with information on the creditworthiness of any commercial enterprise that wishes to do business with them.

New in 2004 is Xseption, a unique package of information designed to list companies that have exceptional characteristics worthy of closer examination by fraud prevention managers or credit risk personnel.

Overseas reports   A3.61

Graydon can supply online reports for most European countries; they can also obtain reports from Canada, Japan, the Middle East and Africa via this system. They also have a facility for automatically ordering an updated report. Reports from over 150 countries can also be obtained. All their reports are endorsed by all the leading credit insurance companies.

Company Watch

Company Watch was formed in 1998 to evaluate companies' financial health. They can actually predict whether a company will fail within a predicted timescale if no management changes are made to the structure of the business.

Their Technical Director, Malcolm Hiscock, invented the 'H' score some years ago. It is based on the 'Z' score method but it has a number of significant technical advantages over it, as the model can highlight many features apart from companies in danger of financial distress.

Originally this company only analysed public limited companies. When interviewing Guenter Steinitz, their Managing Director, he confirmed that they can now not only check private limited companies but they can also include those who file modified or abbreviated accounts. The only sector in the UK they do not cover is financial services.

There is online access to virtually all the 1.2 million UK limited companies where, through their model, they can produce health profiles.

Company Watch now provide a truly global service.

For the UK, their database of 1.2 million companies covers virtually every single company including those with abbreviated accounts. They now have models purpose built for all other countries across the world and a database of the majority of US listed companies plus all other listed companies on Standard & Poor's international database. The only companies not covered are those in the financial sector such as banks, insurance and investment companies.

The company data is held on their secure file server and is available online via the Internet. The system that manages and presents the data is available either as a locally installed system using Windows or on browser via the Internet. This makes it possible for anyone anywhere in the world to gain immediate online access to the in-depth health profile of any company in the world together with the full functionality of the Company Watch system. All they need is a password.

The system now falls into two categories:

- UK+ with access to all 1.2 million public and private UK companies;

- global, covering listed companies from all countries in the world.

Both provide an extremely reliable measure on any company's financial health and its trend over time. Both include a graphical interface unique to Company Watch that has been designed to take the user through a series of screens to provide a detailed explanation and evaluation of any company's strengths and weaknesses. The browser system includes a 'Diagnostic Walk Through' with an online step-by-step interpretation guide of what to look out for as the user progresses through each screen.

The UK+ database now contains a wealth of supporting data, including county court judgments, history and warning flags for late accounts filing, qualified audit reports, post-balance sheet events and contingent liabilities. New for 2004 are credit limits, common directorships, charge register, shareholders and company advisers.

The Global system displays the information of any company in its local currency or, at the choice of the user, in any of $US, £Sterling or Euros. A data search is possible across the complete international database.

Another new development lies in the application of the Company Watch system. Most companies find that typically around 80% of their sales come from around 20% of their customers. This distribution permits the use of statistical techniques to enable companies to focus scarce credit management resources on areas that require most attention. Companies with a combination of low exposure and good financial strength require the least attention and vice versa. Company Watch have developed a technique where companies with a normal distribution of customers can cover 69% of their risk by focusing on only 5% of their customers. Ranking customers by sales (or exposure) and using the data search facility to rank them by financial strength enables the user to identify those with the combination of high exposure and high risk. The portfolio management system provides the means of a structured, regular and comprehensive monitoring of the customer base. The diagnostic power of the system helps the user to understand the nature of the risk of each high-risk/high-exposure company, providing the necessary information to help them make the best possible business decision in each case.

This technique has also been successfully applied for purposes of supply chain management. Losing a key supplier without warning can be just as damaging as losing a key customer.

Company Watch's policy continues to be the provision of a highly reliable, immediate and readily understood in-depth measure and understanding of any company's financial health. It achieves this with the combination of powerful purpose-built mathematical models with a carefully designed graphical presentation that imparts the complex information in a structured yet simple way in order to achieve the maximum understanding of any company's finances in the shortest possible time.

Further information can be obtained from: Company Watch Limited, 308 Coppergate House, 16 Brune Street, London, E1 7NI. Tel: 020 7721 8460.

Creditsafe.com   A3.63

Creditsafe is one of the newcomers in the credit information industry in the UK. Creditsafe.com is a Scandinavian-owned Internet business and consumer credit information provider. They were established in London in 2000, and in 2002 moved to Caerphilly as they gained a Welsh Assembly Grant. They now employ 123 staff, and have over 11,000 clients.

Their database covers over 4 million businesses and 44 million consumers. Because the entire system is delivered by email their least-expensive reports only cost approximately £5.00. This is one of the most reasonably priced credit reports the author has come across in the UK.

The author reviewed an operating limited company and in seconds had three years' accounts details, and key ratios, before viewing under ratings to see that the company had a credit limit of £20,000 and were rated at 75 (very good creditworthiness). This report also showed how the rating had changed over the last four years. In addition there was an explanation on how the rating system worked.

Within the Limited Company search, county court judgments and group structures can be researched. A full listing of directorships is also available.

Under the Non-limited Company search, credit limits, ratings, county court judgments, full proprietor names and address details are available.

In May 2004 a new service was launched where customers of Creditsafe can input their own criteria in order to evaluate their customers in their sales ledger.

Further information can be obtained from Creditsafe.com via email: ukinfo@creditsafe.com. Their address is: Bryn House, Caerphilly Business Park, Caerphilly CF83 3GG, South Wales. Tel: 0292 0886500. Website: www.creditsafeuk.com.

Credit bureaux worldwide   A3.64

It is estimated that there may be about 40 reputable credit bureaux established throughout the world. In some countries one bureau is the sole source of information. In other countries credit bureaux such as D&B (see **A3.16–A3.26** above), Equifax (see **A3.27–A3.40** above), Experian (see **A3.5–A3.15** above), ICC Credit (see **A3.41–A3.52** above) and Graydon (see **A3.57–A3.61** above) have either branch offices or liaise with other specialised agencies overseas.

Burgel   A3.65

To illustrate the benefits of using a country-based credit information agency, the chapter's author interviewed Burgel, the German agency which was founded in 1885 in Berlin. Burgel now employs 1,000 staff who operate from 60 offices in Germany.

They have information on more than 3 million companies and on more than 12.5 million private individuals stored at their head office in Hamburg.

In addition to standard reports, Burgel can report on:

- bankers' details;

- business relationships and credit recommendations;

- solvency ratings;

- financial information on managers and shareholders; and

- consumer information.

As they have such a large network of offices in Germany they can also report on any debt collection actions by their staff.

Further information can be obtained from: Burgel Wirtschaftsinformationen GmbH & Co, KG Gasstrabe 18, 22761 Hamburg, Germany. Tel: 0049 40898 03000.

CMR Insurance Services   A3.66

CMR Insurance Services can provide an opinion of credit worthiness on businesses in the UK and on 177 overseas countries. The price of a limited company status report is £15.00, a non-limited company report is £35.50, and an overseas report costs from £55.00 upwards, depending on location and the difficulties of obtaining the information.

For further information contact: CMR Insurance Services Limited, Central House, 3–4 Chalice Close, Wallington, Surrey SM6 9RU. Tel: 0208 835 2567.

Data Protection Act 1998   A3.67

In the credit industry, there still seems to be some confusion on the requirement under the *Data Protection Act 1998* that businesses who wish to obtain credit information from credit information bureaux or banks, must first obtain prior consent from the businesses they are thinking of trading with. It is particularly important that all the reasons for requiring the information are clearly noted on the new business form. For example, if a tracing agency might need to be employed to search for an individual or sole trader, or a partner in a partnership, the added words 'for tracing' must be included on the request form to authorise that consent has been given. Searches may have to be made on directors of limited companies and although the limited company financial data is 'public information', the search on how a director pays their domestic bills at their home address is personal information, therefore a consent must be first obtained.

Companies House   A3.68

The two main functions of Companies House, which is the official Registry of limited companies in England, Scotland and Wales, are:

- registration, which includes the incorporating and striking off of companies and the registration of documents required to be delivered under company, insolvency and other legislation; and

- to make available to the public their database of nearly five million live and dissolved limited companies.

Online information   A3.69

Over the last few years there has been a dramatic change in the way Companies House services are delivered. In the past, everyone relied on microfiche copies of accounts and documents which sometimes were of rather poor definition. Now the emphasis is centred on electronic methods of receiving, holding and disseminating company information.

Companies House provides electronic access to its database through two web-based services: Companies House Direct which serves customers paying a regular subscription, and WebCHeck which serves customers who use their services less frequently.

There are also facilities to view online companies' accounts, Annual Returns and the Mortgage Index and charge details. These vital documents are often the only way to prove who actually owns the assets of a company. This intelligence is especially useful when it appears that a company may be running into difficulties. If a debenture holder has a fixed charge or charges on the assets of a limited company, provided the debenture is registered within the time specified by the *Companies Act 1985*, in the event of an insolvency he has a prior claim against all other preferential claimants. The Company Directors Disqualification Index is also available online, and is free of charge to users.

For businesses who may still not have the facilities to receive online information, Companies House at Cardiff can still post or fax any of their products or services.

New developments   A3.70

Companies House has already introduced electronic filing for some of their documents and web filing for Forms 287 and 288a, b, and c, which are recent changes of the registered office and directors. The Electronic Shuttle was introduced at the end of 2003. Through authentication codes it will also become far more difficult for fraud to be committed by placing false information on a company record.

The electronic incorporation of companies was launched in October 2001. There is now a brand new CD-ROM Companies House Directory containing 1.4 million limited companies on the live register, the cost is £30.00. There is also a CD-ROM on Change of Name and Dissolved Companies Index which costs £30.00.

There are now plans to replace their core mainframe computer system which is more than fifteen years old, the project started in 2002 and will probably not complete until 2006.

Companies House publications   A3.71

Their booklet, *Company Directors and Secretaries*, explains the responsibilities of directors and company secretaries in filing accounts and other documents. The booklet also outlines the main differences between a private and public limited company and refers to the various sections of the *Companies Act 1985* and other Acts that relate to directors' and secretaries' duties.

Companies House publishes a set of 16 guidance booklets (three of which have Scottish equivalents) that are available through the Companies House website and can be obtained in hard copy form. Their titles: Company Names, Company Formation, Accounts and Accounting Reference Dates, Annual Returns, and Auditors Returns will be particularly useful for credit personnel staff.

These publications can be obtained free of charge by calling their contact centre or faxing 029 2038 0517 or writing to their head office in Cardiff.

Companies House has an office at: 21 Bloomsbury Street, London WC1B 3XD. Their Head Office is at: Crown Way, Cardiff CF14 3UZ. The national telephone number for all enquiries is: 0870 333 3636.

There is a Registry for limited companies registered in Scotland, which is located at: 37 Castle Terrace, Edinburgh. There is a further Registration Office for limited companies registered in Northern Ireland which is at: Registry of Companies, IDB House, 64 Chichester Street, Belfast BT1 4JX. Tel: 029 9023 4488.

Credit circles and industry groups   A3.72

These groups are normally formed by senior credit personnel in certain sectors of commerce and industry who wish to exchange information on a strictly confidential basis.

Having been a member of an international group for a number of years the author of this chapter can confirm how valuable these meetings are in supporting credit decisions for any amount. Discussions at these groups can also cover technical matters including:

- legislation;

- banking; and

- new methods of marketing and distribution.

It must be emphasised that membership of these groups is by invitation which is normally based on the experience and the reputation of the individual candidate. There is little or no publicity on how to find these groups; however, often interested members of trade associations or high profile credit managers sometimes create groups to exchange ideas, especially when wrongful trading or fraud suddenly occurs in a sector of trade.

The *Competition Act 1998* came into force on 1 March 2000. There are heavy penalties of up to 10% of a company's turnover if any anti-competitive behaviour occurs at credit circle meetings and attendees should approach these meetings with caution and should seek to have the meetings minuted.

The Office of Fair Trading has issued several booklets on the *Competition Act 1998* including: *The Major Provisions* (OFT 400), *The Chapter I Prohibition* (OFT 401) and *The Chapter II Prohibition* (OFT 402).

I would recommend that readers obtain the above publications, (free of charge) from the Office of Fair Trading, Field House, 15–25, Bream's Buildings, London, EC4A 1PR. Competition Act enquiries, telephone: 020 7211 8989.

Under the Institute of Credit Management's umbrella, three Special Interest Groups meet on a regular basis. These groups are not credit circles. If credit circles or special interest groups do meet and if they do discuss relevant data, they should comply with the *Data Protection Act 1998*. Minutes should *not* be sketchy and should demonstrate that nothing likely to offend against the Act was discussed. The OFT also pointed out that the exchange of information on sensitive matters such as pricing data, the amount of credit offered or the terms on which it is offered or any element of pricing policy is forbidden.

The three special interest groups are:

● Petroleum Group;

● Secured Lending Group; and

● Building and Allied Trades Group.

Further information can be obtained from: Institute of Credit Management, The Water Mill, Station Road, South Luffenham, Oakham, Leicestershire LE15 8NB. Tel: 01780 722900.

Information on credit management and training   A3.73

The Institute of Credit Management is the largest professional credit management organisation in Europe. Its 9,000 members hold important credit related appointments throughout industry and commerce. Many of its members grant credit on a secured and unsecured basis.

During the year 2003 the Institute responded to 16 Government consultation exercises and, through its membership of national working parties and the Government's Better Payment Practice Group it continued to play a full role in public life.

Members and students of the Institute can use their special 'bulletin board' on the Institute's website. This is currently being used by over 18% of the membership.

Its membership has skills and knowledge in every area of credit assessment, collection and insolvency, on domestic and overseas markets.

Over 100 seminars are run by the training department each year on all credit management subjects, and the Education Department supervise the 2000 students who are studying for their professional qualifications.

Their staff bureau is available to all students and members, and the Institute's monthly journal *Credit Management Magazine* features leading articles on every sector of commercial, financial and retail credit.

For further information: Institute of Credit Management, The Water Mill, Station Road, South Luffenham, Oakham, Leicestershire, LE15 8NB. ICM Website: www.icm.org.uk. Tel: 01780 722900.

Customer visits   A3.74

There is no better way in gaining information on a customer than to pay a personal visit. However, often due to the pressures of trade, fewer visits are now made than was the case some years ago. This problem may be due to staff reductions and increasing technology. Some credit personnel seem to think that a visit is only necessary when payments are greatly delayed or when it comes to their notice that there are massive accounting problems. If a visit is made when there is a crisis, it may be too late to rescue the situation. Although many businesses rely on their suppliers and live off their credit, an actual personal visit should not be considered as a negative action. It is the author's belief that visits to customers are part of the professional routine of credit managers and controllers. Often when a company has many bad debts, credit controllers are overruled by marketing decisions and are left to deal with any problems. This is not a partnership that will increase profitable sales.

By firstly developing good relationships with the sales and marketing departments, the normal conflict between sales and the credit department can disappear. Joint visits with the sales representative are a helpful way of enhancing sales. Sometimes the technical requirements of the customer need the two strands of sales and finance to support the sale and improve the business relationship. Visits can be structured to increase credit limits or credit terms where increased sales are being negotiated. Sometimes a visit can be made just to create a better working relationship between the staff of buyers and sellers. When initially visiting a customer, the objective is to understand more of the customer's business, so that profitable future business can be maintained. Coming away with a further order can be another bonus!

The call reports of the sales force contain information that can help to prepare for the visit. This is all part of the pre-planning that is necessary for a successful visit. Before calling on a customer it is also advisable to re-examine the past sales records to see if sales are constant, rising or falling and finally check to see if any credit notes or other sales queries have been resolved.

When entering the premises of a customer an immediate impression is gained. The attitude of the receptionist or switchboard operator can often reflect the way the entire business is being run. It is worthwhile observing the state of the premises and the condition of the vehicles. If products are stored, it is useful to see the warehouse, as this often gives a better picture of the business. With shorter lunch breaks it is perhaps a little more difficult to take the purchasing manager or bought ledger staff out to lunch. It is, however, useful to offer lunch, as often accounts staff do not get these opportunities to talk to their suppliers. An occasional comment by suppliers can completely alter what was previously a fixed view of a customer. For instance, it may be discovered on visits, that sales could easily be increased as customers were only ordering when a competitor failed to deliver, staff overtime was being cut, or a large expansion of a business was being planned.

Incidentally, businesses in the UK can still be reticent about releasing current financial information, but if a question is framed, 'May I ask you what your monthly sales are?', a positive reply will normally be received.

Improving credit management A3.75

There have been developments within the last four years which may help industry and commerce, not only to improve their credit management skills but also to increase payments and cashflow throughout the UK, and details of the Better Payment Practice Group are noted at **A3.76–A3.77** below.

The Better Payment Practice Group A3.76

The Better Payment Practice Group (BPPG) was formed in 1997 by the Labour administration to create a partnership between the public and private sectors. Its aim is to improve the payment culture of the UK business community and reduce the incidence of the late payment of commercial debt. Barbara Roche, who was the Minister for Small Businesses, was the driving force changing the traditional slow payment pattern.

In October 1997, the BPPG launched their new *Better Payment Practice Code* to enable companies to identify themselves as prompt payers. They also issued a new *Guide to Credit Management*. This is a 37-page guide which includes a highly useful wall chart which illustrates how to plan a credit management programme to minimise late payment. With this pack are two other booklets, *Factoring and Discounting* and *Credit Insurance*. Copies of this pack, reference URN00/1308, can be obtained free of charge by telephoning 0870 1502500.

The BPPG launched in September 2001 a Credit Application Form on its Internet site www.payontime.co.uk as part of its ongoing campaign to help small businesses to protect themselves against incidents of late payment.

This form records information on the customer's identity and ability to pay. It also sets out, on the reverse, the supplier's trading terms. By signing the completed form, the customer provides the information, and agrees the terms.

In April 2002 they created on their website notes to help businesses on a range of prompt payment and credit management related issues which include:

- credit vetting methods;

- risk reduction procedures;

- setting credit limits;

- effective collection techniques; and

- the *Late Payment of Commercial Debts (Interest) Act 1998.*

In December 2002 the BPPG launched an extensive new glossary of credit management terms for UK business owners and managers, available at: www.payontime.co.uk.

Payment performance tables   A3.77

In April 2004, a further edition of the *Private Sector Payment Performance Tables* was published showing the payment performance of public limited companies and their subsidiaries. Copies of this most interesting survey can be viewed on their website.

Information is available on BPPG's website at: www.payontime.co.uk.

Trade press   A3.78

It is a sad fact of life that in some businesses the *Financial Times* or other key national newspapers or trade magazines are not seen by the credit department until days or weeks after reported events.

PIMS UK Ltd, the media directory publisher, confirm that there are 115 daily and regional newspapers, 1,073 weekly newspapers, and an amazing 5,974 technical and trade magazines in their directory. PIMs, in their guide, actually list every publication that is published in the UK under subject and publication index with addresses and editors' names. There is now an enhanced online version of this Directory.

Credit managers and controllers must keep up-to-date with every piece of business intelligence which helps them to monitor current activity in their sector. This guide will help any business manager to review every technical publication.

The author emphasises the need to constantly read publications, and to retain a budget for them, as when a downturn in trade occurs, the first action management often take is to completely cut the money spent on publications.

Further information on PIMS can be obtained from: Mildmay Avenue, London N1 4RS. Tel: 020 72261000.

Also recommended is a cutting service Romeike & Curtice, who employ 160 readers, who scan and read 4,000 weekly and national publications, and who also scan 2,000 technical publications and newspapers using key words to identify news items. They are now scanning websites and the Internet for additional information which their clients require. Tel: 0800 289543.

Conclusion

A3.79

Credit managers and controllers and their staff spend a high percentage of their time on collection activity. This was the conclusion of Professor Nicholas Wilson (who holds the ICM Chair of Credit Management at Leeds University Business School), when he surveyed a number of SMEs to assess how much time was spent on various credit management tasks. If more time is spent on assessing the risk by gathering credit intelligence information, the task of collecting debts becomes easier, and the constant anxiety of wondering if one is going to be paid is greatly reduced.

Mike Barry (a well known consultant with many years' experience in the legal profession and a lecturer for the Institute of Credit Management) was asked his thoughts on UK credit management in 2003 during a recent interview. He said:

> 'It's only when the economy is in decline when a business suddenly realises that they have not been paid. Companies seem to take the view that if they purchase the best telephone and marketing system with a superb computer system, this will solve their credit and collection problems.
>
> However, they often completely forget that staff have to be trained, and importantly they also forget to consider that the quality of the debt impacts on their collections. You cannot collect bad debts!'

The author of this chapter believes that these two concise statements highlight what has to be carried out to create profitable sales.

Since 2003 it has been confirmed that businesses are not paying their creditors any faster. It is reported that it takes a plc 46 days to pay their suppliers, this being the average over a 4-year period.

The Better Payment Practice Group reported in February 2004 that 63% of businesses never checked the creditworthiness of new customers.

A4

Credit Assessment and its Uses

Introduction

When asked what he does for a living, the likelihood is that a credit manager will say, 'I am a credit manager'. It is equally likely that the questioner has no idea what a credit manager is and will like as not respond with a knowing look, 'Oh, you're a debt collector'. Those with the barest of knowledge are just as likely to say, 'you're the one who is always stopping orders'. In spite of what may be seen as a grain of truth on both counts, the reality is wrong on both counts. Collecting money owed forms part of the duties of many credit management functions, and assessing credit risk is undoubtedly the cornerstone of the role, but 'always stopping orders'? Absolutely not.

Credit management is at the heart of any effective marketing operation, finding ways of accepting every *profitable* order so as to increase sales and profitability. It is also at the heart of asset management, protecting the seller's investment in receivables, and managing that asset in order to achieve the best possible return. There will always be customers who either cannot or will not pay, just as there will always be unexpected failure. During a recession, pressures on cash for both buyer and seller become acute, and hitherto satisfactory accounts become problematical. Outside influences can lead to results that could not have been predicted – floods and the foot and mouth outbreaks of 2001 inflicted immense damage on rural and tourist economies in the UK, the tragedy of September 11, 2001, the ensuing terrorist threat and the fallout from the bursting of the dotcom bubble of the late 1990s instilled uncertainty in the minds of investors which remains today.

Nonetheless, as far as it is possible to predict, it is the role of the credit manager to assess all potential customers for risk, and set terms and conditions which are commensurate with that risk. To only accept the alleged cast iron certainties, to only accept terms of cash up front, would quickly lead to a dramatic fall in sales, and hence income. Every order has potential merit, and to judge that merit is risk assessment. Not everyone is worthy of credit, and of those that are, not all are worthy of large amounts of credit.

The credit manager is just as eager for the new customer as the salesman. The only difference, perhaps, is that the credit manager would like a modicum of reassurance that the new customer will be of profitable benefit to both himself and the salesman.

Why assess customers for credit worthiness? A4.2

There are great benefits in allowing customers time to pay, but the facility carries cost and risks (see **A2 CREDIT RISK ANALYSIS**). Credit terms promote more sales than 'cash only' terms would allow and sellers are able to compete creatively with credit offers and promotions. The downside is the risk of not being paid for the wealth transferred to customers, either on time or not at all. Meanwhile, until customers pay, the interest on the funds borrowed by the seller severely depletes the net profit margin.

Since it is common practice to allow all customers time to pay, with the exception perhaps of a small minority of really bad risks where facilities would not be granted at all, the seller is faced with a range of customer attitudes to paying, as well as a similarly wide, but quite different, range of customers abilities to pay. This is the well-known dilemma of 'can't pay – won't pay'. The same costs and losses are incurred by the credit grantor with both types of debtor, but the collection remedies are different in each case. It is important, therefore, that both types of debtor are identified.

In essence, this requires the same level of expertise being applied to managing the credit granting process as is applied by most companies to the selling function. Expertise also means resource, and to expend large budgets on sales and marketing without adequately matching the resources available to credit management would simply be throwing good money after bad. The granting of trade credit facilitates sales, but credit sales are pointless without due payment – therefore the sales and credit functions have to work closely together. The joint aim is 'maximum profitable sales unpaid over the shortest possible time with the minimum of bad debt'.

While the credit manager's duty is to look for ways of accepting every order, really confident companies are happy to reject those orders for which payment may be difficult to collect. This avoids a situation where such orders reduce the profits derived from all the sound business. Some credit managers will say 'let the competition have the bad sales – the losses will damage their competitiveness'.

High risk sales   A4.3

Marginal, or 'high-risk' sales are a different matter. Some companies accept that a number of customers are bound to fail (failure means loss of identity, which would include being merged or taken over, as well as actual insolvency) but that profitable sales can be made to such customers before they lose their identity or become insolvent. The credit management skill is in giving these accounts special attention, closely controlling levels of sales so that exposure is gradually reduced and funds are collected in good time. If the credit assessment is correct, the customers identified as 'high-risk' will fail within a matter of months. For the most part, therefore, emphasis in this chapter is on seeking a strategy for managing marginal risk customers.

Positive risk assessment   A4.4

Too many companies accept every possible order, and indeed chase after every possible order, regardless of potential risk. Under the influence of the great god 'turnover' and his number two 'sales commission', every order is taken on standard credit terms and no awareness or consideration is given to the financial standing of the customers, how they pay other suppliers or indeed anything at all to do with their solvency or otherwise. It is worth repeating that credit management is not out to stop sales – on the contrary, well-organised risk assessment is totally positive, i.e. the purpose is to:

- direct sales resources towards customers worth cultivating;

- advise sales staff on the maximum volumes possible within the credit terms;

- identify customers between categories of low, average and high risk; and

- assist in day-to-day actions regarding customer problem situations.

Approaches to credit ratings

Terminology   A4.5

Terminology varies in different organisations. 'Credit limit' is the most widely used expression, but it sounds restrictive, especially to sales staff and customers. The fact that credit limit sounds restrictive is one reason why some companies do not use them, just as the concept of credit control is mistrusted by some commercial people. The term credit management sounds more constructive, and is used widely by the more progressive companies who see 'credit rating' or 'credit line' as being more appropriate. Credit ratings and credit lines are terms which can be used by sales staff directly to increase business, so clearly have a more positive ring to them.

The informal approach to credit ratings   A4.6

Not all companies adopt specific credit ratings for customers. They operate quite happily without quantifying values, by running checks on customers, deciding whether they are a good or bad credit risk, then allowing credit accordingly. This is often the approach when credit is given to the sales area and it is usually carried out only when an account is opened. The weaknesses in this informal approach are:

- subjective decision making occurs, with little or no consistency or explanation;

- little record is kept for use in problem situations;

- subsequent changes in customers' fortunes are not tracked;

- there is often no strong belief in the credit decision, when subsequent disagreements arise; and

- junior staff remain untrained in company credit decision-making.

Advantages of formal credit ratings A4.7

The benefits of calculating and recording credit ratings are:

- decisions to allow time to pay are quantified and based upon information;

- the decision-making process can be operated consistently and can be explained;

- the credit data examined can be condensed into a credit figure;

- there is little need to keep re-examining paperwork;

- credit ratings are easily shown and automated on computer files, e.g. sales ledger, order processing systems, customer lists, etc;

- staff tend to respect the credit ratings and can operate them with confidence; and

- credit ratings are easily justified to customers and can help in negotiations.

How is a credit rating calculated? A4.8

There is no standard agreed method for calculating a credit rating in commercial credit and any gathering of credit managers or credit analysts will produce different views on the most useful criteria. Opinion also differs on whether a rating should just support present levels of sales or whether it should be a maximum per customer, regardless of present sales. More experienced credit staff take the maximum view, exemplified by the question 'how much are we happy to be owed by this customer?' To arrive at an answer to this question, a seller can:

- purchase a recommendation from a credit agency (see **A4.9** below);

- obtain a credit limit decision from a credit insurer (see **A4.10** below); or

- make his own calculations, by a well trusted method which can be easily explained to colleagues (see **A4.11** below).

Recommended credit ratings from credit agencies, via purchased reports A4.9

Reports purchased from credit agencies have considerable merit in saving time by trusting the recognised expertise of the agency. Indeed, some busy people barely read the pages of financial results, trading data and corporate information (all included in the total report charge), going instead straight to the stated credit rating and entering that rating into their own system. For companies that take the credit rating of an agency, it is important to understand how the rating has been calculated. The agency may not be willing to explain in detail the methods used to arrive at their conclusions, but it can be assumed that the rating is a composite opinion derived from all sources open to the agency, and in particular the last three years of balance sheet data. However, the credit manager should know whether the agency's figure is a 'maximum exposure' or 'a monthly sales amount'. If the printed or online report does not show the basis for the recommendation, at the very least, the credit manager should be sure to ask (see **A3.2–A3.61** above).

A credit limit from a credit insurance company A4.10

There can be no doubt that this is a useful guide to the credit manager, since it is derived from the insurer's vast database, using all the same sources that the credit manager could approach, plus any topical experience of claims or near-claim warnings from other policy-holders. The insured credit manager should be aware that the suggested credit limit from a credit insurance company may err on the low side, since it may have to pay claims for that amount. It is for this reason that the credit manager should always negotiate the limit needed for the proposed sales, using his brokers' expertise in the negotiations. Where a credit manager holds up-to-date credit information which suggests a higher level of credit than the insurer's limit, this should always be passed on to the insurance company and used to negotiate an increase. A seller is not bound to observe the insured limit, but that limit should be clearly shown on all company listings as it defines the limit of recovery of loss. In the same way, when the insurer responds to a credit limit application with a much lower figure than the seller needs, the credit manager should always ask, 'is this disappointing credit limit due to bad information or a *lack* of information?' The answer makes quite a difference to the seller's risk attitude to the customer.

The seller's own calculation   A4.11

For those who decide the credit ratings for themselves, there are two main approaches:

(a)   if the bank and trade references look good enough for the seller's proposed sales, then the credit rating shall be the monthly sales figure (or two to three times this, as a cushion); or

(b)   regardless of the seller's intended sales, a maximum credit exposure level shall be set that is believed to be safe.

The approach described in (a) is unsafe, because it ignores the customer's financial trends and requires constant revision if sales grow or if payment problems occur. The only advantage is that it is a trigger to review payment records and references if sales begin to exceed the rating thus set.

The benefit of using the approach in (b) which sets a maximum credit exposure limit, irrespective of actual sales, is that it encourages sales staff to sell up to the published figure without the need for prior credit approval. With approach (*a*), nobody knows at the point of sale, whether the credit rating can be increased or not.

Setting a maximum exposure level   A4.12

Where the approach described in **A4.11**(*b*) above is used, there are a number of ways of calculating the amount of that level. The key point is to set a limit within the financial capacity of the customer, as shown in the latest available balance sheet. Financial capacity can be expressed as net worth or working capital, net worth being the total of all assets minus all liabilities. Any assessment based on net worth should call for extra prudence since, in a final break-up, assets are never worth their ongoing value while the debts always are. A more generous view can be taken of the working capital of a customer, simply because working capital, being the total of current assets less current debts, is more immediately available.

A typical broad sweep approach is to take a proportion of the customer's balance sheet worth, such as the lesser of 10% of net worth or 20% of working capital, with an overriding maximum of 25% of total creditors. The rider is given because it is unwise to become too prominent as a single creditor.

'Working worth'   A4.13

In his book, *Credit Analysis* (Simon & Schuster, 1989), John Coleshaw invented the concept of 'working worth', whereby he averaged working capital and net worth. In his trial cases, he found it gave an acceptable and reliable figure on which to base the above percentages. Working worth is a good description of capital available for further credit.

Risk codes   A4.14

In **A4.15** below, risk codes are explained. These are quite different from the credit value ratings which do not affect the risk of a customer going out of business, as these risks may vary. Low or negligible risk may be coded as 'A', average risk as 'B' and high risk as 'C'. A more refined way of using a percentage of net worth or working capital to calculate a credit rating is to vary the percentage according to the risk code (see Figure 1.00 below).

Figure 1.00 – Risk codes

Risk code	Net worth	Working capital
High risk ('C')	5%	10%
Average risk ('B')	10%	20%
Low risk ('A')	15%	30%

The approach of assessing a credit rating as being a proportion of the customer's net working capital (see **A4.12** above) is enhanced in some companies by computer based scoring systems. The credit analyst loads items from the customer's balance sheet and profit and loss account for the last two (or three, if available) years. Based on pre-set parameters, the data produces a score which is then applied to the net worth, working capital, or working worth figure. Figure 2.00 illustrates this approach which, if kept simple, can also be achieved easily with pencil and paper!

Figure 2.00 – Credit rating using scoring from four ratios

Middling Ltd *(has working worth of £165k)*	Percentage of working worth
Current assets/current liabilities	1.2
Quick assets/current liabilities	0.9
Net worth/current liabilities	0.4
Net worth/total liabilities	0.4
Score	2.9

Scale to produce percentage of working worth		
Score	*Percentage of working worth*	*Credit rating*
4.5 or worse	= 0%	£0
–3.2 to –4.5	= 5%	£8,250
–1.8 to –3.2	= 10%	£16,500
–0.4 to –1.8	= 15%	£24,750
+0.3 to –0.4	= 17.5%	£28,875
+0.3 or better	= 20%	= £33,000

Another simple way of 'scoring' is to use a combination of latest year and year-on-year figures. The case for this is that poor ratios that have improved over the last two or three years are better than good ratios that are deteriorating. This method can be used by a trade association, which checks prospective members for both technical performance and financial capability. Once admitted, a member can boast of its membership to take, for example, deposits from the public, so it is important that they are able to complete orders without risk of loss by consumers. (See Figure 3.00.)

The scoring method was derived from a random selection of 100 trade firms who were in business three years earlier. Every relevant performance ratio was listed and applied to the list, which was then divided to show the companies which had failed and those still trading. It showed clear differences in certain ratios between survival and failure. Their relative importance was given a subjective weighting from 0 to 3 and then applied to actual membership applicants. A few adjustments in weightings were made in the first year. After that, the next ten years showed that only one company that 'passed' this test actually went out of business.

Figure 3.00 – Credit scoring basis for risk assessment

Trade association risk assessment of Advance Builders Ltd (score = ★)		
NPBT %	over 8%	0
(average 3 years)	5%–8%	1
	2%–5%	2
	below 2%	3★
NPBT trend	increases years 2 & 3	0
	mixed	2★
	decreases years 2 & 3	3
Interest to NPBT %	below 50%	0★
(latest year)	50%–90%	1
	over 90%	3
Creditors to net/worth %	below 75%	0
(latest year)	75%–100%	1
	over 100%	3★
Current ratio %	over 150%	0
(average 3 years)	100%–150%	1
	85%–100%	2★
	below 85%	3
Current ratio trend	increases years 2 & 3	0
	mixed	1★
	decreases years 2 & 3	3
Acid test ratio %	over 100%	0
(latest year)	75%–100%	1
	below 75%	3★
Collection period	below 60 days	0★
(days – latest year)	41–90	1
	over 90	3
Stock turnover	below 60 days	0★
(days – latest year)	60–110	2
	over 110	3
Stock trend	reduction years 2 & 3	0
	mixed	1★
	increase years 2 & 3	2
Personal assessment	excellent status	0
(from overall scan of data)	good status	1
	slight concern	2★
	serious concern	3

Possible Score Range		0–32
★Applicant Score		17 = FAIL

(Applicant company asked to re-apply the following year if results are better, otherwise to supply financial guarantee of third party company who pass this test).

The lower the score the better. The basis for admittance is 16 or less.

Why have risk codes? A4.15

Whereas credit ratings indicate liquidity, the solvency of companies is quite different. Customers have different levels of insolvency and instead of treating all customers as equally valuable, a coding to indicate their likelihood of survival, helps both sales and credit staff to deal with them appropriately.

Some companies use *only* risk codes (or categories), and do not bother with credit value ratings, in the belief that the risk codes decide priorities for pricing, delivery and after-sales service, and that strong collection action takes care of any overdues. The case for those who believe in credit ratings is that problems and costs are avoided without friction by selling only up to calculated limits of ability to pay.

Defining risk codes A4.16

Typically, credit managers who believe that risk codes are worthwhile use a simple group of three, e.g. A, B and C, indicating good, average and poor risks. A fourth code, 'D', could be added for credit control and order processing purposes – this code may be useful simply to mean 'no credit – cash only'. These are then easy to apply to vetting procedures and easy to explain to sales staff and senior management. However, there are companies who use a greater number of codes or categories, e.g. A to L, meaning various shades of opinion between the main categories. The number of categories, and the 'greying' of the areas in and between each code make this difficult to administer. More importantly, perhaps, more codes mean more explanations to sales staff and senior management and the greater the possibility of misunderstanding and confusion.

Common definitions of the four codes are as follows.

● 'A' – no risk, for example, Government departments, official bodies and blue chip customers. It should be remembered, however, that no risk does *not* mean that the customer is necessarily a good payer. It means that slow payment is a collection task, not an insolvency risk.

● 'B' – an average risk, and includes all customers who are not in categories 'A', 'C' or 'D'.

● 'C' – a high risk, for example, persistent slow payers, or those with recent County Court judgments, or distinctly worsening solvency, or poor interest versus profit ratios (their bank will not be backward in coming forward to act in such circumstances).

- 'D' – No credit – cash only.

By applying a rating of A, B and C to all credit accounts on the ledger, a clear pattern will emerge and no insolvency will then be a surprise, since all will be 'C' accounts. Typically, some 30% of credit accounts by number have a 'C' rating, about 10% are code 'A', leaving about 60% in the average 'B' bracket. No seller is happy to have so many high risk accounts in their portfolio but the facts of business life dictate that at any one time many companies actively trading are in danger of failing. Sellers can rarely get all the sales volume they need from customers with 'A' and 'B' ratings. By identifying the 'C' credit customers, more expert sales effort can be applied to the 'A' and 'B' accounts, i.e. those accounts with a future – hence the need for good credit controls at the front end of business.

Show the credit opinions on customer lists   A4.17

It is highly efficient to show the credit rating and risk code alongside each other on documents and screens where staff are reviewing performance or deciding priorities for sales or collection actions. A very clear picture emerges of capacity, risk, and ability to pay or indeed to survive (see Figure 4.00 below).

Figure 4.00 – An example of credit ratings shown alongside risk codes

Customer name	Credit rating	Credit limit
A/c 63942 Bloggs Engineering Ltd	B	£50,000
A/c 82615 Western Electrical Ltd	C	£1,000
A/c 86811 Ministry of Defence	A	Unlimited (or, £99,999,999)

How to decide risk codes by calculation   A4.18

Instead of defining 'no risk' and 'high risk' accounts as described in **A4.16** above, some companies use actual ratio analysis, from the official audited accounts lodged at Companies House. Rather than visit Companies House, sellers normally take the data from credit agency reports (see **A4.9** above). Figure 5.00 shows a method used by a major UK corporation. It is regarded as reliable for credit management and useful to commercial staff. This corporation uses a fourth risk code, 'U' for no risk. Having calculated customers' risk codes, it then produces credit ratings using proportions of worth for each category (see **A4.14** above).

Figure 5.00 – Calculating risk codes and credit ratings from the balance sheet

	C High risk	B Average	A Low risk	U Undoubted
Current ratio	<1.25	1.26–2.00	>2.00	'A' ratios plus Net
Quick ratio	<0.50	0.5–1.00	>1.00	Worth above £10 million
Current debt/net worth	>1.25	1.24–0.75	<0.75	
Total debt/net worth	>2.00	1.99–1.25	<1.25	

C risk is where *any* of the four ratios apply.

B risk is where there are *no* ratios in the high risk bracket.

A risk needs all four ratios to be achieved.

From these results, the credit manager also calculates credit ratings, as:

C are rated at 5% of working worth

B are rated at 15% of working worth

A are rated at 20% of working worth

U can have unlimited credit

A retrospective test for risk codes   A4.19

It is worth the time and effort involved to test risk codes against actual customer failures already experienced. Credit staff should make the time to go back into the records for the last six to ten accounts which went into liquidation or receivership. They should pull any credit reports held on file at the time, plus the sales ledger account experience up to the insolvency.

It should be decided objectively whether the failed companies should have A, B, or C risk codes, and it is almost certain that they will all be found to have been 'C' types. In other words, if there had been a risk code system in place at that time, the insolvent companies would all have been in the high risk group and subject to special controls. How much sales and credit effort and bad debt cost would have been saved? Put another way, how much net income was lost by not categorising those accounts as being at risk?

Use risk codes to decide priorities   A4.20

It is clearly more beneficial to cultivate the better customers for sales and for cash, than investing expensive resource in poor risk accounts, and it follows that risk codes are a convenient and highly cost effective method of best utilising the resource available. If the risk codes are respected as sound indicators of stability, internal procedures can be established to fit the codes. For example, instead of giving all customers equal priority and processing all orders and customer service queries in chronological order, the codes can give preference to those customers who are so identified as representing good future buying prospects. For example:

- Delivery dates – where the standard time is three weeks, quote one week to customers with A/B risk codes, and six weeks to those with 'C' codes.

- After sales service – this should be immediate for 'A/Bs' and as time permits for 'Cs'.

- 'Hold orders' list for late payers – 'As' should not appear on the list as a general rule, with 'Bs' being listed when 30 days late. 'C' accounts should be listed when only 7 days late.

If there are some 'C' accounts which are uncomfortably large, extra controls might include the following.

- A monthly review of payment experience – how are they responding to reminders?

- A regular review with sales staff – what can we do together to improve risks?

- A monthly discussion with customers' senior staff – closer contact for early warning.

With a well-defined sales credit policy for risk codes, the customer profile comes to life, with everyone realising that the customers' differing viabilities can be used objectively by the company. All customers are important, but a seller's expense and future planning should vary with their prospects for survival and growth.

Ways to reduce the risk assessment workload

Quick-start credit rating   A4.21

Decide a quick-start credit rating which can get a small account started *with no credit checking*. This figure will be dependent upon both the nature of business, minimum order values and other considerations, but should be as painless as possible, say £100 to say £500. It will not matter greatly to the seller's financial circumstances if it is lost, but will be big enough to accommodate typical small first orders. Make it clear that further orders will be subject to the normal credit checks. This approach wins friends in the sales area and allows more time to deal with important cases.

80/20 ratios   A4.22

The 80/20 rule, or Pareto principle, states that 80% of business is done with 20% of customers. Use the 80/20 ratio to identify the 20% of customers who account for the 80% of business, and so provide 80% of cash. Identification should be easy – list all debtors in descending value, drawing a line where the cumulative value reaches 80% of the total debtors figure. (It may suit some credit managers to identify the accounts which represent 50% of sales.) There will then be a large number of accounts which together buy only 20% of sales. A full credit check must be done on the few large accounts but the mass of lesser accounts can be checked as time and resources allow. Below a relatively small value, some credit managers *never* credit check, as any losses would never exceed the cost.

As the ledger account is produced monthly (or as frequently as is required), the debtors listing can be regularly reviewed, with smaller customers growing, and larger customers diminishing. As the make up of the 80/20 ratio can alter, so the customers requiring credit checks will follow.

Assess largest accounts first   A4.23

Assess credit on the largest accounts first, and never start an assessment system on an alphabetic or account number basis. Size *is* important and when a credit manager selects customers by size, he will never then be guilty of running out of time to deal with the large exposure which goes bust.

Risk codes to decide priorities   A4.24

Use the risk codes to decide priorities. Since the 'A' and 'B' customers are by definition the more creditworthy, checks can be confined to payment experience and sales reports. It is sensible, of course, to be aware of any changes, and be prepared to go for a full information update if there develops any cause for concern.

Changing risk codes   A4.25

Always be prepared to move accounts between risk codes. It used to be a rare occurrence for an 'A' to fall from grace in such a way that it moves to 'C', but it does happen – and in recent years there have been some spectacular failures creating popular press headlines. More common is the movement between 'B' and 'C', both promotion and relegation. The criteria is credit performance.

Dealing with high risk, or marginal customers   A4.26

The inexperienced credit manager usually works to fixed procedures related to credit limits and stop lists. Supplies may be stopped to all late payers and accounts are looked at in chronological order, as time permits. The result of such a rigid approach is that there will be overdues and bad debts because of the lack of priorities.

Good credit management has a *commercial* approach, which earns respect from sales colleagues, as well as extra income for the company. A commercial but risk-aware approach should:

● gain information on customers;

● identify risky customers;

● tell the sales people who the risky customers are (and why); and

● encourage sales people to sell up to the ratings indicated.

In return, sales staff should support the controls the credit manager has put in place, because of the risks being taken with the company's money.

A significant advantage of identifying high risk customers is that orders from all other customers can flow quickly, uninterrupted by controls. Far from being accused of losing orders, a marginal risk policy can demonstrate extra sales and profit obtained.

Identifying high risk accounts   A4.27

Credit information should answer the three key credit questions.

● Solvency – is the company likely to go bust?

● Liquidity – can the company pay its proposed commitments on time?

● Growth – will the company be there next year?

Negative answers will mean a high risk probability, and for those sellers with a risk coding system, these will be 'C' accounts.

Control techniques for marginal or high risk accounts   A4.28

There are three major ways to control marginal or high risk accounts. These are:

● pre-delivery controls;

● collection actions; and

● risk reduction measures.

Pre-delivery controls include referral of an incoming order to the credit manager to add its value to the existing balance and to compare that total with the credit rating. Also included is the need to update credit data at defined intervals.

Collection actions will obviously depend upon the size of the debt, but will no doubt require telephone contact at intervals, to judge customer situations. After a first reminder of an overdue debt, supplies must be held back until the account has been paid. Payments in advance, either total or partial, should be encouraged.

Measures to ensure risk reduction include:

- guarantees from acceptable third parties;

- credit insurance;

- special short payment terms;

- cash discounts;

- retention of title; and

- offsetting payables.

All of these measures and others are explained in some detail in **A12 RISK MITIGATION AND SECURITY FOR COMMERCIAL CREDIT TRANSACTIONS**.

Special short terms, such as 7 days instead of 30 days, allow the customer to receive the goods and start to use them for profit, but keeps the risk horizon very short.

Cash discounts to encourage prompt payment from risky customers are usually a false step since the customer may well take the discount and still pay late, leading to problems in respect of disallowed discount balances left on the ledger. It is only a worthwhile incentive if the seller's margin is really high, since 2% is probably the minimum attractive rate for earlier settlement. One major problem when offering a cash discount selectively, such as to high-risk customers only, is that other customers may hear of it and demand the same effective price reduction.

The payables ledger should be checked regularly to see whether any high-risk customers are also suppliers, including to other group companies. No money should be paid out to a high-risk customer while debts are still owed by them. It should be noted, however, that withholding amounts due to suppliers, even if they are high-risk customers, does present legal difficulties, for example if an Administrative Receiver is appointed and demands payment (see **A12.63** below.)

An action plan for high risk accounts may consist of the following steps:

- identify the high risk customers;

- obtain information on them;

- sell to them – with extra controls;

- monitor them and make time to get involved where needed; and

- stop trading with them well before they fail.

Credit control at order entry   A4.29

Businesslike controls can only be effective if the credit manager has the authority to approve, hold back or totally reject orders, within a properly set out credit policy (see **A1 CREDIT POLICY**). With that authority comes the responsibility to do everything possible to arrange terms to suit risks, to reject the bare minimum, and to communicate fluently with the relevant sales area staff.

In computerised systems, orders can flow uninterrupted into the order processing disciplines if they meet set parameters, such as 'credit rating less existing balance plus order'. Orders that fail this test or those orders from customers currently on a 'stop list' *must* be extracted from the process for expert action. By assessing risks in good time for *prospective* customers and by keeping assessments updated for the *active* ones, almost all orders each day should flow quickly into the order processing system.

Stop list   A4.30

There are basically two kinds of stop list:

- the *refer list*, where the credit manager is alerted to incoming orders from accounts where any movement needs appraisal; and

- the *actual stop list*, where credit has been withdrawn because of a serious debt situation. In this case, holding back an order may be a good lever to obtain payment if the customer is desperate for more of the supplier's product.

There should be a daily review of all orders that have been put on hold to see what needs to be done to release them. Whenever a stop list operates, the sales force should also be given a 'go list', which shows the relatively few customers who pay their accounts really well, and whose extra orders would be welcomed as producing faster cash inflow for the company.

Bad debt reserve policies   A4.31

The final element of good risk assessment is to be able to make the smallest possible provision for lost sales revenue when bad debts occur. It is important here to appreciate and understand terminology. The term 'bad debt' should only be used for an irrecoverable debt of an insolvent customer and not just a badly overdue debt of a solvent customer.

Having categorised some accounts as high risk, it makes business sense to allocate debt provision out of profits. Provisions are expensive and deplete current profits but are necessary because debtors are a current asset, i.e. capable of liquidation within twelve months. Auditors expect any doubtful debts to be fully provided for, so that the net balance sheet figure for debtors is considered to be collectable and is anyway less than twelve months old.

In the rush that is the hallmark of most financial year end processes, accountants may make provision based on historical losses or as a flat percentage of total debtors. As the credit manager knows the probable collectability of high risk debts, it is more accurate, and have usually less impact on profits to base the bad debt provision on these specific accounts. The general provision can add to specific by a percentage in order to cover the unexpected bad debt loss which might hit out of the blue.

Debts which are disputed should not be cleared by writing them off against the bad debt reserve. Writing off a dispute should be by sales credits against the sales credit provision, since the question of credit risk loss does not apply. Furthermore, misuse of the bad debt reserve distorts any measurement of the company's risk assessment and credit controls. Such bad practice also distorts the real cost of errors and defects being handled by sales or customer service functions.

There are several different ways to make bad debt reserves.

- 100% with reversal – each month, the *total* value of all 'C' category accounts is reserved, i.e. a transfer is made from the profit and loss account to the bad debt reserve. As accounts are paid, the value is reversed, i.e. transferred back to the profit and loss account. In practice, all that is needed is to keep a bad debt reserve for the total high risk accounts and adjust it each month to the new total balance.

- Reserve according to age – this method recognises that risk of loss increases with age. A reserve is made as a percentage of the age analysis of 'C' accounts, e.g. 25% of balances one month overdue, 50% of balances two months overdue, 75% three months overdue and 100% at four months. The percentages are derived from the seller's experience of the collectability of its marginal accounts at various ages. This method provides an extra incentive to collect overdue 'C' accounts, to avoid too heavy a depletion of profit.

- Annual write-off experience – this method recognises a company's bad debt experience each year. For example, if the company lost 1% of sales in bad debts last year, it may reserve 1% of *all* sales this year. A quick study shows that its *actual* bad debts occurred only in the 'C' accounts, for whose billings, the bad debt losses were, say, 5%. So instead of tying up 1% of all revenue, the company can gradually build a reserve through the year of 5% of sales value to 'C' accounts only.

Where credit insurance cover is held, it is normal to reduce the bad debt reserve expense by applying provisions to only the *uninsured* portion of 'C' accounts. This obvious reduction can offset the premium cost of the insurance cover.

Credit risk assessment – the future   A4.32

Interest rates will always fluctuate to a greater or lesser degree, which means that credit will be cheaper or dearer, depending upon the economic cycle. What will remain constant, however, is the fact that borrowings are very expensive as a proportion of meagre net margins, which means that the risk of slow payments will remain the top credit management priority, followed by bad debt losses. The way forward will demand better and more liaison between credit and sales managements, helped by continuing and ever quickening advances in office technologies.

Order processing, information displays and communications will only get faster, mobile phones, the internet and laptop computers in the forefront. The downside of faster transactions will be less time available for humans to deal with credit risk problems.

The best organised companies will, now or tomorrow:

- have top management support for risk assessment processes and procedures;
- have topical data on all key customers (financial status, trends, industry positions etc.);
- use e-mails and faxes for opening accounts (credit application form and customer commitment to payment terms);
- use e-mail to make early contact with payments contacts and send out ongoing reminders;
- use computerised calculation of credit ratings and risk codes;
- use computerised commercial scoring techniques; and
- use automated credit approvals and fast processing of acceptable transactions.

As a blanket agreement on conditions of sale, electronic forms of the credit application form will continue to grow in importance. Apart from the routine data of customer name; address; phone; fax; e-mail; contact names; bank details etc, it will become the main way to get acceptance of payment terms to apply to all orders.

Credit control and customer service continue to move closer together as it is recognised that credit control *is* a service to customers, with major customers already being seen as too important to be just names on invoices or an entry on the ledger. The credit/payables relationship will come to match the sales/buyer one, with many more customer visits by credit staff.

Much of the required data for risk assessment is already available online, and this growth will continue. Instant decisions are fast becoming the norm, as is downloading from websites selected data for loading into own PC based calculation modules for producing risk analysis spreadsheets and reports. There is a fast expanding range of credit analysis software available for purchase by credit managers for calculating credit ratings, and loading directly into order processing system. Many software packages on order and stock control will contain credit related sections.

Controlling high risk accounts will benefit from ever more sophisticated insolvency watch and insolvency prediction services, including the standard use of 'flash reports' of external events. Many agencies will e-mail and fax subscribers with any events affecting risk, (such as judgments, appointments of Administrative

Receivers, profits warnings, a Chairman's adverse news statements, etc.), automatically linking in with the sellers' computer systems and so built into order processing and debt collection.

Automated credit approvals will improve by building in events such as accounts approaching limits, orders in from a specified problem customer, and accounts automatically put on stop and taken off stop according to set parameters. The test of all good automated systems will be their growing acceptance by sales staff, who recognise that in return for faster approvals, occasional rejected cases must be serious and deserve combined action with the credit manager.

Top management support will increase the importance of company risk assessment in preserving profits and directing sales efforts to the right customers is recognised. When developing credit rules, credit managers must continue to ensure that such rules should be confined to a one-page documents as far as possible, to be signed-off and circulated by the Board.

Summary   A4.33

In summary, good credit management means:

- knowing exactly who the customers are;

- checking their ability to pay the proposed billings on time;

- purchasing the best affordable credit data;

- organising a smooth way to speed orders and deliveries through, to create time to deal with really risky cases; and

- above all, getting company-wide acceptance of why risk control matters.

Appendix A4

Appendix A4.1 – Sales and credit management use of risk codes

This is an extract from the credit manual of one large UK manufacturer, it spells out the separate approaches for sales staff and credit staff, using the computerised risk categories.

Sales use of risk codes

- A customers   More sales time to be spent with these than B or C customers.

  First priority for phone calls and correspondence.

  First priority for delivery dates.

  Best price discounts to be given (subject to volumes, etc.).

  First priority after-sales service.

  Fastest response times on claims and disputes.

- B customers   Standard performance levels.
- C customers   Minimal sales resource.

  No advance expense.

  No special production/procurement actions.

  Observe 'stop list' from credit departments.

  Lower priority on service, claims, etc. than A and B customers.

  Inform credit staff urgently of any adverse news.

Credit management use of risk codes

- A customers   Unlimited credit ratings.

  Never on stop-list, unless fully discussed.

  Always personal contact for collections – no standard letters.

  Same-day action on queries and disputes.

  Maximum support for sales requirements.

- B customers   Standard credit and collection actions.

  Stop supplies if accounts are a specified number of days overdue.

- C customers   Mark as high risk on all listings.

  Debts never to exceed credit ratings.

  Stop supplies immediately payment is overdue.

  Special actions to control risks (e.g. guarantees, etc.).

  Notify sales staff of collection steps.

A5

New Business

Introduction

The dictionary defines agreement as 'the act of agreeing', 'a settlement, especially one that is legally enforceable', or 'a contract or document containing such a settlement'. There are others, the English language being famously rich in its diversity and complexity, but 'contract' and 'document' are relevant in the context of this chapter. The same dictionary offers an equally relevant definition, among many alternatives, of contract, namely 'to enter into an agreement with (a person, company, etc.) to deliver (goods or services) or to do (something) on mutually agreed terms'. Contracts and agreements come in many shapes and sizes, from marriage to mortgage, hire purchase to holidays, vehicle rental to volume discount – the core being the undertaking to do something by both sides in the agreement. If one pays the money, the other supplies the service.

In days of old, when supplier and customer were well known to each other, such a contract or agreement may have been no more than a nod and a shake of the hand. The spread and increase in the volume of trade called for a more formalised approach to inter party dealings as knowledge of both buyer and seller decreased in direct proportion. For many, the handshake lost its credibility and to paraphrase the 20th Century Hollywood mogul, Samuel Goldwyn, the view prevailed that a verbal agreement was not worth the paper it was not written on.

In addition, the business environment of today, along with society as a whole in the industrialised West, has become increasingly litigious. Either party in a contract or agreement is now much more ready to resort to law to enforce their rights and expectations under such agreements. All the more reason, therefore, when two parties enter into a contract, both sides are fully aware of the requirements placed upon each by the contract, and the consequences of failure to comply.

Terms of trade

Business transactions usually involve two parties, the buyer and the seller. Common sense should dictate that the participants have some idea of what they are getting themselves into when dealing together, and what both sides expect of each other. It follows that the most effective way of ensuring that there is clarity between the two parties is to structure the transaction so that possible issues are understood and accounted for and that agreement is reached at the outset.

This is not to say that every contract of sale must be painstakingly recorded in indelible ink on parchment, a seal affixed thereon and witnessed by an officer of the Crown. All it does mean is that a framework for trade is established at the outset and that the ensuing business relationship is formalised.

It is important, therefore, that terms of trade are agreed by seller and buyer at the time that the sale is agreed, if not before, and that the terms themselves are both legally enforceable and clearly defined. Legally enforceable means that the terms must comply with the law current at the time and can stand the test, if necessary, in a court of law. By implication, such terms should also be considered reasonable, i.e. it could be reasonably expected that both parties be able to comply with them under normal circumstances. Clearly defined terms reduce the possibility of misunderstanding or dispute. It is also worth remembering that both the seller and the buyer will operate under terms of trade, so clarity and understanding refers to both parties in the transaction – all the more reason for agreement at the outset.

Terms and conditions of sale   A5.3

The normal answer to a general enquiry as to terms would probably be something along the lines of 30 days or net cash monthly. These are 'payment terms' (see **A5.4** below), and whilst they do in fact form part of general terms and conditions of sale, they are themselves specific. Terms and conditions of sale are familiar to many as the mass of small print on the reverse of *pro forma* invoices, quotes, delivery notes or even the invoices themselves. As such they can be overlooked or ignored, and only referred to in the case of a subsequent dispute. They are, however, the fundamental rules under which the seller operates. Being the seller's prerogative, allowing for the rights of the buyer as protected by law, they set out in detail the seller's conditions under which business will be allowed with the buyer, together with the duties and responsibilities of both seller and buyer.

Parliament oversees trading activities with a view to allow and create fairness in dealings between parties, with:

- laws of contract;

- legislation concerning restrictive trade practices;

- the *Consumer Credit Act 1974*;

- the *Sale of Goods Act 1979* and similar.

Normal terms and conditions of sale operate within that legislative framework. Conditions of sale will cover all aspects of the seller's operation and would normally include buyer responsibilities in respect of shortages, delivery, breakages, returns, returnable pallets or packaging, together with the seller's declaration on performance guarantees or warranties, and the handling of complaints or disputes. In addition, it is not uncommon for the seller to include a specific clause establishing retention of title, the goods remaining the property of the seller until they have been paid for in full (see **A12 RISK MITIGATION AND SECURITY FOR COMMERCIAL CREDIT TRANSACTIONS**). More specific conditions may well be included in particular trades or industries, relating to such things as perishable or hazardous goods, temperature control and storage and handling – the seller would not want to be responsible for the buyer's mishandling or errors. Conditions would also stipulate the rights of the seller in respect of the insolvency of the buyer, and would include a statement as to the choice of law governing the conditions.

As previously stated, terms and conditions of sale are often the small print on the reverse of order acknowledgements or *pro forma* invoices, quotations etc, and it would be wise to draw the buyer's attention to any particular condition which it would be the seller's intention to enforce in the event of the buyer's non-compliance, which under normal circumstances the buyer may not have read or appreciated. Examples would be retention of title, or the intention to charge interest on overdue accounts. Subsequent arguments or disputes can be greatly reduced or eliminated entirely by the evidence of the buyer's signature in the relevant box.

Payment terms A5.4

Payment terms, themselves forming an integral part of the terms and conditions of sale, are a clear statement as to the:

- time the seller agrees to allow for payment;
- methods by which payment will be accepted; and
- rights of the supplier in the event of late payment or non-payment.

As such, they should be clear and unambiguous. Not only is it important that the terms are known and understood by the prospective customer, but they should also be well understood by all personnel employed by the seller. All too often, the marketing and finance departments do not appear to be 'singing from the same hymn sheet' and if the seller does not know his own terms, it would be hardly surprising if the buyer was confused.

It should be made clear, therefore, what is defined by the seller as net 30 days, net cash monthly, strict 30 days or such other terms as may be stated. There would be a number of factors dictating the seller's choice and use of terms, not least of which would be the seller's own financial position and requirements, taking into account the amount of capital likely to be tied up in accounts receivable and the seller's ability to finance such sales on credit. The seller will also have to be aware of the competition and what is regarded as the norm for that particular trade or industry, together with the nature of the product sold and the profit margins to be expected. Fundamental to the choice of payment terms being offered to buyers, the seller needs to balance terms given to customers against terms he has to experience with his own suppliers – giving customers 90 days whilst having to pay suppliers on 30 days is a recipe for financial difficulties. It is equally true to say that it is easy for the seller to fall into the trap of increasing credit terms given to buyers in order to promote sales, without having carried out the necessary evaluation of finance costs and not having a full appreciation of all that is involved.

Unsustainable credit terms change the recipe for difficulties into a recipe for disaster. The nature of the product or service, not just the market place, will influence the terms given.

Production lead times and costs, the complexity of the goods produced or services provided, and the anticipated or expected performance after delivery or installation, all point to the need to be clear and unambiguous in stating payment terms. Of particular concern would be those 'bespoke' products – made specifically for an individual customer, which would be of no use to any other customer, or of any value to the seller if not taken up or not paid for.

It is important, therefore, to establish payment terms at the outset, and to distinguish between terms which are associated with time to pay, and terms which are connected to delivery. For example:

- time:
  - net 7 (10, 15, 30 etc.) days – payment is required 7 (10, 15, 30 etc.) days after delivery,
  - monthly – payment for the full month of supplies to be made by a date stated in the following month (examples would be February invoices due for payment by 10 (15, 25, 30) March),
  - two monthly – (often used in export and referred to as 60 days) – as above but payment for February invoices would be due by 10 (15, 25, 30) April,
  - strict 30 days – payment is due 30 days after date of invoice;

- delivery:
  - cash in advance,
  - cash on delivery,
  - cash with order,
  - cash next delivery.

In other words all terms of payment are governed by being tied to payment expected by a specified date, and/or by a specified event, such as delivery. It is worth remembering that the setting of payment terms should also take into account the practicalities of administering such terms. In many trades, for instance, it is common practice to collate all invoices rendered by a supplier during the course of the month and to issue one payment at the end of the following month covering all such invoices. This can be the case even when the supplier has stated terms of strict 30 days – a large customer with 20 deliveries in a month hardly wants to issue 20 cheques. It may be practically expedient for both the supplier, from a collection standpoint, and the customer from the payment angle, to accept this arrangement, as it is less costly for both parties to administer.

Contract A5.5

Terms and conditions of sale, including payment terms, form part of the contract between the seller of the goods or services and the buyer. The contract can be quite informal in its creation, under English law, there is no formal requirement for the contact to be in writing. Verbal contracts are quite common, as evidenced by the popularity of telephone orders and sales. There are exceptions to this rule, notably contracts for the sale of land and contracts of guarantee, both of which are required by law to be in writing in order to be enforceable. Agreements regulated under the *Consumer Credit Act 1974* (see **A14.6–A14.15** below) must also be in writing. Notwithstanding these exceptions, legally enforceable contracts are created verbally every day, sometimes without a word actually being spoken. It may not be appreciated by many people, but calling at the corner shop on the way to work, picking a pack of mints from the display, and handing over the money to the shopkeeper to pay for them is in fact creating an enforceable contract between the purchaser of the mints (the buyer) and the shopkeeper (the seller).

Verbal contracts are quite common and legally enforceable if all the essential elements of a contract are evident. However, to avoid misunderstandings and to make clear whatever obligations and responsibilities are expected and required from both buyer and seller, it is particularly useful to operate under written contracts. It may be desirable, for example, to draw the buyer's attention to particular terms or conditions within the contract and have signed agreement to those clauses, such as reservation of title or interest on overdue accounts, as well as the signed acknowledgement of credit terms and, where applicable, the credit limit.

By definition under English law, a contract is a legally binding agreement which the law will recognise, and every contract, whether oral or in writing, has three essential elements:

- offer and acceptance;
- intention to create legal relations; and
- consideration.

Simply stated, an order for goods and acceptance of that order is offer and acceptance, it is clearly the intention of the buyer and seller to create a legal relationship by way of trading with each other, and the consideration is what of value the buyer and the seller agree to give to each other – payment or promise of payment by the buyer and delivery or promise of delivery of the goods by the seller.

It could well be that little or no negotiation takes place in respect of order and acceptance. The customer has seen the catalogue and price list, wants the goods and places an order. On the other hand, some negotiations may well have taken place which may have been complicated and protracted. What is important, whatever the extent of negotiations, is that such discussions involve the principle of offer and acceptance. The contract is made when an offer is put forward by one party and accepted without reservation by the other party. Only then does the contract come into being as recognisable and enforceable under the law.

Distinction should be made by what constitutes an offer and what is simply best described as an invitation to treat. Advertisements in newspapers or magazines, for example, and the price displayed on the washing machine in the shop window are not of themselves offers. They are in fact invitations to treat. Going into the shop, choosing the washing machine and arranging to pay is an offer. Taking the money and arranging delivery of the washing machine is an acceptance. The principle of distinction between an invitation to treat and an offer is well tested in English law – see *Pharmaceutical Society of Great Britain v Boots Cash Chemists (Southern) [1953] 1 All ER 482* and *Fisher v Bell [1961] 3 All ER 731*.

Once the buyer and seller have negotiated and agreed, the contract thus entered into becomes binding and places responsibilities and obligations upon both parties. In other words, there are consequences. Both sides are bound by the undertakings that they have given to each other, and failure of one side to perform under the agreed terms of the contract leads to the other being able to sue for breach of contract. Credit managers will be well aware that a common breach of contract by the buyer is failure to pay, either to the terms agreed or indeed failure to pay at all. It is worth also noting that once a breach of contract has occurred, that contract is in effect complete and subsequent negotiations mean the forming of a new contract. In other words, no new or revised terms can be introduced without the agreement of both parties to those new terms. Again a good example experienced by credit managers would be the arrangement of a new repayment schedule following default by a customer.

Legal standing – whose terms apply?   A5.6

One of the most commonly asked questions in respect of contracts, especially in respect of payment terms, is that which wants to establish exactly whose terms prevail – the buyer's or the seller's. The seller operates under his standard terms and conditions of sale, but the buyer will want to perform under his conditions of purchase.

The previously outlined principle of offer and acceptance applies (see **A5.5** above). Both parties are in the process of making offers through the various stages of contract negotiation, and the final acceptance could come from either seller or buyer. It is often argued that the final document to pass between the two parties before the goods are delivered, or the service provided, is regarded normally as the indicator as to whose terms now prevail. Put simply, if the seller states in his paperwork that his selling terms are 30 days and receives an order from the customer whose paperwork indicates a payment policy of 60 days, then unless the seller contacts the buyer again, it could well be that the buyer's terms govern the contract. In the normal course of trading, it would be not untypical to see the following course of events. A potential customer approaches the seller with an enquiry, perhaps involving product, price and delivery. The supplier then produces a quotation, which should contain not only the price and delivery details, but also the supplier's terms and conditions of sale, including payment terms. The customer then places an order, and that order documentation may well quote a payment policy which does not tie in with the supplier's terms. What should happen next is the issue by the supplier of either an order acceptance or order acknowledgement which in turn establishes again the supplier's own terms and conditions. The goods are delivered, an invoice produced and sent and payment made.

Two points are worth noting. Firstly, in the case of telephoned orders, the customer may well confirm his order in writing subsequent to the telephone call – if an order acknowledgement is issued before the written confirmation has been received, then the confirmation of order is the last document to pass between the parties, not the supplier's order acknowledgement. The obvious result is that the customer will view the contract as being governed by his terms. Secondly, terms printed on an invoice, or terms and conditions detailed on the reverse of an invoice can only be regarded as being for information only. An invoice document is not part of the contract negotiation, the process of offer and acceptance etc. As the invoice is produced after the delivery of the goods or the provision of the services, it is too late and therefore has no legal effect on the substance of the contract.

The difficulties clearly arise when it is not common practice by the supplier to issue order acknowledgements or confirmation of order acceptances. If the last document to pass is the customer's purchase order, then such terms as are contained in that order are invariably those terms under which the contract will be governed, the purchase order itself being the last act in the offer and acceptance process of contract negotiation.

Cash discounts   A5.7

In an attempt to promote prompt or early settlement it is not uncommon in some industries to offer cash discounts. However, before considering such a policy it is important to take into account such factors as price and profit margin. Cash discounts should not be confused with trade discounts, where goods are offered to customers at a discounted price. In such circumstances, the margins may already have been trimmed and to offer further discount by way of cash settlement is uneconomical. In any case the costs of cash discounts are high, frequently much higher than many realise, and the implications of such costs are not readily understood. It may well be that in actual fact, the real cost of allowing cash discount is greater than it actually costs the supplier to borrow. For example, if borrowing costs were 15% per annum with a normal DSO (no discount) of 60 days, if the supplier were to offer 2.0% discount for payment in 30 days, the calculation would be:

$$\frac{365}{30} \times 2.0 = \text{approximately 24\% per annum.}$$

Similarly, 2.0% discount for payment in 50 days would be approximately 15% per annum. Therefore, from the standpoint of cost alone, offering the above discounts in the circumstances outlined would not be worthwhile. There would, however, be a case for the selective use of cash discounts to closely control high risk accounts, where premium prices were being charged in the first place, and to offer a discounted 'price' to those accounts where, for whatever reason, terms of trade were restricted to cash on delivery, cash on dispatch or cash with order.

Even if the cost is not fully appreciated, a common argument against cash discounts is the question of abuse. When cash discounts are included as part of normal terms and conditions of sale, trouble arises when customers take discount to which they are not entitled, for example, when paying late. The supplier then has the administrative problem of small balances on the ledger which have to be cleared by attempting to collect from the customer. The real question is whether such balances are worth pursuing at the expense of customer relations or whether they should be written off. If the latter, one is bound to wonder as to the value of including a discount provision in the first place.

Interest   A5.8

In the last quarter of the 20th Century the debate on the right to charge interest on overdue accounts raged relentlessly. Supporters of full blown legislation always argued that the weight of the law would bring about a change of payment culture and promote prompt payment as best practice. What was often forgotten was the existing right held by suppliers to charge interest on overdue debts, provided such intention was included in the supplier's standard terms and conditions, and that these terms and conditions were those under which the contract between seller and buyer was conducted. The rate of interest which the supplier proposed to charge should be clearly stated, and should be sufficient to act both as a deterrent against slow payment and not be seen by the buyer as a source of cheap borrowing. It should also not be of a level which may be interpreted by the courts as being oppressive or excessive.

In practice, the application of interest in trade credit is often as fraught with difficulties as the granting of cash discounts. Established customers who normally pay more or less to terms and have a good track record, may well feel upset if they found themselves subject to interest charges on the odd times when the cheque was later than usual. There is also the administrative problem of customers who pay the capital balance, but not the interest. The supplier has to decide whether pursuing the interest would be commercially the right thing to do – much depends on the hoped for value of ongoing business and the likely damage to be caused by chasing up interest payments.

Legislation   A5.9

The *Late Payment of Commercial Debts (Interest) Act 1998* came into force on 1 November 1998 and was introduced to give business a statutory right to interest on late payment. The legislation was designed to reverse the bad practice of deliberate late payment, often ascribed to large companies and organisations using their power over small business and was planned to be phased in over six years. The original timetable was as follows.

- 1 November 1998 to 31 October 2000 – small businesses (under 50 employees) able to claim interest from large businesses and the public sector on debts incurred under contracts agreed after that date.

- 1 November 2000 to 31 October 2002 – small businesses able to claim interest from other small businesses on debts incurred under contracts agreed after that date.

- 1 November 2002 onwards – all businesses and the public sector able to claim interest from all businesses and the public sector on debts incurred under contracts agreed after that date.

The timetable was brought forward, following the requirement to bring the Act into line with the European Directive on Late Payment, so that the final phase came into force on 1 August 2002 (see **A13.57** below).

The rate of interest stipulated under the Act is the official dealing rate of the Bank of England, otherwise known as the base rate, plus 8% (for example, if the base rate was 5%, interest could be charged at a rate of 13%).

Most credit management professionals took the view that whilst welcoming measures designed to improve the payment culture, this particular legislation would have little or no effect. Take up has been little more than modest, and data from the Credit Management Research Centre (CMRC) at the Leeds University Business School in its regular Quarterly Reviews has consistently shown that although increasing numbers of businesses are aware of the late payment legislation, take up by businesses remains low, with the CMRC showing 5% of those eligible year on year since 1999 actually using the legislation. Some increase has been noted since large companies came into the frame in August 2002, but this is not of any great significance. Indeed, large companies who do utilise the provisions of the legislation do so quite selectively – they too take the same commercial marketing decisions as any other business when it comes to deciding when to apply late payment interest and enforce it through the legislative process.

Informing the customer A5.10

It is good practice for the supplier at the outset to inform the customer of the process which will be undertaken in respect of fulfilling the customer order. This keeps the prospective customer aware of the steps to be undertaken by both buyer and seller, what will be expected of each and what further needs to be done at any point in the negotiation or procedure. This will include:

- product price and availability;

- delivery;

- terms and conditions, including payment terms and method; and

●   any steps to be taken by the supplier to establish credit worthiness.

Any customer ordering goods on credit should know what is required to be provided so that the account can be established, he should also be kept up-to-date on progress. It is worth repeating that the vital element of payment terms has to be clear and at the end of the process no surprises should await either side.

Confirmation – customer contact   A5.11

At the conclusion of the negotiations and the establishment of the new trading relationship, the supplier confirms in writing to the customer all:

●   terms;

●   conditions;

●   arrangements;

●   product price;

●   delivery details; and

●   other relevant matters.

In many cases this will simply take the form of an order acknowledgement or order confirmation, that document itself containing all that the supplier and customer have agreed in respect of the customer's order. If there are any errors, or alterations requested by the customer, and these are agreed by the supplier, then a further order acknowledgement is produced – in effect this is a new contract. It is extremely important that such alterations are confirmed in this way, as this will ensure that the contract remains governed by the terms and conditions of the supplier.

Special terms (payment)   A5.12

As outlined in **A5.4** above, every business should have terms of payment known and understood by both the supplier (sales and finance departments) and the customer. There will be circumstances, however, when it is commercially expedient to deviate from those standard terms, and offer the customer special deals. This may be when there are:

●   specific marketing promotions taking place;

●   deals on slow moving or obsolescent stock;

●   new customer branches being opened; and

●   the need for substantial restocking orders.

Special terms include, major capital contracts, with down payments, progress payments, retention and performance clauses and sale or return arrangements. Such special payment terms need to be carefully negotiated, agreed in detail and confirmed in writing. Apart from ensuring that payment is made when due, the supplier has to carefully operate the account, aside from the general day to day accounts, so as to correctly record the sale and age the debt and avoid the issue of reminders and final notices if in this case they were not appropriate.

Special payment terms may also be linked to special price deals, and as such it is equally important for the business to be aware of margins and the level of debt to be supported. As with cash discounts, it is easy to erode the profit twice in one bite with a discount and extended terms.

There are always seasonal factors to be taken into account which may mean that at particular times of the year or trading cycle, terms other than standard will be available to customers as part of smoothing out the peaks and troughs of seasonal trading. However, the overriding factors remain business need and the ability to support financially the level of accounts receivable.

Temporary terms (payment) A5.13

In circumstances similar to those outlined in **A5.12** above, there may be situations when it is beneficial to offer temporary payment terms. The opening by a customer of a new branch or depot or the setting up or acquisition of a new subsidiary may require terms different from the standard for a temporary but fixed period of time. It is also possible that in the process of account collection (see **A13 COLLECTING OUTSTANDING ACCOUNTS**) a repayment schedule is instigated for existing debt, and new business is conducted on different terms for such a period of time as may be required to bring the account back into line.

The same criteria as mentioned in **A5.10** above apply. Flexibility is desirable in all business transactions, but control is vital to ensure that any existing risk is minimised and overall exposure remains manageable.

References A5.14

When dealing with a customer for the first time, knowledge of that customer and the potential risk involved is of the utmost importance (see **A2 CREDIT RISK ANALYSIS; A3 GAINING INFORMATION TO SUPPORT CREDIT DECISIONS** and **A4 CREDIT ASSESSMENT AND ITS USES**, which detail the value of risk analysis and assessment, together with sources of information). Long standing business practice has been the request by the seller to the buyer to supply a bank and two trade references when wishing to open a credit account. Dependent upon the expected level of exposure, many businesses regard the provision and follow up of these references to be sufficient to establish credit worth. This view is not universally shared but such references confirm the existence of the customer and give some indication as to reputation. In the past, suppliers have regarded such references as quick and cheap, though there are limitations which should be appreciated and cheapness may not now be regarded as applicable. In any event, bank and trade references, at best, form only part of the picture in risk assessment and should be interpreted with care.

Bank references or banker's opinions

Rules A5.15

Prior to 1994 it was common practice, upon receipt of bank details from the prospective customer, for the supplier to approach his own bank and request:

> 'Bank reference please Anycompany (Anywhere) Ltd £5,000 monthly account. Customer's bank – XYZ Bank Ltd, address etc.'

The supplier could even approach XYZ Bank direct. In due course, the reply would come back: 'Anycompany (Anywhere) Ltd considered good for your figures and purpose'. The fee, if any, would be nominal and debited to the supplier's account. This was the situation which prevailed for many years and bank references were, for many, the most common form of credit checking and indeed for many businesses, the only form of credit checking. Such references were quick, inexpensive and standard business practice, even though the value and reliability of them was often called into question and the subject of heated debate whenever two credit managers met. The process was confidential, being between the supplier, his bank and the customer's bank, and no authority of the customer was required by his bank before a reference was produced. In 1994, the rules in respect of bank references changed fundamentally. These changes are detailed below.

- Express written consent must be obtained from the subject of the enquiry. This must be signed by an authorised signatory under the customer's bank mandate.

- Normally, the authority of the customer is specific to a particular enquiry, known as 'specific authority'. However, the customer could also give his bank what is known as 'blanket authority' for the bank to reply to each and every enquiry, from whatever source, without further reference by the bank back to the customer.

If the business relationship between the supplier and the customer is likely to be ongoing, and, therefore, there is a likelihood that the supplier will want to obtain further bank references in the future on the same customer, there is a further authority available to the customer. This is known as 'continuing specific authority', where any future enquiry from that specific supplier can be supplied without further reference back to the customer.

- If so wished, the subject of the bank enquiry will be supplied with a copy of the reference.

- The request for the bank reference is sent to the account holding bank on a standard form supplied by his bank and recognised by all clearing banks. The bank receiving the enquiry will reply direct to the enquirer.

- The fee (which varies from bank to bank and includes VAT at the standard rate) should accompany the request for the reference, the replying bank should issue a VAT receipt with the reference.

● If the subject of the enquiry refuses to consent to his bank issuing a reference, the fee is returned to the enquirer, together with a note of explanation. (It is for the enquirer to form his own opinion as to the significance of such a refusal.)

After the introduction of these rules, the banks made some concessions to the enquiring business community, such as the use of credit cards to purchase the references. Nevertheless, a major fall in bank reference requests was the inevitable outcome, credit managers generally agreeing that this was the aim and intention of the banks in the first place; and certainly there has been no sign of a revival in popularity – indeed, in many industries, the practice of obtaining bank references has all but disappeared.

Interpretation of wording   A5.16

When replying to bank references, there is a general language used, the format being appropriate to the particular circumstance. Commonly used phrases can be subject to interpretation, more often than not because the skilled enquirer is looking just as much for what the bank does not say as for what it does say. Examples are shown in Figure 1.00.

Figure 1.00 – The wording of bank references

Bank reply	Meaning
Undoubted	More or less what it says – certainly the best reference given
Respectable, considered good for your enquiry	Probably the most usual good reference
Private limited company, considered good for your figure and purpose	Much the same as above, with the added confirmation of limited company status
Respectable, but unable to speak for your figure	Guarded, and the enquirer should be wary
Unable to speak for your enquiry	A bad reference

Different variations of wording have been used, which in themselves may give some insight into the real state of play that might not be shown from the wording used in Figure 1.00. There is a deal of difference in emphasis and meaning by using variations of 'could', 'would', and 'should', and the enquirer should be alert to any deviation from the norm. For example, where the replying bank uses the phrase, 'would not enter into a commitment he could not see his way clear to fulfill', it is more an expression of doubt in the bank's mind than a show of confidence. Equally, the use of, 'capital fully employed', is more a statement of the customer's indebtedness to the bank than anything else. Banks can also indicate their prior claim to the customer's assets in the event of insolvency by stating that the bank holds a charge.

After a pattern of bank replies which had been fairly constant over a good many years, recipients began to notice certain changes in wording beginning to appear from time to time from individual banks. This began late in 1998, and at first there was a degree of confused puzzlement. For example, the word 'likely' was used in phrases such as, 'likely to prove good for the amount of your enquiry'. One bank began saying in bank status reports things as definite as, 'the customer is able to meet the commitment'. This departure from the hitherto usual phraseology was explained by the banks concerned as simply modernising the language used with the intention on their part of removing any hidden meaning to bank replies. This initial attempt to remove ambiguity was more puzzling than helpful, but as the modernisation process became more widespread, a greater degree of commonality developed, together with a better understanding by recipients of what was being said.

Only an opinion

A5.17

It should be remembered that a bank's reply to a status enquiry is in the form of an opinion, and that opinion is based upon the account holding bank's current knowledge about the subject of the enquiry, using its own records as the source. A bank reference has never been intended to be definitive in the sense of a statement of the account holder's financial well being and should never be interpreted as anything other than an opinion. The customer may well have other bank or building society accounts, assets and holdings which the bank does not know about (many businesses maintain a current account for meeting normal obligations, but deposit excess funds elsewhere) – it can therefore only speak in opinion terms based upon its own records. It is for this reason that a bank reference should only be treated as one source of information, adding to the whole picture that the credit manager is trying to develop in respect of the customer. It should not be the only source, and it should also be worth considering that the bank may have at least some sort of vested interest to take into account, which could have an influence on any opinion offered. One valuable purpose served, however, is actual confirmation of the existence of a relationship between the customer and the bank – the customer has told the credit manager where he banks, and the bank have confirmed this to be correct. It should be noted that most bankers' opinions carry a form of wording which seeks to absolve the provider from any liability. (See also **A2.27** above for information on bank references.)

Trade references

A5.18

The use of trade references is widespread and a long standing practice across the whole range of industrial and commercial activity. Essentially inexpensive, often quick using telephone or fax, they have formed the mainstay of the exchange of business information for many years. Like bank references, however, they can be viewed with scepticism from some quarters of credit management and should be subject to the same level of careful scrutiny and interpretation in order to be of value.

As trade references are requested by the seller to be supplied by the prospective buyer, the opinion is often expressed that such references have little or no value because the buyer is hardly likely to quote the names and addresses of those of his suppliers who would be liable to provide adverse credit information. Equally it is argued that the buyer will only supply those names and addresses which he treats well in payment terms – in other words, there is inbuilt distortion at the outset. There is a great deal of truth in this, though credit managers are constantly surprised by negative trade reference replies received. Independently sourced trade references, as those obtained by the salesman have more validity from the point of view of the credit manager, in that they are less likely to be 'cultivated' or 'favoured' references.

There is also the value of the trade referee to the customer himself. A manufacturer of glass could well supply the name of his sand supplier as a trade reference, which turns out to be a good, high value and well conducted account. At the same time, the customer is being sued by the local office supplies firm for non-payment for pens and stationery. The customer *needs* his sand supplier far more than he needs his stationery supplier – without sand he cannot make glass. References from associated, subsidiary or parent companies should be avoided – the close connection and relationship between the customer and his referee render the reply and comments of that referee valueless.

The worth of the trade reference lies in its independence and in the high standing of the referee. If the referee can show that the customer has been able to pay for amounts near or over the credit transaction that the enquirer has in mind, so much the better. The use of trade references also brings credit managers into contact with each other, opening up new lines of communication and sources of information. The informal link that is created can be cultivated, and the better the credit managers know each other, the more candid the exchange of information between the two.

It is always advisable to approach the prospective reference in writing, informing the referee that his name has been given by the customer and that information is being sought as to how long the referee has known the customer, payment terms, amount of credit and payment performance. Always offer to reciprocate at any time, and enclose a stamped addressed envelope with the request.

Clearly, the closer the reference to the enquirer's own terms, amount and line of business, the better the information received is likely to be. However, as with bank replies, such information has to be taken in the context of all the data obtained, and not be regarded by itself as definitive.

The credit manager in any particular trade has his own contacts, and insight into the prospective customer can be gleaned by who the customer has actually quoted as his trade referees. If the contact is well known to the credit manager, so much the better, but the fact a referee unknown to the credit manager has been quoted can be both enlightening in itself and open up a new line of contact for the seller. The credit manager's own contacts in the trade can confirm or add to the information received from the referee and act as a form of validation of that information. (See **A2.28** above for more information on trade references.)

Personal references   A5.19

A guarantee is a form of security, and it may well be that in the absence of any reliable information some kind of guarantee is sought. All businesses start somewhere and in the early days of trading it may not be possible for the customer to supply trade references, and the bank reference is unhelpful other than confirming the existence of the account. There could also be circumstances where commercial pressure is such that business is undertaken with a prospective customer when the perceived risk, according to bank and trade references, would deem the need for some form of security.

Sole traders and partnerships apart, many small limited companies are run by the owner or director, and in the absence of adequate information in respect of the limited company, a personal guarantee is obtained from the owner or director. This way the risk is spread, as in the event that the company does not perform as agreed in the contract in respect of payment of the account, then the owner or director is responsible by way of the personal guarantee he has given. The prime responsibility lies with the debtor company to meet its obligations to pay the creditor, the guarantor (in this case the owner or director) is only responsible if the debtor company does not pay.

The guarantee must be in writing, detailing the parties to the guarantee (the guarantor and the creditor) and the obligation which is being guaranteed (the obligation between the debtor and the creditor), and be signed by the guarantor. Banks often secure directors' personal guarantees in respect of the company's overdraft facility, though trade creditors in the normal course of events frequently encounter more difficulty in securing such guarantees. However, there may be no other option available if ongoing business is to be undertaken, and personal guarantees in trade credit are not uncommon. (See **A12 RISK MITIGATION AND SECURITY FOR COMMERCIAL CREDIT TRANSACTIONS** for more information on guarantees.)

Opening the account   A5.20

It is important to ensure that new accounts are 'opened' promptly and efficiently in order to ensure that there is as little delay as possible between enquiry, order and completion. This will be subject to such enquiries as are deemed necessary (see **A5.2–A5.19** above), however, unnecessary delays in establishing accounts can be a constant source of friction between the credit and sales departments. The opening of an account simply means the setting up of the customer account on the sales ledger.

Cash only accounts

It is common practice, when stipulating cash only terms, to either set up the customer account as cash only, or to establish one or more general cash sale accounts. The former may be for customers where regular trade is to be ongoing but where the customer himself stipulates a preference for cash sale (the driver collecting a cheque or cash on delivery is common in the catering trade).

It may also be that cash sale is stipulated until confidence in the account has been established, such as in the case of new businesses, or where there could be an unavoidable delay in establishing the credit account, cash transactions being used in the meantime. Alternatively, cash may simply be insisted upon by the seller due to the account being a bad credit risk, even though ongoing business is both sizeable and profitable.

For small, over the trade counter type transactions, or one off sales, many businesses employ the use of general cash sale accounts, perhaps one for each warehouse or depot or one for each sales representative or sales region. It is vital, however, to be able to produce the necessary VAT invoice for the buyer, even though the buyer may not enjoy the privilege of his own account with the seller.

Cash in the context outlined above need not, of course, necessarily be 'coin of the realm', or actual cash. There are important issues of security and insurance for delivery drivers, for example, handling actual cash. Cash, as opposed to credit, simply means 'payment', i.e. payment is secured before the goods are handed over or collected.

Credit account

Until the credit has been set up on the sales ledger any orders have to be held and no goods supplied, unless processed through the cash sale account (see **A5.21** above). Setting up the account follows the process of credit checking, the establishment of the credit limit and/or risk category (see **A5.26** and **A5.28** below) and other verification of the data supplied by the customer. Having set up the account, the processing of orders can proceed.

Payment terms

Integral to the account, now opened on the sales ledger, are the payment terms in force for that account, whether the normal terms or those specifically agreed for that customer. Such terms will drive the account handling process from that time onwards, subject to review and amendment, and govern the way in which the sales ledger account is conducted.

Prices and conditions

Each account when opened will contain details of prices specific to that account. It is usual for commercial organisations to have a product catalogue and price list, but it is equally usual to negotiate prices in the environment of the competitive market place on a one to one basis, according to projected volumes, product type or other influences. There may also be specific conditions attached to that customer over and above the seller's normal terms and conditions which have been negotiated, such as packing and delivery requirements. All such details, which form part of the account at the time of opening, are subject to alteration during the life of the account, and again govern the way in which the account is conducted.

Confirmation – customer contact   A5.25

When opening a new account, it is good business practice to confirm details in writing to the customer. Many companies write a welcome letter to new customers which serves the purpose of detailed confirmation of all those points raised above (see **A5.21–A5.24** above), but also provides the opportunity for the customer to draw attention to any errors in name and address and where invoices and statements should be sent (see **A2.8** above). The customer now also has a point of contact in the event of any query and has been given at the outset a favourable indication of the quality and efficiency of the organisation with which he will be dealing.

Credit limits   A5.26

In consumer credit the customer is aware from the outset that he will be given a credit limit, based upon a range of factors including status, earnings and outgoings. It is therefore part of the consumer credit culture and accepted that each individual will be so classified by the lender or credit grantor. The use of credit limits is widespread in commercial or trade credit, but not as readily appreciated or understood by the buyer, or sometimes even by the seller.

Limits – why?   A5.27

The purpose of credit limits in trade credit are in essence twofold. Firstly, it is the role of the credit function to minimise the risk of exposure to bad debt, and limiting the amount of credit given at any particular time to customers where it is perceived that the risk is greater than normal makes reasonable sense. Secondly, the operation of the account within an agreed credit limit enables the account to be conducted with the minimum of interference and consequent delay. Credit management can therefore focus attention where required and not waste time and resource where it is not needed.

Credit limits impose disciplines upon both buyer and seller – the buyer ensures that payment of his account always keeps him trading within the agreed limits and the seller ensures that action is taken if the limit is breached. In other words, the limit acts as a brake, to be applied or released as circumstances allow – no limit at all would mean that no restriction was ever placed on order levels, and therefore no ongoing re-evaluation of the account would take place. In such circumstances, non-payment of the debt, however large, could be the first and only indication of a problem with the customer.

Unlike consumer credit (see **A10 CONSUMER CREDIT OPERATIONS**), where credit scoring based upon statistical probability if certain predetermined characteristics are present makes the setting of credit limits a comparatively straightforward undertaking, in trade credit the establishment of absolute and meaningful limits is problematical.

For meaningful limits, the first point of contact has to be the sales department. They have the knowledge of the proposed level of business with the customer, and it is the function of credit management departments, in effect, to check the credit worthiness of the customer and advise sales accordingly. If the prospective customer is deemed to be a higher than normal risk, and therefore would warrant a lower limit than would have hitherto been anticipated, then informing sales may enable them to alter their strategy for this customer. Equally, if the customer presents a less than average risk and is potentially a good account, this can prompt greater efforts to sell more.

The credit limit should be set with ongoing trading in mind and therefore at a level to accommodate the likely amount of exposure according to the terms of trade operated. For example, on monthly terms the limit should be sufficient to cover three months sales, i.e. those not due, those currently due and those one month overdue. More often than not, credit limits are used as guidelines rather than being strictly enforced, being flexible to act as an alert procedure to credit management as opposed to causing the automatic barring of orders. Such flexibility is a matter of judgement and circumstance, however, and the guideline can be an enforced rule when the element of risk is deemed to be high. Limits should not dictate the level of business, except where they are required to act as a barrier, but should assist the credit department to control customer accounts, especially if used in conjunction with risk categories. (See **A4.5–A4.13** above and **A6.14** below for more information.)

Risk categories – why?   A5.28

If credit limits are used as a means of ensuring that no credit is given without at least some element of control, then risk categories are the practical means by which the risk factor is supervised in a semi-structured way. In practical terms this means that those accounts which warrant constant supervision and referral to credit management receive the attention they require, and those accounts which in effect look after themselves operate smoothly without time consuming and costly interference. Some industries are themselves regarded as high risk and customers in such industries may well be defined in risk category terms differently from customers of a similar size in other industries. Typically, trade credit risk categories would adhere to the following pattern.

Category A – undoubted or low risk A5.29

Government bodies, local authorities, nationalised industries, large multi-national companies, large well known national companies, these organisations would be seen to be financially sound, and therefore the risk of failure and not being paid is minimal. They would have no upper credit limit imposed, or at least a very substantial limit, and often enjoy special terms or prices. This is not to say that slow payment will not be experienced with customers in this category – departments of central and local Government, schools, hospitals and so on can be a bureaucratic jungle, as indeed can large commercial companies. It simply means that in the normal course of events orders are processed without referral and the minimum of attention is required by the credit department.

Category B – ordinary trade risk A5.30

Limited companies, partnerships and sole traders where the financial standing is sound and credit checks indicate a good reputation. The majority of customers would fall into this category, and be given credit limits relative to the anticipated level of business in each case. The limits would be for guidance, not mandatory, and involve referral to credit management on an exceptional, rather than a regular basis.

Category C – high risk A5.31

Small and/or new businesses where there is little or no trade experience or where credit checks have indicated a poor reputation for payment and financial weakness. Customers in this category represent a higher than average risk and would be set credit limits which would be mandatory, acting as a bar against orders which would lead to over exposure. All orders would be referred to credit management for approval or otherwise. In a highly competitive market place such customers may be necessary to the seller, but would be dealt with in a strictly controlled way so as to ensure minimum risk.

Category D – cash only A5.32

Any customer who could not be placed into categories A, B, or C would fall into this category, together with known bad accounts where previous experience has been of dishonoured cheques, legal proceedings, or the owners have been involved in a business which has failed. The category would also include one off transactions where no credit account was being established. All accounts would have a zero credit limit, orders being referred automatically to credit management for the appropriate action.

Monitoring A5.33

As outlined in **A5.26–A5.32** above, the use of limits and categories together enable the credit function to focus attention where it is most needed. Referrals to the credit department for whatever reason or from whichever category, need immediate attention. No order should be processed until the credit department has satisfied two fundamental criteria:

- whether the account is overdue for payment; and
- whether this new order takes the customer over his credit limit (guideline or mandatory).

The overdue element is of particular relevance if the credit limit is more of a guide than a barrier, and in both cases the risk factor overrides. Close monitoring of the accounts allows an immediate response in the event of any exceptional circumstance, such as a cheque being returned unpaid or a direct debit or standing order being cancelled. It also allows for the general performance of the account to be kept under review, with order levels and payments indicating movement in the account.

Risk categories are not set in stone once established. Movement of customers between categories should be possible, both up and down the scale, dependent upon account experience. A sudden returned cheque, for example, can move any customer instantly from B to D, with an immediate reduction of any previous credit limit to zero, and it will only be when confidence has been re-established that the restoration of a credit limit and the return to another category would be considered.

Confirmation   **A5.34**

The welcome letter (see **A2.19** and **A5.25** above) above should also inform the customer at the time of opening the account of any credit limit attached to that account. This may not be either appropriate or necessary for category A accounts, but is certainly relevant for other categories and high risk customers should always be told of their limits. This avoids the likelihood of problems later if an order has to be held pending a payment to bring the account back under the credit limit. Informing the customer of his limit also invites the customer to discuss with credit management his requirements, if different, and to establish terms and processes which would have to be undertaken for that limit to be increased. As previously stated (see **A5.26** and **A5.27** above), it is not easy to achieve accurate meaningful credit limits in trade accounts and trade customers often see limits as contentious, however, on balance it is better for the customer to know that a credit limit exists rather than be faced unexpectedly at some future date by an urgently required order held up by the credit department.

Regular update   **A5.35**

A danger inherent in credit limits and risk categories in many organisations is that once in place, they are never looked at again. Not only is this bad business practice, it is a misuse of a perfectly satisfactory aid to pro-active and effective credit management, and renders both category and limit as being totally without meaning. It may be argued that it is better to operate without either than to render them superfluous by not keeping them under review. Throughout the life of an account the success of the business can vary – big companies can fall on hard times and are no more immune from changing circumstances than any other. Equally, big trees from little acorns grow, so today's small account could be tomorrow's major customer.

It follows, therefore, that the limits and categories of all accounts should be regularly reviewed and not just be looked at in reaction to some particular event. A regular update of limits and categories can enable business trends to be acknowledged and exploited – confidence in an account and an increase in the customer's financial standing and reputation should promote increased sales effort.

Any change in the customer's credit limit should be notified in writing to the customer for exactly the same reasons as sending him the welcome letter in the first instance, with the added advantage of re-establishing person to person contact and promoting the seller's own efficiency and professionalism.

A6

Organisation of the Sales Ledger

Introduction A6.1

Ask any auditor, and he will tell you the nightmare tale of the 'shoe boxes'. For many businesses, some large as well as the very many small enterprises which are now such an integral part of the business scene, the keeping of records varies from the ordered to the haphazard. At the end of the accounting period, or at the time that the tax returns are due, into the accountant's office staggers the client, with supermarket carrier bags and shoe boxes stuffed full of purchase invoices, receipts for petrol and calculator tally rolls, bank paying in books, cheque books and myriads of other bits of paper relating to trading activities. The auditor, having an eye on his final audit fee, can see some mileage in employing one of the office staff to unravel this storm of paper, try to flatten out those that have been 'inadvertently' screwed up and put them into some kind of category and order. Then comes the task of matching these to the accounts record book (not always entered up in ink by the client, if entered up at all!) and from this chaos establish how the business has actually done in the last twelve months.

Keeping records has to be the basis of any regularised operation, and not just for the purpose of being able to meet statutory obligations and deadlines, such as Inland Revenue and VAT. To know where we want to be tomorrow, we have to know where we are today, and the only way we can do that is by knowing where we came from yesterday. Not to keep records breaches a mountain of regulations, but it also prevents proper focus on the needs and requirements of an ongoing business.

Keeping records is one thing, but orderly and accurate records is another. Credit control cannot be conducted from a shoe box. Who owes what? When from? What is it for? When did they pay? How much did they pay? How did they pay? And what did I do with it? It may all sound very basic, but that is only because it *is* very basic – the rock on which the edifice of credit management is constructed is an accurate sales ledger.

Sales ledger A6.2

The sales ledger lies at the heart of the credit management function, representing as it does a record of all the sales transactions of the business. Debtors, or accounts receivable, account for anything up to 35–40% of the total assets of the business and it is the control of that asset which is the purpose of risk management, regardless of industry sector. Not to successfully manage that asset spells disaster and it is the sales ledger which provides the key to this, both as a useful record and as a useable tool.

Purpose of the ledger A6.3

The dictionary definition of ledger is, in book keeping terms, 'the principal book in which the commercial transactions of a company are recorded'. The purchase ledger records all that is bought, the sales ledger all that is sold, and the nominal or general ledger translates all into balance sheet and profit and loss terms. The sales ledger, therefore, is fundamental to the business operation, recording:

- invoices raised to customers (sales);

- payments made by customers (receipts);

- credit notes for goods returned or allowances;

- write offs;

- write ons; and

- transfers etc.

At any moment in time, the difference between what has been invoiced to a customer and what has been paid by that customer is the balance owing, and is the amount which the business has outstanding on risk (i.e. at risk of not being paid).

The ledger has an importance beyond the role of a record of transactions. It acts as a source of information to both seller and buyer, being the actual statement of account, informing the seller of his expectations and the buyer of his obligations. In the collection sense, if the invoice can be described as the first request for payment (see **A6.9** and **A6.16** below), then the statement, derived from the sales ledger can be regarded as the second or confirming request. In many organisations, the statement to the customer is no more than the customised version of the sales ledger, specific to that customer and containing the same details of invoices rendered and cash received as shown on the seller's version of the ledger. It is also worth noting that many buyers will use the statement of account sent to them by the seller as a reconciliation document, balancing their purchase ledger to the seller's sales ledger to agree outstanding items, payments made and to highlight any errors or omissions.

Importance of good housekeeping A6.4

The criticism often aimed at the finance function, more than likely emanating from the sales department, towards the credit manager and to accountants in general, is that 'accounts people' seem to have an obsession with the need to maintain what can be best described as a tidy ledger. The criticism is unfair, not because the credit manager wants to keep a tidy ledger at all costs, but simply because it is of paramount importance to maintain accuracy in detail and in fact. The credibility of the function is dependent upon the ledger, as it is an accurate reflection of the true state of the customer's account and shows that the account is as up-to-date as circumstances and systems will allow. No one wants to work with out-of-date data. Trying to collect money from an account already paid, or collect payment for an invoice credited in full (while at the same time stopping supplies because the invoice is 'overdue'), is damaging to customer relations and a poor reflection on the skill and efficiency of the seller's credit department. It should go without saying that once that damage has been caused, retrieving credibility and trust is a much more difficult task.

Entries to the sales ledger come from sources both within and outside the seller's organisation. Internal sources obviously include invoices and credit notes, journal entries and adjustments, the external source principally being payments received from the customer. Entries from either source can lead to a cluttered ledger, in so far as entries from various sources might not at first sight be matched to existing entries or readily identified as being connected.

What is meant by good housekeeping, therefore, is periodic review and vigilance. Regular attention should be given to the correction of any posting errors, and the removal, where appropriate, of invoices cancelled by matching credit notes – some sales ledger systems will automatically connect credit notes to the respective invoices but this is not always the case and they may need to be identified and the contra entries removed. Part of the exercise in identifying credit notes and the relevant original invoice also involves checking that the credit note is correct. This includes, not only confirming that the items credited refer to the items disputed or returned, but also seeing that the price credited was the price originally charged. It is not uncommon to find that since the goods were originally invoiced, a price increase has taken place and been input to the computer system, and it is easy for the credit note to be raised at the new price instead of the old one.

Good housekeeping also involves clearing the ledger, where appropriate, of small debit and credit balances. Such balances may be the result of small overpayments or underpayments, perhaps involving miscalculated discounts, or transposed figures, which themselves are not worth the time or effort in contacting the customer. There is also the question of unallocated cash, often a difficult area. Payments from customers in normal circumstances should be in respect of debits existing on the ledger (or about to exist, such as in the case of deposits or payment in advance or with the order), but from time to time customers do make payments which are not readily identifiable. There is pressure on the cash allocation process to see that the payment is reflected on the customer's account without delay, to which end the payment is placed 'on account'. This may be expedient, but every effort should be made in the first instance to identify and to add some explanatory notation to the entry. As part of the housekeeping process all unallocated cash entries should be identified and correctly applied, and this should be an ongoing process. More often than not, contacting the customer at the outset before the cash is actually posted to the ledger provides the necessary explanation.

The aim of good housekeeping is not to be fussy or awkward, but simply to ensure that the ledger accurately reflects the genuine position of the account – clearing the trees to reveal the wood makes for clarity to both seller and buyer and indicates what needs to be collected and what needs to be paid. Pages of mispostings, unallocated cash and unmatched items are confusing and unprofessional. In addition, audit charges are often higher where there is a great deal of unallocated cash and credit notes on the ledger which have not been reconciled.

Customer name and address A6.5

In addition to the sales ledger being a record of transactions with customers, the ledger also contains the basic details of customer name and address. Each account is given an account number or unique reference for ease of identification and all relevant information in respect of name and address is established.

The legal identity of the customer is of paramount importance, so accuracy is essential. It is often the case that the initial details supplied by the sales department are subject to verification by the credit management function as part of the credit assessment process, and that the account is actually opened on the ledger under a name perhaps different from that originally supplied. Sole trader, partnership or limited company may not mean a great deal to personnel outside the credit department, but in terms of legal standing, liability and therefore credit risk, there is a world of difference. The customer name is at the heart of the customer file and at the very least the seller should know exactly with whom he is dealing.

During the trading life of the account the customer's name may be subject to change. Businesses are acquired or disposed of, new trading names adopted, and/or customer requirements alter. Part of sales ledger management is to reflect those changes, keeping the customer file accurate and up-to-date, in line with the changed status or legal identity of the buyer and correctly following customer instructions as to how he should be invoiced and to whom statements should be sent.

The customer file includes the address – full postal address, including postcode where appropriate. In trade credit, the address file should be set up to accommodate three basic addresses per customer, namely:

- invoice address;
- statement address; and
- delivery address.

In many cases, all three will be the same, but often not and with large customers there could be a varied combination of delivery, invoice and statement addresses. Sending invoices to the wrong address delays payment and delivering goods to the wrong address causes confusion and delay. It is often said that the removal of impediments to payment speeds cash flow, so creating unnecessary obstacles by the use of incorrect addresses is both foolish and costly. The customer order will contain specific invoice and delivery instructions which should be followed in order to ensure the smooth flow of the payment paperwork. These instructions may well change at any time, so each order must be scrutinised for any divergence from already established details – changes of address are as important as changes of name (and are more frequent) and sales ledger maintenance incorporates the adoption of those changes promptly and accurately as they occur. Such changes may be specifically notified by the customer by way of a general circular to all suppliers, but could also simply be an alteration on the order, or a notice accompanying the remittance. It should be part of the credit management routine to keep a close watch on all correspondence.

In large organisations, with a number of branches or depots, it is quite common for the order to give clear invoicing and delivery instructions. Many groups have centralised accounting and accounts payable centres where all invoices and statements should be sent, regardless of which depot received the delivery, and the supplier's customer name and address file has to be capable of incorporating all such instructions. (See **A8 COMPUTER ACCOUNTING SYSTEMS AND MONITORING OF THE SALES LEDGER** for information as to how computerisation of the sales ledger can assist.)

Customer history   A6.6

The customer file should record the date that the account was opened and from then on build up a history of relevant events related to the account. This will include the:

- original bank reference and trade references;

- original status report;

- customer credit application and signed acknowledgement of terms;

- credit terms and credit limit allocated;

- invoice, delivery and statement instructions;

- contact name(s), telephone and fax numbers and e-mail addresses;

- bank details and payment method;

- trade and settlement discounts;

- all changes to any of the above, together with the source and date of the change;

- queries, disputes and/or complaints; and

- purchases and payments.

Maintenance of the file   A6.7

All of the items listed in **A6.6** above can be computer stored (see **A8 COMPUTER ACCOUNTING SYSTEMS AND MONITORING OF THE SALES LEDGER**), although some documents may be considered worth filing or keeping in their original form, such as those containing customer signatures. The file, therefore, builds up a history of the account regarding significant events or changes, including periodic credit status and credit limit reviews, taken in conjunction with the record of how the account has been conducted over a period of time. The maintenance of the customer file and the subsequent development of the history of that customer is subject to information received from the customer, and to updates generated by internal review procedures – it is useful, therefore, not just to note the date of any change, but also to record the source of the amendment. It is worth remembering that if e-mails are the source, then an adequate e-mail storage process is required, and it may simply be expedient to retain a printed copy. Following any internal review, where an amendment to credit limit or credit terms materially alters the way in which business is undertaken with the customer, then the customer should be informed.

The customer history may well also be expanded to include information not directly connected to sales ledger operation, but of interest or concern to other personnel outside the sales ledger. Details of product type, size, colour, quantities etc, marketing information, press reports or reports from sales or delivery personnel can be a valuable source of information for marketing purposes, as well as being useful data to credit management.

Businesses can grow by mergers and acquisitions, and product diversification can bring new marketing opportunities. Few successful businesses fail to adapt to changing needs and circumstances, however, diversification can also lead to problems, for example, cash flow strained by rapid expansion, or entry into markets without previous knowledge of that market place.

Both credit management and marketing departments can develop a good insight into the customer by looking at the customer history, identifying what took place and when, and taking the steps required to act accordingly.

Record of events A6.8

The sales ledger can, in effect, be regarded as a complete diary of transactional events taking place between seller and buyer on an ongoing basis. The ledger is updated by such events at regular intervals, such intervals being dictated by the volume of business. Invoices and cash can be posted daily, with weekly summaries and sub-totals and statements of account produced on a monthly basis, according to customer demand. Production and maintenance of the ledger triggers all related activities – telephone collections, reminder letters, final notices etc, all geared to the cycle in operation. As an accurate record of events, the ledger serves an invaluable purpose in illustrating, at any given moment in time, the position in respect of receivables, allowing prompt release of orders, an explanation of amounts due and overdue and the totals owed by customers. Good housekeeping (see **A6.4** above) eases interpretation and therefore minimises confusion.

Principal sales events A6.9

The principal events recorded on a regular basis on the sales ledger revolve around:

- invoices (debits to the customer account);

- credit notes (credits to the customer account);

- cash allocation (usually credits, but includes debits such as deductions for discount or debit notes); and

- journal entries (debits or credits).

Invoices A6.10

The invoice is a record of the sale made to the customer, whether for goods supplied, services provided, or both. It should be issued as quickly as possible after delivery of the goods or provision of the services – any delay is adding to the cost of financing credit. The sooner the invoice is produced and sent to the customer, the sooner the invoice enters the customer's payment process and the greater the expectation of being paid on time. It is in fact the seller's first request to the buyer for payment, indicating that the seller has discharged his side of the bargain and drawing the customer's attention to his obligations under the contract. Many small businesses suffer from cash related problems simply because they fail to appreciate the need to invoice quickly – many are craftsmen who lay out hundreds of pounds in time and materials installing central heating or erecting a conservatory, but leave the invoicing until either they or a partner has time 'to catch up with the paperwork'. The customer is certainly not going to even begin to think about payment until the invoice arrives, and giving extra credit by way of late invoicing benefits only the buyer not the seller. The time gap between doing the work and receiving payment should be governed only by agreed credit terms, not by the lax timetable of invoice production.

Equally prompt attention should be paid to posting the invoice to the sales ledger. The ledger can only be as up-to-date as entries made to it, and there is nothing to be gained from failing to accurately record sales as and when they take place. Failure to post invoices to the ledger leads to a distorted picture, both in terms of actual customer indebtedness at any given moment in time, and in relation to the customer's credit limit. It might be that a new order is taken, which would in fact exceed the credit limit, but at the time the order was taken the previous invoice had not been posted to the ledger thus increasing the exposure and ultimate risk.

The same time disciplines should apply to the production and issue of monthly statements. As a record of transactions for a specific accounting period, the statement should be with the customer as soon as possible after the month end. The statement is taken by many as the second request for payment, as well as being used as a reconciliation document, delays cost money and are to be avoided. In short, at any given moment in time, the customer should be able to ask 'what do I owe?' and the finance director should be able to ask 'what do they owe?', with the answer being readily available to both, and the answer being exactly the same.

Credit notes   A6.11

In many organisations there is a tendency to deliberately delay the production and issue of credit notes. For some, the negative effect that the credit has on the sales figures overrides the need to satisfy the customer requirement, whilst for others credit notes are likened to giving money away and are therefore to be avoided if possible, and in any event delayed if need be. This is not good practice. All businesses strive to meet customer needs and part of that is to deliver the right goods, at the right price, to the right place, and at the right time, and for every aspect of the delivery and subsequent charge to be correct. If, however, for whatever reason it is agreed that the customer is entitled to receive a credit note, then the document should be raised promptly, posted to the ledger and sent to the customer without delay. The customer could well be withholding payment of the original invoice pending settlement of his claim and is not going to release his cheque until he is satisfied that his complaint or request has been dealt with. Not issuing the credit note only means that the debt remains outstanding on the ledger, with knock on effects on the customer credit limit, overdue reminder letters, stop list and even recovery action. There is the added negative impact of the customer taking the view that he is not dealing with an efficient organisation and to lose a customer simply to satisfy sales manager's concerns about his figures, or the accountant's wish to hold onto his company's money at all costs would be the height of folly.

The credit note should also refer to the original invoice in text and invoice number, in order that the customer is able to identify, and the seller's sales ledger reflects, true indebtedness. In some organisations this is not always possible – credit notes can be produced for a variety of reasons, including those which could be regarded as diplomatic credit notes, and are therefore not necessarily referring to any specific invoice. In such cases, the text of the credit note should be clear enough for the customer to identify and acknowledge the original query, enabling the document and accompanying invoices to be processed without delay.

Cash   A6.12

Payments should be allocated accurately to the ledger as soon as they are received. It must be the first real function of the day to take all incoming payments, bank the cheques and post the cash to the ledger. Using the sales ledger to highlight collection targets for the day, or ongoing targets for the week or month, means that as well as having the complete picture in respect of invoices and credit notes, all cash movements are shown as they occur so that the ledger is always as up-to-date as it is both possible and desirable to be.

Not every customer will enclose with his payment a remittance advice and in some industries it is not unusual simply to receive a cheque and nothing at all with it. A frequent occurrence is for the customer to write on the back of the cheque the invoice number he is paying – this highlights the need for the cashiers department, if separate from the sales ledger, to be vigilant when handling cheques and to ensure that the correct information is passed to those actually posting the cash to the ledger.

As shown in **A6.4** above, there are circumstances when it is not possible to directly allocate the cash to specific invoices, however, any unallocated items should be followed up straight away and not left languishing in a suspense account. The whole point is for the customer's account to always reflect the true position, and the month end, before statements are sent out, should be the deadline for clearing unallocated items. It is also more than likely that the longer an oddity is left on the ledger, the less chance there is of it being satisfactorily resolved and the greater the possibility of the item having to be written off.

Care should also be taken to ensure that the invoices being marked as paid are those which the customer has indicated he is paying. A common mistake is to clear the 'older' items first, especially when the customer has a number of repeat or same value invoices. The older items may have been overlooked, or they could be being withheld for a reason, perhaps in query. To remove such invoices could cause problems later when credits are to be raised, or when the customer's next cheque appears to pay invoices already paid. Most customers like to see that their payment has been received and correctly applied, so the movement should be reflected on the ledger and hence on the customer statement.

Effective credit control depends upon the accuracy of the ledger and the fact that the ledger is up-to-date. Nobody would consider it sensible to sit on cheques and not bank them, so why sit on remittances and not allocate them?

Journal   A6.13

From time to time movements will take place on the sales ledger which have not themselves been generated by the production of invoices or credit notes, or by the allocation of cash, although in the case of cash there can be a direct connection. These small differences occur, for example when:

- the customer has overpaid or underpaid;

- discounts have been wrongly taken or interest not paid and the commercial decision is taken not to pursue;

- an invoice has been transferred from another account or to another account; and

- there is effective contra of sales and purchase ledger items and an agreement exists to offset on a regular basis.

Journal entries are as much a part of the updating process as invoices and cash, and as such need to be promptly and accurately applied.

Credit limits   A6.14

Credit limits form an integral part of the management of the sales ledger and of the customer file. The question of the need for and use of credit limits has been discussed earlier (see **A5.26** and **A5.27** above), but in the context of the organisation of the sales ledger, it is the relevance and the maintenance of credit limits which is to be addressed.

It is a fact that consumers fully accept that when applying for credit, the successful outcome will include being given a credit limit, and that credit limit will be amended (increased, reduced or removed) according to the way in which they conduct their account. It will be also subject to alteration according to any change, for better or for worse, in personal circumstances. Therefore it is also a consequential fact, in consumer credit that the customer is regularly notified of his credit limit, whether or not any amendment has taken place. A good example would be the store or bank credit card monthly invoice or statement, which clearly shows purchases and payments in the month, the amount owed, the amount available to spend and the credit limit. A separate additional letter will be sent notifying any change in the credit limit. The organisation and management of the consumer sales ledger is therefore very much centred around the regular review and constant use of the credit limit.

The trade credit sales ledger is more problematical in the use and open display of credit limits. Many suppliers inform the customer of the credit limit assigned to the account at the time of opening, although not many would continue to show the limit on monthly statements and fewer still would regularly write to the customer informing him of changes to the limit in the normal course of events. Placing a stop on the account (see **A8.19**, **A8.33**, **A13.21** and **A13.55** below), because of non-payment or removal of credit facilities for whatever reason, should lead to the customer being informed, however, it is not unusual for a trade customer to be actually unaware of any credit limit allocated at any given moment in time. On the other hand, it is surely better to keep the customer informed of regular reviews of his credit limit, both from the standpoint of promoting further business and the awareness of the customer as to his order potential.

Whether credit limits are used as a barrier or as a guide (see **A5.27** above), they perform a key function within the organisation of the sales ledger, allowing resource allocation and effort to be focussed, and as such require constant monitoring and review. As a record of events in respect of the customer account, the sales ledger also records:

- limit;

- frequency of change;

- the reason for the change; and

- customer notification.

Records of query and dispute to be flagged   A6.15

The sales ledger records invoices issued and payments received. It should also register any query raised by the customer, particularly if that query means that the invoice in question is not going to be passed for payment. It has often been argued by collection staff that they can only collect that which is collectable and an invoice under dispute is deemed not collectable until the customer complaint has been satisfactorily resolved. Only then can the item resume its collectable status and be returned to the general total of cash to be collected this month.

The ledger should therefore be clearly marked, for example, with a 'Q' alongside the invoice number, this being placed so that reminder letters or stop list procedures are not instigated by queried invoices, or the customer repeatedly asked for payment of an invoice he has already been in contact about. The marker should remain in place until the query has been satisfied – this may be by way of a credit note, replacement goods free of charge or simply a letter of explanation with a copy of the sales ledger file. Once the flag has been lifted, the invoice can be paid.

It is good practice for the query flag also to be evident on the customer's copy of the sales ledger (the statement), if the item remains in dispute over the accounting month end, and is still unresolved at the time of the production of monthly statements. It is then clear to the customer that his complaint has been noted, that he is not being asked for payment of that particular item and that he should not hold up payment of any other invoices. It illustrates the supplier's efficiency and commitment to customer service and that matters raised by the customer have not been ignored. A monthly statement, liberally dotted with query flags may of course say something about the customer, but also may well say a lot more about the supplier. (See **A6.17–A6.22** below for more information on queries.)

Open item format   A6.16

In days of yore, before the advent of mechanised accounting let alone computerisation, books of account, including the sales ledger, were literally books. Entries were laboriously entered on the page, including sales, payments, adjustments and all other items. As far as the sales ledger was concerned, it was standard practice at the end of the accounting period to close off, total up and bring forward the opening balance for the new accounting period. In some businesses the brought forward sales ledger balance is still in use and such a statement shows:

- the brought forward balance;
- a listing of transactions in the current month; and
- the new closing balance at the end of the month.

The big disadvantage of this procedure is that unpaid or disputed individual items from the previous month are listed together in the closing and brought forward balance, and as such are immediately lost to view.

The best format for the sales ledger is known as 'open item'. This means that at all times the ledger shows all the items that make up the total outstanding balance, with cleared invoices and credits disappearing, leaving only unpaid and uncleared records. Computerisation of the sales ledger makes this possible (see **A8 COMPUTER ACCOUNTING SYSTEMS AND MONITORING OF THE SALES**

LEDGER), and the availability of cheap sales ledger software packages should mean that even a small business should be able to operate a computer generated sales ledger system. An open item clearly shows what has been invoiced this month, what is still outstanding from last month and before, what is under query and what is actually owed in total.

The sales ledger serves two prime purposes:

- to tell the supplier what is owed by the customer; and

- to tell the customer (when the ledger forms the basis of the statement) what he owes.

So two things should be crystal clear on the ledger – the invoice (for both the supplier's benefit as well as the buyer's) and on the statement version, the address to which payments should be made (for the buyer's benefit). The invoice line on the ledger should give:

- the date;

- invoice number;

- amount (usually inclusive of VAT at the appropriate rate);

- customer order number; and

- balance outstanding.

Each month outstanding is sub-totalled and a grand total should be shown for each customer. The statement version contains the same information together with details of how and where payment can be made, perhaps incorporating a tear off remittance advice. Clarity of both the invoice amounts to be paid and where to pay them is one of the means of removing at least some obstacles from the path of customer prompt payment, and ledger clarity allows the collection activity of the supplier to be unimpeded by the need to carry out time consuming tasks before getting down to the nitty gritty of collecting money owed.

Dealing with queries A6.17

It has to be the aim of every business organisation to get it right first time and to completely satisfy customer requirements. It is inevitable, however, that mistakes are made – the supplier delivers the wrong size or colour, shortages, damage in transit, wrong price or no discount etc. The error could be on the part of the buyer, ordering incorrectly, not matching quotation and purchase price, being unable to take delivery or no longer requiring the goods. In many high value, high technical specification industries there can be customer dissatisfaction with the goods not performing to specification, or indeed the equipment not doing what the customer thinks he was led to believe it would do. Whatever the circumstances or reasons, there are bound to be queries and disputes which will arise in respect of invoices on the ledger.

Frequently such disputes or queries are not discovered by the sales ledger or collection teams until collection activity has already begun, even though the customer may have previously contacted the sales office, the representative, dispatch or some other department within the company. Often the cry will be heard from the credit manager of anguish and despair when politely informed by the customer that 'your representative called three weeks ago, collected the offending part, and must still be driving around with it in the boot of his car'. Often too it is the collection team who make the first contact with the customer after the goods have been delivered or the service provided. The customer has been waiting for just such contact from somebody within the supplier's organisation to register his complaint, so the sales ledger is very much in the front line when it comes to unearthing disputes.

Customer queries are serious on more than one level. In terms of cash flow alone, they can be very damaging, tying up as they do amounts in accounts receivable which are rendered uncollectable until the dispute is resolved. They can be costly in man hours, involving time and effort in sorting the problem out and thus diverting attention away from the prime function of collecting cash. They clutter up the ledger with unpaid amounts, deductions or query flags obscure the overall picture of the account and where collection targets have been set, act as a barrier to collection staff in achieving them, leading to demotivation and low morale.

As if all this was not enough, great damage can be done to customer relations, giving the impression of inefficiency and lack of customer care or focus. In any business, losing customers is much easier than gaining new customers, and months of hard work can come to nothing in a trice. It should go without saying that every customer query should be taken seriously, acted upon promptly and resolved. There is no alternative but to adopt a structured approach to queries, developing processes and procedures within the seller company which are centred within the sales ledger or credit control function, but which also encompass all departments of the company.

This structured approach serves more than one purpose. The level of queries may indicate problems within the seller company, whether administrative, product or price related. They could highlight problems with certain products in specific market sectors or suitability or otherwise of the products in other sectors. They could also point to individual customer problems and the need to be particularly vigilant with customer A or customer B. Apart from experience, or what could best be described as a gut feeling, no pattern or general picture would emerge if all queries were simply dealt with in an *ad hoc* manner without form or structure.

Query register   A6.18

The purpose of the query register is to:

- formalise basic rules for recording disputes;

- identify the personnel or departments responsible, both in terms of cause and resolution; and

- instigate follow up procedures to finalise and resolve the query.

It is important that disputes are not forgotten and allowed to languish, hence the need for follow up procedures, and there should be a reporting line established to highlight areas of concern. The register also serves the purpose of definition and analysis of customer queries into areas, categories and frequency, so that objective decisions can be taken to prevent the same mistakes being constantly repeated. The query register, and the routines surrounding its operation and function, should be incorporated into the company's credit policy and included in the company's manual of credit operating procedures (see **A6.23–A6.34** below). This will have the effect of involving everyone in the business, so that even though the register is maintained centrally by the sale ledger or credit control team, input to the register is from all areas of the company. In other words, whoever receives the first notification from the customer that there is a problem with an invoice, be it salesman or warehouseman, delivery driver or telesales clerk, it is incumbent upon them to log the query.

Record   A6.19

By whatever means the query is received, it should be recorded. The log record should be made up of:

- date;

- customer name;

- invoice number(s);

- nature of the complaint or dispute;

- who the matter has been passed to for action (and when); and

- date and nature of the outcome.

There should also be included a reminder or follow up procedure to ensure that the complaint is being dealt with. Such a process should impose disciplines on all personnel concerned, and enable the customer to be informed, if needs be, of the progress in respect of the query raised. It also avoids the damaging effects of a customer raising a query with a member of staff who takes the view that it is 'nothing to do with me' and ignores it. Small businesses run by a well knit team may not feel the need to formalise the process in such a way, but larger companies do need to. It is good practice to instigate processes at the outset so that as the business grows the processes are already in place to deal with such eventualities.

It may well be that some queries are extremely simple and can be dealt with straight away by whoever takes the call, however, the query should still be logged as it could form part of a pattern. Other complaints may involve complexities requiring specialist attention from various areas, so the need for the log is much more obvious. It is the discipline, however, which is important, as is the need to see that such a query is not constantly repeated.

As has already been seen, the invoice under query needs to be flagged on the ledger to avoid embarrassment to the collector, and equally important is to remove the flag on resolution. This means that the register should be controlled from within the sales ledger department and that all lines of communication to other departments remain open and free.

Define   A6.20

If notation of the query is vital, equally so is the definition as to nature of the query. The list can appear endless, and at first sight, quite daunting. Just a few are:

- price;
- discount;
- shortage;
- damage;
- colour;
- size;
- model;
- performance;
- credit terms;
- credit limit;
- early delivery;
- late delivery;
- wrong delivery;
- special deals arranged with sales;
- wrong address;
- customer order number;
- erroneous description;
- unable to match to quotation;
- unable to match to order;
- insufficient details;
- errors in extension; and
- wrong rate of VAT.

Definition of the customer query identifies to whom the query should be sent for action and also forms the base data for ongoing analysis of frequency and type.

Analysis   A6.21

The more cynical may see customer queries as simply delaying tactics, in the same way that they may view requests for copy invoices. This may not be true and can only be verified, if at all, once some form of pattern has been established. Analysis of the query register provides the answer. In many ways, such analysis simply reinforces what some people in collection already feel – 'there is a major problem in our own packing department'. If this is true, then documentary evidence is surely the best way to start the process of putting right the wrongs. It is also true to say that if analysis reveals major problems within the seller's own organisation, then it is for the facts to be laid before senior management and for senior management to take such steps as are deemed necessary to cure the problem.

In some respects the query register will follow much the same pattern as a purchase ledger system – the incoming query (purchase invoice) is logged to the system and the person or department who will be responsible for resolving the problem (passing the invoice for payment) is identified and the document passed to them. The date and name is noted, and following a set period of time, the matter is followed up. The major difference will be that time scales for resolving queries will be much shorter than for processing purchase invoices, and that follow up will be urgent and final. If there is still no response, then the matter is automatically escalated to senior management. Apart from perhaps not having got it right in the first place, there can be nothing worse than ignoring a problem in the vain hope that it will go away – it will not, and for all the reasons stated it cannot be allowed to happen.

Having identified the problem, and resolved it, the manner of that resolution should also be noted, along with the date satisfied. Analysis of the query register serves not only to identify areas of concern, but also to illustrate how long it takes to settle dispute. The time taken may well be associated with the nature of the query, which would be taken into account when analysing the register and it could well be that such time scales are themselves identified as a problem.

Sales ledger personnel need to know that the dispute has been settled so that query markers can be removed and collection continued. Such settlement can take various forms, including credit note, free of charge replacement, letter of explanation or some other alternative. In the case of letter or replacement goods, a copy should be filed with the customer record and the customer contacted to confirm that the matter has been resolved and that the invoice will be paid.

Any credit note should be posted to the ledger without delay and matched to the original invoice for ease of identification by both seller and buyer. It is useful to be able to age both the invoice and the credit note together, though some systems will not allow this, but in any event to clearly refer to the invoice in dispute is essential in order to remove the obstacle to payment by the customer. If the original invoice contained the customer order number, then so should the credit note.

Crediting an invoice in full does from time to time produce the occasional problem for some people engaged in sales ledger maintenance – pressure to comply with good housekeeping principles sees the matching of and removal from the ledger of the invoice and credit, only to see from the customer's next payment that he has taken the credit note but not paid the invoice. This is not a problem, simply reinstate the invoice, but ensure that the file contains all the required back-up documentation.

Summary A6.22

In summary, the purpose of the query register is to:

- keep a tight rein on disputes, in order to minimise their effect on cash flow;
- identify areas which require attention; and
- maintain good customer relations.

The cost of such a system is minimal, but the cost of ignoring queries can be devastating.

The credit manual A6.23

A credit policy should be as much a part of the operation of a business as sales, safety, health and environment policies (see **A1 CREDIT POLICY**). As the sales ledger and the way it is managed within the business is fundamental to profitable health, it should be clear to all concerned not just why it is done, but equally just how it is done. Explanation of procedures to other departments, to new staff, to customers and to management, serves the purpose of creating clarity and understanding, adapting to meet changing needs as they occur and setting benchmark standards to be followed and continually improved upon.

Several disciplines exist within the sales ledger and credit control function including:

- efficient processing of documents, including invoices, cash and correspondence;
- communication and interface with other departments;
- working to targets and requirements;
- maintaining and adapting to new systems;
- responding to changing needs;
- developing existing staff and training new personnel;
- understanding company policy and working within that policy framework; and
- upholding business ethics at all times.

In addition to the need for a written credit policy, there should also be a credit manual, clearly stating all matters relating to the operation of a sales ledger and credit control department, both in general terms and in the matter of detailed procedures. This written manual of processes and procedures is the department's handbook, available for all to see, and subject to update, amendment and improvement as circumstances both allow and dictate. Ideally, the manual should be maintained by the credit manager, in cooperation and conjunction with other department heads who are likely to be concerned with the contents. It should be in a format that allows pages to be replaced by the updates as and when they are introduced.

Rules and guidelines   A6.24

Some operational functions within the credit department will be governed by rules which are to be enforced and in principle are not likely to change. An example may be the separation of duties which involve the actual handling of cash received and the preparation of cash received listings from those of actual cash allocation and posting – auditors frequently like to see this division for security reasons. In other operations, there may simply be guidelines in place to assist, although these are not written in stone and allow a certain flexibility when need dictates. This may include discretion in respect of order release on the promise of payment – the *guideline* may allow the customer to have one such order at the discretion of the collector, but the *rule* could stipulate only one order, with no further order release until payment is received.

Expressing, as they do, the practical application of the company's written credit policy, rules and guidelines in the credit manual should cover all aspects of the credit and sales ledger operation, including:

- credit assessment;

- new account procedures;

- invoicing;

- collection;

- management reporting (see **A6.29** below);

- management structure (see **A6.31** below);

- duties and responsibilities (see **A6.32** and **A6.33** below); and

- specimen letters, documents and forms.

In some organisations, the manual may well contain a re-statement of the objectives of the company's credit policy, the objectives of the credit function specifically in achieving those objectives and the role played by the credit department in cooperation with other departments. On the other hand, it should be sufficient to view the manual as an operating document, with the credit policy itself stating overall aims and objectives.

Credit assessment

A6.25

Attempting to determine the ability of a prospective customer to pay, as well as establishing his reputation for paying accounts with other suppliers, begins with credit assessment. The credit manual lists in broad outline the sources of information used in the process and the procedure to be followed in assessing risk. This would apply both to new accounts and to ongoing review of existing customers. It should be company policy to credit check, and the application of that policy should be outlined in the manual. Sources of information would include bank and trade references, credit agencies, Companies House, salesmen's reports and other relevant sources (see **A3 GAINING INFORMATION TO SUPPORT CREDIT DECISIONS**).

The use of credit limits and risk categories should not be a mystery to credit personnel and how they are arrived at, applied and used should be contained in the manual. This also serves the purpose of confirming to sales and other departments that appropriate limits are established and the manner in which limits and categories are applied for the benefit of profitable sales growth. (See **A4 CREDIT ASSESSMENT AND ITS USES**.)

Terms of payment may be subject to change from the company norm, according to the results of the assessment process or experience with an account. Guidelines for the use of payment terms as appropriate, alternative or special terms, any requirements to be used in respect of credit insurance for home or export trade or both should be contained in the manual.

New account procedures

A6.26

The credit policy will lay down the criteria under which new credit accounts will be established – put another way, the value level below which credit accounts will not be opened. The process for opening new accounts will be clear to all concerned in the operating manual, beginning with the correct completion of the credit application form, opening the account on the ledger with the appropriate payment terms, credit limit and risk category, through to notifying the customer of the outcome of the credit application. Implicit in this process are the authority levels and limits of the personnel concerned, both within the credit function and outside. (See **A6.31–A6.33** below.)

Invoicing

A6.27

The manual illustrates the process for producing invoices and credit notes, from order input through to completion and delivery. The process will also cover quotations and the issue of *pro forma* invoices, and in addition will stipulate minimum information requirements for the production of such documentation (e.g. customer order number). In the event of any minimum order value restrictions, the process for handling such orders will be shown, together with the relevant invoicing requirements. Invoicing may also include the delivery schedule, particularly if actual invoicing of the customer is dependent upon receipt of the signed delivery note.

Collection   A6.28

The credit manual will define the collection methods employed, including:

- reminder letters;

- telephone calls;

- the use of fax and e-mail;

- personal visits; and

- if appropriate, the assistance of sales and delivery personnel in the collection of cheques.

According to the payment terms agreed in the credit policy and agreed with the customer, this section will also state the collection timetable (invoice, statement, telephone call, first reminder letter, second telephone call/e-mail/customer visit, final letter). It is true to say that the conduct of this activity and related timetable can be at the discretion of the credit department, often in cooperation with sales, and there can be any number of examples in most organisations where strict adherence at all costs to such a timetable is not carried out. However, the important point is that there is a policy in respect of the collection of monies due and overdue, and that this is reflected in the procedures manual – there should be no possibility of anyone in the company, particularly from sales, being unaware of the practice of sending reminder letters or making telephone collection calls.

Companies dealing with particular types of customer who may be subject to what is best described as 'special treatment', should ensure that the manual includes procedures for such treatment. Special customers may well be local authorities or Government departments, schools or hospitals, where deviation from the norm is considered appropriate.

Order referrals and stop list procedures are laid out clearly – no one should be in doubt as to the company's use of such sanctions. Equally clear are the criteria by which a referred order is released, or a customer is removed from the stop list and deliveries allowed. In many companies, the stop list can be one of the most contentious documents produced by the credit department, and one of the major causes of friction between the sales and credit departments. As often as not this friction can be avoided by both sales and credit having the same understanding as to when, why and how the stop sanction is used and its inclusion in the manual is mandatory.

There will be guidelines for the use of third party involvement in the collection process, such as collection agencies and solicitors. According to company policy, the manual should also contain the rules in respect of future business with customers who have been stopped previously and referred to collection agents or solicitors for action.

The manual should also contain the procedure for the operation of the query register (see **A6.17** above), and the timetable stipulated for the resolution of customer disputes. Its inclusion as an operating procedure emphasises the value placed on maintaining good customer service ethics and also reinforces the recognition of the financial impact of unresolved queries.

In the event of customer insolvency, there is often the need to move quickly, whether to halt deliveries or recover goods. It is also necessary to be able to bring together all the required paperwork for submitting claims, writing off bad debts and recovering VAT bad debt relief. Inclusion in the manual clarifies the procedure, although the technicalities of the differences between the various forms of insolvency need not be detailed. (See **B10 INSOLVENCY** for more information about the different types of insolvency.)

Management reporting   A6.29

This entry in the credit manual covers the content, frequency and format of reports to the management of the credit function. The management should have a requirement to know what is going on and the level of debtors being maintained. It is also the forum in which to highlight particular problems, such as individual problem accounts of significant substance, or difficulties arising from other departments which are impacting on cash collection. Management are then able to take the appropriate action.

In addition to format and frequency of the reports, the manual also stipulates the responsibility for production of the reports and the sources required to compile and complete them. This would include budget control reports as well as debtor management reports, together with plans and forecasts.

Specimen letters, documents, forms   A6.30

The manual should also contain copies or masters of all the regular documents in use in the credit department including:

- terms and conditions of sale;
- credit application forms;
- customer welcome letters;
- order acknowledgements;
- invoices and credit notes;
- statements;
- various collection letters;

- telephone record forms;

- standard computer prints (aged debt analysis etc.);

- query forms and query follow up forms;

- credit note authorisation forms;

- credit limit review forms;

- budget forms; and

- standard report forms.

Management structure   A6.31

The credit policy contains a clear statement as to the function of the credit control department and how that department fits into the overall organisational structure of the company. It also gives the authority of the credit manager in relation to other departments, with the appropriate reporting line to the board, through the finance director, sales and marketing director or commercial director. The management level organisation chart forms part of the credit manual, together with the specific credit department organisation chart.

The organisation of the credit department will, of course, be governed by:

- the size of the operation;

- the number of active accounts;

- whether the business has domestic and/or export trade;

- whether the trade is centralised or at local level;

- the level of computerised support; and

- the nature of the business.

Of fundamental importance, however, will be the position in respect of the functions to be performed – sales ledger maintenance (customer file, records, cash receipts and allocations) and credit control (credit appraisal, establishing new accounts with credit limits and risk categories and cash collection) – that is to say should the functions be distinctly separate, or should all these activities come under the remit of the credit control department?

Separating sales ledger maintenance from credit control has the advantage of allowing less specialised staff to operate the more clerical sales ledger duties, leaving the specialised risk assessors and collection personnel to concentrate on their particular tasks. Ledger work is routine, calling for accuracy and attention to detail, and can be time consuming. Ledger clerks may not automatically be good credit clerks, the latter needing different skills which would involve personality, fluency, the ability to interface with the customer and to negotiate and achieve acceptable results. It could also be argued that too much time can be tied up in sales ledger maintenance, eating into the time required to contact customers by telephone or letter, collect cash and resolve problems. Similarly, credit clerks do not necessarily make good ledger clerks, the talents of the latter being channelled in other directions.

On the other hand, it is argued that an accurate and up-to-date ledger is fundamental to the success and efficiency of the credit clerk, and confidence in the ledger is the backbone to confidence in customer contact – credibility can soon fly out of the window if sales ledger inaccuracy undermines the credit clerk or collector. The situation can be further exacerbated if the credit manager and the sales ledger manager work in different physical locations, with different line managers. Errors or inefficiency by one department can have a seriously damaging impact on the other department, with the company being the ultimate loser in terms of cash flow and customer relations.

The compromise solution would be to separate the functions of credit control and sales ledger maintenance within the same department, both reporting to the credit manager, who has overall responsibility for the total function. In this way, the credit department has the advantage of the best of both worlds, the credit manager can organise the right personnel for the right task and there exists maximum cooperation and minimum disruption.

Whichever option is chosen, the credit manual contains the organisation chart for the credit department, with the credit manager at the head, supported by supervisors, section leaders, and clerks, according to the size of the business. (See **A6.32–A6.34** below for information on authority levels, duties and responsibilities.) If the ledger is to be split into geographical areas, size of account, sales region, or any other breakdown, that should be reflected in the organisation chart for ease of reference, both within the department and in the rest of the company.

Decision tree   A6.32

The organisation of the sales ledger and credit department can be based upon a number of variables and combinations (see **A6.31** above). There should, however, be a clear reporting line within the function, with the decision process allocated according to areas of authority and responsibility. The level of authority equates with that reporting line, with the credit manager at the top, being responsible for all the decisions made within his department, including those made by personnel below, to whom certain levels of authority have been delegated. Typically, a clerk would be able to make credit decisions up to a set amount within his section of the ledger, referring up to section leader, supervisor or credit manager, according to value. The section leader has decision authority from the clerk's upper limit to a higher level, again referring up to supervisor or credit manager for values in excess of this amount.

Supervisors work directly under the credit manager, with wider ranging authority levels, referring up to the credit manager for major decisions. The credit manager looks after the most important individual accounts, taking business direction and functional guidance from the Board and passing that back down the line through the delegation tree.

The decision tree is laid out in the credit manual, detailing job title and authority level, with reference to an established arbitration procedure to be followed in case of dispute. This procedure also includes senior management outside the credit function, with the finance director, or managing director as the final arbiter.

The ultimate authority of the credit manager is shown in relation to other management functions in the business, as stated in the credit policy and repeated in the credit manual.

Clarity on individuals' responsibilities   A6.33

It is important that there is a clear understanding, both within the department and in the business as a whole, of the duties and responsibilities of each job function. The general authority levels have been covered in **A6.31** and **A6.32** above, but the credit manual should detail job titles together with a description of the areas covered by those posts. These would include the following:

- credit approval limits;

- setting up new accounts;

- identifying risk categories;

- customer file maintenance;

- cash allocation;

- order referral;

- customer contact and negotiation level authority;

- reminder letters;

- special arrangements (payment plans and debt rescheduling);

- stop list maintenance (including placing customers on stop and circumstances for removing customers from stop);

- stop list override;

- instructions to collection agents and/or solicitors;

- changes to credit terms, credit limits, risk categories (temporary and/or permanent);

- reporting requirements; and

- arbitration.

In whatever manner the sales ledger and customer base is subdivided (by value, geographic region, sales area or product), the role of each sales ledger or credit clerk is defined with the above duties and responsibilities clearly attributed, according to predetermined and defined parameters.

Update   **A6.34**

It will be the responsibility of the credit manager to ensure that the credit manual is regularly updated to accommodate changes as they take place, both in company policy and in management and department structure. All systems and processes in use should themselves be under constant review to achieve best practice and optimum performance at all times, and such changes may well be reflected in aspects of the credit manual. Where such changes have an impact outside the credit department, or where changes elsewhere have repercussions within credit control, other department heads need to be involved in contributing to amendments and updates. No single department in any business organisation should operate in splendid isolation, and as the credit function is central to profitable success, so the manual is at the heart of the whole credit process.

A7

Staff Training and
Staff Recruitment

Introduction A7.1

A Prime Minister of modern times once said 'Education, education, education'. No one can doubt that being ill-equipped to face the competition and the traumas of the modern world leads to disadvantage and to more difficulties in finding and keeping that rewarding job, both in terms of financial reward and job satisfaction. In the decades following the Second World War, the United Kingdom economy has gone through radical upheaval, along with similar Western industrialised economies. The demise of what were regarded as traditional industries was both dramatic in its speed, and far reaching in its consequences. Generations of men (and women) had worked in the shipyards of the Clyde, Tyne, Wear, Tees, Mersey and Belfast, the steelworks of South Wales, Teesside, Sheffield and North Lincolnshire and the coalfields throughout the country. Almost overnight, it seemed, this way of life, founded way back in the Industrial Revolution, came to an end.

It did not disappear completely, of course – there are still shipyards, coalfields and steel works, the West Midlands produces cars by the million – but a shadow of their former selves, and no longer able to offer secure long-term employment to large bodies of men and women. The service sector – hotels, shops, catering, tourism, financial services etc. – have taken the lead role in terms of employment, and these sectors require different levels of expertise. It is one thing to toil in the filthy blackness of the South Yorkshire pit, and quite another to answer the telephone with a pleasant 'Good morning, how may I help you?' Equally, it is not simply a matter of handing in the token at the pithead at the end of the last shift on Friday, and walking into the air-conditioned office on the Business Park on Monday. The Prime Minister's exhortation in respect of education, aimed at equipping today's young for tomorrow, could just as easily have been 'Training, training, training', aimed at equipping today's workforce for today's work needs.

The pace of change does not slacken, and the need to remain efficiently ahead of the competition never falters. Like painting the Forth Bridge, getting to one end simply means starting again at the other end. To maintain sales, the department store needs the latest fashions, the newest gadgets and the up to the minute marketing techniques. In the drive for profitability, the manufacturer must invest in plant and machinery so that he can produce more, higher quality products at lower unit cost. Not to invest in machinery and techniques might bring savings in the short term, but would inevitably lead to long-term decline against the competition who do invest. Training the greatest asset that any business has, its workforce, is an investment of equal importance, with the same short and long-term consequences. Not to invest in staff training and development is to waste a precious resource and to limit the ability of any business to survive and prosper.

Employers should not use the excuse of 'training for the benefit of someone else' to justify not investing in staff development. Equally importantly, staff should not confuse training and employer loyalty. Employers benefit from staff development, whomsoever has paid for it, and it is a fact of career progression that people will move on and take their newly acquired skills with them. New staff will be appointed, and they will bring their newly acquired skills with them. Training benefits all, and should be seen as such. The member of staff should be aiming to better himself in all ways, regardless of whether it benefits his current employer in the long term. A highly motivated, well trained employee will be much sought after by all employers, and again, everyone is a winner – the only losers are those who do not educate and train.

The importance of training A7.2

The granting of credit is a practice that dates back a very long time, although consumers in the 21st Century could be forgiven for thinking it a more recent innovation. Ancient Egyptians knew about trade credit and the business cycle, as did Mediaeval merchants, Georgian speculators and Victorian industrialists. The concept of the provision of goods or services on the promise or expectation of payment at some future agreed date is not new, nor is the need to understand the consequences of not being paid. Essentially, all that has changed over the centuries has been the scope and sophistication in all matters appertaining to credit, and the complexity of laws, rules and regulations regarding the conduct of business affairs in a credit granting environment. However, although the ideas may be the same, the technology and development of required knowledge would be unrecognisable to our forbears.

Alongside the progress in technology and scope, there has developed a recognition of the unique skills required to navigate the world of credit. There has been rapid growth in specialist industries, dedicated to credit insurance, risk management, the provision of credit information, debt collection and receivables management. The scope of credit management has also expanded to incorporate accounting in general and the interpretation of balance sheet information in particular, together with hands on practical knowledge of the workings of the civil courts and insolvency. The level of sophistication in consumer credit, call centres and computer-based credit granting and support procedures would have bewildered the Victorian bank manager, but is commonplace to the credit manager of today.

Less than a generation has seen credit management move from being a 'cinderella' operation, overlooked and under resourced, to that of a core function, vital to profits and liquidity. There are still a great many businesses, some large, who regard credit control as a necessary evil (or even an unnecessary evil), to be viewed simply as debt collection and not having any pro-active contribution to make to business growth and profit. Such organisations relegate credit management to second or third tier importance at their peril, and are less likely to succeed in today's competitive environment. The holder of the ICM Chair in Credit Management, Professor Nick Wilson and his team at the Credit Management Research Centre, Leeds University Business School, have shown repeatedly in the light of their research that 'front end' pro-active credit management adds significantly to the financial success and stability of business.

Recognising the importance of the function means, at the same time, an appreciation of the skills required to perform the multitude of tasks to obtain maximum benefit, and the key is in recruiting the right staff and training them.

Training is not an afterthought. Sales people are not sent out into the field until they have been product trained and the company's books are audited by trained and qualified accountants. It would be unthinkable to board a jumbo jet at Heathrow knowing that the pilot had never gone through flying school and was only there because there were no vacancies with the bus company. Managing a substantial proportion of the company's asset base, as represented by accounts receivable, demands knowledge and understanding of a range of issues and should be approached with professionalism. Credit control should never be second place to selling or completing the job, with staff catching up with the paperwork when time allows, and something that 'Elsie can do on Fridays'.

It has been argued that credit management is more of an art than a science, and there is no substitute for experience. This may to some extent be true, and working knowledge acquired through experience plays an invaluable part in the day-to-day working environment. Not everything in the cut and thrust 'real' world is done 'by the book', and it would be wrong to assume that training covers all eventualities. However, training for the role lays the right foundations and ongoing guidance hones existing skills and encourages development. People benefit from the encouragement given through training, and that benefit repays the company for its investment in those people. The added bonus is that new talents can be discovered within existing personnel, achieving flexibility of labour and multi-skilling.

Square pegs and round holes   A7.3

Credit control holds the financial future of the business in its hands and those hands must be capable. To leave it to untrained and unskilled staff would be disastrous, and the long-term return far outweighs the financial cost of employing the right people in the right positions, suitably skilled and trained to do what is expected of them. As has already been seen, the function covers a variety of specialities, which together make up the complete department – these specialities would include:

- credit assessment;

- sales ledger maintenance;

- legal procedures;

- company law;

- contract law;

- insolvency law;

- account collection;

- book keeping and accounting; and

- the ability to effectively communicate by telephone, letter, fax or visit.

Interpersonal skills extend beyond the department and its relationship with customers to include the ability to work with other departments, outside agencies such as debt collectors, solicitors, insurers and factors, and the ability to communicate at all levels. Such varied duties and responsibilities demand a diverse skill base to support the operation and it is of the utmost importance to ensure that each member of the team is suited to their particular allotted task.

It is perfectly normal for some personnel to be more comfortable and achieve their full potential in some roles rather than others, and it would not be helpful to try to force a member of staff to undertake a role which was clearly beyond their capabilities. There is an obvious distinction, for example, in the skills required to carry out telephone collection work, compared to the clerical expertise needed for cash allocation and sales ledger maintenance. For the former, good communication ability is required, and for the latter, accuracy and attention to detail, numeracy and a methodic approach. As has already been discussed, the two roles can be combined, but it is important to recognise the differing skills required, and to provide training and support where it is seen to be needed.

Telephone   A7.4

Notwithstanding the fact that the telephone has now been with us for a good many years, it is still an instrument to be treated with both respect and caution. Not everyone is able to use the telephone effectively as its use requires special skills. (See **A13.31–A13.37** below for a detailed look at the use of the telephone as a tool in cash collection, the emphasis in the context of this chapter being on the training required to ensure correct use.) It would be wrong to assume that everyone knows how to use the telephone, not only because everybody is different, but also because telephone collection work is specific. Ringing to invite friends round to dinner on Friday is not the same as calling a customer in respect of his outstanding account, and being comfortable with the former does not guarantee being at ease with the latter. Similarly, the ability to make occasional calls does not lead automatically to the ability to undertake the set task of making a minimum number of collection calls each day – the number of calls depends upon the size of the business and customer base, but could run into dozens. It is important, therefore, that the employer recognises the need for specialist selection, training and support for the telephone collector, and that the activity is monitored and disciplined to achieve both the desired results and to identify where additional training and support may be needed.

Selection   A7.5

The telephone is an instrument which can distort, change or hide personality. It is well known that once behind the wheel of a car, the meek and mild mannered gentleman can become an aggressive monster, protected inside the steel box by an artificial anonymity, which allows him to do things he would never normally do. It is power and invulnerability, coupled with the feeling of being untouchable. The driver is less tolerant, less patient, determined to occupy and dominate his space to the exclusion of all others and certainly not the man we thought we all knew. Parked in his allotted place and out of the car, the driver is now the gentleman once more, courteous and well mannered. An exaggeration, perhaps, but the parallel with the telephone is worth noting. The telephone can also alter personality, providing as it does, cover to hide behind and because contact is not face to face, the communication between caller and recipient can appear to be quite impersonal. Aggression, rudeness, an offhand attitude, even vulgarity can result, leading to the loss of a valued customer.

There is also a developing resentment towards the telephone as an instrument of communication, brought about by the growth of computerised telephone systems which require the caller to, 'press one for orders', 'press two for service' etc, leading to an assumption that human beings no longer exist in the company – a situation aggravated by the subsequent run through the 1812 Overture while holding for somebody to be free to take the call. Equally irksome can be the patter phrases 'thank you for calling, my name is … how may I be of service to you?' – delivered by someone who has clearly learned the words, but not the meaning. Situations exist where a telephone user feels, for some reason, the need to speak in loud tones, so that not only does the recipient have to hold the instrument away from the ear, but everyone within the vicinity of the caller can hear every word of at least one half of the conversation.

The telephone represents immediate contact, with the caller needing to establish very quickly the purpose of the call in order to achieve a successful result. There has to be a disciplined approach which does not alienate, but which at the same time develops a satisfactory rapport so that objectives are met.

All of this points to the need to both carefully select those members of staff whose task it will be to use the telephone as a tool of their trade, and to support them with ongoing training and development. The time and money invested in such training and support will be repaid handsomely by results, as use of the telephone is a proven success in the effective collection of cash, and the business benefits by improved cash flow and skilled, motivated personnel. Once the new staff have been selected and installed, training and support continues, as it does for existing telephone collection staff, so that there is scope for continuous improvement.

The telephone collector's role should be clearly specified, with a full job description which would include details of to whom the employee will be reporting, whether he will work as an individual or part of a team, his responsibilities and his level of authority. It should also be clear as to what is expected of the collector in respect of daily or weekly call targets, and the way in which such targets will be monitored and amended. Selection (and training) begins with attitude. It is important to establish the ability to control emotion, leave domestic problems at home, and to adopt a positive and professional approach to the task in hand. Equally vital is the ability on the part of the telephone collector to be able to speak clearly and with authority, without sounding superior and he also has to be able to listen to what the customer is saying. Being able to listen to what is being said is not automatically the same as hearing what is said.

It is often stated that a smile, unseen by the recipient of the call, is nevertheless conveyed to the listener by the voice of the caller. The reverse is certainly true – a miserable, bored collector is not encouraging the right feedback and the call will not be as effective or successful. From the outset, therefore, the collector has to be confident, comfortable and at ease on the telephone.

The specialist techniques required for telephone collection come with training, but the personality must fit the role. The collector must be able to communicate at all levels (the customer contact may be anyone from the managing director downwards), and not feel outfaced by any person encountered when making the call. Politeness and courtesy go a long way to creating the right environment for collections, and are achievable without losing firmness and authority. Selection of the right staff for any role is never easy or foolproof, but forcing the wrong personality into a position for which they have no aptitude is both damaging and self defeating. The right attitude and ability, backed by training and ongoing support, will prove beneficial to both employer and employee.

Training   A7.6

All staff involved in customer contact, whether collection or customer service, should know about their company's products or services and the market place in which they operate. They are going to be asked questions by customers which will require answers, and they are going to need to be aware of the environment in which both their company and its customers carry on business. For example, selling tins of baked beans to supermarkets is not the same as supplying steel girders to civil engineering contractors, the only similarity being that they both have to be paid for.

The collector also needs to be able to distinguish between the sole trader and the corporate body – whether in effect trying to collect the customer's payment from out of his own pocket or dealing with a purchase ledger clerk whose job it is to look after someone else's money.

All personnel should undergo an induction process when joining a company to become familiar with:

- the company's product or service;

- the way the company is structured;

- the role of the various departments; and

- where their own particular function fits into the overall organisation.

To become really familiar with who does what, how and why takes time and experience of course, but a general introduction is valuable background to enable acclimatisation to be more comfortable and meaningful. That induction is extended to an introduction at department level, so that new collectors or transferees from other departments can be made aware of what the job entails and what will be expected of them. In addition, the introduction to telephone collection activity includes an explanation and an appreciation of the importance of the part played by telephone collection in respect of the financial well being of the business. The contribution to cash flow, and the subsequent profitable growth which it encourages, should be made clear, as should the alternative consequences of poor cash flow and an unacceptably high level of unpaid accounts.

The introduction to the department and the activity may also include the opportunity to accompany a member of the sales department on customer visits. Such visits are a useful connection, both between the credit and sales departments and the collector and the customer, where they can be introduced personally as the individual who will be looking after the account from now on. It is also useful on an ongoing basis as a means of both collector and customer putting faces to voices and names and assists in the ability of both to understand each other better. It is appreciated that in many organisations, such an option to visit may be logistically difficult, but the value of the exercise is immense and fully justifies the effort.

Telephone collection work is disciplined and structured, not just a pick up and dial approach. Initial training in techniques equips the collector to be professional in his attitude, both to the task in hand and to the end result. Such techniques are discussed in detail at **A13.31–A13.37** below, and are necessary for a successful outcome to any telephone collection call, and few if any of the skills are natural. More often than not, they have to be learned, and experienced collectors will testify to having developed skills over a period of time.

Training can be undertaken in-house, on the job, or can involve outside courses and seminars. In-house training can utilise senior experienced personnel, though there should be an element of supervisory control to ensure that bad habits are not passed on. It is often an advantage to bring in third party specialists to undertake the training, as they can bring a new face and fresh ideas to the function and are not constrained by company politics or culture.

Care should be taken to choose the right environment if the tuition is undertaken on company premises as the trainees need to feel comfortable and not harassed by constant interruptions. Equally they have to feel free to contribute and question and not be held back by the feeling of senior management watching their progress. Courses and seminars held away from the workplace provide an ideal environment for freedom of expression, as well as the opportunity to share experiences and problems with other delegates – there is often a belief that one's own problems or circumstances are unique, and sharing with others reveals a commonality which can be quite comforting.

Provision of training for both new staff, and for continuing development of existing staff involves the utilisation of the best resources available, and a mixture of in-house and outside involvement, with course content chosen to meet the specific needs, usually provides the right balance.

Monitoring   A7.7

The purpose of ongoing training is twofold, on the one hand there is the development of learned skills, with a view to continually improving performance, secondly as collectors settle into their roles, weaknesses and strengths in the individuals will become apparent and training will help overcome those weaknesses and further develop the strengths. If the collectors are properly monitored in their roles, then faults can be identified early, and the training programme designed to rectify them before they become ingrained bad practice. Taught correctly, the driver does not cross his hands on the wheel, and more advanced driver training not only picks up faults developed, but teaches more skills with increasing relevance to the current driving conditions.

It will be for the training manager or credit manager to see that all duties are being performed in line with department policies and procedures, all forms correctly completed, calls followed up where required and the results, by way of payments received, duly noted. It is better for this supervisory role to be undertaken by the department head, rather than the collector's own colleagues, especially in the case of new starters, simply because assessment of standards and achieved results has to be objective and constructive and not subject to personal influences, friendly or otherwise.

Each collector will have targets set, usually based upon effective telephone calls (i.e. calls which result in payment being made), and evidence of success or non-achievement will guide management in the direction of the most appropriate form of support training for the particular collector. In large organisations, collectors may form part of large groupings or teams, each team having its own targets, and collectors will be encouraged to work as a team.

Many call monitoring systems exist to help management see and hear what is going on, giving the supervisor or the training manager the opportunity to listen to both sides of a telephone conversation. This has obvious advantages over the situation where listening over the shoulder of the collector only reveals what the collector is saying but not precisely what is being said to the collector. If the collector is failing to respond to the customer in the right way, this can be identified and put right at the next training session. There are systems available to record and time calls, both outgoing and incoming, with the obvious benefits for training purposes. We never see ourselves as others see us, only in the mirror, in a photograph or on a video recording and we never hear our own voices in the exact same way that others hear us. Therefore listening to a tape of our own conversations can be quite illuminating.

Staff appraisals   A7.8

Staff appraisals, or discussions of contribution together with objectives for the next year, are now quite common in many companies and form part of the pay review and promotion process. In order for that procedure to be meaningful, in so far as it relates to staff training and development, each collector should have a training file. The file contains all matters concerning the various training courses attended and schedules set, together with relevant management comments and appraisals, updated on a regular basis, with outcomes and expected outcomes noted. This is not the same as the personal file which may be held on the employee by the human resource department, but is specific to training and development and is confidential to the collector and his supervisor or manager. In this way attention can be focussed on a regular basis on those aspects of the collector's job which are important to both the collector's own success and satisfaction and to the overall benefit of the business itself.

Summary   A7.9

In summary, telephone collecting can appear both easy and daunting, depending upon the approach. Management needs to ask the following questions.

- How many quality calls are expected each day?
- To whom does the collector report?
- What is the authority and responsibility of the collector?
- What is the collector's role in the team?
- What level of training is required?
- Who should undertake staff training?
- How is the collector motivated?
- What can be done to sustain ongoing interest and enthusiasm?
- What prospects exist for advancement?

Each question requires a positive and constructive answer. Giving somebody a telephone and telling them to get on with it is just as fruitless as expecting a bus driver to fly a jumbo jet to New York.

Customer visits   A7.10

There can be a variety of reasons for people from different areas of the business to have occasion to visit a customer – each visit could be for a specific purpose, and the visitor needs to have the necessary expertise to carry out whatever may be required. The salesman wants to sell the product or service, and to that end has been trained in all aspects of the seller's offerings. The salesman knows the technical specifications, shelf life, performance capability, price, company back up service, warranties, terms of payment, and what leeway there may be for negotiation in order to achieve the sale. Ongoing visits by sales and marketing could be for public relations purposes, keeping the customer up-to-date with the latest developments and innovations, new products and product upgrades, and to make sure that the customer's needs are being met. The salesman has also to be aware of the customer's personal likes and dislikes and be able to judge suitable entertainment programmes which help seal the buyer/seller relationship.

The service engineer has been fully trained in problem solving, trouble shooting and repairs, knows how the product is made up and what parts are needed to ensure continual operation.

Both the salesman and the service engineer may also need to have detailed knowledge of health and safety issues, environmental concerns and other statutory regulations. They are trained to be aware of the competition, on the look out for competitors' products on the shelves, or equipment which may be compatible to their own and where there may be an opportunity for conversion.

It is true that credit personnel, as a rule, tend not to be involved in visiting customers to the same extent as the sales or service departments, but that is not to say that visits should not be made. There can be varied reasons for credit personnel to visit customers and skills are required for such visits to be effective. As with telephone collection, not everyone will be suited to the role, and much will depend upon the purpose of the visit to determine the knowledge necessary. However, the credit visitor must have sufficient confidence in his ability to carry out the task and be suitably equipped for the purpose.

If the visit is in respect of credit assessment, then knowledge of all the elements covered in **A2 CREDIT RISK ANALYSIS, A3 GAINING INFORMATION TO SUPPORT CREDIT DECISIONS** and **A4 CREDIT ASSESSMENT AND ITS USES** is essential – it would clearly not do to be faced by a customer with all his books, management accounts, trial balances and cash flow forecasts and not know what they mean and how they should be interpreted. Equally, if the visit is in respect of collection, the options available and subsequent courses of action need to be fully understood. It may also be necessary to show some concern and understanding for a customer's problems and to be able, if circumstances permit, to offer some assistance and a range of solutions giving longer or shorter credit terms and re-negotiating existing contracts. At the same time, being alert to what is going on around, observing levels of activity, attitude or morale of staff, and how much (and whose) stock is on the shelves, is all part of the visit process, so awareness of surroundings is a prerequisite.

Many people are natural 'back room' types, and do not take readily to operating 'front of house'. Regardless of training in the technical substance of the role, unless the personality is confident and to a degree outgoing and therefore comfortable in the company of customers, it would not be appropriate to try to force the issue. Credit personnel will have to deal with people at all levels, and any weakness will be quickly exploited. Nevertheless, it is possible to learn 'people skills', and training courses are readily available to develop interpersonal qualities, negotiation skills, and those facets necessary to achieve the best out of face-to-face meetings. Such skills are also of great value internally, in relationships with other departments, and in the setting of meeting agendas, controlling the agenda and contributing fully and constructively to the proceedings. (See also **A13.19** below for more information on customer visits.)

Self motivation   A7.11

The dictionary states that to motivate is 'to give incentive to'. The thesaurus offers a range of other definitions of motivation – ambition, desire, drive, hunger, inspiration, interest, wish, impulse, incentive, incitement, inducement, inspiration, instigation, motive, persuasion, reason, spur and stimulus. It would be over simplistic to generally define what motivates people in given circumstances but many would regard adequate reward for a job well done as a good motive for continuing, and a degree of job satisfaction adds to the experience.

Cash bonuses, good salaries and comfortable working conditions are all incentives designed to motivate staff, as is good people management, but the credit function with its emphasis on delegation of authority and defined responsibilities is to a greater extent dependent upon a degree of self motivation among personnel. Self motivation is itself dependent upon personality, but can be encouraged by support and training. Trying to force someone to undertake a role which is clearly beyond their capabilities will demotivate the individual concerned, as will being given a role for which he has had no guidance or instruction. The person concerned may well have been able to do the job given the right backing, but left to his own devices, has encountered insurmountable obstacles and been unable to find a way through the difficulties. Training identifies strengths and weaknesses, develops the former and helps eradicate the latter.

Obstacles which prevent the collector or the credit clerk from giving of their best should be removed. These impediments could well be simple and straightforward, for example an uncomfortable chair or a broken desk. However, they could be more complex – an antiquated accounting and/or computer system, or a telephone system with too few lines so that obtaining outside lines to undertake collection activity is difficult. Stringent rules about when outside calls can and cannot be made do not apply to credit collectors, who have to call at the best time to contact customers, not when it best suits the employer. Over bureaucratic procedures for the issue of office stationery, long hikes to the photocopier or the fax machine, inadequate lighting and ventilation, noise and dirt all contribute to the mound of obstacles preventing employees doing a good job, and should be rectified without delay.

Open discussion should be encouraged in order to involve people in contributing to the improvement of both their working conditions and practices, and in the improvement of results to be achieved. When staff feel that they have a positive contribution to make, and that their ideas and opinions are worthy of consideration and perhaps implementation, their involvement and their attitude becomes more constructive – they are being motivated on the one hand, and engaging in self motivation on the other. Many companies reward staff suggestions, in the hope that financial gain will spawn new ideas and a fresh approach but even without such rewards the satisfaction gained from having made a worthwhile contribution which has been recognised by the fact of its adoption enhances attitude and encourages further commitment.

The team environment   A7.12

Self motivation extends beyond the individual. Working in a team environment, with team targets and objectives to be met, encourages cooperation between individuals as well as creating friendly rivalry. Members of a team support each other, filling in the gaps and assisting in the training process by mutual self help. Rivalry can of course develop beyond the friendly and it is important for the manager to be aware of the different personalities which make up the team, watching out for friction and also for any situation where one person is doing more than his fair share under pressure from colleagues. Choice of the right people for the right roles in the first place should have gone a long way to preventing any friction, but it can arise at any time, often for the most trivial of reasons, and needs to be spotted and sorted out straight away.

In-house training may involve several members of the same team being trained at the same time, and the help they give each other in tackling something different or new can greatly assist the learning process. Training from external sources away from the place of work also adds to the mutual support that exists in the team, removing as it does any barriers of inhibition which may exist in the place of work and encouraging active participation in the training process.

Rewards   A7.13

Credit personnel are frequently, if not always, expected to work under their own initiative, and one of the least used management tools which promotes motivation, as well as job satisfaction, is the recognition from time to time of a job well done, rewarded by a thank you and a pat on the back, as nothing succeeds like success. Supportive training itself can often be seen by personnel not just as a means of improving and developing skills, but also as a recognition by the employer that the role has a value which is well worth the investment, and the people concerned are motivated by the confidence expressed in them.

Development of confidence and contacts   A7.14

Most motorists will agree that their first driving lesson was something of an experience. It all seemed so easy watching somebody else do it, but that very first time behind the wheel was no doubt a little daunting. However, after the requisite number of driving lessons and the ordeal of the driving test, that very first time alone behind the wheel was exhilarating, though perhaps a little nerve-racking. More practice, and the acquisition of experience saw the confidence behind the wheel improve, and it becomes harder to remember a time when it was all so new and mysterious. No matter how much initial training has been given, the first telephone collection call or the first customer visit will be nerve racking. In the beginning much effort will go into remembering all that has been taught, who to ask for, what to say, how to respond and what to do next. Everything and everybody will seem strange and unfamiliar and the feeling will be one of isolation. Ongoing support will help and, over a period of time, the routine and the process will begin to take on some shape. Standard responses will become familiar, as will the way to deal with them, and customer voices will be recognisable.

Ongoing training   A7.15

As time goes by and the individual becomes more comfortable with the process, there could be an element of complacency, adopting bad habits (rather like crossing ones hands on the steering wheel) and perhaps looking for short cuts. In order to ensure that this does not happen, ongoing performance is monitored and evaluated with the dual purpose of correcting errors as, or before, they occur and guiding the staff member in the correct approach and attitude. It is just as easy to acquire good habits as it is to acquire bad ones, and if the good habits can be shown to achieve both better results and be easier to cope with than bad habits, so the confidence of the collector or credit clerk is increased. At the same time, feedback is important and both managers and trainers need to be able to capitalise on the staff member's own contribution to the benefit of both the business and of the individual. The learning curve in any function is steep to begin with, but enthusiasm with support can make the process easier and coincidentally more enjoyable. Regular discussions, analysis of results and additional training in those areas identified as in need of further assistance will add to the growing confidence of the collector or clerk.

Building a relationship with customers   A7.16

The new collector or credit clerk will begin to get to know his customers better, be able to build up a relationship and therefore an understanding of the customer's needs and the customer's problems, if there are any. That relationship can be important, not just to the business in respect of cash flow and avoiding failure, but also to the collector or clerk himself. Building relationships and becoming more at ease with the customer contact, at whatever level, adds to confidence. It also adds to the growing number of people with whom the collector or clerk is able to hold a meaningful business conversation, and increases the awareness of what is going on in the world outside the confines of where they actually work. The credit control function is very much one of customer service, and in many businesses credit control is actually located within the customer services department. It will not be long before new starters or transferees realise that their customer contact is more frequent and more regular than probably any other department in the company, and that they perform a wider role than setting credit limits or collecting cash, often being the troubleshooter and problem solver. The emphasis on ongoing development, therefore, is one of multi skills, such as the ability to communicate, negotiate, persuade, resolve and understand. What began as an apparently straightforward telephone collection, or clerical role has developed into a multi-faceted operation, and the skills acquired along the way, both by experience and by targeted training has highlighted new talents and opened up new horizons which perhaps were not evident in the beginning.

Promotion of awareness company wide   A7.17

As has been seen, credit control does not, and cannot, work in splendid isolation. It may well be that everyone in any business has a specific job to do, and a job description which spells out in detail all their duties and responsibilities. The van driver may think that he is just a van driver, but perhaps the name of the company is on the side of the van, which makes the driver just as much a representative of the company as the salesman or the managing director. Visitors are existing or potential customers, and the image of the business is enhanced by cleanliness and neatness, so cleaners play an important role in promoting the best image. In other words, everyone within the company has a part to play.

Part of the induction training for every new starter should provide some background as to the business and its products or services, but also to have a general introduction as to the business structure, who does what, where, why and to some extent, how. Acting as it does in a key position between business and customer, the credit control function, and its staff in particular, play a pivotal role.

All training must incorporate the concepts of quality and customer care. Fundamental to all aspects of quality is the principle that every organisation serves 'big C customers' and 'little c customers'. The big C customers are those outside the business who actually buy the product or service – they are the ones who provide the income, enable the wages to be paid and the profits to be made. The little c customers are the internal departments which are served by other internal departments, upon whom they rely, and the whole work as an integrated team meeting each others' requirements in order to satisfy big C customers' needs. Obvious examples would be all employees being little c customers of the wages department, and users of computer systems being little c customers of the computer department. In any business organisation, even quite small businesses, there is therefore a chain of suppliers and little c customers, leading to the ultimate big C customer and each role has some bearing, directly or indirectly, on each other and the eventual ability of the business to thrive and prosper.

This connection can often be perceived by some as remote and without relevance, but the reality is that even the most apparently disconnected departments have both a common interest (the big C customer) and a direct effect on each other. For example, credit control and production departments on the face of it do not appear to be two areas of the business where the actions of one would impact on the other. However, take the scenario where the customer orders 50 items for delivery in 6 weeks. After 7 weeks, 38 items are ready and delivered, with 12 marked 'to follow'. The customer is not pleased, his order is incomplete and he may not have been told when the 'to follows' are going to follow. The invoice for the 38 falls due and payable, the credit collection activity comes into action, and the customer's happiness is about as complete as his order. Complicate the issue further by having 2 of the 38 delivered being the wrong colour, and it can be seen that the task of collecting what is genuinely due has been made infinitely more difficult by the actions of another department.

Quality, and getting it right first time, should be part of the ongoing training programme and can be approached from both ends of the spectrum. It can be management motivated, with the quality ethic and awareness driven from the top down through the organisation. It can be developed at employee level, with quality groups meeting and discussing issues, formulating solutions and making recommendations to management. Ideally it should utilise both, so that there is full involvement and commitment by both staff and management in partnership, with the joint aim of continuous improvement. In order for everyone to be customer focussed, there has to be an understanding and an awareness throughout the business of the part each plays in the whole, otherwise each constituent member will concentrate only on one aspect, their own, to the exclusion of all others. Each department doing a good job is a start, but if the various roles do not come together for the total benefit of the whole business, then however good each may be the result is less than the sum total of all the parts.

There is an added bonus in training which involves company wide awareness, which lies in the degree to which the individual has his own horizons extended beyond the confines of their own particular function. On the one hand job satisfaction can be improved by a greater understanding of the individual contribution that can be made by that job being done professionally and well. On the other hand, benefit is derived by the knowledge of the valued contribution to the total company effort and performance made by personnel in areas outside their own and to the increase in their own knowledge of what makes a business a success and the part that they play in that success. Added to that, there can be an introduction to a wider range of job opportunities which may become available both inside the company and beyond.

Sales and credit control – a difficult relationship   A7.18

Of all the relationships within an organisation which can be fractured from time to time is that which exists between the sales and credit control departments. The sales and the credit control departments need to collaborate in order to achieve optimum sales and profits. There is certainly the need to ensure that initial and ongoing staff training and support recognises the vital connection between the two roles as well as the part that each play in working together. The company's customers are not in the ownership of one particular department as they are in fact customers of the company as a whole and, therefore, shared between all the functions. It may be that in precise terms the objectives of sales and credit could be seen to be different, each with specifically defined tasks to perform, although the overall objective of maximised profitable sales with the minimum of bad debt is shared. For the two areas to be at loggerheads, unable to co-operate or to communicate, leads to one inevitable result – the customer suffers, which means that the company suffers. There are simple reasons why sales see credit control as an adversary as the department might:

- stop the customers' supplies without discussing this with sales;
- reduce credit terms or credit limits;
- not allow a credit account in the first place;
- take legal action against customers without discussing this with sales;
- send nasty reminder letters;
- make harassing telephone calls; or
- take weeks to open accounts.

There are equally simple reasons why the credit control department regard sales as being on the wrong side, for example they may:

- do deals regarding payment terms without discussing it with credit control;
- take orders from known bad accounts;
- change terms and/or prices without telling anyone;
- tell customers they can have credit when credit control say they cannot;
- carry goods returned from customers around in their cars for weeks; or
- not authorise or agree to genuine credit notes because 'they affect sales figures'.

The list on either side could go on and on and it is sad but true that there are long standing prejudices held by both the sales and credit control departments, based upon lack of appreciation and understanding of each other, which is deeply rooted. This problem has to be addressed, the simple matter being that at some point the two have to be aware of what each actually does, and exactly why they do it. It is this understanding and awareness which is at the heart of the relationship, and on which good communication and cooperation are based.

Much of the prejudice comes from the different methods and perceptions of levels of remuneration for the two areas. The credit control department often see sales as having large salaries and even larger expense accounts, company cars and all the trappings which allegedly go with sales and marketing. These include long lunches, competition winning trips to exotic locations and much gift receiving around the Yuletide season. At the same time, credit control see sales as being driven to sell at all costs, and hang the consequences, and if credit are feeling a little charitable, they may concede that this desire to sell, sell, sell is chiefly because salaries in sales are boosted by the earning of vast amounts of commission. Indeed some credit personnel would like to see sales commissions deducted where payment of the account has not been made and a bad debt has been incurred.

Sales may see credit controllers as pen pushers, money counters or at best overgrown clerks who have no idea of what the competition is like and how difficult it is to actually sell. Credit impose stupid rules, delay paperwork or create yet more paperwork, refuse to open accounts for obviously good customers or send rude reminders to their very best accounts. It is not for sales to become involved in the sordid aspects of money, their job is to persuade the customer to order and all their hard work and effort comes to nothing just because credit says some 'i' is not dotted or some 't' not crossed.

Educating the departments   A7.19

The answer to the problems mentioned above at **A7.18** lies in education and training for both areas. Credit need to understand the trials and tribulations of selling – being out on the road all day, living out of suitcases and the only connection with the office being by phone, fax or e-mail, with the very occasional visit for a sales meeting or product presentation. Sales need to understand the actual cost to the company of granting credit, what slow or non-payment means in terms of profit and what happens when a debt goes bad. An excellent way of getting the message across would be to train credit staff in selling, and sales staff in credit! This may not be possible in its entirety for many practical reasons, but some cross fertilisation of processes and procedures is possible. By this means, staff can develop a better understanding of what each other's role actually entails, and what the outcome of each other's actions mean in terms of results. The educative process can be eye opening and chin dropping for both participants – going out on the road with the sales representative can be quite an experience for the credit controller. This is how it *really* is, and the credit representative is now looking at the potential customer through the eyes of the salesperson, taking into account those things that the sales representative looks for and why they seem to be important to the sales department. The long drive, the hassle, the frequent mobile phone call interruptions, the sales pitch, the demo, the effort put into clinching the deal, the waste of time when the deal does not come to fruition, can all be appreciated by one credit controller.

Taking the sales manager along to a meeting of creditors can be an equally enlightening experience, this time for sales. Now the sales manager is looking at the customer (because, creditors meeting notwithstanding, customer is what the sales manager sees) through the eyes of the credit control department – the reality behind the outward appearance of the debtor company. The acrimony of creditors crying for blood, no assets beyond a word processor keyboard and a half box of copy paper, equipment leased or subject to hire purchase agreements and the realisation that there will be no dividend payable to unsecured trade creditors. The realisation in fact, by the sales manager, that he actually works for an unsecured trade creditor!

Both scenarios should be encouraged as common practice, being regarded very much as part of the full training exercise, involving both sales and credit, and not seen as just a trip out or a one off happening. For both sales and credit control departments seeing the realities of the respective roles gives a clear insight into the why and how of the equation, emphasising the need for working together to achieve the same end.

Sales and credit conferences　　　　　　　A7.20

Sales conferences and credit conferences are ideal opportunities for sales and credit to get together and to publicly discuss all manner of issues. They are also the perfect opportunity for credit and sales personnel to be exposed to a wider range of topics than would normally have been the case. For credit, the sales conference is often the only time that they will be able to have the full sales team together under one roof, face to face and hanging on every word if credit department is scheduled to make any sort of presentation. Making the presentation user friendly, by way of graphics as well as anecdotes, can get the message across with maximum effect – a good example would be to equate the cost saving to the business by reducing DSO by two days to the difference in price of replacing all the 1.6 sales cars with 2.0 models. Equally startling for the sales department can be a demonstration of exactly how much has to be sold just to recoup the loss from one bad debt.

For the credit control department, the reality of sales targets can be revealed – what it means for the sales representative to have a next year's target of 110% of this year's, which itself was 110% of the previous year. New products, promotions and campaigns can be shared, as can economic trends, failure rates, cash flow and finance. Now everyone is 'singing from the same hymn sheet', faces are put to names and voices, and misinterpretations and misunderstandings can be ironed out.

Sales and credit are shown to be working towards the same goal, directed by management. The more one function understands the other, the greater the level of respect and cooperation. Conferences are therefore very much part of the training programme, benefiting all who attend and take part, as well as being an often enjoyable opportunity for some social mixing of hitherto separated teams.

Career progression　　　　　　　　　A7.21

Whatever the chosen career or profession, the 1980s witnessed a fundamental final switch from what had been expected, and accepted as the norm for many generations previously – namely the notion of a job for life. Old industries faltered and died, modernisation and mechanisation, once seen as the solution to all work-related problems, did of themselves create new uncertainties and anxieties, replacing the use of intensive labour with fewer, more skilled and more adaptable staff. Multi-skilling came into vogue, not just because it had economic benefits for employers and employees alike, but also because it was a prerequisite for adaptability and therefore employability.

Alongside this movement the need for education and training was increasingly recognised as the basis for a qualification, the qualification itself in turn being the recorded proof that the applicant for any post had obtained at least the minimum standard needed to carry out the function. The modern employee has to be educated, trained and qualified in order to be successful in a fluid and competitive jobs market and to obtain optimum performance in any role. Such training and qualification is now seen as the new norm which has replaced the old. It is important to be aware of differing ambitions and expectations in that not all see the work role in the same light. For many it is simply something which has to be done in order to earn money to live, or as a second wage to supplement the partner's income which can provide extra luxuries. Others look for something more rewarding, not just in the economic sense, but something more fulfilling with prospects for future advancement, perhaps to a managerial or an executive position.

Credit management is not immune from all of this, and in many ways has been at the forefront of adapting to the changing circumstances and equipping itself to operate effectively in the modern environment. The whole range of functions performed by credit management allows for a broad spread mixture of career ambitions, including management and executive staff, as well as a large number of second income jobs. Education and training is therefore aimed at equipping for particular roles and encouraging development of staff to achieve optimum potential. Through this process, there can be seen evidence of career progression and those who have been identified as being potentially able to further their careers and those who see themselves as willing and able to make credit management their chosen profession have a wide range of training options and opportunities available to them.

Credit clerks   A7.22

As has already been seen, the clerical level requires skills to be acquired in order to achieve the best results. This level, which encompasses the credit clerk, sales ledger clerk or collections clerk (or a combination of these) is often the beginning of a career in credit management. The credit clerk deals with risk analysis and risk assessment, and in addition to numeracy and communication skills, has to have an understanding of basic accounting and book keeping so as to be able to look at balance sheets and accounts and interpret their meaning. Training is designed to develop that knowledge and to provide the confidence as well as the ability to meet, discuss and decide on a variety of issues relating to the granting of credit facilities, with customers and other staff members at all levels. Levels of authority and responsibility increase with experience and ability, and exposure to the wider world of businesses large and small which make up the customer base adds to growing maturity.

The collections clerk has to be equipped with telephone skills, the ability to create effective collection letters and to undertake, often difficult negotiations, at different levels. The collections clerk also has to thoroughly understand the litigation process and the options available to the creditor in the event of non-payment.

The sales ledger clerk has to reconcile accounts and balances, allocate cash accurately and maintain the customer ledger and file, so needs to know not just the how, but also have an appreciation of the importance of the accuracy and prompt attention to detail – in other words, the why. To combine the three skills into one successfully, which is often necessary for smaller businesses, takes time and effort and this means training and support. As the basic skills outlined form the core of credit management, there can be no question of taking short cuts and hoping for the best – the best is only attainable by investing in staff development. It also means that the skills and experience acquired in all three roles opens up the opportunities for advancement within the organisation, or becoming equipped to undertake a more senior position elsewhere. It is this latter point that often prevents the less enlightened employer from investing in training, in the belief that staff are being trained for the benefit of someone else. There may be truth in that, in so far as the ambitious will always want promotion, and if there are no openings within the existing company, they will look elsewhere. This is no bad thing in itself, as the traffic runs both ways. New employers can benefit from the training given to an applicant by their existing employer, who in turn have the advantage of training given by the previous employer to the new starter replacing the recent leaver – the end result is a flexible, experienced and well trained labour market from which all employers can gain advantage.

Team leaders   A7.23

Higher up the ladder, staff are developed into team leaders, learning the techniques of people management and being responsible not just for their own actions, but for the actions of others in their team. People management is not a 'natural' skill, although some managers may well be instinctively more capable than others. Essential in a good team leader is an ability to be able to adapt and to learn how to:

- get the best out of people;

- make and implement decisions; and

- be the leader of the team at the same time as being a member of the team.

Managers   A7.24

From the team leaders come the managers, combining all that has gone before with the wider responsibilities of target setting, budget controls, forecasting and reporting. This may now be at senior management level, involving the credit manager in wider business issues both internally and externally. These could include:

- the choice and implementation of new computer systems;

- evaluating the performance of outside agencies such as solicitors, debt collectors or credit insurers and credit factors; and

- reporting to the board of directors with findings and recommendations.

The need for a clear career path   A7.25

In large organisations the opportunities should be made available for all employees to see a career path ahead of them, backed at all stages by training and the availability of courses, seminars and conferences which are designed to develop existing skills and enhance performance. Membership of a professional body is to be encouraged, as is the achievement of professional qualifications and awards. Continuous professional development is now regarded as a boost to career prospects – the field of credit management is wide ranging and does not stand still, with constant changes in legislation, practice and market circumstances making it imperative for the ambitious credit manager to try to keep up with all that is going on at any time.

Trade, consumer and export credit   A7.26

There is another aspect to the widening of horizons and the prospects for career progression which may not be immediately evident in any particular business organisation. Within credit management, though the basic requirements outlined above and elsewhere in this publication remain constant through various disciplines, there are three distinct divisions:

- trade;

- consumer; and

- export.

Many working in credit are deeply involved in one, with little or no experience of the other two, principally because each is seen to have its own specific requirements in terms of knowledge and understanding. There are many who are actively engaged in two of the disciplines, but few who operate across all three, though more and more have developed a thirst for knowledge of all three.

There is, of course, quite often a merging of all three types of credit in some businesses. Commercial companies with markets overseas as well as at home will be involved in export credit related matters as well as domestic trade. Some companies will have a customer base which includes sole traders as well as corporate bodies, which would entail some consumer credit knowledge. There are, however, businesses which operate almost entirely under one of the three headings of trade, consumer and export, and credit staff within those businesses would have little or no practical experience of any discipline other than that to which they are normally exposed. It may well be that specialising in consumer credit offers sufficient career opportunities for staff working for large companies engaged in the provision of finance facilities, for example credit cards, finance houses etc, in so far as the large organisations have structured processes for career progression. On the other hand, it could be argued that the overall field of opportunity is narrowed by lack of knowledge or experience of trade or export credit, and indeed *vice versa*. Professional qualifications in credit management are designed to give a broadly based understanding of all relative matters which the credit manager would be likely to encounter during a career in credit, including trade, consumer and export, and also embracing law, insolvency, micro and macro economics, accounting and finance. As such, the holder of that qualification can be regarded as having a wider understanding beyond his own immediate work experience and therefore prospects of a change of direction and hence advancement become greater.

Summary   A7.27

It may be that there could well be some way to go before companies in general have credit directors sitting on the Board alongside sales directors, but movement in that direction is happening and it is training and education at all levels which is bringing it about.

A8

Computer Accounting Systems and Monitoring of the Sales Ledger

Introduction
A8.1

'I am sorry about that – it's the computer, you know'. We live in a world dominated by information technology (IT) and there has grown up a whole language and sub culture which can be utterly meaningless to the less well informed. These days, we have come to expect that we will phone a call centre, speak to a computer, receive recorded instructions from a computer, and complete whole transactions without ever involving any kind of communication with another human being! The internet, dot.com shopping, booking holidays and cheap flights and endless other services have transformed the way we live as well as the way many do business.

The credit manager of today has to understand the benefits, as well as the drawbacks, of computerised systems, and how to make those systems work for him. It may appear daunting, modern technology can be quite mind blowing, but computerisation is little more than a technological development, in the same way that a 747 to New York is a giant step from an outside cabin with en suite facilities on the *Mauretania*.

Background
A8.2

The principles of granting credit and collecting payments due have their roots back in ancient times and the assistance available to the grantor and the collector remained unchanged for centuries. Advances in printing and book keeping gathered pace but slowly, and methods of communication were restricted to the best speed of the horse on land or the sailing packet at sea.

Probably the first major innovation to have a significant impact was the introduction and widespread adoption of the telegraph, but it was the reliable postal service, the typewriter and the telephone that really got things off the ground. The computer, which had its beginnings back in the Second World War, is the innovation which more than any other has changed beyond recognition the way that business is conducted. It is now taken for granted that cash is available anywhere in the world from a hole in the wall, that the pressing of a key illustrates the latest up to the second status of an account, or that interrogating the database provides a full history of trading, going back as far as capacity allows. It is also taken for granted that such a service is instantaneous, with response times measured in nano seconds and that millions of items of data, whatever that may be, can be stored on disks taking up less space than an inexpensive box of chocolates.

It is often said that computers are merely magnificent adding machines or calculators, crunching numbers at mind blowing speed, and that what comes out is entirely dependent upon what goes in – 'garbage in, garbage out' is a favourite phrase. Of course, to an extent this is true, but the degree of sophistication in dealing with masses of data, and the techniques available for optimum use take number crunching to a higher plain. What was once unimaginable is now commonplace, with improvements and innovations in the design and control of systems and processes taking place almost daily. There can be little doubt that the possibilities now seem endless.

Credit management is about control – control of the risk, control of the cash and control of the sales ledger. Computer systems and applications are the means to exercise that control to the full. The development of systems in large organisations was often undertaken by in-house computer departments, designing and implementing tailor made applications which suited that particular business.

However, as costs of maintaining such facilities increased, the availability of 'off the shelf' packages at less cost has grown. Such packages are intended to meet most needs for businesses large and small, being designed to require the minimum of modification to adapt to a particular business application or environment. Whether the package is developed internally or bought in, it is essential to be clear as to actual requirements and to adopt systems which enhance the credit function from both the standpoint of customer interface and internal job efficiency. Buying a sales ledger package may be cheap compared to designing a tailor made package, and certainly easy, but if it does not do the task effectively and efficiently and is not user friendly for the credit controller then difficulties will soon arise.

Similarly, the customer needs to be able to understand the output from the package which directly affects him. For example, product description on the invoice should be recognisable to the customer, and not just a meaningless series of reference numbers which mean everything to the seller but nothing to the buyer. It is important, therefore, to be able to clearly specify requirements at the outset and to know what the computer systems can (and cannot) provide to assist the credit function.

It is at best unfortunate, and at worst incomprehensible, for any system to be acquired and installed simply to facilitate some internal processes without any reference or regard for customer impact or customer interface. It is far too easy to be persuaded by the big business of computer software and hardware suppliers and manufacturers that no organisation can survive and prosper without 'their' product. Any computer system, and credit control is no exception, *must* fulfil the dual role of meeting both seller and buyer requirements.

It is vital to be aware of some real down to earth fundamentals. For example, there should be enough character field to accommodate the full names and postal addresses of customers. It is not acceptable to shorten names in order to make them fit fields which are not adequate for the purpose. Leaving 'Ltd' off so that it fits, or missing the name in brackets, or even shortening 'George' to 'Geo' corrupts the data filed throughout the system. In the event of subsequent legal action, the seller may well find himself suing the wrong buyer, with dire consequences. Similarly, a system which suits domestic trade may not be suitable for export, where postal codes and towns can be placed in a different order in the address section to that in use in the UK.

Fixed or variable data   A8.3

Much of the information used by credit control is also needed by other departments, such as customer name and address, so a large requirement is for an easily accessible and easily maintained data base. Data kept on computer systems falls into two categories:

- fixed; and

- variable.

Fixed does not mean set in concrete, because fixed data needs to be updated (the customer changes name or address), but rather it is a constant for all company needs. Variable data, such as current outstanding balance owed, will change from day to day. Identifying fixed and variable data is therefore the first step in establishing the system requirements.

Fixed data   A8.4

Fixed data includes:

- customer name;

- customer address for invoices, statements and delivery;

- customer account number;

- customer telephone, fax and telex numbers;

- customer e-mail address;

- terms of payment;

- customer contact name;

- customer contact special instructions (e.g. phone a.m. Mon–Thurs);

- credit limit;

- order limit;
- risk category;
- date account opened;
- sales division;
- representative code;
- product group;
- price and trade discount structure;
- delivery instructions, packing instructions and shipping marks;
- currency; and
- any special instructions (e.g. fixed holiday shutdowns).

Variable   A8.5

Variable data may include:

- current sales ledger items;
- orders on hand;
- orders ready;
- turnover year to date;
- turnover current month;
- credit hold;
- queries;
- payment history; and
- telephone collection call record.

Computerisation of fixed and variable data   A8.6

Paragraphs **A8.4** and **A8.5** above illustrate the kind of data that can be stored on a computer and accessed, but also serve to show the breadth of assistance to the credit function afforded by computerisation. All that data, in hard copy paper and file form, would have been monumental in storage and a nightmare in retrieval in days gone by.

Both fixed and variable data are dependent upon accuracy of input, and each item of data has a source. In simple terms, the customer name and address comes from the original credit application form which has been completed by the customer and the salesperson, checked and amended if necessary by credit control and thereafter subject to update by customer file maintenance. Variable data, such as invoices, cash received and balances can be fed into the system from a variety of sources, but still with the same need for complete accuracy.

Online features A8.7

Any computer system will have capacity restraints. Apart from filing and storage, the real benefits in computerisation lie in the information which can and should be provided online. That is to say that the answer to as many questions as possible, and as much information as possible should be at the touch of a keyboard, or click of the mouse, with the data displayed for the operator to see the situation immediately at any given time. The computer should also produce all the documents necessary to conduct business transactions speedily and accurately, so that time is freed to devote to positive credit activities and not spent in the preparation and issue of paperwork. (See **A8.13** below.)

Producing paperwork A8.8

The following paragraphs look at the ways in which different elements of paperwork can be produced by a computer.

Invoices A8.9

The invoice is a record of the transaction which has taken place between supplier and buyer. It is, in effect, the first request for payment in that it is the first document issued after the goods have been supplied or the work undertaken, and as such it should tell the customer everything he needs to know in order to arrange settlement. It should be issued as soon as possible after delivery or completion, certainly within 24 hours and this is easily achieved by its production on the computer system. It should be clear, error free and jargon free, with the following essential features:

- customer name and invoice address;
- where the goods were delivered to;
- description of the goods;
- unit price;
- quantity;
- trade discount (if applicable);
- correct extension and total (i.e. quantity price, 2 at £10.00 = total £20.00);
- VAT (at appropriate rate);
- VAT registration number;
- customer order number;
- supplier's name and address;
- where to pay;
- how to pay;
- payment due date and payment terms; and

- cash discount (if applicable).

One of the major causes of payment delay is the omission of the customer order number. It is accepted practice in large commercial organisations to submit orders with an official company purchase order number and to reject supplier invoices which do not quote that number. In Government and local authority transactions it is mandatory, and a rejected invoice often loses its place in any payment queue even when re-submitted containing the correct data. Not to include this is literally to invite delay and it is also an illustration of the supplier's failure to meet customer requirements.

The invoice address and the delivery address may well be different and the customer's order will have contained precise invoicing instructions which have to be followed. Sending an invoice to the wrong address adds to the payment period and can lead to the invoice being lost altogether.

The speedy production of a clear, error free invoice, promptly dispatched facilitates prompt payment. First class mail should always be used where appropri-ate – why send an invoice dated 31 May second class on 2 June and expect it to arrive in time to be included in the customer's May purchase ledger? It should be no surprise if the customer claims to have closed off his May books and has included the item in his June balances.

Correct input to the computer system in the first place ensures that the invoice is accurate, and online production ensures that it is timely.

Statements A8.10

The statement of account is often a document which many businesses find superfluous and therefore either do not produce at all or only produce as an afterthought. It is true that many companies process invoices and pay on invoice only, but a great many still use the statement, both as a payment document, and as a means of reconciling their purchase ledger with the supplier's sales ledger. When used for reconciling the ledgers, missing invoices can be identified and copies requested, at which time both customer and supplier are aware of differences between their respective ledgers. Another view is that the statement is simply the customer copy of the supplier's own sales ledger, and that therefore at any time both the supplier and the customer are looking at exactly the same information when discussing issues together on the telephone. More importantly, from the supplier's point of view, issuing a statement of account is in effect a second request for payment, giving the customer a second opportunity to read payment instructions and be reminded of terms and due dates. In listing current month transactions and totals, the statement also allows attention to be drawn to any items uncleared from the previous month, giving amounts due and overdue and therefore reminding the customer again of his obligations.

Whatever the purpose to which statements may be put, by either customer or supplier, they do provide a useful service, and require the same careful input and attention to detail as in the case of invoice production.

Essential features of a statement are:

- open item status;

- customer name and address;

- supplier name and address;

- address to which payment should be made (perhaps incorporating a tear off remittance advice portion);

- bank details for payment by credit transfer;

- invoice number, date and amount;

- customer order number; and

- total outstanding by month, indicating those items which are due or overdue.

The statement should be produced as soon after the closing of the accounting month as possible, allowing more time for the various reconciliations to take place, and certainly not more than three days after the month end.

Open item listing is by far the most preferred type of statement, giving clarity to any items left outstanding from the previous month and is much easier to both read and reconcile than the brought forward balance type of statement. Clarity is essential and if invoices are still outstanding from previous months due to unresolved queries, they should still be visible as individual entries so that attention can be focussed on dealing with them as a matter of urgency.

Order documentation   A8.11

On receipt of an order from a customer, the data is input into the system, which will then produce an order acknowledgement to be printed off immediately and issued to the customer. This confirms the customer order, containing all the information contained on that order, including any special order instructions. It is at this stage that the customer has the opportunity to correct any errors or make additions or amendments and it is also at this stage that the system can prepare further documentation relating to this works order (internal order documentation). Once delivery has taken place, the works order set is actioned, which triggers the production of the invoice. All the basic data relating to quantity, description, price etc. is the same through the various outputs, up to and including the invoice itself. This negates the need to make duplicate or triplicate entries to the system. The more entries that have to be made, the greater the chance of input error, so getting the order input right first time saves considerable time and effort.

Such systems can accommodate off the shelf orders or orders which have to be placed on to a production schedule process, again highlighting the importance of accuracy at the outset of the procedure, because one system is now feeding another, and the aim is not just to supply the correct documentation quickly, but also to ensure that the right product is made and delivered.

Stock availability and downdate   A8.12

An important feature of any busy order office is the knowledge that the goods which the customer is now ordering are actually available. Finished goods placed on the warehouse shelves should be entered into the computer system at once, so that upon any incoming enquiry the real level of stock can be ascertained at a glance. Supplying from stock means that as the customer order is input, the program selects the available stock for allocation to that order, prepares a picking list for the warehouse to action, and a load list for dispatch to complete. The moment the goods are allocated to the incoming customer order, even if not yet picked and packed, the stock is downdated, and those goods are therefore not available for the next customer. The same principle is involved in producing to order, in that the production schedule is fed from the order input system so that product is produced in the right quantity at the right time and in the right order (though for production purposes, schedules may amalgamate orders in to product types or sizes for optimum production efficiency).

The process can have additional features to greatly improve the interface with the customer in the event of stock not being readily available, production and delivery schedules input by production or by the buying department can indicate when such stock can become available. The order clerk is thus in a position to be able to give the customer a realistic delivery date for his order.

Aged debt analysis   A8.13

The aged debt analysis, or report, is the credit control or collection clerk's basis for further credit granting decisions or collections activity (see **A13.16** below for more information in respect of collections), and should be available at the same time as the monthly sales ledger and monthly statements, as well as on request. The report lists customers and their balances, aged from current to one, two, three months and three months and over. This enables the controller and/or collector to see the position of the account as it relates to the customer's credit limit, how much is past due and how much is required to keep the account up-to-date and within the agreed limit. The ageing element of the report indicates due dates and within the system there should be an additional facility for the credit manager to re-age accounts if required. If special terms have been agreed on one particular order for a customer, which is different to that customer's normal terms and is a one off arrangement, then it may well be that no amendment has been made to the customer master file in respect of credit terms. The effect of this would be to show an incorrect due date on that particular order, which may have a knock on effect in respect of overdue reminders and other collection activity. Similarly, special arrangements in respect of agreed payment schedules may need to be reflected in the ageing process. The facility has to be closely controlled, however, a feature of many computer programs is that they can only be password accessed, providing a safeguard against misuse.

Screen display   A8.14

The big advantage of using computers in business is being able to retrieve, at the touch of a button, all the information needed when talking to a customer on the telephone, or when making various decisions about the customer. Before computerisation, all the necessary information was there, but in paper file format, often in different files, maybe even in different offices or buildings. It was not possible to make customer contact without considerable physical preparation and answering a customer question often involved taking the telephone number and calling back later. None of that is now necessary, and the right combination of information on one screen, or easy access to a variety of screens, is all that is now needed.

Customer name and account number   A8.15

Establishing a customer on the sales ledger involves the allocation of a unique customer account number. It may be that the customer is a subsidiary of an existing customer or part of a group of companies, more than one of which are already customers, in which case it is possible to allocate an additional account number, designated major group account, which links together all members of the same group, and gives sight to any group exposure in accounts receivable. The particular customer, however, has an account number relating only to that customer's account, and it is that number which is the key to all information relating to that individual account. The number is likely to stay with the customer throughout dealings with the company, even though the customer may undergo more than one change of name and perhaps several changes of address. Enter the correct account number, and the correct account name and address will be displayed on the screen. Not all customers have their account number to hand when calling, so a search facility is a must, usually based upon some form of short code and location. For example, A Smith & Sons (1999) Ltd, Wolverhampton would be allocated account number S12345, sort name (or short code) SMIWOL – entering either S12345 or SMIWOL will bring up the same account.

Contact name and extension number   A8.16

The contact name will vary according to which department needs to access the customer account. Credit control require the name of the person who deals with the payment of accounts, sales will want the buyers' names and numbers, and transport may require the name of the goods inwards or warehouse man.

In addition to the name, the position should also be recorded, as knowing who to talk to, and that person's position within the organisation and authority, go together. Extension numbers, direct line numbers, fax numbers and e-mail addresses are also needed.

Contacts may of course change. People leave, or are promoted to other roles and new people join – part of the function of customer file maintenance is to keep all these records up-to-date, including job title and responsibility. Purchase departments can be amalgamated with other functions within the customer's organisation, centralised to a new head office, or even out-sourced. The contact name and number section of the customer file should also have clear details on the best times to call or visit, so that the employee making customer contact should not waste time and effort.

Credit limit   A8.17

It is paramount that the customer credit limit is visible to the seller, more so if the limit is used as more than just a guide, but as an actual barrier to the granting of further facilities. Display of the credit limit assists the order intake procedure in so far as the customer can be forewarned at an early stage that acceptance of the order is going to prompt further action which will be required if that order is to be processed. It also gives the collector valuable information when talking to the customer about his account and what needs to be paid in order to prevent any order difficulties in the future.

Part of the credit limit display should show order status (see **A8.18** below), but should also include an exception report facility, available online and also as a hard copy print. The exception notification is part of the record of the customer's account, and can be analysed for reasons and remedies. It also gives a record of how many times the credit limit has been exceeded, and the consequences which resulted, either good or bad. It is often the case where the credit limit is more of a general guide that exceeding the credit limit simply prompts a warning to credit control that it has taken place. It will then be for credit to take the appropriate steps, which may range from withholding supplies and contacting the customer, to actually reviewing the existing credit limit to see if it should be increased. Its strength lies in the objectivity of the review process and in providing meaningful information to substantiate any necessary changes.

Risk category   A8.18

The purpose of risk categories are explained in **A5 NEW BUSINESS** and in the context of screen display, they are closely linked to credit limits. Access to the customer file online gives the operator a full picture of the customer according to his limit and category. A customer in the undoubted or low risk category clearly warrants a different approach as far as the credit limit is concerned to the customer in the ordinary trade risk or high risk categories. Both the credit clerk and the collector will be better equipped for whatever approach is to be adopted if that information is readily available. It is also a displayed indicator for other departments with access to the file, sales and marketing can see at a glance that sales efforts directed at low or ordinary risk customers would be more profitable. Provided that they are fully aware of issues of confidentiality and sensitivity, there is no reason why sales personnel should not be able to see the category and limit established for their individual customers, as sales should be able to understand how the decisions had been arrived at and this knowledge should be of assistance to them in their contacts and negotiations with customers. Trading conditions in all industries can be volatile, some more than others, and it follows that the fortunes of companies can rise and fall. Risk categories can go up and down, and moving customers between categories according to trading experience (or in the event of information received) is common practice. The screen display shows the current risk category and the customer file contains the history of category movements and reasons for this.

Stop list   A8.19

Anyone accessing the system (for example warehouse and distribution staff, sales representatives, collectors or credit clerks) will need to see at a glance whether or not the customer is on the stop or credit hold list and the reason they are on it (use of the stop list as part of the collection process is outlined in **A13.21** and **A13.55** below). Ideally, the stop list is fully integrated into the order processing and invoice system so that on receipt of the customer order there is both visibility of a stop situation and a system prompt for action to be taken. Degrees or levels of 'stop' are also preferable. For example, ordinary stop prompts the order department or warehouse to contact credit control and/or the customer to arrange for payment, but the stop category can be overridden for the order to be taken and a works order processed. Whereas real stop, or super stop, prevents the order from physically being input into the system and means that there is no way that goods can be supplied unless and until credit control have taken the required steps to arrange payment and released the customer from the stop list.

Exception reports are produced for credit control to determine where stops have been overridden and to ensure that the follow up action has taken place and payment has been made or promised. Changing the category from 'ordinary' to 'super' gives the credit control department the overall control of the customer's credit facility so that if the depot or warehouse have overridden once and no payment has been forthcoming it will not be possible for it to happen again.

Sales are also made aware of the customer being on stop, both by notification by credit control and by their own access to the system and the stop situation being visible to them. In addition, each sales representative can receive a print out of all his own customers who are stopped, in order that they may be aware when calling on the customer and can be prompted to assist in the collection process. This is all the more useful if the sales commission is linked directly to the account being paid.

Queries   A8.20

Accounts where invoices are held in query can be a problem in distorting the facts about what may be overdue for payment and included in the total outstanding balance on the customer account. Having looked at the setting up and maintenance of a query register (see **A6.17–A6.22** above), an online display feature should incorporate an indicator or notation that invoices are subject to query. This allows the operator to ensure that the customer is not placed on stop because of an outstanding invoice (which may be overdue), as well as prompting follow up action to see that the matter is speedily resolved. It also allows the collector to be aware of a problem with the account and to carry that awareness through to the customer when discussing the account in general. It is good for relations for the customer to be confident that his query is being looked into and not ignored, and that the rest of the account can be settled knowing that there will be a speedy outcome to the problem raised. The matter of identifying genuine queries as opposed to excuses for non-payment is covered later (see **A13.29** and **A13.30** below), but at the very least any query that has been notified and as yet remains outstanding should be noted on the ledger, and hence displayed online for all to see.

Current balance   A8.21

At any time it should be possible to ascertain exactly what the customer currently owes. This figure will include payments which are not yet due, currently due as well as any overdue amounts. The figure simply indicates at any given moment in time the total exposure and risk. This figure should include VAT, where applicable, and be in the currency in which the customer was invoiced. The information links in with the credit limit and risk category data referred to earlier (see **A8.17** and **A8.18** above and **A4.5–A4.25** above), and also connects with any stop list scenario (see **A8.19** above and **A13.21** and **A13.55** below).

One of the most commonly asked questions internally, whether from sales or from elsewhere in the company (very often from senior management) is, 'how much does so and so owe us?'. The answer should be swift and clear, as it should to the customer himself enquiring about his balance.

Two other items worthy of note under the heading of current balance, are major group exposure, and turnover year to date. Both are useful front screen displays not least because they put the current account balance into perspective set against other criteria and give the credit clerk or collector a better idea of the organisation being dealt with.

Overdue balance – amount and age   A8.22

The importance of being able to display overdue balances should be self evident. However, if more than one invoice, covering more than one accounting period make up the total overdue, then they should be displayed as grouped and aged totals. The only point to note is that as mentioned above in respect of queries (see **A8.20** above) – it should always be possible to filter out collectable and non-collectable balances at any given time.

Cash allocation   A8.23

Fundamental to all credit control activities remains the prompt and accurate posting of cash received to the ledger. Cash allocation should always be a priority, not just for good housekeeping purposes, but also to be sure that at any given moment in time, the account reflects the actual state of play and is as up-to-date as it is possible to be. Future orders, further deliveries, collection action, legal proceedings and risk decisions will require knowledge of the account as it is, not what it may be if someone gets round to posting cash to the ledger. Not only that, but it must make sense to receive the cash, bank it straight away and update the account – it may save work that need not be done, such as chasing the customer for an amount he has paid, as well as avoiding any embarrassment that such action may cause.

Updating the ledger   A8.24

Two principal features which update the ledger are available with most systems, these are real time or overnight update. The latter is sometimes possible during the day if computer time allows batch processing during quieter periods, such as over lunch, but this would depend upon a number of factors, including volumes, and overnight processing is much more usual.

Real time   A8.25

Real time is to all intents and purposes instantaneous. The sales ledger clerk can call up the customer's account on the cash allocation program, enter the amount of cash received and match it against the invoices to be paid. Once agreed and balanced, the transaction is entered as completed and the matched invoices are paid and removed. At that moment in time, the customer account reflects the fact that those invoices have been paid, and anyone looking at the customer account will be shown the current balance, if any, or a nil balance. All the more reason to give cash allocation priority – the sooner the customer's account reflects the true state of affairs, the better.

Overnight processing   A8.26

Batch processing overnight means that the input to the system is done during the day, whether undertaken by sales ledger staff, or done by computer staff using documents prepared by sales ledger, but processed later by the computer system. This means that the customer ledger reflects today's cash tomorrow, rather than immediately. This is perfectly satisfactory in many environments, the only point to consider is that everyone should be made aware of the fact that there is a 24 hour delay in updating the customer account. Real time processing (see **A8.25** above) is becoming more common since the capacity of modern computer systems has greatly increased along with their capabilities, and the actual costs in real terms has dropped dramatically over the years. It is now, therefore, possible to own and operate a computer system with levels of sophistication unheard of in the past.

Balancing and reconciliation controls   A8.27

Common to both methods of cash allocation are the establishment of balancing and reconciliation controls. The cash received from the customer is the amount to be posted to the ledger, and the invoices to be removed are those which the customer indicates from his remittance advice that he is paying. This is particularly important when there is more than one invoice with the same value, it should not be assumed that the customer is paying the older invoice first, because there may be a very good reason why he is not. Taking out the wrong invoice only complicates the issue later if it is established that a query exists. It may be that the customer does not actually send a remittance advice with the payment, in which case it is extremely important that staff opening and sorting post keep a look out for compliment slips with invoice numbers written on them, or for invoice details written on the back of cheques. If it is not immediately possible to reconcile the payment to the items on the ledger, the customer should be contacted to determine what the payment covers. This is equally true of BACS (Banks Automated Clearing System) payments, where either the customer has failed to send a remittance advice or the entry on the bank statement is not sufficient to identify. A call to the bank usually produces more information. Only if all this fails should a payment be placed on the customer account as an 'on account' payment (unless of course that is exactly what it is, e.g. deposit, instalment, part payment etc.). The system of payment allocation also requires a check mechanism to balance the total received to the total posted and allocated. It is frequently the case that there are minor differences, for example the supplier's pricing system working to a different number of decimal points to the purchaser's system which can result in odd pence differences. Tolerances can be defined which allow automatic write off of such differences and save time and cost in dealing with small sums. However, it is necessary to determine a sensible tolerance feature so that such write offs are insignificant in proportion to the money volumes and average invoice values, otherwise amounts will be being written off automatically which cumulatively have a value worth considering.

This is also the case when sales ledgers are designed to handle currencies in addition to Sterling, invoices raised in a foreign currency at an exchange rate established at the time of issue will be paid in the fullness of time at an exchange rate which could well be different, resulting in a gain or a loss. Such cash allocation requires more careful attention, and although programs can handle conversions and currency differences, control needs to be exercised so that gains or losses are not automatically lost, but are accounted for in the nominal ledger.

The sales ledger, the nominal or general ledger and bank records must all reconcile, and it is far better for the reconciliation to begin at source, i.e. at the point of cash posting, than to try to recreate actions later. In other words, if the cash received and the cash posted balance for each entry and for each day's sub-totals and totals, then there can be confidence in the belief that the process has been undertaken correctly.

The customer account is therefore updated immediately in real time, or overnight, so that the next operator, when viewing the account, has the latest information to hand. No unallocated or unmatched cash should be left in abeyance. The ledger should show what has happened, and reference to the customer file will show what action has been taken in contacting the customer for information, or requesting a credit for goods returned or wrongly priced.

The real time or overnight situation refers equally to journals and other adjustments made to the ledger account, so that the clearance of debit notes, writing off of small differences, matching off credit notes and invoice balances, and removal of invoice and on account payments are subject to the same disciplines and the same processes. The customer's account should be up to date and truly reflect the actual position.

Orders   A8.28

At all times there will be a requirement to have up-to-date information on all matters relating to the customer and the current order situation. Both credit limits and stop lists are closely linked to orders, so that at any given moment in time operators will need to know what orders are in hand, which are ready for shipment, what is being held and why, and what has been shipped and perhaps not yet invoiced.

At the time of order input there is the need to know if this order takes the customer over his credit limit, the limit being based on order values, total exposure or a combination of the two. If the customer is on the stop list this too has a bearing on whether or not of the order is processed, and in either case, action needs to be initiated by credit or sales staff to contact the customer with a view to finding a way to bring the account back to order. Unless sight can be had very quickly of the total order situation, the customer could very easily become deeply indebted to an unacceptable level without the supplier being aware of the situation having arisen. By looking at the orders which are on hand, ready, held or have been shipped, the credit or order clerk can see exactly what is happening. Investigating the orders which have been 'held' to ascertain the reason (which may be perfectly innocent, for example, the order is not fully completed), and looking at the actual customer account to confirm that those orders that have been shipped have also been invoiced, will help clarify and ease the decision making process. Looking at the customer account will also show payments that have been received, which will have a bearing on both credit limit and stop list problems.

It is also possible to incorporate into the order display, a form of progress report, with suggested completion and delivery dates, which is another form of guidance to both operator and customer. Although this chapter is chiefly concerned with matters relating to the sales ledger and the customer file generally, and therefore is assumed to be aimed at the sales ledger, credit control or collection personnel, it is worth remembering that any computer system, adequately protected as far as access is concerned by password controls, should be as comprehensive in its capabilities as capacity and costs will allow. It is therefore not unreasonable to display the kind of information which would be useful to more than one department and to authorise such access as is deemed justifiable in order to offer the customer the fullest possible service.

Payment history   A8.29

Collection activity is greatly enhanced when full knowledge of the customer's trading history is readily available and understood (see **A13.8–A13.15** above). An extremely valuable online feature of a computerised sales ledger and customer file is therefore a record of payment and a history of activity which has a significant bearing on the approach to be taken with the customer. Experience of ten transactions with the customer over a period of time is a more meaningful guide to the customer's probity than just one, and equally one instance of a payment difficulty among ten satisfactory dealings does not of itself necessarily mean trouble. What is important is to be able to build up a pattern of payment behaviour over a period of time, together with a record of events which have a bearing on the manner in which the account has been conducted.

As will be seen later, the payment history itself is significant (see **A8.31** below), and it should be available online to view at a glance. A rolling twelve months is more beneficial than a year to date display, the latter only becoming useful in the second half of the trading year – before that there is not enough real data to provide worthwhile analysis. The display can be in the form of number of days taken to pay (DSO), or in the number of days each transaction is overdue. Care should be exercised to ensure that any apparent distortion is due to the customer's payment itself and not caused by any special event, such as the customer being allowed an extra 30 or 60 days for a particular purchase. In other words, the pattern is based upon standard information and can be judged as reflecting the actual payment behaviour of the customer.

It follows that the customer who always pays his account close to terms warrants treatment of a different kind when in an overdue situation, to the customer who only ever pays after two reminder letters and three telephone calls.

Record should be kept of dishonoured cheques – the system can display the frequency and, by use of suitable codes, the reason for cheques being returned. It is extremely important to be able to distinguish between a cheque being returned by the bank due to lack of funds and one which is returned requiring a second signature, and to record that distinction accurately in the computer file. The second signature scenario, for example, may not be a real problem in itself in a one off situation, whereas lack of funds is immediately more serious even the first time it happens. Repeated return of cheques for second signatures, however, is perhaps indicating at best sloppiness by the customer and at worst a deliberate ploy to delay payment. It is the frequency which guides the collector, and to have the full data readily to hand when speaking to the customer prompts the right questions and the right responses.

Frequency of appearance on the supplier's stop list in the previous twelve months (again better than year to date) also augments the actual payment pattern history and is a sign of the degree of seriousness to be attached to the customer's promises or offers. It is also of significance for sales personnel, who have a role to play in developing the relationship between the supplier and the customer and who need to be informed of problems which will have a direct impact on their own relationship with the customer. It all too often happens that the sales representative is told one thing by his customer, which is believed, and only on returning to the office does the actuality become evident. The saying 'forewarned is forearmed' works just as much for the sales department as it does for credit control.

Taken together, the payment pattern, record of dishonoured cheques (and reasons), and appearances on the stop list paint a more complete picture of the customer and his account, giving the collection team the right background against which to carry out their function more effectively.

Use of the ledger in predicting problems   A8.30

It is well known that early signs of difficulties to come lie in the supplier's own sales ledger, and being able to pick up those signs, interpret them and take action can prevent losses from bad debts. Not all losses are either predictable or preventable and the nature of credit granting as a calculated risk always carries with it the danger of getting it wrong or being unexpectedly caught out. However, there are many indicators of impending trouble, and use of a computerised ledger and all the accompanying facilities that it provides improves the chances of spotting problems early and building up a picture of things going wrong. Analysis of all the relevant data should be part of the continual review and monitoring process, added to which the occurrence and frequency of particular events greatly enhance the possibilities of making the right decisions at the right time. More positively, being able to spot problems early enough enables the supplier to be in a position to assist the customer through what may simply be temporary difficulties. It is an accepted fact that in real terms the costs involved in keeping existing customers is far less than the amount spent on attracting new customers, and every effort made to retain the customer base is of real benefit. There is the added bonus of developing customer loyalty through the customer care programme, which in turn not only retains the customer and his turnover, but also adds to the armoury when fighting off the competition, the customer is almost bound to ask himself if the new proposed supplier is likely to try to look after him in the same way as his existing supplier has done.

History of the account   A8.31

Payment history and the pattern of customer payment behaviour is just as important to the credit clerk when assessing potential risk as it is to the collector when contacting the customer for settlement of the account. An account, hitherto paid more or less to terms, which becomes later and later each month is saying something, and taken in conjunction with other information recorded along the way, may be telling the credit controller something quite specific. It is always a danger to generalise, and there can be many factors which have to be taken into account when assessing risk by analysing the conduct of the sales ledger account. The customer may well be the first to point out difficulties by being upfront about current problems being encountered. For example, a manufacturer whose production is principally for export, may well be going through a difficult time due to the strength of Sterling, these difficulties will be temporary and will ease as the exchange rates move more to his benefit. The art of risk assessment is to judge the seriousness of such circumstances, the real financial strength or weakness of the customer and his inherent ability to weather the storm. The boom and bust trade cycles of the years since the Second World War have shown that the weak will go to the wall, and that even the strong are subject to trying periods of cash shortage and depressed conditions. Nevertheless, the payment history itself does reveal trends and is of immense value, giving as it does, the supplier the opportunity to decide on the appropriate course of action, for example, a supplier may ask, are we in a position to help, or do we need to act promptly to collect the debt?

Over the rolling twelve months, the pattern of payments shows:

- invoices paid to terms;

- the number of days by which a payment is late; and

- changes that have taken place to the payment pattern.

Increasing delays in payment, and instances of part payment or payments on account, point to a deteriorating cash flow position, and that the customer is finding it increasingly difficult to meet obligations as they fall due. In the absence of industry or seasonal circumstances which may be affecting everybody, this would have to be taken as a sign of impending failure, and such steps as are required to protect the supplier's investment will have to be taken.

The credit assessor needs to be aware of the history of the account – how long have they been a customer? – to which end every customer file should contain the date that the account was opened and that date should be readily accessible on the system. In addition, there should be recorded in the file significant events and dates, such as mergers and acquisitions, disposals and restructuring. The customer may have sold loss making subsidiaries, been taken over by a large conglomerate, or undergone re-financing. Sole traders or partnerships may have become limited companies, private companies may have gone public, changed bankers or experienced major changes in key personnel. Companies can diversify their product range, attacking new markets, or can rationalise and retrench in those markets and products which they know best.

The other aspect of customer history to be considered is the reliance, or otherwise, of the customer on the supplier and *vice versa*. Many suppliers use customers for trials of new products or as reference sites, combining the supply of both chargeable and free of charge materials with the use of customer feedback to promote product development and marketing. Equally, the customer may be reliant on the supplier's product to keep in business, using the supplier's product as an integral part of his own finished product, and restriction or stoppage of supply could cause immense problems. In those circumstances, the supplier would expect to remain at the top of the customer's payment priority list, and therefore any deterioration in payment days would have a greatly added significance as far as predicting difficulties is concerned. It would also influence the supplier's approach to assisting the customer on a temporary basis so that the *status quo* can be restored to the benefit of both parties. Any change in the buying and ordering pattern of the customer should be noted. Order levels falling may be an indication of the customer buying from an alternative source, however, it could also reveal trading problems for the customer. This may be predictable from general economic conditions prevalent at the time, or may be more specific to that particular customer. When assessing risk it is for the credit analyst to take all factors into account, isolating those relevant to the customer in order to arrive at an accurate assessment.

Similarly, the reverse is worth noting – an increase in order levels has to be seen in the context of the ability of the customer to pay, and the supplier needs to be conscious of the dangers of overtrading and of carrying too high a level of stock. Changes in the pattern of ordering may be seasonal and can be analysed quite easily as such, or one off large orders from time to time can simply be because the customer himself has a large order to fulfil. It is not unknown for production schedulers to query a customer order which is larger than normal with the order department, if that blip is evident to production, it should also be visible to credit control.

Changes in product type are noteworthy as this may have ramifications of cost and exposure risk. For example, the supplier of consumables to company A may be aware from articles in the trade press of the purchase of new manufacturing equipment by company A which will result in either the potential supply of a different product, or increased volumes of existing products. The purchase by the customer of expensive capital equipment can itself send messages to the supplier, for example, has the customer dug deep into his reserves or borrowed heavily to finance the purchase and will this have an effect on his ability to pay the supplier's account when it falls due? This may be another occasion when temporary help is going to be needed, and the supplier needs to be ready for this. Alternatively, this may be an opportunity for sales to increase trade. Or it may be possible that it will be a combination of both the need for help now and the opportunity for increased business later.

Business information and memo record pads A8.32

Many businesses operate a marketing function which includes running a business information library, where such deals and announcements are noted and entered into the company database. Access by the risk assessor is adding to knowledge already readily available from the customer ledger file, and contributes further to the prediction and assessment process.

All contact with the customer should be noted, and most computer systems incorporate a memo record pad facility (or diary facility usable online). More often than not, this is principally maintained by the collection function, noting dates and times of requests made for payment, copy invoices and proof of delivery. That is not to say that other functions do not record customer contact, and certainly queries and customer responses are noted by more than just collectors.

From the memo record pads, it can be seen how often the customer has undertaken to do something, such as send a cheque, and how often that has or has not taken place. The real judge of a customer's commitment is not just the instances of what can be described as broken promises, but what the outcome or following action may have been. The customer may have promised payment in full the following Tuesday, but either before or on the day, he contacted the supplier to say that something had gone wrong and payment would be made on Friday. What the supplier should do is dependent upon a number of factors, but the point here is that the customer made the next move before Tuesday came and went, not leaving the supplier to carry out the follow up in the knowledge that a promise had been made and broken. It may be argued that the customer's action was no more than a delaying tactic, but it may have been a genuine attempt to try to meet an obligation made in good faith.

The inclination to be able to assist can be influenced, therefore, by two apparently similar situations seen in different ways. On the one hand, the customer makes a promise, breaks it and does nothing, leaving the supplier to continue to chase for payment, only this time with less respect and greater cynicism. On the other hand, the customer makes a promise, realises it cannot be kept, and tries to find a way to repair any damage that may have been done and make a new undertaking. In the latter case, the supplier can be appreciative of the customer's efforts in trying to deal honestly with the situation, and all other things being taken into account, this customer may be a better prospect for temporary help to the benefit of both concerned.

Therefore, in effect what both the collector and the credit assessor are trying to do from the memo record pad is to differentiate between the genuine customer who needs help and the habitual promise breaker who is not to be trusted. Full analysis of the memo record pad over a period of time will no doubt ease that identification, and subsequent actions will have largely been dictated by previous experience.

Stop lists   A8.33

The system records each and every time a customer is placed on the stop list. The number of times a customer is placed on stop is principally determined by two factors:

- when the stop list is produced; and
- when the customer pays.

Timing of the stop list is crucial and is going to vary from industry to industry according to terms and current accepted practice, what the competition is doing and the supplier's position in the market place, to list just a few factors. If the example of net cash monthly is taken, and generally interpreted as payment being due at the end of the month following the month in which the invoice was issued, then the supplier would be looking for his January invoices to be paid on or by 28 February. On the basis that most customers in the supplier's particular industry pay one month's invoices at a time at the end of the calendar month and post cheques second class, it follows that a stop list produced on 1 March, when accounts are only one day overdue, will have nearly all the supplier's customers on it. A large number of customers would be off the stop list by 2 or 4 March, and more each day as March progresses. In such circumstances, appearances by customers on the stop list may be taken as the norm, rather than the exception, and therefore perhaps not too much should be read into the number of such appearances over the preceding twelve months.

Taking the same supplier, but this time producing the stop list for January accounts at the end of the second month following the month in which the invoice was issued, say 1 April, there would be appreciably fewer customers on the stop list, and each one would be one month overdue. Further, those accounts would have had reminder letters and telephone calls, and be fully aware that non-payment will lead to supplies being restricted, and therefore fully understand the consequences of non-payment. Appearance on the stop list would now have more significance, so that the record of appearances from the point of view of the collector or the assessor now has real meaning. If the customer always pays his account on the 20th of the month following the month of invoice, he will always appear on the first stop list example, but never on the second. In other words, stop list entries for that customer become important to note and to analyse as being indicative of something untoward which is happening.

Reminder letters   A8.34

Reminder letters and telephone calls can reveal patterns. Much would depend upon frequency and timing of reminder letters and telephone calls (see **A13.5–A13.7** and **A13.17** and **A13.18** below), but the system records when such reminders are issued, and analysis reveals how many and how often. It is a fact, sad though it may be, that many will wait for the reminder before issuing payment, and this of itself is not necessarily serious, but coupled with the payment history file, it is possible to identify those who pay on reminder, and those who do not. Changes to the pattern of events are important, rather than just the events themselves, as are the responses to the reminders. It is this that decides the course of action following analysis, and may indicate that help is required.

The final letter stage is more serious, for obvious reasons, and much as some always wait for the so called 'red letter', it is in effect very much the end of the collection process. By this stage all the usual reminders have been issued and telephone calls made, and the customer now knows that he is on the stop list. No further goods will be delivered or orders accepted, and in many cases, all credit facilities will have been withdrawn. Even if this action has not been taken, it may well be about to be taken and certainly any decisions about the future of the account will depend very much on how many times this situation has arisen before. It would normally be hoped that if the previously good customer was in trouble and in need of some assistance, this would have come to light before this stage, but it is not always the case, and even at this late stage some help may still be possible. However, much will depend upon whether the customer has been in this position before and if so, how many times. Swift reference to the computer system should provide the answer, for each time a customer is the subject of a final notice, the fact is noted on the file.

Third party collection   A8.35

The final element in the customer record is the notation of being placed out into third party hands for collection. This may or may not mean inevitable legal action and most would say that introducing a debt collection agency has to be the end of the road as far as the customer's account is concerned. If all of the business world paid according to terms, that would probably be so. However, in the real cut and thrust world of the competitive business environment, it is by no means unusual to carry on trading with customers who have been in the past the subject of third party collection activity. They are still in business, and provided that the terms and the prices are right many suppliers will feel obliged for commercial reasons to find ways of continuing to trade with customers with whom their experience has not been good. It is often for that reason that suppliers choose debt collection agencies carefully, and look to the agency to collect the debt and hand the customer back to them in one piece. The right terms and the right price could mean that the customer now pays the list price, with no trade discount, and does not enjoy the usual credit terms, if indeed any credit terms at all.

Experience has shown that there could be much to be gained by allowing the current debt to be paid off in instalments, with current or new supplies on a cash on delivery basis. The customer still trades, and the argument is that the chance of a successful outcome, i.e. the debt being paid in full, is greater if the business continues as a going concern, than if it were to fail and payment became part of the distribution of assets on a *pro rata* basis from an insolvent estate. The circumstances will undoubtedly vary from case to case, and indeed from industry to industry, some trades being much more vulnerable and accustomed to the aforementioned scenario than others, but it is true that even at this seemingly hopeless eleventh hour, something can be salvaged, and firmer foundations laid for the future. The key is once more an accurate record of all activities being recorded on the system and used by both the risk assessor and the collector as the basis for the decision making process.

Need for a complete record   A8.36

The common thread through all the processes which may be considered, is the availability of a complete record of events – the more comprehensive and easily accessible the better. To throw away potentially profitable business by shutting down an account that could be saved would be just as foolish as allowing unlimited credit to an account which was out of control and heading for collapse. The foundation for success is reliable information, which can be used to the best advantage of all concerned.

Compliance 2000   A8.37

The end of the 20th Century saw a worldwide flurry of activity as computer experts, accountants, financial institutions and Governments warned of the change from 1999 to 2000. In retrospect, the likelihood of most major systems not being able to cope with 2000 and beyond seemed unlikely to many, but there was a danger of smaller companies, and those with older systems, finding anomalies and even crashing altogether.

The publicity focused many minds, and the opportunity was taken not only to check and ensure, but also to upgrade systems. The end result was that many companies spent heavily on 'modernising' their systems, but also included all the latest upgrades to enhance their activities at the same time as guaranteeing that the change from 1999 to 2000 would cause no problems.

The change over, when it came, was for the most part satisfactory, with little or no disruption. The only point now for credit managers to bear in mind is that their systems can still recognise 1999 and prior for historical analysis purposes.

Euro symbol   A8.38

The single European currency (the Euro) was officially launched on 1 January 1999, with coins and notes entering official circulation in the Euro member countries on 1 January 2002. This introduced a new international trading currency to world markets. Exports are usually conducted in an internationally recognised currency, such as United States Dollars, or Pounds Sterling, for which established symbols existed on computer systems – $ or £. Many companies, having previously dealt in Deutsche Mark as DM or DEM, or French Francs as FRF or FFR, undertook to handle the Euro as EUR, simply because the Euro symbol had not been incorporated into many systems. With the adoption of the Euro as national currency by twelve 'Euroland' countries (Germany, France, Spain, Italy, Belgium, Holland, Greece, Portugal, Ireland, Luxembourg, Austria, and Finland), and the Euro becoming an accepted internationally recognised invoicing currency for exporters, the Euro symbol (€) should now be an integral feature on all systems.

The introduction of notes and coins into circulation in the participating countries emphasised the need for recognition of the importance of the Euro, and other countries (Sweden, Denmark and the United Kingdom) may still join in the future. Ten other countries joined the European Union in May 2004, with more to follow in the next few years, and these could well want, and qualify for, Euro membership.

User friendly systems   A8.39

There are aspects of all computer systems which should be paramount in the process of choice and installation (see **A8.2** above). The package or system is going to be used by credit controllers, sales ledger and collection personnel who are trained and competent credit management professionals, but not by definition experts in information technology. This means that the system must be as easy and as straightforward for them to use as possible, and that they are not outfaced by unnecessary complications. It should be user friendly, speak a reasonably simple language, have a series of functions and facilities which are readily accessible with the minimum of fuss, and will be robust enough to cope with errors in operation without tying up or crashing the whole system.

In the allocation of cash, for example, the operator can be asked at various stages 'are you sure? – yes/no' giving the check facility and the opportunity to stop without having made a final and binding commitment which could incorrectly update the ledger balance or alter a cash total. Mandatory fields to complete, guide the user down the right track, as do regular confirmation requests. The screen displays should be clear and easy to read, and not resemble the wiring diagram for an aircraft carrier – there is nothing more off putting for any normal user than to be faced by a complicated array of seemingly meaningless data which can only be interpreted by an expert in computer jargon. The user also needs to be able to retrieve the required information with ease. When the customer is on the phone, the clerk needs to be able to find the right screen display, move from screen to screen and back again with the minimal of key operations in order to answer whatever questions are being posed and not keep the customer hanging on endlessly. Windows based displays can solve some of these problems, but it is easy to have too many windows opened at one time, and like the key function, the fewer the better.

Retrieval is often a problem in so far as many businesses operate more than one system, with certain data going through one and other data through another. The sales ledger or credit control package should be designed to contain all that the operator is likely to require on one system so time is not wasted logging off one, logging onto another, and then logging out of that and back to the original once more. There are now a number of search and retrieve programs available which are designed to act as the link between various systems using pre-set parameters to find and store centrally such information as may be required at any time. All too often packages are bought and installed without either full evaluation having been undertaken by those who are actually going to use the system, or without adequate training having been given to those users. Evaluation means testing out all the features in the real work environment, running in parallel with the existing system to iron out anomalies and then training the personnel in all aspects of use. Switching off the old on Friday, and switching on the new on Monday and expecting business to carry on as usual is not a good idea. Involving the users in the evaluation process, and offering meaningful training and support, increases confidence and smooths the change over to the benefit of the business, its employees and its customers. That has to be the more sensible approach.

Summary A8.40

There is a myth and a mystique about computers which needs to be overcome, though it is often perpetuated by computer experts themselves and by the IT departments of many businesses. The computer, glorious adding and calculating machine that it is, is the servant – the operator, manager, proprietor, businessman is the master. The system chosen and used is for the benefit of the business and the customer, not something cosmetic. It needs to do specific tasks, designated by the business for the business, adding value and contributing to profitable success. Fit for the purpose, easy to use by properly trained and supported staff, the computer is an invaluable asset and as such should be chosen with due care.

A9

Cash Flow Planning

Introduction A9.1

Everyone who is employed has an income, paid weekly or monthly. For the hourly paid, that income may vary according to the hours worked, or for those paid on results, the income may vary according to what they have produced or what they have sold. Whilst ever employed, however, the commonality is a regular income. Matched against that income, are the outgoings, much of which is known in advance – the rent, mortgage, car payments, insurance etc. There are variables, such as the weekly shopping bill (much bigger those weeks when re-stocking of basics takes place, or seasonal purchases for the Christmas holiday), and extras like holidays or birthdays. The end of the week, or end of the month, however, is the time when the amount left (or not) is revealed.

In normal circumstances, some forward planning is therefore possible. The income is known, the expected outgoings are known, and what is left can go into the holiday fund or towards the new furniture. It does not always work that this week, or this month, something can be put away – this is the month for paying the house insurance, or the car tax, or the phone bill – but over a period of time, the ups and downs can be accounted for.

Planning cash flow in business, knowing what is going out and what is likely to be coming in, is part of the preparation process for what is to come. Businesses can prepare for 'busy' periods (the January sales, school half-term, the summer season, or whatever), and so too they can look ahead to the highs and lows of cash inflow and cash outflow. Knowing when to have the capability of meeting obligations as they fall due, against expectations of receipts as they also fall due is just as important for UK plc as it is for Tommy Atkins.

Cash flow – a dynamic tool for improving profits A9.2

Negative cash flow means that more money is going out of the business than is coming in. For many firms, the subject of cash flow does not feature high up in the agenda unless and until that very thing happens. Then, all of a sudden, cash flow becomes the overriding topic of the day. The consequences of negative cash flow are serious, the problem becoming acute when the bank refuses to increase the overdraft or demands that it is reduced immediately. It is vital, therefore, that companies address the subject of cash flow professionally, and use the good times to plan carefully.

Very positive results can be achieved by planning cash flow. In addition to giving the confidence that the business is soundly financed, it involves every business function in a regular system of forecasting net cash and takes corrective actions when fluctuations occur. Involving all managers in contributing to planning cash flow, places the business in a better balanced shape to forge ahead of competitors who are still struggling with cash gaps and leakages.

The various stories of entrepreneurial millionaires who went 'from rags to riches' invariably reveal that they succeeded by keeping a close watch on cash flow. In particular this enabled them to avoid accumulating excessive stocks and focused their attention on collecting money due to them on time. Those failed geniuses who litter the pavements of Carey Street, by comparison focused all their attention on technical excellence or sales volume and neglected their cash flow.

Since sales activity is usually planned in advance, it makes sense to plan the cash results of those sales to ensure that assets, as well as borrowings and interest expense needed to support those assets, are kept to a minimum.

Cash flow and net profit   A9.3

Businesses like to measure their profits in terms of sales exceeding costs. That is not the same as sales cash flowing in and expense cash flowing out. The measurement of profit depends on the accounting treatment of assets, liabilities, sales and expenses, with a variety of accruals, provisions and depreciation, all valued cautiously.

Actual cash flow is much more simple. It is the total of customers' payments flowing in to the bank account minus the total of payments for suppliers, wages, taxes, etc. flowing out of it in a given period.

Bank overdrafts are to cope with temporary spells when more funds flow out of the account than in. In an ideal world, it may be said that this shortfall should not happen – it is easy to control wages, taxes and other fairly fixed items, so there should be no need for an overdraft to cope with temporary spells of shortfall, which should not happen. This is not an ideal world, however, and the fact is that more bank funds than intended are needed to support unsold stocks and uncollected debtors. Stock control needs time and skills in managing procurement and manufacture to meet order levels, with minimal excesses. The real hazard for most businesses is uncollected debtors.

The largest asset on most balance sheets is debtors (also frequently referred to as accounts receivable, or simply, receivables). Debtors are in fact unpaid sales. If customers are allowed a month's credit, the seller should have just the latest month's sales total unpaid at the end of the month. In practice, of course, companies are usually owed between one and three months' total sales in excess of the latest month's sales. This means that either extra credit has been allowed for some sales or, more often than not, that collection procedures are very lax.

Planning cash flow, therefore, should always concentrate on the collection of sales revenue as near to terms as it is commercially possible. Once that is reliable and regular, the rest of the cash flow and borrowings become much easier to plan. Additionally, it will enhance customer relationships, aid future sales efforts, and at the same time improve internal procedures and the relationships between internal departments.

Cash forecasts should be enforced by top management as serious commitments, not just form-filling. They should be published, as appropriate, and their contributors required to explain variances between forecasts and actual results. As months go by it is the published variance analyses which motivate people to improve their performance in sales, collections and expense controls.

Sales and cash   A9.4

Sales are made in order to produce cash. Salaries and suppliers are paid with cash, and are not simply book entries in a ledger – expense has to be covered by income, and without income, there can be no expense discharged. Companies need cash profits to pay dividends or to re invest in the business itself, or both. It follows that the seller must have a level of management expertise to get cash equally as good as the expertise required to obtain orders. Every order should be seen as a means to valuable cash and then managed all the way through until the customer's cash is in the seller's bank. The attitude in every business has to be that a sale is simply a cost to the company until it has been paid. It is for that reason that credit terms should be kept as short as possible and why no sales commission should be paid until the cash is in.

Net profits and the effect of interest
on borrowings   A9.5

The cash needed for salaries and suppliers can be borrowed from the bank, but borrowing carries an interest charge, and that interest expense has to be covered by even more sales. Even if the company does not actually have to borrow money, it still faces interest expenses, i.e. the lost interest on funds that could have been invested if customers had paid. Therefore, credit sales mean debtors, which also means borrowings, at a cost of interest.

Interest rates can be high compared to net profit margins. In the past, publications such as the D&B *Key Business Ratios* have shown that the average net profit on sales for UK companies ran at about 4.5%. Some were higher, but many, especially those engaged in export, were lower. Pressure on end user prices, and the fierce competition on the High Street means that margins are under constant pressure, irrespective in many ways of actual interest rates. The proliferation, for example, of out of town shopping complexes and so called 'Designer Outlets' means that the consumer expects the lowest possible end user price, which is reflected all the way back through the delivery and manufacture chain.

On profit and loss statements, the final cost deduction before profit is declared is 'interest expense'. It follows that minimising this cost will directly increase net profits. For most businesses, the cost of interest is less than 10% of profits, a typical target for cash planning. When the cost of interest grows to 50% or more, the business is almost certainly doomed to fail because the assets are so excessive in relation to sales being made that the cost of financing them can never be recovered in trading profit. Cynically, it is then said that the company is making more profit for the bank than for the shareholders. However, even the bank will be concerned when the cost of interest exceeds the 50% level because the same message of inevitable failure is picked up by the bank, who will then appoint an Administrative Receiver to recover its loan.

Return on capital employed (ROCE) A9.6

This is a cash flow ratio, popular with City analysts and finance directors alike. The ratio compares the profit before tax made by a business with the borrowings needed to operate in the period. ROCE is usually calculated as:

$$\frac{\text{Return (net profit before tax) x 100}}{\text{Capital employed (borrowing)}}$$

Successful businesses know that faster cash collections improves the ROCE twice:

- the return figure is increased by the reduced interest expense; and

- the capital figure is reduced by fewer assets to be financed.

Long and short-term financing A9.7

If a business arranges its borrowings to suit its cash flows, it would be adopting the generally accepted normal procedure. Borrowings to suit cash flows means in essence that long-term, or fixed, assets which generate wealth over future years should be financed by long-term liabilities, such as share capital and mortgages. The more dynamic short-term assets, such as stocks and debtors, should be financed by short-term money such as overdrafts and supplier liabilities. The objectives in matching the short and longer term nature of assets and liabilities are to:

- remove any pressure of having to repay long-term debts before the related assets have matured; and

- be able to manage working capital (short–term assets less liabilities) from day to day through the overdraft.

A major dread of any finance director is having to borrow time and again in the 'short-term' to pay off instalments and interest on long-term loans.

Cash flow forecasting and sample worksheets   A9.8

Cash forecast should be kept as simple as possible. Not only does it make the forecast generally more readily understood by users, but as so often in life, the simple cash forecast is most likely to be the most accurate. Cash forecasts should be seen as a discipline, on the one hand, and a motivation on the other, by all the functions involved in their preparation and use. Functional heads benefit from focussing their experience on the assumptions and data needed for their input and may even subtly amend the way they do things for the better.

In managing the daily working capital, which is based on the different costs of sales and the sales revenue itself, a company has ready access to data on debtors and creditors. It is relatively simple to forecast cash needs over a very short period of a few weeks, and worth risking a small error rate in forecasting further ahead. The cash forecast can be used to check that the overdraft is adequate and to oversee actions to make sure that the forecast is achieved. A great ally is a reliably performing cash collection structure – one which brings in the cash at a given rate to sales volumes. This means that the cash needed to pay suppliers is reliably available, helped by a policy of negotiating the best possible credit terms from suppliers, *and honouring them.* This avoids the chaos of losing discounts, having supplies stopped, incurring penalty interest charges and having court orders published for all to see.

It is a good company discipline to create a cash flow forecast form for a rolling twelve month period. Trying to build up in an accounting year means that meaningful data is only available in the second half of the accounting year. The rolling twelve months means reliable data from day one. All the relevant departments should be responsible for their inputs and be expected to act on any subsequent variances. In this way, future forecasts become far more finely tuned and therefore more reliable. Actual month-end figures should be published alongside a comparison to the original forecast and any significant variances should be subject to immediate action to put things right. Significant variances may cause difficulties with the existing arrangements in respect of bank borrowings, hence the urgent need to identify and react.

The items shown on a summary cash forecast for a rolling twelve months are as follows.

- Opening bank overdraft:
  - plus collections from customers,
  - plus other receipts,
  - minus payments to suppliers,
  - minus payroll,
  - minus VAT,
  - minus other taxes paid, and
  - minus other payments.
- Closing bank overdraft.

Figure 1.00 shows an example of a cash management forecast.

Figure 1.00 – Example of a cash management forecast

Cash Management Forecast								
Item	Jan	Feb	Mar	Apr	May	Jun	Jul	Aug
Opening overdraft	4785	6023	6319	6924	6293	6517	5094	5206
Receipts								
Cash collected	1203	1200	1445	1308	1197	1645	1498	1344
Other receipts	599	978	978	1819	888	965	1543	596
Sub-total receipts	1802	2178	2429	3127	2085	2610	3041	1940
Payments								
Creditors	2442	1689	1640	1682	1261	503	2052	1239
Payroll	529	685	1311	735	961	601	1019	750
VAT	25	30	21	26	32	20	13	15
Other payments	44	70	62	53	55	63	69	46
Sub-total payments	3040	2474	3034	2496	2309	1187	3153	2050
Net receipts (payments)	(1238)	(296)	(605)	631	(224)	1423	(112)	(110)
Closing overdraft	6023	6319	6924	6293	6517	5094	5206	5316

Cash intake from customers should be forecast by collection staff. They know the 'behaviour' of their own accounts, and should be encouraged to make 'bottom-up' forecasts of expected cash. The credit manager should simultaneously make a 'top-down' calculation of the cash needed in the month to achieve the intended DSO (days sales outstanding) result. Any discrepancy between the total cash needed and the collectors' forecasts can be ironed out so that the cash inflow figure becomes locked into the total cash forecast. In this way, collection staff feel better recognised in terms of their important contribution to the whole process and therefore are much more likely to be committed to their task.

Equally, payables staff should estimate amounts needing to be paid in the period, with the total compared to an overall ratio of creditors to sales, or to cost of sales.

Other expected receipts, such as grants, subsidies, parent company transfers etc, as well as any special outgoings, should be known to the finance director. The net VAT sum payable should be available from accounts records and payroll totals should be readily available.

Measuring debtors as a basis for planning better cash flow   A9.9

It is important that every business granting credit to its customers should have a simple way of measuring debtors. Regardless of the size of the business, it should be a matter of policy to be able to see at any given point in time, not just how much is owed, but what that debt represents in terms of a proportion of sales. By seeing on a regular and constant basis how debtors are performing, and therefore how the cash is flowing, it will be possible to take immediate corrective action in the event of any cash flow problems.

There are two very useful measurements, namely:

● the DSO, or collection period, to show the speed of cash inflow; and

● the aged debt analysis, to show the collectability of debts.

Days sales outstanding ratio (DSO) – the way to faster cash   A9.10

The ratio between sales and debtors, also called the collection period, is decided by credit terms and collection performance which combine to give the time it takes for sales to turn into cash, and this can be expressed in days, weeks or months.

That DSO is the prime tool to measure efficiency in managing debtors. The existing ratio, applied to the sales budget, can produce a reasonably accurate debtors budget, as well as interim forecasts.

Count-back method   A9.11

The DSO is usually calculated at each month-end using a method called 'count-back' (or 'add-back'). This method takes the *total* debtors (not yet due, current, overdue and disputed, awaiting credit, etc.), and deducting *total* monthly sales going back in time until the debtors figure is used up. See Figure 2.00 for the method.

In Figure 2.00, August debtors equalled all the sales for the last 65 days which equals 65 DSO. This means that sales take an average of 65 days to be paid. The DSO is not affected by sales volume in so far as more sales produce more debtors and less sales produce less debtors. It is certainly affected, however, by the credit period allowed to customers and by the efficiency in collecting cash.

The benefit of the count-back method, over other methods, is that it uses the latest sales figures, since debtors relate mostly to the latest sales. This method of calculating DSO is the one most commonly in use in the UK and the USA.

Figure 2.00 – Calculation of DSO by count-back method

31 August	– total debtors	£1,200,000		
	August Sales	(£650,000)	=	31 days
		£550,000		
	July Sales	(£490,000)	=	31 days
		£60,000		
	June Sales (total £600,000)	£60,000	=	3 days
				65 days

Quarterly averaging method   A9.12

Another method is 'quarterly averaging', which can be useful if monthly sales totals are not available, or are not accurate. For example:

$$\frac{Debtor}{Sales\ last\ 3\ months} \quad x\ 92 = 68.0\ DSO$$

This averages the sales per day and is less accurate than the count-back process because it levels out peaks and troughs in sales.

Annual averaging method   A9.13

There is an alternative averaging method known as 'annual averaging'. This can be used when only year-end figures are known. For example:

$$\frac{Year\ End\ Debtors}{Annual\ Sales} \quad x\ 365 = 71.0\ DSO$$

This averaging method compounds the weakness of averaging, because the only data available is the total for the year, evenly calculated, thus levelling out even more generally.

Aged debt DSO   A9.14

The 'aged debt DSO' is a method preferred by a number of credit managers, combining as it does the total credit taken with the ages of debts. The total debtors is made up of the unpaid sales of each month in which the sales were made. For example:

£000	August	July	June	May	April	March	Total
Total Sales	650	430	600	550	510	620	
Sales p/day	21	14	20	18	17	20	
Unpaid	630	310	120	85	30	25	1200
Debt Days	30.0	22.1	6.0	4.7	1.7	1.3	65.8

In this example, August total debtors equals £1,200,000, which is 65.8 DSO.

Summary   A9.15

The four methods described in **A9.11–A9.14** above show the same total debtors collection periods of 65, 68, 71 and 65.8 days respectively. It can be seen that the methods using averaging are in excess of the others.

DSO and cash targets   A9.16

The DSO makes it easy to set cash targets to improve the speed of cash flow. Taking the earlier described 'count-back' method and example (see **A9.11** above), if the actual DSO for August was 65 days, and the requirement is to reduce it to 64 days by the end of the next month, the calculation is as follows.

August DSO	65 days	
Add September Sales	30 days	
Total	95 days	
Deduct September DSO target	64 days	
Cash required in September	31 days	sales value

The 31 days equivalent sales value to be collected by the end of September will be 3/30 of June sales plus 28/31 of July sales, i.e. £60,000 plus £442,580 respectively, a total cash requirement of £502,580. If that sum is collected by the end of September, a DSO of 64 is guaranteed.

Setting a cash target is simple arithmetic, but achieving it needs specific approaches to encourage larger customers to pay a little earlier. Success with two or three large accounts has a far more dramatic effect on cash flow than getting several smaller ones to pay sooner.

DSO and reducing borrowings   A9.17

Using cash targeting based upon DSO calculations in order to achieve a reduction in borrowings significantly increases profitability. For example, a UK company has:

- sales of £22 million;

- the national average profit margin of 4%; and

- unpaid sales at an average of 72 DSO.

If the company collected its cash just 10% faster, at 65 DSO, or achieved 38 DSO (the one time average rate in Germany, and the target for many businesses in Europe), its net profit and balance sheet borrowings would improve in the manner illustrated below:

£000	At 72 DSO	At 65 DSO	At 38 DSO
Sales	22,150	22,150	22,150
Debtors (= borrowings)	4,370	3,945	2,306
Profit before interest (7%)	1,542	1,542	1,542
Interest expense (at 10% pa)	437	395	231
Net profit before tax	1,105	1,147	1,311
NPBT as % of sales	5.0%	5.2%	5.9%
Increase in profit	–	42	206
Reduction of borrowings	–	425	2064

It is relatively easy to collect cash 10% faster, given top-level support, and the right processes and procedures. Much greater than 10% needs targeted improvements as well as fundamental changes in procedures and resources.

DSO and industry averages   A9.18

There are clearly variances in DSO between industries, with accepted and acceptable levels for one sector being higher (or lower) than another sector. For example, foodstuffs (perishable goods, with a short shelf life), would be low, whereas construction and civil engineering would be much higher. Every company, however, should aim to have its own DSO as better than the average for its industry. This entails finding out what the industry is, and then making plans to exceed it. There are numerous publications, Government statistics and European statistics which can provide the information – D&B publishes *Key Business* ratios, there are frequently published surveys from Experian, and accountants such as KPMG or PWC, as well as the output from the Credit Management Research Centre at Leeds University Business School and the Better Payment Practice Group. (See also **A3 GAINING INFORMA-TION TO SUPPORT CREDIT DECISIONS**.)

Using the DSO for a competitive advantage   A9.19

Improving its DSO also gives a company a head start in competing with rivals. For example, Company X sells £14.6 million a year, which is an average of £40k per day. The company has debts of £2.4 million, at 60 DSO. Its main competitor has similar sales but debtors of 70 DSO. Company X has therefore £400,000 more cash to use (i.e. 10 days at £40,000 per day). To compete for profit, its competitor must borrow an extra £400,000 at, say, 10% per annum, costing £40,000 off its net profits.

Aged debt analysis   A9.20

The only point in producing aged debt lists is to act on them, so they should be designed for easy visibility of priority accounts. Although usually produced monthly, they should be available on demand, and be segregated by types of customer, e.g. Government, home and export, with foreign debts grouped by country and home accounts divided between major customers (those accounting for 80% of sales and cash) and ordinary customers. It should also be possible to print, or have visually displayed, the listing in value order, with the largest debts first.

Analysis of overdues ageing within total values   A9.21

This shows the totals of all debts overdue in monthly groups, e.g. 1–30 days, 31–60 days, and 61–90 days etc, all expressed as a percentage of total overdue debtors. See Figure 3.00 below.

Ideally, any overdues should be *only just* overdue, i.e. 100% 1–30 days overdue. The real world is, of course, different, so collection activity should aim to increase the left hand columns percentages at the expense of the right hand columns percentages. Some credit managers budget certain percentages for each category.

The golden rule is that the overdue percentages should reduce with age. In Figure 3.00, too much money has eluded collection after four months.

Figure 3.00 – Ageing analysis of total overdues

Total O/due	Overdue Ageing (days)				
	1–30	31–60	61–90	91–120	121+
£120,000	83,000	21,000	12,000	1,000	3,000
100%	69.2%	17.5%	10.0%	0.8%	2.5% *(cont'd)*

Budgets, reports and control of cash flow   A9.22

Most financial planning begins with a budget for sales, usually for 12 months ahead. By using the sales budget and the DSO, it is possible to budget a debtors total. From this, it is relatively simple to plan cash inflow and how much borrowing is needed.

Where good budgets exist, reports on actual results should include explanations of variances from budget, where applicable. Reports for action purposes should highlight only those items needing attention, known in some companies as 'red flag' or 'action' items. It is good management practice to issue action assignments to individuals, making them responsible for correcting adverse trends by stated deadlines.

Reporting upwards should show selected items of interest and/or concern to top management. Such reports should include:

- minimal key data which is not obscured by masses of detail;

- highlighted variances from budget and previous periods; and

- brief reasons for any variations from the budget etc.

It makes sense to add a few lines of actions under way, to show firm control of the asset and especially to mention any major customers giving severe payment problems or credit risk worries, so that the board:

- is forewarned of possible shocks; and

- may contribute useful advice or even 'hands-on' assistance.

A monthly debtors report should compare the main debtor items with the budget and previous periods. Variances may be due to sales variances or collection performance, but usually represents a combination of the two.

Measurement of debtors and creditors   A9.23

The total debtors figure on the balance sheet is a snapshot on one day of the year. It gives no idea of the age or collectablity of individual debts, although the DSO ratio will indicate the speed of cash intake. The creditors figure alone gives no idea of the imminence of liabilities, although showing the ratio of creditors to cost of sales will indicate the speed of settlements generally.

Some of the more experienced in the analysis of collectability of debts apply percentage probabilities to the age of debts. For example:

Age	Worth
Current, i.e. within terms	100%
60 days overdue	80%
180 days overdue	50%
12 months overdue	10%

It is worth analysing the percentage of debts paid at the different stages of overdue, to add more precision to cash inflow forecasting.

Control of cash flow   A9.24

In most companies, it is fair to say that debtors provide 99% of cash. It is therefore vitally important that the size and quality of debts are regularly reviewed. This can be done by:

- daily control by the credit manager;

- an overview, as needed, by the finance director; and

- a regular report to the main Board, for action as needed.

A cash forecast sheet, showing total amounts of cash expected, split by type of account, divided into daily or weekly totals for the month ahead, is useful to flag up unexpected shortfalls and also show the DSO which would result from the forecast being achieved.

The 'law of ten to one'   A9.25

When customers fail, the temperature in many finance and sales offices can rise, especially if it is perceived by those 'upstairs' as unexpected. Enormous amounts of noise and steam are generated – profit is written off and sales outlets lost. Writing off bad debts visibly reduces the profit and loss account, but the interest cost of payment delays from customers still trading is often unnoticed as a cost effect as it is rarely measured. However, if companies *actually measured* the cost effect of delayed payment, they would be surprised, more often than not, to find that the cost of waiting for overdue payments can be many times the bad debts written off.

Burt Edwards, the well respected expert in credit management, now retired, and author of many related publications, including the highly successful '*Credit Management Handbook*' has in the past undertaken much research in this area, and quotes two prime examples of the cost of delayed payment as compared to the cost of bad debts written off.

- An engineering firm in Hampshire was proud of its loyal customer base with sales of £14 million and bad debts of only £15,800, i.e. 0.1% of sales. On the face of it, this would appear to be an excellent situation, and no doubt many a finance director or accountant would consider the position more than satisfactory. However, the company's debtors were £3.2 million, which equated to a DSO of 83. On 30 days terms, debtors should only have been £1.2 million. With borrowing at 8% p.a., the excess debtors cost £160,000 – more than ten times the company's level of bad debts.

- The finance director of a well known public company manufacturing DIY products was under the impression that he had no need to employ a credit manager. This was on the basis that only £30,000 had been written off in bad debts in the year under review. When asked the cost of late payments, he realised that he did not actually know, because this was a measurement that had never been undertaken. On investigation, it was learned that past due accounts averaged £3.5 million, and, borrowing at an average of 9% p.a., and the finance director realised that slow payments were hitting his profit and loss account to the tune of some £310,000 per year.

In his research, Edwards found that the ratio of interest expense being ten times bad debt losses was far from unusual – indeed, normal was nearer the mark. Those companies with fast DSOs and exceptional controls on risky accounts proved the case by not experiencing the same cost relationship.

Figure 4.00 – Effect of bad debts on sales

Bad Debt	Pre-tax Profit Percentage			
£	5%	8%	10%	12%
50	1,000	625	500	417
500	10,000	6,250	5,000	4,170
5,000	100,000	62,500	50,000	41,700
10,000	200,000	125,000	100,000	83,400
50,000	1,000,000	625,000	500,000	417,000

Value of previous sales on which profit has been lost, or extra sales needed to recoup the bad debt total.

Figure 5.00 – Effect of overdues on profits

Cost of Borrowings	Net Profit on Sales				
	10%	8%	6%	4%	2%
5%	24.0	19.2	14.4	9.6	4.8
6%	20.0	16.0	12.0	8.0	4.0
8%	15.0	12.0	9.0	6.0	3.0

Cost of Borrow-ings	Net Profit on Sales				
	10%	8%	6%	4%	2%
10%	12.0	9.6	7.2	4.8	2.4
12%	10.0	8.0	6.0	4.0	2.0
15%	8.0	6.4	4.8	3.2	1.6
	Months overdue after which profit is absorbed by interest				

Buying and paying   A9.26

What follows is a checklist for buying and paying.

- Are there clear, written instructions to accounts and purchasing staff on agreeing terms with suppliers and then paying them?

- Is the head of payables primed to ensure that there are no embarrassing arrears which may cause a stop on supplies or worse?

- Is there a clear responsibility for resolving disputes quickly and are technical and customer service staff properly monitored for this?

- Is the payment policy monitored to ensure that it works and is properly funded?

A good payables system is proved by the smooth flow of purchases and the scarcity of suppliers chasing for payment. It has been shown many times that the interest cost saved by playing delaying games with suppliers' money is outweighed by the costs of staff, paper-chasing, supply interruptions, lost discounts and delivery priorities, and in some cases, penalty interest for paying later than agreed terms. This latter possibility could become more prevalent according to the take up of the late payment legislation now in force (see **A5.9** above and **A13.57** below).

The credit period needed should be seriously negotiated and then honoured. If a company does not bother to negotiate the seller's terms when ordering, it should not then just pay as late as it suits them.

A good cash flow policy includes tight negotiation of credit terms with suppliers, then proper funding to meet the liabilities.

The real costs of cash discounts for faster cash   A9.27

It is a very common misconception that cash discounts are inexpensive to the supplier, and do not affect profits in any appreciable way. Apart from all the arguments of debtors taking discount to which they are not entitled due to late payment, cash discounts *are* expensive. To offer cash discounts as an incentive to prompt payment is of dubious value, and cannot be afforded for the most part, *unless they have already been costed into the price of the goods.* Experience has shown that this is extremely rare. Just as a customer would be foolish not to take an offered discount, so a supplier would in fact be unwise to offer one in the first place. The rate must be high enough to be attractive to the buyer, say 2%, but may still be abused by being deducted by late payers, to whom it is in effect seen as a price reduction.

The annualised cost of a cash discount is always much higher than the seller's cost of money. It would be cheaper to suffer a 90 day overdue account than to give away 2% for payment in 30 days. It is far better to establish firm net terms with customers and follow them up efficiently. Discounts for paying earlier than the net terms have a cost to the seller best seen as an annualised rate of interest, as per the following formula.

$$\frac{\text{Rate of discount x 360}}{\text{Credit period less the discount period}}$$

By way of illustration, terms of '2% 10 days, net 30 days' would be:

$$\frac{2 \times 360}{30 - 10} \qquad = \quad 36\% \text{ p.a.}$$

Staff incentives for faster cash A9.28

In the same way that sales operations can be targeted and incentivised, so too can the same motivational principle be applied to staff converting those sales into cash. Total cash targets, based perhaps on DSO improvements, should ideally be decided by the actual collector using personal knowledge of individual account behaviour. The credit manager should verify that the target is adequate (and realistically achievable), but once accepted, it becomes the month's commitment for the collector – a considerable motivation to deliver.

Many companies incentivise collectors by means of cash, products or high profile recognition. Faster collections bring in thousands of pounds of extra profit for the company whereas staff need only a fraction of that as a reward for exceptional endeavour. It is both inefficient and unreasonable to incentivise sales staff to bring in extra orders, regardless of risk, and then expect an underpaid, unrewarded credit clerk to collect the sales revenue from often over-sold and illiquid customers.

Credit manager's report A9.29

Every credit manager should convert their knowledge and information about the vital debtors asset into a regular, brief report. Even if the boss is not interested, the report serves as an excellent self-management tool. In due course, ways will be found to distribute the report, and there are almost inevitably going to members of top management who will take an increasing interest as the performance of the profitability of the company varies. The report should show selected items of interest to top management, but also be used every month for a working discussion with collection staff on upcoming priorities. Always on a single sheet, the report should show the speed of turning sales into cash, the quality of unpaid sales in terms of age, and any major problems. Comparisons should be made with the budget, if any, and with relevant previous periods. Apart from demonstrating the credit manager's control of the asset, the data is extremely useful in adding reality to the cash flow forecast.

Summary A9.30

Planning and managing cash flow is the opposite of depending on the bank overdraft to cope with the ups and downs of business. That is a lazy, expensive and dangerous approach. Apart from the interest cost, bank borrowings can be cancelled or reduced at very short notice, leaving the borrower unable to continue. Growing a business into the future means adjusting the levels of assets to produce good performance ratios. Adequate cash is essential to cope with the topical need of suppliers and customers. If cash flow is sensibly planned, targets can be set for maximum short-term borrowings. This then forces the right decisions onto asset management.

A10

Consumer Credit Operations

Consumer and trade credit A10.1

Trade credit is the act of a supplier allowing time for a trader to sell goods. The time given reflects the likely period between delivery of the goods to the trader, and the trader effecting a sale to a consumer. For fast-moving cash-generative goods, such as cigarettes or confectionery, trade credit may be given for relatively short periods of up to a month. Supplies of goods that move more slowly, such as white goods or clothes, may receive the benefit of longer trade credit, typically for up to three months. In most cases the supplier will include a clause in the contract retaining ownership of the goods until the sale proceeds are received. This is known as 'reservation of title' and gives the supplier an element of security (see **A14.48** below).

Some suppliers also provide trade loans to customers. These can be linked with agreements to purchase minimum amounts of product at an agreed price over the term of the loan. Breweries offer trade loans to the free trade on an interest free basis (usually up to £20,000 on an unsecured basis and up to £250,000 on a secured basis) and petroleum suppliers operate similarly. Ice cream suppliers may offer loans to purchase freezer display cabinets.

The underlying motive of the supplier extending trade credit or trade loans is always to sell more goods.

Consumer credit, on the other hand, is provided to individuals by credit grantors with a view to making profit. Profit is determined as the margin between the interest charged and the costs of funds, less the cost of administering the transaction and after making adequate provision for bad debts. Consumers tend to use credit as a method of making a purchase earlier than would otherwise be possible by saving to accumulate sufficient cash from earnings.

Trade and consumer credit have many similarities. In both cases, an assessment is required of the borrower in terms of creditworthiness and ability to repay. Both are subject to the risk of fraudulent applications, and to the risk of bad debt. When the risk appears high, additional security may be called for. Both trade and consumer credit grantors may seek guarantees or charges over assets as security.

The differences are less obvious. Trade credit grantors may deal with companies, which publish annual accounts in a format prescribed by the *Companies Acts*. These help trade credit grantors to assess creditworthiness and the ability to repay. Unlike individuals, companies may give mortgage debentures offering fixed and floating charges over all assets. Changes of controlling directors of companies may mean that the risk may change during the term of trade credit.

Trade credit is usually provided interest-free, whereas consumer credit is routinely provided at a rate of interest linked loosely to prevailing money market rates. Consumers are also provided with extensive protection from abuse by lenders across a wide spectrum of risks under the *Consumer Credit Act 1974* (*CCA 1974*), whereas trade credit takers are protected only from extortionate credit bargains under the Act.

Consumer Credit Act 1974 A10.2

The *CCA 1974* covers all aspects of consumer credit, from advertising and canvassing to default and termination, and is examined in depth in **A13 COLLECTING OUTSTANDING ACCOUNTS**, together with the supplementary regulations concerning advertising, rebates on early settlement and guarantees. In this chapter the operational requirements of the Act are summarised.

Licensing A10.3

Prior to trading in consumer credit or hire, a credit grantor must be licensed under *CCA 1974*. To obtain a consumer credit licence, a prospective credit grantor must submit a completed application form to the Consumer Credit Licensing Bureau at the Office of Fair Trading, Craven House, 40 Uxbridge Road, London, W5 2BS. Tel: 020 7211 8608. It is not possible to apply online.

If the applicant is considered fit to hold one, and subject to the trading names being deemed as not misleading or undesirable, the credit grantor is granted a standard licence by the Director General of Fair Trading, which is valid for five years. The licence recites the name of the credit grantor, the principal place of business, together with its registered office if a company, and lists all of the trading names used. The licence is not assignable nor transmissible to another legal entity, such as if a partnership decides to incorporate, when a new licence is required. Approximately five million standard licences have been issued under the Act to date.

Licences may be obtained for the separate activities or any combination of consumer credit, consumer hire, credit brokerage, debt adjusting and counselling, debt collecting, or operating a credit reference agency. In each case, this may or may not include the right to canvass third party financed deals, known under *CCA 1974* as debtor-creditor-supplier (DCS) agreements, and regulated consumer hire agreements 'off trade premises'. As the fee for registration is the same, irrespective of the number of activities registered, the Office of Fair Trading encourages applicants to apply to be registered for all activities.

The current fee for a five year licence, whether for a new application or for renewal, is £110 for a sole trader, and £275 for most others. Debt counsellors and debt adjusters who do not charge for their services together with registered loan societies and credit unions do not have to pay any fees.

Once issued, the licence holder is under a duty to notify the Office of Fair Trading of any changes, such as changes in main business addresses, changes to partners or company officers and changes to controllers. Licences are not amended to reflect such notifications.

In contrast, amended licences are issued upon other notifiable events. These include a change in the name of the licence holder, the addition of new trading names or deletion of old ones, the addition or deletion of a category of business activity or the addition or deletion of authorisation to canvass off trade premises.

Licences are terminated upon death or bankruptcy of an individual licence holder, or dissolution or striking off of a company.

Any regulated credit or hire agreements that are entered into by a credit grantor when not properly licensed may be unenforceable. The Director General of Fair Trading has the power to grant a validation order to permit such agreements to be treated as if they had been entered into under a valid licence.

Marketing of credit A10.4

Oral efforts by a credit grantor to encourage a prospective consumer to borrow or hire goods are called 'canvassing' and the *CCA 1974* forbids the canvassing of consumer credit 'off trade premises' without a prior invitation, which may be verbal or in writing. General discussion on financial matters is permitted in all places subject to the third party instigating the discussion and the credit grantor not visiting the prospective borrower with a view to canvassing credit.

When marketing credit, credit grantors must not approach minors. All marketing material must follow the principle of 'truth in lending' and must not mislead or misrepresent. The APR – Annualised Percentage Rate – must be quoted and given the same prominence as any other interest rate quoted in advertising and marketing material. If an introductory rate is offered, the long-term rate that applies after the expiry of the introductory period must be given the greater prominence. The total cost of credit is also required to be shown, to include all costs which surround the availability of credit, such as arrangement fees and security charges, but not those which would have also been payable by a cash purchaser, such as delivery charges.

The advertising and marketing requirements extend to all deals caught by the *CCA 1974*, known as 'regulated credit' and also to any credit to individual consumers secured by a charge over land, irrespective of the size of the borrowing.

Quotations and agreements   A10.5

Once attracted by marketing efforts, a consumer is entitled to seek a written quotation that must again follow the above principle of 'truth in lending'. All aspects, terms and conditions of the proposed borrowing must be clearly laid out.

If taken up, a regulated agreement is required to be supplied in a form and content defined by the *CCA 1974* and containing compulsory detail – 'prescribed terms'. To be effective it must be signed by the credit grantor and by the borrower, and copies given to every person who may be liable under the agreement whether as main borrower or as a guarantor or as a third party provider of security. Copies of any related documentation, such as security forms, must also be provided at this stage.

Some types of regulated agreement are non-cancellable, such as borrowing secured on land, but most forms of revolving consumer credit are defined as cancellable agreements that allow a cooling off period of five days for the borrower to back out of the deal. The right to cancel must be communicated to the borrower within seven days of the agreement being signed. If the right to cancel is taken up, the borrower must advise the credit grantor in writing within five days, which starts with the day of receipt of the notice of the right to cancel.

Administration of the credit facility   A10.6

Any modifications to the terms of the deal must be recorded by way of a modifying agreement. Typically, modifications are any new or release of security, any change in the term, or upon default and agreement of new repayment proposals. The procedures required under the *CCA 1974* are cumbersome and most credit grantors issue an entirely fresh regulated agreement.

During the term of the regulated agreement the borrower is entitled to ask for a statement of account. For revolving credit, statements must be supplied regularly to each borrower, although a borrower may elect to receive only one statement for each account. For a fee, a borrower may also ask for further copies of the underlying regulated agreement or of any connected security documentation, which must be supplied within twelve working days.

Guarantors and third party givers of security are entitled also to ask for copies of documentation and a statement of the state of the regulated borrowing, the amount remaining payable under the agreement by the principal debtor, and the amounts and due dates of any future payments required to be made.

Termination of a regulated agreement   A10.7

Borrowers who wish to repay a regulated agreement early must be advised of the amount required and also how the sum has been calculated, to include any rebate for early settlement.

Credit grantors who wish to terminate a regulated agreement usually do so upon default of the repayment programme or upon bankruptcy of the consumer. A warning notice is required to be served in such circumstances, setting out the consequences of failing to put right the default, and advising that the full amount outstanding will become due after a specific period has elapsed, which must be not less than seven days. The warning must state the specific date and the full amount that will be quoted in the formal default notice.

Great care is required in the drafting of the warning notice and of the default notice to ensure that the requirements of the *CCA 1974* are fully met before any further action is taken to recover debt or realise security. This is a fertile area for dispute and challenge by solicitors, money advisors and debt adjusters.

Making quick and accurate decisions using online systems   A10.8

Technology is now an important aspect of granting credit. Tasks which are substantially aided by technology include marketing, the capturing of application data, the supply of credit reference information, the assessment of credit and fraud risk, the selection of appropriate pricing, terms and conditions, and the issue of regulated or non-regulated agreements. Once a borrowing is in place, further systems may be employed to account for transactions, apply interest, seek direct debit repayments, prompt collection actions, issue statements and deal with requests for early repayment.

As credit grantors have different views on which aspects are undertaken in-house, and which are outsourced, it is rare to find all processes integrated into one technological solution. Also, the components of account processing may have been purchased from different suppliers and at different times, or have been developed in-house. For example, the relatively recent innovation of fraud prevention systems will need to be interfaced with existing new business systems.

Further, the basic platforms of proprietary system or software components may be different. Some may be delivered only to mainframes, some to PC-based technology, and others may be delivered over the internet. The size of the credit grantor's new business and the nature of the underlying deal will influence the types of technology employed. A typical mortgage lender will deal in hundreds of applications each day and will have weeks to process the application pending release of money. In contrast, a retail store will deal with thousands of transactions each day, all of which will require a decision and release of funds at the point of sale.

This section examines the systems available in the four broad areas of marketing, application processing, account maintenance and collections.

Marketing   A10.9

The marketing of credit cards and personal loans is now heavily dependent on mailshots to potential clients, known as 'prospects'.

Mailing lists are purchased and screened against the Mailing Preference Service, where individuals may elect not to receive unsolicited mail, and against credit reference agency data to remove those that are likely to be unacceptable on the grounds of credit risk. Scoring techniques may also be employed to measure the probability of a prospect responding to an offer, known as 'response modelling', and the likelihood of a responder subsequently using a credit facility, known as 'propensity modelling'. Together, these 'pre-screening' practices reduce the cost of acquisition of accounts, minimise unwanted mail and identify creditworthy prospects who are most likely to respond to mailshots and subsequently use the credit facility on offer.

The Internet is also emerging as an important channel for attracting consumer credit applications. Sites such as www.moneysupermarket.com and www.give-mecredit.com, generate many thousands of applications for all types of credit. Credit companies may bid directly for search terms such as 'credit card' or 'mortgage' in search engines, to obtain a high listing, to increase the likelihood of being found by applicants, and pay in excess of £5.00 per click for top ranking. More frequently, applications are obtained from affiliate marketing schemes, which use 'banners' to attract internet surfers to apply online for credit. Typically a credit card company may have in excess of 10,000 affiliates, and the most successful affiliate site will forward in excess of 1,000 applications per month to the consumer credit grantor. Credit grantors will pay affiliates a fee ranging between a few pounds per application and up to £50 per activated card, or up to 8% of the loan amount for loans drawdown that are introduced to them through this medium.

Some affiliates use credit scoring to assess the creditworthiness of the applicant and match lenders to the credit score. Websites such as www.checkmyfile.com enable consumers to obtain a free credit score and offer three likely sources of credit, depending on the credit rating of the applicant.

Response rates will vary depending on the market and the extent of pre-screening undertaken, but typically will be in the region of 1 to 3% for direct mail, and up to 45% for internet-based introduction schemes.

Online systems are available for both small and large credit grantors. For small credit grantors these are PC-based systems that deliver credit reference agency data in accordance with the Rules of Reciprocity (see **A14 COMPANY AND CONSUMER LEGISLATION AND CODES OF PRACTICE**) together with a 'bureau score', which may either be generic, or tailored to a specific segment of the credit industry. Bureau scores are those derived from credit reference agency data and not from samples taken from a credit grantor's own portfolio, which therefore enables new entrants to the market to operate quickly.

By manual interrogation of the online system, the name and address of the prospect can be checked and any unacceptable risks, defined as those who fail to meet the bureau scorecard criteria, can be eliminated from any marketing effort. This system may also be applied to telemarketing operations and is used by the retail outlets of mobile telephone companies.

Large credit grantors will typically ask a credit reference agency to supply a list of prospects based upon target market criteria, using its own resources or by compiling from several lists purchased elsewhere. The agency will merge the lists, remove those who appear more than once, known as 'de-duplication', take out any known existing clients of the credit grantor, remove any Mailing Preference Service people, remove any persons known to have died, pre-screen the list for credit, response and propensity, and then finally check all addresses against the Royal Mail Postcode Address File for accuracy. It will then either undertake the mailing on behalf of the credit grantor, or hand back the list in electronic form, on disk or tape, to enable the credit grantor either to undertake its own mailshot or to pass it to a third party who will fulfil the mailing process.

Application processing   A10.10

This process commences on receipt of a telephoned or written application form and ends with the decision to grant or refuse credit.

Upon receipt, data is required to be captured to a database. For telephone applications this is a manual keying process, but for written applications manual keying may be supplemented or replaced by the automatic reading of application data. For typed or partially typed applications this is undertaken using optical character recognition (OCR) and, for hand-written applications, using intelligent character recognition (ICR). In both cases, a degree of manual intervention is required for characters that cannot be fully recognised by the software, and interfaces with other reference databases, such as the Royal Mail Postcode Address File, may also be used to validate the spelling of addresses and the correctness of postcodes. Pre-printed mailshots, which are returned, may also contain barcodes that will enable OCR to take application details from existing marketing databases to either supplement or validate applicant details.

The ICR and OCR process involves the scanning of the original document that can be inexpensively retained for future reference either alongside the paper-based document as a contingency or in lieu of it to save storage space. This can be useful if a signature comparison is required during the term of the borrowing. Disadvantages of scanning and character recognition processes include the inability to spot applications from 'Mickey Mouse' or other suspect data and the relatively high cost of investment in the underlying equipment. Advantages include speed, lower headcount requirement and less premises overhead.

Manual keying of application data can also be validated using similar reference databases and for logic, such as ensuring that applicants are over 18 and that the bank account numbers quoted are consistent with the bank sort code. Manual keying is sometimes undertaken twice, on a 'key and verify' basis, to reduce the incidence of errors. The disadvantages of manual keying are the practical difficulties of varying the size of the team to cope with fluctuating levels of response, the relatively high labour and overhead costs and the training lag. Advantages include flexibility in making small amendments to the process during mailing campaigns, lower capital cost and the human ability to spot and remember some types of fraudulent application that are difficult to automate.

For all manual data capture operations the content, size and layout of the application form are important considerations. Systems should capture information in the precise form and order given on the application form. The form should be big enough to be completed legibly and read easily. If more than one application form is in use, the system should have the flexibility to recognise the type of form used and to adjust the keying screen to follow its content and order.

Internet-based applications involve little or no manual intervention and a response is given direct to the applicant online.

Either during the data entry process or immediately afterwards a credit reference agency search is usually undertaken. To reduce search costs, some systems firstly apply credit scoring systems and rule-based selection processes to remove those applications which will never be acceptable whatever the outcome of the search, known as 'super declines'. Some applicants may also be deemed so creditworthy that the contribution from search data to a scorecard would not affect the decision to lend. These are known as 'super accepts'. The majority of applications are searched at a credit reference agency. The four principal reasons for using credit reference agency data in application processing are to:

- verify an applicant's identity;

- assess the credit risk;

- prevent losses from fraud; and

- leave a search footprint to inform others of impending credit usage.

There are over 300 million records on a credit reference agency's database, including 180 million account performance records supplied and shared by over 250 credit grantors from all sectors of the credit industry, (see **A14.38**) plus public domain information, such as the 44 million voters roll records and 9 million judgment records.

In order of size, the principal credit reference agency databases in the UK are as follows.

- Shared account performance information (CAIS (Credit Account Information Sharing) from Experian, Share from Callcredit, and Insight from Equifax) which are only available to subscribers of the schemes.

- Register of electors ('the voter's roll').

- Public information (bankruptcies and insolvencies).

- Companies House data.

- Geodemographic segmentation tools (marketing information given generally at postcode levels giving a snapshot of the type of area).

The following data is not currently available:

- car ownership;
- employment records;
- bank current account records (although some new banks and internet banks are now reporting accounts and there are plans to expand this to all banks); and
- medical records.

In addition, the credit reference agencies have access to data matching services that are designed to prevent fraud. These take several forms, but may check application data against all previous applications submitted to other lenders to highlight inconsistencies and irregularities, or may return warnings if a piece of data appears to have been used before in a suspect application. These are described at **A10.13** below.

Once application data has been loaded and verified against the credit reference agency data and fraud checks, it is passed through a system to assess credit risk, sometimes referred to as a 'decision engine'.

Decision engines may take several forms but are likely to contain:

- rule-based checks to ensure that the credit grantor's lending policy has not been breached;
- logic checks (such as checking that 'time at address' is less than age);
- options to search other credit reference agencies if data is sparse or suspect;
- credit-scoring tools to measure risk and propensity;
- limit-setting for revolving accounts, based on measured risk;
- the ability for manual intervention in the process, sometimes known as 'overrides'; and
- hand-off files to print agreements or decline letters.

There are many vendors of application processing systems. Some contain data capture capabilities, the decision engine and an accounting processing system. Most comprise only part of the process and require integration with in-house or other supplier systems. Some support online connections to the credit reference agencies.

With effect from the end of 2004, lenders are required to give applicants the option to be considered solely on their own merits, rather than on a 'household' basis. This is the principal outcome of a credit industry voluntary code, known as the Third Party Data Rules, which has been drawn up by lenders, in conjunction with the Information Commissioner, to address the historic practice of including within the credit assessment all people living in the same household with the same surname, or known to be financially associated with the principal applicant.

The use of 'third party data' – meaning data relating to other than the principal applicant – was permitted following a Data Protection Tribunal ruling in 1992 which was aimed at encouraging lenders to consider the financial position of all people living in the same household, to prevent families from becoming over-burdened with credit. The need for social responsibility in lending has now been somewhat displaced by the increasing need for the privacy of individual data. One of the consequences of allowing lenders to view the financial history of an entire household is that under *section 158* of the *CCA 1974* (and also under *section 7* of the *Data Protection Act 1998*) any person is able to seek from a credit reference agency a copy of all information used by a lender when assessing credit. This means that any person is therefore able to view the financial history of all persons in his or her household. This has been widely criticised as an invasion of personal privacy, yet ironically is the outcome of a Data Protection Tribunal ruling.

Once the option to be considered only on personal merits has been exercised, the credit file will contain only that individual's data.

To prevent fraud and to enable people with thin credit files to be more favourably dealt with, the Third Party Data Rules have retained the ability for lenders to continue to view the entire household credit file in certain, well-defined, exceptional circumstances.

The introduction of the Third Party Data Rules will necessitate major changes to both application systems and credit reference systems and will also require options to be added to application forms with suitable guidance for consumers. Consumers are unlikely to be able to make an informed decision as to whether opting to be considered on personal merits only is beneficial, although a comparison of personal and household credit ratings and scores can be obtained from websites such as www.checkmyfile.com.

Account maintenance A10.11

The accounting of credit, namely the calculation and application of interest due, the production of statements and the collection of repayments by direct debit or otherwise, have long been automated.

During the life of a credit facility, supplementary online systems can be useful to help manage risk and to identify cross-selling opportunities. Examples include:

● setting limits on revolving facilities, such as personal loans and credit cards;

● giving early warning of impending default or other difficulties; and

● predicting a requirement for additional borrowing facilities.

Risk is managed using behavioural scoring. This uses account behaviour and repayment history, together with credit reference agency information, to re-assess the overall risk on an existing account on a monthly basis.

Credit reference agency information requires to be adjusted to exclude the performance of a credit grantor's own account performance to ensure that an external picture of the account holder's financial fortunes is obtained.

The aggregate of a consumer's borrowings and available credit lines can also be mapped over time to see whether there is increasing or decreasing reliance on credit. This may identify the most likely time that an existing customer will be receptive to a marketing approach and may also help identify over-commitment.

When viewed against the background of default, this information may be used to accelerate or modify collections' activities.

Behavioural scoring using online systems in the UK is currently the preserve of the larger credit grantors although systems are available to suit any size or type of credit portfolio.

Collections   A10.12

Online credit reference agency data continues to be useful in the collections and recovery processes. It can help to trace the whereabouts of a gone-away and to assess the reasonableness and affordability of offers to repay arrears by instalments. During the litigation process, the data can also be used to help select the most suitable and cost effective post-judgment remedy. For historic unrecovered bad debt, it can also help to determine the correct timing of an approach to salvage previous written-offs.

Using either internet access, or through a Windows-based package available from the credit reference agencies on a dial-up basis, collectors within both small and large credit grantors may interrogate the raw data contained on the significant databases held. This may be networked with existing systems or held on a stand-alone basis by installing the software on desktop PCs or individual laptops.

Some credit reference agencies offer an online tracing service. The name and last known address of a gone-away is keyed in to the system, which then checks various sources including whether any other credit grantor has had notice of a new address, or whether any recent application for credit has been made which quotes a new address. If so, this is reported immediately online. If not, the system continues to search for the gone-away each week for two years and will report a new address, again online, when found. Charges are only applied if a successful trace is obtained. Compared to the process of using external debt collectors, online tracing is cheaper and faster.

In the assessment of offers by debtors to repay arrears by instalments, a collector is able to examine each account entry on a credit file to see how their financial affairs are being conducted. It may be possible to see an existing HP or loan commitment coming to an end, which may indicate that disposable income will increase that may then be used to help repay the credit grantor's own debt.

Recent or increased levels of search activity can indicate the availability of further disposable income, assuming that the borrower applies for credit with intent to repay.

Bank statements or income and expenditure statements are usually the first choice for interrogating the financial position of a defaulting borrower, but if supply is refused by the borrower, account performance databases and search data provide a unique insight and are relatively irrefutable. Account performance data provides the current balance and detailed account performance over periods of up to four years, depending on the credit reference agency used.

Careful examination of raw credit file data can help to select the most appropriate post-judgment remedy in the recovery process. Search activity can often be interpreted to identify the recent purchase of a motor vehicle that may then become the subject of a levy of execution. A mortgage account will point towards the possibility of a charging order. The sudden re-start of searches may indicate new employment and the possibility of an attachment of earnings order. In each case further investigation is necessary, but data can help to focus upon the most cost-efficient remedy.

Using Internet searches through sites such as www.hpi.com, or www.carwatch-uk.co.uk or using the same Windows-based package, it is possible to search for vehicle details if a registration number is known. This can identify the existence of any HP on a vehicle before levying execution and confirm its colour and type to help bailiffs.

Written-off debt can be partially recovered in an economic way if the timing of the approach is made carefully and providing the debt is not statute-barred. Using the bureau scores mentioned previously, these are a useful surrogate measure of the debtor's financial health. A 'cut off score' needs to be established, and when a debtor's bureau score exceeds this it is an indication that the financial circumstances are sufficiently recovered to enable collection action to be recommended with a reasonable prospect of success.

Screening for fraudulent applications   A10.13

All credit grantors are potential targets for fraudsters. As redress and recovery of fraud losses is highly unlikely, prevention is a better option. There is a credit industry specific fraud prevention screening scheme – CIFAS (see **A10.14** below) – and several commercially available online fraud filters. These are all delivered via the credit reference agencies.

Hallmarks of fraudulent consumer credit applications include heavy pressure to grant a credit facility, unexpected complaints or praise, undue urgency, unexplained absences from the UK, inability to find an applicant on the electoral register, an application for the maximum amount permissible and declaring a round sum salary. As it is now possible to purchase payslips and P60s through magazines such as *Exchange & Mart*, or even reproduce these using inexpensive payroll software, such as *Sage Instant Payroll*, *Quickbooks*, and as many documents such as driving licences and even passports can be easily obtained by a professional fraudster, verification of application details through secure databases has become common underwriting practice.

Credit grantors should also remain conscious of the high and rapidly increasing incidence of impersonation fraud, whereby an innocent victim's identity is stolen and used to obtain credit. In 2003 over 101,000 cases of identity theft were reported and impersonation fraud is widely reported as the fastest growing crime in the UK. Traditionally, a recent change in the applicant's address together with a change in banking details would highlight an increased risk of identity theft, but increasing sophistication by fraudsters requires a significantly more vigilant approach by credit grantors. Identity thieves now tend to hijack the identities of recently deceased or temporarily absent creditworthy persons, using mail and telephone redirection services, untraceable IP address email accounts (such as hotmail or yahoo) and pre-paid mobile phone accounts. If called upon to authenticate themselves, the fraudsters will have access to a passport, birth certificate and driving licence, each of which has been obtained fraudulently from the correct sources.

CIFAS   A10.14

CIFAS (formerly the Credit Industry Fraud Avoidance System) was incorporated in 1991 following initiatives put in place by the Consumer Credit Trade Association to encourage credit grantors to exchange information regarding attempted fraud.

Membership is open to credit grantors, leasing and hire companies, mortgage providers and 'others who share the same concerns regarding the prevention and containment of fraud'. Its offices are at 4th Floor, Central House, 14 Upper Woburn Place, London WC1H 0NN. It also operates a useful website at www.cifas.org.uk. Its telephone number is ex-directory.

Members are bound by a regulatory framework, *The Rules of CIFAS*, which seek that information is lodged to a database, managed by the credit reference agencies, recorded in a coded manner and classified under strictly defined categories. Access to the CIFAS database is open only to CIFAS members who contribute such information. There were more than 240 members as at March 2004.

A Board of Directors oversees CIFAS, comprising an executive director employed by CIFAS, directors from specific market sectors, and co-opted directors from the participating credit reference agencies, which at the time of writing were Callcredit, Equifax, Experian and MCL Software. A police observer and a representative from the National Consumer Council also attend Board meetings. A number of management committees handle operational issues relating to specialist issues such as the Organised Fraud and Intelligence Group (OFIG) and the Ports Anti-Theft System (PATSY), which helps detect stolen cars that are subject to finance.

Several security alerts are issued each year, and a regular quarterly Fraud Discussion Forum attracts around 200 delegates, including several observers or prospective members. Training seminars are also held around the country.

The database itself is address-based, and any suspected data match requires telephone contact between members' designated senior staff, who number 2,300 in total. Automatic declining of applications using CIFAS data is not permitted. In the year ended December 2003, CIFAS identified 310,056 frauds, issued 4.5 million security warnings and claims to have prevented £487m of fraud losses for its members in that year.

CIFAS has the advantage of being inexpensive (it is a non-profit making company limited by guarantee) and available on a low technology basis. It currently has the greatest number of contributors of all available fraud prevention data sharing schemes and spans the entire credit market, which commercially available databases are striving to achieve.

Commercially available fraud prevention systems   A10.15

In contrast, the commercially available fraud prevention systems, such as *Hunter* from MCL Software, *Navigator* from Equifax and *Detect* from Experian, do not base themselves on a suspect address file. Instead, all application data is captured, pooled and matched, both against all previous application data in the pool and in some cases against all other databases held by the credit reference agencies.

Some of the systems also seek out suspect data, such as telephone numbers used in previous fraud attempts, apply logic checks, and use statistical techniques to measure the probability of fraud. It is not possible to automate the systems to decline applications without reference, as data protection requirements require manual intervention of any decline.

Because each of the systems work in different ways, some credit grantors purchase as many systems as their processing capacity will accommodate, as the savings obtained from any of the systems often justify the cost many times over.

Manual systems   A10.16

Manual screening of applications for fraud is a labour-intensive process but again the investment in the overhead is often very easily justified, even for large volume credit grantors. In-house teams can be focused on industry sector risks, can deal with fraud on an objective basis and can respond quickly if a large fraud ring is discovered. Investment in the in-house team should include:

- PC links to raw data from the credit reference agencies;

- CD-ROMs of business and personal telephone numbers, the electoral roll and other telephone directories; and

- access to newspaper search software.

Independent scorecards have been developed to help predict the incidence of fraud based on application data. These are not as powerful as credit scorecards but are useful supplements to help filter highly suspect applicants to an in-house investigation unit.

Internal security   A10.17

Credit grantors should also remain alert to the risk of internal fraud from employees, who should be carefully screened if employed in sensitive positions. The physical security of buildings, account records and computers is also of increasing importance as the incidence of application fraud becomes more comprehensively addressed by credit grantors and fraudsters move to other methods of obtaining credit by deception.

Credit scoring   A10.18

Compared to subjective lending, credit scoring is quicker, cheaper and more efficient at differentiating 'goods' from 'bads'. It is fair, unbiased and based on specific experience. Champion/challenger tests comparing subjective judgement against a properly developed custom scorecard have consistently shown that the scorecard will accept a greater proportion of applicants and reduce the incidence of bad debt.

Credit scorecards were originally constructed with relatively few questions – known as characteristics – all of which were derived from application data. These were built specifically for each lender, based on the premise that past performance is a guide to the future. Great care was taken to ensure that any overlap of predictive power was duly compensated for and that the information from each characteristic was properly weighted.

Performance of simple scorecards may be tracked every month, using tests such as:

- whether the type and mix of applicants had changed significantly from the historic customer base – the 'development sample' – upon which the scorecard had been built (a test known as 'population stability');

- whether the percentage of new additions to the portfolio in arrears, at a certain age of account, remained consistent, or was improving, or declining – presented in a table known as a 'dynamic delinquency matrix'; and

- monitoring the average score of all applicants – a sudden shift may mean that something may be amiss, a gradual shift may mean that the card is moving away from the type of applicant it was designed to measure.

Only six characteristics are often capable of providing significantly greater differentiation between expected 'goods' and 'bads' than would be achieved using subjective assessment. These vary, but usually consist of a selection from the following list.

- Time in job.

- Home phone.

- Years at address.

- Other credit cards/store cards held.

- Age.

- Occupation type.

- Homeowner or tenant.

- Annual income.

- Age of motor vehicle (for motor finance).

- Amount sought (for a mortgage lender, loan to value ratio, for example).

Separate scorecards, or additional characteristics, are sometimes used to reflect the source of the application, with variations such as 'leaflet pick up' or 'branch recommendation' or 'mailshot response', or past relationship, such as 'new customer', 'previous customer' or 'current customer'.

The 'cut-off score' is varied by the lender to reflect any changing appetite for risk, or to compensate for seasonal variations in risk. For example, applications for credit cards received in December can be significantly more risky than others and a higher cut-off score can be used to compensate.

Later developments in scorecard history introduced credit reference agency information in the form of a simple characteristic, such as 'all derogatory', 'no record', and 'one performing loan'.

Scorecards were also developed by consumer credit reference agencies and known as bureau scorecards, offering a different approach to scoring but based on the same principles. Bureau scorecards are not built on application data but on data available at the credit reference agency, which is less prone to being 'adjusted' by the applicant. Bureau scorecards are available with or without age as a characteristic, with age providing greater predictive power, but as such data is not always collected in some high volume quick dealing retail situations, a suitably weighted 'without age' model is also available.

Bureau scores distil all of the data available at the credit consumer credit reference agency into one easy-to-manage risk-ranking score. They are cheaper and quicker to install, so are ideally suited to start-up situations, when new credit grantors have no historic portfolio upon which to build a traditional scorecard.

The shared account performance databases such as CAIS (Credit Account Information Sharing), Share and Insight grew enormously in the 1980s and significantly greater (and more powerful) information became available to the credit reference agencies. This, together with the availability of cheaper computing power, to crunch greater masses of numbers, enabled bureau scorecard developers to construct cards which are specific to sectors of the consumer credit industry. They may also be refined to be further specific to the required uses of the scorecard, such as pre-screening prospect lists, evaluating propensity to use a credit facility, or measuring credit risk.

In application assessment, sector-specific scorecards now make use of very complicated 'hierarchical' characteristics. This is the combination of several answers in an application form to construct a composite characteristic that gives a better insight of underlying risk. For example, compare the insurance risk of an 18 year old purchasing a red sports car to that of a 45 year old purchasing a white estate car: age, type of car and colour of car are each important influences; together they form an even more powerful predictor of risk and drain more power from available data. Such scorecards will have in excess of 50 characteristics.

Scorecard developers who are not credit reference agencies, such as Fair, Isaac Inc, (www.fico.com) promote the combining of consumer credit reference agency scores and custom scorecards to get the best of both worlds. Such companies also heavily research the self-learning tools now available, such as artificial intelligence and neural networks.

There is a body of thought that believes that complexity in scorecard construction has produced scorecards that are less robust and more prone to error than the very simple models that were first developed. Simple scoring models are easier to implement, to understand and to monitor, so the benefits of a complex model are required to be significant to overcome the obvious overheads associated with its complexity. To make this comparison, side-by-side tests are undertaken on recently approved applications where the outcomes are known, referred to as 'retrospective analysis'.

There have been a number of incidences both in the UK and the US where lenders have employed complex scorecards without having the will, skills, or knowledge to monitor the desired outcomes. Errors can occur in the interfacing of the card with account processing software, which may then lead to losses that will be uncovered many months or years after implementation.

Most scorecard developers produce monitoring tools that are user-friendly and virtually self-diagnostic. A user may sometimes decide to leave this 'ancillary' product on the shelf, on the grounds of cost of both the product and the additional manpower required to learn and operate the monitoring systems, which may never have factored in the original purchase justification. This is false economy and in breach of the *Guide to Credit Scoring* mentioned in **A14 COMPANY AND CONSUMER LEGISLATION AND CODES OF PRACTICE.**

The power of different cards and their components A10.19

The precise power derived from the individual elements of any scorecard is commercially sensitive and will vary from scorecard to scorecard. Nevertheless, there is some published research available to examine frequently asked questions, such as whether a custom scorecard generally outperforms a bureau scorecard, and how a simple scorecard may appear in practice.

Bureau scores versus custom scores   A10.20

Firstly the power of bureau scorecards against custom scorecards is compared using samples taken in the very different sectors in the US of direct personal loans, premier bankcards, and agent introduced motor finance.

	Bureau – accepts	Bureau – bad rate	Custom – accepts	Custom – bad rate
Personal loans	62%	2.1%	60%	1.7%
Premier cards	37%	1.9%	40%	1.8%
Motor finance	57%	4.1%	58%	1.9%

From this it can be seen that whilst the first two sectors are broadly similar in acceptance rates and bad rates, there is a significant difference in the bad rates for motor finance, with bad debt over twice as prevalent with bureau scorecards.

This study concluded that:

- there is consistent agreement of scores between custom and bureau score cards;

- used alone, custom score outperforms bureau score;

- opportunities exist to improve 'grey area' decisions; and

- the cost of bureau scores is relatively low.

A further observation from a practitioner's viewpoint is that the bureau scorecard, which ostensibly relies on a wide range of information taken from many sources and which is less prone to 'adjustment' by the applicant, had, in this instance, failed to outperform the custom scorecard.

Illustrations of credit scoring   A10.21

The information values of individual components of a custom scorecard vary in accordance with the market application. However, some reasonably general observations are possible.

This is probably best illustrated by a published scorecard intended for the US retail market, incorporating credit reference agency data as a characteristic.

Characteristic		Score
Time in job	Less than 6 months	5
	6 to 18 months	15
	19 to 29 months	18
	30 to 77 months	20
	78 to 125 months	27
	126 to 245 months	39
	246 months plus or retired	53
Home phone	Yes	35
	No	0
	Close by	30
Years at address	Less than 6 months	2
	6 to 29 months	8
	30 to 65 months	19
	66 to 149 months	19
	150 months plus	30
Other cards held	None	0
	Storecard	11
	Storecard + major	27
Age of car	No car	0
	1/2 years	22
	3 years	10
	4/5 years or, 1 year	9
	5 years plus	9
Previous lender's reference	Yes	5
	No	11
Source	New customer	5
	Present customer	5
	Former customer	18
Consumer credit reference agency information	All derogatory	−15
	No record	−4
	One record OK	0
	Two records OK	8
	Three records OK	18

The above scores have been adjusted for correlation and it is quite clear to see that derogatory information at the credit reference agency can be offset by the power of individual characteristics in some cases. Despite this, some lenders override similar scorecards to ensure that derogatory information results in a decline. Some consumer lenders in the UK will accept applicants with County Court judgments (CCJs) if these have been declared and explained on the application form. Others take a different view, and the existence of CCJs results in an automatic decline irrespective of any other information or scorecard outcome.

Some characteristics are closely correlated with age, such as loan-to-value ratio, or existence of a savings account, or time in job. Age in itself can be used as a characteristic and generally as a person gets older, he or she becomes more creditworthy, although this is not a linear relationship as there is often a dip in the heavy spending years of 35–45. Younger borrowers are also discriminated against by a simple age characteristic.

An applicant's gender can no longer be used in credit scorecards, although this was once a discriminating characteristic, with females performing marginally better than males.

It is important to stress that consumer scorecards cannot be universally applied to all sectors and, even within a specific sector, different products may require special attention. To illustrate, in consumer finance, a US bank has used credit scoring extensively to handle its 650,000+ applications per annum with just a handful of staff. It uses separate cards to reflect the purpose of each loan application. The worst performing loans relate to RVs (recreational vehicles, or motor homes), which have a high degree of abandonment after twelve months, and which has an entirely separate scorecard.

The power of individual *consumer* scorecard characteristics is measured in terms of weight of evidence, which is the natural logarithm of the percentage of accepted applicants divided by the percentage of those rejected. As a rough guide, these are listed here in descending order of strength:

- age;

- time in job;

- loan–to–value ratio (or loan to purchase price ratio);

- home telephone;

- other cards held;

- savings/deposit account held;

- homeowner, tenant or living with parents; and

- marital status.

Interaction of several screening tools   A10.22

The use of automated policy rules in underwriting effectively adds a filter to the front end of the process. If such rules reduce the 'through the door population' of applicants, then the scorecard will be less accurate than intended, as it would have been developed on samples which included all applicants. The pool of applicants being presented to the scorecard will therefore be biased.

Fraud screening products have much the same effect, yet it is not uncommon for the bureau score, custom score, application rules system and fraud prevention tool to have each been supplied by separate companies. The interaction and correlation required to make the most of all components is an essential exercise in such situations.

Types of consumer credit accounts   A10.23

The principal types of credit accounts held by consumers are credit charge and store cards, personal loans and overdrafts. Other types of consumer credit regulated under the *CCA 1974* include hire purchase, lease arrangements, TV rental and mail order.

Credit cards   A10.24

In the UK, most credit cards are issued under the Visa or MasterCard schemes that enable worldwide usage. Credit card borrowings represent the largest proportion of unsecured consumer credit. The largest card issuers in the UK are MBNA, Barclaycard and RBS Advanta.

Following a successful application to a card issuer, a credit card is issued to the consumer and any additional cards on the account are issued to named persons as agents of the principal debtor, who is liable for all debts incurred by all cardholders. Revolving credit is granted subject to a credit limit that is advised to the cardholder on issue. The card issuer may amend the credit limit at any time, giving notice to the cardholder.

On issue the cardholder is also provided with a Personal Identification Number (PIN) to permit the use of the card in cash machines. From 2004 the PIN will also be used as a fraud prevention tool to authenticate the cardholder at the point of sale when making retail purchases, under an initiative known as Chip and Pin. All credit cards are being modified to contain an embedded electronic chip to enable Chip and Pin to be rolled out throughout the UK. The signature portion of the card also contains a tamper-proof security code so that losses through 'card not present' transactions (i.e. for purchases made using the card by telephone, mail order or internet) can be minimised. It is no longer possible to use lists of stolen credit cards fraudulently without knowledge of the PIN or the security code.

Interest is calculated daily on the balance outstanding and added to the account on a monthly basis. A monthly statement is sent to the cardholder detailing all transactions on the account and requiring a minimum payment, typically 3% of the balance outstanding or £5, whichever is the greater. Depending on the issuer, payment may be made by direct debit, by post, or through the banking system.

In the event of the card being used fraudulently with the cardholder's permission or as a result of negligence, the cardholder is liable for all transactions posted to the account. Otherwise there is usually a limit on liability for fraudulent use of £50.

Cards are renewed after a period set by the card issuer, depending on perceived risk, historic use of the card and the issuer's policy. Credit cards may attract an annual fee of up to £20 but most are free. Certain events will trigger additional charges. For example, a returned cheque or late payment may typically result in a charge of £20 per incident. Because such charges are not contained in the calculation of the APR, they are colloquially known as 'stealth charges'. There are moves to have all such charges displayed more prominently in the Consumer Credit Agreement, in a table similar to that in use in the USA, which is called a 'Schumer' box.

Some credit cards have dual purpose in that they may also be used to guarantee cheque payments. Card issuers refer to the habits of cardholders as 'inactives' (which may include cards issued for cheque guarantee purposes), 'full payers' or 'extended credit takers'.

Company credit cards issued to employees are similar in appearance, although the connected lender liability protections given under the *CCA 1974* for personal credit cards are not extended to authorised cardholders, and the balance is expected to be cleared in full each month. The company is primarily liable to pay the card issuer in full each month, and the employee is contracted to pay the company. In the event of failure by the company, some credit card authorisation slips reserve the right to pursue the authorised cardholder for repayment.

Charge cards A10.25

These are similar to credit cards with two important exceptions:

- there is no extended credit facility — statements are expected to be paid in full each month; and

- there may be no advised credit limit.

American Express and Diners Club are the largest issuers of charge cards and do not carry Visa or MasterCard logos, unlike all other charge card issuers.

Sometimes called 'T&E' cards (travel and entertainment), charge cards may attract annual fees ranging between £38 and £275, in return for which a package of services, such as travel insurance, may be provided to the cardholder. Interest does not usually apply to transactions applied to charge card accounts if they are paid by the due date, unless they are for currency purchase or cash withdrawal. Interest applies to overdue balances at rates that are in line with credit card interest rates.

Some Visa and MasterCard gold cards are charge cards, such as those issued by NatWest and Barclays, but other bank-issued gold cards, such as that issued by the Cooperative Bank, are credit cards. The 'gold card' descriptor therefore cannot be taken to determine the underlying nature of the card.

Retail store cards   A10.26

Retail cards are not usually issued under the Visa and MasterCard schemes but instead may only be used in the stores that issue the cards, such as Marks and Spencer and Next. The reason is that all transactions purchased by charge card or credit cards attract a 'merchant service charge' of between 1 and 5% on the value of the purchase, which the retailer pays to the card issuer. By issuing its own cards, the retailer can avoid the merchant service charge and instead assumes the credit and fraud risks, unless of course it outsources the provision of its store card operation to a third party, such as GE Capital, which is the largest issuer of store cards in the UK.

In most other respects, retail store cards are similar to credit cards. Interest rates tend to be significantly higher – indeed this is the subject of an Office of Fair Trading enquiry in 2003 and 2004 – and credit limits lower.

Retailers may also offer instalment credit, which is an unsecured non-revolving credit facility, usually lent for a specific purpose and requiring regular monthly repayments ('instalments') over a period of typically two years. The amount borrowed by UK consumers on retail instalment credit is broadly the same as that on retail store cards.

Personal loans   A10.27

This form of credit is a loan given by a lender for a specific purpose and requiring repayment by regular instalments by a specified date.

Personal loans may be secured or unsecured. If secured, this is normally obtained by a second mortgage over the family home. The total cost of credit is usually less than an unsecured credit card account and more than a first mortgage from a residential lender.

Such loans may be maintained either in sole name or jointly and severally with another, such as a spouse, and are used for many purposes including consolidation of credit card and other revolving credit, car purchase or holidays. Repayment periods are typically between two and five years.

Early repayment of personal loans will usually involve a penalty that can be expensive for the consumer if the loan is paid off during the early life of the loan term.

Overdrafts   A10.28

An overdraft is a negative balance on a current account at a bank or building society. It is quick to arrange and relatively cheap and is intended to be a flexible buffer zone pending receipt of an expected salary payment. It may be authorised up to an agreed limit, or unauthorised. All overdraft facilities are subject to general terms and conditions published by the lender and are exempt from certain sections of the *CCA 1974* in relation to the entry documentation required for other types of credit.

Authorised overdrafts are subject to lower interest charges than those that are unauthorised and are usually subject to a monthly maintenance fee. If the bank holds a mandate on the account, the account holders will be jointly and severally liable for the debt.

Overdrafts are repayable on demand from the bank. Following demand, the bank may exercise a right of set-off over any credit balances held in any of the account holder's other accounts.

Bank loans   A10.29

Bank loans are a flexible method of financing and may be unsecured or secured by charges over land, life policies or shares. Interest is charged at a margin over the bank's base rate, which varies from time to time, and may be subject to a minimum rate. The margin is set by the bank on an individual loan basis to reflect perceived risk and therefore should be lower for secured loans than unsecured loans.

No early repayment penalties are usually charged although the loan may attract an arrangement fee of up to 2% and an annual renewal fee of up to 1%.

Repayments are usually on a monthly basis for terms of between one and eight years.

Mortgages   A10.30

Building societies, banks, insurance companies and specialist residential lenders provide finance to consumers for the purchase of their homes, taking a first legal mortgage over the property as security. The largest home loan lenders are the Halifax, Abbey National and Nationwide.

Loans are extended over periods of up to 40 years but typically for 25 years. The interest rate payable is varied as Bank of England base rates change, although there is no specific link. Typically mortgage rates are around 1% above the Bank of England base rate. Mortgage lenders often provide options to borrowers to take fixed rates, or rates that are capped, which are variable up to a specified maximum rate, or collared, which may vary within a specific range of rates.

Repayment may be made by equal monthly instalments of capital and interest over the term of the loan (a 'repayment mortgage'), or by monthly instalments of interest if the capital sum is to be repaid by another source, such as the proceeds of an endowment policy (an 'endowment mortgage'), or a pension fund (a 'pension mortgage'). Repayment mortgages are often taken with the benefit of life assurance that decreases over the term of the loan as the size of the loan diminishes.

Some finance companies specialise in second mortgage finance for the purposes of car purchase, loan consolidation and holidays. Loans are extended for periods from two to ten years at interest rates that are slightly lower than credit card rates. Repayments are usually effected by monthly direct debit and additional accident, sickness and redundancy insurance is often sold alongside the credit facility.

Administration, management and accounting aspects A10.31

All credit grantors should ensure that, as far as possible, their marketing literature, application forms, and most forms of regular communication with the consumer are fully compliant with the *CCA 1974* and all other relevant legislation. These, together with best practice guidelines, should be enshrined in published manuals as a reference point for new staff, for consultation by existing staff, and in case of need as a record for the courts.

Procedure manuals A10.32

Detailed procedure manuals should be scripted to include:

- credit policy;

- administration and operational procedures; and

- collections and recovery procedures.

These should be reviewed carefully by the credit grantor's legal advisors prior to use, then regularly reviewed and updated as required.

An historic archive of obsolete manuals should be retained for future reference.

The credit policy manual should contain:

- general instructions relating to lending;

- detailed credit policy and explanations for limitations where appropriate;

- general instructions relating to security;

- detailed instructions for taking security;

- authorisation levels and procedures for the control of lending;

- descriptions of the various classes of customer and how they should be treated;

- a list of events requiring attention and the action required to be taken;

- security procedures;

- extracts from appropriate legislation;

- draft notices and specimen letters; and

- a record of base rate and charging rate changes.

The administration and operations manual should contain:

- communications policy, both internal and external;

- maintenance of records;

- authorisation levels for all matters other than for the control of lending;

- the security of buildings, people and data;

- extracts from appropriate legislation, such as health and safety and data protection; and

- procedures for events requiring attention during the term of a credit facility, such as calculation and advice of early repayment settlement figures, action required on death or bankruptcy of a consumer and the issue of interest certificates.

The collections and recovery manual should contain:

- clear definitions of default;

- specific triggers requiring action;

- general guidelines on collections and recovery;

- detailed recovery policy;

- authorisation levels for specific collections and recovery actions;

- list of authorised third parties, solicitors, tracing agents, valuers, receivers;

- guidelines for accepting offers to repay by instalments;

- guidelines for realising security;

- specimen letters and notices;

- extracts from appropriate legislation, such as the *Insolvency Act 1986* and the *CCA 1974*;

- write off procedures and the subsequent salvaging of written off debt; and

- methodology of calculating provisions for bad debt.

Application forms A10.33

Application forms used by credit grantors are often a compromise between the need to gather sufficient information to evaluate credit and fraud risk and the wishes of the marketing department to make the form as simple as possible to encourage completion and application.

There is no set format. Generally, the larger or cheaper the credit facility, the more comprehensive the application form.

1. Name and address details

Title, gender, full first and middle names, surname, house number, address and postcode are all required. If an applicant has been at the current address for less than one to three years, previous addresses are sometimes requested, although this practice is becoming less prevalent. If a credit grantor cannot find an applicant on the electoral roll at the address given, he is now likely to telephone the applicant to ask why and to seek the previous address.

Gender is required as a fraud prevention measure and is particularly useful for those using titles such as Doctor or Reverend. Under the *Equal Opportunities Act 1975* it cannot be used as a credit scoring characteristic.

On a credit grantor's database (but not necessarily on the application form itself), foreign and BFPO (British Forces Post Office box) addresses must be specifically flagged as such.

2. Personal details

Date of birth, age, number of dependent children, marital status (with prompts of single, married, divorced, separated, widowed and living together) and mother's maiden name are required here.

Date of birth and age are required together as a verification check. Age is often a scorecard characteristic. The date of birth helps differentiate between people with the same or similar names living at the same address that may have very different credit file histories. The mother's maiden name is used in fraud prevention and is also useful when tracing gone-aways.

3. Home details

Whether an owner, tenant (distinguishing between furnished and unfurnished accommodation) or living with parents, home telephone number and the number of years at current address are sought. These are powerful 'stability' characteristics used in credit scoring. The home telephone number is also used in fraud prevention, with mobile and non-geographic numbers arousing suspicion, and also if the telephone number is 'out of area' to the address given.

4. Financial details

Most prudent lenders attempt to assess the ability to repay in addition to using credit scoring to evaluate the risk of default. This section seeks annual income, partner's income (to assess household income), specific credit cards used and the number of years held, bank or building society name, account number and sort code, the number of years in account with the bank and the types of account held.

The number of cards held will give the credit grantor an indication of likely usage.

Most volume credit grantors are able to check the majority of this information with the shared account performance databases held at the credit reference agencies, enabling a veracity check to be undertaken if required. Information given in this section is also useful in the data matching techniques used in fraud prevention systems.

Details of bank accounts held are also useful in the recovery process. The details given are sufficient for the credit grantor to apply for a garnishee order should the applicant default in future, and recovery action is required.

5. Additional cardholder

Only sufficient information to issue a card is usually requested; whether male or female is asked for future fraud prevention checks on manual authorisations. ('Is the person presenting the card a male or female?').

The additional cardholder may or may not be required to sign the form, depending on the policy of the card issuer. Only the principal applicant is liable for debts incurred on any card issued on the account. Some issuers ask for the relationship between principal applicant and additional cardholder, but this is not essential.

6. Employment details

Whether full or part-time, and the nature of employment, such as civil servant, other public sector, retired, unemployed, private company, homemaker, or self-employed. Also whether permanent, temporary or contracted, professional, manual/shop worker, skilled or semi-skilled, supervisory, nursing, clerical/ secretarial or other. The employer's business or company name and address is required, including postcode, the employee's job title, the time with employer and the business telephone number.

This is fertile data for credit scoring and fraud prevention.

7. Cross-selling opportunities

This heading is not used on application forms, of course, but instead, options are given to the applicant to apply for lost or stolen card protection insurance, and also accident, sickness, unemployment and death insurance.

Such offers must not be mandatory to the credit facility.

8. Declaration section

This starts with the clear statement 'Credit Agreement regulated by the *Consumer Credit Act 1974*'.

A number of warranties and consents are then listed, including:

- that the information is correct;

- that the credit grantor may make enquiries of credit reference agencies and others, in a standard format which the Information Commissioner suggests, and giving the applicant the ability to be considered only on his or her personal merits rather than on 'household' credit data; and

- that the applicant has read and agreed to the terms and conditions of use.

The signature box follows, which has to be dated. This is prefaced by the warning required under the *CCA 1974* that the agreement is regulated under the Act and with the statement: 'Sign it only if you want to be legally bound by its terms'.

Prominently beneath the signature box is a reminder that the cardholder will be given the right to cancel within a short period.

A further space follows for signature by the credit grantor, in accordance with the requirements under the *CCA 1974*.

Credit card application forms tend to use the reverse of the form to display the terms and conditions applicable to the issue of the card but others may prefer to have a more explicit list of warranties and declarations as is shown here.

Credit Agreement regulated by the Consumer Credit Act 1974 – Declaration

(1)   I hereby apply for a personal loan from XYZ Trust plc.

(2)   I am 18 years of age or over.

(3)   I confirm that replies to questions and all information provided by me are true and accurate and are complete in all respects.

(4)   I understand that this application and the information provided by me will form the basis of a contract between me and XYZ Trust plc.

(5)   The rate of interest and monthly repayment on the loan can be varied by XYZ Trust plc from time to time.

(6)   I authorise XYZ Trust plc to make enquiries of credit reference agencies and others to take up references as in its absolute discretion it considers necessary to process the application. The information provided by me may be disclosed to a credit reference agency which will retain a record of the search. If the loan is granted I irrevocably➡

authorise XYZ Trust plc to pass on information to third parties regarding me and the conduct of the account. This information may be used by other lenders in assessing applications from me and other members of my household and for occasional debt tracing and fraud prevention.

☐   Tick here if you wish your application to be considered only on your personal financial information and not on that of your household and any persons known to be financially connected to you.

(7)   I understand and consent that XYZ Trust plc may at any time assign its interests in the loan and does not warrant to provide the required monies either in its own name or on behalf of third parties.

This is a legal requirement – sign only if you wish to be legally bound by its terms

In this case, clause 6 is a form of consent enabling the credit grantor to record a search at a credit reference agency and to submit monthly reports of the payment history to shared data schemes such as Credit Account Information Sharing (CAIS) share, or Insight. The wording of this is based upon the recommendations given in *Data Protection Guidance on Credit Referencing,* issued by the Office of the Information Commissioner (then called the Data Protection Registrar) in March 1996. The additional tick box in this section is now required to give the applicant the option to be assessed entirely on his or her own merits, or in conjunction with others in their household. The wording of this section is not currently subject to the guidance of the Information Commissioner.

Clause 7 enables a lender to assign, sell or securitise the loan, or to broke the loan application to another lender if it wishes to do so. Guidelines are issued by the Bank of England in its *Banking Supervision Guide* in respect of further notification required to the borrower in the event of a securitisation. The regulation of securitisation is now to be harmonised across Europe, following the recommendations of the Securitisations Group of the Basel Committee published in October 2001, and further changes may arise.

Accounting and taxation aspects

Ability to collect interest on a gross basis   A10.34

Banks, building societies and most registered lending institutions have a dispensation to collect interest from borrowers on a gross basis. In the absence of a dispensation, credit grantors are required to collect interest on a net basis; if collected gross, then the borrower must provide the credit grantor with a certificate confirming that the appropriate level of tax has been paid to the Inland Revenue. Failure to obtain and retain certificates can render a credit grantor liable to pay the full tax due.

Provisions for bad debts A10.35

Credit grantors should undertake detailed audits of their portfolio on an annual basis, and more regular interim audits as considered necessary, to determine the level of bad debt which is considered irrecoverable.

To withstand the rigours of an accounting audit, it is best if clearly defined criteria are published to define when a provision for bad debt is necessary. The criteria should be consistently and logically applied during the audit process. An example of provision criteria is as follows:

- any debt where there are three or more monthly instalments overdue;

- any debt where a provision for bad debt has already been made and no improvement has been seen;

- any debt where the credit grantor has reason to believe the borrower is or will become insolvent; and

- any debt which is subject to legal action or in the hands of external collections or tracing agents.

Provision should be raised for all connected accounts and guarantee liabilities less the value of any credit balances or security held. Larger provisions should be fully explained in standard format to help external auditors to assess the appropriateness of the provision.

Once all accounts at risk have been identified, the aggregate bad debt provision is called a 'specific provision' as it relates to specific, identifiable debts. Specific provisions are tax deductible. General provisions for bad debts are not tax deductible without a specific dispensation from the Inland Revenue.

Once a bad debt has been 'written off', it no longer forms part of the credit grantor's assets in the balance sheet. This is an accounting convention and does not mean that the underlying debt is no longer due or irrecoverable. The act of recovering written off debts is termed as 'salvage' and suitable 'adding back' of provisions should be made for any sums received in the salvage process. The borrower should therefore not be advised under any circumstances that a borrowing has been written off in accounting terms.

Payment collection options A10.36

The most efficient repayment options are those which coincide with a borrower's income. For example, if a borrower is paid on the first day of each month, then a direct debit, which debits the bank account on the same day that the salary is received, will have the best chance of success.

Direct debits are the preferred method of regular repayment, followed by standing orders. In the event of variable repayments, the direct debit can be amended by the credit grantor without the need to seek specific, amended authority from the borrower, although the credit grantor is required to notify the borrower in advance of the amended payment.

Under a standing order arrangement, a credit grantor must advise the borrower of the revised payment, the borrower will need to authorise the bank to amend the existing instruction, and the credit grantor will then verify on the due date that the amendment has been properly effected. Some accounting systems used by credit grantors permit only a limited number of direct debit 'runs' per month, or limit the collection frequency to monthly or weekly, in which case a standing order is a more flexible alternative.

Cheques may be requested to be sent by post with a tear-off slip from a monthly statement. This method suits credit agreements where the repayment is variable at the borrower's discretion, such as credit cards. The tear off slip is often in the form of a bank giro credit, enabling any combination of cash and cheques to be paid in at most banks and building societies or forwarded by post.

The same principles apply to the collection of payments from borrowers in arrears. For those borrowers where salvage activity is undertaken, (i.e. where the underlying debt has been written off in accounting terms), a small paying-in book of personalised bank giro credits should be provided regularly, to encourage voluntary payments to be made, whether or not an agreed repayment programme has been negotiated.

Confidentiality   A10.37

A borrower's affairs must be kept confidential at all times. Information should not be disclosed to any third party without the prior written consent of the borrower, and any requests for information regarding the account from the borrower should only be released when identity has been verified.

The only exception is where the credit agreement permits certain disclosures, such as the monthly extract of account performance to credit reference agencies.

Information may be released when it is in the interests of the credit grantor to do so, such as when a borrower is in default and details are required to be forwarded to solicitors or tracing agents.

Credit grantors may also reveal information when under compulsion of law, but 'fishing expeditions' are not permitted. Requests for information from the police should not be disclosed without sight of an order under the *Bankers' Books Evidence Act 1879*, or a witness summons specifying the extent of information required.

Data may also be requested by the police under *section 29* of the *Data Protection Act 1998*, when the underlying reason is the prevention or investigation of fraud. In such cases a written request by an officer of the rank of inspector or greater should be sighted, the officer presenting the request must explain the need for the information, and the credit grantor may only provide information which is sufficient to assist in the investigation or prosecution. In this situation the police will advise whether the borrower may be informed of the investigation. If not, the credit grantor must take every care to maintain the secrecy of the investigation to avoid falling foul of 'tip off' regulations.

On the rare occurrence of requests for information from the military police, HM Customs and Excise, Department of Trade and Industry inspectors, the Inland Revenue or the Director of Public Prosecutions, immediate reference should be made to legal advisors prior to the release of any information. Legislation exists for such persons to have access to personal data in specific circumstances which must be first demonstrated to avoid a case being brought against the credit grantor by the borrower for wrongful disclosure, or breach of privacy.

Consumer credit collections A10.38

To be effective, consumer credit collections action must have immediate impact, consistency of approach and proper regard for social responsibility.

No two collectors will handle a particular situation in an identical manner but it is possible for them to be guided to take a similar professional approach which helps to gain the best results.

The initial default A10.39

Collectors can sometimes underestimate the seriousness of the initial default due to the volumes handled each day and the repetition of hearing similar excuses for non-payment. As a general rule, the earlier an arrears problem is identified, the better chance the borrower has to put matters right. Also workload and costs are minimised and the borrower becomes aware of a prompt, efficient and caring approach which probably goes hand-in-hand with a commitment to provide service to the borrowers at the time when needed most.

When a monthly direct debit is returned unpaid or a standing order is not received as expected, the underlying reason must be ascertained without delay.

If a borrower's banker returns unpaid a direct debit, or stops payment of a standing order in favour of an important commitment such as a mortgage, pension or life policy, he is most likely to have undertaken a very thorough appraisal of the borrower's financial position. He will be very conscious of the potential consequences on his customer's overall financial fortunes as a result of his actions. His efforts to encourage his customer to find monies to meet payments may well have included several letters and telephone calls, and the return of other cheques and other direct debits in a continued attempt to avoid damaging the borrower's financial reputation.

In some cases a banker may have advanced monies to meet payments over recent months and repayment arrangements for that temporary accommodation has not been honoured. With that in mind, the initial default of any important financial commitment is a very serious matter and must be viewed against that background.

Even if payments are of a discretionary nature, then a banker will not return cheques lightly. In general, he will only do so to avoid an increase beyond acceptable limits for the bank's own lendings.

Common errors   A10.40

Poorly managed collection procedures are based solely on automated letter production – a sequence of letters which become increasingly curt and threatening as the matter becomes closer to legal action. Letters do have their place in the collection of debts but are not the most effective recovery action. Letters merely reinforce the message that is already known by the borrower, specifically that a cheque has not been paid. Compared with chasing by letter, telephone contact is faster, more positive, less expensive and affords an additional opportunity to gain more information by way of instant two-way communication that cannot be achieved by letter.

Before making contact, it is absolutely essential to make thorough and proper preparation and to plan the presentation of the call to enable the initiative to be maintained. It must be fully understood why the call is being made and all relevant information must be readily at hand to enable any questions to be answered relating to the history of the account as they may arise.

Most importantly, the objectives of the call should be clearly before the collector, examples of which are as follows.

- To contact the borrower.

- To ascertain why the default has occurred in the first place.

- To return the account to order and to endeavour to keep it in order.

- If appropriate, to educate the borrower in terms of the consequences of failure to co-operate.

- Weighing all the above factors together, to consider a repayment programme, if appropriate, in the light of any adverse financial situation the collector may discover.

Having said this, the overriding objective that the collector must keep in mind at all times is to ascertain why the account is in arrears. If the collector remains unaware of the reason for the initial default, then any action taken is unlikely to address the cause of the difficulty and the probability of further default is increased.

Establishing telephone numbers   A10.41

Telephone numbers should be obtained from the files, for instance from the original application form, from telephone directories, from specialist CD-ROMs, or even possibly from the original introducer of the business who may have contact numbers which are not available from other sources. As a last resort, in view of its relative cost, directory enquiries can also be used.

If there are no telephone numbers available from other sources, then consideration should be given to sending a suitable and simple Telemessage:

> Please contact me urgently.
>
> John Collector
>
> 0207 000 0000

To increase the chance of the borrower contacting the collector and to reduce the possibility of wrongful disclosure, no mention should be made of the sender's identity. It should be borne in mind that the borrower's bankers are likely to have already advised the borrower that the payment has not been made and the borrower will be expecting contact from the collector. The telephone number should be a direct line number, and if the STD code is synonymous with the credit grantor, consideration should be given to using a non-geographic number (details are available from British Telecom).

Upon contact   A10.42

Preparation is important and a collector should endeavour to plan the call in advance prior to making a call.

When the collector has established contact, he should introduce himself on a personal level giving only his first name and without making any reference to the corporate identity or the nature of the call. He should address the borrower by his or her first name, using his or her surname only when absolutely necessary.

Confidentiality is of paramount importance. When the collector is entirely satisfied that contact has been made with the borrower, he must then disclose his full identity as a representative of the company.

If the borrower is out, the collector should ask when they are expected to return and if possible, should leave a message.

If the borrower is working from another office or work location, the collector should tactfully seek the telephone number. If the recipient of the call refuses steadfastly to disclose any information, the collector's first name and direct line telephone number should be left. No deliberate inference should be given that the collector is a social contact, friend or relation, but on the other hand no inadvertent disclosure of the nature of the call can be given as this may breach confidentiality. A balance is required to provide the minimum factual information that is possible when leaving a message with a third party. Any questions asked must be answered truthfully but care always taken to retain confidentiality.

If a spouse, who is not a joint borrower, becomes inquisitive, care must similarly be taken not to disclose any information but a sense of urgency can be instilled as this can lead to the spouse urging the borrower to contact the collector.

Timing of telephone calls A10.43

Contact at home is generally more productive especially if made at breakfast time or to a slightly lesser extent if made in the early evening. Care must be taken not to harass the borrower by continually telephoning during unsocial hours. Occasionally it may be necessary to remind the borrower that the reason for ringing outside office hours is because the collector wishes to help to resolve the default with the minimum of disruption to the borrower.

Harassment is a criminal offence under the *Administration of Justice Act 1970*. An offence is committed if demands for repayment are made which 'in respect of their frequency or manner or occasion of making any such demand, or of any threat or publicity by which any demand is unaccompanied, are calculated to subject him or members of his family or household to alarm, distress or humiliation'. Under the *Protection from Harassment Act 1997*, harassment is incurred when any distress is caused by an action which a person knew or ought to have known was wrong.

Despite the above comments on the most effective timing of calls, in practice, the majority of attempted telephone contact will be made during office hours when borrowers are working. Every effort must be made to preserve confidentiality. When telephone messages are left for the borrower to telephone the collector, every care and effort must be made not to disclose the source or nature of the call. Simply leave the first name and direct dial telephone number and say that the matter is urgent. Remember that the person that the collector is calling may well be in the employ of the borrower.

The content of the call A10.44

The collector should ask why the direct debit or standing order has not been paid and encourage the borrower to discuss fully their financial and personal circumstances by asking open questions.

Possible reasons or excuses should not be volunteered, as they will be quickly adopted. Instead, the collector should encourage the borrower to speak, should act as counsellor and endeavour to update records wherever appropriate in respect of employment, income or contact numbers.

Overcoming objections **A10.45**

Most reasons offered by borrowers for failing to make a repayment have been heard before and collectors should be guided by their company policy for the most appropriate response.

These may be along the following lines.

'I have been ill'	Response: 'I'm sorry to hear that; how does your sickness affect your income, then?'
'I've lost my job'	Response: 'Sorry to hear that. Are you claiming unemployment benefit, or do you expect to find another job soon?'
'I'm ill/busy/housebound at the moment and can't get to the bank'	Response: 'I'll send you a standing order form to make regular payments easy for you. When you've filled it in, send it back to me with a cheque and I'll sort it out for you.'
'The cheque's in the post'	Response: 'What's the cheque number? I'll look out for it for you and if it isn't here tomorrow I'll ring you again.'
'You should have had the cheque. I sent it ages ago'	Response: 'It's definitely not here. Please send another one today and let me know the cheque numbers of both cheques whilst you are on the phone. You need to ring the bank to stop the cheque in case it's lost. I'll do the rest.'
'I'm fed up with your company. I spoke to someone about this earlier today. Can't you people talk to each other?'	Response: 'That's strange because I look after your account and there's nothing on your file. Who did you speak to, and when did you call? I'd like to put this right as soon as possible.'

Abusive or aggressive calls may be handled using silence until the borrower stops to wonder whether the collector is still on the line. Continually abusive borrowers should be warned to calm down, and if the warning is unheeded, the collector should hang up and call again later. If a collector feels bullied by a borrower, the simple act of standing up can help restore confidence and can indicate to a supervisor that help is required.

Coached borrowers A10.46

Collectors should be sensibly aware of the likely motive behind unexpected letters of praise, cheques marked 'in full and final settlement' and offers made subject to the removal of adverse credit information. All such actions point to the borrower having been coached by less-reputable debt counsellors. Only the most experienced collectors in any team should deal with coached borrowers.

Failure to effect telephone contact A10.47

If the collector is unable to contact the borrower by telephone, contact by email or sending a Telemessage may elicit a response from the borrower. If all else fails, a letter or even a visit to the borrower's home may be necessary, although this should always be accompanied and in the vast majority of cases such action is rarely cost-effective.

Acceptance of offers A10.48

On initial contact the major objective is to find the reason for the default, and then to obtain a payment from the borrower to put matters right. Failing this, a collector must weigh up all the circumstances of the borrower and to come to a compromise where a repayment programme is re-established at a different level to that contracted in the credit agreement.

To have the greatest chance of success, timing of the payment or subsequent payments should coincide as closely as possible with the borrower's income expectations. Cheques can be requested to clear arrears, but at all times the collector should bear in mind that this is an inferior option to seeking immediate settlement by credit card, SWITCH or DELTA, or collection by direct debit. This is because the borrower has to write the cheque and send it in the post, leading to the classic excuse. Secondly, there is little chance of presenting the cheque to arrive at the borrower's bankers on a specific date. It should also be borne in mind that a cheque has no advantage over direct debit payments. It may be countermanded, wrongly dated or otherwise wrongly completed or alleged to have been lost, thereby securing further delays.

The collector must appreciate that borrowers will not always be in a position to clear arrears in one payment. Some may seek to clear arrears by increasing monthly payments over the following six months or so. Others may seek to suspend payments for a period and increase all future payments to compensate.

There are no hard and fast rules and each case must be considered on its merits on a common-sense basis. The company may well have established maximum guidelines in terms of the percentage of the contractual payment which the collector is permitted to accept or the maximum time over which arrears may be repaid. Whatever the rules and regulations are, the most efficient and successful arrangements are those which are acceptable and reasonable both to the collector and to the borrower.

It is for the credit grantor's own policy-makers to decide precisely what limitations are placed on acceptability, but as general guidance:

- arrears should be cleared by instalments within a period of twelve months;

- payments should not be suspended totally for any period; and

- capitalisation of arrears to the principal debt should only be undertaken on a most exceptional basis.

Reservation of rights   A10.49

Extreme care must be taken with all offers to ensure that all verbal promises are 'subject to retention of all rights and remedies in the event of default'.

Clear and concise notes of the telephone conversation must be recorded as a matter of course.

All telephone contact must be followed up immediately with a letter confirming what was said, what arrangements have been made and setting out the precise amounts and deadlines to avoid any question of any ambiguity arising in the future.

A suitable diary note should be made to ensure that payments are received as promised, preferably by both automated and manual methods.

Empty threats   A10.50

In all matters relating to arrears collection it is imperative that when collectors say they are going to do something, they do it precisely as advised to the borrower and precisely on the day promised. If the borrower can be led to believe that the collector will not follow through on advised action, then recovery efforts are weakened.

Involvement of third party introducers   A10.51

In general, the collector should not seek to call upon the introducers of the business or other agents to undertake visits to the borrower to enable the return of the account to order. Even if the introducers come within the own organisations, the collector should leave them free to pursue new business and keep them protected from specialist and time consuming debt counselling. Also, once the collector establishes the precedent of collection of payments by visit, this can become an extremely cost-inefficient method of keeping a performing loan on the books.

Involvement of debt counsellors   A10.52

There are good debt counsellors, such as those under the umbrella of Money Advice Trust, but some are poorly trained, if well-intentioned.

The collector needs to be guided by company policy as to whether the collector may negotiate with debt counsellors or not. Company policy may even differentiate between 'fee paid' debt counsellors, and the 'advice for free' sector debt counsellors.

If the collector is unsure as to whether the debt counsellor, or the offer of repayment, is properly respectful of everyone's interest, but primarily that of the borrower, then bank statements should be sought in preference to prepared income and expenditure statements. If the debt counsellor does not have these immediately to hand, then the collector should call into question the extent of investigation undertaken by the counsellor.

Acceleration of action   A10.53

If all the right action is taken and the account remains in arrears with no satisfactory arrangement or co-operation, then the need arises to examine more closely the severity of the difficulties and in particular whether they are of a temporary or long-term nature. Some people regard the position of being two months' in arrears as a turning point for a borrower's financial fortunes and action taken at this juncture is often critical to the success of collections and recovery processes.

Temporary difficulties   A10.54

These may occur for many reasons including loss of employment or ill health. In such cases State benefits may be available. For example, the Benefits Agency is prepared to pay support direct to mortgage lenders under certain circumstances.

If difficulties are generally of a temporary nature then borrowers often seek time and flexibility. These are not unreasonable requests, but as a *quid pro quo*, the borrower must be prepared to co-operate fully, preferably by submitting bank statements and full details of their current financial position. These will enable the collector to ensure that the borrower is not promising a commitment which they have little hope of fulfilling. The seeking and examination of bank statements is the easiest and most reliable method of doing this.

On the return of the bank statements, a careful appraisal must be undertaken and if repayment proposals are acceptable this should be confirmed in writing, remembering to reserve all rights and remedies in the event of default. For regulated agreements, consideration should also be given to issuing a modified or fresh credit agreement.

Long-term or persistent difficulties   A10.55

When it is clearly evident that the borrower is unwilling to co-operate, or unable to adhere to a reasonable repayment plan for whatever reason, then recourse to any security held, or to the court, needs to be considered.

It is a fact of life that many promises made to collectors are broken. In the event of continued broken promises and failure to respond to the initiatives, a final letter should be forwarded to the borrower setting out in plain English that legal proceedings will commence in seven days in the continued absence of co-operation.

The first solicitors' letter should give the borrower several options to avoid legal action.

Immediate restoration to order   A10.56

In the event that a payment is received to cover arrears to date it is necessary to reinstate the direct debit request or standing order instruction and to monitor the account for at least three months to ensure that subsequent payments are made without the need for reminder.

Voluntary sale of any security held   A10.57

In such cases, control of the sale proceeds is of paramount importance and the security must not be released until monies are held and cleared.

Full repayment by another lender   A10.58

Most borrowers will be unaware of the number of 'sub-prime lenders' who specialise in providing finance to distressed borrowers. A simple fact sheet of contact addresses and telephone numbers may be provided in appropriate cases.

Action should not be deferred on verbal promises of monies being advanced by another lender unless an unfettered commitment letter is sighted.

It is essential that cleared funds are obtained prior to release of any security. Also possible rights of subrogation and contribution must be borne in mind. These are covered in greater detail in **A14 COMPANY AND CONSUMER LEGISLATION AND CODES OF PRACTICE.**

Training aid for effective collection action   A10.59

An *aide memoir* of best practice collection rules are contained in the following 'ten golden rules' and 'seven deadly sins' used in collections training.

Ten golden rules

Always:

- define collection periods and specific actions required within that collection period by scripting detailed collection procedures and policies and ensure that all collections staff are fully trained;

- use telephone collection techniques in preference to all others;

- make concise and unambiguous records of all telephone calls by letter which are sent to the borrower promptly after each call;

- use envelopes without the company logo or franking machine mark at all times;

- write a suite of standard letters and Telemessages and rarely deviate;

- use a double diary system for both payments and responses;

- monitor what works and what does not for your particular credit niche;

- preserve confidentiality and retain rights and remedies in the event of default;

- seek legal help if at all uncertain; and

- read the file again before taking any significant action.

Seven deadly sins

Never:

- allow the borrower to have two points of contact;

- advise the borrower of an action that it is not proposed to undertake;

- simply seek adjustment of an arrears position and always find out why the account has defaulted;

- talk about the borrower's affairs to any third party without the borrower's specific written authority to do so;

- accept any offer to pay by reduced instalments without seeking bank statements;

- make light of the borrower's predicament or volunteer possible excuses; nor

- transfer the file to the solicitors without having re-read the entire file to ensure that no aspect has been overlooked.

Tracing borrowers   A10.60

It is often tempting to employ professional agents to trace a 'gone-away' borrower but in many cases sufficient information to find the borrower will already be on file. The original application form, references and bank details can usually point to the borrower's current whereabouts. Failing this, relatively simple methods such as checking with directory enquiries or consulting the local electoral roll using websites such as www.192.com can produce good results.

There are also computer-aided methods that enable the collector to interrogate automated databases, details of which the collector can obtain from credit reference agencies such as Callcredit, Experian or Equifax. Membership of GAIN, the Gone Away Information Network, can also help credit grantors when an absconding debtor resurfaces.

Persistence is the key to successful tracing of borrowers and second to this is the preference in following a warm lead rather than a cold lead.

In general, it is far more difficult to 'skip' an address, without leaving a forwarding address, than most collectors think.

It is comparatively easy to return all mail marked 'gone away'; buying valuable time, removing the letters from the inspection of a worried spouse, and not always with the criminal intent of avoiding debt.

There are several reasons why a borrower may have genuinely 'gone away'. The borrower may have:

- died;
- been confined to hospital;
- gone on holiday; or
- started studying at college or university.

Alternatively, in a small minority of cases, the borrower actually may have skipped to avoid creditors or family, or both.

In a significant number of cases the borrower is still living at the address the collector has on file. Studies have shown that around a quarter of alleged gone-aways are still 'living as stated'. The use of 'contact cards' can help identify these. Contact cards are anonymous greeting cards that simply ask the recipient to call a specific, dedicated telephone number. Calls to that number are trapped on an answering machine with an anonymous message asking the caller to leave their name and contact telephone number. Some lenders send such cards on days when the likelihood of opening the cards is high (e.g. to reach the borrower on Valentine's Day).

Half of other gone-aways are with friends or family, usually within seven miles of the old address.

In all but the first instance, most gone-aways return to the neighbourhood within twelve months.

In-house or outsourced debt tracing   A10.61

The bureaucracy of filling in tracing enquiry forms, sending them to trusted and experienced tracing agents, monitoring for responses and then making sense of the result between a month and two months later, is extremely longwinded. This is especially so when compared with the online alternative of simply submitting a name and address and receiving an immediate trace in the majority of cases from an automated database solution from a credit reference agency.

If the online tracing system fails to find a gone-away on the date of keying, then it continues to search for the data every week for two years and returns an up-to-date address as soon as it is known. This means that the process is significantly quicker – over 70% of gone-aways have been traced on day one in tests and 50% is not untypical. Administration is considerably reduced and, as the collector pays only for hits, the process is cheaper than instructing agents.

In-house tracing can be very cost-efficient, full control of the process is retained, but more staff are required and tracing is not a job for the novice. Outsourcing can buy time and skill for a busy arrears department, and payment of fees often relates only to successful traces.

For most credit grantors, in-house tracing should be tried first, using an agent only when own efforts fail. This requires a small investment in CD-ROMs and access to credit reference agency automated tracing services. For the best results, staff should be rewarded by bonus for every successful trace achieved that leads to a single payment.

Basic steps for in-house tracing   A10.62

The following steps should be followed when tracing gone-aways in-house.

- Read the file and ring every telephone number found to get leads, remembering all that has been said before about confidentiality.

- Check the borrower's credit file. Think about contacting other lenders – there is a common interest.

- Use Internet people-finding services such as that available on www.192.com.

- Use CD-ROM directories to find people with the same surname in the same locality.

- Send a Telemessage, or a contact card.

Before engaging the services of an external tracing agency, the following steps are recommended:

- Visit the prospective agent's premises.
- Get references in writing and also speak to other lenders who use the agent.
- Agree methodology, prices and timescales for reporting.
- Appoint two agents contractually and give each 50% of workload.
- Measure success rates and publish them internally and to the agents.
- After a suitable testing period, give the most successful 70%, the other 30%.
- Regularly audit. And/or:
- Keep measuring and review workload allocation every six months.

A11
Exporting

Even greater competition for sales A11.1

In January 2004 Experian, the credit information company, reported that UK companies' profitability had entered a fifth year of decline. At the same time our manufacturers and service industries have been cutting jobs as the high pound hits their profitability.

The tumbling dollar may have cut earnings as our sales to European countries have slowed.

However, in March 2004 it was reported by Anna Fifield in the *FT* that 'corporate profits bounced back sharply at the end of last year (2003)'.

In reviewing our major exporting markets, the *Export Times* confirmed in their survey of the 200 countries to which the UK exports that there was a 13% downturn in our sales to the USA, Germany and France between 2002 and 2003. They also reported that some caution should be noted in our trade figures due to the impact of VAT fraud.

With the new candidate countries having joined the EU in May 2004, with their lower labour and production costs, there will be even greater competition to not only capture our domestic markets, but also attack markets in other EU countries.

Due to low margins in the UK, there is still a need for British businesses to increase their sales by exporting goods or services where their margins could be considerably higher.

Global movement of trade A11.2

Since April 2003 there has been a huge movement to transfer manufacturing to overseas countries such as China, where labour costs are far lower and regulations less severe. In the service industry it has already been reported that callcentres are becoming too expensive, therefore the Philippines and China are the new locations for outsourcing and offshoring.

Brazil, which traditionally has lower labour costs, has moved some of its manufacturing to China. This is a warning for all traders as China is the second largest importer of oil after the USA.

Why export? A11.3

Even now a trader with plenty of orders, may ask the question, why trade overseas? The answer is simple, basically, selling overseas can not only increase sales and profits but it can also increase production runs and lower the total operating cost. If it is a seasonal business the overhead costs can be spread and new markets can create repeat orders.

Some traders only consider exporting either when there is a downturn in the domestic market or when they cannot achieve any further increase of their sales in Britain. In the author's view this is the wrong attitude. Exporting should be a natural expansion of any business provided that it has the management skills and finance to increase extra sales. However, the exporter must have the products or services that the buyer requires, which are tailored for the buyer's market, at a price which is acceptable and are delivered at a date that the importer requires.

The extra task the prospective exporter has to carry out to gain profitable orders is thorough research. There also has to be an understanding of the cultural differences in any one of the 240 countries where it is possible to export. It is important to remember that there may be different legal jurisdictions within one particular country risk. At the same time the exporter will need to have enough information to make a commercial decision based on the political, economic and commercial risks which relate to any particular country.

Coupled with this rather large checklist, an exporter must have a banking facility available to service the production of the goods and services, especially when buyers in many parts of the world are demanding far longer credit terms than are required in the UK. For example, in the USA buyers are now demanding 90 day terms or longer, and in this market and many others throughout the world buyers are also demanding far lower prices.

The 11 September alarm A11.4

Since 11 September 2001, there has been a general downturn in world trade. Terrorist attacks have created a lack of confidence, therefore businesses have suffered due to lower investment, world tourism has declined in some areas but share prices have improved throughout the world. The other uncertainty is the increasing cost of oil and the political impact of the USA, the UK and the other countries that supported the war in Iraq. Sudden changes in trade patterns may take place due to terrorism.

A further political aspect which was not a consideration when the previous edition of this book was written are the number of changes of government that have taken place in Europe. These new governments could reverse economic and trade policies in 2004/5.

The USA's economy has suffered, but they still generate some 40% of the world's trade. We still need to export, but due to the lack of strength in some economies, a far greater amount of research and assessment must now be carried out to check all the risks, including whether different payment terms may now be required.

However, the fundamental principles of exporting remain unchanged.

Longer credit terms – the advantages and costs   A11.5

Different payment terms still have to be agreed to suit the risk, and the business must have the ability to monitor and collect any outstanding overseas debts. (See **A11.52** below.) The author of this chapter would again emphasise that the positive aspect of exporting is that production runs may be far greater, as many countries overseas have enormous populations with high demands and spending power. The negative aspect, which must be remembered, is that there are many extra costs in exporting which it takes time to understand.

It may seem impossible to make a profit at a time when, in many parts of the world, raw material and labour costs are lower, and in some countries there is the worry of deflation. However, it is still possible to make profits, as many overseas countries admire our manufacturing and service skills. In a number of countries they will buy our products because of the design and superior technology.

The biggest mistake for exporters to make is to accept an order without having any information or little independent data on the buyer, so that it is impossible to assess the commercial and financial strengths, which include whether they will get paid. (For information on obtaining overseas reports on buyers, see **A3.62–A3.66** above.)

The second problem area for newer exporters is not realising that in an export transaction there may be certain costs for which they are responsible, and other costs which the buyer incurs. Provided traders understand the trading conditions and international transportation terms when negotiating the sale, there will be far fewer problems. (See **A11.9** and **A11.47** below.)

Success stories   A11.6

There is still a certain glamour in exporting, and a true commercial friendship can definitely be developed when a real partnership is created between the exporter and the buyer or their agents or distributor. However, a number of UK manufacturers are now transferring part of their entire production to overseas countries where labour costs are far lower. They can then export their products from, for example, the Czech Republic and make a profit. This is an adaptation of inward investment which many global companies are using to counter high costs. In an interview with Mr Ian Campbell, the former Director General of the Institute of Export and now an export trade advisor, he mentioned that 'China is looking much more closely at manufacturing outside the USA, because of the high cost environment. Many UK companies are looking to outward investment. Japan, France and Germany are moving parts of their motor industry to other countries. This is because global companies will manufacture in the most cost effective way. Trade Partners UK (now known as UK Trade & Investment), in conjunction with the Foreign Office, is aiming to increase the number of active exporters by using the "Passport to Exporting" subsidy scheme'. (See **A11.15** below.)

Meanwhile, due to the number of acquisitions and mergers in the UK, it is now believed that there may be only a core group of between 50,000 and 60,000 exporters who are selling overseas with constant repeat orders. However, the other way companies can now start exporting is by using a website to advertise, and using the Internet to sell.

Research   A11.7

When researching, it is first necessary to check if a licence is required for exporting, and then to confirm what customs barriers exist. The other segments of an export contract, such as local government regulations, translations of instructions, labelling, certificates of origin, health certificates, legalisation and certification of invoices are further elements that have to be examined.

Other factors which must be understood are:

- the complex documentation;
- transportation;
- location of the buyer;
- time differences;
- the currency and its fluctuations in the buyer's country; and
- the languages of those countries.

Finally, remember that there may be extra translation and packaging costs which must be calculated.

Provided that the trader has costed all these extra charges that they will incur in exporting to a particular country, or a number of countries, it is then possible to calculate whether a real profit can be made.

Starting the research – is a licence required?   A11.8

Before carrying out an immense amount of work to decide whether it is possible to sell a manufactured item or a service to any country, it is first essential to know whether a licence is required to communicate and trade. There are many types of licence, however the Export Control Organisation (ECO), which is part of the Department of Trade and Industry (DTI), issues notes on how to apply for a licence and in what sectors licences are required. The ECO are responsible for administering strategic export controls and the United Nations and EU trade sanctions in the UK. The rules concerning the exportation of goods, technology and services can change very quickly so the exporter must keep up-to-date by contacting the ECO Helpline or visiting the ECO's website (www.dti.gov.uk/ export.control). The Helpline provides a list which outlines the UK's policy commitments with regard to sanctions and embargoes.

As at April 2004 there were 43 countries where trade sanctions applied. Apart from restrictions on arms and oil embargoes there are also a number of countries where there are restrictions on travel, flights of aircraft, engineering, maintenance and servicing. Financial controls, withdrawal of preferential trade tariffs, visa restrictions, freezing of funds to individuals, and freezing of assets of companies, and measures against terrorists are just some of the restrictions.

Due to the large increase of countries which have been added to the list since May 2000, they are not listed here as the author suspects other countries will be added to the UN embargoes list as more actions are taken to counter terrorism.

There are detailed rules which relate to exporting military equipment, arms, ammunition and related materials as well as dual-use goods suitable for military purposes. The ECO general guide points out that exporters should be suspicious about an enquiry or order if the customer is reluctant to offer information about the end-use of the goods, and will not provide clear answers to commercial or technical questions which are routine in normal negotiations. There are also new controls to prevent proliferation of nuclear, chemical and biological weapons and missiles capable of delivering them. The *Export Control Act 2002* came into force in late 2003. This Act gives new powers for the control of exports of military and torture equipment, long-range missiles and weapons of mass destruction.

Further information can be obtained from: ECO Helpline, Department of Trade and Industry, 4th Floor, 4 Abbey Orchard Street, London SW1P 2HT. Tel: 020 7215 8070. Fax: 020 7215 0558. E-mail: eco.help@xnpd.dti.gov.uk.

Will the supplier be paid? A11.9

Help is at hand as there are a number of publications which give up-to-date information on the current payment delays which relate to individual countries.

International Risk and Payment Review A11.10

D&B's *International Risk and Payment Review* is a monthly publication which shows the risk factors and the payment delays of 132 countries. For example, in the February 2004 issue, 24 countries were listed under risk pointers. It highlighted for example, the Paris Club rescheduling on the Kenyan debt, the Egyptian EU trade agreement, and the Kuwaiti new banking sector laws. The *Review* also states the 'Regional Risk Indicators' for each region of the world, and there is an extensive economic and political commentary and a risk indicator for each country which is graded into seven bands. Macroeconomic and external risk, and a trend arrow to show improving or deteriorating economic, political, commercial or external developments are also included. For exporters, payment performance of companies, GDP growth, import cover and local currency charts are some of the extra data which if available, is noted against the country reports. (See **A3.16–A3.26** above for more information on D&B.)

Journals and magazines   A11.11

There are a number of journals which are helpful to exporters.

Trade Finance. This is a monthly magazine (published by Euromoney Publications) on trade and commodity finance which highlights the credit risks and credit finance available in a number of countries. In a recent edition trade finance to Russia was highlighted, plus a cover story on the insurance hot spots throughout the world. The magazine also states forfeiting rates (discounting of bank guarantees). In June 2003 factoring and trade documentation and processing was featured, and in October 2003 there was a review of political risk in trade.

Further information is available from: Trade Finance, Nestor House, Playhouse Yard, London EC4V 5EX. Tel: 020 7779 8888.

Export Times. This is published monthly and issues a schedule in May and November listing the UK's total value of exports and imports for the preceding year in descending order to cover 200 countries. There is also a comparison with previous years and a commentary on the findings of their survey. This survey is a highly valuable source of information for any trader as it shows with which countries the UK is trading at a surplus, and therefore indicates which countries have foreign exchange to pay for their imports. Subscribers are targeted in the automotive, chemical, construction, food and drink, engineering, and machine tools sectors.

Further information can be obtained from: Export Times, Nexus House, Swanley, Kent BR8 8HU. Tel: 01322 660070.

Overseas Trade. This is UK Trade & Investment's publication for UK exporters, aimed primarily at SMEs. It is available free of charge to approximately 32,000 readers around the country and is also distributed to Chambers of Commerce, Business Links, Embassies and other intermediaries. *Overseas Trade* contains updated market reports, sector analyses, dates of forthcoming export events, news, expert trade finance pieces, success stories and news of developments in e-commerce. *Overseas Trade* also publishes a monthly supplement giving a broader outlook on a specific market. There are two extra pages devoted to key export-related events worldwide and details from the diary of the Institute of Export.

Further information can be obtained from: The Editor, Overseas Trade, 102 Sydney Street, London, SW3 6NJ. Tel: 020 7368 9600.

International Trade Today is a new publication for exporters. However, Tony Bush the Editor and Ian Campbell the Editorial Consultant (who was the Director General of the Institute of Export), have years of experience in international trading and finance. This well-written magazine has regular features on export successes, country profiles, transport updates, freight and finance news, customs regulations, economic reviews and background briefings on our government's export promotions and policy.

Further information can be obtained from: Jo Beecroft, International Trade Today, Impromptu Publishing Ltd, 11th Floor, Portland Tower, Portland Street, Manchester M1 3LF. Tel: 0161 238 4942.

In the *Second Annual International Business Owners Survey* issued by Grant Thornton, the International Accountants, they surveyed business-owners in 26 countries and 6,900 companies worldwide. They noted that late payment may be reducing in Europe.

They show in their research that the average figure in the EU has improved from 65 days in 1993 to 55 days in 2004.

The EU *Late Payment Directive* may now be having an effect. See Figure 2.00 and Figure 3.00 at **A11.54** below.

Further information on this superb 51-page report, which also covers economic prospects, export expectations, employment, and EU business trends can be obtained from Grant Thornton, Grant Thornton House, Melton Street, Euston Square, London NW1 2EP. Tel: 020 7383 5100.

A strategic approach to exporting A11.12

Once a decision has been made to consider selling overseas, it is necessary to conduct research to confirm in which country or countries a particular product or service will sell. The initial research will depend on the amount of capital, personnel and time that is available within the business.

After seeing a number of overseas transactions come to grief, the author of this chapter would emphasise that when planning the export strategy, overseas sales should be a commercial decision and not a commercial gamble. For instance, if a competitor is already selling the supplier's type of product or service, the supplier should consider whether they are making a profit and if he sold in the same market would he have to decrease the price or perhaps increase the credit terms to gain the order? It all depends on the technical quality of the supplier's product or service and whether any modifications have to be made to reflect customer preference in any particular country.

When beginning to research marketing, it is strongly recommended that, if the supplier is considering selling overseas for the first time, he plans to sell to one or two countries in the first instance. However, once a market is established, it is dangerous just to rely on a few markets as world trading conditions can completely change without any prior notice.

New methods of marketing and selling for exporters   A11.13

With the massive expansion of advertising via websites, and the ability of buyers all over the world to send enquiries and orders, it might seem that an exporter's life would now be easy. This is not so as the economic, commercial and political risks still have to be considered. (See **A11.21** below.)

The major change for all traders is that the speed of the transmissions of these enquiries is instantaneous. However, caution is still necessary. The reason for still being cautious is that it takes many hours of careful research to decide which is the right market for you, but help is at hand.

UK Trade & Investment   A11.14

UK Trade & Investment is the leading government trade support service for British companies trading in world markets. Its principal role is to seek out and help UK companies who wish to develop new opportunities in overseas markets. Its vast international service network enables it to provide sales leads, market information, consultancy services and contracts. It has teams of advisors – in the UK and overseas – on issues in all major markets throughout the world. Within the UK, it has teams of experts dedicated to the major sectors of business. It also has local international trade teams situated at Business Links throughout England as well as in the devolved administrations of Scotland, Wales and Northern Ireland.

It may seem an impossible task to decide how to begin selecting the right market for your goods or services, but exporters need not spend many thousands of pounds on research to find the right markets, as UK Trade & Investment has a number of schemes and services which will assist them. Here is just a selection of ideas that could help an exporter.

UK Trade & Investment's Information Centre   A11.15

The UK Trade & Investment Information Centre is a free self-service reference library for exporters and it holds the most extensive collection of reference books, statistics, directories and market reports on overseas markets in the UK. Many of the publications have been obtained by using the network of over 200 British embassies and High Commissions throughout the world – information that is not generally available under one roof. Statistical, contact and market information can also be found in the valuable online services available via high-speed ADSL connections in the Information Centre.

The Information Centre provides much more than unlimited access to the very latest export intelligence. Experienced staff can also help you find the information you need to assess and compare export markets, and locate valuable contacts.

Exporters and their representatives, market researchers, consultants and business students can use the Information Centre free of charge and without prior appointment. If you wish to use the online resources available in the Centre it is advisable to telephone in advance to book one of the terminals.

The Information Centre is open from 9.00 to 17.30 from Monday to Friday. Last admissions are half an hour earlier. (Hours are subject to change so please telephone the day before visiting to avoid disappointment.)

For further information on all the above services, contact: UK Trade & Investment Information Centre, Kingsgate House, 66–74 Victoria Street, London SW1E 6SW. Tel: 0207 215 8000.

Internet: http://www.trade.uktradeinvest.gov.uk/information_centre.

Your Passport to Export Success   A11.16

UK Trade & Investment's Your Passport to Export Success is an assessment and skills-based programme that provides new and inexperienced exporters with the training, planning and ongoing support they need to succeed overseas.

The Your Passport to Export Success programme includes:

- a free export health check, which provides an objective assessment of a company's capability to export;

- free export mentoring;

- a training subsidy to develop skills of staff;

- UK Trade & Investment's export services – market research, export sales leads, foreign language trade literature, all provided at subsidised cost;

- market visit – a subsidised visit to an overseas market;

- customer service – aftercare services to help a company continue its successful development in international trade.

Further details on the programme are available from International Trade Advisors based in Business Links and Devolved Administrations or from UK Trade & Investment's website at http://www.trade.uktradeinvest.gov.uk.

Export Explorer   A11.17

The Export Explorer scheme is designed specifically for smaller firms with limited or no experience of markets outside the UK.

To join Export Explorer costs £99.00. That includes all the hands-on help a business requires, including information, briefings on the market and administration. Travel and accommodation are extra, but there are normally special rates that can be arranged.

International business schemes   A11.18

UK Trade & Investment uses overseas events to develop trade for small-to-medium-size UK businesses (SMEs) with an interest in exporting to new foreign markets. Support is wide-ranging from grants to help companies attend events such as exhibitions, trade fairs and seminars, to free, invaluable, current and local information.

All support is delivered through UK business support organisations; full details are available on UK Trade & Investment's website: www.trade.uktradeinvest.gov.uk.

Tailored market research   A11.19

Many UK exporters do not realise that they can obtain tailor-made reports prepared by Commercial Officers at Embassies and High Commissions. Reports can include:

- basic market information;

- identification and assessment of potential agents/distributors;

- customised local contact lists;

- market assessments;

- advice on the market approach;

- general information on local investment opportunities.

The cost of these reports ranges from £50 to over £1,000, depending on the information required and the number of hours of research involved.

Sales leads   A11.20

You can also register for free business opportunities from abroad, matched to your interests, and these will be emailed direct to your desktop if requested. You will need to profile your firm, indicating the kinds of opportunities you want to receive and from which overseas markets. Business opportunities are sourced from UK Trade & Investment staff in British Embassies worldwide. For more information and to register, visit: www.trade.uktradeinvest.gov.uk.

A review of world trade   A11.21

Over the past two years there have been significant changes in the patterns of world trade, not least because of heightened awareness of security, fair trade, corporate social responsibility issues, and by developing countries with increasing export market penetration.

Global economic confidence is at a ten-year high, according to the results of the latest ICC/Ifo World Economic Survey (January 2004), with sustained growth expected in all regions of the world. The poll found that the favourable global conditions are also expected to have beneficial effects on export/import performance worldwide and thus on world trade.

Adriaan Vickery FIEx, the National Chairman of the Institute of Export who, last year, commented on economic conditions and certain overseas markets, with an eye to export potential, has since updated the picture, and this is reflected in the text below.

A regular visitor to overseas markets, Adriaan Vickery operates Roade International Ltd – export managers and consultants – and is also busy arranging overseas catalogue and information shows for UK companies through a sister company, Britcom Services.

The euro and EU enlargement   A11.22

The strength of the euro presents opportunities for exporters. However, the accession, on May 1 2004 of the new EU members – Cyprus, the Czech Republic, Estonia, Hungary, Latvia, Lithuania, Malta, Poland, the Slovak Republic and Slovenia – although they do not immediately join the euro, may test the currency and EU stability. Certainly, the movement of labour and, significantly, a substantial proportion of highly qualified job seekers will positively affect competitiveness and, possibly, standards in those countries that become target areas for migrants.

Certainly, the EU aid and benefits package will now have to be more widely distributed. The potential benefit to exporters to the acceding countries will be better funding to support requirements, assuming always that exporters have previously developed initial relationships in those countries.

Generally, the EU is dependent on a global recovery to shake off the current and ongoing period of flat cyclical performance and a relatively high-value currency. A continued rise in the euro against the US dollar would be extremely harmful to Europe's prospects of economic growth.

World Trade Organisation (WTO)   A11.23

Global trade is expected to gather pace this year, after a weak dollar and a robust Chinese economy helped to create some encouraging activity in 2003. However, uncertainties about the US and European economies coupled with volatile oil prices could temper further optimism. During 2003 world trade is estimated to have expanded by a higher than expected 4.5%, a second successive year of growth since 2001 mainly due to a number of Asian countries and the USA. Clearly currency movements contributed strongly to this trend caused by the weaker dollar and strengthened euro and yen.

Markets

Middle East

Consumer and financial markets have become more lucrative as a result of a move away from oil/petrochemical and construction markets. More than half of the Middle East population, with its attendant purchasing power, is under the age of 25 years. Modern communications, technology and the purchasing power within this group offer immense opportunities as governments struggle to keep the sector within their own borders, and to maintain as much as is possible, traditional and cultural values. Radical values, and a leaning towards democracy in a benevolent yet authoritarian environment, now threaten to disturb the status quo.

Since 9/11 anti-US/UK sentiment is increasing at a popular level, without any appreciable effect on business levels in general, although travel safety and official travel advice have become inhibitors to market visits. Real wealth and power remains in the hands of the few. Nevertheless US intransigence in its support for Israel and its antipathy to Palestinian rights, affords some Arab states somewhat of a dilemma in their approach to their trading partners.

Iraq (and Kuwait/Jordan) **A11.25**

Iraq affords enormous opportunities in what is, effectively, a major new market. Whilst basic business infrastructure within Iraq, in terms of the general ability to trade internationally, is in its inception, it is vital that even the smallest exporters begin the introduction process.

Whilst it is true that major contracts are issued mainly to US companies, or others with strong US connections, exporters are asked to consider the 'spin-off' – lucrative sub-contracts for non-US products or expertise.

By virtue of their geographical position, both Kuwait and Jordan, and to a lesser extent Iran, the United Arab Emirates and Saudi Arabia, are in prime position to benefit from (often urgent) requirements for transport and essential goods and services including portable and temporary accommodation, water supply, electricity generation and security. Entry to Iraq is normally via these two countries, and even if visiting the country is not an option, involvement in these influential neighbouring countries will bring its own benefits.

United Arab Emirates **A11.26**

Unlike many of the surrounding countries, the United Arab Emirates forges ahead with major construction and development programmes. Dubai, particularly, continues to develop diversified non-oil sector activities including tourism, Internet and media services and real estate.

Saudi Arabia   **A11.27**

Less diversified, Saudi Arabia remains a major market for UK exporters, although travel to the market is severely inhibited by security issues.

Iran   **A11.28**

Despite ongoing US-inspired perceptions, Iran continues to be a much more open and desirable market. It has a strong, well-managed economy with a burgeoning private sector. The non–oil related sectors are benefiting from the emergence of a new, younger generation of well-educated entrepreneurs, who are geographically spread throughout the country. They are not generally party to the fundamentalist attitudes of the revolutionary period, and are responsible for a growing and active private sector. There are good opportunities for UK exporters in all sectors.

Central and Eastern Europe   **A11.29**

After a period of difficulty and uncertainty, Russia is now stabilising and new opportunities are being sustained in line with the growing experience of open market global trading. Caution is still the watchword for exporters. Russia is certainly not a suitable market for the novice exporter or investor.

The Czech Republic, Poland and Hungary, as part of their need to impress to support their EU entry, are progressively opening up their markets.

South and Central America   **A11.30**

The Argentinian 'melt down' has had its effect on Brazil and the other regional markets. In response, Brazil and the other emerging markets (Colombia, Chile) are looking to other markets, including Europe.

Brazil, since devaluation two to three years ago, has a growing economy, – the world's 8th largest. The UK's trade balance is in Brazil's favour. The UK's products are well accepted but we only hold 2.3% of their import market.

Chile offers considerable scope for UK exports, particularly in the building and transport infrastructure sectors through public-private partnerships.

Mexico, which is part of the NAFTA bloc, greatly fears the competitive challenge of the new WTO members, China and Taiwan. Mexico is an improving market for UK exports, particularly in view of reducing tariff protection.

North America   **A11.31**

As previously anticipated, during 2003 there was substantial growth in the US services sector and some upturn in the job market, reflecting increased yet cautious confidence in economic prospects. US import growth beat the world average for the third straight year but continued to rise faster than exports, further widening a worrying trade deficit in one of the world's major economies.

After-effects of 9/11 manifest themselves particularly with regard to security issues concerning the physical movement of goods, particularly to the USA. Having to deal with the regulatory aspects will tend to favour the regular exporter, and may be so stringent as to discourage the less committed. In pursuing opportunities in the USA, exporters need to recognise this aspect and the cost, both direct and as a result of lengthy delays for incorrect procedure, in what will certainly be a quite rigid regime.

Despite the optimism expressed above, it is conceivable that the weakness of the dollar, particularly against the yen and the euro, and the unpredictable, now increasing, price of oil could contribute to the possibility of a 'slower than expected' import growth in the USA.

India   A11.32

India has a fast-growing market economy, expansion of the service sector being the main contributor to growth. With a population exceeding 1 billion, India is already the UK's 10th largest export market, and the UK is India's 2nd largest trading partner. With a bulging foreign exchange reserve and increasingly liberalised attitudes to imports, India presents a further and wider range of opportunities for UK exporters.

India's growing international reputation for software development and business process outsourcing (callcentres) is well documented, and is contributing significantly to the rapid growth of an 'upwardly mobile' grouping with increased disposable income and an appetite for Western products.

South East Asia/Asia Pacific   A11.33

In one or two areas, the region is recovering from recession, although the weakness of the dollar, which is oft-quoted in pricing, has served to depress revenues in real terms.

Malaysia   A11.34

This country has a stable economic outlook and a vibrant business culture which creates attractive opportunities for UK exporters. Malaysia has coped with and has minimised the effect of the Asian financial crisis. Pro British sentiment is still strong and the 'Made in Britain' logo remains prestigious.

Australia   A11.35

Their economy is carrying a significant amount of momentum in the private consumption, housing and public spending sectors. It is expected that Australia will maintain this continued domestic economic growth.

Japan   A11.36

Recent surveys have raised optimism that an export-lead recovery will, crucially, benefit the weaker sectors of the economy, although a solid trend has yet to be established. In response to a recovering world economy, Japan's trade surplus surged on the back of mainly Asian demand. Exports are likely to continue growing faster than imports, but as a pro-British market, particularly for high-quality consumer and leisure equipment, it is recommended that UK exporters revive their interest in this market.

China   A11.37

China is now arguably the world's largest economy, and since joining the World Trade Organisation (WTO) has been irrepressible in its influence on international trade.

With its goal of quadrupling its gross domestic product by 2020, China's economy is modernising and continually expanding.

China's economy grew at its fastest pace for six years in 2003, adding 9.1% to gross domestic product. China's strong performance is due to growth in trade, foreign investment, and consumer spending.

Upon joining the WTO, China made significant, one-way market-opening concessions across virtually every economic sector, including increasing access to its markets for agriculture, services, technology, telecommunications and manu-factured goods. China also agreed to eliminate 'unseen' barriers, such as exclusive rights to import and distribute goods, and to cut major tariffs by 2005.

China will phase in more liberal trading rights over three years, and also open up sectors related to distribution services, such as repair and maintenance, warehous-ing, trucking and air courier services. This will allow exporters to export to, and to have their own distribution network in China, rather than being forced to set up factories there to sell products through Chinese partners.

China will participate in the Information Technology Agreement and will eliminate tariffs on products such as computers, semiconductors and related products by 2005. The IT industry will benefit hugely from a vast, expanding and information-hungry market.

Whilst much of the world's business sector is worried about the threat posed by China's rapid development, there is no doubt that the market, above all others, generally presents the major opportunity for many UK exporters.

Emerging markets   A11.38

The UK government is tending to move away from the idea of target markets, preferring instead a sectoral approach and support for businesses involved in products and services at the higher end of the 'value-added' chain. This policy tends to lessen SME support, particularly in overseas posts.

Emerging markets, other than those previously described, in which it is felt that opportunities exist for UK exporters, include:

- Brazil;

- Mexico;

- Colombia;

- Chile;

- Turkey;

- Hungary;

- Poland;

- The Czech Republic; and

- Romania

The Institute of Export   A11.39

The Institute of Export was established in 1935 by licence of the Board of Trade and was incorporated as a registered charity. A professional association for exporters, their main role is to train and educate those who are engaged in international trade. They achieve this by utilising multimedia technology and techniques alongside the more traditional methods for the delivery of skills training and knowledge. Topical global information and news on the Institute's activities is published in their own official bi-monthly membership magazine, *Exporting World*, which also carries in-depth practical articles on every imaginable aspect of international trade.

Student members are supported in their quest for the Institute's professional examinations which eventually confers upon them the right to use the suffix MIEx(Grad), an internationally respected and recognised professional qualification.

Run in parallel with these qualifications, the Institute offers its Short Course Training Programme – a web of half-to-four-day seminars – delivered by JETS (Joint Export Trading Standards) accredited trainers in convenient locations nationwide. This programme addresses the need for essential, up-to-date know-ledge and skills development requirements. It covers every aspect of international trade management; sales and marketing, logistics, documentary requirements and international trade finance, delivered in courses to suit all status levels.

The programme is regularly revised and offered in two half-yearly series. These Short Courses can also be delivered in-house and can be bespoke to suit individual company requirements.

As is now the case with most national organisations, the Institute has its own website which is regularly visited by people from all around the world. Traffic to the Discussion Forum is particularly heavy and has created a 'fount of all knowledge' style environment; it is currently open to non-members.

The Institute of Export has a diverse branch network and its members are encouraged to take an active part in their events and activities. This provides members with an unrivalled method of networking and of obtaining mutual advice and assistance.

There is a comprehensive range of membership grades ensuring that everyone involved with international trade will be at home with The Institute of Export.

The Institute of Export's address is: Export House, Minerva Business Park, Lynch Wood, Peterborough, Cambs PE2 6FT. Tel: 01733 404400; Fax: 01733 404444; E-mail: enquiries@export.org.uk; Internet: www.export.org.uk.

Export Clubs   A11.40

There are over 100 Export Clubs that meet regularly throughout the UK which help new and established exporters to carry out research, meet specialists and visit overseas markets.

In March 2004 the author of this chapter again interviewed Brian Trehearne, who is now not only the chairman of the very successful South London Export Club but in the process of launching and developing a number of Export Clubs within the London region.

The South London Export Club has arranged 13 trade missions covering the West Indies, Guyana, Poland, the Czech Republic and South Africa over a 5-year period with the support of the Croydon Corporation and the local Croydon Chamber of Commerce. Some 300 companies have participated in these visits and many millions of pounds worth of orders have been gained.

Brian Trehearne emphasised that the Tailored Market Information Reports which all mission members commission from our local Government Commercial Officers based in our Embassies and High Commissions abroad are absolutely essential when selling to a new market; these reports cost £600. In Brian's words, 'you hit the ground running'. The Commercial Officers can also arrange interviews with prospective buyers.

Brian Trehearne also confirmed that in the West Midlands all the Export Clubs have been brought together through a virtual website, based on a password; and through the South East Development Association, where 18 Export Clubs are in existence, a similar scheme of co-operation will be launched shortly.

He confirmed that since 2003 the conditions for overseas trade have changed. The rate of the pound against the US dollar has made selling, particularly in the West Indies, too expensive. Basically, finding the correct price for the product or service is essential. What many mission members are doing is to add extra value to their particular product, allowing them to sell it at a slightly higher margin. Innovation is now the word, whether it be in the manufacturing or service industry.

Market units   A11.41

The initial point of contact with UK Trade & Investment is still the Victoria Street, London W1 office, where a number of very helpful members of staff who really understand their markets are based – most visit the countries under their responsibility. These members of staff cover all countries where it is possible to export. General background information on a country's economy, market opportunities, basic facts on tariffs and export regulations can be obtained from UK Trade & Investment's website at www.uktradeinvest.gov.uk. If the website does not contain the information that you require, then further information and advice is available from the market unit staff. The switchboard operators at the DTI will be able to direct readers to a particular market unit. Tel: 0207 215 8000.

Editorial note. The author can confirm that there is a pilot scheme to locate some desk officers to posts overseas. There also appears to be yet another government reorganisation of the export promotion information services, and some export consultant staff may be relocated to Regional Development Agencies. Many changes are taking place with Business Link Offices, and care should be taken when using some of these franchise operations.

Exporters who wish to carry out individual research or elect a specialist to carry out this work should contact the UK Trade & Investment Information Centre (see **A11.15** above).

Checking the status of agents or distributors A11.42

With over 240 countries who may be persuaded to buy from the UK, it is never easy to decide whether to sell direct or through an agent or distributor. In some countries it is only possible to sell through an agent, therefore first check the country regulations. It is essential to check the agent's or distributor's reputation and to meet them before signing any agreement, as they may be trading with your competitors. They may also try to offer even longer credit and demand very high commission.

Through UK Trade & Investment the commercial officers of UK overseas posts may be able to identify agents and distributors and assess their potential. This is an extremely useful service which the author of this chapter would thoroughly recommend.

Export trade mission list and research   A11.43

The British Chambers of Commerce (BCC) issued their *Directory of Overseas Trade Missions in 2004–2005* in June 2004. This publication gives the dates and destinations of all trade missions organised by Chambers of Commerce, with contact names, full addresses and telephone numbers of the Chambers involved. The handbook is available free of charge, and also online at www.chamberonline.co.uk.

The BCC also run an 'Export Marketing Research Scheme' on behalf of UK Trade & Investment. This scheme is designed to help British companies undertake research prior to developing a market entry strategy. Companies with less than 500 employees are eligible and grants of up to £60,000 are available.

Further information can be obtained from: British Chambers of Commerce, 4 Westwood House, Westwood Business Park, Coventry CV4 8HS. Tel: 024 7669 4484.

Export documentation – understanding rules and regulations   A11.44

The object of an export transaction is to make a profit, but to do so both the principles and the fine detail of an export contract must be understood.

When reviewing an order, if the offer and acceptance is carried out too quickly, the exporter may not realise that the terms of the contract are unworkable. It can become exceptionally expensive if documents have to be amended as goods or services may be delayed, and the buyer may not purchase again or may just refuse to pay. For example, the instructions from the buyer may say that only one named national shipping line should be used. However, when checking the buyer's instructions for delivery, the date required cannot be met because the shipping line does not call at a defined port until later in the month. This type of problem often occurs when there are numerous clauses in a letter of credit (see **A11.61** below). There must be absolute proof that the goods or services have been supplied as per the buyer's or agent's requirements. A considerable number of documents are required to prove the export's origin and, depending on the terms of trade, who is responsible for transport and insurance. Again, the author would emphasise that the agreed payment terms and conditions must be clearly shown so that each party fully understands what their responsibilities are within the transaction. (See the *Incoterms 2000* and **A11.46** below.)

Week after week there are notifications from countries spread across the world that there are changes of customs duties, government documentation amendments, or sudden exchange control or shipping requirements. It is therefore essential to keep up-to-date on international documentation requirements. Again, help is at hand from many sources. Particularly recommended are publications by the International Chamber of Commerce, which was formed in 1919 by business leaders to try to get the world's economy moving and now has over 7000 members drawn from more than 130 countries, and SITPRO (Simplifying International Trade). (See **A11.49** below for details of their services to traders, also see **A12.34** and **A12.53** below.)

Documentation   A11.45

A major part of any export transaction is the precision of its documentation which is totally unlike the domestic despatch of an order. Within that documentation, terminology is used which may often confuse traders, as there are various shipping terms or delivery terms and there are also terms of payment which are internationally known by their initials.

Incoterms   A11.46

The International Chamber of Commerce (ICC) have issued *Incoterms 2000*, which specifies the obligations for delivering goods in international contracts. Incoterms are the standard terms which are known throughout the world by traders, shippers and bankers.

Incoterms 2000 was published in late 1999 and came into force on 1 January 2000. This revision takes into account the changing commercial environment.

One of the great advantages of using these terms is that the buyers and sellers can be sure of defining their responsibilities by simply looking at the guide. Under each shipping term the guide defines what the seller and buyer must do to complete the transaction.

The ICC confirm that their guide has been drafted to show traders when they have to provide various documents, such as:

- commercial invoices;

- documents needed for customs clearance; or

- documents in proof of delivery of the goods, as well as transport documents.

With the development of multimodal transport, faster air freight services and the increased use of the Channel Tunnel, goods can now move from border to border at great speed. It is therefore essential to know who has good title to the goods being exported. In Figure 2.00 below, the 13 shipping terms are listed in four categories. These different groups of shipping terms describe from what point in the transaction the sellers and buyers are required to pay the freight, insurance and other charges.

Figure 1.00 – Incoterms

Group E		
EXW	Ex Works——(named place)	The exporter places the goods at the disposal of the buyer. Carriage and insurance has to be arranged by the buyer. It should be noted that the seller is not responsible for the loading of goods onto the buyer's transport. The buyer has now to obtain the export and import licences and pay any costs.
Group F		
FCA	Free carrier in——(named place)	In this group the exporter arranges for the customs-cleared goods to be available to the buyer by arranging with the importer to transfer the goods to a carrier which has been nominated by the importer. If delivery occurs at the seller's premises, the seller is responsible for loading. If delivery occurs at any other place, the seller is not responsible. This new Combined Transport Incoterms replaces FOB (see below), where combined transport is used. When the buyer requires goods to be containerised or air freight is used, then FCA shipping terms are used. With the amount of multi-modal transport, the exporter and importer must highlight where the actual transfer of the goods takes place. When using FCA shipping terms it is far safer to add after FCA a named place.
FAS	Free alongside ship	Again, with the named port of shipment being noted after FAS, it makes it easier to distinguish that the importer is responsible for all the freight cost up to the point where the goods are loaded on to the ship. However, unlike in the previous terms, the seller is required to clear the goods for export. *(cont'd)*

FOB	Free on board	The exporter agrees to pay all the freight cost up to the point when the goods pass over the ship's rail at the named port of the shipment. The buyer has to pay all the freight and other cost including customs clearance and the transport cost in the importing country.

It should be noted that importers may not realise how many methods of moving goods there are in the UK. Exporters and importers should discuss with their agents and/or freight-forwarders all the implications of the delivery terms so that both parties can make a profit.

Group C		
CFR	Cost and freight to——(named port of distribution)	In this term the exporter agrees to pay all the costs and freight on the consignment to the named port of destination. Loss or damage to the goods after delivery are the buyer's responsibility.
CIF	Cost, insurance and freight	In this term the exporter agrees to include marine insurance in addition to being responsible for cost and freight to a named place of destination.
CPT	Carriage paid to——(named place of distribution)	In this term the exporter pays all the freight cost to the named place of destination.
CIP	Carriage and insurance paid to——(named place of distribution)	In this term the exporter, in addition, agrees to pay the insurance to the named place of destination.

With the above terms if any goods are damaged or delayed the exporter must check before the contract is signed, to see at what point responsibility moves from the exporter to the buyer.

Group D		
DAF	Delivered at frontier	Delivery at a named place (but the goods have been cleared for import).
DES	Delivered ex-ship	Delivery at port of destination.
DEQ	Delivered ex-quay	Delivery at a named port of destination.
DDU	Delivery duty unpaid	The seller delivers the goods to the buyer. They are not cleared for import. The buyer has to bear all costs and pay all charges. (Under the 1990 Incoterms the exporter was responsible for clearing the goods.)

DDP	Delivered duty paid	Delivery at a named place of destination. The seller delivers the goods, which have been cleared for import, to the buyer and bears all the costs. This is totally different from Ex Works terms where the buyer bears all the costs. It should be noted that if the exporter requires the buyer to bear all the cost of importing, the DDU terms should be used.
In the above group it may seem that the terms are self-explanatory as the exporter has to pay for the cost of carriage to the named port of destination. However, the greatest care has to be taken with all these terms where goods are being delivered to countries where there is corruption and where cargoes can vanish in the night.		

Example. The following example shows why it is essential to completely understand these terms. An exporter who was selling to the USA did not realise that the importer thought that the exporter was responsible for paying the freight to Houston. Whereas the exporter thought he was not responsible for paying any of the freight charges once the machinery was lifted from their premises in Liverpool. If on the original offer and acceptance documentation or on the *pro forma* invoice the shipping terms had stated 'EXW–Ex Works, Liverpool' then the importer would have realised that they had to pay the freight charge and take responsibility for the insurance from the exporter's premises in Liverpool. Ex Works basically means that the supplier makes the goods available to the buyer at the exporter's designated premises.

Who pays the freight cost? – a warning. In a perfect world it would be expected that if a buyer confirms that they would pay all freight charges then they would carry out their obligations. Regrettably, due to a number of countries, who have severe shortages of foreign exchange, shipping and freight forwarders are demanding that the transport charges are paid before the goods are accepted by the carrier. Research carried out in May 1999 confirms that shippers delivering goods to Russia and a number of countries in West Africa have special payment terms.

The author of this chapter warns exporters that the party responsible for the contract of carriage under the Incoterms should ensure that the carrier is instructed as to which of its charges are to be levied against the seller and which against the buyer to mirror (as best as the shipping line's tariff allows) the division of costs under the Incoterms.

It should be emphasised that if the terms of sale are agreed between the buyer and seller before the contract is made with the carrier, it may be discovered that the carrier has its own policy as to which charges must be prepaid and which they will concede to be collected. The latter is always at the discretion of the carrier. The carrier's concern is only the contract of carriage and not the contract of sale.

Exporters who feel that there may be difficulties should instruct a shipping agent who has worldwide experience. It may be necessary to check the status and experience of the importer's agent or representative in the UK (especially when the buyer is responsible for all freight costs), as this is sometimes where an export order comes to grief even before the shipment has been despatched.

In reviewing all these shipping terms, the key to remembering their importance is to understand from what point costs are incurred when the goods are transferred between buyer and seller.

On all orders, contracts or *pro forma* invoices, it should be noted that *Incoterms 2000* is being used. The author of this chapter would advise all exporters to read carefully all 13 items in the ICC's Guide as Figure 2.00 is an attempt to summarise 316 pages into a small chart.

ICC also publish a *Wall Chart* showing which parties bear the responsibility for costs of the carriage of goods. This is publication No. 614.

The full description of these shipping terms is published by the International Chamber of Commerce in their publication No. 560 called *Incoterms 2000*. Their *ICC Guide to Incoterms 2000* (No. 620) is a most useful training guide as the various shipping terms are illustrated in a pictorial form. Their *Guide to Export/Import Basics* (No. 543) will help any business to understand the financial, legal and transport aspects of international trade.

A new publication on combating '*Trade Finance Fraud*' ICC No. 643 was issued in December 2002. This study helps traders and financiers to recognise and interpret the many risks, and how they can protect themselves. The ICC's Commercial Crime Service combats all types of crime affecting business, from piracy on the high seas to fraud, counterfeiting and cybercrime.

ICC published a supplement to *Letters of Credit, Electronic Presentation* (UCP 500) (see also **A11.61** below) in January 2002. Among other key issues that eUCP addresses are:

- the format in which electronic records are to be presented;

- the consequences if a bank is open but its system is unable to receive an electronic record;

- how notice of refusal of an electronic record is to be handled;

- how original documents are to be defined in the electronic world; and

- what happens when an electronic record is corrupted by a virus or other defect.

It should be noted that within these new rules both a mixture of paper and electronic documents can be presented to a bank.

In 2003 ICC published *Fighting Corruption – a Corporate Practices Manual* and they also produced a series of booklets on the ICC Tools for E-business.

Information on their many publications can be obtained from: ICC United Kingdom, 12 Grosvenor Place, London SW1X 7HH. Tel: 0207 838 9363. Internet: www.ICCUK.net.

The correct documentation A11.47

There are a considerable number of documents required for any overseas transaction. For example, if the exporter despatches a *pro forma* invoice or order confirmation to the buyer, giving full details of the transaction, it will help the buyer to obtain foreign exchange, an import licence, or to raise a letter of credit, if required.

If the products have to be pre-inspected, the supplier should allow plenty of time for this administrative procedure. Pre-inspection is often used by importing countries who are exceptionally short of foreign exchange, and again the supplier should be aware that these rules can suddenly change with little notice.

Consular and legalised invoices may be required to be obtained and normally a certificate has to be issued by UK Chambers of Commerce before a consular invoice can be issued. Each document that has to be obtained is costly and it can take an immense amount of time as Embassies often work restricted hours and allowance should also be made for their national holidays.

It is vitally important to check that the correct number of invoices have been raised. Some countries require anything from six to ten copies. These copies may have to be personally signed by an authorised person and in many countries they will not accept facsimile signatures.

Certificates of origin are required especially if exporting to the Middle East. The Arab-British Chamber of Commerce is a particularly good source of information at: 6 Belgrave Square, London SW1X 8PH. Tel: 020 7235 4363.

Transport documentation A11.48

Various types of transportation documents are required for a number of different methods of shipment. However, again it is necessary to understand the difference between a bill of lading, which is also a document of title, and a sea waybill, which is not a negotiable instrument. An air waybill is also not a document of title, and regrettably if the contract states 'CAD' (cash against documents) and the freight costs have been paid by the importer, the consignment can often be released before payment has been made, so beware. (See **A11.58** below.)

Often the security offered by using different methods of transport will give greater protection to the exporter. For example, the road and the rail consignment notes are not documents of title and are not negotiable.

The multimodal transport document, or combined transport bill of lading, does give more security to the exporter as the carrier accepts the liability until the consignment has been delivered to the importer. However, the supplier should be certain to check the status and experience of the freight forwarder and the carrier, as there are many small operators in the UK and Europe.

In times of political instability the only way to gain extra security is to either nominate a secured warehouse, or instruct an inspection company or name a bank or agent to act as the consignee. However, other help is available to enable international traders to raise the correct documentation. (See **A11.54** below and **A12 RISK MITIGATION AND SECURITY FOR COMMERCIAL CREDIT TRANSACTIONS.**)

SITPRO (Simplifying International Trade)   A11.49

SITPRO was originally formed in 1970, and is now a company limited by guarantee. It is the UK's trade facilitation agency, sponsored by the Department of Trade and Industry and supported by British business.

Its aims are to use its unique status to improve the competitive position of the UK through:

- identification and removal of barriers in the international trade process;

- identifying and promoting best trading practices;

- delivery of practical, value for money trading solutions including the application of electronic commerce; and

- influencing future policy.

SITPRO offers independent advice and information through publications, *Briefings*, a free newsletter called *SITPRO News* and individual Country Spotlights. SITPRO can also help on developing an export business strategy as well as the day to problems associated with the cross–border movement of goods, the international payment cycle and export trade finance.

SITPRO *Briefings* are available free of charge, on the website.

Other services   A11.50

Over the years SITPRO has developed the UK Aligned Series of Export Documents. The aligned system, which is based on the UN Layout Key is a series of official and commercial documents used in international trade. The main feature of this system is that the same piece of information appears in the same place on every document where that piece of data is required.

However, whilst Electronic Data Interchange (EDI) and other electronic commerce techniques are becoming more and more frequently used, paper documents still form part of the international trade transaction.

SITPRO has developed WebElecTra which was launched in late 2001. The system allows the compatibility of paper documents and electronic ways of handling and transmitting data.

SITPRO's priority areas for 2004 will be the security requirements of international trade including all the additional requirements when selling to the USA, and the Trade Facilitation Agreement in the WTO. In the UK the Customs Blueprint Programme aimed at implementing fast-track trade and electronic transmission of data is also a development which SITPRO is studying.

The Helpdesk   A11.51

SITPRO also operates a free of charge Helpdesk, the telephone number is 020 7467 7280. The service is available from 9.30 to 16.30 Monday to Friday. Help can be given on specific procedural and documentation issues in international trade.

Further information on their other services can be obtained from SITPRO, Oxford House, 8th Floor, 76, Oxford Street, London, W1D 1BS. Tel: 020 7467 7280. Fax: 020 7467 7295.

Payment terms   A11.52

As a result of shortening world trade cycles with boom and bust economies and intense competition to gain orders, there are no standard rules that can be applied to selling overseas. Unless a business has a unique product or service which many buyers throughout the world require, it may be impossible to demand the shortest payment terms as there is always someone in the market place who will not only give longer payment terms but may also capture the market.

From an exporter's point of view, he must safeguard his cashflow and guarantee his profits. Therefore, he must have enough current credit information on the buyer to confirm that they have sufficient funds to pay for the proposed transaction. It is also important to establish, from credit reports or other information, that the buyer has in the past paid to terms the amount of the proposed transaction to an exporter. It is important to remember that unlike in the UK, it is often far more difficult to gain overseas business information, but the question must always be asked, is the buyer's business expanding, declining, or is it stable? (See **A3 GAINING INFORMATION TO SUPPORT CREDIT DECISIONS**.)

While considering any new market the exporter must also:

- check whether there are any restrictions on the release of foreign exchange;

- confirm whether exchange control authorisation is required; and

- research to confirm in which currency the sale should be invoiced.

Finally, if there are currency fluctuations, negotiations with the exporter's bank may be required for the buying forward of currency to protect the profit margin.

Research in March 2004 with members of the Institute of Credit Management confirmed that most businesses in the UK are now invoicing in the euro. There is an advantage in transacting in the euro in that it means a large reduction in bank charges as the majority of EU countries are now trading in the euro. There are now some indications that inter-country trading is increasing between a number of EU members.

Payment periods in Europe   A11.53

When the UK joined the European Union, an impression was given that there would be harmonisation in many areas of trade. There has been a slight improvement in paying accounts in a number of countries over the last seven years. However, there is still a vast difference in the average payment period between the Northern and Southern regions of Europe. An underwriter from Atradius confirmed that anyone supplying in the building, construction or textile trades will wait many more days than the average payment time for any particular European country. Figure 2.00 below shows the schedule of the average payment time for 19 European countries in the period 1993–2002; Figure 3.00 below shows payment period in average days, plus payment period for sales invoices over three time periods, for 26 countries worldwide (both tables by courtesy of Grant Thornton).

The EU Directive on Combating Late Payments in Commercial Transactions   A11.54

The EU Directive on *Combating Late Payment in Commercial Debts* has now been incorporated into the UK's *Late Payment of Commercial Debts (Interest) Act 1998*. In the UK apart from being able to charge the 8% interest plus the current rate of the Bank of England's base rate (as at April 2004 is 4%), a further compensation fee from £40 to £100 can be claimed by creditors for overdue debts which depends on its size.

It should be noted that each country in the EU seems to have a slightly different rule to enforce this Directive.

Figure 2.00 – European Business Survey 2002 – Average Payment Periods in Days – 9-Year Trend Data (source: Grant Thornton)

Country	1993	1994	1995	1996	1997	1998	1999	2000	2001	2002
Austria		44	43	44	38	39	34	30	33	31
Belgium		57	60	55	53	53	52	53	52	52
Finland			26	24	29	27	26	27	28	26

Country	1993	1994	1995	1996	1997	1998	1999	2000	2001	2002
Austria		44	43	44	38	39	34	30	33	31
France		70	66	65	65	63	58	60	56	58
Germany		42	42	38	38	34	35	30	30	31
Greece		73	78	82	85	77	87	90	88	83
Ireland		60	60	58	59	58	57	55	60	56
Italy		89	89	86	83	81	81	77	78	78
Luxembourg		69	60	52	56	56	50	45	49	47
Netherlands		49	50	46	45	41	44	40	44	43
Portugal		64	59	58	58	70	67	65	68	70
Spain		79	72	73	73	74	72	72	70	71
EU (Euro Zone)								54	54	52
Denmark		38	34	36	35	32	33	31	33	30
Sweden		39	38	36	36	36	37	34	36	36
United Kingdom		50	49	49	49	49	46	45	47	41
EU (Non-Euro Zone)								54	48	40
EU	65	66	64	62	62	59	55	54	52	50
Norway					33	33	31	30	30	30
Poland					31	40	41	45	49	
Switzerland			53	49	49	49	48	46	45	44
Turkey					47	48	52	54	58	51
Survey Average		65	62	61	61	57	55	54	51	50

Figure 3.00 – Payment periods for sales invoices (source: Grant Thornton)

Country	Average (days)	Under 30 days (%)	30–89 days (%)	Over 90 days (%)
Russia	20	74	15	4
Indonesia	27	65	31	2
Pakistan	33	49	39	6
Germany	36	44	53	3
Australia	37	36	61	1
New Zealand	37	32	63	1
Sweden	37	33	64	0
Poland	39	38	53	2

Country	Average (days)	Under 30 days (%)	30–89 days (%)	Over 90 days (%)
Russia	20	74	15	4
US	40	29	60	1
South Africa	42	26	64	4
Canada	43	25	73	2
India	43	33	52	7
Turkey	43	36	47	11
Mexico	44	31	60	8
Global average	*46*	*29*	*56*	*9*
UK	46	21	73	3
Netherlands	47	17	74	3
Philippines	47	34	48	15
Taiwan	52	28	53	16
France	57	21	63	15
Hong Kong	58	18	63	17
Ireland	59	8	77	9
Singapore	61	16	64	21
Japan	62	16	56	28
Greece	70	19	40	38
Spain	76	9	50	40
Italy	83	6	45	44

EU Invoicing Directive   A11.55

The EU *Invoicing Directive* came into force on 1 January 2004. There is a long list of new requirements which must be studied, but included in the regulations are the rules for electronic invoicing.

With ten new countries having joined the EU on 1 May 2004, it should be remembered that when invoicing it will be necessary to obtain the VAT registration number from those customers to comply with the rules for zero rating within the EU.

Full details of the regulations can be obtained from Customs & Excise.

Payment methods

When a business decides in principle to sell to a new market or buyer, the decision still has to be made as to which payment methods will be used and the agreement of the buyer gained before any goods or services are despatched. This action can only be taken when there is up-to-date knowledge of the buyer's background and their country's economy has been studied. The exporter must be confident that, whatever payment method is chosen to reflect the risk, the buyer can and will pay.

Within the last two years there has been a gradual change in the methods of payment due to the collapse of banking systems in Russia. However, the Russian economy is now strengthening, although there are still payment problems when dealing with Russia. There are still some concerns in South East Asia, some countries in Latin America and Eastern Europe where the economies are weak. Previously more transactions were on open account and documentary collections, but recently there have been indications that as these markets are opening again, buyers are demanding even longer credit. To protect their risk, UK companies are therefore demanding more security by gaining their buyer's agreement to raise letters of credit and other less risky forms of payment.

Payment methods and levels of risk

The following are the most common forms of payment along with the level of risk they represent:

- open terms – highest risk;
- cash against documents – medium to high risk;
- documentary collections – medium risks;
- unconfirmed irrevocable letters of credit – some risk;
- letters of credit – some risk;
- confirmed letters of credit (CILC) – no risk;
- cash against order – low risk;
- cash before order – no risk.

(For notes on the main differences in using the above payment methods, see **A11.58–A11.62** below.)

Open terms

Open terms is the easiest and riskiest payment method, as apart from the invoice and statement of account, there is little extra payment documentation to be raised and low bank charges. However, on agreeing these terms there must be confirmation that there are no exchange control regulations in the country importing the goods and there must be absolute trust by the exporter that the payment will be sent by the due date. Often open terms are offered, after a period of successful trading, when the history on the sales ledger shows prompt payment when either letters of credit or documentary collections were previously used. Open terms can also save the buyer considerable bank charges and this can be used as a bargaining tool if the buyer also demands a longer credit period.

Beware, it is a buyer's market and buyers all over the world are demanding open terms. This can be a real risk to anticipated profits.

Cash against documents   A11.59

This method of payment is widely used throughout the world when the export documentation is consigned to the importer's bank with exact instructions that the documentation must not be released by the bank to the importer or their agent until payment has been made. This system is extensively used in Europe as the costs are far less than when raising letters of credit. Before considering cash against documents transactions, there must be absolute confidence in the bank's ability not to release the documents until the buyer has paid the amount due to the exporter.

There can be numerous problems if there are any discrepancies in the documentation. Buyers can, and often do, demand the release of the documents, thus leaving the exporter with little or no control.

Documentary collections   A11.60

With this method, both the exporter's and importer's banks are used to transfer the documents which include a bill of exchange. In some countries there are heavy stamp duties on bills of exchange, so sometimes there may be a reluctance by the buyer to accept these terms. Documentary collections can be paid at sight or at an agreed future date, and once the buyer signs a bill of exchange there is a greater chance that they will honour the agreement, but it is not a guarantee of payment. (See **A12.44–A12.47** below.)

Letter of credit   A11.61

This is a far stronger form of payment as the bank will pay the credit provided that there are no discrepancies in the documentation. The confirmed letter of credit is the strongest form of payment as a second bank adds their guarantee. However, there are additional costs which sometimes can be split between buyer and seller.

Care should be taken with irrevocable letters of credit, as payment is often only made when the importer's bank has funds available. With this type of credit it may be necessary to check out the status of the bank. (See **A12.49–A12.57** below.)

Standby letter of credits originated in the USA as in a number of States banks were not allowed to issue guarantees. Standby letters of credit have become more commonly used in Europe and other parts of the world.

Standby letters of credit should not be confused with letters of credit. A standby credit is really used in international trade as a substitute for a guarantee.

For further information on the way the documentation interacts with the payment terms, HSBC Trade Services publish *International Trade* and *Documentary Credits*. Barclays Bank also publish *Documentary Letters of Credit*, a booklet which describes the workings of letters of credit and the documentation that may be required in relation to UCP 500, being the ICC rules.

The ICC under their publication 590 have issued rules covering standby letters of credit, and within Citibank's 122 page booklet on *An Introduction to Letters of Credit* there are some first class illustrations on various types of standby credits.

Cash against order or before order   A11.62

If little is known about the buyer the following payment methods may be the safest way of trading:

- cash against order;
- cash before order; or
- part deposit

can be used. Where countries have severe currency shortages they may impose exchange control restrictions, therefore payment before shipment may not be possible. Exporters must always check the regulations with their bankers.

Successful transactions   A11.63

This chapter highlighted the number of segments of an export transaction that have to be considered so that a profit can be made, these include:

- thorough research;
- the development of a product or service that the overseas buyer desires;
- ensuring that the buyer, agents and distributors are advised when shipments are arriving; and
- constant communication with the buyer, agents and distributors.

First class communication can save and increase orders. Provided that exporters have the time to read and research, there are opportunities day by day to sell UK goods and services throughout the world.

A12

Risk Mitigation and Security for Commercial Credit Transactions

Introduction A12.1

The ability of a company to grant credit to its customers is fundamental to its ability to continue trading. If it cannot grant credit when its competitors can, it will more often than not lose that order to the competition. It therefore behoves the company to seek ways to mitigate unacceptable credit risks in such a way as to enable it to win the order.

There are several ways in which the seller can arrange to reduce all or part of the risk of the customer failing to pay. Some measures, such as third-party guarantees or forfeited bills of exchange, require the cooperation of the customer. Others, such as credit insurance and confidential invoice discounting, can be arranged without the customer's knowledge. Indeed, most credit insurance policies specifically forbid the seller from letting customers know of the cover in case of abuse. There is usually a cost impact involved in reducing credit risk because the third party may require recompense for taking the risk of loss instead of the seller. (This is not always the case, as in some circumstances selling down to a third party may be less expensive overall.) There is also the less measurable cost of administration, since some human effort is required to set up a security and then monitor it. This time and cost element and the belief of some sellers that customers will be upset by being thought risky, leads to many high-risk transactions going ahead without adequate security.

This chapter looks at ways of mitigating the credit risk to suit differing commercial trading situations, both in domestic trade and in cross-border business, including:

- credit insurance;
- third-party payment guarantees;
- reservation of title;
- bills of exchange;
- letters of credit;

- forfeiting;

- factoring;

- offset agreements;

- bonds for bids, performance and retentions;

- stakeholder accounts; and

- special payment terms.

Credit insurance

The facility and its purpose   A12.2

Credit insurance is an insurance product like any other, where, in exchange for a premium, a company can protect itself against loss. It is concerned mainly with the non-payment of sales revenue, which can be due to many events, not just the more obvious one of customer insolvency. It is surprising that, since the trade debtors asset is usually the largest on a balance sheet, only a minority of companies purchase this form of security, believing that they are better off self-insuring using their own bad-debt provision.

Normally, slightly different policies are sold for domestic and export sales. In fact these days, the domestic market is treated as not just the UK but the European Union as well, which in May 2004 increased in size to include ten new countries in the Mediterranean and Central Europe. The features of cover are more varied for foreign trade, to meet the complex conditions found in selling to a mix of up to 200 independent markets. As with any insurance product, there are several providers to choose from and the premiums and degree of cover vary from provider to provider. A seller with excellent credit control systems in place should be able to obtain a lower premium rate than one who takes every available order, regardless of risk. In fact, those who take everything regardless of risk may find the insurance market is unwilling to cover them.

The origins and development of credit insurance   A12.3

The two principal bodies in the UK were traditionally the Trade Indemnity Company (TI), who were formed in 1918 to insure domestic trade, and the Export Credits Guarantee Department (ECGD), who have insured exports since 1919.

The 1980s brought major changes to the credit insurance market when:

- competitive forms of secured financing were being promoted by specialist banks; and

- monopolies in credit insurance underwriting were being removed across western Europe.

Previously, only national credit insurance companies could insure sales from their own country, as a way of supporting its export effort. It had been the view that political risk losses, especially the non-transfer of hard currency from weak markets, could be so massive that only governments could carry the burden. The UK Government's provider was ECGD, the industry's world leader and a benchmark for other governments.

The 1990s freedom of trade encouraged the creation of several new insurers as well as mergers of some existing ones. Some 95% of UK exports are on short terms up to 180 days and this high-volume part of ECGD was sold to NCM, a Dutch company in September 1991. As a UK Government department, ECGD has retained responsibility for insuring capital goods exports and their related financing. TI is now owned by the German group Euler Hermes (for more information on Euler Hermes, see **A12.9** below).

In 2001 NCM itself was acquired by Gerling Namur to form a group which is now known as Atradius. A number of other insurers are also now active in the market.

Credit insurance for domestic trade   A12.4

A company supplying trade customers in the UK and EU runs two main credit risks, normally referred to as 'commercial' risk:

- that a customer becomes insolvent before paying (insolvency cover); and

- a customer who is still trading does not pay for goods or services properly supplied, despite requests for payment over many weeks (protracted default).

Credit insurance may be arranged, whereby a rate of premium is set by the insurer for either the seller's whole turnover or specifically agreed buyers (although certain safe sales, such as cash in advance and confirmed letters of credit, can be excluded).

Some insurers set credit limits and payment terms for every customer. These are known as 'with limits' policies. To reduce administration for small low value buyers, a 'discretionary credit limit' on each policy is allowed. Up to this value, the supplier can decide his own credit limit on any account without reference to the insurance company, as long as it holds references or credit reports vouching for that figure. Such evidence would be needed for any subsequent claim. As any new customer comes along, or sales to an existing account take it over its established credit limit, a request is made to the insurer for an insured credit limit. The seller may, of course sell higher than the insured limit but claims would be limited to that level. Each month or quarter, the supplier declares his total sales for the period and pays the appropriate premium. He also completes an early warning report of any debts overdue by three months and shows the action taken to collect. At that point, under the conditions of the policy, the underwriter is entitled to specify collection action, such as to sue the customer or to join in talks with other suppliers. When a customer begins to default with one supplier, there are usually others suffering as well. The insurer usually has a better overall view than a single supplier. When the insurer's instructions to collect involve expenses, such as legal fees or collection agency fees, these are borne by the insurer in the proportion of the claim settlement. For example, if the level of cover is 85% of loss, the insurer would pay the first 85% of the relevant collection costs, the supplier bearing the other 15%. If such legal action were to prove a valid claim in the event of a dispute, in those circumstances, the seller would pay.

When insolvency occurs, e.g. an administrator or a liquidator is appointed (see **B10 INSOLVENCY**), the insured supplier must obtain written confirmation of the appointment, and confirmation of the debt and can then make an immediate claim. Claims are normally settled promptly. When a claim is paid, two things must be remembered:

- the debt is subrogated to the insurance company, so they are quite entitled to take whatever action they think fit against the defaulting customer; and

- if there is a subsequent salvage recovery, such as a dividend from a liquidator, it must be repaid to the insurer in the proportion of the original claim settlement, e.g. 90%, and not fully retained by the supplier.

It is often the case that claims are made for payment default while a debt is disputed, for example for shortages or defects. The position is that any commercial dispute must be settled and a claim only made when the debtor still does not pay after that.

Cover is rarely for 100% of any loss. It is normally for between 80% and 90%. The principle is shared liability, so that the supplier retains a strong interest in getting debts paid, especially if his own net margin is less than, for example, the 10% self-retention.

Some insurance companies now offer a form of credit insurance policy whereby it relies on the expertise of the seller's own credit management processes, including credit analysis and limit setting and collection process. The insurer effectively underwrites the seller's credit policy and process. Providing that policy and process is followed, in the event of any claim, the insurer will pay.

Another form of policy, which is appropriate for the more sophisticated organisation, is the 'excess of loss' policy. Here the seller is happy to cover a significant level of loss itself but above that level, it would prefer to protect itself against a major or series of smaller losses in one year. For example, ABC plc is happy to cover the first £100,000 of bad debt loss in any one year, but above that it wants to protect its interest. It arranges an excess of loss policy for £500,000 over the first £100,000. This means that if the total losses in the year where over £100,000 the policy would pay out. If the losses exceeded £600,000, (£100,000 uninsured plus £500,000 excess layer,) the company would cover those itself. As the seller is taking a significant loss before any claim is paid, premium levels are typically much lower than in a traditional whole turnover policy. Furthermore, within the excess layer, the indemnity level (the percentage insured) is often 100%.

There are also a number of insurers who will cover single buyers but as they are not benefiting from a spread of risks over a number of buyers, premium rates are higher. These policies normally cover only insolvency, rather than insolvency and protracted default.

There is also a form of cover referred to as 'top buyer' cover, which covers the seller against a catastrophic loss caused by the default or insolvency of one or more of its major buyers. This takes account of the 80/20 rule, in which 20% of most companies' customers account for 80% of its turnover. Therefore, any failure to pay will have a significantly greater impact on the seller's business than one of the other 80% of customers. Many companies use this to cover their top 10 or 20 customers, which, as they tend to be bigger more creditworthy companies, may result in lower premium cost.

Credit insurance for short-term exports   A12.5

A number of different insurers provide cover against either the political risks and/or commercial risks involved in selling overseas.

Atradius credit insurance   A12.6

The basic Atradius export policy is their 'International Policy', designed for all types of exporters who sell on short-term credit. It suits companies with ordinary sales to a variety of markets, as well as those who need to protect high value transactions. A standard low premium rate is applied for all markets on a total turnover basis, but policies can also be tailored to suit particular selections of markets and buyers. Cover normally starts from invoice but can be from the date of contract for specialised goods, which could not easily be re-sold if the contract went wrong. There is a small extra premium for this pre-credit risk contract cover.

The standard range of insurable risks included in the International Policy is divided between customer and governmental events, as follows.

- Buyer (or, commercial) risks, include:

  o   the insolvency of the buyer,

  o   the buyer's failure to pay within six months from the due date for goods accepted, or

  o   the buyer's failure to accept goods despatched which comply with the contract.

- Country (or, political) risks, include:

  o   delays in transferring hard currency from the buyer's country,

  o   any action of the government of the foreign country which wholly or partly prevents performance of the contract,

  o   political events or economic, legislative or administrative measures occurring outside the UK which prevent or delay transfer of payment,

  o   war, civil war and the like, outside the UK (other than war between the five major powers i.e. USA, UK, China, Russia and France) preventing performance of the contract,

  o   cancellation or non-renewal of an export licence or the imposition of new restrictions on exports after the date of the contract, or

  o   for public buyers, the failure or refusal to fulfil any of the terms of the contract.

Cover is normally for 90% of the amount lost for commercial risks and up to 95% for political risks. Claims are paid at different times, depending on the cause of loss:

- insolvency – immediately on proof;

- political risks – in OECD countries, four months after loss;

- political risks – outside of North America, Australasia, and the European Union, the period can be much longer and 180, 270 or even 360 days may be included in the policy for those countries;

- protracted default – six months after due date, (unless an extended claims waiting period applies).

A schedule is issued with each policy to show, market by market, various limitations on cover and different claim waiting periods, according to current market experience.

Other policies are available to cover:

- services rather than goods;

- royalties on licensing and franchising;

- sales through overseas subsidiaries; and

- goods sold from stock held overseas.

Cover is available for exports in hard currencies other than Sterling.

Premium is calculated each year based on export turnover and administrative expense, with the addition of a flat-rate monthly premium on the value of exports declared. For a few high-risk markets, an additional premium is levied to recognise the existing high risk of loss.

Although the vast majority of exports are on terms less than 180 days (a standard recognised by most foreign governments), sales on longer terms may be covered by an 'Extended Risk Endorsement'.

Lloyd's of London   A12.7

Lloyd's is not a company but a place in the City of London where many insurance syndicates operate. A few of those write policies for credit risks. Lloyd's are less well-known than other providers because for many years they did not cover commercial credit risks in addition to their existing range of political/governmental credit risks. Now a number of syndicates offer commercial as well as political risk cover. Lloyds is one market where specific risk or single buyer risk insurance is available, rather than on a whole turnover basis. These are usually on much more stringent conditions, but do offer a good tool to credit managers where the sale is deemed attractive, but the risk either too great or too concentrated.

Risks such as import/export embargoes, non-transfer of monies, war, and default by government buyers can be covered. The indemnity is usually 90% but premium rates, claims waiting periods and the precise nature of the policies issued are very much the subject of individual discussion to reflect the exporter's particular needs.

The separate import and export parts of counter-trade deals can be covered, usually with a linked contract for both parts.

Pure barter, the exchange of goods for goods, is fairly rare in that it is very difficult for the parties to agree a common value in hard currency, and to pin-point agreed delivery dates from unstable markets. Insurance cover for these transactions at Lloyd's normally requires the less creditworthy country to supply first. Barter cover is usually for loss of profits or for extra costs due to non-delivery or non-acceptance resulting from governmental actions.

Overseas investments can be covered at Lloyd's, with indemnity up to 100% and cover for three years, extendable annually where experience so far has been good.

Contingency cover is available for a wide variety of specific events in connection with an exporter's overseas contracting, including kidnap and ransom, cancellation of exhibitions, product extortion, etc.

Lloyd's reputation has been second to none for its policy precision and thoroughness, however some concern has been expressed over the market's solvency due to a number of large claims and catastrophic events in the recent past. The rating agencies still view Lloyds as an investment grade insurer, and their reserves appear sufficient to meet their liabilities. In addition, Lloyds has taken actions to ensure the central fund is sufficient to meet any potential liability.

To save everyone's time, Lloyd's underwriters will only deal with specialist brokers, who prepare proposals in the way the underwriter needs, and does not directly deal with traders.

AIG Europe (UK) Ltd (AIG)   A12.8

This American owned underwriter also offers the exporter protection against losses from political events, either for specific cases or for total turnover or an acceptable spread of markets. In effect, AIG underwrites the seller's own credit management process, rather than providing a limit writing service provided by the traditional whole turnover underwriters. However AIG does have an online limit approval process if required.

Multi-sourced contracts can be included and the risks insured parallel those covered through Lloyd's. The indemnity is usually 90% and premium rates, claim waiting periods, etc. reflect the individual requirements of the exporter. Insurance for risks in barter and counter-trade arrangements, overseas investments and other contingencies are available, although they are sometimes conditional.

AIG caters for the larger sophisticated exporter who wishes to select cover from:

- insolvency only;

- insolvency and default;

- insolvency and import/export licence cancellation;

- political risk insurance for export transactions;

- comprehensive export credit insurance;

- annual excess of loss.

The 'insolvency-only cover' applies in countries where buyers would not be in default for long without one of its creditors pressing for insolvency, e.g. in North America, Australasia and Western Europe. Much reliance is placed on the seller's own credit control efficiency, and a large minimum insured turnover is normally required.

AIG's 'comprehensive export credit insurance' covers a wide spread of markets and takes into account the policyholder's credit control procedures by allowing a high discretionary credit limit per account.

The 'excess of loss cover' particularly suits exporters with good credit management which only wish to be protected against unacceptably high losses. While this form of cover may be cheaper and protects the balance sheet, it provides little day-to-day contact between policyholder and underwriter.

Just as with Atradius (see **A12.6** above), policy-holders with AIG have not only insurance cover to replace cash flow losses, but also ready access to a vast database of credit information, sources of debt collection services and highly topical dialogue with experienced underwriters and brokers.

Euler Hermes   A12.9

Euler Hermes is a large insurer of UK domestic receivables and also covers exporters against both the risks of insolvency and protracted default in overseas markets and political causes of loss. It is considered to be a very flexible underwriter for exports, agreeing cover in some cases for longer terms of payment than usual. Like AIG (see **A12.8** above), they will take into account the particular merits of a transaction and an exporter's expertise in the territory.

Euler Hermes is part of the Allianz Insurance Group which has recently been rebranded worldwide to incorporate both arms of the business Euler and Hermes. Hermes no longer writes credit insurance *per se* in the UK.

Coface UK Ltd   A12.10

Coface is the French Export Credit Agency. It was established in the UK in 1993, taking over the business of London Bridge Finance. Whilst its usual products are whole turnover based, it will consider more limited risks in certain circumstances.

Coface has two valuable networks. The first, its information alliance, Infoalliance, spans most of the world. This is the backbone of its credit limit writing service. Using this local information, Coface has also developed its '@rating' through which it is possible to obtain ratings (of the likelihood of insolvency) of companies and also economic reports on countries. Coface's other network is its alliance of credit insurers around the world – the Globalliance. Through this alliance, a multinational company can, with a single policy wording world wide, negotiate protection for each of its local operations. This solution is particularly suitable for a company with sales offices world wide that sell mostly to the local market.

Coface has a specialist political risk underwriter 'Unistrat' which has a reputation for writing good risks in difficult political markets. It places great weight on the skill and expertise of the exporter, and on the reasoning behind the structure of particular contracts and projects.

Other insurers   A12.11

There are a number of players in the credit insurance market including the following:

- Ace Europe;

- De Montfort Insurance Company plc;

- Exporters Insurance Company (TUA);

- Amlin (Lloyd's of London);

- CIFS (Lloyd's of London);

- QBE;

- Royal & SunAlliance;

- Zurich;

- various Lloyd's syndicates (the various syndicates at Lloyd's are actually separate legal entities in the same way as Coface and EULER are).

In addition, some of the banks and factoring companies offer credit protection, through 'without recourse' factoring which provides finance on invoice as well as protection against credit risk loss (but not political risk), ECGD and credit insurance for capital goods on medium terms and longer.

ECGD and credit insurance for capital goods on medium terms and longer   A12.12

After NCM acquired its short-term business, ECGD continued to cover the 'long and large', referring to terms of payment between two years and seven years, or longer in a few cases, involving capital or quasi-capital goods.

Buyer credits   A12.13

Policies for buyer credits are individually produced to protect loans arranged by banks to support high-value contracts for UK capital goods and/or services. Typically, a UK bank will make a loan to an overseas buyer (or more usually to its bank), to fund purchases from a UK supplier, where there is a major sales contract, usually heavy with pre-conditions, and a matching bank loan agreement. Once the contract is effective, the exporter is paid from the loan soon after each shipment. ECGD issues a buyer credit guarantee to the UK bank against non-repayment of the loan. There is also a recourse agreement between ECGD and the exporter to allow ECGD to recover any claim monies paid to the bank if the overseas loan default was due to the exporter's non-performance under the sales contract. As a result of contract and loan complexities, qualifying sales contracts must usually exceed £5 million.

Lines of credit   A12.14

These operate similarly to buyer credits, except that one line will fund a number of contracts, often of small values. Lines of credit may be:

- general, popularly called shopping basket loans, to finance a number of UK sales to a variety of buyers in the market to which the bank lends the money; or

- project line, which finances sales by various suppliers into a specific project.

Supplier credit financing facility
A12.15

This is an ECGD policy for 100% cover to banks who fund medium-term credit transactions, normally by purchasing bills of exchange drawn by exporters and accepted by their foreign buyers. The important security for the exporter is that there is no recourse on them for funds received from the bank. Normally there must be a trade credit period of two years and a 15% down payment by the buyer before shipment.

Supplier insurance policy
A12.16

Whereas the financing policy discussed at **A12.12** above, covers the bank, the exporter may wish to have separate cover for costs and expenses in the pre-finance period, i.e. after the contract is signed but before the bank finance comes on stream. The exporter may also cover war for the contractual down-payment.

Specific guarantee
A12.17

As the name suggests, ECGD may cover an exporter against particular named risks on a capital goods contract, such as any segment not being financed by the bank, or a pre-finance period event. It can apply to services or to construction works.

Bond risk cover
A12.18

Where an exporter is insured for the sales contract, ECGD will, for an extra premium, provide cover against the unfair calling of tender or performance bonds by the buyer or his government, where it can be shown that the exporter has performed properly under the contract. This security can be assigned to the exporter's bank which may otherwise be reluctant to write the original bond.

Overseas investment insurance facility
A12.19

UK companies can obtain cover for long-term equity and loan investments made overseas, where a risk is perceived of expropriation, war or restrictions on remittances.

Tender to contract cover/forward exchange supplement
A12.20

Exporters can be covered against the risk of exchange rate loss during the tendering process for major contracts, allowing them to commit to firm currency prices. However given the relative cost, this is not normally an option taken by many exporters.

Specialist credit insurance brokers   A12.21

Compared to pre-1980, there are now a growing number of providers of credit insurance. It is therefore advisable to use a specialist broker to help find the most suitable cover. There are only a handful of broking firms that specialise in this field. They know the topical marketplace and are expert in negotiating cover with underwriters, getting claims paid faster and re-negotiating cover at the renewal date. Since the insurance companies pay their commission, it makes sense for a seller to nominate a broker instead of going it alone. One of the main services of a specialist broker is to do the research on behalf of a potential client and to find the right kind of cover at the right price. Any company about to obtain credit insurance protection should expect a broker to get at least two quotations and explain their key features. Similarly, as renewal dates approach, policyholders should require their brokers to obtain the best alternative quotations for them.

These days, with credit insurers reluctant or unable to give the level of limits many companies require, engaging a broker can work favourably, to the extent that they can better negotiate higher limits than the company may be able to do itself.

Third-party payment guarantees   A12.22

A third-party payment guarantee gives its beneficiary access to, or up to, a sum of money if the debtor fails to pay at the agreed contractual date. Trade debts can be made more secure if the seller obtains a suitably worded written guarantee from a creditworthy third party who undertakes to be legally liable for another's debt. The entities most usually called upon for such guarantees are:

- banks or other financial institutions including insurance companies;

- parent companies of the debtor businesses;

- other companies, associated or not with the debtor businesses; and

- directors of the debtor businesses or other private individuals.

As a general principle, the guarantees of limited companies may be preferable to those of individuals, since the wealth of individuals can be difficult to check and it is not possible to verify how many other guarantees have been issued by an individual, or their total value. The net worth of a business can readily be seen from its audited accounts and any existing guarantees given by a company should be visible as contingent liabilities in the notes to the accounts.

Individuals who are sole traders or partners are personally liable for their business debts, so there is no point in requesting their personal guarantees, unless this can be tied into a charge over property. With limited liability companies, since directors are not responsible for the debts of their businesses, it may be tempting to involve their liability by obtaining their personal guarantees, especially when they are known to be wealthy people in their own right. However, such guarantees have the defect mentioned above, of being difficult to verify as to their inherent worth. In case there are good reasons for believing that a director's guarantee is worth obtaining, Figure 1.00 below provides a suitable wording which has proved successful in past cases. Again tying this into a charge over their personal assets does seriously enhance the security value.

Guarantees from parent companies   A12.23

Contrary to popular belief, parent companies and group holding companies are not automatically liable for their subsidiaries' debts in the UK. (This is not necessarily the case in other countries, where parent companies may be responsible for subsidiaries under consolidation rules.) Often sellers do not realise that the debtor company, although a subsidiary of a rich group, is a limited liability company in its own right. In the heady insolvency days of the 1980s and 1990s, there were several cases of rich groups allowing ailing subsidiaries to go to the wall, leaving many unpaid creditors feeling shocked and poorer. When a supplier believes that a parent company guarantee is necessary, the group's chief financial officer should be approached. If the group wishes its subsidiary to succeed, yet recognises it has a poor credit reputation, it may well issue its guarantee of payment. Often, such a request is refused. An initial refusal may, however, be a test of a supplier's willingness to do business without a guarantee, so a firmer request, making the supply position quite clear, often achieves a positive response.

Figure 1.00 – The wording of a suitable third-party payment guarantee from a parent company

(To the supplying company)

Dear Sirs

We confirm that we are the parent company of _____ Ltd which has applied to you for a credit account, for estimated supplies of £___ per month.

In consideration of your willingness to supply _____ Ltd we hereby guarantee all their liabilities to yourselves and undertake to indemnify, upon demand without set-off or deduction, for any losses, claims, damages, costs or any form of indebtedness which may arise.

This guarantee is a continuing security and primary obligation which shall not be affected by any waiver, release or indulgence allowed to _____ Ltd.

Yours faithfully

Figure 1.00 gives an example of a letter of guarantee from a parent company for supplies to its subsidiary.

Figure 2.00 – Suitable wording for a letter of guarantee from a director of a debtor company

(To the supplying company)

Dear Sirs

I confirm that I am a director of _____ Ltd and that in consideration of your continuing to supply them I hereby guarantee all liabilities of _____ Ltd to yourselves howsoever arising and I undertake to indemnify you immediately on first demand without set-off or deduction in respect of all losses, claims, damages, costs and any other indebtedness which may arise.

This guarantee is a continuing security and primary obligation which shall not be affected by any waiver, release or indulgence allowed to _____ Ltd.

Yours faithfully

Letters of comfort A12.24

When refusing a payment guarantee, some group headquarters offer a 'letter of comfort' instead. Such comfort letters are meant to reassure a supplier that there is no risk of not being paid by the subsidiary. Comfort letters usually confirm the shareholding, state that there is no intention of disposing of the subsidiary and reassure the supplier that the customer is able to pay the amounts involved for the envisaged purchases. From a well-known and powerful quoted plc such a letter may be considered to be adequate backing for a debtor. However, the letter is not a guarantee. If it were, it would say so. It is not enforceable in law and should be rejected. Where there have been successful court actions to uphold suppliers' claims that comfort letters were a powerful reassurance and that the issuers should settle the debt, these were overturned on appeal on the simple basis that the letters were not actually guarantees.

Whilst the letter of comfort has no real legal strength in the UK, outside of the UK, in Germany for example, letters of comfort may have much stronger legal standing, and may in some cases amount to an enforceable guarantee.

Guarantee from a bank A12.25

Banks sometimes issue payment guarantees to suppliers when debtors are considered to be worth supporting, or where they hold other security such as cash deposits.

The guarantee takes the form of either a bank guarantee or a standby letter of credit (see **A12.26** below).

Any guarantee that is supporting a credit facility needs to be as unconditional as possible for the beneficiary, to ensure the asset or credit is as protected as possible.

The best form of bank guarantees are those payable 'on demand' and 'on first call', preferably without any prior conditions, 'unconditional'. These are the guarantees a prudent lender or exporter would wish to be in receipt of.

Standby letters of credit   A12.26

Standby letters of credit are more common in the USA, as guarantees are an anathema to US banking regulations. Standby letters of credit also have the unfortunate facet of being conditional. They are similar to normal letters of credit inasmuch as they have documentary requirements against which a bank is obliged to make a payment, but are 'standby' in nature as they are normally only called on when a default has occurred. They are useful to support open account trading where otherwise a letter of credit or deposit would be required.

Surety bonds   A12.27

A further type of security, similar to the bank guarantee, is the insurance-based 'surety bond'. These are more popular in the USA due to the idiosyncrasies of the banking regulations related to bonds and guarantees, and tend to be highly conditional in nature. Many require an arbitration award or court judgment to be in the beneficiary's favour before the beneficiary may call on the surety to pay. In addition, they may require the explicit support of the buyer's owners, be they individuals or companies. However, they do protect against the insolvency of the buyer or default against certain types of contract performance. They have the further complication that they are not well understood outside the USA, so are often not as acceptable to the beneficiary as an on-demand bank guarantee, especially in the developing world and to banks who have a very rational fear of get-out clauses.

Guarantees must be in writing   A12.28

Payment guarantees are an exception to the rule under English law that a contract may be oral. They must not only be in writing but must be self-explanatory and set out the guarantor's obligations precisely. Sample wordings for guarantees can be obtained from solicitors, credit insurance companies and various publications on credit risk management. The key elements are that:

- there must be a 'consideration' involved, the most obvious one being the supplier's willingness to continue the supply of goods or services to the customer;

- the guarantee is for unlimited amounts and has no expiry date, this is the optimal position, but it may suit a supplier to accept a maximum liability and an expiry date which is enough for the intended deliveries;

- the non-negotiable obligation is to pay the supplier under the guarantee on first demand, i.e. not after a prescribed delay or set of actions;

- the liability must be met without any offset or deduction, even if the supplier is separately a debtor to the customer or guarantor; and

- the guarantee is a continuing security, to apply even after the customer's debt is paid in full, in case any further debt arises.

It is usual for the supplier to prepare the guarantee wording and ask the customer to ask the guarantor to issue it on his own letter-heading.

Figure 3.00 gives the wording of a suitable third-party payment guarantee which has been used successfully for many years, including in court actions. It is a wording insisted upon by a leading credit insurance company before they will insure a credit level much higher than justified by their own risk assessment.

Figure 3.00 – Suitable wording for a third-party payment guarantee

---

(To the supplying company)

Dear Sirs,

In consideration of your readiness to supply goods or services to _____ (hereinafter referred to as 'the buyer'), we hereby guarantee the due payment of all sums which are now or may hereafter become owing to you by the buyer.

Our liability shall not in any way be diminished or affected by your giving time or indulgence to the buyer, nor by any release, agreement not to sue, composition or arrangement of any description granted or entered into by you to or with the buyer and we shall be liable to you in respect of any obligation accrued hereunder as if we were principal and not surety.

This guarantee shall be a continuing guarantee, subject to our right to give notice of revocation thereof. Any such notice shall be in writing and become effective upon its actual receipt by you at _____ [address] but no revocation shall in any way diminish or affect our liability to you in respect of any indebtedness of the buyer incurred under any contract or obligation entered into between you and the buyer prior to your receipt of such notice.

Yours faithfully,

Witness to the signature of _____

(Signed) _____

Address _____ Date _____

Using guarantees in daily credit management work   **A12.29**

It may be considered prudent for a seller to seek third-party payment guarantees in the following circumstances.

- A customer established for less than two years, places a very large order and requires time to pay. Since about half of all newly-formed businesses fail within their first two years, it makes sense to get payment guarantees for any particularly large orders from firms less than two years old.

- Routine updates of risk assessments show worrying deterioration in the fortunes of some established customers.

- A customer account is proving very troublesome to control, e.g. due dates are missed, polite collection reminders are ignored and credit references show worrying trends. (A minimum value level should be established for this policy, i.e. it should only apply to accounts above a defined 'pain level', which would hurt the seller if lost.)

- A schedule of repayments for a sizeable overdue account needs third party support to be justified.

- Sales volume requirements mean over-selling, for a period, to accounts assessed as 'high-risk' in the seller's risk assessment drills.

- Exporters replacing letter of credit payment terms with limited guarantee supported open account trading.

- The buyer represents a highly concentrated risk compared to the seller's portfolio of debtors as a whole, and could present a catastrophic loss if insolvency of the debtor occurred.

As the guaranteed seller knows that the guarantor hopes he will never be called upon to pay up, the seller's policy should be to collect always from the customer and not bother the guarantor every time there is a slight delay. From time to time, when the credit collector is in contact with the payables staff, it is worth mentioning politely the existence of the guarantee, it being almost certain that they have been told to pay promptly any guaranteed accounts, to avoid upset. However, if the customer begins to default more seriously, the seller should ask the guarantor to intervene, to get payments flowing from the customer rather than be called on themselves to pay.

The credit manager should clearly note guaranteed accounts on the sales ledger, so that they can be collected somewhat differently from the mass of others. For example, it would be wrong to send out routine and escalating letter threats to guaranteed accounts. They should always be telephoned, using the subtle comments mentioned earlier. (See **A7.4–A7.9** above and **A13.18** below.) The same notes can help with periodic reviews for bad debt provisions. Whether a company's approach to provisions is specifically account by account or on a broader basis, such as by aged analysis, profits can be saved by excluding debts which are guaranteed. Similarly, when credit insurance is held, a seller can decide whether to exclude guaranteed accounts from credit limit approval and premium expense.

Calling for guarantors to pay   A12.30

If normal collection attempts fail and it is deemed wise to call in a guarantee, the approach should be made, in writing by recorded delivery, to a director of the guarantor company, or to the manager of the guaranteeing bank. In the case of a personal guarantee, the letter should be addressed to the actual individual at his home address. Although there is no legal requirement to set out the steps already taken to try to collect from the debtor, it may be expedient to let the guarantor know what has taken place. Figure 4.00 gives an example of a letter claiming payment from a guarantor.

Figure 4.00   Suitable wording for a claim for payment under a guarantee

(To the guarantor)
Dear Sirs,
Re: _____ Ltd   A/C _____ Debt overdue £ _____
By your letter of guarantee dated _____ a copy of which is attached for your convenience, you undertook to pay us on first demand in the event of the failure of the above company to pay us for goods supplied.
Despite our attempts to collect the due payment we have not received the required amount. We have made a full check to ensure that there is no dispute and that the account is properly due.
In accordance with the terms of the guarantee, we now call upon you to honour your legal obligation by sending us your cheque by return of post. If this amount is not received by _____ [note: specify a date seven days ahead], we will instruct our solicitors to begin proceedings against you for the full amount.
No further notice will be given.
Yours faithfully,
Credit Manager.

International guarantee agreements and the problems of enforcement   A12.31

Credit managers and others involved in international trade must add some extra knowledge-based skills to their normal working portfolio. As a result of geo-political influences on world trade, there is an array of international conventions, such as those managed by the International Chamber of Commerce (ICC) and those for the main transport methods, as well as banking, documentation and all the underlying legal bases.

Rather than trying to become an expert in the practices of all countries, the person managing his company's foreign credit operations should at least know the wider economic and political situations for the countries to which his company is selling.

The main conventions supporting cross-border trading which assist management of credit in international trade include the following.

- International Chamber of Commerce:
  - Incoterms,
  - UCP,
  - URDG,
  - URC, and
  - ISBP.

- For transportation:
  - Incoterms,
  - Hague-Visby Rules,
  - Warsaw Rules,
  - CIM Convention, and
  - CMR Convention.

- For cross-border enforcement of judgments and jurisdictions of courts:
  - Brussels Convention,
  - *Foreign Judgments (Reciprocal Enforcement) Act 1933*, and
  - *Administration of Justice Act 1920*.

- Arbitration awards:
  - UNCITRAL rules for Arbitrations,
  - Geneva Protocol on Arbitration Awards,
  - Geneva Convention on the Execution of Foreign Arbitration Awards, and
  - New York Convention on the Recognition and Enforcement of Foreign Arbitration Awards.

Other Information   A12.32

A prudent credit manager would require information on the following items to ensure his security was valid and he mitigated any risk in the contract:

- currency;
- payment terms;
- essential documentation;
- import licences;
- trade bloc relationships;
- embargoes;

- blacklists; and

- the general atmosphere of risk and governmental involvement.

International Chamber of Commerce (ICC)   A12.33

The ICC, based in Paris but with offices in London and all the major world trade centres, promotes the collaboration of governments and legal institutions in standardising the approach to issues which otherwise would create every day trading disputes. Its publications are used by exporters, importers, banks and transport organisations for top-level guidance. For example, a contract will state that its price is 'subject to *Incoterms* 2000'. (See **A11.46** above.) Other ICC publications include *ICC Uniform Customs and Practice No 500* (for letters of credit), *ICC Uniform Rules for Collections No 522* (for bills of exchange), and various model clauses for contract situations. The ICC wordings are not legally binding as such, unless incorporated into the contract, but are generally agreed guidance which the courts would take into account when deciding issues. In many countries, certain ICC rules are incorporated into law as the basic law concerning that aspect of international trade.

- Incoterms – the internationally agreed shipping terms which define the obligations of buyer and seller. These also define when risk passes, a key element in determining liability for loss and subsequent credit note claims. Issued by the ICC, the current version is Incoterms 2000 (ICC Publication Reference ICC 560).

- UCP – Uniform Customs and Practise for Documentary Credits – the internationally agreed rules under which letters of credit are regulated. The current version is UCP 500.

- URDG – Uniform Rules for Guarantees. These rules regulate 'on demand' guarantees but unfortunately are not in widespread use.

- URC – Uniform Rules for Collections – These rules, issued by ICC, are in widespread international use, and regulate the obligations and responsibilities of banks undertaking collection of payments for bills of exchange of cash against documents. If a bank is required to follow the rules when it receives the instruction from the exporter's bank and fails to do so, it will probably be liable for damages in negligence. This is a potent protection ensuring the buyer does not obtain control of the goods without making the necessary payment on cash against document terms. ICC publication No URC522 refers. This document is now in process of review and an updated version is expected by the end of 2005.

SITPRO   A12.34

SITPRO is a Government funded body in London which has, over the years, produced a mass of guidance for exporters, particularly on documentation. In recent years, SITPRO has specialised in reducing the high error rate in letters of credit and in moving funds more efficiently across national borders. It has worked closely with international lawyers, Government staff and banks to produce excellent laminated guidance sheets and checklists for exporters.

The current SITPRO venture is in the field of electronic documentation, to eliminate paperwork and delays by the use of e-mail for contracts, letters of credit and most of the export documents. Besides the massive security hazard in not having hard documents and actual signatures, there is the considerable task of agreeing standards which will have the approval of all the major trading nations and their legal systems. (Also see **A11.48** and **A12.4** above.)

Country reports   A12.35

All the main banks issue free country reports compiled by their economic and legal experts in collaboration with correspondent banks in the countries concerned. In giving valuable national data on imports and exports, with substantial commentary, they also show:

- borrowings;
- reserves;
- FX earnings and debt ratios;
- licence restrictions; and
- current government plans which may affect future sales to that market.

International risk and payment information   A12.36

D&B is the world's largest provider of corporate and country risk information. Of all its many credit publications, the star product is the *International Risk and Payment Review*. (See **A11.10** above.)

The credit insurer, Coface, also provides similar information free of charge via its online service www.cofacerating.com.

Transport of goods   A12.37

Payment disputes often arise over delays, errors and losses in the transport of the goods. There are international conventions for all transport methods and reference to these should be enshrined in sales contracts, as they certainly will be in the carriage contracts between carrier and exporter. The following are the most important conventions.

- Transport by sea is subject to the Hague-Visby Rules of 1968.
- Transport by air is subject to the Warsaw Rules of 1975.
- Transport by rail is subject to the CIM Convention of 1961.
- Transport by road is subject to the CMR Convention of 1956.

Most sales out of the UK by road and rail now go to other European Union countries. The original Treaty of Rome is being elaborated all the time to provide a framework of law on transport responsibilities and liabilities.

In addition the ICC Rules, Incoterms, define the obligations of both buyer and seller. This is of particular importance where claims for short delivery, damage in transit and pilferage are concerned. Many suppliers incorrectly believe that they are responsible for loss on CIP, CIF and CPT contracts until the goods are delivered to the customer, whereas in fact the customer is responsible from the time the goods are loaded. The seller may thus enforce payment in full from the buyer, or assist the buyer in making an insurance claim to cover the loss. The seller itself may even be covered by the 'seller's interest' clause of its own global freight insurance. Understanding the international delivery terms is therefore very important in protecting the debtor book asset from erosion.

Contracts made subject to English law and their enforcement abroad   A12.38

Experienced exporters use their order confirmation to show that their contracts are made subject to English, Scots or Northern Irish law (not UK law, which does not exist). This certainly helps the seller if any contractual points need clarification. It also gives a seller the confidence of clarity in the contract, and enables him to threaten and take court proceedings when the customer defaults.

However, an English court judgment may have to be enforced abroad, if it alone does not produce the right customer response. While it is technically possible to arrange local enforcement of an English judgment, it is sometimes unproductive for all but the largest cases, because of the need to appoint and brief a local law firm, pay them substantial fees in advance, and then wait a disappointingly long time for the local courts to act. It is important to note the wasteful effect of long drawn-out proceedings. When action begins, the invoiced debt may be converted into local currency and frozen at that value for the duration of the case, so that in a market whose weaker currency steadily devalues against, for example, Sterling, the passage of time will have made the final award worth much less than the intended debt value. Other reasons why English judgments may become unenforceable include:

- interpretations of warranties;

- conflict with local laws; and

- local prejudice, perhaps connected with potential unemployment, competition or even international politics.

This is not always the case in those countries where the UK has long standing reciprocal enforcement conventions, such as certain Commonwealth countries and the EU Member States. The key is whether the local court system is efficient and free from interference. Under the Brussels Convention, UK judgments are easily enforceable in all European Union countries, and relatively inexpensively following registration. The question is whether it is more effective to have a contract which permits the action to commence in an English court, in the English language and the client must come to England to defend the action, rather than the reverse.

The lesson, therefore, is to assume that legal action for debt recovery abroad is long, drawn-out, expensive and disappointing. Instead, it is far better to have strong, clear conditions of sale, explain them to all new customers (and existing ones whenever a minor dispute arises), and make it clear that they will be enforced where necessary. It is also important to note that in many countries which use the Napoleonic code of law, enforcement of judgments or debts against State entities or parastatal corporations is difficult or impossible, as the law may not permit the court to seize the State's assets. This may be avoided by taking out political risk insurance.

Arbitration clauses   A12.39

An arbitration clause will help to resolve disputes, even without going to arbitration because one or other of the parties may fear an unfavourable decision. Even though the Brussels Convention makes it possible to register judgments in other EU Member States, cases have shown that some disputes may obviate enforcement and remain unsettled for a long time. Rather than suing under the law of the contract, it is often more effective to enforce an international arbitration award, such as that of the ICC Court at The Hague.

Arbitration is of particular advantage in many countries as the rights of the losing party to challenge the award are very limited, and in many cases the award can be immediately registered for enforcement. However, the value of any such award is clearly dependent on the efficacy of local enforcement procedures.

Conditions of sale   A12.40

For sales outside one's own national boundaries, the conditions of sale are naturally protective against a variety of events. Apart from technical conditions, the main matters in the area of credit risk and payment are:

- payment terms, showing the credit period and method, place and time of payment;

- that it is clear that any payment received must be free of all deductions, including bank charges and confirmation fees;

- penalty interest for late payment, showing a rate or basis for a rate;

- cost escalation, usually by reference to an agreed neutral index;

- retention of title (particularly for Germany and Holland, where its use is commonplace);

- local currency responsibility, whereby the customer must supply enough of his own currency to his remitting bank to pay the invoice at date of transfer;

- arbitration, where the parties agree in advance that a major dispute will go to a stated arbitration body and that their decision will be accepted by both sides;

- law of the contract, in which language and whose courts have jurisdiction; and

- delivery terms and definition of where and when title and risk pass.

Reservation of title (retention of title or reservation of property)   A12.41

A seller's conditions of sale should always include a reservation of title (ROT) clause, provided the product (*not* service) is capable of intact recovery. When a customer is known to be in difficulties, it is clearly better for a supplier to recover resaleable goods now, rather than to try to sue a bankrupt company later for the price.

The intended sense of a clause is, 'the goods remain our property until paid for', but the actual wording needs legal advice in case of problems occurring if the right is challenged. It is vital, however, for a credit manager to instruct his legal adviser to keep the wording as brief as possible. The clause has to be notified to customers and it is important that it receives smooth acceptance and does not become a lengthy negotiating matter.

For example, it is important that the wording of such a ROT clause does not inadvertently give rise to the buyer having a right to reject or return the goods, thus cancelling the contract and leaving the seller with the goods and no profit. Whilst this is not normally an issue in the UK, it may be in a foreign jurisdiction.

At least one major claim has been lost in the courts when it was ruled that a supplier's clause was so complex that it would have been too difficult for the customer to have free use of the goods and yet observe the ROT obligations. Figure 5.00 gives a suitable ROT wording in a standard set of conditions of sale.

Furthermore, the wording and efficacy of any ROT clause is of particular importance for those companies using credit insurance. Most credit insurers, in their standard policy conditions, now require an effective enforceable ROT clause to be incorporated within the sales contract worldwide, so credit managers must be mindful of this. If this is impractical or undesirable, or simply because the buyer refuses, the policy must reflect this. As such ROT clauses may cover many different countries, the wording for each local law is likely to be different and should be checked for each country.

Figure 5.00 – Sample wording of a retention of title clause in conditions of sale

This standard condition of sale may precede or follow the seller's other conditions. The number 8 is just an example.

8.   Risk and Property

8.1   Risk of damage to or loss of the goods shall pass to the buyer:

(a)   when goods are to be delivered at the seller's premises, at the time when the seller notifies the buyer that the goods are available for collection; or

(b)   when goods are to be delivered to the buyer or to his order, at the time of delivery, or attempted delivery if the buyer fails to take delivery.

8.2   Notwithstanding the passing of risk, the property or title in the goods shall not pass to the buyer until the seller has received full payment of the goods and all other goods sold by him to the buyer where payment is already due.

8.3   Until the title of the goods passes to the buyer, he shall hold the goods as the seller's fiduciary agent and bailee, and keep the goods separate from those of other suppliers and his own goods and keep them properly stored, insured and identifiable as the seller's property. Until ownership passes to the buyer he shall be entitled to resell or use the goods in the ordinary course of business, but shall account to the seller for the proceeds of sale and shall keep all such proceeds separate from the funds of the buyer or third parties.

8.4   Until title to the goods passes to the buyer, provided the goods still exist and have not been resold, the seller shall be entitled to demand the return of the goods and if the buyer fails to do so, to enter the buyer's premises or those of any third party where the goods are stored and repossess the goods.

8.5   The buyer shall not be entitled to pledge or charge for security any goods which remain the property of the seller but if the buyer nevertheless does so then all amounts owed by the buyer to the seller shall become payable immediately.

The recent history of introducing a ROT clause
A12.42

The general rule under *section 17* of the *Sale of Goods Act 1979*, is that ownership of goods passes when the parties intend it to pass, e.g. at manufacture, inspection, delivery, payment or whenever else ownership was intended to pass. However, taking together the seller's wish to supply goods to a customer with that customer's wish to pay for them, it seems equitable that a buyer should be put in possession of the goods, but not actually own them until the supplier has been paid. Thus, existing law under *section 19* of the *Sale of Goods Act 1979* already allowed a seller to incorporate the right to retain ownership until paid, and yet it took the actions of a Dutch seller into the UK to alert British companies to the possibility.

That case was *Aluminium Industry v Industrie Vassen Romalpa Aluminium Ltd [1976] WLR 676*, usually known as the *Romalpa* case. When a liquidator was trying to dispose of stocks for the benefit of creditors in the usual order of priority, a Dutch seller won a court action to enforce their little known ROT clause. UK companies were astonished that one particular supplier could recover goods in an insolvency ahead of the mass of unpaid creditors. This led to the production of a brand new condition of sale in UK contracts and order confirmations.

With a more international outlook, UK companies would have known that the operation of ROT was, and remains, quite routine in countries such as Holland and Germany (where it is called *Eigentumsvorbehalt*). At an international credit gathering, a major German credit manager stated that he believed the miraculous German post-war recovery was helped, in part, by suppliers giving very generous credit ratings, in the knowledge that they could recover their products if their trust was misplaced. It has also been said many times that English suppliers do not take back their goods when a German company fails. German suppliers also have the benefit of extended ROT in two ways. There is 'lengthened' ROT which gives the right to recover goods that have been sold on, and 'widened' ROT, when goods have been mixed in with others. In the latter case, the liquidator allows the ROT creditor a priority in pay out, because he has been able to work with extra stocks and raise more money for the creditors generally.

Dealing with receivers and liquidators A12.43

In the UK, the power of the insolvency profession has achieved the opposite effect of that on the continent, by restricting the rights of unpaid suppliers. Limitations have been placed on the operation of ROT clauses in voluntary company arrangements, administration orders and elsewhere. For example, the *Insolvency Act 1986*, as amended by the *Enterprise Act 2002*, allows an administrator, with leave of the court, to dispose of goods subject to retention clauses if it appears to help in saving the insolvent business, albeit that the administrator would need to convince the court that the supplier was placed in no worse a position than if they had exercised the right of repossession. In practice, therefore, this provision is rarely exercised.

In general, despite the clarity of the law and of suppliers' own clauses, it is often difficult for a supplier to recover stocks from an administrative receiver or liquidator, who refuses right of entry onto premises, is not available for discussion and who demands evidence that a ROT clause, not only exists, but was properly notified to the company before it failed.

The lessons learned from experience with receivers who are reluctant to release suppliers' property in their control, are that:

- the goods must be easily identifiable, e.g. with a serial number or unique feature; and

- there must be evidence that the seller's ROT clause was known to the buyer before the insolvency, e.g. via contractual conditions of sale.

As it is not safe to rely on a customer spotting the insertion of a new or amended ROT clause, it is recommended that each buyer is notified separately of such additions. If possible, the customer's confirmation of receipt of the ROT clause should be obtained.

Bills of exchange   A12.44

A bill of exchange can be used in any commercial transaction if the parties agree. However, it is usually applied to export sales, where it adds more firmness to the credit arrangement and gives the seller the benefit of being processed by the banking system, instead of just waiting for a customer to pay on the due date. In terms of payment security, a bill of exchange does not guarantee payment, nor does it give any priority over an unsecured debt in an insolvency but, properly managed, it is an excellent 'enforcer' for the seller. In most jurisdictions, it is clear evidence of the acceptance of the debt, and is legally enforceable as such. Failure to honour a bill, or draft as it is known after it has been accepted by the debtor, is proof of insolvency in many countries, so customers are very reluctant to cause this situation. In France, for example, it is an offence to dishonour a bill and the central bank investigates each case. Not a situation many clients wish to be in.

History   A12.45

Bills of exchange were devised in the Middle Ages, so that after a mobile trader moved on, a written acceptance of a debt obligation remained until his return. Thus, bills dealt with evidence and time. In the vast expansion of world trade, goods were sent on precarious sea journeys over thousands of miles to often unknown customers. Bills of exchange were drawn up by sellers and sent by their banks to correspondent banks, in two identical sets by different ships in case one sank. The foreign banks then collected the funds, or obtained signed acceptance from the drawee or importers to pay at future due dates, before releasing the goods to them. Thus, bills dealt with distance and risk. The use of bills was fairly routine for world trade until the Second World War, since then the concept of trust has expanded to the point that firms allow time to pay to customers they know little about, for reasons of expediency and competition.

Key features   A12.46

The key features of bills of exchange in English law are that they:

- are separate contracts related to, but independent of, the sales contract;

- show the obligations of the parties mentioned;

- are payable to the order of the beneficiary and may be transferred by endorsement, or where payable to bearer, by mere delivery;

- give their holder the right to receive a specific sum of money; and

- are negotiable instruments of credit or of debt as specified in financial agreements.

The *Bills of Exchange Act 1882*, gives one of the most famous wordings in legal history in that its brevity has stood the test of time despite many challenges to its interpretation. The standard definition of a bill of exchange, under *section 3* of the Act is:

> ' … an unconditional order in writing, addressed by one person to another, signed by the person giving it, requiring the person to whom it is addressed to pay on demand or at a fixed or determinable future time a sum certain in money to or to the order of a specified person or to bearer.'

This section has been copied by the USA, Commonwealth countries, much of Latin America, the Republic of Ireland and Israel, while most of Europe uses the Geneva definition of 1930, which is similar except that it does not allow a bill to be payable 'to bearer'. In certain of the Geneva Convention countries, the bill of exchange is not a separate contract and non-performance of the underlying contract by the seller may give rise to a defence in court for non-honouring of the bill on presentation.

A bill is called a 'sight draft' if payable on demand, i.e. on its arrival (not the arrival of the goods, although the bank may be told to defer the demand until then), and a 'term draft' if a period of credit has been allowed. The word 'draft' instead of 'bill of exchange' indicates the raw state of a bill before it is accepted or paid. In everyday use, the terms 'draft' and 'bill' are interchangeable.

Typically, the bill of exchange is made out on a plain piece of paper by the seller, sent to his bank with a formal instruction sheet and sent on to a bank in the buyer's town. The standard instruction sheets, supplied by banks or by SITPRO (see **A11.49** and **A12.30** above and **A12.49** below), show that the collection is governed by the ICC Uniform Rules For Collections No 522. This convention, which is accepted by most banks in the world, puts a strict obligation onto banks to act in the best interests of the drawer (seller, usually) in several specific ways, and it is up to credit managers to hold the banks to their obligations where unsatisfactory service occurs.

Figure 6.00   Example of a term draft (bill of exchange) prior to acceptance

---

Bill of Exchange

Ref: 280635

Sleepytown, 30 March 2003.......   ***Amount*** US$10,000.00 ......

At ... 60 days after date................. ***pay against this Sole Bill of Exchange***

To the order of.... ourselves ....

the sum of...... ten thousand United States dollars ....

for value.......... Received ....

To: ... Ying Tong Songs Ltd ....   ***For and on behalf of***

      Feng Shui Square   English Widgets Ltd

      Victoria, Hong Kong

                                          (Financial Director)

Figure 7.00 – Example of a term bill of exchange after its acceptance

A bill of exchange can be used in a 'clean' collection or a 'documentary' one. A clean collection simply uses a bill on its own to reinforce an open account obligation, by using the banking system to process the bill and collect the funds. With a 'documentary collection', the essential export documents, which the importer needs to get hold of the goods on arrival, are attached to the draft. The foreign bank, acting for the seller's bank, will ask the buyer to pay the bill if it is a sight draft, or 'accept' it, as payable at a specific future date, by signing it across the face, if it is a term draft (or 'tenor bill', or 'time draft'). The accepted term bill may or may not be returned to the seller at that point, but it is certainly presented to the drawee as 'acceptor' at the due date for payment. Non-payment is called 'dishonour' and is a serious matter in many countries, tantamount to an act of insolvency in some.

The seller can make the bill payable to another party if that is convenient, e.g. in a financing arrangement where funds have been advanced. The use of 'bearer' is comparatively rare, since it can be cashed by any finder if it goes astray. Once the 'drawee' has accepted the bill, he is legally bound to pay it. Action can be taken in a court on the evidence of an accepted bill alone, i.e. there is no need to prove a sales contract or delivery of goods, nor is a commercial dispute a defence against non-payment of an accepted bill of exchange.

An actual guarantee of payment can be achieved on a bill of exchange by the buyer arranging for a third party, often a bank, to sign ('endorsing') the back of the bill. When a party other than the drawer or drawee signs a bill, they take on the liabilities of, 'an endorser to a holder of the bill in due course'. The guarantee is only as good as the creditworthiness of the endorser.

In Europe, and for many financing schemes, such as forfeiting, the endorsement is called an 'aval'. With modern-day Anglicisations, the bill is said to be 'avalised'. An aval is an irrevocable and unconditional guarantee of payment for the bill amount or a part of it if the wording of the aval says so. The advantage of an aval over other payment guarantees is that it cannot be separated from the bill of exchange, i.e. it is not released by reason of a sales dispute or any problem with the commercial contract. The usual wording on the back of a bill is, 'per aval for account of the drawee'. In the financing technique of forfeiting, which provides the seller with the full value of the bill without any subsequent recourse if the drawee defaults, the forfeiting bank will usually insist that the aval is given by the buyer's bank. Rarely is the aval of a non-banking entity accepted, unless it is one of the major blue chip corporations. When arranging an aval, the credit manager should ensure that the:

- signing body is acceptable to the forfeiting bank;
- guarantor's corporate constitution allows it to avalise trade bills; and
- country's foreign exchange authority will allow the transfer of hard currency immediately on payment.

Protesting a bill for non-payment   A12.47

If a bill of exchange is dishonoured, the collecting bank must give notice to the drawer and any endorser. It is usual to give the reason at the same time. For a foreign bill to be sued on separately from the sales contract, it must be strengthened by being 'protested'.

A bill is protested, or in the home trade, 'noted', by a public notary appointed by the collecting bank. He records the drawee's non-acceptance or non-payment on a slip of paper and attaches it to the bill. Where a bill has not been accepted, protest has little value and is rarely done. There may be a good reason for not taking up the goods and a remedy lies in the sales contract. By the same token, there is little point in protesting a non-accepted bill for its eventual non-payment. However, for accepted obligations, the protest action has serious consequences and is a powerful collection tool. The instruction to the bank to organise protest action has to be given when the bill is sent out. There is no time to discuss the matter when dishonour occurs, since most local jurisdictions require protest to take place within two days of a default. So, for experienced credit managers, a policy on protesting unpaid bills might be to give the instruction for all new or high-risk customers but never to give it for long-established, trusted customers or inter-companies (or other group companies). Where credit insurance cover is held, the policy conditions normally insist that unpaid bills are protested, to improve the collection chances of insurers when debts are subrogated.

Protest action is usually followed by automatic publication in the local business gazette and can lead to a reduction in confidence by other suppliers. It is seen as an inability to pay rather than unwillingness. The fact that the customer knows this may happen is a useful collection tool, so that a customer with limited resources may well pay a bill of exchange to a bank, and leave open account suppliers unpaid.

Given the propensity for allowing open credit around the world regardless of customer risk, there is no doubt that more exporters should review their credit terms and negotiate hard to arrange documentary bill collections in all cases where customers are not fully creditworthy or do not have a prompt payment record.

Promissory notes   A12.48

A promissory note is an unconditional and irrevocable written undertaking to pay a stated amount at a stated date. It is not a bill of exchange, but can be useful as a collection tool. It is raised, often in a series, by the debtor and frequently used to support a repayment schedule. Like a bill of exchange, a promissory note may be payable at sight or at a future date, it can also be endorsed or guaranteed by aval. Figure 8.00 gives an example of a promissory note.

Figure 8.00 – Example of a promissory note

PROMISSORY NOTE

Place and date of issue Hong Kong .... 10 April 1999

On 31 July 2002 .... AGAINST THIS PROMISSORY NOTE WE PROMISE TO PAY

to: English Widgets Ltd, Orchard Hill, Sleepytown, Blissex, England ...... or Order

the sum of US$10,000 .... (in words) ten thousand US dollars ....

for value received .... Authorised signature ....

for YING TONG SONGS Ltd

payable at ... Barclays Bank plc ....

...... Feng Shui branch, Victoria, Hong Kong ....

Letters of credit A12.49

Documentary letters of credit have become very much in demand as a means of being paid by customers in countries short of hard currency. They represent a strong guarantee of payment from a bank on behalf of the customer, but may be expensive and unsuitable for small value deals. (Also see **A11.61** above.)

A letter of credit is simply a written undertaking by a bank, issued at the request of their client, to pay a stated amount against stipulated documents within a prescribed time.

The three main types of letter of credit are:

- revocable;
- irrevocable; and
- confirmed irrevocable

Revocable letters of credit A12.50

As the name implies, the revocable letter of credit (RLC) can be amended or cancelled by the buyer or his bank at any time up to payment, thus diminishing its security. An RLC is rare these days and used mainly with traditional markets merely as an instrument of payment. In fact, it is suggested that in the next UCP revision, revocable credits are abolished due to their lack of use!

Irrevocable letter of credit A12.51

The irrevocable letter of credit (ILC) is by far the most common type in use. The customer's bank (the 'opening' or 'issuing' bank) gives the exporter its undertaking to pay provided the conditions of the credit are met. Thus there is no longer any customer credit risk but there is still the risk that the foreign bank will not be able to pay when the time comes. The ILC is advised to the exporter by a bank in the UK, usually in London, and payment will be made by that bank in due course, but only if it has the funds from the other end by then. The issuing bank is in the country of risk that caused the exporter to ask for the letter of credit in the first place. It may be prevented or severely delayed by its government in remitting hard currency to the UK. Exporters should be wary of ILCs from countries with a known currency transfer delay.

Confirmed irrevocable letter of credit A12.52

The confirmed irrevocable letter of credit (CILC) is more expensive but removes the country risk, since another bank in the UK (or another hard currency country) adds its commitment to the letter of credit payment. For example, a

CILC opened by a bank in Bangladesh and advised and confirmed by HSBC in London, means that the exporter can be confident of payment regardless of the customer and the country risk.

Documentary credits   A12.53

Exporters should ensure that letters of credit they receive show that they are issued under the International Chamber of Commerce (ICC) *Uniform Customs and Practice for Documentary Credits*, known as *UCP 500*, which govern the obligations of all the parties and are accepted by banks and courts in almost every country of the world.

However, a major risk remains with letters of credit, regardless of the bank involved – that of the exporter not complying with the letter of credit's conditions. Having gone to all the trouble and expense of getting a bank undertaking for an order, there is a 70% chance (the national average) that, because of lateness or errors in documents, the exporter will not be paid by the advising bank. Banks paying under letters of credit operate to a doctrine of strict compliance and, regardless of common sense or previous practice, an exporter must make sure that he presents to the bank exactly what the letter of credit specifies, including correct spelling and punctuation.

SITPRO (see **A11.49** and **A12.34** above), a Government-funded body, has an excellent set of checklists for letters of credit. They recommend the following three stages of control to achieve smooth payments and avoid customer upsets.

- When asking the customer to open the letter of credit.

- When receiving the letter of credit from the advising or confirming bank.

- When presenting the documents to the bank for payment.

Requesting the letter of credit   A12.54

When notifying a customer, on a quotation or order confirmation, that a letter of credit is required, the exporter should send a standard advice of the details he expects the letter of credit to show, especially:

- description of goods;

- weights and prices;

- Incoterms basis (see **A11.46** above);

- port of shipment;

- normal documents for that market;

- whether part shipments and/or transhipments will be made; and

- final shipment date required.

All these points should reflect the sales order, but the customer will find them useful to give to his opening bank (issuing bank).

On receipt of the letter of credit   A12.55

Letters of credit arrive by mail or fax in different shapes and sizes from different banks selected by customers, not by the exporter. They will vary in addressee, such as the MD, sales or product contact, shipping manager, credit manager, cashier, and so on.

The exporter should appoint a single person to centralise the handling of all letters of credit. That person should immediately:

- cross-refer the letter of credit to its order;

- photocopy it five or six times;

- stamp each copy with a request 'please check this for accuracy and let me have any points for amendment within 7 days';

- send the copies to the people who will produce the documents, such as, shipping information, insurance certificates, invoices, technical certificates, sales items and accounts.

A few days later, when all parties have had the chance to spot any difficulties, the customer should be faxed amendments of any unworkable documents or dates. (If this is in several separate requests over the weeks, especially at the last minute, the customer may justifiably complain about the bank amendment charges. There is also the real danger of not having enough time to alter the letter of credit before shipment.) The letter of credit controller should put the letter of credit expiry date in the diary two weeks earlier than the actual date, to allow time to get documents in, errors corrected and avoid the danger of lateness.

Presenting the documents   A12.56

A single person, either the original checker, or a member of credit staff, should be responsible for accumulating the specified documents from their various sources in good time to claim payment before the stated expiry date. The final check should be that:

- documents are exactly as called for in the letter of credit;

- there is consistency between the documents; and

- the presentation to the paying bank meets the instructions in the bank's original covering letter.

Summary of letters of credit   A12.57

In summary, an ILC (see **A12.51** above) and particularly a CILC (see **A12.52** above) is an excellent guarantee of payment, but the exporter should remember that the bank acts as a fair broker between the parties. They will pay the exporter quickly and safely, but they protect the foreign customer by ensuring the exporter has done exactly what the buyer has specified.

Exporters can obtain the highly recommended *Checklists for Letters of Credit* from: SITPRO, 8th Floor, Oxford House, 76 Oxford Street, London. W1D 1BS. Tel: 020 7467 7280. Fax: 020 7467 7295.

Forfeiting

What is forfeiting? A12.58

This expression comes from the French *a forfait,* which means to forfeit something, in this case the right to a customer's payment in exchange for having the funds in advance from a forfeiting bank.

Forfeiting is a secure method of export financing in that it is without recourse. The technique is often used by larger companies undertaking capital goods contracts where payment is by a series of bills of exchange over several years. However, it is also valid for single payment transactions and for terms as short as 60 days, as long as the transaction is acceptable to the forfeiting bank.

Forfeiting banks are usually specialist subsidiaries of the major banks. They undertake to purchase trade bills which have been accepted by the buyer and endorsed, i.e. they carry the aval (see **A12.46** above), of a major bank in that country. It is also possible to forfait open account invoices if the forfeiting bank agrees, and also obtain separate written bank guarantees instead of the aval on bills. As a result of the official backing given to such debts, it is easier to forfait bills for sales to a government or with a government connection. For example, if the Ministry of Health in Jamaica purchased equipment for a major hospital project, it would almost certainly arrange for a Jamaican bank to avalise suppliers' bills if so asked. Equally, an exporter's sales to a sub-contractor involved in the project could also probably be avalised, since the government would recognise the need for the equipment in its project. In many cases the aval or guarantee of the Ministry of Finance is acceptable as an alternative to a local bank.

How does forfeiting work? A12.59

An exporter asks his contractual buyer to confirm that he can get the commitment of a major bank to avalise the bill or bills of exchange after acceptance. The exporter then approaches a forfeiting bank, usually by telephone, to ask if they will buy the bill when it is returned to the UK after acceptance and avalisation. The forfeiting bank will quote a fee for doing so, which combines the bank's view of the default risk with its cost of borrowing the funds and its administration costs. The quotation is usually held open for several weeks to allow the exporter to make his sale and receive back the accepted and avalised bill of exchange. Should an extended period be required before the bills are available for discounting, the exporter can arrange a 'commitment' by the forfeiter, for a fee, guaranteeing it will discount the bills on presentation. This is particularly useful where the exporter has a long manufacturing period prior to shipment and wants to ensure the facility will still be available when it finally ships. On presenting it to the forfeiting bank against its earlier quotation, the exporter is paid the face value less the agreed percentage. The payment is without recourse, the exporter has no risk and can count the sale as fully paid.

Why does a forfeiting bank take on such a significant risk? A12.60

Forfeiting banks take the risk because the aval of a major foreign bank moves the risk from a commercial buyer, which the forfeiting bank does not know well, to that of a financial institution, of which it has greater understanding and creditworthiness. The forfeiters take up positions in certain country debts, such as African or Eastern European and sell the purchased bills to each other in a secondary market which is of no concern to the exporter.

Bills expressed in US dollars, Swiss francs, Japanese yen or Euros may be preferred as they carry a lower fee than those in Sterling, because of lower interest rates in those countries.

An obvious advantage of forfeiting, apart from the cash flow and no-risk benefits, is that no credit insurance is needed so the premium saving can be offset against the forfeiting charge.

Factoring and invoice discounting

Factoring A12.61

Factoring is a 'credit management plus finance' service from subsidiaries of the main banks. The service includes:

- credit ratings assessed for each customer;
- sales ledger management of suppliers' invoices;
- advances against suppliers' invoices; and
- collecting customers' payments.

A seller who is interested in this service, which obviates the need for credit management resource in-house but may be seen as expensive, should discuss his needs with his own bank, who will introduce him to its factoring subsidiary. A bank which is trying to enforce its overdraft limit on a struggling business may insist that it follows the factoring route to improve its cash flow.

An annual agreement will be signed, showing the mechanics of the service and stating the fee basis, which will be between 1% and 5% of turnover, plus an interest charge on funds advanced at a rate similar to the existing overdraft rate.

Following the setting up of the facility, the seller sells as usual and sends copies of his invoices to the factor, usually in weekly batches. In many cases this is now done on an online basis, updated each night. Up to 80% of the invoiced value is advanced 'without recourse' if sales have kept within the credit limits set. The balance of 20% is paid when customers pay or, more occasionally, in bulk at an average due date. The seller tells his customers to send their payments to the factoring company who pursues them at due date if they do not pay. The 'without recourse' basis means that the seller has reliable revenue that never has to be repaid, provided he has sold within the set limits. Only irrecoverable debts for sales above the credit limits have to be repaid.

The factoring service at, say, 4% may well be seen as expensive when compared to net profits, but cash-flow is better, debts are 'insured' and administration is much reduced. As sales increase, many companies find it cheaper to come out of factoring and operate their own credit management function.

Another perceived disadvantage is the interposing of a third party between seller and buyer, especially when billings are disputed or when the factoring bank takes a harder line on past due debts than the seller would have. For these reasons and others, the facility can be 'non-disclosed' or 'confidential', whereby customers are not told and continue to pay directly to the seller, who has the task of collecting to the satisfaction of the factor.

Invoice discounting   A12.62

Factors and banks also offer an invoice discounting facility, whereby the seller does his own credit management and sales ledger maintenance and simply receives advance funds on his invoices, often with recourse in the event of customer default. In many cases, for a larger exporter, the invoice discounting facility can be without recourse and undisclosed to the buyer, and even off balance sheet if the buyer's name is strong enough or credit insurance available.

Contra and offset against payables   A12.63

It is not legal, and also inefficient, to withhold payments to a supplier just because they are overdue for their own purchases. Where debtors are also suppliers, it is important to run sales ledger and payables accounts separately, since they represent separate legal contracts to sell and to buy. For example, the receiver for an insolvent customer can require a supplier to repay amounts already so offset or withheld.

The more efficient approach, which can improve relationships anyway, is to discuss the common account situation with the customer and make a written agreement that debts may be offset. In this way, for example on a monthly settlement basis, the two companies would send each other statements as usual and the one owing the most would pay the excess amount only. Both companies would then adjust their books to cancel the common amount between receivables and payables. The exchange of statements is important for account reconciliation purposes of detailed amounts.

In the event that the customer becomes insolvent, the agreement should be shown to the receiver or liquidator to justify retaining the offset debt.

Tender and performance bonds   A12.64

A small proportion of international trade, usually for high value capital goods, depends on processes of tendering and, for the successful bidders, proper performance of the contracts awarded. To protect a buyer from frivolous tendering by any supplier who withdraws after the buyer has made all the effort of adjudicating bids, and also against unsatisfactory performance under a contract, suppliers are usually asked to arrange guarantees that buyers will be recompensed in those cases.

The guarantees are issued on the exporters' behalf by banks (as bonds normally payable on demand or standby letters of credit) or by surety companies (conditional bonds). Although most buyers insist on 'on demand' bonds, they are disliked by exporters because of the risk that they can be cashed at any time without justification, even after the exporter has performed properly. This is known as 'unfair calling', for which insurance cover may be available, at a premium, although it is often more difficult to insure against an unfair calling by a commercial organisation rather than a State entity or foreign government. The reason for this is that the unfair bond calling insurance was developed to protect against the action of governments who called whole portfolios of bonds to enrich their national treasuries, rather than against beneficiaries who called the bond incorrectly. Thus standard cover protects against the actions of governments and State entities including State owned corporations and is arranged through the political risk markets. Cover can be extended to cover actions by a commercial organisation, but the underwriter will take into account the standing and reputation of that organisation before agreeing to it.

Types of bond   A12.65

The following are the most common type of bonds.

- *Tender or bid bonds* – these guarantee that the bidder will not walk away from an accepted bid and can be for as much as 10% or 15% of the contract value. Typically, 2.5% to 5% is more usual.

- *Performance bonds* – these guarantee that the exporter will perform as per the contract and are usually between 5% and 10% of contract value, but are sometimes a lot higher.

- *Advance payment bonds* – these ensure that any payment made in advance, under a contract's terms, can be recovered by the buyer if the supplier does not comply with the contract.

- *Maintenance bonds* – these are necessary where a contract calls for expert maintenance services after commissioning, and the buyer fears the exporter may not perform these satisfactorily once the main contract work is finished.

- *Retention bonds* – these are suggested by the exporter rather than the buyer where a contract allows the buyer to retain a percentage, usually 5% or 10%, of the price until satisfactory commissioning or for a number of months after completion. Rather than have a cash flow squeeze during this waiting time, the exporter can be paid in full. The bond gives the buyer the confidence of knowing he can recover the contractual retention percentage if a defect occurs.

Stakeholder or escrow accounts   A12.66

A seller can both generate customer confidence and reduce credit risk by using a neutral body, such as a bank, to hold the funds until the buyer is happy, as evidenced by an agreed document such as a certificate of completion. There are many forms of trusteeship, secure deposits and escrow accounts to achieve this equitable state.

In building work and related contracting, for example, there are problems of credit risk, quality disputes and cash flow. However, the contractor may need working funds. A stakeholder account will give the client confidence that his money will not be released until he is satisfied. It will keep the contractor up to the mark and may encourage a bank to advance money for the work. For example, where contract terms are 'one-third on signing, balance on satisfactory completion', the client can be asked to deposit the initial third into a nominated bank acting as trustee for the seller. That bank, as stakeholder, will only release the funds when the client signs a 'release docket'. The seller will be keen to satisfy the client to obtain payment. If the seller is at fault, the stakeholder bank may refund the advance.

In all relevant industries, where a contract allows a customer to prove satisfactory completion of work before making payment, sellers should be always ready in advance with:

- a stakeholder account with a respectable bank;

- good wordings for contract terms which require advance payments using the stakeholder account; and

- a confident explanation of the scheme for clients.

Special payment terms, including prepayment A12.67

When a clearly risky customer wants time to pay, every seller should have the confidence to insist on some form of security. If the risk assessment is correct, there is little to fear and it is unlikely that the request is the first one to the errant customer.

The simplest starting point is to reduce the normal credit period to, for example, 7 or 14 days. This is better for the customer than having to pay cash and also indicates to all concerned that the supplier perceives a risk in allowing any longer. Accounts on special terms should be grouped together in the ledger for constant collection attention. Any default on special terms should lead to 'cash only' terms.

Many suppliers ask risky customers for an advance before releasing goods or providing a service. Normal credit is then allowed on the balance, e.g. '20 per cent before despatch, balance at 30 days from invoice date'. The mean risk is thus reduced and the customer still has time to organise the funds for the balance.

The use of load over load terms may simply manage the risk at an acceptable level.

Cash discount for prompt payment A12.68

This is a very expensive inducement to obtain payment from a customer who might become insolvent before normal terms mature. It is only viable when a seller's net margin is high and it has the staff resources to recover unauthorised deductions, i.e. discounts taken even when payments are made late. If only bad payers are offered cash discounts, all the good payers may demand the same benefit, effectively a price reduction for all customers.

Terms of say, '2% 10 days, net 30 days' should produce fast payment because a customer would be silly to ignore the lower net price. However, the seller's annualised cost is huge (36% per annum for the example above) and more expensive than waiting an extra two months for late payment. Also, it is difficult to recover deductions from payments made too late to qualify.

It is worth noting however that some countries standard commercial payment terms include an attractive discount level for early payment, for example after 10 days, but normal credit terms are 90 days. These longer credit markets also tend to delay actual payment further. In these circumstances granting a further 2% discount may be a valuable consideration in the administration process as managing the extended term debts can be a considerable additional burden. Building the 2% discount into the pricing for these local markets would cover the cost.

Prompt payment rebate scheme   A12.69

Far better than discounts (see **A12.62** above) for supposed prompt payments is to arrange a well-structured rebate scheme, which also encourages more purchases. If a seller invoices staged price reductions according to volumes purchased by customers who then pay late, he suffers a double cost, the interest cost of waiting for payment as well as the price reduction.

A popular scheme in many industries is for sellers to agree each year with a list of major customers to rebate the sales discounts by quarterly credit notes, but only for invoices paid on time. This is popular with purchasing staff because they are usually rewarded for savings, so they will make sure that billings are paid on time in order to qualify.

Legal expenses insurance   A12.70

In the building contracting industry, where technical disputes often delay payment, the fear of large legal costs deters many supplier firms from suing for their money. Some debtors are suspected of extending disputes because they know a supplier cannot afford litigation, so it is important that unpaid sellers feel confident of having disputes settled in court if needed. Insurance cover is available for such legal expenses and the help of an experienced broker is advised in negotiating the terms of a policy. When debtors are told that legal costs are not a barrier to proceedings, experience shows that disputes are settled more quickly without even going to court.

Summary   A12.71

As stated in the introduction, there are several ways available to sellers to take care of the risk of not being paid by customers. A security always means a cost, and the need for some degree of monitoring or administration. Good credit management, as practised by successful companies of all sizes, assumes that a sale is only a cost until it is paid, and that therefore information and communication skills are needed to preserve the intended profit margins, using security options wherever relevant and necessary.

A13

Collecting Outstanding Accounts

Introduction

The ideal world would be one in which there were no accounts outstanding, one in which all credit account customers paid their bills on time, and overdue was not a word in common use in accounting circles. This is not an ideal world, and the reality is that even if most customers 'behaved', many would not. The unknown factor for many is knowing which is which. That unknown factor can be minimised by risk analysis, up front credit management, and assimilation of all the available facts, but nevertheless it will remain to some extent.

For many businesses, as for many people, there is something slightly distasteful, even 'not British', about asking for money. It is seen by some as an almost grubby activity, beneath dignity, and to be avoided if at all possible. Perhaps it is more to do with the word 'debt' itself, which has connotations of unpleasantness, Carey Street and Dickensian poverty. Perhaps it is also to do with our expectations of others, and our profound disappointment when they fail to live up to those expectations. In reality, debt is only the condition of something owed by one to another. Many a Sales Director can be offended by his customers being referred to as debtors, but angry with them himself if they are reported as 'customers who have not paid'!

We live in a world now governed by 'rights'. Rights should be balanced by obligations, or responsibilities, and the process of collecting outstanding accounts is simply one of reminding the customer of his responsibilities and ensuring that he meets his obligations. The seller's side of the bargain has been fulfilled by supplying what was ordered at the agreed price, at the right time to the right place, and now the seller has the right to be paid. There is nothing grubby or 'not British' about that – on the contrary, rights and obligations underpin society as a whole.

A positive view, and a positive approach, is all that is needed.

Background

The purpose of being in business is to make a profit, and that profit is to be achieved by making and/or selling goods, or providing services, and being paid for those goods or services. The well known cycle of raw materials to finished goods or stocks to sales to debtors to cash to raw materials etc. holds the key to success in so far as the flow is regular and not slowed down or stopped by some failure along the way. Turning debts into cash is not the easiest part of the cycle, but for profits it is the most important. Not to be paid at all would soon bring the whole cycle to a grinding halt and to be paid slowly and constantly beyond terms would have a negative effect on profits and just as surely lead to the same inevitable halt. Cash needs to be collected (for the main part it does not collect itself), otherwise it is not cash at all, and the collection of what is owed is both basic to survival and the key to profitable success.

Collection is not haphazard. Doing the work, or supplying the goods, and then sitting back and waiting for something to happen, such as being paid, may work in some cases, but it is not good enough to be sure of payment. Nor is it good enough just to have a contingency plan which says that after sitting back and waiting with the result that nothing happens, something will be done. Collection is pro-active, not reactive, with a planned approach based upon a considered policy and a defined business need. Any plan in business is based upon where the business is at the current time, where it wants to be, and how it will get there. So too with the collection of cash.

The planned collections policy is part of the credit policy of the business (see **A1 CREDIT POLICY**), and defines:

- the collection methods to be employed;

- the collection timescale;

- responsibility and authority of collection personnel; and

- alternatives or sanctions available in the event of non-payment.

Collection methods would include invoices, statements, reminder letters, telephone calls, faxes, e-mails and visits. Sanctions would include the stop list, retention of title, charging interest and using debt collection agencies, solicitors and legal proceedings. The approach is therefore structured and planned, known to all personnel, including sales, and written into company policy.

The planned approach to collections begins with timing and priorities. If the trade in which the supplier is involved operates principally on a monthly cycle (i.e. monthly payment runs against invoices raised in the previous month, or whatever the terms may be), then the collection cycle follows that pattern. The question is how the collection sequence runs through that pattern, and the timings of the different actions to achieve optimum results. Using a combination of collection methods, the activity flow could be:

- invoice;

- statement;

- first reminder letter;

- first telephone call;

- second or final letter;

- stop list;

- second or final telephone call; and

- collection agency, solicitors or legal action.

Actual timings would depend upon individual businesses and their terms, or terms agreed with specific customers and interspersed could/would be faxes and e-mails where appropriate. The fax and/or the e-mail may replace the reminder letter or the telephone call in certain circumstances, but the balance and frequency would be determined by the nature of business and business culture. The collection cycle would begin at the earliest opportunity, starting early enough in the month to ensure payment within that month. Whatever the mix of phone calls, faxes, e-mails and reminder letters, the framework should be:

- constant;

- part of the company credit policy; and

- a process which is clear to everybody.

Priorities begin with the biggest and most significant values first, the smaller and less significant later. Working alphabetically through a sales ledger would mean that the 'A's and 'B's receive the most attention and the 'W's and 'Y's never hear from the supplier at all. The Pareto Principle (20% of customers account for 80% of sales) is an accepted fact in commercial terms, so emphasis on the 20% of customers who account for 80% of business makes more commercial sense than trying to trawl through the whole sales ledger in the limited time available.

Invoices and statements   A13.3

Invoices and statements are requests for payment, the former being the first request following the supply of goods or provision of services, and the latter being a summary at month end of all the transactions which have taken place in that month. (See **A8 COMPUTER ACCOUNTING SYSTEMS AND MONITORING OF THE SALES LEDGER** for a discussion on the clarity and accuracy of these documents and the need for promptness in their production and issue.)

In the context of account collection, the sooner the customer receives invoices or statements, the sooner the payment process begins. Accuracy is a prerequisite, as is getting it right first time. Initially the invoice should include the correct:

- name and address;

- delivery details;

- order number;

- type, quantity and price of goods delivered;

- VAT amount; and

- totals.

Delivering the right goods, at the right price, at the right time, to the right place, reinforces the right to be paid – failing to do any of the former will only weaken the latter.

Making it easier for the customer to pay is part of the exercise, so the use of detachable remittance advice slips on invoices and statements adds value to the documents. So too do clear instructions as to where payment should be made, and the variety of payment options available, such as credit transfer or credit card. Including the payment due date on the invoice is a useful additional guide and reminder, though strictly speaking the invoice and statement are produced after the contract has been negotiated and agreed, so that date is not of itself necessarily binding.

Using only second class post as a matter of policy can be self-defeating in terms of savings on postage set against costs incurred in delayed payments. There should be a flexible approach to the policy on post, there being many occasions when use of first class post has a distinct advantage in ensuring the invoice reaches the customer in time for inclusion in his current month's purchase ledger.

Getting it right first time is part of any quality operation, as any extra time and expense incurred in making sure at the beginning of the trade cycle that everything is correct is more than repaid at the conclusion of the transaction. Delay costs, promptness pays, and delays caused by the inefficiency or sloppiness of the supplier cannot be blamed on the customer.

Aged debt reports   A13.4

For many businesses, the aged debt report is the principal collection tool for the collector (see **A8.13** above). Used as either a hard copy print, or online screen display, the report gives the collector the full listing of all customer balances and their ages, in a format determined by the collector. The report can show the full customer name, address, contact name and telephone number, together with individual invoices and totals, or a summary with just customer name and outstanding balances by monthly total. Format is according to need and volumes and will vary from business to business, but the purpose is to show debts which need attention as well as those which may not.

Customers can be sorted by geographic location, turnover, balance, representative, sales area, or whatever combination is required, and split between different collectors according to their seniority, responsibility or authority. Using the report on a day to day basis and updating it as cash is received forms the base document on which collectors can work.

Similarly the sales ledger itself, in effect the supplier's copy of the customer statements, can be the base document, sorted and distributed among collectors in the same way as the aged debt report and containing the same information. It is interesting to note that in many businesses, no matter the level of sophistication reached in full computerisation, many collectors still prefer to work from hard copy print outs, and make notes and comments on these at the same time as making memo record pad entries into the system.

Collection plans – use of letters   A13.5

The use of reminder letters in the collection process has been the subject of debate for many a year. Rather like statements (or indeed trade and bank references), they have their enthusiastic supporters and their detractors – some would not consider undertaking any collection activity without them, and others would use them very rarely, if ever. The argument revolves around the effectiveness of the reminder letter, it being destined immediately on receipt to 'File 13' (the waste paper bin), or it being the prompt to pay that the customer has been waiting for. The waste paper protagonists found allies in the early days of computerisation, when computer produced reminder letters were pre-printed on flimsy paper, complete with sprocket holes down each side, and did nothing to encourage the customer to think that he was anything but an unimportant tiny cog in a much bigger and far more important wheel. Indeed, not only were these letters pre-printed, but the wording was standard, everyone got one if they were overdue, regardless of the size of the debt or the customer or circumstance, and there was no evidence of them even having been seen or vetted by the issuing supplier. The phrase 'Sorry about that, it's the computer' certainly devalued the reminder letter as a means of collection and caused much stress between credit and sales departments.

However, even with such difficulties, supporters argued that the reminder letter ensured that at least every customer who was overdue was certain to be contacted, including those whose accounts were small and did not in truth warrant a telephone call or visit. Added to that, the reminder letter spelled out the supplier's intentions in the event of the account not being paid, so the customer would know that not paying the account would lead to a suspension of supplies and, possibly, further more serious action. Supporters would also maintain that for businesses with a very large number of customers, especially those with a high number of accounts with low individual value, the letter was the most cost-effective way of issuing reminders. There is middle ground, as in all debates, and reminder letters have an accepted place in the collection process.

Variable content and timing   A13.6

Notwithstanding the comments at **A13.5** above regarding reminder letters and computerisation, one significant way of improving the effectiveness of the letter is to vary the content. This is now infinitely more possible than in the past due to the growth of computerisation and the levels of sophistication now achievable. Downloading data from mainframes to PCs, and using word processing functionality, enables the production of letters which can be tailored for specific accounts and which look individually produced. A letter, written on good quality notepaper, addressed to an individual person, or at least to a job title, and actually signed by the issuer, looks more professional, and is therefore far less likely to find its way automatically into the waste paper bin.

Actual variation of the wording means that priority accounts, significant customers or those where special circumstances exist for whatever reason, receive a reminder letter which has an impact beyond the standard reminder. Addressing to a named individual emphasises the importance of the customer to the supplier, as does the letter carrying both the signature and name of the writer. In addition, that signature and name gives the customer a point of contact and may help to uncover or isolate a problem which has caused payment to be delayed but which has yet to be resolved.

Even if the customer does not warrant what may be described as a 'special reminder letter', there is much to be said for varying the content and format of general reminder letters from time to time. Familiarity with form and content breeds complacency in the attitude of the customer, as he may feel he knows the system, knows the boundaries and can play the game up to the wire. A change in the format and content can be something of a jolt to the customer and keeps the initiative with the supplier.

The same is true about the timing of reminder letters. It is for the supplier to decide when to issue the first reminder letter and how soon after the due date, and therefore how many days overdue the payment is. As previously stated, it is advantageous to begin the collection process as soon as feasible in the prevailing trading and economic conditions. It is not unusual for a form of 'reminder' letter to actually be sent *before* the account is due, reminding the customer that the account will be due for payment on a given date and trusting that all is satisfactory and payment can be expected on time. Such a letter could also add that should there be any problems the customer should contact the writer etc. However, certainly once an account is a week overdue the customer should be contacted.

Calendar months and accounting periods vary in length, and allowing for capacity and user constraints, some variation in the timing of reminder letters can be a useful method of making the customer aware of the obligation to pay the account. The same type letter, on more or less the same day every month dilutes the impact – the customer knows the timetable just as well as the supplier and can gear his payment pattern accordingly. It should be borne in mind that collection of accounts is not just a matter of collecting overdue debts, but is also intended to be an educative process as far as the supplier's terms with the customer are concerned. That is to say that the idea is always to find ways of bringing the customer into line with the agreed terms. The customer should be made aware that a reminder this month does not mean by definition that the same credit is allowed next month or the month after that. The ideal situation is to remind the customer just the once, and thereafter payment is made when it is due. This is a noble ambition, and possibly very difficult to achieve, but by sticking rigidly to a well known and predictable timetable it is undoubtedly impossible.

Number of reminders before the final notice   A13.7

The actual number of reminder letters which a supplier is prepared to issue to a customer in respect of his overdue account is a matter very much for the supplier to consider carefully. There are factors to take into account, such as:

- the size and importance of the account to the supplier;

- the importance of the supplier and/or his product to the customer; and

- the level of accounts receivable which the supplier is prepared, or able, to sustain.

Competitive issues, price and other factors may be considered, but the overriding concern has to be the cost impact to the supplier of carrying the debt for any appreciable length of time. Low margins, for example, dictate rapid action, as do the cash needs of the business, and it could also be that the resources available to the supplier for cash collection are limited, meaning that collection has to be prompt and effective.

The collection process begins with the issue of an invoice, followed by the production of a statement. Any customer therefore in effect receives at least two requests for payment. Most businesses would conclude that one, and at the most two, reminder letters before the final notice was issued was quite sufficient. If it is assumed that the collection process also includes reminders by telephone, fax and/or e-mail (see **A13.18** below), then in reality one reminder letter before final notice is enough. The more reminder letters that are sent, each one at a cost to the supplier, the more time the customer has to pay, unofficially giving the customer extended credit at an additional cost to the supplier which was not taken into account in the original pricing of the goods or services. Add to that the non-variation of content and timing (see **A13.6** above), and the result is a charter for delayed payment.

Reminder letters should be polite but firm, clearly defining what is expected of the customer and by when, and equally clearly informing the customer of the consequences of ignoring the reminder. The final notice should be just as polite, but firm in its resolve, and again should clearly explain the consequences resulting from non-payment by the specified date. Of course, no letter should make illegal threats, but nor should any letter contain the threat of some action that the supplier is not prepared to carry out and follow through at the stated time. Idle threats are as ineffective as idle promises, and knowing the supplier has no intention of doing what he says he is going to do leaves the customer in the safe and comfortable knowledge that he can pay whenever he wants to. The deadlines set out in reminder letters and final notices should be clearly shown (the best way is to specify an actual date), and should be adhered to at all times.

There will be circumstances where the timetable goes adrift following a customer response to the reminder, for example, he may make a promise to pay, a part payment or a query. This is not necessarily a bad thing in so far as the customer has at least responded to the reminder, so some progress has been made. The customer has probably also acknowledged that he owes the debt which may prove very useful later on. What is not going to happen, however, is that the whole process starts again from the beginning – the reminder letter procedure has been followed and the account is now at another stage of the collection process.

Predicting problems   A13.8

The computer provision of data available to the collector and the credit clerk, in the form of a history of the account, puts the collector who is in constant contact with the customer in a unique position to be able to recognise signs of impending trouble (see **A8.29–A8.36** above). The collector by experience over a period of time can be aware of how difficult it can be to make contact with the right person, how often promises have been made and not kept, or cheques returned dishonoured and how many times the customer has come up with some excuse or reason for not being able to pay. Each occurrence is recorded on the memo pad or record card and can be brought up on screen or on file each time the customer is contacted. This history of the account, which also includes dates of payments actually received, reminders and final notices sent, goods stopped and debt collection agents instructed, gives an accurate feel for the account and for the customer, and is invaluable in assessing steps to be taken to safeguard the investment in receivables. It also guides the collector as to the approach to be taken on subsequent contact and the need for a higher authority (such as middle or senior management) to be involved in the collection process. There is the additional advantage of continuity – a new collector can take over from a colleague and be brought up to date speedily by having all that information and history to hand.

Frequency and variety of excuses   A13.9

Excuses are plentiful and varied, and many a credit controller or collector will enjoy a subdued chuckle on hearing the same excuse from different customers, a new variation on an old theme or a brand new reason not heard before. New ones do crop up from time to time, but usually they are constant and subject to recycling with slight variations, a few examples include:

- 'My cheque is in the post';
- 'We have already paid this account';
- 'We need a copy invoice';
- 'Can I have proof of delivery?';
- 'The director who signs the cheques is on holiday';
- 'The director who signs the cheques is off sick';
- 'There is a postal strike down here';
- 'Our customers have not paid us yet';
- 'The computer is down';

- 'The auditors have my books'; and

- 'Your rep said he would sort it out'.

It is the constant use and repetition of excuses, as well as the different excuses themselves, which indicate to the collector that all is not well and further action is going to be needed. Each excuse has the necessary response, which may be sympathetic in some instances when used for the first time, but account history reveals whether or not that particular, or any other, excuse has been used before.

A previously reasonably well conducted account may have run into difficulties for the first time, and rather than facing up to the fact and looking to the supplier for some understanding and possible assistance, the customer may try to hide behind a reason which is in fact transparent to the supplier. The situation may improve and the payment may be made, in which case all is well until the next time. Alternatively things may get worse, excuses becoming more usual than payment. One excuse for non-payment is in itself not bound to be a bad sign, but seen in the light of previous trading history and of prevailing economic conditions at the time, it could be serious.

Customers who are awaiting payment   A13.10

Much is made of the strength of so called big business and its ability to put pressure on smaller customers, who in turn are reluctant to press their own customers for payment. Hence the 'we are still waiting for our customers to pay us' response. Whatever the rights and wrongs of that argument, it is often a genuine reason rather than an excuse as such, and the supplier should be looking for ways to educate the customer in his own credit control and collection procedures to ensure that both parties reach a satisfactory outcome.

Requests for copy invoices   A13.11

Constant requests for copy invoices may be a delaying tactic by the customer or a sign of his own inefficiency. The same is true for repeated requests for proof of delivery. However, it may just be that the supplier is in fact doing something wrong, not having noted the customer's precise invoicing and delivery instructions. It would be beneficial for the supplier to check to be sure that his own house is in order before attaching doom-laden interpretations to such customer requests. It is, however, comparatively easy to spot the excuse rather than the reason, and the frequency and the variety is the trigger to alert attention.

Broken promises   A13.12

The customer making a commitment to pay and then failing to do so, is a much more obvious and serious sign of problems. The history of the account should have notations regarding promises of payments made, and the date of that undertaking, together with a note of when payment was actually received and what follow-up action had been required to achieve settlement. When somebody says they are going to send the cheque, and they do, then the next time a request for payment is made, and a promise is given, that promise is going to be taken at face value. However, the reverse is true and a promise to pay followed by nothing means that the next time the collector is less likely to accept any future undertaking as being genuinely meant. That being the case, all subsequent dealings will be under the cloud of distrust and arrangements for settlement will have to be more carefully scrutinised and more strictly enforced.

Attempts should be made by the collector to try to establish why promises have not been kept. If the customer is having some difficulty in obtaining payment from his own customers, it is possible that at the time the promise of a cheque was made, it was made in good faith, on the reasonably confident expectation that he would be collecting some of his own accounts and therefore be in a position to issue a cheque to his supplier. It may be argued that a promise not kept under such circumstances may be better than the customer having blithely issued a cheque, knowing that at the time of issue, funds were not available to clear the cheque (see **A13.13** below).

Again it would be the frequency of such events which would alert the collector to the genuine quality of the promise or otherwise, and in any event the broken promise itself is yet another sign of trouble. It is the record of such events which establishes a pattern.

Post-dated/dishonoured cheques   A13.13

Unsolicited post-dated cheques represent a problem, although this is not necessarily the case when arrangements have been made to accept post-dated cheques. Although the practice is not to be actively encouraged, there are circumstances when the receipt of post-dated cheques by prior agreement is an acceptable way of reaching settlement of an account. For example, sale of a large amount of redundant stock to a particular customer may be possible if that customer can have the opportunity to pay for that larger than normal purchase over a longer credit period, and in good faith offers a series of post-dated cheques to cover the balance. It may also be that an agreement to settle a large debt by way of post-dated cheques can be a satisfactory compromise to avoid legal proceedings and perhaps force the customer into insolvency. Under normal circumstances, however, the receipt of a post-dated cheque has to be viewed as a sign of difficulty. It has not been pre-arranged, therefore it was not known to the supplier that this was going to happen, and it must mean that at the time that the cheque was issued, the issuer knew that there would be insufficient funds to cover the payment, but hoped that there would be by the date of presentation. It is just possible that if the date is only one or two days hence, the cheque can be kept and presented on the specified date, but this would be seen as an acceptance of the customer's further delaying tactic and should therefore be discouraged. In any event, the customer should be contacted and challenged as to the reason for post-dating without prior consultation, and told that acceptance of the cheque was not to be taken as approval or as a precedent. There would also be the need to establish an assurance that if the post-dated cheque was accepted, then it would be honoured upon first presentation, and no further orders would be accepted, or goods delivered until the cheque had actually cleared. The history file should be noted, and reference to any previous instances of post-dated cheques, pre-arranged or otherwise, would add to the evidence that the customer is in trouble and that care is needed.

Dishonoured cheques are serious, for perhaps more than anything else, they could indicate real cash problems and are therefore a great cause for concern. The use of the word 'could' is deliberate because, on the one hand, there are a number of reasons why a cheque can be returned by the bank, and on the other hand, there could be a genuine error. The various reasons, and the appropriate action to take are covered in **A13.51–A13.53** below, but it is worth noting here the possibility of genuine error. There are circumstances when banks make mistakes, especially at a time of changing of accounts, or where a new overdraft limit has been agreed but for some reason not notified correctly to the customer account. There can also be genuine mistakes by the customer as it is becoming increasingly common, especially among small businesses, to maintain current accounts with enough in them to service day to day needs in general, but to move surplus funds to interest-bearing deposit accounts. If the customer miscalculates, what he thought would be enough turns out not to be so, and much to his embarrassment a cheque will be returned. Of course, in either situation, the matter can be rectified quickly and satisfactorily, but the circumstances should be noted in the history record file in order that such a returned cheque is not taken as a sign that the customer has no funds at all.

More often than not, however, dishonoured cheques *are* a bad sign, and repeated instances with the same customer must tell the collector that he is trading very much on the edge, and considered to be of high risk.

The degree of difficulty in contacting the payer

A13.14

A sure sign of trouble is not being able to contact the person within the customer organisation who is responsible for the authorisation and/or the release of payment. On asking for a named contact when telephoning, a hesitation before being asked who it is that is calling and then being told that the contact is not in or not available, even though the caller knows that he is, quite clearly indicates avoidance. That the contact is constantly in meetings, and not returning calls when messages have been left, all point to an unwillingness to take a call which it is known is going to be about the account. If letters or faxes are not answered either, the collector is left with no alternative but to suspect the worst, and to take action accordingly. Analysis of the telephone record cards or memo pads and a review of previous attempts to contact will soon reveal the extent of the problem. If the account warrants more attempts at contact, a visit by collection staff, or the assistance of the sales department might be sought, but the warning signs are clear, and at the very least supplies should be stopped. This can have the effect of the customer's buyer becoming involved, and acting for the supplier's collector in trying to get some response from the payer contact.

The importance of being alert to changes   A13.15

All the warning signs will be there, dutifully recorded in the payment history and memo records, including:

- persistent avoidance;

- dishonoured cheques;

- post–dated cheques;

- on account or part payments;

- broken promises;

- excuses;

- payments becoming later and later each month; and

- requests for extended credit or temporary help.

It is even worth recording opinions on attitude and morale, and noting high turnover of purchase ledger staff or the unexpected resignation of the managing director or the finance director. It is important for the collector to be alert to changes and be on the look out for early warnings of trouble. Equally, the collector has to distinguish between the beginning of the end and what may only be a temporary problem, and he should be in a position to seek help and guidance.

Collection methods   A13.16

The background to this chapter outlined the principle of a planned approach to account collection and the mixture of methods available to the business in undertaking the task (see **A13.2** above). It is not the aim here to define or describe any particular method as being better or worse than any other, as each has its place in the collection process, and it has to be more effective to dovetail various types of collection activity into one cohesive process. A typical flow has already been described (see **A13.2** above), and much will depend upon volumes and values, but on the basis that getting paid is the objective, it follows that all avenues must be considered and such resources as are available should be utilised. The prime tools to hand are:

- letters;

- telephone calls;

- faxes and e-mails;

- customer visits;

- assistance from sales personnel; and

- use of the stop list as an aid to collection.

Letters A13.17

The timing and content of reminder letters has already been discussed (see **A13.5–A13.7** above), it is their place in the overall collection context which is the subject here. The weakness is obvious, they can simply be ignored, though it has to be repeated that many companies do in fact wait for the reminder letter and pay on that, and that the sending of reminder letters to all and sundry does ensure that all customers have received written notification of the position regarding their account. It is also a recorded event on the system, noted for future analysis and can be regarded as the first serious attempt to collect the outstanding debt. Customers often react in an aggrieved manner to a telephone call, fax or a visit, and of course they are most distressed at the knowledge of being on stop. Often they vehemently maintain that this is the first they knew about the debt. They have had the goods, they have had the invoice, they have had the statement *and* they have had the reminder letter – have they lost *all* those pieces of paper? One is inclined to think not, and if they have, then something somewhere is seriously wrong. As far as the supplier is concerned, a polite and courteous reminder letter is an established cost effective method of trying to make contact with the customer to nudge him towards meeting his obligations, and to indicate what happens next if payment is not made. It is far better to specify actual dates by which payment should be made, though more often than not, the first reminder letter tends to be more generalised than the second or final notice. A reminder letter is cost effective to produce and issue in large numbers – it covers the whole of the overdue balances and ensures that no customers are missed, unless by specific design.

Responses to letters vary – some will in fact prompt payment and a measure as to whether or not they are being effective is easy to achieve. Over a period of time the supplier can analyse payment dates in relation to reminder letter issue dates and draw general conclusions. What can be said is that in many busy sales ledger departments, staff will know when the reminders have been sent because there is an increase in incoming cash. Customer service will know too because the telephone lines will be busy with customers calling with queries or questions. For many collectors, their first telephone call seems easier if they know that the customer has already been reminded by letter and their first call is in effect a follow-up call.

The choice of letter content, timing and number of letters is a business decision, as already discussed (see **A13.5–A13.7** above), and it may be that some businesses take the view that an invoice and a statement is enough of a notification in writing, and that the real reminder and collection process begins with the telephone call. It is for that reason that most businesses find a combination of letter and phonecall the best method of collection. The right letter, correctly worded, and the personal impact of the telephone call get closer to achieving the right result. (See **APPENDIX A13** for examples of letters.)

Telephone, fax and e-mail A13.18

The telephone is now regarded as the most effective method in collecting accounts. The strength lies in the immediacy of contact (notwithstanding the comments in **A13.14** above) – it is personal, creating one-to-one contact, and has to be dealt with by the recipient. Before embarking on a policy of telephone collections, indeed a policy of telephone only collections, a business has to assess costs and resources available. The number of accounts on the ledger, and their average values, together with the number of trained and qualified staff needed to carry out this specialist role, need to be taken into account. There is a relationship between the number of accounts and the volume of calls which staff would be expected to be able to make on a daily basis and the number of trained staff who can make those calls. It may not be possible to ensure that every single customer with a balance on the ledger can be called (hence the need for a mixture of telephone calls and reminder letters), and many of the balances themselves may not in reality justify the cost of trained staff calling. In working out the resources needed to collect accounts over the telephone, it has to be remembered that:

- each call will involve a certain amount of planning and preparation;

- some calls will take longer than others; and

- a number of calls will involve queries and disputes, as well as discussion of problems and negotiating agreements.

In addition, notes have to be made to ensure follow up, and perhaps it will be necessary to involve other people, like sales or dispatch. In other words what may appear to be a reasonable relationship between numbers of accounts and numbers of trained collectors may subsequently be discovered to be out of balance, with the department in fact lacking in the resource for the activity planned. In real terms, the cost of telephone calls is now much cheaper than ever before, but staff may have to hold from time to time, and make more than one call to the same customer in order to contact the right person. If the credit control department does not have specified collectors and that function is just one of the credit controller's roles, then they cannot, for instance, telephone collect when allocating cash received, and they cannot do their ledger updates when making telephone calls.

Telephone collection work requires special skills (see **A7.4–A7.9** above). In untrained hands the telephone can damage customer relations, produce no tangible beneficial result and prove to be expensive. If the issue of a reminder letter is defined by some as a clerical role, the opposite is true of telephone collection. The collector must have:

- company and product knowledge;

- the right telephone technique;

- the authority to discuss and negotiate with customers; and

- the responsibility to make agreements and arrangements with customers within defined parameters.

With all that in mind, the use of the telephone has a central role in the collection process, either following on from the first reminder letter, or being the first reminder in its own right. The call produces a promise by the customer to pay (the best result) and highlights a query which has to be identified as genuine and followed through to resolution, or identified as a delaying tactic and overcome accordingly. Equally, the call could result in no payment, either because the customer:

- will not pay (the collector needs to establish why); or
- cannot pay because he has no money, in which case the collector has to decide on the next course of action.

Using fax messages as a reminder tool is not as effective as it was when fax machines first became a common feature of business offices. They were seen to be more immediate than a reminder letter, though less immediate than a telephone call, and produced a customer response by fax or phone. Over recent years, however, they have diminished as an actual reminder weapon, though they do play a vitally important role in speedily getting copies of documents to customers in order to shorten the payment delay time. Faxed reminders now tend to be on a par with reminder letters in the results achieved, so they do have their place in the overall activity.

More recent developments in the reminder and collection field include the use of e-mails as a method of immediate contact. This has proved to be quite effective in making immediate and personal contact with the right person, and there is every reason to believe that the use of e-mails will continue to grow. However, some care should be taken to ensure that familiarity does not breed contempt and that e-mails are specifically targeted to the right person at the right time. More and more large organisations use e-mail indiscriminately to circulate all manner of internal documents, safety briefings, organisational changes, rules and regulations, and more often than not mixed in with the important messages are the trivia, referring to birthdays, leaving parties or forthcoming social events. The forwarding and re-forwarding of notes and messages substantially increases their length, even more so with large circulation lists attached or headed, and the trash folder becomes a recipient's favourite.

The sender of an e-mail should ensure that there is clarity for the recipient as to exactly who has sent him the e-mail – 'anyperson@anyservice.com' may be insufficient. More professional is to set up an e-mail template which incorporates senders name, job title, company name, telephone and fax numbers and e-mail address:

Glen Bullivant

Credit Manager

XXXXXXX Ltd

Direct Phone 0123 45678

Direct Fax 0123 45679

E-Mail glen.bullivant@.......co.uk

It follows that though the recipient may be alerted to the fact that he has received a message, no guarantee exists that a reply will be forthcoming. Therefore, all the usual follow-up diary procedures apply equally to e-mails as they do to telephone calls or letters. There is a further pitfall to consider – updating the customer file. Copies of letters in the file may be old fashioned, but the computer notepad is an up-to-date way of keeping the file current. Therefore, it is important to note date and contents of e-mails on the file so that it is clear to anyone with access to the customer file just what is the latest situation.

There is a tendency for many operators to assume that sending an e-mail is in itself sufficient. On the contrary, the mere fact that it is quick and easy to utilise the function can be self-defeating if no record is kept other than that locked away in the operator's own password protected system. In the drive to paperless offices, the reality for many has turned to the concept of a *less paper* office, and many a customer paper file now contains e-mail print outs! It can also be tempting to include others on a circulation list either to confirm that action is being taken or to nudge the recipient into taking the message more seriously because someone else may become involved. The credit controller may well want to alert the customer finance director to the lack of action on the part of the customer purchase ledger department, but user beware – relationships can be severely damaged by thoughtless attempts at scoring points at someone else's expense.

The same careful thought should be given before putting finger to keyboard as applies to pen to paper, or face-to-face encounter. Many e-mails are riddled with spelling mistakes, bad grammar, ill constructed sentences or phrases. Very often in the heat of the moment, things are said which in the cold light of re-reading should not have been said. It is very easy indeed to press 'send' and almost instantly regret it. Creating a word document memo appears to have an editing discipline attached to it which e-mail senders neglect. As methods of communicating, the telephone and the fax were revolutionary in their time – the e-mail is another method of communication, and requires the same measure of care and attention.

Customer visit   A13.19

Whilst it is clearly not possible for credit control and collection staff to visit every customer, and it could be argued that it would not be a good thing for customers to receive constant visits by such staff, such visits do have a part to play in the collection process. Very often the best way to reconcile accounts or resolve outstanding queries is face to face, and combining the visit with the collection of a cheque for the agreed balance can prove worth the effort and the expense. A large and valuable customer, for example, could be a problem with constant and continual requests for copy invoices and proof of delivery, which may be due to both the complexities of their internal bureaucracy and the supplier's failure to understand the requirements necessary to ensure a swift passage of their invoices through the customer's payment procedures. Such visits can also be good for the relationship between supplier and customer on a personal level, putting faces to names and voices, and fostering goodwill.

Visits have to be planned carefully, making appointments with the people to be seen and making the travel arrangements so that the visitor arrives in plenty of time. The collector should be well prepared, with all the facts and figures to hand and with the authority and responsibility to carry out the negotiations and agreements which may be required. As a matter of courtesy, the sales department should be informed of the intended visit and invited to accompany the credit controller, if the visit is mainly a public relations and goodwill exercise the representative will want to be there, however, if it is all about money, sales may not wish to attend. (See **A13.20** below for more information on the involvement of sales personnel.) They will, of course, be interested in the outcome and will expect and be entitled to a report of the meeting upon return to the office.

Visits to the same customer regularly to pick up cheques should be avoided. The customer can become used to the fact that the credit controller will call to collect, and begin to save himself the cost of postage, the supplier footing the bill each time to collect his own money. (See also **A7.10** above.)

Sales personnel   A13.20

The use of sales personnel in the collection process can be described as contentious. In some businesses, involvement of sales in credit collection matters is frowned heavily upon on the grounds that their role is to sell and that any function which detracts from that is bad for business. Others take the view that commission is earned on paid for sales, and it is in their interest to assist, where required, in obtaining payment. It is certainly true that sales are more regular visitors to the same customers than any of the credit staff, and therefore know people within the customer's organisation on a more personal level, which may give them greater powers of persuasion. On the other hand, the people they know are not necessarily the people who authorise and sign the cheques. That is not to say that sales should not be aware of credit or collection issues concerning their customer – on the contrary, they may be in the ideal position on their next visit to resolve outstanding queries, pick up faulty goods or confirm free of charge replacements.

Frequently, however, sales will feel it useful to be involved and to offer assistance. Future sales may be dependent upon getting the account back up-to-date and on an even keel. In addition, it can be quite enlightening for sales to have promises of payment made to them which have subsequently not been kept, as it gives them an insight into the difficulties faced by credit control in such circumstances.

Relationships between sales and credit control can be fragile, as can relationships between credit control and the customer from time to time. It is important therefore not to do anything to worsen that relationship, but to work constantly towards improving it. It is for each business to judge the value, or otherwise, of involving sales in the collection process, and much would depend on the mutual trust and understanding of the credit and sales departments.

Stop list   A13.21

The stop list, contentious document that it may be in many organisations, can serve as a useful collection tool (see **A4.30** above). For example, if a customer who is on the stop list wants an order, and the depot and the warehouse know that the customer is on stop because they have a listing which tells them so, a system will be in place which will not allow them to process an order without some appropriate action having been taken. That appropriate action could be for the depot or warehouse to arrange with the customer for the delivery driver to pick up a cheque when he makes a delivery. Once this has been cleared with credit control, another outstanding account will have been sorted out. The driver may have instructions not to accept cash (for insurance and security reasons) and not to unload the van until he has been into the office and collected the cheque.

There are pitfalls, as one might expect. The driver will have a schedule of deliveries to make, with the van loaded and the route arranged, in such a way as to make optimum use of the time available. Each delivery where such a cheque collection has to be made may slow down the delivery process and cause problems with the delivery schedule. It is also true to say that delivery drivers are delivery drivers and not debt collectors, and may not feel comfortable with the role of asking for payment before the van is unloaded. On the other hand, if the practice is part of the company culture and the role is expected of them, delivery drivers can become extremely useful to credit control as reliable collectors of cheques and, equally, useful sources of information. Back in the office at the end of the day, the cheques will be handed over, often with interesting pieces of information about the customer, for example, picket lines, locked warehouse, staff standing around doing nothing, new cars in the directors' spaces, a competitor delivering at the same time and also picking up a cheque. In such organisations as these, many depot and warehouse managers become proxy credit controllers, getting to know the regular stop list accounts and being prepared to make arrangements without being asked – further than that, they will try to persuade such customers to pay the next due amount at the same time so as to avoid next month's stop list.

For collectors back in the credit office, the stop list may also be the base document for the final round of telephone calls to try to avoid debt collectors and legal action.

Analysis of accounts will show every month A thousand statements, followed by B thousand reminder letters, resulting in C hundred final notices, D hundred stopped accounts and E number of debt collections or legal action accounts. What began as a flood ends as a trickle, due to the collection contribution made by letters, telephone calls, faxes and e-mails, visits, sales, and the stop list.

Dealing with problem customers   A13.22

Every supplier will have accounts which, for some reason or another, become a problem. The definition of problem is broad and far reaching, late payment is experienced for a variety of reasons, and collecting cash is very closely linked to understanding what those reasons are and how they should be tackled. Problems cannot be directly connected to the inability to pay as such, though they may directly impinge on payment performance. Queries or disputes allowed to build up and remain unresolved will cause the customer not just to hold back on the payment of disputed invoices, but also to freeze the whole account until somebody does something about it.

Lack of money is an obvious reason for non-payment, or delayed payment, though businesses will go to great lengths to hide the fact, or even not be prepared to face those facts themselves.

Inefficiency can be a prime factor in late payment, both in the customer's organisation and also in the supplier's. Some processes are cumbersome and bureaucratic, even more are simply sloppy, and invoices, goods received notes and other documentation is lost among chaotic offices or stuffed into drawers somewhere and forgotten about.

Where it is deliberate company policy to take as long as it is conceivably possible to pay accounts, the customer will delay payment to the supplier every time. The task of the collector is to identify and handle each account accordingly.

The right person   A13.23

The 'right person' is the one who can pay the account, or at least the one who can see that the account is paid. The right person is also the one who is preventing the account from being paid. They may be one and the same, they may be different people, and it is part of the collection process to identify them.

The identification process may well depend upon the size of the customer organisation. A small business run by the owner will mean trying to talk to the owner himself every time. This is itself not always an easy thing to achieve – the collector phones from the comfort and *privacy* of his office environment, but the owner may not have an office, the phone being in the shop or café and in full public view and hearing. Sole traders and partnerships require a different approach in so far as the collector is in effect trying to get the owner to dig into, what is to him, his own pocket to pay the account. The owner is therefore key to the account being paid, and probably controls his business personally – he is thus aware of every transaction, every reminder or call and is personally involved in the business every step of the way. It is also not unusual for the owner to be totally involved in the actual running of the business, 'working at the coal face' as it were, being an expert in whatever his business sells or produces, but not good at paperwork, and leaving, what is to him, the chore of the books to be done later when time permits. Perhaps he employs someone part-time, or is helped by his wife or by his accountant, and in the latter situation, the collector may have to speak to the accountant more often than not.

On the other hand, dealing with a large company usually means contacting the purchase ledger department, where staff are dealing with their company's money and are simply following instructions and procedures. The collector in this situation has to establish the right person to contact on either a regular basis, or on those occasions when particular problems need to be resolved. The purchase ledger clerk may suffice, but it may have to be the purchase ledger manager. The circumstances may dictate the financial controller as the contact, or even the finance director. Much will depend upon the reason for the problem with the account (see **A13.24** below). Alternatively it could also be that with the assistance of sales, the customer's buyer or even someone in the customer's production department could be identified as the key contact.

To differentiate between the types of customer organisation, and hence establish the right person to contact, requires the collector to have prepared beforehand and to have accurate customer file information which guides the approach to be taken.

The right question   A13.24

The obvious question revolves around 'When will I get paid?'. However, having already accepted the fact there are a number of reasons why accounts are not paid on time, collection activity needs to establish at the earliest opportunity just what the particular cause is in each case. The causes of non-payment or slow payment fall broadly into three categories:

- inability;
- inefficiency; and
- policy.

(See **A6.15** and **A8.20** above and **A13.29** below for further information on the problem of accounts queries.)

Inability   A13.25

A customer who has no cash is a customer who cannot meet obligations when they fall due. Shortage of working capital, cash tied up in debtors, and an imbalance between terms on which payments should be made to suppliers and terms given to their own customers are prime causes. The fundamental concept of cash flow may have been lost on the customer, or ignored, and in his eagerness to do business and generate turnover he may have failed to set up adequate controls. The result is shortage of liquid funds, and on the basis that he is working to the limit of his available or negotiated overdraft, and is unable to obtain additional support from the bank, he sees the supplier as the only source of finance open to him.

The original 'right question' may have been the simple one in respect of the account being overdue, and when will the cheque be sent. The customer may be open with the supplier on this issue, in which event the next right question will not be aimed at discovering the reason, but at finding out what needs to be done about it, or even what assistance may be offered.

The customer may, however, be trying to put the collector off, without revealing the real reason behind his failure to pay the account when due, in which event the collector will now try to discover exactly why this situation exists. Questions are therefore aimed at:

- isolating the root cause;

- discarding excuses which are not causes; and

- isolating the real reason.

Inability to pay clearly dictates the ensuing course of action, whatever that may be, and gives both collector and customer clear objectives to be achieved to return the account to normality. This may well include the collector now going beyond the purchase ledger clerk, or manager, and dealing direct with senior management or the owner.

Inefficiency   A13.26

From responses to the initial question about payment, the collector can identify problems of inefficiency within the customer company with comparative ease. Frequent references to staff shortages by the customer, or excuses about their computer system, coupled with constant requests for copy invoices or proof of delivery, are good signs of an organisation being disorganised. Getting to know the customer's invoice processing system is invaluable, not only because being forewarned is being forearmed, but also because there may be actions which the supplier can adopt to make the invoice processing procedure more effective. It is always a very good idea for sales ledger and collection staff to be able to spend some time in their own purchase ledger section, both to see how they operate in the clearance of supplier invoices and also to see what questions are asked of their own purchase ledger clerks, and how they are handled.

In many organisations there are often two very distinct methods of handling supplier invoices as far as it concerns purchase ledger.

- Register *all* incoming purchase invoices on to an invoice register as they are received at the centre, and then book them out to each relevant buyer or department for agreement and clearance. When received back duly signed and authorised, they can be passed on to the invoice payment system, coming up automatically for payment at due date. This has the advantage of knowing at any time where an invoice is in the company, such as awaiting authorisation or under query with the buyer. It also allows for cash planning, the invoice register giving full details of total liability in respect of unpaid invoices at any given time. Additionally, such a process gives an impression of efficiency at the outset, in that anyone calling about the account can have an immediate and accurate update of the true state of play, and not be fobbed off with, 'I can't find your invoice' or 'Can I call you back?' Equally, a request for a copy invoice in these circumstances is much more likely to mean that the invoice has never actually been received in the first place, and that frequent requests for copies might be more indicative of the supplier doing something wrong in the first place, rather than the customer being inefficient.

- Only register purchase invoices onto the ledger system when they have been received in the department as passed for payment, and they are then paid on due date. In large organisations, where there are numerous delivery and invoice points and one central payment, and therefore contact point, this can have enormous problems for people trying to establish when they will be paid. Enquiries of purchase ledger staff invariably call for copy invoices, because unless it has actually been approved and passed for payment, purchase ledger staff will have no idea as to whether or not it has been received, or indeed where it might now be. It could well be that purchase ledger want a copy so that they themselves can identify what the invoice was for, and therefore who may be responsible for authorising the approval of the invoice. Such a system is by no means uncommon, and the ramifications for the supplier can be costly.

Either scenario requires the supplier to be sure that they are doing everything correctly, invoicing and delivering according to customer instructions, that they have the correct addresses and postcodes and always quote customer order numbers etc. It is also worth checking to be sure that deliveries to the customer are as per the originally agreed schedule – it is all very well for the supplier to deliver early and ahead of schedule, but the customer has agreed delivery dates for a purpose. That purpose may well revolve around his own cash forecasting, and taking delivery early, and thus being expected to pay early may not be possible according to his own cash flow, and should be considered unreasonable. This is especially true where cash flow is critical, and in these circumstances the supplier is creating a situation which may not have existed before.

Small businesses can be inefficient when it comes to handling supplier invoices. Visiting the customer, the collector or the credit clerk can view an untidy and disorganised office, with papers bunched up on bulldog clips with no apparent system in place, a confused or flustered owner rummaging through box files or mounds of paper, opening drawers looking for the offending document, and not being altogether too sure of what it is he is looking for. The question the supplier will now be asking is 'What can be done to rectify the situation?'. It may be that the supplier regards the customer business as valuable enough to simply be aware of the customer's chaotic inefficiency and live with it, or perhaps take steps to let the customer know that it cannot be tolerated and that he must ensure that he takes care to see that these invoices are dealt with promptly or face the consequences.

Policy   A13.27

There is no doubt that some businesses do undertake, as a matter of policy, not to pay invoices when they are due, and to seek the maximum credit period which the supplier will apparently tolerate. In some cases, this is well known, and indeed the customer goes out of his way to notify that his payment terms are X days, whatever the credit terms that may have been stipulated by the supplier. Often, too, the customer will complain that a particular supplier, chasing payment on 30 days, is out of line with all his other suppliers, who give him 60 days. When the Government introduced the *Late Payment of Commercial Debts (Interest) Act 1998* (see **A5.8** and **A5.9** above and **A14.34** below), which brought onto the statute book the right to statutory interest on overdue accounts, there were attempts by some companies to officially notify all their suppliers that they were changing their payment terms. This was irrespective of previously agreed contractual arrangements and the clear purpose was to avoid falling foul of the legislation, by either ensuring that their own inefficiencies did not give rise to 'late' payment, or simply taking the opportunity, under cover of that reason, to take advantage of extended credit. Success or failure of that tactic was very much dependent upon such companies' relative strength in their own market place, but it certainly flew in the face of the spirit of the legislation.

The customer may not openly advertise the fact that it is policy to take as much credit as will be allowed. The policy is carried on under the smokescreen of various excuses given to collectors when seeking settlement of the account, such as 'we can't sign cheques here, they all go to head office' or 'all cheques need to be countersigned by the managing director' or 'we only have one payment run each month, the third Thursday and you have missed this month's run'. A common indicator of the company's policy towards payment is the request for cash discount, with the undertaking that if such discount was allowed, payment would be made sooner. In other words, it *is* possible to pay more quickly, but the customer has no intention of so doing unless it is made worth his while. The supplier's attitude to such payment policy has no doubt to take into consideration the value of the account, both in terms of the value of the supplier to the customer, and the value of the customer to the supplier, as well as the competition in the market place and prevailing economic conditions.

However, it is the initial approach by the collector, the responses to the questions regarding payment and the developing history of the account which identify the characteristics of the customer and show the way forward. In other words, there is more to just asking the question 'when will you pay me?' – it is more a question of 'why are you not paying me on time and what are we going to do about it?'.

Listening as well as hearing A13.28

Asking the right person the right question is the beginning, but being able to hear what the customer says, and actually listen to what he is saying holds the key to knowing exactly what is being dealt with. Put another way, customer responses can in some way be likened to bank replies to credit reference enquiries (see **A5.14** above), what is not being said is as important as what is being said. In attempting to identify the real nature of the problem with the customer, and to correctly identify the route to be taken to resolve the problem, the collector needs to be receptive to the customer's words. Late payment taken at face value is simply that, late payment. Looking deeper, however (see **A13.24–A13.27** above), reveals more to late payment than initially met the eye. The differences would be missed, however, if the collector had both a closed mind, and rattled off a pre-arranged form of words to the customer without a pause for breath, giving the customer little or no opportunity to respond. Analysis of that response means listening to exactly what is being said and applying the necessary interpretation to the meaning – missing the point does irreparable damage, and may not result in the account being paid. Even less certain would be the possibility of putting the account back on an even keel, and future trading amicably to terms, if indeed there is to be any future trading.

It is, of course, true that it is the supplier's money and the supplier has a right to be paid, but in order to deal effectively with problem customers, the real problem has to be known. The only way that initially the collector can gain that knowledge (which will be confirmed or otherwise by subsequent events) is to be in a position to be able to analyse all the meanings of what is being said. That calls for listening and hearing, and is a skill, which for some, needs to be acquired. The question of training was dealt with earlier (see **A7 STAFF TRAINING AND STAFF RECRUITMENT**), and it is as well to bear in mind that the purpose of collection activity is basically to seek payment of money due, which can only be done effectively if the collector is alert to all situations – that alertness may require more than just a natural talent.

Queries – genuine or not?   A13.29

The need to monitor and analyse customer queries, the maintenance of a query register and the importance of speedy resolution are dealt with elsewhere (see **A6.15** and **A8.20** above). When dealing with customers where problems are being experienced with payment, one significant issue may well be the question of customer disputes. Unless the collector is in possession of information to the contrary, it has to be assumed at the outset that the query is genuine and that the collector will find out from the customer the exact nature of the dispute. At first sight, it should not be automatically assumed that the query is spurious, and merely a delaying tactic, unless again the collector is aware of other factors. Such other information may well be that there is a long history of this customer raising insignificant queries on all or most of the invoices rendered to him, and that past experience has shown that in the end, the dispute cannot be substantiated and payment has to be made. In those circumstances, it may be reasonable to presume that disputes are delaying tactics. On the other hand, even with a long record of invoice queries, this particular one may be genuine, and needs to be resolved.

The collector should have confidence in his own company and product and in the company's ability to deliver to order and specification. The nature of the goods or services may well be of a type which is prone to dispute, such as product performance. Expensive capital equipment, with sophisticated specifications, may be perceived by the customer as not doing all that the sales representative led him to believe it would do (computer hardware and software is a favourite in this category), and the collector should be aware of the vagaries or otherwise of the company's own performance in this respect.

Special prices or discounts are also favourite areas of conflict, and again the collector should know his own sales force and pricing department, as well as the systems used and thus have a ready feel for potential problems. Price increases or alterations made to the product file, and meant to be applied to new orders from a certain date, all too often are applied retrospectively, wrongly pricing orders already in the system. In addition, the problems that can be created by the installation of new sales ledger software and systems can be manifold. All this has to be taken into account when contacting customers for settlement of accounts and from the very start of the process there should be an awareness of the likelihood of disputed invoices due to the supplier's own actions.

On the basis that all is well at the supplier company, the raising of a dispute by a customer requires immediate attention. If this is the first time that the customer has been approached for payment, any dispute must be taken as genuine. There is no track record to indicate otherwise, and the query must be followed up and resolved without delay. Prompt action will soon separate the genuine from the not so genuine and may also give the collector an early indication of the customer's efficiency (see **A13.26** above). Following swift resolution of the query, the next test will be to see how quickly the customer now settles the held invoice. Early payment would tend to support the contention that the dispute was in fact genuine. Protracted payment, only after more contact by the collector, would lead to the view that it was indeed a delaying tactic. The next time, the collector will have a better idea of the nature of the customer being dealt with.

Knowing that the dispute is spurious simply means that the collector knows how quickly to act to settle the matter and the course of action to be taken. In effect that is calling the customer's bluff, confirming that the invoice is correct and seeking immediate payment. Full use of the updated customer history file and the analysis provided by the properly maintained query register add weight to the collector's conclusion and subsequent action.

One of the most difficult types of query to deal with, certainly as far as its effect on the ledger is concerned, is where a customer withholds payment of a large invoice due to a small error on one line of the document (for example, not paying the full value of £22,557.36 because an item on line 4 was charged at £36.39 instead of £31.39). There is a school of thought which urges collectors to try to persuade customers to pay that part of the invoice not in dispute, with the suppliers undertaking to quickly investigate the query, and if correct, raise a credit note to cancel the remaining outstanding debit. This is perfectly feasible and many will do just that. On the other hand, some companies will not raise debit notes, nor will they process invoices containing errors and it is not always easy, if indeed at all possible, to persuade them to do otherwise. The opinion as to whether this represented a delaying tactic would again revolve around the number of times this had happened before and how quickly the full-value invoice was paid once the error line had been corrected. There is another school of thought which insists on every aspect of every invoice being right first time (and so it should be), and that no customer should be expected to process an incorrect document (see **A13.3** above). As with most things, the answer lies between the two.

What should never happen, however, is that 99% of the goods are delivered, with 100% invoiced and the working of the 99% dependent upon the delivery and installation of the 1%. For example, a customer is hardly likely to want to pay for the new car if it is delivered without wheels. Everyone is entitled to make mistakes, it is the frequency of those mistakes which is the giveaway, either in encouraging the collector to believe that mistakes are symptomatic of something seriously wrong internally, or that the number of mistakes pointed out by the customer are not genuine and that it is the customer who is looking for another way out of his present difficulties.

Making clear the alternatives or consequences   A13.30

Whatever the problems with the customer, it is for the supplier to make it crystal clear to the customer what is expected of him next. The query has been resolved, the invoices have been agreed as correct and going to the right address and containing all the right information and the customer agrees that the balance should be paid. All that could and should have been done, has been done, including speaking to the cheque signer. What is now required is payment.

There will be a date set for payment, an instalment plan agreed, an action to replace faulty goods to be followed by a settlement date, a credit note raised to be followed by a settlement date or a final date set beyond which the supplier will not extend terms. Now the customer must be made absolutely aware of what the consequences will be of non-compliance, from stop list to legal action, the withdrawal of all credit facilities and the recovery of property. Efforts will have been made to assist the customer through his difficulties – recognition has been given to his complaint or his problems and there is nothing more that can be done. All that will remain is payment, and failure to meet that obligation will have an inevitable consequence – the customer must be aware that action *will* be taken. Not to carry the process through to the logical and decided conclusion only creates the illusion for the customer that having got away with it once, he can do the same again in the future. It is for the supplier to ensure that this is just what it is – an illusion. The supplier means business and will carry out the detailed action explained to the customer at the time of making the final agreement, nothing less will be acceptable.

Telephone techniques   A13.31

The telephone is now recognised as the principal collection tool in the following up of outstanding accounts, having its advantages in direct contact with the customer and obliging him to do or say something to satisfy the caller that the objective of the call has been achieved (see **A13.18** above). That objective is the collection of the payment, but at the same time maintaining customer goodwill. The telephone collector is very much part of the total customer service team, in just the same way as the telephone sales office order clerk, or indeed customer service personnel themselves. This chapter deals specifically with general techniques to be employed by telephone collectors in order to successfully carry out their role. (See **A7.4–A7.9** above for a discussion on the training requirements and qualities necessary to carry out telephone collection work.)

Preparation A13.32

Telephone collection is about structure, control and thorough knowledge of the situation. This all begins with preparation. Before making the call, the collector needs to have to hand essential information, taken from the customer file screen display or manual telephone record card, which would include the following:

- the correct telephone number;

- name, extension number and job title or position of the customer contact;

- hours of availability and/or best time to contact;

- details of the outstanding account, which includes the items which are overdue, due and about to become due;

- invoice numbers and values;

- relevant customer order numbers;

- the customer credit limit and risk category;

- details of the last payment, date and value;

- details of the last telephone contact, including any undertakings given; and

- details of any queries raised and resolved and dates.

The last three items give the collector an idea of the nature of the customer being contacted, and also enable any new collector to easily pick up where the last collector left off. This is especially important in the event of sickness and holidays, and provides continuity of contact even if the regular collector is not available for any reason. The customer record includes notes on incoming calls, as well as outgoing collection calls, so that the collector can see at a glance, for example, where and when the initiative came in respect of requests for copy invoices or proof of delivery. Experience has shown that an unsolicited request for a copy invoice is more of an indication of a genuine need than a tactic for delay.

Facts A13.33

Every collector needs to avoid the situation of being wrong-footed. Being in possession of all the relevant facts of the account before actually making the call lessens that possibility. The customer can still come up with the unexpected, but the more the collector knows beforehand, the less likely he is to be caught unawares. Such facts will not just be those contained on the record file as outlined above (see **A13.32** above), but all other relevant information known about the supplier's:

- own invoicing and delivery process;

- price file and how it operates; and

- procedure adopted in raising and issuing credit notes.

Open or closed questioning

A13.34

The biggest mistake made by the untrained or inexperienced telephone collector is the inability to distinguish between open and closed questions, and allowing the customer simply to answer 'yes' or 'no', leaving the collector with nowhere to go. The responses 'yes' or 'no' in effect close the question, and what follows is supplementary and usually clumsy. By way of illustration, the question, 'Will you be sending me a cheque?' can be answered by 'yes', but the customer is not required to say when the cheque will be sent, or for how much it will be for, or whether it will be sent first class. Similarly, 'Have you sent a cheque?' produces exactly the same result. The object of the exercise is to obtain payment, or a commitment to payment, and the collector wants to know the value of the payment proposed, when it will be sent, and by what method. It is therefore necessary to ask a question which gives the recipient no alternative but to answer with the information requested, or to reveal his intentions or non-intentions, by the way the specific questions are answered. In other words, questions asking:

- when, where, how, and which, are those which bring an informative answer; and

- will, can and could only require the affirmative or the negative.

Controlling the conversation

A13.35

It is important to be in control of the conversation, not only to achieve the required result, but also to underline the fact that the collector has every right to be asking for the supplier's own money. Too often there is a feeling of hesitancy among some people when telephoning in respect of accounts, as if they were intruding or doing something wrong. It is not uncommon for small businesses to feel very ill at ease at the prospect of contacting their customers in respect of money, believing that to ask for payment in some way jeopardises the business relationship and might lose them their valuable customer. It is quite simply not true and experience has shown quite the opposite as being the case. In practice, it is far easier to upset small businesses by asking for payment, as the owner or manager may be personally involved, it is his money, and paying or not paying has greater personal significance. Dealing with the purchase ledger department of a large organisation is far less likely to cause upset as they deal with collection calls all day long, and indeed expect to be called if the account is overdue and not yet paid. The purchase ledger clerk does not differentiate in his own mind between the collector from a small business or a multi-national — the account is not paid, and the caller is asking for what is rightfully his. A small business must have a positive attitude towards collection. It may be that not asking the right questions, or failing to appreciate the value of controlling the conversation is actually perpetuating the myth believed by the small businessman. Therefore, he too could benefit from training in telephone collection techniques (see **A7.4–A7.9** above).

There is nothing wrong with being friendly on the telephone, and in fact it should be actively encouraged. Part of the collector's technique is to get to know his contact, and to cultivate a relationship which, while remaining on a business footing, is nevertheless comfortable enough for both the caller and the recipient to feel at ease. A collector should be polite at all times, in control of his emotions and never lose his temper. The professional approach also precludes chewing gum or eating when calling, and the call should come from an environment which is itself quietly efficient – there is nothing more off putting than to take a call which sounds as if it is coming from a war zone, the caller having a mouthful of cotton wool!

It may be that at this stage, the customer raises some form of objection to payment, whether because of a dispute with the invoice itself, a complaint about the goods delivered, or simply an excuse not to pay. The collector must listen to what is being said, all the while judging from the customer's words, voice and attitude the genuineness of the complaint or dispute. At the same time he must make notes on what the customer is saying. It is important to remain neutral in this situation, at least until the full facts have been established, but it is equally important to acknowledge what the customer is saying and so give him the feeling that he is being heard and that somebody has taken time to listen. If the customer has a genuine point, no-one should be afraid to apologise if such an action is called for, especially if the situation has arisen because the supplier has not done what he said he was going to do. Being sympathetic and helpful is not a sign of weakness or an admission of guilt, rather it is part of remaining calm and in control.

There is a place in any telephone conversation for a pause – the occasional silence can encourage an answer and there can be times when the customer needs to offload some of his anger and frustration, especially if he has a genuine complaint. Remaining calm, no matter how agitated, or even downright rude or offensive the other party may be, can have a quite disarming effect, and soon calms the customer down. Really offensive or obscene behaviour cannot be tolerated, however, and most collection departments have the support of a policy which allows such a call to be transferred to a superior or terminated. In such a situation at least the collector has remained in control. It is the debtor who has lost control, and the supplier now knows the nature of the beast he is dealing with. There is an old adage which states that the debtor who shouts the loudest has the most to hide and there can be truth in that.

The collection call ends with a commitment from the customer to pay the account, and is closed by the collector on obtaining confirmation from the customer that he has agreed to pay the amount requested, on the day agreed, to be sent by first class post. The collector equally gives an undertaking to do what it has been agreed that the supplier needs to do, in respect of any query or dispute, and both parties now will be clear as to what is expected of them.

Follow up A13.36

All promises and commitments should be entered onto the record card or the memo record pad on the system, and entered as a diary notation, so that subsequent follow-up action can be taken at the appropriate time. If any action has been agreed, such as query resolution, or a credit note issued, this should be done as soon as possible. Equally if no satisfactory outcome has occurred, then any consequences outlined to the customer, such as putting them on the stop list or taking legal action should be confirmed to the customer in writing. If the collector has undertaken to take further steps to assist the customer, such as checking delivery dates or product availability, this should be done quickly and again confirmed in writing to the customer.

In addition, any further information obtained from the customer during the telephone conversation, such as an intended change of address, change in bankers or other financial arrangements, or any changes to key personnel or the contact name, should be entered on to the customer file database. It will also be necessary to inform sales and marketing of any significant change in customer details or status as a result of the telephone call, especially if the ultimate outcome is likely to lead to legal proceedings and/or closure of the account.

Summary   A13.37

In summary, when carrying out telephone collection work, the credit controller should always:

- prepare for the call;

- be in the right frame of mind;

- have all the facts and figures, as well as past records, to hand;

- be friendly, courteous but firm – the supplier is entitled to the money;

- understand the customer's invoice authorisation and payment process;

- speak to the right person, but be prepared to go higher if the contact cannot or will not help;

- ask open questions;

- control the conversation;

- cultivate relationships and use first names where and when appropriate;

- keep calm;

- leave pauses;

- listen carefully to any complaint or dispute;

- obtain a firm commitment to pay, and reach agreement as to when and how this will be made;

- confirm any actions in writing;

- update the record file and diarise forward for next action; and

- always remember 'please' and 'thank you' – politeness costs nothing and pays dividends.

Special arrangements   A13.38

The collection process may well involve coming to special arrangements with customers in respect of payment of their account. In some cases, special arrangements already exist, having been agreed with sales at the outset of trading as in the case of one-off promotions or sale of redundant or obsolete stock. It is not unusual, for example, for customers to buy stock which would otherwise be scrapped, in return for a deal involving special prices or longer terms, or a combination of the two. It is also not unusual for goods to be delivered and invoiced early by arrangement with the customer on the understanding that payment would be delayed to the time when it would have been due had the goods been delivered according to the original schedule. Such arrangements should already be noted on the ledger file and the customer file, and therefore taken into account during the collection process.

The other type of special arrangement is that which comes to light as a result of collection activity, when the customer has been asked to pay his account and has indicated the need for extra time and/or assistance (see also **A12.67** above).

Payment plans   A13.39

Payment plans are frequently agreed when the customer is not able to pay on normal terms or meet this current monthly commitment at due date. It may be a request that he makes to the collector, or it may be mutually agreed between the collector and the customer that a payment plan could prove beneficial to both and is a practical alternative to taking further more drastic steps.

Payment plans can be a useful method of striving towards the goal of achieving ultimate settlement of the account, retaining the customer as a viable business and developing a degree of customer loyalty. It is important, however, to be sure of the ground and to keep the arrangement under strict supervision. It will also be necessary to establish how subsequent supplies will be made and paid for as the original account is being paid off. Before the plan can be agreed, the collector needs to have confidence in the customer's financial ability to meet the proposed commitments, and that the situation is not beyond redemption. To establish this confidence, the customer should supply up-to-date financial details, such as internal management accounts and cash flow forecasts, which may entail the collector actually undertaking a customer visit (see **A7.10** and **A13.19** above). The customer is far more likely to agree to supply this information in person, rather than through the post or by fax. If the customer is for any reason unwilling, he should be politely reminded that the supplier is offering, or being asked to offer, financial assistance, and it should go without saying that if the customer were approaching his bank for this help, the bank would certainly be seeking financial details.

There should always be an end in sight of a payment plan – it should not be allowed to go on and on for years, but in agreeing a time span, account should be taken of the realistic figure which the customer can afford to make and the supplier can reasonably be expected to accept. In normal trade credit, such plans would not be expected to last for more than six months, although they often last longer, or are made back to back, with new plans being agreed as the previous plan is completed. Direct debit or standing orders are the best methods of fixing regular monthly instalments (post-dated cheques should not be accepted, though the customer can draw up a series of bills of exchange to cover the payments – see **A13.47** below). Again, the customer should be made aware that if he received this assistance from his bank, they would stipulate secured payments and would also charge interest – there is no reason why the supplier should lose out altogether and interest should be negotiated into the plan.

To finally draw the plan together, the customer should be under no illusion as to the consequences of default. The agreement becomes null and void in the event of default of any one instalment and the whole account is due for payment.

If ongoing trading is considered during the course of the repayment schedule, then the terms and prices available should be agreed as part of the agreement for a repayment plan. Many companies will agree to trade on a cash on delivery (COD) basis at list price, though some will offer a form of price discount or even limited credit. Whatever the arrangement, it must be closely monitored to avoid abuse, and action taken immediately if any deviation from the agreement is experienced.

Incentive schemes   A13.40

Companies can offer incentives to customers, both to boost sales and to promote prompt payment. (See **A12.67–A12.69** above for information on how incentive schemes affect staff and account collection targets.) Obvious examples exist in the field of consumer credit, with utility companies offering discount for customers who pay their accounts by direct debit, or where special offers exist allowing two for the price of one. Most commercial companies have trade price lists, with sales personnel being given authority to negotiate sales based upon the price list, less a trade discount. It is usual to tie such negotiated deals in with trading terms so that prompt payment in fact earns greater trade price flexibility, though not necessarily offering cash discount for early settlement.

More companies are seeking to have their accounts paid by direct debit (see **A13.48** below), and can either offer one-off incentives to customers who are prepared to switch to that method, or continue to give higher trade discount for direct debit customers.

There are also trade promotions, aimed at moving old stock, or at the launch of new products where specially selected customers can be offered special deals to encourage them to use the product or service. All such promotions should be linked to payment terms, so that both supplier and customer benefit, and the ledger file should be clearly marked so that collectors know that special arrangements exist.

It is important to differentiate between any special one-off incentive deal for a customer and the rest of his trade, so that advantage is not taken. This should be done at contract negotiation stage, and start and finish dates should be clearly marked. Long-term deals can easily be taken as the norm and this pitfall should be avoided.

Penalties   A13.41

Penalties for late payment exist by way of interest on overdue accounts (see **A5.8** and **A5.9** above). In the case of special arrangements, however, the consequences of non-compliance with the agreed deal should be made clear to the customer at the time the deal is negotiated. Payment plans should carry interest, as already discussed at **A13.39** above, and the customer should be left in no doubt as to what will happen if the arrangement is not adhered to, or if he defaults on any one instalment.

Additional penalties exist, however, which are designed to make it easier for the supplier to have offered a special arrangement, or agreed to a special arrangement in the first place. If the customer is continuing to trade and to buy the supplier's products at the same time as paying off an existing debt, then the prices and terms are in the supplier's favour. Such prices could be at the list price, with no trade discount, and delivery may be dependent upon cash with the order, cash before delivery, or cash on delivery. There could be an exclusivity clause, or a maintenance contract, a policy of no returns (except in the case of damage in transit or defective product) or a retention of title.

Methods of payment   A13.42

In domestic trade, for large value and for large volume transactions, there are a variety of ways in which payment can be made. These include:

- cash;
- cheques;
- bankers' drafts;
- bank transfers;
- bills of exchange;
- direct debits;
- standing orders; and
- credit cards.

This list is not complete because there can be the question of offset or contra (see **A12.63** above), but for the purpose of this chapter the focus is on those methods most commonly in use.

Cash   A13.43

Cash is not the common unit of exchange that it once was, not even in the 'high street'. Certainly in commercial transactions cash is rarely used because of the security problems posed by handling large sums of cash and the need for it to be counted and banked as quickly as possible. Money laundering regulations have also focused the mind on the need to know the source of funds and not to be party to any doubtful transaction. It is unlikely that large commercial transactions would ever involve actual cash unless the source of that cash was clear, unequivocal and beyond doubt. No-one likes to leave cash overnight on premises for insurance reasons, and certainly delivery drivers do not want to be driving about with their vans carrying cash. In addition, since banks make charges for all transactions conducted over the counter, even paying in cash at the bank costs money. It is for this reason that terms such as, 'cash with order', or 'cash on delivery', really mean 'payment' with order or on delivery. There are circum-stances, however, in commercial transactions when cash is accepted. The trade counter at the depot or warehouse, where the customer comes in to purchase a few items (although the credit card is being used increasingly for such transac-tions), is more geared up to take cash, operating like a retail outlet. There are also those customers who have been specified as cash only, because of previous difficulties experienced with cheques.

Cheques   A13.44

The cheque remains one of the most common forms of payment and is universally recognised as a method of getting funds out of one account and putting them in another. The cheque is a negotiable instrument, and as such is not in reality payment until the instrument has been negotiated, and the cheque cleared. In other words, whereas cash obviously represents cleared funds, the funds negotiated under the instrument of the cheque will not be cleared until that negotiation has been concluded. The major clearing banks have moved towards 24 hour clearance in recent times, but two to three days is still a common time scale. Cheques drawn on those banks, formerly mutual Building Societies, can take longer. Payment by cheque is therefore conditional upon the funds being cleared, and as such, acceptance of a cheque in settlement of an account is likewise conditional. Cheques are crossed and payable only to the payee (the person/company to whom they are made out), a move undertaken by the banks to prevent fraud and misuse.

Bankers' draft   A13.45

A bank or bankers' draft is in effect a cheque drawn on the bank's own account and as such can be treated as safe. Much used in export, and often used in home trade where the supplier is not prepared to accept the risk of a cheque, the draft can be 'bought' from the bank and issued in payment of a commercial transaction.

Bank transfer   A13.46

Bank transfers, or BACS payments as they are known, are increasingly replacing cheques, just as cheques have increasingly replaced cash. If the supplier gives the customer details of his bank account (bank name, branch, sort code, account number and account name), the customer can arrange for payment to be made via the Bank Automated Clearing System (BACS). The supplier should establish the bank transfer date to be used by the customer, ensuring that it complies with the customer's given credit terms, and should also require the customer to provide a remittance advice when payment is being made so that the supplier knows that the amount is being paid, and how the cash should be allocated. Though a safer method than cheques being lost in the post, and beneficial in that they are cleared funds when they arrive, BACS payments can be delayed and not necessarily received by the supplier on the same day as the customer has released payment.

Bills of exchange   A13.47

Used primarily in export, bills of exchange are not uncommon in domestic trade, and are often used as a method of payment when a payment plan has been agreed (see **A13.39** above). The *Bills of Exchange Act 1882* defines a bill of exchange as:

> '... an unconditional order in writing, addressed by one person to another, signed by the person giving it, requiring the person to whom it is addressed to pay, on demand or at a fixed or determinable future time, a sum certain in money to, or to the order of, a specified person or to bearer'.

It is in effect a written request to pay, and having been accepted by the customer, is a given undertaking or assurance that it will be paid on the date specified. It has the advantage of maturing for payment on the date pre-fixed by the supplier, and unless the customer is insolvent, it is more than likely to be paid without further intervention by the supplier. (For further information on bills of exchange see **A12.44** and **A12.47** above.)

Direct debits   A13.48

Direct debits are useful for both fixed and variable amounts due for payment at regular intervals on about the same time each month or each year, and are commonly used in consumer credit for the payment of household bills, TV licences, insurance premiums and subscriptions etc. Their use is also now becoming widespread in commercial transactions. A direct debit is set up when the customer gives authorisation to the supplier's bank to go into his bank account to collect payment direct. The supplier then gives notice each month of the amount to be collected, listing invoices and values, and giving the customer time to query or dispute any amount.

The supplier raises a direct debit mandate, which goes to the customer for completion with bank details and signature, and it is then returned to the supplier, who then sends it to the customer's bank. Once agreed by the customer's bank and returned to the supplier, it is now possible for the supplier to put the collection process in place, making sure that at least 14 days elapse between the date of the last invoice to be collected and the date of collection. Indemnity against errors must be given, and the supplier must specify the collection date (collection can be on that date or after it, but not before).

As no cheques need to be raised or banked, there are advantages to both the supplier and the customer – for the supplier, not the least advantage being certain knowledge of payment on the certain date (unless there are no funds or the account with the supplier is disputed and the customer has cancelled authorisation).

Standing orders   A13.49

An older cousin of the direct debit, the standing order is initiated by the customer who gives his bank instruction to pay a fixed sum on a fixed date each month to the supplier's bank account, usually over a specified period of time. More commonly used in consumer credit for the payment of HP instalments or other fixed monthly payments, standing orders are still used in commercial transactions where the deal is for a fixed sum over a fixed period of time. An example would be the repayment of payment plans (see **A13.39** above).

Credit cards   A13.50

Although dominated by the consumer credit industry, the use of credit cards in commercial transactions has grown rapidly over recent years. Over the counter transactions, one-off purchases of low value items, such as stationery and office requisites, are now utilising credit cards as a method of payment in preference to cash. Credit cards are also being preferred to opening actual credit accounts where the turnover is not likely to have any real significance, representing fundamental cost savings to both the sales ledger department of the supplier and the purchase ledger department of the buyer. Payment is secure and guaranteed, and the transaction is free from any problems.

Dishonoured cheques   A13.51

Cheques can be dishonoured for a variety of reasons, not necessarily because of lack of funds and not necessarily due to some intentional act on the part of the customer.

Reasons   A13.52

Having a customer's cheque returned by the bank can cause some alarm, but each time it happens, the first step is to identify the reason for the return. These may include the following.

(*a*) The cheque is returned marked 'refer to drawer' – if nothing else is written or stated, it has to be taken that there are no funds available at the time of presentation to honour the cheque, and further, the bank does not see the likelihood of sufficient funds in the immediate future.

(*b*) The cheque is returned marked 'refer to drawer – please represent'. It may alternatively be marked 'uncleared funds'. This shows that at the time of first presentation there were insufficient funds to clear the cheque, but by the time that it is represented the bank feels that there is a likelihood of sufficient funds being available.

(*c*) The cheque is post-dated. If the post-dating is only a day or so, the bank may not return the cheque, but present it at the right date, or presume that it will have the right date by the time it goes through the clearing system. Otherwise, it is returned to the supplier.

(*d*) The cheque is returned marked 'no A/C held' or 'account closed'. Obviously if there is no account held by the customer at the bank on which the cheque was drawn, then it cannot be cleared.

(*e*) The cheque is returned marked 'countermanded by order of the drawer', or 'countermanded by drawer'. The customer has stopped the cheque, and the bank will not process it.

(*f*) The cheque is out-of-date. The life of a cheque to be presented at the bank for clearance is six months, beyond that it is stale and cannot be honoured.

(*g*) The cheque is not signed at all, or is not signed in accordance with the mandate held at the bank, e.g. a second signature is required.

(*h*) Words and figures on the cheque do not correspond with each other.

(*j*) The cheque is not made out to the person or company who has banked the cheque.

(*k*) The cheque has got mangled up in the post, dropped in a pot of steaming coffee or is any event unreadable, and is thus defined as mutilated.

(*l*) The cheque is returned marked 'account holder deceased'.

(*m*) The cheque is returned marked 'administrative receiver appointed' or 'liquidator appointed'.

Action to be taken A13.53

In all cases shown in **A13.52** above, except (*f*), (*g*), (*h*), (*j*), and (*k*), the cheque should be kept by the supplier. The original cheque is evidence of the unpaid debt, and if legal action is to follow, then the cheque will be required. For cheques returned for the reasons shown above, the following action should be taken.

• If the cheque is marked 'refer to drawer', as discussed at **A13.52**(*a*) above, the customer should be contacted at once and advised that his cheque has not been honoured. Another cheque is not acceptable, and payment must now be made immediately by bankers' draft or by cash. The customer should also be informed that a dishonoured cheque has serious consequences, and that until the matter is satisfactorily resolved all deliveries will be suspended. It may also lead to legal proceedings.

- If the cheque is marked 'refer to drawer – please represent', as discussed at **A13.52**(*b*) above, the customer should be contacted at once and told that his cheque has not been honoured on first presentation, and is being presented for a second time. He should also be asked to ensure that there will be sufficient funds to meet the second presentation, because to be returned again would have serious consequences (see above). The customer should also be invited to be open about any problems he is experiencing, and dependent upon the size of the account, a visit might be appropriate.

- If the cheque is post-dated, as discussed at **A13.52**(*c*) above, the customer should be contacted at once and invited to explain why the cheque was post-dated. It should be pointed out that this was not by prior arrangement, and that it is not policy to accept post-dated cheques. The supplier should ask for a current cheque immediately (not on next month's cheque run), and if necessary restrict supplies until the new cheque is received, presented and cleared.

- If the cheque is marked 'no A/C held' etc, as discussed at **A13.52**(*d*) above, the customer should be contacted at once and asked to explain. It may be a simple error, in that he has changed banks and got the timing wrong. Alternatively it could be a deliberate ploy. The supplier should ask for a current cheque from the correct bank account immediately, and if necessary restrict supplies until the new cheque is received, presented and cleared.

- If the cheque is marked 'countermanded by order of the drawer' etc, as discussed at **A13.52**(*e*) above, the customer should be contacted at once for an explanation, unless the supplier knows already that the account has been paid twice, and that the customer had already said that the second cheque would be stopped. On the other hand, the customer may know that the bank would not clear his cheque if it were presented, and it would be better to stop it before that happened. The supplier needs to be clear as to the reason, and if necessary be prepared to take appropriate action.

- A cheque being returned because it is out-of-date, as discussed at **A13.52**(*f*) above, is a common occurrence at the beginning of a new year, and it is usually sufficient to telephone the customer, tell him that the cheque will be sent back to him for alteration and ask him to send it back to the supplier straight away.

- If a cheque is not signed or has an incorrect signature, as discussed at **A13.52**(*g*) above, the customer should be contacted and either he should be asked to issue an immediate replacement cheque, or to contact his bank to arrange for this particular cheque to be honoured in spite of the errors. The same action should be taken for the scenarios discussed at **A13.52**(*h*)–(*k*) above.

- If the cheque is marked 'account holder deceased', as discussed at **A13.52**(*l*) above, the supplier should get in touch with the deceased's bank and obtain the name and address of the executors of the deceased's estate.

- If the cheque is marked 'administrative receiver appointed' etc, as discussed at **A13.52**(*m*) above, all orders on the system should be cancelled, credit facilities withdrawn and deliveries stopped at once. An attempt should be made at contacting the customer for information as there will usually be someone from the insolvency accountants on site who can update the supplier on the present situation.

Follow-up procedures A13.54

Having gone through the collection process, from the first issue of an invoice to the end of the cycle (i.e. the final notice), there will be accounts which have not yet been paid, for whatever reason. It is inevitable that, not only does not everyone pay on time, but there will always be some who ignore all the collection processes, waiting until the bitter end before paying – some may not pay even then. There are still options open to the supplier to put final pressure on the customer, and at this stage it could be argued that customer goodwill is not an overriding factor as it was earlier in the process. Nevertheless, there is still time to salvage the situation, and even at a very late stage, customers can be brought back from the brink and returned to the fold.

Stop list A13.55

As has already been seen at **A13.21** above, the use of the stop list as a collection tool can produce payment, and it remains one of the last and most powerful of the non-legal action sanctions available to the supplier. In effect the stop list serves two main purposes.

- As far as the supplier is concerned, it prevents any further risk in the event that the customer is in serious trouble and likely to fail. If nothing further is delivered, then the debt is in effect capped. At worst then it is damage limitation.

- On the other hand, it can be seen as a means by which pressure is put on the customer to pay his account, and his failure to obtain continuing supplies may well cause him serious problems.

The supplier may use the threat of the stop list to entice payment, and may use the actual placing of the account on the stop list as notice of his serious intent. Due consideration has to be given to the value placed on the account overall, and to whether there is still goodwill to be preserved. No account should go on stop without both the customer and sales departments having been informed. There can be circumstances where sales can intervene on the collector's behalf and make their own approach to the customer in the full and certain knowledge that supplies will be stopped if payment is not forthcoming.

In many organisations the stop list is probably regarded as the most contentious document produced by credit control, and as such it must not only be produced with care, but it must also be clear and unequivocal. The mere fact that an account is overdue is not of itself a sufficient reason for inclusion on the stop list. It would neither be sensible or good business practice to put the largest blue chip customer on the stop list for one overdue unpaid invoice of £25.22, when the customer's annual turnover with the supplier is £300,000. Equally, it would do nothing for the relationship between the sales and the credit departments.

It would also be true to say that an account does not have to be overdue to appear on stop. Trouble with a cheque (see **A13.51–A13.53** above) can cause an immediate stop placement, and the surest way to be absolutely certain that nothing more is delivered until the full facts are known and understood is to use the stop list.

No customer *likes* to be on stop. It can disrupt workflow and production schedules, cause embarrassment with other suppliers and their own customers, and can have a damaging effect on reputation. Both the supplier and the customer should be aware of all this as the time comes for the sanction to be applied. The supplier needs to weigh up the profitability of the business against the cost of giving extended credit, albeit unofficially, and the customer needs to weigh up the value of the supplier to his own business and the likelihood of finding alternative sources and what this would cost. The customer's buyer may not even know that there is a payment due and his new-found knowledge of the potential effects of not being able to procure the goods needed may just be enough to secure the payment. Putting a customer on the stop list may be near the end of the collection process, but it is a worthwhile sanction, and produces many a cheque in settlement.

Where the supplier goes from there, as far as the future of the account is concerned, is up to him and his business needs, but it is a course of action worth pursuing, and provided he has remembered to include a restriction of supplies clause in the event of late or non-payment in his terms and conditions, it should be used. (See also **A4.30** above.)

Collection agencies and legal action   A13.56

At the end of all the collection processes, including the stop list, there will still be unpaid accounts, and the supplier has to decide what to do next. It may be that the customer, by now regarded and described more accurately as the debtor, does not need further supplies, so the stop list has not galvanised him into paying. Perhaps he is still under the impression that the supplier will not take the matter further, and that he can wait a bit longer to pay. Or perhaps he is still short of cash and not in a position to pay and is merely waiting for the inevitable. Whatever the reason, the supplier now needs to decide whether it is cost effective and worthwhile carrying on with trying to collect the debt himself or should he now seek outside help.

Collection agencies   A13.57

It may well be that ultimately, legal proceedings will be taken as the final act of debt collection, but there is an option open to the supplier that could have the desired effect and stops short of potentially expensive litigation. Debt collection agencies, specialising in the collection of commercial debts, are an option to be seriously considered.

Third party intervention alone is often effective in showing the debtor that the supplier really does mean business and that he has every intention of following the recovery trail to the end. It is now no longer just a question of late payment – the issue is serious. It may also mean that the debtor has now damaged his credit reputation, and he may find it difficult to obtain supplies from elsewhere in the future. The introduction of the collection agency in to the relationship between the supplier and the customer is to be ignored at his peril.

The supplier should see the agency as an extension of his own credit and collection department. His own staff can concentrate on current customer collection issues, as the agency has the resources and the expertise to concentrate on the matter of the debts passed to them for collection.

In choosing an agency, the supplier needs to know that they will be effective, but equally important (if not more so), that the methods employed will be both ethical and legal. The agency will in fact be working on behalf of the supplier, and the supplier's reputation for good business practice and ethical behaviour is important to him, and therefore to the agency. The agency should be able to offer a range of collection services, combining letters, telephone calls and visits, keeping the supplier up-to-date at all times with progress reports. The agency should also pass on money collected without delay.

At the eleventh hour, commercial pressures are such that even a debtor, now in the hands of a debt collection agency, may still be a customer in the future. What the supplier will want, therefore, is the debt collected, and the debtor handed back in one piece as a potential future customer. With this in mind, the supplier should look for an agency with:

- a good reputation;

- a verifiable track record;

- testimonials from other suppliers; and

- an audited client account for collected funds.

It is also important that the agency itself is well established and financially sound. It should be licensed by the Office of Fair Trading, have professional indemnity insurance and have all directors, partners and staff fully bonded (i.e. insured).

Commission rates are variable and usually negotiable within certain parameters. The *Late Payment of Commercial Debts (Interest) Act 1998* did not originally allow for recovery of collection costs in addition to the interest charged. The *EU Directive* on *Combating Late Payments in Commercial Transactions* (passed by the European Parliament on 15 June 2000) does allow for reasonable recovery costs to be claimed, and all EU Member States should have brought their domestic legislation into line by August 2002. At the time of writing (April 2004), two EU

Member States (Luxembourg and Spain) still had to comply, all other states, including the United Kingdom, having brought their legislation into line with the EU Directive. The UK legislation has been modified to include reasonable recovery costs to be claimed according to size of debt, limited to three main bands – debts up to £999.99, the recovery costs allowed are £40, debts between £1,000 and £9,999.99 the costs are £70, and debts over £10,000 the allowable recovery costs are £100. It was not the intention of the EU Directive to become a supplier's charter or debt collector's bonanza, but simply to allow 'reasonable' compensatory recovery costs.

It should go without saying that the use of an agency is going to involve additional cost for the supplier, even allowing for the compensation element in the legislation, but this should be seen as a debt collection cost. As such, it should be part of the overall collection budget, and be set against the costs incurred in supporting a debtors ledger.

Legal action   A13.58

Many agencies utilise the services of their own solicitors, who are themselves specialists in the field of debt recovery through the courts. Legal proceedings have to be seen as the final option when all other options have been used to no avail. The supplier needs to be aware of what this final action really means. This will be to all intents and purposes the end of the road and there will now be little or no chance of the customer coming back, or even the perceived need of the supplier to have him back. The supplier needs to be sure, however, that his house is in order, all that should have been done has been done and that there are no outstanding or unresolved disputes to cloud the issue. It will also need to be ensured that the debtor has received all the right paperwork and all the right notifications, and has been given every opportunity to pay the account and to avoid the present situation. (See **PART B: DEBT RECOVERY** for a full discussion of the litigation process.)

Recovering property   A13.59

Recovering property is an option available to the supplier, provided of course, such an option has been included in his terms and conditions and the clause has been made known to the customer at the outset.

The option may or may not be worthwhile. The supplier has to be able to correctly identify his goods, and correctly identify the goods as being those covered by the unpaid invoice(s). He also has to set the cost of recovery against the value left in the goods themselves. It may be that the property can be correctly identified, is easily recovered and can be resold at a profit, in which case the exercise is worth pursuing. On the other hand, this may not be the case and it may also be that recovering the goods actually forces the customer out of business, and therefore completely removes any possibility of either full settlement or ongoing business. For many businesses, recovery of property is not an option, even though they may reserve the right. The goods have lost their identity, been incorporated into another product, and sold on. The supplier is left once more with the recovery of money owed as the only feasible avenue open. (See **A12.41–A12.43** above for a full discussion of this area.)

Appendix A13

First reminder letter

For the attention of ...., Purchase Ledger Manager

Customer Name
Customer address 1
Customer address 2
City
Postcode

Dear Sir/Madam

Overdue Account ... £ .... [month]

We are unable to trace receipt of your payment of £ .... in settlement of our [month] account, which became due for payment on ....
This is now .... (days/weeks) overdue, and we look forward to payment by return.

Should there be any problem, please contact the undersigned without delay.

Yours faithfully

Credit Manager

Second reminder letter

For the attention of ...., Purchase Ledger Manager

Customer Name
Customer address 1
Customer address 2
City
Postcode

Dear Sir/Madam

Overdue Account £ ....

We regret to note that we have not received any reply to our letter of ...., and the amount of £ .... remains unpaid.
This is now well overdue, and outside our agreed terms of trading. In order to avoid the cessation of supplies and withdrawal of credit facilities, please remit by return of post.

Yours faithfully

Credit Manager

Final reminder letter

For the attention of ...., Finance Director

Customer name
Customer address 1
Customer address 2
City
Postcode

Dear Sir/Madam

Overdue account £ ....

Despite previous reminders, the above account remains unpaid. Please note that unless payment is received by .... [day/month], the account will be passed to our solicitors for the commencement of recovery proceedings in the .... Court.

Yours faithfully

Credit Manager

A14

Company and Consumer Legislation and Codes of Practice

Companies Acts   A14.1

The *Companies Act 1985* (*CA 1985*) was introduced with the aim of bringing together in one document all previous legislation governing companies. Prior to this, company law was enshrined in the various *Companies Acts* of *1929, 1948, 1980* and *1981*.

The four main types of company are:

- private companies, limited by shares;

- public companies, limited by shares;

- private companies, limited by guarantee; and

- private companies, unlimited.

The limitation refers to the amount of the liability of the members in the event that the company is wound up and relates to the amount unpaid on shares held by them, or the amount of the guarantee given by the members.

One person may form all types of company other than public companies, which require a minimum of two directors. The authorised share capital of public companies must be £50,000 or more, one quarter of which must be paid on incorporation.

The Registrar of Companies strictly controls the name of a limited company. A name cannot be used if:

- it has been used already;

- it includes 'limited', 'unlimited' or 'public limited company' (or the Welsh equivalents) anywhere other than at the end;

- it is 'too like' that of an existing company;

- it offends; or

- its use constitutes a criminal offence.

Secretary of State approval is required if a name sounds like a government office or if it contains a prescribed word, such as 'police' or 'university'. There are also sensitive words that may only be used with valid justification and prior sanction, such as 'national', 'royal', and 'Post Office'.

Memorandum and Articles of Association   A14.2

The memorandum of association is a document which sets out:

- the precise name of the company;
- the country in which it is registered;
- the purposes for which the company has been formed, known as 'objects'; and
- unless unlimited, the limitation of liability of members of the company and the share capital.

If the company is a public company the memorandum must say so.

The Articles of Association are the internal rules of the company. Under the *Companies Act 1985*, prescribed sets of model rules automatically apply to all companies unless a modified version is substituted. The standard prescribed set of model rules are:

- Table A for companies limited by shares;
- Table C for companies limited by guarantee; and
- Table E for unlimited companies.

These are set out in full in the *Companies (Tables A to F) Regulations 1985 (SI 1985/805)*, as amended by the *Companies (Tables A to F) (Amendment) Regulations 1985 (SI 1985/1052)*.

The original Memorandum and Articles of Association are separately signed by the subscribers and witnessed, then combined into one numbered document before being lodged, together with a fee of £20 and two standard registration forms, at Companies House, an executive agency of the Department of Trade and Industry (see **C1 USEFUL ADDRESSES**). Form 10 sets out the full names of the directors and the company secretary, their home addresses (unless the directors have special sanction to protect their home addresses for security reasons), dates of birth and other directorships held, together with details of the registered office. Form 12 is a declaration of compliance by a director, witnessed by a solicitor or commissioner for oaths.

Standard forms of Memorandum and Articles of Association are available from law stationers such as Oyez, which provide a ready-made document incorporating modifications reflecting common practices, such as stating that *section 293 of CA 1985* does not apply, which then allows directors to remain in office after age 70.

Registration can also be undertaken by formatted e-mail under the Electronic Incorporation Service for those persons who have registered to do so. In this case the Memorandum and Articles of Association are sent as printable attachments to the e-mail.

Upon registration, a Certificate of Incorporation is issued and a registered number allocated to the company. A company cannot trade until this is held and a copy must be available for inspection at the registered office.

Limitations on company powers   A14.3

Clause 3 of a typical Memorandum of Association is called the principal objects clause, and describes the purpose, or the 'objects', of the company. The objects clause contained in the Memorandum of Association is of vital importance. If a company trades in purposes beyond those contained in its objects then it may be held to be trading *ultra vires* ('beyond its powers') and such transactions may be voided.

Other clauses of importance to credit grantors include those giving specific power to borrow monies and to charge assets as security.

Directors' duties   A14.4

Company officials include:

- subscribers to the Memorandum and Articles of Association;
- members;
- directors;
- the company secretary; and
- shareholders.

There must be at least one director and one company secretary appointed for every company.

In addition to signing the Memorandum and Articles of Association, subscribers must take at least one share and normally appoint the first directors of the company.

Members are created by subscribing to the Memorandum of Association or by allotment or transfer of shares. Members are therefore always shareholders. Shareholders own the company and may or may not have voting rights, depending on the class of share held. Typical classes of shares are:

- ordinary;

- preference, which has a preferred fixed dividend payable before any ordinary dividend, and which may or may not append voting rights;

- redeemable preference; and

- deferred.

Shareholders may also receive dividends if permitted by the Articles, subject to the company declaring a dividend and the directors recommending the amount payable. Shareholders can reduce the recommended amount, but not increase it.

Directors hold a special position of responsibility as they are empowered under the *CA 1985* and:

- are officers of the company and agents of it;

- have a duty of good faith and care;

- are appointed to manage the affairs of the company in accordance with the Articles; and

- have a personal responsibility to ensure that statutory documents are delivered on time, such as accounts, annual returns and notifications of changes.

Directors may be fined up to £5,000 or convicted for failure to lodge accounts or to supply annual returns, which is a criminal offence. Fines are levied for late accounts on a sliding scale, depending on severity, starting from £100. Directors may also be disqualified from acting as a director in certain circumstances (see **A14.5** below).

In contrast, the company secretary has no similar powers under the *Companies Act 1985*, but is allowed to sign most forms and returns required to be submitted to the Registrar of Companies, and:

- is an officer of the company;

- may be criminally liable for defaults committed by the company;

- is required to prepare a statement of affairs if a liquidator or receiver is appointed;

- is required under *CA 1985, s 283* for every company;

- cannot be the sole director of a company; and

- must be suitably qualified if appointed in a public company.

The duties of the company secretary under the *CA 1985* include:

- maintaining the statutory registers, such as the register of members under *section 352*, the register of directors and secretaries under *section 288*, the register of directors' interests under *section 325*, the register of charges under *section 407* and, for public companies, the register of interests in shares;

- filing statutory forms on time, including Form 287 for change of registered office, Form 288 for change of directors, within 14 days, and the annual return, Form 363s;

- providing members and auditors with 21 days' notice of an annual general meeting, or with 14 days' notice of other meetings, (except for unlimited companies when the time limit is seven days), and with copies of draft accounts 21 days before a meeting is called to discuss them;

- sending the Registrar of Companies copies of special and extraordinary resolutions under *CA 1985, s 80*;

- keeping minutes of meetings;

- supplying accounts to all persons entitled to receive them; and

- keeping the company seal.

On 16 July 2002, the Government published its first White Paper entitled *Modernising Company Law*. The White Paper sets out the Government's response to the independent Company Law Review, which published a series of reports between March 1998 and July 2001. Its final report, *Modern Company Law for a Competitive Economy: Final Report* URN 01/942 and URN 01/943, on 26 July 2001. The recommendations seek to modernise the law, to simplify it, to encourage enterprise and to provide a degree of continuity. Other aspects to be reformed are new means for company formation and a new type of company for small businesses which is not subject to the full rigours of the *CA 1985*.

Company Directors Disqualification Act 1986 A14.5

Directors, or shadow directors ('a person in accordance with whose directions or instructions the directors of the company are accustomed to act' (*Company Directors Disqualification Act 1986, s 741(2)*), may be disqualified from holding office, without leave of the court, for a minimum of two years and a maximum of 15 years. During the disqualification period, the director may not be involved in the promotion, formation or management of a company.

Disqualification arises when the director concerned is believed to be responsible for fraudulent or wrongful trading, defined in *section 214* of the *Insolvency Act 1986*, whereby the director knew, or ought to have known, that the company continued to trade whilst insolvent, with no reasonable prospect of avoiding insolvent liquidation. In such circumstances the court may order the director, following an application by a liquidator, to make a personal contribution to creditors.

Directors may avoid personal liability if it can be shown that every step was taken to minimise the potential loss to creditors. Therefore, the aim of this legislation is to focus the minds of directors when trading in an insolvent position.

Liquidators or administrators may also report to the Secretary of State that the director's conduct makes him unfit to manage a company. Such conduct may include misfeasance, breach of duty or misappropriation of assets, failure to submit statutory returns or to keep adequate statutory records. If the Secretary of State believes it to be in the public interest, he may apply to the courts for a disqualification order.

Directors may also be disqualified if they are involved in two companies that have entered into insolvent liquidation in any five-year period, under *CA 1985, s 295*.

Under *CA 1985, s 18*, disqualified directors who continue to act as directors, and those who act willingly on the instructions of a disqualified person, become personally liable with the company on a joint and several basis for the company's debts and are guilty of a criminal offence.

The bankruptcy of a director automatically prohibits them from continuing to remain in office without the consent of the court.

Consumer Credit Act 1974   A14.6

The law surrounding consumer credit developed in the UK in a very fragmented way but always with the intention of making the relationship between lender and consumer more fair and equitable. Examples include the *Moneylenders Acts* of *1900* and *1927*, which attempted to protect the poor by various means, including placing a maximum interest rate on borrowings of 48 per cent. Similarly, the *Hire Purchase Act 1938* gave better protection to borrowers regarding 'snatch back' of goods provided under hire purchase agreements.

A committee under Lord Crowther was commissioned in 1968 to undertake a thorough review of consumer credit and the regulation of security, acknowledging existing law to be 'gravely defective'. The Committee reported in 1971, recommending totally sweeping revision, including redressing the bargaining inequality between individual and lender, controlling malpractices and regulating default remedies. The report also recommended:

- a new 'credit commissioner';

- the licensing of brokers and lenders;

- regulated advertising and canvassing of credit;

- new documentation;

- the compulsory introduction of an easily compared price of credit – the Annualised Percentage Rate (APR); and

- exclusive jurisdiction of the County Court in consumer credit matters.

A White Paper was published in 1973, followed by the passing of the *Consumer Credit Act* in 1974 (*CCA 1974*). The US principle of 'truth in lending' pervaded the Act. The *CCA 1974* is published in twelve parts (see **A14.7–A14.14** below).

Part I – Duties of the Director-General of Fair Trading

A14.7

The principal duties of the Director-General of Fair Trading under the *CCA 1974* are to:

- administer the licensing system;

- enforce the *CCA 1974*;

- supervise its workings;

- continually review the relevance of the *CCA 1974*; and

- advise the Secretary of State on any changes required.

He is also responsible for communicating the *CCA 1974* to consumers and is required to make an annual report to Parliament.

The 'credit commissioner' recommended by the Crowther Committee was never appointed. Instead, the Director-General of Fair Trading's existing responsibilities were extended to embrace the role envisaged.

Part II – Definition of what is covered under the CCA 1974

A14.8

The *CCA 1974* introduces the concept of regulated agreements. All consumer credit bargains are regulated by the *CCA 1974* unless specifically exempt. The main exemptions are:

- credit agreements to companies;

- credit over £25,000 (originally credit over £15,000 in the *CCA 1974* and raised to current levels in 1998; the Government has now announced an intention to remove the £25,000 ceiling for specific purposes);

- credit given by local authorities under certain conditions;

- credit secured on land;

- certain credit agreements where instalments are few; and

- credit given for the purchase of mortgage guarantee indemnity policies and very cheap finance.

Other exemptions include agreements involving a connection abroad, credit relating to utility meters and non-commercial agreements, which are 'made by a creditor not in the course of business carried on' (*CCA 1974, s 189(1)*).

Provisions contained in the *CCA 1974* which are designed to protect consumers from overcharging, known as the extortionate credit bargain provisions, apply to all deals, whether regulated or not.

Distinction is made between unrestricted use credit, where the borrower has free disposition of the money loaned, and restricted use credit, where a lender ensures that the credit applies to a specific purchase or transaction. The regulations apply differently to each. Restricted use credit gives rise to the concept of debtor-creditor-supplier (DCS) agreements and also to connected lender and joint venture issues. Transactions linked to cancelled DCS agreements are automatically cancelled and Consumer Credit Licences of those lenders engaged in DCS transactions need to be specifically endorsed to allow canvassing off trade premises, which otherwise is not permissible under the Act.

Part III – Licensing   A14.9

Sections 21 to *42* of the *CCA 1974* deal with the licensing of those who are engaged in the provision or selling of consumer credit or hire. Over 5 million licences have been issued to date, the vast majority for credit brokerage (see **A10.3** above).

Part IV – Seeking business   A14.10

The compulsory publication of the Annualised Percentage Rate (APR) was one of the most visible elements of the *CCA 1974*. Based on the principle of reflecting the total charge for credit, this must reflect the total interest payable, together with any other charges payable at any time under the transaction by or on behalf of the borrower, whether to the creditor or to any other person.

There are some exclusions permitted from APR calculations, including:

- default charges;
- charges payable by both credit and cash purchasers, such as installation or delivery charges; and
- incidental charges, such as maintenance contracts.

In 1998 the European Commission established a working party to consider the harmonisation of the components of APR and reported that sufficient comparability already exists across Europe.

Part V – Entry into credit and hire agreements   A14.11

Written agreements are required under the *CCA 1974* to ensure that the deal and all negotiations leading up to the deal are documented for future reference. *Part V* concerns:

- the disclosure of information prior to signature;
- the content of agreements;
- withdrawal and cancellation by the consumer; and the effect of agreements which breach the *CCA 1974*.

Some agreements are exempt from *Part V*, including:

- commercial agreements, which are those 'not in the course of a business carried on by the creditor' (*CCA 1974, s 189(1)*);

- current account overdrafts from banks and building societies;

- agreements to finance payments on death; and

- certain small DCS agreements for restricted use credit.

Any representation made orally or in writing during the negotiation of a credit facility by the credit grantor or by a credit broker or a supplier under a DCS agreement, is binding upon the credit grantor. Notice of withdrawal of an agreement by a consumer may also be made orally or in writing to the credit grantor or to the credit broker or supplier if they have negotiated the agreement.

The precise form of credit agreements are contained in the:

- *Consumer Credit (Agreements) Regulations 1983 (SI 1983/1553)*;

- *Consumer Credit (Cancellation Notices and Copies of Documents) Regulations 1983 (SI 1983/1557)*; and

- *Consumer Credit (Guarantees and Indemnities) Regulations 1983 (SI 1983/1556)*, as amended.

Agreements that do not follow the form and content of the provisions are deemed to be improperly executed. Improperly executed agreements may be unenforceable, or enforceable only with the leave of the court. Unenforceable agreements include those:

- that are not signed by the consumer;

- that do not reflect the express terms of the deal, including those agreed by an agent under a DCS agreement;

- failing to include the required cancellation rights; and

- which do not contain all of the 'prescribed terms'.

Prescribed terms include how the credit facility is to be repaid by number, amount, frequency and dates of instalments, and if repayments are not for fixed amounts, how the amount may vary, and the reasons for this, such as a variable rate of interest. Any other powers of variation of the agreement by the credit grantor are required to be detailed.

Improperly executed agreements which are enforceable with the sanction of the court are those where information required by the regulations has been omitted, which are called 'non-prescribed terms'. Examples of non-prescribed terms include:

- the APR;

- the rate of interest;

- the duration of hire agreements;

- details of security;

- details of default charges;

- names and addresses of the parties; and

- the total charge for credit when calculable.

Consumers must receive copies of regulated agreements to enable the terms and conditions to be carefully considered and for right of cancellation and obligation of acceptance to be fully appreciated. For regulated secured loans, copies must be provided seven days prior to signature.

Part VI – Matters arising during the currency of agreements A14.12

The concept of 'connected lender liability' arises in *CCA 1974, Part VI*. In any deal where the supplier of credit is different to the supplier of the goods or services, then the credit grantor and supplier are considered to be undertaking a joint venture and may be liable for each other's liabilities for any breaches or misrepresentations.

Under *CCA 1974, s 75*, if a consumer has a right of action against a supplier for misrepresentation or any other breach of contract, he may hold the creditor jointly and severally liable if the agreement is:

- regulated under the *CCA 1974*;

- made under pre-existing or contemplated contracts; or

- is subject to a restricted use DCS agreement.

Exceptions to connected lender liability include:

- non-commercial agreements;

- claims relating to single items under £100 or over £30,000;

- individual users of company credit cards; and

- non-regulated agreements, such as charge cards and debit cards.

Part VII – Default and termination A14.13

A default notice is required to be served on the borrower:

- before a credit grantor can take action to terminate a regulated agreement;

- to demand earlier payment of any sum;

- to recover possession of any goods;

- to treat any right conferred on the debtor as terminated; or

- to enforce any security.

The default notice must be in a prescribed form, as set out in *Regulation 2(2)* of the *Consumer Credit (Enforcement, Default and Termination) Regulations 1983 (SI 1983/1561)* and must include:

- the nature of the breach;

- if the breach is capable of being remedied, the action required to do so and any specific deadlines, which must be not less than seven full days after service of the notice;

- if the breach is not capable of being remedied, the sum required to be paid and latest payment date, which again must be not less than seven full days after service of the notice; and

- a statement of intended action detailing the consequences of failing to comply with the notice.

If a credit grantor fails to serve a default notice, serves a defective notice or takes enforcement action before expiry of a notice, then the borrower may regain possession of any land or premises and claim damages for trespass, sue the credit grantor for conversion in respect of any goods seized, recover the goods, or may apply for an injunction and time order to prevent unlawful enforcement. Default notices are not required where:

- the agreement is non-commercial (i.e. not in the ordinary course of business);

- the credit grantor seeks to stop the borrower from drawing further credit by returning cheques, recapturing a credit card, or does not authorise transactions;

- a breach by the borrower crystallises a floating charge or triggers another provision of an agreement; and

- the credit grantor is suing only for arrears.

The *CCA 1974* also gives detailed guidance on early termination of an agreement by a borrower.

Remaining parts of the CCA 1974   A14.14

CCA 1974, Part VIII deals with the enforcement of mortgages, and with security, pledges and pawnbroking.

Part IX places judicial control over credit agreements in the County Court.

Under the Woolf reforms, the *Civil Procedure Rules 1998* (*SI 1998/3132*), effective from April 1999, place no restriction on where procedures may be issued, other than that they may not be issued in the High Court for less than £15,000. (See **B3.6** below.) Claims under the *CCA 1974* must generally commence in the court of the borrower or defendant (the defendant chooses the location of the court, but not the type of court).

Part X deals with ancillary credit business and is largely relevant to credit brokerage and credit reference agencies.

Part XI confers authority to the Director-General of Fair Trading and to Trading Standards Officers to enforce the *CCA 1974* and sets out offences, defences, penalties and compensations payable.

Part XII embraces a number of miscellaneous issues, such as matters of interpretation and requirements for the service of documents under the *CCA 1974*.

Future reform of the CCA 1974   A14.15

In June 1994, the Office of Fair Trading published *Consumer Credit Deregulation – A Review by the Director General of Fair Trading of the Scope and Operation of the Consumer Credit Act 1974*. Its main recommendations were to:

- remove all business lending from the scope of the *CCA 1974*;

- extend the relaxation permitted in *CCA 1974, Part V* relating to entry into overdraft agreements to other types of agreement;

- increase the limit for regulated agreements to £25,000, and the lower cash price limit for connected lender liability to £150;

- remove the need to show an APR for agreements up to £150;

- revoke the quotation regulations (*Consumer Credit (Quotations) Regulations 1989* (*SI 1989/1126*));

- simplify the advertising regulations (*Consumer Credit (Advertisements) Regulations 1989* (*SI 1989/1125*));

- have only one permitted formulae for calculating APR; and

- revise early settlement rebate calculations and remove the 'Rule of 78' (see **A14.20** below).

Further aspects have been identified as requiring attention, including revisiting extortionate credit provisions, (consultation published March 2003), introducing a single form of open-ended licence with variable fees, (consultation closed April 2003), the impact of e-commerce (consultation closed March 2003), and re-examination of the form and content of agreements.

These reforms will now be implemented on a gradual basis. An implementation plan is due to be published in 2004 and will determine the regulatory vehicles to be used. These may require primary and secondary legislation, Regulatory Reform Orders or *European Communities Act 1972, s 2(2)* amendments, so it will undoubtedly be some time before they will take full effect.

Money Laundering Regulations 2003 (SI 2003/3075)   A14.16

The *Money Laundering Regulations 2003 (SI 2003/3075)* significantly extend the scope of the law to apply to a wider range of 'relevant business' beyond that originally specified. 'Money laundering' means an act which falls within *section 340(11)* of the *Proceeds of Crime Act 2002* or an offence under *section 18* of the *Terrorism Act 2000*.

The Regulations seek that relevant businesses must appoint a Money Laundering Reporting Officer, must introduce appropriate internal procedures for reporting incidents and must ensure that staff are sufficiently trained to spot potential cases of money laundering. Relevant businesses must also obtain 'satisfactory' proof of the potential client's identity and residence. This is defined as 'evidence which is reasonably capable of establishing that the applicant for business is the person he claims to be'.

Those failing to file reports risk a prison sentence of up to 5 years, while those who assist in money laundering face jail terms of up to 14 years.

Within the context of the Regulations, 'relevant business' now means the following (these lists have been adapted from *Regulation 2*):

- the regulated activity of:
  - accepting deposits;
  - effecting or carrying out contracts of long-term insurance when carried on by a person who has received official authorisation pursuant to *Article 4* or *51* of the *Life Assurance Consolidation Directive*;
  - dealing in investments as principal or as agent;
  - arranging deals in investments;
  - managing investments;
  - safeguarding and administering investments;
  - sending dematerialised instructions;
  - establishing (and taking other steps in relation to) collective investment schemes;
  - advising on investments; or
  - issuing electronic money;
- the activities of the National Savings Bank;

- any activity carried on for the purpose of raising money authorised to be raised under the *National Loans Act 1968* under the auspices of the Director of Savings;

- the business of operating a bureau de change, transmitting money (or any representation of monetary value) by any means or cashing cheques which are made payable to customers;

- certain activities defined in the *Banking Consolidation Directive* including:

  - acceptance of deposits and other repayable funds;

  - lending;

  - financial leasing;

  - money transmission services;

  - issuing and administering means of payment (e.g. credit cards, travellers' cheques and bankers' drafts);

  - guarantees and commitments;

  - trading for own account or for account of customers in money market instruments (cheques, bills, certificates of deposit, etc.), financial futures and options, exchange and interest-rate instruments or transferable securities;

  - participation in securities issues and the provision of services related to such issues;

  - advice to undertakings on capital structure, industrial strategy and related questions and advice as well as services relating to mergers and the purchase of undertakings;

  - money broking;

  - portfolio management and advice;

  - safekeeping and administration of securities.

- estate agency work;

- operating a casino;

- the activities of a person appointed to act as an insolvency practitioner within the meaning of *section 388* of the *Insolvency Act 1986* or *Article 3* of the *Insolvency (Northern Ireland) Order 1989* (*SI 1989/2405*);

- the provision by way of business of advice about the tax affairs of another person;

- the provision by way of business of accountancy services;

- the provision by way of business of audit services by a person who is eligible for appointment as a company auditor under *section 25* of the *Companies Act 1989* (or *Article 28* of the *Companies (Northern Ireland) Order 1990* (*SI 1990/593*));

- the provision by way of business of legal services which involves participation in a financial or real property transaction;

- the provision by way of business of services in relation to the formation, operation or management of a company or a trust; or

- the activity of dealing in goods of any description by way of business (including dealing as an auctioneer) whenever a transaction involves accepting a total cash payment of 15,000 Euros or more.

Certain exemptions to the definition of 'relevant businesses' apply, including the Bank of England and the Official Solicitor to the Supreme Court.

The extension of the definition of 'relevant businesses' to include lawyers, accountants, casino operators and estate agents came into effect from 1 March 2004. Such businesses are now obliged to report any suspicious activity to the National Criminal Intelligence Service (NCIS) regardless of the amount of money involved.

The extension of the definition of 'relevant businesses' to include businesses that deal in 'high value goods', such as art, jewellery and cars came into effect from 1 April 2004. Companies that handle high value cash payments of more than 15,000 Euros must register with HM Customs & Excise. The term 'cash' applies to notes, coins and travellers' cheques in any currency. High value dealers will be obliged to report any suspicions they may have relating to the source of the money.

Supply of goods and services legislation   A14.17

The *Sale of Goods Act 1979* protects a purchaser of goods such as he may imply that a seller has title to and the rights to sell the goods, which are also implied free of any encumbrances. Goods must also correspond with any description made by the seller.

They must be also of merchantable quality, if sold in the course of a business, and free from defects unless these are specifically drawn to the attention of the purchaser before the contract of sale. The goods are considered merchantable if they are fit for the purpose for which they are sold.

For services that are supplied, the *Sale of Goods Act 1979* allows a purchaser to imply that the services will be supplied within a reasonable time, at a reasonable price and that the provider of services will carry these out with reasonable care and skill.

The *Sale and Supply of Goods Act 1994* (*SSGA 1994*) removed a distinction between a contractual condition and a warranty, and redefined both with the word 'term'. This has important consequences as, unlike a breach of warranty, a breach of any condition of sale enables a purchaser to reject goods, repudiate the contract and claim damages. In addition, the *SGGA 1994* replaced 'merchantable quality' with 'satisfactory quality', indicating that goods may not be satisfactory but may nevertheless be fit for sale.

For goods supplied on hire, the *Sale of Goods Act 1979* and the *Sale and Supply of Goods Act 1994* apply similarly. The hirer may be implied to have the right to hire, goods must correspond with any descriptions given by the hirer, and the goods must be fit for purpose.

When credit is extended for the purchase or hire of goods or services, then in the event of a breach of the above Acts (for example, faulty goods are supplied), then the credit grantor may be jointly and severally liable with the seller under the terms of the *CCA 1974*. Similarly, the seller and the credit grantor may be liable for misrepresentations made by a seller or supplier.

Consumer Credit (Advertisements) Regulations 1989 (SI 1989/1125)   A14.18

SI 1989/1125 controls advertising and quotations for consumer credit. Developed in conjunction with trade associations and consumer bodies, the Regulations were first brought into operation in 1980. They were simplified and extended in 1989 to clarify their application to brokers and to introduce appropriate warning statements about the risks of secured loans and foreign currency mortgages.

CCA 1974, Part IV (see **A14.10** above) regulates advertisements with the intention of ensuring that the form and content conveys a fair and reasonably comprehensive indication of the nature of the credit facilities and the true cost to borrowers. In addition, advertisements may not mislead. Breaches are criminal offences and the advertiser, the publisher, the author and the person procuring the publication may all be held liable. Regulated credit, together with mortgages of any size, advertised through any medium are covered by the *CCA 1974*.

SI 1989/1125, made under *sections 44, 46* and *47* of the *CCA 1974*, specify three categories of advertisement – simple, intermediate or full – and set out the information which is required, optional or prohibited in each category. Expressions such as 'overdraft', 'no deposit' or 'interest-free' may not be used except in specific and limited circumstances. There are also restrictions on any claims that the cost of credit is cheaper than that of competitors.

Prescribed information must be clearly shown and legible. The APR must be as prominent as any other rate quoted, and the required warning statements must also be presented prominently. In March 2000, the Office of Fair Trading issued further guidance on the APR. In brief:

- the cost of payment protection insurance (PPI) must be reflected in the APR when it amounts to a condition of a loan – this is aimed at those lenders that offer discounted interest rates, which are only available if PPI is taken out;

- advertising a *minimum* APR is only acceptable if a *typical* APR is also given – the latter should be more prominent.

Failure to comply with the above guidance may leave a company open to prosecution under the *CCA 1974*. Local Trading Standards Officers take the lead on such cases. Offenders can be tried either in a Magistrates' Court or a Crown Court. Those found guilty in the former can be fined up to £2,000. The maximum sentence in a Crown Court is two years' imprisonment or a fine, or both.

This was the first major step following an announcement, earlier in April 1999, when the Office of Fair Trading sought views from trade associations in connection with a review of the *SI 1989/1125*. It had been concluded in their report of June 1994 (entitled *Consumer Credit Deregulation* (see **A14.20** below)) that the complexity of the Regulations was out of proportion to the benefits given to consumers. Consultation is now underway with a view to simplify the Regulations and to make them more sharply focussed on requiring informative and truthful advertising. In all the time that the Regulations have been in place, not a single prosecution has been brought successfully.

Consumer Credit (Guarantees and Indemnities) Regulations 1983 (SI 1983/1556)   A14.19

SI 1983/1556 ensure that any third party guarantor or indemnifier of credit regulated under the *CCA 1974* is made aware of the nature of the obligation being entered into, and is kept informed of any materially adverse events as they occur. The guarantee, indemnity, or agreement by a third party to pay if a principal debtor fails to do so must contain:

- a description of the principal regulated agreement;

- a statement of rights;

- the names and addresses of any other parties to the guarantee, indemnity or agreement (see **A14.36** below regarding rights of contribution and subrogation);

- details of any other security taken; and

- prominent warnings such as 'do not sign unless you wish to be legally bound' or 'important notice – please read this carefully'.

Copies of the agreement and security forms must be given to the third party. If the agreement is signed after the security is executed by the third party, a copy of the agreement must be provided to the third party within seven days. In the event of default by the principal debtor, a copy of the default notice must be issued to the third party at the same time as it is issued to the principal debtor.

Consumer Credit (Rebate on Early Settlement) Regulations 1983 (SI 1983/1562) A14.20

A consumer is entitled to a rebate of interest if the whole amount due is paid. The relevant provisions are contained in *SI 1983/1562* (as amended by *SI 1989/596*) and the *Consumer Credit (Settlement Information) Regulations 1983 (SI 1983/1564)*.

There are five formulae permitted in *SI 1983/1562* to calculate rebates. The most common is known as the 'Rule of 78' which is proposed to be removed under the Consumer Credit Deregulation proposals (see **A14.15** above). This is calculated as follows:

$$\frac{M\,(M+1)}{N\,(N+1)} \times K = \text{amount of rebate due}$$

Where:

- M = total number of instalments not yet due;

- N = total number of instalments; and

- K = total charge for credit.

A credit grantor must supply an early settlement statement within twelve days of a written request which is then binding on the credit grantor.

Although the 'Rule of 78' was held, at its introduction, to be a fair way of calculating early repayment penalties, it is now widely thought that it is unfair and in particular can generate extortionate penalties in some cases, which is why revision is now being canvassed.

Data Protection Act 1998 A14.21

The *Data Protection Act 1998 (DPA 1998)* is aimed at regulating the use of personal information by third parties. It is built around eight data protection principles which are summarised as follows, which require that personal data shall be:

- fairly obtained, and processed fairly and lawfully;

- only held for purposes notified to the Office of the Information Commissioner (formerly the 'Data Protection Commissioner');

- used only in a manner compatible with the notified purpose;

- adequate, relevant and not excessive;

- accurate and kept up-to-date;

- kept no longer than is necessary;

- made available to the data subject who, where appropriate, can correct or erase it; and

- kept securely.

Credit grantors collect and process a great deal of personal information and often relay this to credit reference agencies and other third parties if parts of the credit function are outsourced. Achieving compliance with the principles is discussed in the following paragraphs (see **A14.22–A14.29** below).

Principle 1 – Fair obtaining   A14.22

Seeking free, fair and informed consent is the most common course of action for most credit grantors. This is usually obtained by the insertion of standard clause statements in application forms, for example:

> 'Data contained in this form will be passed to a credit reference agency and shared with other credit grantors for the purposes of credit risk assessment, account management, fraud prevention, and occasional tracing.'

For trade credit applications an additional clause may be added:

> 'The person signing this form hereby authorises such disclosure and confirms that he or she is authorised to disclose all corporate and personal information contained on this form.'

There is no set clause, although the Information Commissioner gives some examples at the back of Guidance Notes on Credit Referencing (available free from the Office of the Information Commissioner (see **C1 USEFUL ADDRESSES**), alternatively they are on the Commissioner's website at: www.informationcommissioner.gov.uk), and is happy to be consulted on the adequacy of the wording.

Principle 2 – Held only for notified purposes   A14.23

The *DPA 1998* changes emphasis from registration to notification. Credit grantors should regularly re-examine existing register entries to ensure that for each notified purpose, including all credit risk, collections and fraud prevention activities, all of the following areas are adequate:

- the types of data subjects about whom data is held;
- classes of data to be held;
- sources of data; and
- countries where data may be transferred.

Any amendments must be lodged on Form DPR2. Once adequate notification has been lodged, compliance of this principle is achieved.

Principle 3 – Held for intended purpose A14.24

Given proper attention to free, fair and informed consent (see **A14.22** above) and a review of existing notification, this principle should be reasonably addressed.

Principle 4 – Adequate, relevant and not excessive A14.25

Adequacy may manifest itself in the preferred practice of collecting dates of birth to ensure that people with the same surname can be differentiated from one another. Relevance and measures of excessiveness can be subjective. Credit grantors should establish clear guidelines for deleting and removing data which is no longer required.

Principle 5 – Kept accurate and up-to-date A14.26

Immediate responses to notification of changes are expected, as are quality control measures. Procedures should be documented to set out the actions required to keep records both accurate and up-to-date.

Principle 6 – Not kept longer than necessary A14.27

This is self evident, records of closed accounts should be kept for no longer than six years to ensure that any dispute raised by the borrower within the *Limitation Act 1980* period may be defended. Records of declined applications may be retained for a much shorter period.

Principle 7 – Subject access A14.28

Most borrowers wishing to access personal data held by credit grantors tend to exercise their right to obtain information on all credit files by making a single application under *CCA 1974, s 158* to one of the three credit reference agencies for the statutory fee of £2.

A request for information sent direct to a credit grantor, seeking copies of all personal data held, and exercising rights held under the *DPA 1998, s 7*, requires payment of a fee of £10, is comparatively rare, and must be dealt with within the statutory 28-day period.

Principle 8 – Appropriate security A14.29

The company's operational security issues, such as physical security precautions for premises, and hierarchical password protected access to the database, should ensure compliance with this principle.

Other information   A14.30

The Information Commissioner has published some useful guidance notes for credit grantors including *Data Protection Guidance on Debt Tracing and Collection* and *Data Protection Guidance on Credit Referencing*. These are based on the *DPA 1984* but the principles still apply, pending revision.

Third Party Data Rules 2001   A14.31

The Third Party Data Rules 2001 provide a voluntary code which:

- affect the extent of information that may be considered when assessing credit applications;

- give the applicant the choice of whether the assessment is to be undertaken on a household or individual basis; and

- seek immediate improvement in requirements regarding the minimum information to be collected from an individual on application forms.

The practice of revealing on credit files the credit history of all people with the same surname, within the same household, or anyone known to be financially connected to a person, arose from a Data Protection Tribunal ruling in 1992. The underlying motive of the ruling was that it is necessary to consider the financial fortunes of all people within a household to ensure social responsibility in lending. Since then, the Information Commissioner has increasingly voiced concerns that the practice is unsafe and is in conflict with concerns over privacy of personal information.

The practice of assessing applicants on a household basis is particularly offensive to privacy issues when the matter of individuals seeking copies of their credit files from credit reference agencies (under *CCA 1974, s 158* or under the *DPA 1998* – see **A14.28** above) is considered. Such credit files must return all the information that a lender may see. This will include all people deemed to be financially connected to the individual. 92% of credit files contain details of third parties, and 56% have defaults or late payments recorded which relate to other people.

Typically, for example, an adult son living at home can obtain his credit file and view the detailed financial transactions of his parents without their knowledge or consent, which may be deemed a breach of privacy of the parents' confidential information.

Representatives from the credit industry and from the credit reference agencies have completed protracted negotiations to agree a compromise position with the Information Commissioner on future access to third party information, effective from October 2001.

Lenders may then give an individual applicant the option to be considered only on his merits. If this option is taken, the lender may only consider 'third party data' (i.e. data about people in the same household with the same surname or who are known to be financially connected) if either the information on the individual applicant is so sparse that the election may prejudice his access to credit, or if the lender believes that the election is a deliberate attempt to hide deleterious information, or to defraud the lender.

Once a person has elected to be considered on his merits, then that election is recorded at the credit reference agencies and all future applications are similarly treated, unless the applicant elects otherwise.

An exception within the rules relates to 'transient associations', which is where a joint application is made for a temporary and non-enduring purpose (for example, students living together and applying for a telephone line in student accommodation).

As part of the compromise agreement, the Information Commissioner sought and obtained agreement by all principal credit industry trade bodies to improve the quality of data held by lenders.

From October 2001, lenders must collect the title, full first name, full second name (or initial), surname, PAF (Postcode Address File) validated address, and date of birth for all applicants. Foreign and BFPO addresses must also be flagged as such. This will help to ensure that individuals can be properly identified.

The Information Commissioner has sought that all data controllers bring their systems into line with the new code by the end of 2004.

Guide to Credit Scoring 2000   A14.32

This guide provides a framework for best practice for credit grantors who use credit scoring as part of the risk assessment process. The guide was originally drawn up in 1983, updated in 1993 to take account of the recommendations of a report on credit scoring published by the Director-General of Fair Trading in May 1992, and again updated in 2000 to encompass the issues arising from the Rules of Reciprocity and the *DPA 1998*. The guide contains contributions from all main trade associations in conjunction with scorecard developers and credit reference agencies.

The Director-General of Fair Trading has prefaced the updated guide with a foreword that acknowledges the role of credit scoring in the responsible granting of credit. He goes on to say that consumers need to understand the basis of credit scoring and the procedures involved, and what steps they can take if they are refused credit. The revisions to the 2000 guide help provide greater openness and transparency to this end. The Information Commissioner commends the guide – and the directness it promotes – in a new addition to the preface.

The guide sets out principles to be used when designing scorecards and expresses a preference for bespoke scorecards, which are those developed from the credit grantor's own lending experience. Unless the credit grantor's entire portfolio is used to build the model, any sample should be selected on a representative basis, and in both cases should exclude fraudulent accounts. If it is not practical to develop a bespoke scorecard then a generic scorecard may be used, using data from other credit grantors or credit reference agency data, always based on the same principles as a bespoke scorecard. Scorecard developments must comply with the Rules of Reciprocity (see **A14.38** below), which apply to all credit grantors who share data.

When implementing the scorecard, the guide suggests that:

- likely acceptance and default rates are evaluated;

- adequate testing is undertaken to apply appropriate cut-off scores; and

- data is captured and coded correctly.

If scorecard decisions are to be overridden, then the reasons for doing so require definition, and levels and performance of overridden accounts should be monitored.

All internal departments of the credit grantor should be notified of the implementation and its effects. Access to the scorecard must be strictly controlled. All procedures and the wording of communications declining credit must be agreed prior to implementation and kept under review.

Once a credit scoring system is in operation, the guide suggests that only competent persons may use the system and enter data. Control mechanisms are required to be put in place to ensure compliance with the guide and to ensure that the scorecard is meeting its objectives. Any generic scorecards require periodic revalidation to ensure they remain appropriate, and should be replaced with bespoke scorecards when sufficient credit experience is available.

Scorecards may not discriminate by sex, race, religion or colour. Nor may credit be refused solely on the grounds of area of residence, although this may be included as a properly weighted factor in a scorecard. Credit grantors are also permitted to decline credit in areas where they are not represented or where it is considered that servicing the account may place property or staff at risk.

Credit grantors are not obliged to rely solely on the credit score and may take into account factors such as:

- verification of identity;

- credit reference agency information; and

- any security offered.

The guide suggests that applications which require clarification or further information are not declined, but referred pending investigation. The subsequent underwriting process may be introduced at this point if required.

Appeals and review procedure requirements are given in the guide, seeking, amongst other things, that explanations given to applicants will be clear and not overly technical so as not to deliberately confuse. In automated decision-making, credit grantors must inform all applicants of their right of appeal, and of the process they should follow. Credit grantors are not expected to give details of scorecard attributes or weightings as it is recognised that this could jeopardise the integrity or security of the scorecards, as well as increasing the risk of fraud. Repeat applications must be dealt with as if they are new and may not be rejected solely on the basis of the previous application. Exceptions are where there is an element of dishonesty, or if there has been no change to the credit scoring system, or the cut-off score, and identical information is being processed.

Where a credit grantor is aware that a Notice of Correction, Notice of Comment, or a Notice of Dispute has been filed with a credit reference agency, by or in relation to an applicant, any declined application must be manually reviewed.

The Guide to Credit Scoring 2000 is available from the Finance and Leasing Association, Imperial House, 15–19 Kingsway, London WC2B 6UN, price £1 (minimum order £5).

Insolvency Act 1986   A14.33

The *Insolvency Act 1986* (*IA 1986*) sets out procedures for dealing with corporate and personal insolvencies and includes deterrents to penalise irresponsible behaviour of company directors. It replaced a haphazard collection of statute and case law, including the *Insolvency Acts* of *1976* and *1985* and the *Bankruptcy Act 1914*, and represented the most significant review of insolvency for over 70 years. The *IA 1986* is largely in accordance with a recommendation of the Insolvency Law Review Committee, appointed in 1977 and chaired by Sir Kenneth Cork, in its report published in June 1982 (Insolvency Law and Practice – Report of the Review Committee, Cmnd 8558). The main purposes of the *IA 1986* were:

- to curb the unprofessional activities of some liquidators and receivers;

- to simplify procedures;

- to encourage voluntary procedures to relieve individuals and corporates of unnecessary involvement with the courts and the Insolvency Service; and

- to change the role of the Insolvency Service so that Official Receivers may concentrate on protective and investigative work.

The basic structure of the *Companies Act 1985* in respect of corporate insolvency law was unchanged by the *IA 1986*. (See **B10 INSOLVENCY** for a full discussion of this area of law.)

The *Enterprise Act 2002* introduced significant changes to bankruptcy and insolvency law. The underlying motive is to encourage enterprise by reducing the dishonour related to failure, and in particular to reduce the stigma of bankruptcy.

A distinction between 'honest' and 'dishonest' bankrupts is attempted to be drawn in the legislation, with 'honest' bankrupts being those who have used their best endeavours to succeed, but who have failed due to external influences, such as changes to market conditions. The main changes introduced (which applied from 15 September 2003 for companies and from 1 April 2004 for personal bankruptcy) are as follows:

- the automatic discharge period has reduced from three years to a maximum of twelve months, and to a minimum of three months in some circumstances;

- bankrupts who have abused their creditors and the public will face restrictions of between two and fifteen years;

- the ability of government debt to have priority over others has been revoked ('Crown Preference' no longer applies);

- it is now possible for the trustee to exclude the family home as part of the debtor's assets;

- some powers of trustees have been amended; and

- steps have been taken to try to restrict the ability of debenture holders to appoint administrative receivers to the detriment of other creditors.

Late Payment of Commercial Debts (Interest) Act 1998   A14.34

The *Late Payment of Commercial Debts (Interest) Act 1998* was introduced to address the issue of purchasers paying suppliers late without good reason. As this practice can lead to cashflow problems for suppliers, it can also reduce profits and threaten survival. The introduction of a statutory right to claim interest is expected to encourage purchasers to pay on time. The statutory right passes to liquidators and administrators, who may be more inclined to pursue historic claims than a struggling business.

Up to 31 October 2000, small businesses – defined as those with an average of 50 employees or less over the previous financial year prior to the date of the contract – were able to claim interest from large businesses and the public sector on debts incurred under contracts agreed from 1 November 1998.

From 1 November 2000 to 31 October 2002, the right to claim interest was extended so that small businesses were able to claim interest from other small businesses on contracts agreed on or after 1 November 2000.

The right of all sizes of business and the public sector to claim interest from all others became law for all contracts agreed after 1 November 2002.

Payments are defined as late when overdue any agreed credit period, or in the absence of an oral or written agreement, are outstanding more than 30 days after delivery of goods or after the day on which the purchaser has notice of the amount of the debt, whichever is later. Notice may be written or oral. Clearly, under oral contracts there is greater potential for dispute of the underlying terms.

The interest rate applicable is the official dealing rate of the Bank of England (base rate) which applies at the end of the day on which the contract says that payment is to be made, plus 8%. In the absence of a contract, the base rate reference point is the end of the day of the 30-day default period. Historic base rates may be obtained from back copies of the *Financial Times* or from the Bank of England Public Enquiries Unit. Tel: 020 7601 4878. Interest is calculated on a simple basis until repaid.

Claims should be made in writing within the *Limitation Act 1980* period of six years and may be pursued by:

- the supplier as principal debtor;

- any subsequently appointed liquidator or administrator; or

- any assignee of the debt, subject to notice of assignment of the debt.

Limitation Act 1980   A14.35

The *Limitation Act 1980* (*LA 1980*) places a time limit on the ability of credit grantors to commence proceedings in law.

For simple debts, *LA 1980, s 5* provides that the period is six years from the date when the first cause of action arose, or under *section 6*, from the date of the last acknowledgement by the principal debtor of the liability. For debts where security has been given under seal, *section 8* extends the period to twelve years. For judgment debts, a precedent has clarified a creditor's ability to enforce the judgment. (See **A14.54** below.)

Any right of action to commence proceedings, once statute-barred, cannot be revived by subsequent acknowledgement or payment of the debt, under *LA 1980, s 29*. It is important to distinguish the difference between the ability to commence proceedings and the basic debtor/creditor relationship issue. Once a debt becomes statute-barred, it remains due and normal collections procedures may continue, but the credit grantor is no longer able to escalate the matter to the courts.

Rights of subrogation and contribution   A14.36

These are complicated rights, arising under ancient law, which are designed to ensure that third parties who repay or otherwise help to reduce a debt may subsequently have a right of recourse to the principal debtor, or his estate, or to any security held by the credit grantor. Arising under *section 5* of the *Mercantile Law Amendment Act 1856*, when a guarantor or a third party who has given security, repays a debt in full then he has the right to subrogate to the credit grantor's position. This means he is entitled to take over any other security held by the credit grantor, or receive any dividends due from a bankrupt's estate which would have been due to the credit grantor.

If other third parties have also put up security or given guarantees, then the paying guarantors are entitled to a share in the estate or any other security on a pro rata basis of contribution.

In the event of joint and several guarantees, where contributions have been made by several third parties, including those who may or may not have entered into formal guarantees or have lodged third party security, each contributing party is individually entitled to rights of contribution and subrogation. In such cases any remaining security or dividends should not be released by a credit grantor without the joint written instructions of all paying contributors. In the absence of this, the security or dividends may be surrendered to the courts for the contributor to claim against.

Monetary union legislation   A14.37

To simplify and stimulate cross-border trading within Europe, a common currency, the Euro, has been introduced by the European Commission. This followed the signing of the *Single European Act 1986* and a report from a committee commissioned by the Council of Ministers and chaired by the then President of the European Commission, Jacques Delors. The Delors report was published in April 1989 and its recommendations enshrined in the Maastricht Treaty, which came into effect on 1 November 1993. This amended and supplemented the Treaty of Rome, creating an obligation for all thirteen Member States without an opt-out to merge their currencies if they met four macro-economic criteria relating to:

- inflation;
- exchange rates;
- long-term interest rates; and
- levels of government debt.

The participating Member States were initially selected by the European Parliament in May 1998 and now include:

- Austria;
- Belgium;
- Finland;
- Germany;
- Greece;
- Spain;
- France;

- Ireland;

- Italy;

- Luxembourg;

- the Netherlands; and

- Portugal.

Greece did not satisfy the initial entry criteria on various counts but was later admitted, and Sweden failed to fulfil the exchange rate criteria. Denmark and the UK exercised an opt out.

On 1 May 2004 a further ten countries joined the European Union and also became part of the European Economic Area (EEA):

- Cyprus;

- Czech Republic;

- Estonia;

- Hungary;

- Latvia;

- Lithuania;

- Malta;

- Poland;

- Slovakia; and

- Slovenia.

The currency is managed by the European Central Bank (ECB) in Frankfurt, which was created in June 1998. The ECB has seventeen members, six from the Frankfurt directorate and eleven from the central banks of the participating countries. Extensive statistics can be obtained from their website www.ecb.int.

On 1 January 1999 the Euro became a new trading currency. A transition period allows financial markets to operate in Euros alongside existing currencies, and on a no compulsion, no prohibition basis, companies may choose to deal in either. By 1 January 2002 new Euro notes and coins were circulated. On 1 July 2002 the Euro became the only legal tender for transactions in or with countries opting to adopt the Euro.

Where payments under contracts were due in affected national currencies prior to 1 January 1999, they will now be due in Euros unless otherwise agreed. Businesses which trade principally in affected countries must consider the need to report in Euros rather than national currency to avoid the possible risk of misleading shareholders in annual accounts.

Rules of Reciprocity 1998 A14.38

The use of personal credit account performance data, either in raw format or in scorecards, is now defined by the Rules of Reciprocity. The Rules are complex, but the underlying concept is that account performance data is shared to encourage social responsibility in granting credit. The Rules replaced an informal understanding that credit grantors 'got what they gave', specifically that data sharers may only see the detail of data that reflects the detail of data submitted to the central databases. 'Subscribers' is a term used in the principles to describe credit grantors who are members of the data sharing schemes. 'Rules' and 'principles' are interchangeable terms.

The basic principle still remains that virtually all data can be used for risk assessment. When a subscriber uses shared data for prospecting or marketing purposes, the rules become much more restrictive and generally only data relating to bad payers can be used.

The Rules of Reciprocity are embodied around eleven 'general principles', which are given here substantially as contained in the text of the rules.

- Credit performance data will be shared on the principle that subscribers receive the same credit performance level data that they contribute, and should contribute all such data available. The only exceptions to this principle are that:

  ○ banks will continue with existing arrangements to supply default data and receive default and delinquent data; and

  ○ subscribers offering current accounts will have access to positive and delinquent data when processing current account applications or operating the accounts, providing they are subscribing both positive and delinquent data on all other consumer credit products.

- Each subscriber owns all the data – including positive, delinquent, default and searches – it provides to the credit reference agencies.

- The data may be used or made available by the credit reference agencies only in ways permitted by the principles.

- Data is shared for the prevention of over-commitment, bad debt, fraud and money laundering, and to support debt recovery and debtor tracing, with the aim of promoting responsible lending.

- Notwithstanding anything in these principles, data provided for sharing purposes must meet legal, regulatory and voluntary code of practice requirements before use.

- Subscribers must use data only for purposes for which the required form of consent has been given by the individual.

- The shared data may not be used beyond or within a group of subscribers without the agreement of the supervisory body. A purpose of this rule is to clarify the use of data in bureau scorecards (see **A14.41** below). No shared data should be used for propensity or response models. Geodemographic and other generic scores using shared data may only be made available by the agreement of the supervisory body for credit purposes. Notwithstanding the above, consumer credit reference agency risk scorecards must not be developed from shared data where a subscriber represents 25% or more of the sample on which the scorecard is developed, unless the consent of that subscriber is obtained.

- Subscribers may not screen a mailing list targeted at prospects identified as holding a specific product of another specific subscriber against a shared data file (for example, from a lifestyle list). The purpose of the principle is, for example, to prevent the targeting of another subscriber's customers through lifestyle questionnaires and subsequent screening against the bureaux databases. Detailed lifestyle questionnaires often generate comprehensive information on respondents' credit commitments. Lists derived from responses to such questionnaires can then be screened against existing subscribers' records to remove individuals with repayment problems and so generate 'derived positive' lists of active credit users for mailing offers. This principle specifically outlaws any risk screening of such prospect lists where a specific subscriber has been identified. The shared data is not to be used in ways that specifically target the good customers of the originator of the information.

- Access for all shared data will be restricted or suspended for subscribers who do not comply with these principles. Any restriction will apply to both credit reference agencies. The supervisory body will decide on such restrictions, which will be appropriate in scale and on appropriate notice and will hear appeals. Any such restriction must be made known to all subscribers and the appropriate regulatory body with reasons for the restriction detailed. The Office of the Information Commissioner will be notified as a matter of courtesy if any subscriber's access to shared data is restricted or suspended.

- The uses of data by subscribers and bureaux may be audited independently for compliance with these principles.

- Credit bureaux must insert a statement of adherence to these principles into all contracts with subscribers.

- Should the quality of the data provided by a subscriber prove unsatisfactory, or if the subscriber fails to provide data, then access to the shared databases will be withdrawn. Subscribers and credit reference agencies should take appropriate and timely action to correct inaccurate or misleading data.

There are some important aspects to note from the general body of text that surrounds the rules. Firstly, distinction is made between types of subscriber, i.e:

- full subscribers (positive, delinquent and default data providers);

- default only providers;

- partial subscribers (those who supply limited fields); and

- new subscribers.

Secondly, the types of data are defined precisely. Positive data is all credit performance data that is not delinquent or default data. Delinquent data is defined as those relating to accounts which are:

(i)   currently three months or more in arrears;

(ii)   at least twice three months in arrears in the last twelve months or once four months or worse in the last twelve months;

(iii) closed delinquent; and

(iv)   if settled, at least twice three months in arrears consecutively in the twelve months before settlement.

Default data is defined as when the relationship with the individual is deemed by the lender in a standard business relationship to have broken down. Typically, banks and building societies will issue to individuals at least 28 days' notice if they intend to disclose information to credit reference agencies on undisputed personal debts which are in default and where no satisfactory proposals for repayment have been received following formal demand.

Banks are permitted to continue with an historic arrangement, whereby they supply default data and receive default and levels (ii), (iii) and (iv) of delinquent data as defined above.

Search data relates to credit searches on individual applicants held at credit reference agencies and information recorded in the course of the search.

Complicated rules cover the uses of shared data and these are presented in the rules using matrices. The first matrix relates to the different purposes of data within the credit assessment process. It differentiates between solicited business (outbound) and unsolicited business (inbound). Generally, unsolicited applications can enable the lender to interrogate greater levels of data. The matrix also makes a differentiation between an application for the same sort of product as already held (e.g. a credit card) and an application for a product not already held (a new product, e.g. an existing credit card holder applying for a personal loan).

For the purposes of credit scoring models, the following is an abbreviated summary of the application of the general principles and the matrices.

Prospecting, screening and propensity models   A14.39

Only delinquent, default and search data can be used, but they may be used for both existing and new customers, and for existing or new products. If subscribers only supply delinquent or default data, they may only access similar data.

Application risk assessment A14.40

If unsolicited business is being assessed, then all data may be used to assess the risk for new or existing customers. If solicited, then only delinquent, default and search data may be used. If the customer is an existing client, 'positive bureau risk scorecards' may also be used.

Fraud risk assessment A14.41

The rules specifically do not cover the use of data shared for fraud prevention purposes, which therefore are governed only by any contractual agreement of the underlying scheme. Scorecards used, which derive power from such data, are therefore outside the ambit of the body which has been set up to supervise the implementation and operation of the rules – the Standing Committee on Reciprocity (SCOR).

Unfair Terms in Consumer Contracts Regulations 1994 (SI 1994/3159) A14.42

The purpose of *SI 1994/3159*, which arose following *EC Directive 9/13* in April 1993, is to create a level playing field between suppliers and consumers. The Regulations apply to all contracts entered into after 1 July 1995, with no retrospective application, and apply to any term in a contract that has not been individually negotiated. The latter is defined as a term which has been drafted in advance and where it is part of a pre-formulated standard contract. As borrowers often have very limited scope to exert influence over such terms, most credit agreements will be subject to the Regulations.

A term is rendered unfair if it is contrary to the requirements of good faith and if it causes a significant imbalance in the parties' rights and obligations under the contract to the detriment of a consumer. Contracts must also be in plain, intelligible English – if ambiguous then interpretation in the consumer's favour applies.

When making an assessment of good faith, amongst other things, regard is paid to:

- the strength of the bargaining position between the parties;
- the presence of any inducement; and
- whether the services were tailored to special order for the consumer.

The Unfair Contract Terms Unit of the Office of Fair Trading has responsibility for investigating complaints about unfair terms and policing the Regulations. When undertakings cannot be extracted from suppliers to correct an unfair term, the Director-General of Fair Trading has power to seek an injunction, if necessary, or to refer the matter to courts for arbitration of any disputed issue. If a term is found to be unfair, it will not be binding upon the consumer. Since inception, the Director-General of Fair Trading has secured changes to over 350 contracts. This included a complaint concerning the use of dual interest rates by a sub prime lender (i.e. a lender who accepts a much higher level of risk than mainstream lenders, in return for a greater reward), whereby a concessionary rate of interest no longer applied after default, which was deemed unfair.

Case law round-up   A14.43

There are many legal precedents that are of importance to credit grantors. This section covers some of the most prominent cases, which have guided current practice.

Lending to minors

Coutts and Co v Browne-Lecky and others [1947] 1 KB 104   A14.44

A loan by Coutts to a minor that was guaranteed by a relative was held to be void. As a result of this case, most guarantee forms now contain an indemnity as well as a guarantee, as an indemnifier remains liable always, even if the underlying debt is voided.

Extortionate credit bargains

Castle Phillips v Wilkinson (1992) CCLR 83   A14.45

The borrowers had little understanding of financial matters but were persuaded by the credit grantor to accept an interest rate of 48% on a secured loan carrying little risk. This was held to be extortionate, as the rate was over three times the prevailing building society rate.

The same plaintiff fared differently in *Castle Phillips v Khan (1980) CCLR 1*, where the borrower had been loaned £3,000 for property speculation at an APR of 32%. The borrower was an experienced and mature businessman, had the benefit of advice from solicitors and was under no financial pressure. The courts held that the credit bargain in this case was not extortionate.

Falco Finance Ltd v Gough (1998), unreported   A14.46

Gough, a person with an impaired credit history, obtained a non-status loan of £30,000 from Falco, secured by a mortgage, for the purpose of consolidating two other mortgages that were in arrears. Interest was calculated on the loan at a flat rate of 8.99%, which rose to 13.99% on default. The rebate for early settlement of the loan was based on the 'Rule of 78' (see **A14.20** above), with the settlement deferred for six months, which Gough disputed on the basis of an alleged verbal agreement of three months. Upon default and subsequent possession proceedings, Gough claimed that the interest was in breach of *SI 1994/3159* and *CCA 1974, s 138*. The court held that the dual rate turned the contract into an extortionate credit bargain, given the 'rigid and hard' terms that accompanied the interest rates, and the redemption terms were held to be unfair.

Need to check powers to borrow

Royal British Bank v Turquand (1856) 6 E&B 32 A14.47

A company's Articles of Association required a resolution given at a general meeting to permit the borrowing of money and the giving of a debenture as security. This was not given but the bank lent the money. When the bank took action against the company subsequently, the company claimed that the debenture was invalid. The court held it as binding on the company and that the credit grantor may have assumed that the required resolution had been passed. Despite this, many credit grantors routinely check memoranda and Articles of Association as a belt and braces precaution.

Reservation of title

Aluminium Industrie Vaassen BV v Romalpa Aluminium [1976] 2 All ER 552 A14.48

If reservation of title clauses in supplier contracts are to be fully effective against a liquidator, the underlying goods must be clearly identifiable. If goods supplied have been processed into other goods then the reservation of title is not valid.

Reservation of title clauses are often tested to ensure validity. These require careful inclusion in any supply contracts, repetition on invoice terms and reminders on all appropriate literature. Clauses may be drafted to seek that the supplied goods are kept separate, in order to aid identification, and to give the supplier a right of entry to the purchaser's premises. Clauses, which retain title to the goods until payment has been made, are unlikely to require registration as a charge at Companies House.

Ultra vires

Ashbury Railway Carriage & Iron Co v Riche (1875) 7HL 653 A14.49

The objects of the company included 'to make sell or lend on hire railway carriages wagons all kinds of railway plant fittings machinery and rolling stock'. The company purchased a concession to build a railway in Belgium, which was later assigned to another company. A dispute arose and the question as to whether the object covered the construction of a railway was considered. The court held that this activity was *ultra vires* and the company had no power in law to enter into such a contract nor engage upon it.

The treatment of payments into a running account (the Rule in Clayton's case)

Devaynes v Noble (1816) 1 Merc 529, 572   A14.50

This was a complicated case leading to a very important precedent, whereby a banking partnership of four persons continued to conduct business following the death of Devaynes and subsequently went bankrupt. Creditors, including Clayton, who had suffered a misappropriation of bills deposited prior to Devayne's death, claimed against the surviving partners and also against the estate of Devaynes.

It was held that as business had continued, payments received by the surviving partners had repaid the old debt and payments made by the surviving partners had created a new debt. Known as, 'the Rule in Clayton's case', 'in a running account, payments in are presumed to be appropriated to payments out in the order in which the items occur'.

To avoid this rule working to the detriment of credit grantors upon events such as death of a partner, notice of a second mortgage or termination of a guarantee, running accounts such as current accounts, overdrafts and credit card accounts should be 'ruled off', and a new account opened immediately and all future transactions passed through the new account.

Need for separate legal advice for guarantors

Lloyds Bank Ltd v Bundy [1975] QB 326   A14.51

Mr Bundy junior ran a plant hire company that borrowed from Lloyds. His elderly father, once a farmer, gave a guarantee and a legal mortgage over his home to secure his son's business borrowings. He did this against his solicitor's advice, who advised him to limit the extent of its liability to around half of his assets. Subsequently, additional borrowing was required and the guarantee was increased with a new form being executed at the bank with no legal advice. Mr Bundy junior was bankrupted only months later, but when the bank attempted to rely on its new security, the courts held that they were void as there had been an inequality of bargaining power, brought about by undue influence.

Credit grantors taking security from third parties who may not fully understand the extent of the commitment or who may be in any way subject to undue influence are now routinely asked to seek legal advice, with the solicitor witnessing the execution of the documents. This was reinforced in the Court of Appeal in *Cooke v National Westminster Bank plc and others [1998] 2 FLR 783; The*

Times, 27 July 1998. The bank had requested a wife's solicitors to give separate legal advice to their client who had guaranteed the liabilities of her husband's company, and to confirm it had done so. The bank received no response. Here the bank was held to have had constructive notice of undue influence and could not rely on the guarantee.

Need for all intending persons to complete a security

National Provincial Bank Ltd v Brackenbury (1906) 22 TLR 797

A14.52

A brewery borrowed from the bank which required a joint and several guarantee from four people. One, a Mr Johnson, died before the bank obtained his signature on the guarantee form, which had already been signed by the other three. When the bank sought to rely upon the guarantee, one of the guarantors, Mr Brackenbury, claimed that he had been released from liability because the fourth signature had not been obtained and the bank had not sought permission from the remaining three to rely on the document already executed. This was upheld by the courts.

Credit grantors who face similar situations should prepare new security documentation and renegotiate the security arrangements afresh, to avoid claims.

Family members may have rights which can limit a mortgagee's powers

Williams & Glyn's Bank Ltd v Barnes [1980] 3 WLR 1388 and Williams & Glyn's Bank Ltd v Bolan [1980] 3 WLR 1388

A14.53

Both of these cases involved the family home being vested only in the husband's name, which historically was far more prevalent than it is today. In each case, the husband gave the bank a mortgage over the family home in support of guarantees, and for various reasons the wives in the two situations were not aware of the individual situations.

When the bank called in the guarantees and tried to realise the mortgages, the wives resisted the action, claiming a half share in the home, even though they were not a party to the deeds. It was held that, as the wives had contributed to the home (in money or otherwise, such as in the form of maintaining it), they had obtained a proprietary interest in the property and a right of occupation.

The *Matrimonial Homes Act 1983* later granted to a spouse, who is not the legal owner of a home, rights of occupation in the property which may be registered as a charge on the property and may not be removed without a court order.

Credit grantors should now ensure that all persons over 18 years who occupy a property are consulted in respect of an intended mortgage over that property, and should either be asked to mortgage their interests or postpone them in the favour of the credit grantor. Appropriate separate legal advice should also be obtained, following the principle established in *Lloyds Bank Ltd v Bundy* (see **A14.51** above).

Statute barred debt

Lowsley & Lowsley v Forbes [1998] 3 WLR 501   A14.54

This case ruled that a judgment creditor may execute a judgment after expiry of the six-year limitation period arising under *section 24* of the *Limitation Act 1980*, but is not entitled to recover interest which accrues after a period of six years from the date the judgment becomes enforceable.

Debt Recovery

B 1

Debt Recovery through the Courts

Preliminary considerations

B1.1

Even in the best run and most efficient credit control department there are always a number of customers who will not pay. The only means of obtaining payment is to issue court proceedings, enter judgment and then, if necessary, use one of the methods of enforcement. The most important steps in a claim are those taken before the proceedings start.

If pre-action matters are done properly then the chances of success are increased. Failure to deal with pre-action matters properly could mean losing the claim and paying substantial legal costs.

What is the contract?

B1.2

Although an organisation or person making a claim may consider their action to be the collection of a debt, the court will look at it in terms of a breach of contract. In simple terms, a contract is an agreement to do something in exchange for something else. When seeking payment there will have been an agreement for an individual or a company to supply goods or services in exchange for payment. The goods or services have been supplied but the debtor is in breach of its contractual obligation in that it has failed to make the agreed payment.

The contract may be written down or it may be spoken (an oral contract). If the terms of the contract are written down it is far easier to establish exactly what was agreed. Contracts under the *Consumer Credit Act 1974* must be in writing.

Many companies have standard terms and conditions setting out the terms of the contract. These standard terms and conditions are only incorporated in the contract if they have been made known to the customer at, or before, the time the contract was made.

It is better if there is an agreement at the outset that all orders will be governed by the seller's standard terms and conditions. This is often achieved by ensuring that the customer confirms in writing, when the credit account is opened, that he has received the standard terms and conditions and will place all orders on that basis.

Terms and conditions should be printed or referred to in all brochures, sales literature and, if orders are placed 'over the counter', where they can be read by customers.

A particular problem is created when orders are written on the buyer's order form incorporating the buyer's standard terms and conditions. A 'battle of the forms' may ensue with both sides claiming the contract is governed by their own terms and conditions. If in doubt, an order should not be accepted unless it is clear that the seller's terms prevail. In practice, it may be extremely difficult to persuade sales staff of the wisdom of this approach!

Printed standard terms and conditions must be reasonable especially when dealing with consumers. Any clause that is deemed to be unreasonable by the court may be struck out. The court is more likely to strike out terms in consumer contracts. For this reason, it is advisable to have standard terms and conditions professionally drafted by a solicitor.

Once a contract has been made it cannot be altered by one party without the agreement of the other. A claim for contractual interest, retention of title or any other term is not effective if it is only on an invoice. A contract is made when it is agreed to supply the goods and services to the customer. An invoice is usually sent after that time, often after the goods have been delivered. It is therefore said to be 'post contractual'. If there has been a course of dealing with that customer it may be argued that the terms and conditions were known from previous invoices but it is dangerous to rely solely on this argument.

Is the debtor correctly identified?   B1.3

A common reason for the failure of debt actions is that the wrong person has been sued. It is essential to know the correct identity of your customer. The customer may be an individual or a collection of individuals in the form of a firm or partnership (with no separate legal identity), or it may be a limited company or limited liability partnership (LLP).

A limited company is a separate legal entity and must be sued as a limited company. An LLP is similar to a limited company and also has its own legal identity. For credit control purposes, an LLP should be treated as a company and *not* as a partnership.

Unless the company is a registered charity, the name of the limited company will end in the words 'limited' or 'Ltd' ('cyfyngedig' in Wales), 'public limited company' or 'plc' ('cwmni cyfyngedig cyhoeddai' in Wales).

The name of an LLP will end in the words 'limited liability partnership' (or 'LLP') or, in Wales, 'partneriaeth atebolrwydd cyfyngedig' (or 'PAC').

Details of limited companies and limited liability partnerships are held at Companies House including the registered office, list of directors, list of members, and accounts although these are often in an abbreviated form. The records for a limited liability partnership do not include the Memorandum or Articles of Association. There is, instead, a partnership agreement but this is not a public document.

When a credit account is opened by a limited company or LLP, the supplier should obtain:

- the full name of the limited company or LLP;

- the address of its registered office; and

- its registered number.

Although a limited company or LLP can change its name, its registered number remains the constant. There is no need to ask for the home address of the director or LLP member as the company or LLP has limited liability and such persons are not, therefore, personally liable for its debts.

If any order is received with a different name or a different registered number, credit should not be given on that order until the details have been checked. It is often the case that companies or LLPs owned by the same directors or members have similar names. They are still separate legal entities and should be treated as different 'people'.

When an individual, firm or partnership applies for credit, unless it is a very large partnership, the names of all the partners and their home addresses should be obtained. If this information is not obtained the practical effect is to give the partners a degree of limited liability.

Many smaller businesses that appear to be run by a sole trader are actually a husband and wife partnership. If there is a partnership between a husband and wife, enforcement is often easier if proceedings are issued against both.

The easiest way of finding out the true status of a firm is to ask to see a copy of the last accounts submitted to the Inland Revenue. All partners will be named to ensure the maximum tax benefits.

Partners have joint and several liability for partnership debts. This means that any of the partners are liable for any proportion of the debt. The creditor is not concerned with the 'share' each partner has in the firm.

If there is any doubt at all as to the correct name or identity of the defendants, make sure that is resolved before proceedings are issued.

Is the debtor worth suing?   B1.4

There is little point in issuing court proceedings if the judgment will be unenforceable. If the debtor does not have the ability to satisfy the judgment, court action will be a waste of time and legal costs. It will merely 'throw good money after bad'. A few preliminary enquiries will often save court fees and legal costs.

Court proceedings will need to be served on the debtor. If you know that the debtor has left his last known address he should be traced before proceedings are issued. Proceedings against a limited company or a limited liability partnership can always be served at the registered office even if the company has ceased trading.

Is there a genuine dispute?   B1.5

The *Civil Procedure Rules 1998* (*SI 1998/3132*) (*CPR 1998*), that govern all court proceedings, expect potential litigants to try and resolve disputes before proceedings are issued. In any event, over 90% of court proceedings are settled before the final hearing. Very often settlement occurs at a late stage or even 'at the door of the court'. At this stage both parties have spent court fees, legal costs and a considerable amount of time. It therefore makes sense to try and settle those matters which will eventually be compromised at an early stage. The first step in this process is to identify actions that are genuinely disputed. This does not include matters where the defence is an obvious sham or nothing more than an excuse for non-payment. Also excluded are disputes involving only a small proportion of the overall debt. In these circumstances the undisputed balance should be paid immediately.

It is important to be objective in this assessment and be neither cynical of all customers' complaints nor gullible and accept every excuse for non-payment as genuine. Where there is a genuine dispute every effort should be made to resolve the problem with the customer, and, if necessary, to arrive at a satisfactory settlement.

Pre-action steps   B1.6

One of the stated aims of the *CPR 1998* is to encourage parties to avoid litigation by setting out steps which should be taken by proposed litigants before court proceedings are issued.

Pre-action protocols   B1.7

The rules allow for 'pre-action protocols' to be issued which define these steps in certain types of cases. A number of areas are covered by pre-action protocols but none have been issued for debt or money claims.

However, even where there is no approved protocol, the *CPR 1998* make it clear that the court will expect parties:

'... to act reasonably in exchanging information and documents relative to the claim and generally in trying to avoid the necessity for the start of proceedings'. [Protocols Practice Direction.]

In other words, the courts will generally expect parties to enter into the spirit of the protocols by exchanging information and generally trying to settle matters before proceedings are begun, no matter what the type of claim.

APPENDIX B1.1 shows the practice direction relating to protocols and the notes for guidance and pre-action protocols relating to personal injury matters. Whilst some of the personal injury protocols relate only to insurance claims or personal injuries, they give a flavour of the type of information the court expects to be given before proceedings are issued and reflect the change in philosophy brought about by the *CPR 1998*.

It was originally proposed that a separate pre-action protocol would be published dealing with debt claims. No satisfactory protocol was agreed upon and the idea was abandoned in favour of a general pre-action protocol dealing with all matters not covered by any of the specific protocols in force. That idea has also been abandoned. There is now a general statement of principle in the preamble to the protocols as to how parties should approach matters. This states:

> 4.2 Parties to a potential dispute should follow reasonable procedure suitable to their particular circumstances which is intended to avoid litigation. The procedure should not be regarded as a prelude to inevitable litigation. It should normally include:
>
> (*a*)   the claimant writing to give details of the claim;
>
> (*b*)   the defendant acknowledging the claim letter promptly;
>
> (*c*)   the defendant giving within a reasonable time a detailed written response;
>
> (*d*)   the parties conducting genuine and reasonable negotiations with a view to settling the claim economically and without court proceedings.

(C1003 4.2 Pre-action Protocol Practice Direction (32,003).)

Detailed disclosure, of the type set out in the protocols, is appropriate if there is a genuine dispute. The purpose is to settle disputes without the need for litigation. If, however, there is no dispute the protocols should not prevent court proceedings being swiftly issued.

Notification of claim B1.8

Before proceedings are issued a 'letter before action' or 'notification of claim' should be sent to the potential defendants.

No dispute

Where there is no genuine dispute the letter can be fairly simple. It should notify the debtor that, unless payment is made by a certain time on a certain date, proceedings will be issued. In addition, details of the debt should be given including the date and number of invoice. It would also be helpful to enclose a copy of the outstanding invoice or invoices or a statement. It is a good idea to refer to the previous reminders that have been given and any promises of the debtor to pay the debt, and to record in the letter that there has not been a notification of a dispute. The address where payment is to be made to should also be included as well as the method of payment sought. The pre-action protocol gives the following requirements for a claimant's letter.

4.3 The claimant's letters should:

(*a*)   give sufficient and concise details to enable the recipient to understand and investigate the claim without extensive further information;

(*b*)   enclose copies of the essential documents which the claimant relies on;

(*c*)   ask for prompt acknowledgment of the letter followed by a written response within a reasonable stated period;

(amended claims and a normal reasonable period for a full response may be one month.)

(*d*)   state whether court proceedings will be issued if the full response is not received within the stated period;

(*e*)   identify and ask for copies of any essential documents, not in his possession, which the claimant wishes to see;

(*f*)   state (if this is so) that the claimant wishes to enter into mediation or another alternative method to dispute resolution;

(*g*)   draw attention to the court's power to impose sanctions for him to comply with the Practice Direction and, if the recipient is likely to be unrepresented, enclose a copy of this practice direction.

Disputes

Where there is a dispute the content of the letter of the claim will depend on the nature of the dispute. Relevant documents, which show the debt is owed, should be included.

If the debtors fail to respond to telephone calls or letters this should be stated in the letter of claim, and it should be explained that as a result of the debtor's failure to respond proceedings will be issued. A time and date where proceedings will be issued unless a response is received should also be given.

If a technical dispute has arisen, the court will expect parties to have considered whether a joint expert should be appointed. The protocol for personal injury (see **APPENDIX B1.1**) sets out a procedure for appointing experts.

If the claimant is asked by the debtor to supply documents that are relevant to any dispute, it is important that a copy of those documents are given to the defendant in reasonable time (usually 21 days). Similarly, if the claimant has been notified of a dispute by letter and wishes to see the defendant's documents, a request should be made for the relevant documents to be produced within, for example, a 21-day period. If the defendant fails to respond proceedings may be issued. The defendant's documents, if they are produced, should assist the claimant in evaluating the defendant's case and help him to make a decision as to whether settlement can be reached, and under what terms. Documents disclosed prior to a claim and in particular under the auspices of the pre-action protocols, may not be used for any purpose other than resolving the dispute unless the other party agrees.

The defendant should respond as follows in accordance with the pre-action protocol practice directions.

4.5 The defendant's full written response should as appropriate:

(*a*)   accept the claim in whole or in part and make proposals for settlement;

(*b*)   state that the claim is not accepted. If the claim is accepted in part only the response should make clear which part is accepted and which part is not accepted;

4.6 If the defendant does not accept the claim or part of it the response should:

(*a*)   give detailed reasons why the claim is not accepted, identifying which of the claimant's contentions are accepted and which are in dispute;

(*b*)   enclose copies of the essential documents that the defendant relies on;

(*c*)   enclose copies of documents asked for by the claimant or explain why they are not enclosed;

(*d*)   identify and ask for copies of any further essential documents, not in his possession, which the defendant wishes to see (the claimant should provide these within a reasonably short time or explain in writing why he is not doing so);

(*e*)   state whether the defendant is prepared to enter into mediation or another alternative method to dispute resolution.

If the claimant is in any doubt as to what should be included in a letter of claim a solicitor should be consulted.

It is important to find a balance between behaving in the reasonable manner expected by the court and preventing a defendant entering into a lengthy correspondence, the only purpose of which is to delay a legitimate claim.

The *CPR 1998* introduced a 'front loading' of work in preparing for litigation. Steps that used to be taken after legal proceedings had started should now be taken before the action. This will mean that legal advice should be taken at an earlier stage, especially as the actions of the parties before proceedings are issued can be taken into account by the court in assessing the costs that would be awarded after a trial. In general the question is, have the parties acted reasonably?

Alternative dispute resolution (ADR)   B1.11

The *CPR 1998* encourage parties to try alternative forms of dispute resolution. Whilst ADR is not appropriate in all cases, and is particularly inappropriate when dealing with a debtor who is merely using the court system to delay legitimate payment, ADR can be effective where there is a genuine dispute in promoting settlement and avoiding litigation. It is entered into by agreement, usually as an alternative to court proceedings. It is especially effective where the costs of a civil action through the courts would be disproportionate.

Although ADR cannot be forced upon parties by the court there may be costs consequences if the matter goes to trial and the judge is of the view that one of the parties has unreasonably refused to enter into ADR. The position was set out by the court in *Dunnett v Trailtrack plc [2002] 2 All ER 850, The Times, 3 April 2002, CA*. The party was successful in the claim but failed to get an award of costs as the court decided there had been an unreasonable refusal to enter into mediation. Although that party had formed a view that it was confident of success and therefore felt there could be no benefit in resorting to ADR, it was not felt to be an appropriate reason for refusing mediation. However in *Hurst v Leeming [2002] EWHC Ch 1051* the court accepted that mediation would have had no realistic prospect of success. It did not penalise a party for refusing mediation in these circumstances.

ADR can be used at any stage after proceedings have started. An application may be made to stay proceedings by consent pending the outcome of ADR. There are two main types of ADR, arbitration and mediation.

Arbitration   B1.12

Both parties agree to appoint a person to decide the issues between them and that they will be bound by his decision. The arbitrator, in effect, tries the case and his decision is binding.

Arbitrations are especially useful if the only issue between the parties is a technical dispute. Instead of appointing a judge to decide who is right, a person with the appropriate technical knowledge is appointed. There is usually no need for the parties to appoint an expert as the arbitrator will have specialist knowledge.

Arbitrations are particularly popular in the building and construction industry where there tends to be a significant number of technical disputes. The advantages of arbitrations are that they are usually relatively quick and there is no need, in most cases, for experts to be appointed. The disadvantage of an arbitration is that the arbitrator can give whatever directions he pleases and therefore there is no certainty as to the rules. Although usually quicker than the court proceedings, the construction industry is finding that arbitrations are no less expensive.

Where there is one single technical issue, rather than jointly appointing an expert to assist a judge in making a decision, it is worth considering whether the expert should decide the matter.

Mediation   B1.13

Unlike an arbitration, mediation is not binding on the parties. A mediator's role is not to find for one party or the other or decide the issue, but to facilitate agreement between the parties.

A typical mediation will take place at a neutral venue with the parties in separate rooms. The mediator will then 'shuttle' between the parties assisting them in reaching an amicable solution.

If mediation does not achieve a settlement the dispute between the parties will continue. Therefore, it does not replace litigation but it is a more structured way of reaching a settlement.

Mediation is particularly useful where the amount involved is worth the expenditure on the mediator but not worth long and complex litigation, or where the parties have become entrenched. The trained mediator should assist the parties to think through the commercial reality and the desirability of reaching a settlement.

Other alternatives to court proceedings   B1.14

In addition to these two main types of ADR you may find references to the following methods.

- *Early neutral evaluation* – this is an assessment of the case, often performed by a lawyer, which is not binding on the parties. It can often be used as the basis for settlement or negotiation.

- *Conciliation* – this is similar to mediation, but the conciliator takes a more interventionist role and makes suggestions as to how settlement may be achieved.

- *Neutral fact finding* – this is a non-binding procedure whereby a neutral expert in the subject matter is appointed to investigate and make an evaluation of the merits of the case. It is similar to early neutral evaluation except that an expert is used and not a lawyer. His findings are not binding but can form the basis of settlement or further negotiation.

- *Med arb* – as the name suggests, this is a combination of mediation and arbitration. If the mediation fails the dispute is automatically referred to arbitration. The same person may act as mediator and arbitrator in this type of arrangement.

The Human Rights Act 1998   B1.15

The main provisions of the *Human Rights Act 1998* came into force on 2 October 2000. The Act applies to public bodies, including the courts. The court must now, wherever possible, interpret legislation in a way which is compatible with the *European Convention on Human Rights*.

According to Prime Minister Tony Blair in the Preface to the White Paper 'Rights Brought Home' (Cm 3782, 1997), the *Human Rights Act 1998* is designed to:

'... give people in the United Kingdom opportunities to enforce their rights under the European Convention in British courts rather than having to incur the cost and delay of taking a case to the European Human Rights Commission and Court in Strasbourg'.

The main convention rights are:

- right to life (*Art 2*);
- prohibition of torture (*Art 3*);
- protection from slavery and forced labour (*Art 4*);
- right to liberty and security (*Art 5*);
- right to a fair trial (*Art 6*);
- no punishment without law (*Art 7*);
- right to respect of private and family life (*Art 8*);
- freedom of thought, conscience and religion (*Art 9*);
- freedom of expression (*Art 10*);
- freedom of assembly and association (*Art 11*);
- right to marry and have a family (*Art 12*);
- freedom from discrimination (*Art 14*);
- right to property (*First Protocol, Art 1*);
- right to education (*First Protocol, Art 2*);
- right to free and fair elections (*First Protocol, Art 3*);
- abolition of the death penalty in peace time (*Sixth Protocol, Arts 1* and *2*).

The *Human Rights Act 1998* has had little effect on debt actions. Lord Woolf indicated at the outset that he did not expect that it would be necessary to go further than the obligations under the *CPR 1998* to deal with cases justly (*Daniels v Walker, The Times, 17 May 2000*).

Appendix BI

Appendix B1.1 – Practice direction – protocols and pre-action protocols for personal injury claims

Practice direction—protocols

General

1.1 This Practice Direction applies to the pre-action protocols which have been approved by the Head of Civil Justice.

1.2 The pre-action protocols which have been approved are specified in the Schedule to this Practice Direction. Other pre-action protocols may subsequently be added.

1.3 Pre-action protocols outline the steps parties should take to seek information from and to provide information to each other about a prospective legal claim.

1.4 The objectives of pre-action protocols are:

(1) to encourage the exchange of early and full information about the prospective legal claim,

(2) to enable parties to avoid litigation by agreeing a settlement of the claim before the commencement of proceedings,

(3) to support the efficient management of proceedings where litigation cannot be avoided.

Compliance with protocols

2.1 The Civil Procedure Rules enable the court to take into account compliance or non-compliance with an applicable protocol when giving directions for the management of proceedings (see CPR rules 3.1(4) and (5) and 3.9(e)) and when making orders for costs (see CPR rule 44.3(5)(a)).

2.2 The court will expect all parties to have complied in substance with the terms of an approved protocol.

2.3 If, in the opinion of the court, non-compliance has led to the commencement of proceedings which might otherwise not have needed to be commenced, or has led to costs being incurred in the proceedings that might otherwise not have been incurred, the orders the court may make include:

(1) an order that the party at fault pay the costs of the proceedings, or part of those costs, of the other party or parties;

(2) an order that the party at fault pay those costs on an indemnity basis;

(3) if the party at fault is a claimant in whose favour an order for the payment of damages or some specified sum is subsequently made, an order depriving that party of interest on such sum and in respect of such period as may be specified, and/or awarding interest at a lower rate than that at which interest would otherwise have been awarded;

(4) if the party at fault is a defendant and an order for the payment of damages or some specified sum is subsequently made in favour of the claimant, an order awarding interest on such sum and in respect of such period as may be specified at a higher rate, not exceeding 10% above base rate (cf. CPR rule 36.21(2)), than the rate at which interest would otherwise have been awarded.

2.4 The court will exercise its powers under paragraphs 2.2 and 2.3 with the object of placing the innocent party in no worse a position than he would have been in if the protocol had been complied with.

3.1 A claimant may be found to have failed to comply with a protocol by, for example:

(a) not having provided sufficient information to the defendant, or

(b) not having followed the procedure required by the protocol to be followed (e.g. not having followed the medical expert instruction procedure set out in the Personal Injury Protocol).

3.2 A defendant may be found to have failed to comply with a protocol by, for example:

(a) not making a preliminary response to the letter of claim within the time fixed for that purpose by the relevant protocol (21 days under the Personal Injury Protocol, 14 days under the Clinical Negligence Protocol),

(b) not making a full response within the time fixed for that purpose by the relevant protocol (3 months of the letter of claim under the Clinical Negligence Protocol, 3 months from the date of acknowledgement of the letter of claim under the Personal Injury Protocol), or

(c) not disclosing documents required to be disclosed by the relevant protocol.

Pre-action behaviour in other cases

4 In cases not covered by any approved protocol, the court will expect the parties, in accordance with the overriding objective and the matters referred to in CPR 1.1(2)(a), (b) and (c), to act reasonably in exchanging information and documents relevant to the claim and generally in trying to avoid the necessity for the start of proceedings.

Commencement

5.1 Compliance or non-compliance, as the case may be, with the protocols specified in the Schedule will be taken into account by the court in dealing with any proceedings commenced after 26 April 1999 but will not be taken into account by the court in dealing with proceedings started before that date.

5.2 Where, in respect of proceedings commenced after 26 April 1999, the parties have not had time since the publication of the protocols in January 1999 to comply with the applicable provisions, their failure to have done so will not be treated, for the purposes of paragraphs 2 and 3, as non-compliance.

5.3 As and when an additional protocol is approved, a Practice Direction will specify the date after which compliance or non-compliance with that protocol will be taken into account by the court.

Schedule

1.   Personal Injury Protocol.

2.   Clinical Negligence Protocol.

Pre-action protocols for personal injury claims

Introduction

1.1 Lord Woolf in his final Access to Justice Report of July 1996 recommended the development of pre-action protocols:

'To build on and increase the benefits of early but well informed settlement which genuinely satisfy both parties to dispute.'

1.2 The aims of pre-action protocols are:

- more pre-action contact between the parties

- better and earlier exchange of information

- better pre-action investigation by both sides

- to put the parties in a position where they may be able to settle cases fairly and early without litigation

- to enable proceedings to run to the court's timetable and efficiently, if litigation does become necessary.

1.3 The concept of protocols is relevant to a range of initiatives for good litigation and pre-litigation practice, especially:

- predictability in the time needed for steps pre-proceedings

- standardisation of relevant information, including documents to be disclosed.

1.4 The courts will be able to treat the standards set in protocols as the normal reasonable approach to pre-action conduct. If proceedings are issued, it will be for the court to decide whether non-compliance with a protocol should merit adverse consequences. Guidance on the court's likely approach will be given from time to time in practice directions.

1.5 If the court has to consider the question of compliance after proceedings have begun, it will not be concerned with minor infringements, e.g. failure by a short period to provide relevant information. One minor breach will not exempt the 'innocent' party from following the protocol. The court will look at the effect of non-compliance on the other party when deciding whether to impose sanctions.

Notes of guidance

2.1 The protocol has been kept deliberately simple to promote ease of use and general acceptability. The notes of guidance which follow relate particularly to issues which arose during the piloting of the protocol.

Scope of the protocol

2.2 This protocol is intended to apply to all claims which include a claim for personal injury and to the entirety of those claims: not only to the personal injury element of a claim which also includes, for instance, property damage.

2.3 This protocol is primarily designed for those road traffic, tripping and slipping and accident at work cases which include an element of personal injury with a value of less than £15,000 which are likely to be allocated to the fast track. This is because time will be of the essence, after proceedings are issued, especially for the defendant, if a case is to be ready for trial within 30 weeks of allocation. Also, proportionality of work and costs to the value of what is in dispute is particularly important in lower value claims. For some claims within the value 'scope' of the fast track some flexibility in the timescale of the protocol may be necessary, see also paragraph 3.8.

2.4 However, the 'cards on the table' approach advocated by the protocol is equally appropriate to some higher value claims. The spirit, if not the letter of the protocol, should still be followed for multi-track type claims. In accordance with the sense of the civil justice reforms, the court will expect to see the spirit of reasonable pre-action behaviour applied in all cases, regardless of the existence of a specific protocol.

2.5 The timetable and the arrangements for disclosing documents and obtaining expert evidence may need to be varied to suit the circumstances of the case. Where one or both parties consider the detail of the protocol is not appropriate to the case, and proceedings are subsequently issued, the court will expect an explanation as to why the protocol has not been followed, or has been varied.

Early notification

2.6   The claimant's legal representative may wish to notify the defendant and/or his insurer as soon as they know a claim is likely to be made, but before they are able to send a detailed letter of claim, particularly for instance, when the defendant has no or limited knowledge of the incident giving rise to the claim or where the claimant is incurring significant expenditure as a result of the accident which he hopes the defendant might pay for, in whole or in part. If the claimant's representative chooses to do this, it will not start the timetable for responding.

The letter of claim

2.7   The specimen letter of claim at Annex A [not reproduced] will usually be sent to the individual defendant. In practice, he/she may have no personal financial interest in the financial outcome of the claim/dispute because he/she is insured. Court imposed sanctions for non-compliance with the protocol may be ineffective against an insured. This is why the protocol emphasises the importance of passing the letter of claim to the insurer and the possibility that the insurance cover might be affected. If an insurer receives the letter of claim only after some delay by the insured, it would not be unreasonable for the insurer to ask the claimant for additional time to respond.

Reasons for early issue

2.8   The protocol recommends that a defendant be given three months to investigate and respond to a claim before proceedings are issued. This may not always be possible, particularly where a claimant only consults a solicitor close to the end of any relevant limitation period. In these circumstances, the claimant's solicitor should give as much notice of the intention to issue proceedings as is practicable and the parties should consider whether the court might be invited to extend time for service of the claimant's supporting documents and for service of any defence, or alternatively, to stay the proceedings while the recommended steps in the protocol are followed.

Status of letters of claim and response

2.9   Letters of claim and response are not intended to have the same status as a statement of case in proceedings. Matters may come to light as a result of investigation after the letter of claim has been sent, or after the defendant has responded, particularly if disclosure of documents takes place outside the recommended three-month period. These circumstances could mean that the 'pleaded' case of one or both parties is presented slightly differently than in the letter of claim and response. It would not be consistent with the spirit of the protocol for a party to 'take a point' on this in the proceedings, provided that there was no obvious intention by the party who changed their position to mislead the other party.

Disclosure of documents

2.10 The aim of the early disclosure of documents by the defendant is not to encourage 'fishing expeditions' by the claimant, but to promote an early exchange of relevant information to help in clarifying or resolving issues in dispute. The claimant's solicitor can assist by identifying in the letter of claim or in a subsequent letter the particular categories of documents which they consider are relevant.

Experts

2.11 The protocol encourages joint selection of, and access to, experts. Most frequently this will apply to the medical expert, but on occasions also to liability experts, e.g. engineers. The protocol promotes the practice of the claimant obtaining a medical report, disclosing it to the defendant who then asks questions and/or agrees it and does not obtain his own report. But it maintains the flexibility for each party to obtain their own expert's report, if necessary after proceedings have commenced, with the leave of the court. It would also be for the court to decide whether the costs of more than one expert's report should be recoverable.

2.12 Some solicitors choose to obtain medical reports through medical agencies, rather than directly from a specific doctor or hospital. The defendant's prior consent to the action should be sought and, if the defendant so requests, the agency should be asked to provide in advance the names of the doctor(s) whom they are considering instructing.

Negotiations/settlement

2.13 Parties and their legal representatives are encouraged to enter into discussions and/or negotiations prior to starting proceedings. The protocol does not specify when or how this might be done but parties should bear in mind that the courts increasingly take the view that litigation should be a last resort, and that claims should not be issued prematurely when a settlement is in reasonable prospect.

Stocktake

2.14 Where a claim is not resolved when the protocol has been followed, the parties might wish to carry out a 'stocktake' of the issues in dispute, and the evidence that the court is likely to need to decide those issues, before proceedings are started. Where the defendant is insured and the pre-action steps have been conducted by the insurer, the insurer would normally be expected to nominate solicitors to act in the proceedings and the claimant's solicitor is recommended to invite the insurer to nominate solicitors to act in the proceedings and do so 7–14 days before the intended issue date.

The protocol

Letter of claim

3.1   The claimant shall send to the proposed defendant two copies of a letter of claim, immediately sufficient information is available to substantiate a realistic claim and before issues of quantum are addressed in detail. One copy of the letter is for the defendants, the second for passing on to his insurers.

3.2   The letter shall contain a **clear summary of the facts** on which the claim is based together with an indication of the **nature of any injuries** suffered and of **any financial loss incurred**.

3.3   Solicitors are recommended to use a **standard format** for such a letter – an example is at Annex A [not reproduced]: this can be amended to suit the particular case.

3.4   The letter should ask for **details of the insurer** and that a copy should be sent by the proposed defendant to the insurer where appropriate. If the insurer is known, a copy shall be sent directly to the insurer.

3.5   **Sufficient information** should be given in order to enable the defendant's insurer/solicitor to commence investigations and at least put a broad valuation on the 'risk'.

3.6   The **defendant should reply within 21 calendar days** of the date of posting of the letter identifying the insurer (if any). If there has been no reply by the defendant or insurer within 21 days, the claimant will be entitled to issue proceedings.

3.7   The **defendant**('s insurers) will have a **maximum of three months** from the date of acknowledgement of the claim **to investigate**. No later than the end of that period the defendant (insurer) shall reply, stating whether liability is denied and, if so, giving reasons for their denial of liability.

3.8   Where the accident occurred outside England and Wales and/or where the defendant is outside the jurisdiction, the time periods of 21 days and three months may reasonably be extended up to 42 days and six months.

3.9   Where **liability is admitted**, the presumption is that the defendant will be bound by this admission for all claims with a total value of up to £15,000.

Documents

3.10   If the **defendant denies liability**, he should enclose with the letter of reply, **documents** in his possession which are **material to the issues** between the parties, and which would be likely to be ordered to be disclosed by the court, either on an application for pre-action disclosure, or on disclosure during proceedings.

3.11 Attached at Annex B [not reproduced] are **specimen**, but non-exhaustive, **lists** of documents likely to be material in different types of claim. Where the claimant's investigation of the case is well advanced, the letter of claim could indicate which classes of documents are considered relevant for early disclosure. Alternatively these could be identified at a later stage.

3.12 Where the defendant admits primary liability, but alleges contributory negligence by the claimant, the defendant should give reasons supporting those allegations and disclose those documents from Annex B [not reproduced] which are relevant to the issues in dispute. The claimant should respond to the allegations of contributory negligence before proceedings are issued.

Special Damages

3.13 The claimant will send to the defendant as soon as practicable a Schedule of Special Damages with supporting documents, particularly where the defendant has admitted liability.

Experts

3.14 Before any party instructs an expert he should give the other party a list of the **name**(s) of **one or more experts** in the relevant speciality whom he considers are suitable to instruct.

3.15 Where a medical expert is to be instructed the claimant's solicitor will organise access to relevant medical records – see specimen letter of instruction at Annex C [not reproduced].

3.16 **Within 14 days** the other party may indicate **an objection** to one or more of the named experts. The first party should then instruct a mutually acceptable expert.

3.17 If the second party objects to all the listed experts, the parties may then instruct **experts of their own choice**. It would be for the court to decide subsequently if proceedings are issued, whether either party had acted unreasonably.

3.18 If the **second party does not object to an expert nominated**, he shall not be entitled to rely on his own expert evidence within that particular speciality unless:

(a)   the first party agrees,

(b)   the court so directs, or

(c)   he first party's expert report has been amended and the first party is not prepared to disclose the original report.

3.19 **Either party may send to an agreed expert written questions** on the report, relevant to the issues, via the first party's solicitors. The expert should send answers to the questions separately and directly to each party.

3.20 The cost of a report from an agreed expert will usually be paid by the instructing first party: the costs of the expert replying to questions will usually be borne by the party which asks the questions.

3.21 Where the defendant admits liability in whole or in part, before proceedings are issued, any medical report obtained by agreement under this protocol should be disclosed to the other party. The claimant should delay issuing proceedings for 21 days from disclosure of the report, to enable the parties to consider whether the claim is capable of settlement. The Civil Procedure Rules Part 36 permit claimants and defendants to make offers to settle pre-proceedings.

B2

Starting the Claim

Note

These chapters deal with the law in England and Wales. Scotland and Northern Ireland have a separate legal jurisdiction.

When to instruct a solicitor   B2.1

There is no hard and fast rule as to when the parties need to instruct a solicitor and when they can safely conduct their own litigation. If the claimant has a large number of lower value claims (i.e. less than £1,000) he should consider conducting the actions 'in-house'. Where a debt is over £5,000 this will be allocated to the fast track under the *Civil Procedure Rules 1998* (*CPR 1998*) (*SI 1998/3132*) (see **B5 THE FAST TRACK**), and usually a solicitor should be instructed. For actions between those amounts, whether there is a need to instruct a solicitor will depend on the:

● complexity of the action; and

● claimant's own experience and the claimant's own confidence in legal matters.

If a solicitor is consulted this should be done at an early stage to enable him to draft the letter of claim, if necessary, and give preliminary advice (see **B1.8–B1.10** above).

The claim form   B2.2

All proceedings are started by the completion and issue of a claim form. The party bringing the case is called the claimant.

The claim form is a simple two-page document. The first page identifies the parties and summarises the claim, and the second page is for a description of the claim (called 'particulars of claim') and verification of the details of the claim with a 'statement of truth' (see **B2.12** below).

If the particulars of claim are lengthy, a separate piece or pieces of paper may be used. The particulars of claim must then be attached to the claim form. If that is done a heading should be put on the first page of the additional sheets. The top left-hand side should state the name of the court of issue and there should be a space on the top right-hand side for the case number. There should then be a description of the parties, e.g:

[XXX] County Court	Case Number: [YYY]
Between .... [A–B]	Claimant
and	
.... [C–D]	Defendant

This will ensure that if the attachment becomes dislodged it can be put back with the correct file.

In addition to the claim form, the claimant will obtain notes for claimant (form N1A) from the court. These should be read before completing the form.

The claim form can be typed or written by hand. If it is written by hand claimants are asked to write in black ink using block capitals. (See **B2.3**–**B2.12** below for a more detailed look at filling in a claim form.)

A claim form (Form N1 – see **APPENDIX B2.1**) can be obtained from any County Court office free of charge. A claim form, and any other court form, can be downloaded from the Court Service website at www.courtservice.gov.uk/fandl/forms_home.htm.

In addition, the Court Service is piloting a scheme to allow claims to be made directly online. This is called 'moneyclaim online' and can be found at www.courtservice.gov.uk/mcol/index.htm. You will need to complete the form but payment for court fees is made by credit card. Defendants may also serve a defence electronically if the moneyclaim online system has been used.

The procedures in this chapter describe the 'manual' completion of the requisite documents.

Completing the claim form

The court B2.3

The name of the court at which proceedings are issued should be inserted. This will normally be a county court unless the claim is very large or complex. The claim number will be inserted by the court.

The claimant B2.4

The claimant's full name and address should be inserted.

If the claimant is a limited company the registered office should be given, although the rules do allow for any place of business that has a connection with the claim to be given as the address. It is also helpful to give the registered number of the company so there can be no doubt as to the identity of the claimant.

If the claimant is an individual then their title should be inserted, e.g. Mr, Mrs or Miss.

If the claimant is a firm or partnership the name of the partnership followed by the words 'a firm' will suffice.

The defendant(s) B2.5

The full name and address of all the defendant(s) should be given, including those details referred to above under 'the claimant' (see **B2.4** above). It is important to put the full name of any individual. One of the most common areas of dispute in any litigation is an allegation that the wrong party has been sued. If the defendant is difficult to properly identify there may be problems in enforcing the judgment.

Where there is more than one defendant a separate claim form should be submitted for each of them, identical apart from the defendant's name and address at the bottom of the first page.

If the defendant is a firm with a relatively small number of partners it is better to name the partners as defendants and service each one, e.g. Fred Bloggs and Joe Soap t/a Bloggs & Soap Car Sales. This will make enforcement of any judgment against the individual assets of the partners easier.

Brief details of claim B2.6

This should not be confused with the 'particulars of claim' and should only be a concise description of the nature of the claim and the remedy being sought, e.g. payment of money for outstanding invoices.

The value B2.7

A statement of value need only be given where the exact amount of money that is being claimed is not known. If the amount is known, for instance if the claim is for outstanding invoices, the specific amount claimed should be put in the box on the bottom right hand corner of the form marked 'amount claimed'.

However, where the amount is not precisely known one of the following should be entered (unless it is a personal injury claim when different values apply):

* not more than £5,000;

* more than £5,000 but not more than £15,000; or

* more than £15,000.

If the claimant cannot say what the value is at all, 'I cannot say how much I expect to recover' should be entered in this space.

The defendant's name and address   B2.8

The full postal address of the defendant should be entered here. A separate form should be used for each defendant. The court will use this address to serve the defendant(s) with the claim form.

Court fee   B2.9

The amount of the court fee paid on issue should be inserted here (see **B2.16** below).

Solicitors' costs   B2.10

This can only be completed if a solicitor is acting for the claimant.

Particulars of claim   B2.11

This is a description of the claim that is being made. It should include a concise statement of the facts on which the claimant relies and any claim for interest (see **B2.13** below).

It should be written in plain English and very briefly, in simple terms, the claimant should describe and give details of the basis of the claim. If there is an unpaid invoice the date and amount of the invoice must be given.

Relevant documents can be attached to the claim form. If, for example, there is a written contract and that contract has been breached, a copy should be attached. If there is an oral agreement, details of that agreement should be given, including, if possible, the contractual words used by both parties and where and when these words were spoken.

The function of the particulars of claim is to enable the court and the defendant to know the nature of the claim that is being made. Sufficient details should be given so that this can be understood. This does not mean that a long history should be given with all background details. A statement of case is not the place for putting all the evidence that will be put forward by the claimant. A lengthy statement (a witness statement) can be prepared later in the proceedings. However, if the defendant and the court do not understand the basis of the claim it may lead to costs sanctions or even the claim being struck out.

Statement of truth   B2.12

A statement of truth is required on all statements of case (a generic term meaning all documents put before the court to explain a case), witness statements, and experts' reports. Any document with a statement of truth may be used in evidence, including the particulars of claim on the claim form.

Any document with a signed statement of truth which contains false information given deliberately, that is without an honest belief in its truth, will constitute a contempt of court by the person who provided the information. Solicitors may sign statements of truth on behalf of their clients, but on the understanding that it is done with the client's authority and with the client knowing that the consequences of any false statement will be personal to them. This means that, in effect, if a person knowingly provides false information to a solicitor he or she could be guilty of contempt of court.

Contempt of court actions have, in the past, been very rare indeed. A person cannot be in contempt if they have made an honest mistake. However, the need for a statement of truth does mean that some care must be taken to ensure that deliberately misleading information is not given or that a claim is not deliberately exaggerated.

Interest B2.13

Interest will not automatically be awarded by the court. You must ask for it in the particulars of claim (see **B2.11** above).

If there was an agreement that interest is payable on late payment, contractual interest can be claimed. To be enforceable the term dealing with interest must be incorporated into the contract. Mere notification on the invoice that interest is payable will not usually suffice as that is a post contractual document. In addition, the interest claimed must not be punitive, i.e. it must reflect the actual loss to the claimant or the claimant company.

Late Payment of Commercial Debts (Interest) Act 1998 B2.14

Interest may be implied in a contract under the *Late Payment of Commercial Debts (Interest) Act 1998* (see also **A5.9** and **A14.34** above). This Act gives a right to charge interest, whether or not court proceedings are taken, in certain circumstances.

Where interest can be claimed under the *Late Payment of Commercial Debts (Interest) Act 1998* for contracts made after 7 August 2002 a reasonable compensation can be claimed in addition to interest and court costs. Reasonable compensation depends on the size of the debt:

- For a debt less than £1,000 the sum of £40.

- For a debt between £1,000 and £10,000 the sum of £70.

- For a debt of £10,000 or more the sum of £100 (*Late Payment of Commercial Debts Regulations 2002 (SI 2002/1674)*).

It is important that all terms and conditions are reviewed to ensure that your company is not prejudiced by specifying interest rates which are a 'reasonable compensation' and which are less than the rate specified by the Act.

The present rate specified under the Act is 8% over the Bank of England base rate. This is greater than would be allowed under previous contract law as it would be considered a punitive rate of interest.

Interest under the County Courts Act 1984   B2.15

Even if the contract does not give the right to claim interest, statutory interest can be claimed in the particulars of claim. The *County Courts Act 1984* (or the *Supreme Court Act 1981* in the High Court) allows for interest at a fixed rate, which at present is 8% per annum. Statutory interest is calculated by finding the daily rate of interest by dividing the amount of the debt by 365. The daily rate is then multiplied by the number of days the debt has been outstanding, for example, for a debt of £4,500 the following calculation would take place:

$$\frac{£4,500 \times 8\%}{365} = 0.99\% \,(\text{Daily rate})$$

Lodging the claim at court   B2.16

The claim is started by lodging the claim form at the court office with the appropriate court fee. Any county court in England and Wales will issue a claim up to the value of £50,000.00.

The claim form may be lodged in person or by post. The cheque for the court fee should be payable to 'HMPG' (Her Majesty's Paymaster General).

The following is a list of court fees in force from 26 April 2002. The correct fees should be checked before issue.

Claim size	£
Not exceeding £300.00	30.00
£300.01 up to £500.00	50.00
£500.01 up to £1,000.00	80.00
£1,000.01 up to £5,000.00	120.00
£5,000.01 up to £15,000.00	250.00
£15,000.01 up to £50,000.00	400.00
£50,000.01 up to £100,000.00	600.00
£100,000.01 up to £150,000.00	700.00
Over £150,000.00	800.00

Serving the claim form   B2.17

The court will serve the claim form. This will generally be by first class post. Bailiff service of the claim form is no longer available. The date the claim form is received by the defendant is called 'the date of service'. This is the start of the timetable. The date of service is deemed to be two days after the day of posting. If the claim form is returned by the post office the court will send out a notice of non-service. The court will make no further attempt to serve the proceedings unless an amended claim form with a new address is lodged at court.

Alternatively, claimants may serve their own claim forms having told the court in writing they wish to do this. The court office will return the documents for the claimant to serve. This may be either:

- personally; or

- by post,

or, if the defendant has agreed and is represented by a solicitor:

- by fax; or

- by e-mail or other electronic means.

If the defendant is represented by a solicitor and the solicitor has agreed to accept service, service must be effected on the solicitor.

If service by one of the above methods is impossible, an application to court can be made for substituted service, i.e. service at another address.

If the claimant serves the claim form a certificate of service with a copy of the claim form must be lodged at court within seven days on form N215 (see **APPENDIX B2.2**).

The response pack   B2.18

The court will prepare a response pack, which is sent to the defendant with the claim form. The response pack consists of:

- an acknowledgement of service;

- a defence and counterclaim form; and

- a form of admission.

The notes for defendants on the claim form explain the options the defendant has, which are to:

- pay the claim;

- admit the claim or part of it;

- file an acknowledgement of service; or

- file a defence.

A defendant must respond to the claim within 14 days of service, by lodging the acknowledgement of service at court indicating, if appropriate, that he wishes to defend the claim or part of it, if further time is needed to prepare a defence, or by lodging at court the defence.

If the defendant wishes to dispute the jurisdiction of the court (for example if he alleges it should be tried by a foreign court), the defendant must state this on the acknowledgment of service. The defendant should then take no other step in the proceedings other than to lodge an application disputing jurisdiction, which must be done within 14 days of service.

If an acknowledgement is lodged the defendant has 28 days from service of the claim to lodge the defence at court.

Time to pay   B2.19

If the defendant admits the claim he may make a request for time to pay. The claimant can accept the defendant's request and ask the court to enter judgment in the terms of the defendant's request form. This is done by completing form N225 which will be sent by the court (see **APPENDIX B2.3**).

If the claimant does not accept the proposals, the relevant section of the form N225 must be completed together with the claimant's objections to the payment offered and proposals for repayment. This must be sent to the court together with a copy of the defendant's admission, form N9A. Judgment will then be entered at the time and rate of payments determined by the court. The determination will be made by a court officer without a hearing where the debt is less than £50,000 (including the costs).

Either party may apply for a judge to re-determine the court officer's decision. This application must be made within 14 days of service of the original determination. The application will then be transferred to the defendant's home court if the defendant is an individual and not a limited company.

Contacting the court   B2.20

The court gives each case a separate case number. That is usually found on the Notice of Issue form (N205A). The court uses this number as the basis of its filing system. Courts do not keep the files in alphabetical order.

It is therefore essential that the case number is quoted on all correspondence with the court. If not, the court will be unable to attach the correspondence to the appropriate file.

Documents and correspondence may be 'lodged' by sending them by post to the court or by attending the court office and handing them to the court staff at the counter.

Documents that do not require a fee may be sent to the court by fax.

A list of each county court giving its address, telephone number and fax number can be found at www.courtservice.gov.uk/cms/6718.htm

In addition, the following courts will accept communications by e-mail:

- Basildon County Court
- Birmingham County Court
- Bournemouth County Court
- Carlisle County Court
- The Commercial Court London
- Coventry County Court
- Derby Combined Court Centre
- Leicester County Court
- Lewes Combined Court Centre
- Lincoln County Court
- Nuneaton County Court
- Preston County Court
- Taunton County Court
- Walsall County Court
- Wolverhampton Combined Court Centre

E-mail addresses and guidance relating to each court can be found at www.courtservice.gov.uk/using_courts/email_guidance/courts.htm

Default judgment B2.21

If the defendant does not reply to the claim after 14 days from service of the claim form, by either lodging a defence or an acknowledgement of service, the claimant may apply for a default judgment.

If an acknowledgement of service has been lodged the defendant has 28 days from the date of service to file a defence.

The date of service is not the date when proceedings are lodged at court, but the date when they are deemed to have been received by the defendant. If the court serves the claim the claimant will receive notice of issue or form N205A (see

APPENDIX B2.4). The top half of the form states when the claim was issued, the deemed date of service and the last date for the defendant to respond. Judgment in default cannot be entered until the day after that date, as the defendant has until close of business on the last date to respond. The calculation of time for lodging a default judgment is taken from the deemed date of service, i.e. the date on the form N205A and not the date when the claim was actually received by the defendant (*Godwin v Swindon Borough Council [2002] 1 WLR 997*).

A request for judgment is made by completing the bottom portion of the form N205A, where judgment is claimed for a specified amount.

If the claimant has claimed interest this should be calculated up to the date of judgment and entered on form N205A, together with the court fee. If the claimant has not claimed a specified amount, judgment can be entered in default by filing form N225B or N227. Judgment is final on the issue of liability but the sum to be paid is still to be decided by the court. Directions for assessing the amount to be paid will be given by the court when judgment is entered.

What if the defendant applies to set aside the default judgment?   B2.22

Unfortunately for a claimant, especially in debt collection actions, the defendant may apply to set aside a default judgment.

There are two grounds for such an application.

(*a*)   The first is that judgment has been wrongly entered. This usually means that judgment was entered before the correct time limits had properly expired or where a defence or acknowledgement of service had been lodged with the court but had not been noticed by the court itself or has not been put on the file. It can also mean that the whole of the claim was satisfied before judgment was entered or the claim was not served.

(*b*)   The second ground for applying to set aside a default judgment is that the defendant has a real prospect of successfully defending the claim and it appears to the court that there is some other good reason why judgment should be set aside and the defendant allowed to defend. Applications under this ground should be made promptly, if there has been a long delay in making an application the court may find for the claimant in any event.

An application by the defendant to set judgment aside must be supported by evidence. The claimant also has the opportunity of placing evidence before the court. The evidence of both parties will usually be in a written form – i.e. a witness statement containing a statement of truth – oral evidence is not normally given.

The test that will be applied by the court is whether the defendant has a 'real prospect of successfully defending the claim' (*CPR 1998, rule 13.3*). The court has an absolute discretion as to whether judgment should be set aside so as to ensure that no injustice has resulted from the default judgment. However, the court can impose conditions under its general case management powers and can, for example, set aside a judgment provided the amount claimed is paid into court.

Where the claimant has obtained default judgment and subsequently has reason to believe that the claim form was not served on the defendant, the claimant is under a duty to apply to set the judgment aside and may not take any steps in the proceedings until that is done.

The following is a guide to the meaning of certain legal expressions printed in the *CPR 1998*.

Expression	Meaning
Affidavit	A written, sworn statement of evidence.
Alternative dispute resolution	Collective description of methods of resolving disputes otherwise than through the normal trial process.
Base rate	The interest rate set by the Bank of England which is used as the basis for other banks' rates.
Contribution	A right of someone to recover from a third person all or part of the amount which he himself is liable to pay.
Counterclaim	A claim brought by a defendant in response to the claimant's claim, which is included in the same proceedings as the claimant's claim.
Cross-examination (and see 'evidence in chief')	Questioning of a witness by a party other than the party who called the witness.
Damages	A sum of money awarded by the court as compensation to the claimant.
(Aggravated damages)	Additional damages which the court may award as compensation for the defendant's objectionable behaviour.
(Exemplary damages)	Damages which go beyond compensating for actual loss and are awarded to show the court's disapproval of the defendant's behaviour.
Defence of tender before claim	A defence that, before the claimant started proceedings, the defendant unconditionally offered to the claimant the amount due or, if no specified amount is claimed, an amount sufficient to satisfy the claim.

Evidence in chief (and see 'cross-examination')	The evidence given by a witness for the party who called him.
Injunction	A court order prohibiting a person from doing something or requiring a person to do something.
Joint liability (and see 'several liability')	Parties who are jointly liable share a single liability and each party can be held liable for the whole of it.
Limitation period	The period within which a person who has a right to claim against another person must start court proceedings to establish that right. The expiry of the period may be a defence to the claim.
List	Cases are allocated to different lists depending on the subject matter of the case. The lists are used for administrative purposes and may also have their own procedures and judges.
Official copy	A copy of an official document, supplied and marked as such by the office which issued the original.
Practice form	Form to be used for a particular purpose in proceedings, the form and purpose being specified by a practice direction.
Pre-action protocol	Statements of understanding between legal practitioners and others about pre-action practice and which are approved by a relevant practice direction.
Privilege	The right of a party to refuse to disclose a document or produce a document or to refuse to answer questions on the ground of some special interest recognised by law.
Seal	A seal is a mark which the court puts on a document to indicate that the document has been issued by the court.
Service	Steps required by rules of court to bring documents used in court proceedings to a person's attention.
Set aside	Cancelling a judgment or order or a step taken by a party in the proceedings.

Several liability (and see 'joint liability')	A person who is severally liable with others may remain liable for the whole claim even where judgment has been obtained against the others.
Stay	A stay imposes a halt on proceedings, apart from taking any steps allowed by the *CPR 1998* or the terms of the stay. Proceedings can be continued if a stay is lifted.
Strike out	Striking out means the court ordering written material to be deleted so that it may no longer be relied upon.
Without prejudice	Negotiations with a view to a settlement are usually conducted 'without prejudice', which means that the circumstances in which the content of those negotiations may be revealed to the court are very restricted.

In addition, many people will have heard legal expressions that were used in the old County Court Rules but are no longer in use. The following table shows some of the changes

Old term	*New term*
Plaintiff	Claimant
Writ	Claim form
Summons	Claim form
High Court statement of claim	Particulars of claim
Arbitration	Small claims' hearing
Pleadings	Statement of case
Taxation of costs	Assessment
Calderbank offer	Part 36 offer
Payment into court	Part 36 payment
Order 14 (application for summary judgment)	Part 24 (application for summary judgment)
Chambers	Rooms
Leave	Permission
Discovery	Disclosure
Anton Pillar order	Search order
Mareva Injunction	Freezing order
Minor/or infant	Child
Interlocutory relief	Interim remedy
Interlocutory injunction	Interim injunction
Next friend or *Guardian ad litem*	Litigation friend

Third party notice/Contribution notice

Part 20 claim

Subpoena

Witness summons

Oral examination

Order to obtain information from judgment debtors

Garnishee

Third party debt order

Appendix B2

Appendix B2.1 – Claim Form N1

		In the	
Claim Form			
		Claim No.	

Claimant

SEAL

Defendant(s)

Brief details of claim

Value

	£
Amount claimed	
Court fee	
Solicitor's costs	
Total amount	
Issue date	

Defendant's
name and
address

The court office at

is open between 10 am and 4 pm Monday to Friday. When corresponding with the court, please address forms or letters to the Court Manager and quote the claim number.
N1 Claim form (CPR Part 7) (10.00)

©Crown copyright. Published by *everyform*

Claim No.	

Does, or will, your claim include any issues under the Human Rights Act 1998 ☐ Yes ☐ No

Particulars of Claim (attached) (to follow)

Statement of Truth
*(I believe) (The Claimant believes) that the facts stated in these details of claim are true.
* I am duly authorised by the claimant to sign this statement

Full name _____

Name of claimant's solicitor's firm _____

signed_____ position or office held _____

*(Claimant) (Litigation friend) (Claimant's solicitor) (if signing on behalf of firm or company)
*delete as appropriate

Claimant's or claimant's solicitor's address to which documents or payments should be sent if different from overleaf including (if appropriate) details of DX, fax or e-mail.

Appendix B2.2 – Certificate of Service N215

Certificate of service

In the	
Claim No.	
Claimant	
Defendant	

On the .... *(insert date)*

the .... *(insert title or description of documents served)*

a copy of which is attached to this notice was served on *(insert name of person served, including position i.e. partner, director if appropriate)*

....

Tick as appropriate

☐ by first class post

☐ by delivering to or leaving

☐ by fax machine (.................... time sent)
  *(you may want to enclose a copy of
  the transmission sheet)*

☐ by other means *(please specify)*

☐ by Document Exchange

☐ by handing it to or leaving it with

☐ by e-mail

at *(insert address where service effected,
  include fax or DX number or e-mail address)*

being the defendant's:

☐ residence

☐ place of business

☐ registered office

☐ other *(please specify)* ....

The date of service is therefore deemed to be .... *(insert date - see over for guidance)*

I confirm that at the time of signing this Certificate the document has not been returned to me as undelivered.

Signed ....
  (Claimant)(Defendant)('s solicitor)('s litigation friend)

Date ....

Position or ....
office held
*(if signing on behalf
of firm or company)*

N215 - w3 Certificate of service (4.99)　　　　　　　　©Crown copyright. Published by everyform

469

Notes for guidance

Please note that these notes are only a guide and are not exhaustive

Where to serve   If you are in doubt you should refer to Part 6 of the rules

Nature of party to be served	Place of service
Individual	• Usual or last known residence
Proprietor of business	• Usual or last known residence; or • Place of business or last known place of business
Individual who is suing or being sued in the name of a firm	• Usual or last known residence; or • Principal or last known place of business of the firm
Corporation (incorporated in England and Wales) other than a company	• Principal office of the corporation; or • Any place of business within the jurisdiction where the corporation carries on its activities and which has a real connection with the claim
Company registered in England and Wales	• Principal office of the company or corporation; or • Any place of business of the company within the jurisdiction which has a real connection with the claim

Personal Service - A document is served personally on an individual by leaving it with that individual. A document is served personally on a company or other corporation by leaving it with a person holding a senior position within the company or corporation. In the case of a partnership, you must leave it with either a partner or a person having control or management at the principal place of business. Where a solicitor is authorised to accept service on behalf of a party, service must be effected on the solicitor, unless otherwise ordered.

Deemed Service - Part 6.7(l). A document which is served in accordance with these rules or any relevant practice direction shall be deemed to be served on the day shown in the following table.

Method of service	Deemed day of service
First class post	The second day after it was posted
Document exchange	The second day after it was left at the document exchange
Delivering the document to or leaving it at a permitted address	The day after it was delivered to or left at the permitted address
Fax	If it is transmitted on a business day before 4 p.m., on that day, or otherwise on the business day after the day on which it was transmitted
Other electronic method	The second day after the day on which it was transmitted

• If a document (other than a claim form) is served after 5 p.m. on a business day, or at any time on a Saturday, Sunday or a bank holiday, the document shall, for the purpose of calculating any period of time after service of the document, be treated as having been served on the next business day.

• In this context "business day" means any day except Saturday, Sunday or a bank holiday; and "bank holiday" includes Christmas Day and Good Friday.

Service of documents on children and patients - The rules relating to service on children and patients are contained in Part 6.6 of the rules.

Claim Forms - The general rules about service are subject to the special rules about service of claim forms contained in rules 6.12 to 6.16.

Appendix B2.3 – Request for Judgment and Reply to Admission (specified amount) N225

Request for judgment and reply to admission (specified amount)

In the	
Claim No.	
Claimant (including ref)	
Defendant (including ref)	

- Tick box A or B. If you tick box B you must complete the details in that part and in part C. Make sure that all the case details are given. Remember to sign and date the form. Your signature certifies that the information you have given is correct.

- If the defendant has given an address on the form of admission to which correspondence should be sent, which is different from the address shown on the claim form, you must tell the court.

- Return the completed form to the court.

A ☐ **The defendant has not filed an admission or defence to my claim**

Complete all the judgment details at C. Decide how and when you want the defendant to pay. You can ask for the judgment to be paid by instalments or in one payment.

B ☐ **The defendant admits that all the money is owed**

Tick only one box below and complete all the judgment details at C.

☐ **I accept the defendant's proposal for payment**

Say how the defendant intends to pay. The court will send the defendant an order to pay. You will also be sent a copy.

☐ **The defendant has not made any proposal for payment**

Say how you want the defendant to pay. You can ask for the judgment to be paid by instalments or in one payment. The court will send the defendant an order to pay. You will also be sent a copy.

☐ **I do NOT accept the defendant's proposal for payment**

Say how you want the defendant to pay. Give your reasons for objecting to the defendant's offer of payment in the space opposite. (Continue on the back of this form if necessary.) Send this form to the court **with defendant's admission N9A**. The court will fix a rate of payment and send the defendant an order to pay. You will also be sent a copy.

C Judgment details

I would like the judgment to be paid

☐ (immediately)

☐ (by instalments of £ _____ per month)

☐ (in full by _____)

Amount of claim as admitted
(including interest at date of issue) _____

Interest since date of claim (if any) _____

Period from _____ to _____

Rate ___ %

Court fees shown on claim

Solicitor's costs (if any) on issuing claim

Sub Total

Solicitor's costs (if any) on entering judgment

Sub Total

Deduct amount (if any) paid since issue

Amount payable by defendant

I certify that the information given is correct

Signed		**Position or office held**	
(Claimant)(Claimant's solicitor)(Litigation friend)		(if signing on behalf of firm or company)	
Date			

The court office at

is open between 10 am and 4 pm Monday to Friday. When corresponding with the court, please address forms and letters to the Court Manager and quote the Claim number

N225 - w3 Request for judgment and reply to admission (specified amount) (4.99)   ©Crown copyright. Published by everyform

---

Appendix B2.4 – Notice of Issue (specified amount) N205A

Notice of Issue
(specified amount)

To the Claimant ['s Solicitor]

Your claim was issued on [   ].

The court sent it to the defendant by first class post on [   ]

and it will be deemed to be served on [   ].

The defendant has until [   ] to reply.

The defendant may

- **Pay** you your total claim.
- **File an acknowledgment of service.** This will allow the defendant 28 days from the date of service of your particulars of claim to file a defence or contest the court's jurisdiction.
- **Dispute the whole claim.** The court will send you a copy of the defence.
- **Admit that all the money is owed.** The defendant will send you a completed admission form and you may ask the court to enter judgment using the request below.

✂ — — — — — **For further information please turn over** — — — — —

In the

The court office at

is open between 10 am & 4 pm Monday to Friday
Tel:

Claim No.	
Claimant (including ref.)	
Defendant(s)	
Issue fee	£

- **Admit that only part of your claim is owed.** The court will send you a copy of the reply form and you will have to decide what to do next.
- **Not reply at all.** You may ask the court to enter judgment using the request below.

Note: If the claim is disputed and the defendant is an individual, the claim may be transferred to the defendant's local court.

Request for Judgment

- *Tick and complete either A or B. Remember to sign and date the form. Your signature certifies that the information you have given is correct.*
- *If the defendant has given an address on the form of admission to which correspondence should be sent, which is different from the address shown on the claim form, you must tell the court.*
- *Complete all the judgment details at C*

A

The defendant has not filed an admission or defence to my claim or an application to contest the court's jurisdiction.

Decide how and when you want the defendant to pay. You can ask for the judgment to be paid by instalments or in one payment.

B

The defendant admits that all the money is owed

Tick only **one** box below and return the completed slip to the court.

☐ **I accept the defendant's proposal for payment**
Say how the defendant intends to pay. The court will send the defendant an order to pay. You will also be sent a copy.

☐ **The defendant has not made any proposal for payment**
Say how you want the defendant to pay. You can ask for the judgment to be paid by instalments or in one payment. The court will send the defendant an order to pay. You will also be sent a pay.

☐ **I do NOT accept the defendant's proposal for payment**
Say how you want the defendant to pay. Give your reasons for objecting to the defendant's offer of payment in Part D overleaf. Return this slip to the court **with the defendant's admission** (or a copy). The court will fix a rate of payment and send the defendant an order to pay. You will also be sent a copy.

I certify that the information given is correct

Signed .... Dated ....

(Claimant)(Claimant's Solicitor)(Litigation friend)

N205A Notice of issue (specified amount) and request for judgment

In the

Claim No.	
Claimant (including ref.)	
Defendant(s) (including ref.)	

C   Judgment details

I would like the defendant to be ordered to pay

☐ (immediately)

☐ (by instalments of £   per month)

☐ (in full **by**   )

Amount of claim as stated in claim form (including interest at date of issue) ....

Interest since date of claim (if any)...................
Period   From......................To.......................

Rate ....%

Court fees shown on claim ....

Solicitor's costs (if any) on issuing claim ....

	Sub Total	

Solicitor's costs (if any) on entering judgment

	Sub Total	

Deduct amount (if any) paid since issue

	Amount payable by defendant	

Notes for Guidance

- The claim form must be served on the defendant within 4 months of the date of issue (6 months if you are serving outside England or Wales).You may be able to apply to extend the time for serving the claim form but the application must generally be made before the 4 month or 6 month period expires.

- If the defendant does not file an admission, defence or counterclaim; or if the defendant admits the whole claim with or without an offer of payment, you may ask for judgment. If you do not request judgment within 6 months of the end of the period for filing a defence, your claim will be stayed. This means that the only action you can take is to apply to a judge for an order lifting the stay.

- You should keep a record of any payments you receive from the defendant. If there is a hearing or you wish to take steps to enforce the judgment,you will need to satisfy the court about the balance outstanding. You should give the defendant a receipt and payment in cash should always be acknowledged. You should tell the defendant how much he owes if he asks.

- **You must inform the court IMMEDIATELY if you receive any payment before a hearing date or after you have sent a request for enforcement to the court.**

- Further information in leaflet form can be obtained free of charge from the court.

Part D

Objections to the defendant's proposal for payment   **Claim Number**

B3

The Defended Action

Contents of the defence

If a defence is lodged at court the claimant cannot obtain a default judgment. As with the particulars of claim (see **B2.11** above) the defence should be written in plain English and should give clear and concise reasons why the defendant disputes the claim.

A defence should state which of the allegations in the particulars of claim the defendant:

- denies;

- is unable to admit or deny, but which he wishes the claimant to prove; and

- admits.

A defendant must give reasons for denying an allegation, and if the defendant's own version of events differs he must put forward and give details of this version. The defendant may dispute the statement of value in the claim, in which case reasons must be stated and the defendant's own estimate of value given.

A defence must contain a statement of truth, and the consequences for making a statement and knowing it to be false are the same as for a claimant. (See **B2.12** above.)

There may be a counterclaim as well as a defence, also known as a 'Part 20 claim'. This occurs when the defendant claims that monies are owed from the claimant. When a counterclaim is served, a defence to the counterclaim must be lodged at court within 14 days of receipt. If the claimant fails to lodge a defence, the defendant can apply to court for judgment on the counterclaim. If the claimant is in any doubt it is important to seek legal advice immediately.

Gathering the evidence

If it has not been done prior to the issue of proceedings, it is vital that all the evidence, including documents and witness statements, are gathered together immediately after a defence is received. There are a number of reasons for this, which include the following.

- It is impossible to properly assess the case and consider the terms of any settlement until all the evidence is gathered.

- As time goes by people's memory fades and the quicker witness statements are prepared the better. In addition, employees needed for the case may leave the claimant's company.

- Documents may get lost or be difficult to trace.

- Only three weeks are allowed to complete the 'allocation questionnaire' (see **B3.5** below and **APPENDIX B3.1**), which requires assessment of the case with an idea as to how the case should be conducted.

- The court will order each party to list relevant documents (see **B5.6** below) and exchange witness statements. If the relevant information and documents are gathered at this stage it will ensure that the claimant is in a position to keep to the court's timetable.

The claimant will also need to ascertain whether an application for 'summary judgment' is appropriate (see **B7.8** below). If such an application is appropriate the quicker it is made the quicker the case may end.

The process of gathering evidence may mean a period of frantic activity. In the long run it would be beneficial if the case is properly prepared at an early stage.

If matters are raised in the defence which have not been raised before and were not raised in any pre-action correspondence, an application may be made to the court to stay proceedings as a result of the defendant's failure to follow the spirit of the protocols. (See **B1.7** above.)

Will the action be transferred?   B3.3

Where the defendant is an individual and he has filed a defence and the claim is for a specified amount, the action will be transferred automatically to the defendant's 'home court', i.e. the court for the area, shown by the defendant's address for service of the defence. If the defendant is an individual and is represented by a solicitor, the action will be transferred to the court of the defendant's solicitor's address. If the defendant is a limited company there is no automatic transfer.

Where there is more than one defendant it is the first defendant to file a defence who dictates whether or not automatic transfer will take place. Therefore if there are two defendants to a claim, one an individual and one a limited company, there will be no automatic transfer if the limited company was the first defendant to file the defence, but there would be automatic transfer if the individual is the first to file a defence.

There may also be automatic transfer if other applications are made, e.g. an application to set judgment aside or for re-determination of instalment payments. There will only be one automatic transfer per claim. Where automatic transfer has occurred any further transfer will have to be by an order of a judge. Whether or not a case has been automatically transferred the court may make a transfer order, either on its own motion or after an application by the other party to have the case transferred to another county court. The criteria for making such an order are set out in *rule 30.3(2)* of the *Civil Procedure Rules 1998*. These include:

- whether it would be more convenient or fair for the hearing (including the trial) to be held at another court;

- the availability of a judge specialising in the type of claim in question;

- whether the facts, legal issues, remedies or procedures are simple or complex; and

- the facilities available at the court where the claim is being dealt with and whether they may be inadequate because of any disabilities of a party or potential witness.

A judge will often look at where the majority of the witnesses live.

If the court makes an order of its own motion i.e. on paper and without an application by either of the parties, and one of the parties wishes to apply to set aside the order for transfer the application is made to the court which made the order to transfer.

The court's power to manage the case   B3.4

It is the duty of the court, not the parties or their representatives, to manage cases. (See *CPR 1998, Part 3.*) This means that the court will control:

- the way that the case is conducted;

- the steps to be taken by the parties;

- the length of time each party has to carry out any steps; and

- when the case must be ready for trial.

As soon as a defence is lodged at court, the claim and defence will be read by a judge who can make orders and directions without any application (a request) by either of the parties, and without reference to the parties. These steps can include:

- striking out a claim or defence if it discloses no reasonable ground for bringing or defending the claim, or is an abuse of the process of the court;

- striking out relevant or incoherent parts of a claim or defence;

- staying a claim or defence;

- ordering a party to file and serve further information to clarify a particular part of a case;

- disclosure of documents;

- exchange of experts' reports;

- stating a case for a case management conference; and

- specifying a trial period.

The term 'case management' is not defined in the *CPR 1998* but a non-exhaustive list is given, in *CPR 1998, rule 1.4*, of the elements that make up the concept of case management. Under *CPR 1998, rule 1.4(2)*:

'Active case management includes—

(a)   encouraging the parties to co-operate with each other in the conduct of proceedings;

(b)   identifying the issues at an early stage;

(c)   deciding promptly which issues need full investigation and trial and accordingly disposing summarily of the others;

(d)   deciding the order in which issues are to be resolved;

(e)   encouraging the parties to use an alternative dispute resolution procedure if the court considers that appropriate and facilitating the use of such procedure;

(f)   helping the parties to settle the whole or part of the case;

(g)   fixing timetables or otherwise controlling the progress of the case;

(h)   considering whether the likely benefits of taking a step justify the cost of taking it;

(i)   dealing with as many aspects of the case as it can on the same occasions;

(j)   dealing with the case without the parties needing to attend court;

(k)   making use of technology; and

(l)   giving directions to ensure that the trial of a case proceeds quickly and efficiently.'

The court will always try and deal with cases expeditiously, allocating a proportionate amount of time and cost.

The court will expect its timetable to be adhered to and will not look sympathetically if parties ignore the timetable. Time limits that specify consequences for non-compliance cannot be extended even by agreement of all the parties.

There are a number of sanctions that could be imposed if the court rules are broken or directions are ignored. These include:

- awarding indemnity costs;

- proceeding in the absence of a party;

- staying proceedings;

- ordering the claim to be paid into court;

- disallowing interest for a specific time;

- awarding punitive interest up to 10% over base rate; and

- striking out the claim or defence.

Completing the allocation questionnaire   B3.5

As soon as the defendant files his or her defence the court will serve a copy of it on the other parties, together with a notice that a defence has been filed (on form N152), and an 'allocation questionnaire'. The allocation questionnaire is designed to give the judge sufficient information to allocate a track and to give directions.

The notice that a defence has been filed will give a date for the return of the allocation questionnaire to court. That date will be not less than 14 days after the date when it is served.

The allocation questionnaire is a printed form that the court will provide. When completed it should be returned to the court office by the date specified together with a fee of £80.00. This fee is only payable by the claimant. There is no fee payable if the claim is for £1,000 or less and is a money claim.

If no party files an allocation questionnaire within the time specified on form N152, the file will be referred to a judge who will usually order the claim and the counterclaim to be struck out unless an allocation questionnaire is filed within three days from service of the order. However, he may make a different order.

If only one party files an allocation questionnaire the judge may allocate the claim to a track if he considers that he has enough information. Alternatively he may order that an allocation hearing is listed and that all or any of the parties must attend. It is likely that the costs of the allocation hearing will be payable by the party that fails to complete the allocation questionnaire.

APPENDIX B3.1 shows the current allocation questionnaire (form N150). It is worth considering this form in detail. Although this will normally be completed by the claimant's solicitor, if there is a small claim and the claimant is conducting the litigation on his own account he will need to complete the form.

The first question that is asked is whether the parties wish the proceedings to be stayed for one month to attempt to settle the case. Not surprisingly, most defendants tend to pick yes, the claimants tend to pick no. The court will order a stay only if both parties agree.

The form requires information about the most suitable track and about pre-action protocols.

Both parties are then asked if they intend to make an application for 'summary judgment' (see **B7.8–B7.11** below). A claimant will not be able to answer that question unless he has gathered together all the information. Any application for summary judgment should be made at this stage. In an action for less than £5,000, unless the summary judgment application is heard before allocation, it will not be possible to recover the costs of the application.

The form requires a list of the witnesses that are known at that stage and details as to the evidence they will give. The court does not require a detailed statement of what each witness will say but merely a very brief indication of the area that will be covered by the witnesses. A number of key phrases or one or two short sentences will be sufficient. In addition, the parties are asked, as well as details of any experts and their field of expertise, for an explanation, if there is not to be a joint expert, of why this is the case.

The system envisages most of the preparation work being completed before the action is started. If this is not the case it will be impossible to give information about the experts and time on the allocation questionnaire.

On page three of the form the parties are asked to give an estimate of the hearing time and details of when parties are not available for a hearing. Although parties are not prevented from calling witnesses they do not list, it is an important part of the allocation questionnaire. Unless dates when a particular witness is unavailable are given at this stage, the court may set a final hearing date at a time when a witness cannot attend. Unless the reasons are exceptional, the court will not adjourn a final hearing because a witness is unavailable unless details were given on the allocation questionnaire. The parties are also asked to give an estimate of costs (a costs estimate need not be given if the claim is for less than £5,000 and will be allocated to the small claims track – see **B4.1** below) The litigant in person will find these questions virtually impossible to answer. At this stage it will also be difficult for solicitors to give the required information. However, these are all factors that the court must take into account on deciding the correct track.

Allocating a track   B3.6

The general rule is that the courts will not allocate a claim to a track if the financial value of the claim exceeds the limits of that track. The limits for each track are:

- up to £5,000 for the small claims track;

- £5,000 to £15,000 for the fast track; and

- £15,000 and above for the multi-track.

If the court cannot properly allocate on the information provided in the allocation questionnaire it will hold an allocation hearing.

Although the general rule is that cases will be allocated according to their financial value, *CPR 1998, Rule 26.8* sets out the matters that the courts must take into consideration when allocating the correct track, these are the:

(*a*)   financial value, if any, of the claim;

(*b*)   nature of the remedy sought;

(*c*)   likely complexity of the facts, law or evidence;

(*d*)   number of parties or likely parties;

(*e*)   value of any counterclaim or other Part 20 claim and the complexity of any matters relating to it;

(*f*)   amount of oral evidence which may be required;

(*g*)   importance of the claim to the persons who are not party to the proceedings;

(*h*)   expressed views of the parties; and

(*j*)   circumstances of the parties.

In looking at the financial value the court will disregard:

- any amount that is not in dispute;

- any claim for interest or costs; and

- any allegation of contributory negligence.

Appendix B3

Appendix B3.1 – Allocation Questionnaire N150

Allocation questionnaire

To be completed by, or on behalf of,

who is [1ˢᵗ][2ⁿᵈ][3ʳᵈ][　　][Claimant][Defendant]
[Part 20 claimant] in this claim

In the	
Claim No.	
Last date for filing with court office	

Please read the notes on page five before completing the questionnaire.

You should note the date by which it must be returned and the name of the court it should be returned to since this may be different from the court where the proceedings were issued.

If you have settled this claim (or if you settle it on a future date) and do not need to have it heard or tried, you must let the court know immediately.

Have you sent a copy of this completed form to the other party(ies)?　☐ Yes　☐ No

---

A Settlement

Do you wish there to be a one month stay to attempt to settle the claim, either by informal discussion or by alternative dispute resolution?　☐ Yes　☐ No

---

B Location of trial

Is there any reason why your claim needs to be heard at a particular court?　☐ Yes　☐ No

If Yes, say which court and why?

C Pre-action protocols

If an approved pre-action protocol applies to this claim, complete **Part 1** only. If not, complete **Part 2** only. If you answer 'No' to the question in either Part 1 or 2, please explain the reasons why on a separate sheet and attach it to this questionnaire.

Part 1	The* [＿＿＿＿＿＿＿] protocol applies to this claim.
*please say which protocol	Have you complied with it?　☐ Yes　☐ No

Part 2	No pre-action protocol applies to this claim.
	Have you exchanged information and/or documents (evidence) with the other party in order to assist in settling the claim?　☐ Yes　☐ No

D   Case management information

What amount of the claim is in dispute?   £ _____

Applications

Have you made any application(s) in this claim?   ☐ Yes   ☐ No

If Yes, what for? _____   For hearing on _____
(e.g. summary judgment,
add another party)

Witnesses

So far as you know at this stage, what witnesses of fact do you intend to call at the trial or final hearing including, if appropriate, yourself?

Witness name	Witness to which facts

Experts

Do you wish to use expert evidence at the trial or final hearing?   ☐ Yes   ☐ No

Have you already copied any experts' report(s) to the other party(ies)?   ☐ None yet obtained   ☐ Yes   ☐ No

Do you consider the case suitable for a single joint expert in any field?   ☐ Yes   ☐ No

Please list any single joint experts you propose to use and any other experts you wish to rely on. Identify single joint experts with the initials 'SJ' after their name(s).

Expert's name	Field of expertise (e.g. orthopaedic surgeon, surveyor, engineer)

Do you want your expert(s) to give evidence orally at the trial or final hearing?   ☐ Yes   ☐ No

If Yes, give the reasons why you think oral evidence is necessary:

continue over ▮▮▶

482

Track

Which track do you consider is most suitable for your claim? Tick one box ☐ small claims track ☐ fast track ☐ multi-track

If you have indicated a track which would not be the normal track for the claim, please give brief reasons for your choice

E Trial or final hearing

How long do you estimate the trial or final hearing will take? | days | hours | minutes

Are there any days when you, an expert or an essential witness will not be able to attend court for the trial or final hearing? ☐ Yes ☐ No

If Yes, please give details

Name	Dates not available

F Proposed directions *(Parties should agree directions wherever possible)*

Have you attached a list of the directions you think appropriate for the management of the claim? ☐ Yes ☐ No

If Yes, have they been agreed with the other party(ies)? ☐ Yes ☐ No

G Costs

*Do **not** complete this section if you have suggested your case is suitable for the small claims track **or** you have suggested one of the other tracks and you do not have a solicitor acting for you.*

What is your estimate of your costs incurred to date? £

What do you estimate your overall costs are likely to be? £

In substantial cases these questions should be answered in compliance with CPR Part 43

3

H Other information

Have you attached documents to this questionnaire? ☐ Yes ☐ No

Have you sent these documents to the other party(ies)? ☐ Yes ☐ No

If Yes, when did they receive them?

Do you intend to make any applications in the immediate future? ☐ Yes ☐ No

If Yes, what for?

In the space below, set out any other information you consider will help the judge to manage the claim.

Signed _____   Date _____

[Counsel][Solicitor][for the][1ˢᵗ][2ⁿᵈ][3ʳᵈ][   ]
[Claimant][Defendant][Part 20 claimant]

Please enter your firm's name, reference number and full postal address including (if appropriate) details of DX, fax or e-mail

		if applicable
	fax no.	
	DX no.	
Tel. no. Postcode	e-mail	
Your reference no.		

Notes for completing an allocation questionnaire

- If the claim is not settled, a judge must allocate it to an appropriate case management track. To help the judge choose the most just and cost-effective track, you must now complete the attached questionnaire.
- If you fail to return the allocation questionnaire by the date given, the judge may make an order which leads to your claim or defence being struck out, or hold an allocation hearing. If there is an allocation hearing the judge may order any party who has not filed their questionnaire to pay, immediately, the costs of that hearing.
- Use a separate sheet if you need more space for your answers marking clearly which section the information refers to. You should write the claim number on it, and on any other documents you send with your allocation questionnaire. Please ensure they are firmly attached to it.
- The letters below refer to the sections of the questionnaire and tell you what information is needed.

A Settlement

If you think that you and the other party may be able to negotiate a settlement you should tick the 'Yes' box. The court may order a stay, whether or not all the other parties to the claim agree. You should still complete the rest of the questionnaire, even if you are requesting a stay. Where a stay is granted it will be for an initial period of one month. You may settle the claim either by informal discussion with the other party or by alternative dispute resolution (ADR). ADR covers a range of different processes which can help settle disputes. More information is available in the Legal Services Commission leaflet 'Alternatives to Court' free from the LSC leaflet line Phone: 0845 3000 343

B Location of trial

High Court cases are usually heard at the Royal Courts of Justice or certain Civil Trial Centres. Fast or multi-track trials may be dealt with at a Civil Trial Centre or at the court where the claim is proceeding. Small claim cases are usually heard at the court in which they are proceeding.

C Pre-action protocols

Before any claim is started, the court expects you to have exchanged information and documents relevant to the claim, to assist in settling it. For some types of claim e.g. personal injury, there are approved protocols that should have been followed.

D Case management information

Applications

It is important for the court to know if you have already made any applications in the claim, what they are for and when they will be heard. The outcome of the applications may affect the case management directions the court gives.

Witnesses

Remember to include yourself as a witness of fact, if you will be giving evidence.

Experts

Oral or written expert evidence will only be allowed at the trial or final hearing with the court's permission. The judge will decide what permission it seems appropriate to give when the claim is allocated to track. Permission in small claims track cases will only be given exceptionally.

Track

The basic guide by which claims are normally allocated to a track is the amount in dispute, although other factors such as the complexity of the case will also be considered. A leaflet available from the court office explains the limits in greater detail.

Small Claims track	Disputes valued at not more than £5,000 except
	· those including a claim for personal injuries worth over £1,000 and
	· those for housing disrepair where either the cost of repairs or other work exceeds £1,000 or any other claim for damages exceeds £1,000
Fast track	Disputes valued at more than £5,000 but not more than £15,000
Multi-track	Disputes over £15,000

E Trial or Þnal hearing

You should enter only those dates when you, your expert(s) or essential witness(es) will not be able to attend court because of holiday or other committments.

F Proposed directions

Attach the list of directions, if any, you believe will be appropriate to be given for the management of the claim. Agreed directions on fast and multi-track cases should be based on the forms of standard directions set out in the practice direction to CPR Part 28 and form PF52.

G Costs

Only complete this section if you are a solicitor and have suggested the claim is suitable for allocation to the fast or multi-track.

H Other Information

Answer the questions in this section. Decide if there is any other information you consider will help the judge to manage the claim. Give details in the space provided referring to any documents you have attached to support what you are saying.

5

B4

The Small Claims Track

Introduction   B4.1

The small claims track is the normal track for hearings of £5,000 or less and is dealt with in *Part 27* of the *Civil Procedure Rules 1998*. It is described in the Practice Directions to the Rules as:

> '... intended to provide a proportionate procedure by which most straight forward claims with a financial value of not more than £5,000 can be decided without the need for substantial pre-hearing preparation and the formalities of a traditional trial and without incurring legal costs'.

Not every case where the value is below £5,000 will be allocated to the small claims track. If the case is unusually complex or involves a difficult point of law, the district judge may decide that it is not suitable for the small claims track and allocate a fast track hearing (see **B5 THE FAST TRACK**).

The no costs rule   B4.2

Once the case has been allocated to the small claims track the court will not order the losing party to pay the winners costs, apart from the fixed costs of issue for lodging the claim at court (see **B2.16** above) and the court fees. The only exception to this rule is where the judge decides one of the parties has behaved unreasonably. Merely losing the case will not be held to be unreasonable conduct, and costs orders in small claims track cases are relatively rare.

The court can, however, order the losing party to pay the other side's witness expenses (subject to a maximum, currently £50, for a witness's loss of earnings) and travelling expenses. If a claim for more than £5,000 is allocated to the small claims track, the costs rules of the fast track will apply.

Small claims directions   B4.3

The standard court directions can be seen in Figure 1.00 below.

However, the court has developed standard directions for different types of claims. Figure 2.00 shows some of the standard directions relating to building disputes, vehicle repairs or small contractual claims.

For unusual cases the court may give specific directions.

Figure 1.00 – Standard Court Directions

FORM A — The standard directions

(For use where the district judge specifies no other directions)

THE COURT DIRECTS:

(a)   **Each party shall deliver to every other party and to the court office copies of all documents (including any experts' report) on which he intends to rely at the hearing no later than _____ (14 days before the hearing).**

(b)   **The original documents shall be brought to the hearing.**

(c)   **[Notice of hearing date and time allowed for the hearing.]**

(d)   **The court must be informed immediately if the case is settled by agreement before the hearing date.**

Experts in small claims cases   **B4.4**

No expert may give evidence, whether written or oral, at a small claims hearing without the permission of the courts. Permission to call an expert should be given at the directions stage (see **B4.3** above), and the need for expert evidence should be highlighted by the allocation questionnaire (see **B3.5** above). The rule does not prevent expert evidence in small claims cases. There are many claims on the small claims track which will require expert evidence and which cannot be decided unless an expert is called. However the court will try and ensure that the costs are proportionate. If permission has not been given at directions stage a letter to the court will be necessary if either party wishes to call expert evidence. The judge will normally consider the case and the letter, and should only have a hearing to consider allowing expert evidence to be heard in exceptional cases.

A party who calls an expert to give evidence can, if successful, claim the expert's fees from the losing party subject to an upper limit which is at present £200 (*CPR 27.PD7*).

Preparing for the hearing   **B4.5**

If the claimant is conducting a small claims hearing himself it is important that he prepares for the hearing well in advance, in exactly the same way that a solicitor would prepare.

The standard directions (see **B4.3** above) require that prior to the hearing, each party delivers to the other party and the court office copies of all documents upon which they intend to rely. The time limit given is usually 14 days before the hearing. The importance of documents cannot be over emphasised. In particular, where there is conflict of evidence the documents are likely to be a decisive factor.

Figure 2.00 – Standard directions for claims relating to building disputes, vehicle repairs or small contractual claims

Form C — Standard directions for use in claims arising out of building disputes, vehicle repairs and similar contractual claims

THE COURT DIRECTS:

(*a*)   **Each party shall deliver to every other party and to the court office copies of all documents on which he intends to rely at the hearing. These may include:**

- **the contract;**
- **witness statements;**
- **experts' reports;**
- **photographs;**
- **invoices for work done or goods supplied; and**
- **estimates for work to be done.**

(*b*)   **The copies shall be delivered no later than _____ [14 days before the hearing].**

(*c*)   **The original documents shall be brought to the hearing.**

(*d*)   **The _____ shall deliver to the _____ and to the court office (no later than _____) (with his copy document) a list showing all items of work which he complains about and why, and the amount claimed for putting each item right.**

(*e*)   **The _____ shall deliver to the _____ and to the court office (no later than _____) (with his copy documents) a breakdown of the amount he is claiming showing all work done and materials supplied.**

(*f*)   **Before the date of the hearing the parties shall try to agree about the nature and costs of any remedial work required, subject to the court's decision about any other issue in the case.**

(*g*)   **Signed statements setting out the evidence of all witnesses on whom each party intends to rely shall be prepared and included in the documents mentioned in paragraph (*a*). This includes the evidence of the parties themselves and of any other witness, whether or not he is going to come to court and give evidence.**

(*h*)   **The parties should note that:**

> (i)   in deciding the case the judge may find it helpful to have photographs showing the work in question;
>
> (ii)   the judge may decide not to take into account a document or the evidence of a witness if no copy of that document or no copy of a statement or report by that witness has been supplied to the other parties.
>
> (*j*)   (Notice of hearing date and time allowed.)
>
> (*k*)   **The court must be informed immediately if the case is settled by agreement before the hearing date.**

The claimant should make sure that all the documents that he intends to rely on are readable. If there are more than two or three documents, they should be put in a bundle in date order, and each page of the bundle should be given a number. An index at the front of the bundle describing the documents and giving the page number is the best way of presenting them to the court. This is a method that a solicitor would use and it is the easiest way of referring to documents in court. The judge will be used to seeing documents presented in this way and a favourable impression will be created.

Prior to the hearing the claimant should make sure that he fully understands the issues before the court, and what evidence he will need to call to prove those issues. The judge will prefer to hear direct evidence of what took place. If, therefore, there is a dispute as to what was said by a salesman, that salesman should be called to give evidence. The judge has the discretion to allow 'hearsay' evidence but will not give much weight to the evidence if the person is not at court.

On the other hand, the judge is unlikely to allow the claimant to call a large number of witnesses. The judge will only wish to allocate a proportionate amount of the court's time to a particular case.

The small claims hearing   B4.6

Small claims hearings are held in the judge's private rooms, not in open court. They are designed to be informal and the strict rules of evidence do not apply. The philosophy behind small claims hearings is that the court should make it possible for litigants in person to conduct hearings themselves.

If the claimant is conducting the hearing on his own account the primary objective is to enable the judge to understand the case and the supporting evidence. The issues that are important must be prepared, and it must be ensured that those issues and the evidence to back them up are placed before the judge. The nature of the case should be clear from the papers and, if appropriate, a brief summary of what the case is about can be given at the beginning of the case, as the judge may not have had time to read all the papers prior to the hearing.

A general rule is that small claims hearings are open to the public. A judge may decide to hold them in private if the parties agree, or if he decides that publicity would defeat the object of the hearing or it involves confidential matters. In practice members of the public very rarely attend small claims hearings and many courts do not have facilities for public attendance.

The judge may adopt any method of proceeding that he considers to be fair. The usual procedure is for the claimant to appear first and set out his case and the defendant will then be allowed to cross examine, i.e. ask questions of the claimant and any witnesses. The same procedure then follows for the defendant. However, a judge may decide to adopt a different procedure and may deal with all the main evidence before allowing either party to ask questions, or he can dispense with cross examination and ask the questions himself. Some judges prefer to deal with each issue raised at a time allowing both sides to give evidence on that issue before moving on to the next issue.

In most courts the proceedings are tape recorded.

Although strict rules of evidence do not apply, the usual court etiquette should be adhered to. The hearing must not develop into an 'argument' and the other side or the judge must not be interrupted.

At the end of the case the judge will give a brief summary of the decision and his reasons for it. Once that decision is made no further representations can be given by either party. The parties should take notes of the judge's decision and they can ask the court to provide a copy of any notes that the judge has made.

Non-attendance of parties at the small claims hearing   B4.7

It is always better to attend the hearing in person with the witnesses. This ensures that the judge sees the claimant, hears his evidence and is able to properly assess the weight to be attached to that evidence. However, if the hearing is a long way from the claimant's home or place of business and is for a relatively small amount, it may not be economically viable for him to attend.

In these circumstances the claimant can give the court at least seven days notice before the date of the hearing that he will not attend and ask, in this notice, that the court decides the claim in his absence. The court will then take into account the statement of case and any documents that the claimant has filed with the court before making its decision.

If the claimant does not attend the hearing and does not give the seven day notice the court may strike out the claim. If neither party attends, the court can either strike out the claim and any counterclaim or decide the issues on any documents before it.

If the claimant does not attend it is essential that there is a clear statement of case setting out all the evidence that he wishes to put before the court with a statement of truth (see **B2.12** above), and that all the documents are lodged with the court and the other side.

If both sides agree, the parties can ask the court to deal with the case in the absence of either of them. A letter should be sent to the court explaining that this has been agreed and setting out clearly the issues to be decided. This procedure would be appropriate where there are no real disputes of fact but the parties are asking the court to interpret what has happened.

Is there any appeal? B4.8

Where a party has not attended the hearing he can ask for a re-hearing. Applications on the grounds of non-attendance must be made within 14 days after the judgment was served. This will only be granted if the applicant had a good reason for not attending or being represented or giving written notice, and has a reasonable prospect of success at the hearing. Unless there is a good reason for his non-attendance, e.g. the claimant has not been given notice by the court, it is likely that the judge will say that the non-attendance was unreasonable conduct and award the costs of the abortive hearing to the other side. This procedure is not available if there was an agreement for non-attendance.

An appeal can only be made when a decision is wrong or unjust because of a serious or other procedural irregularity in the proceedings. The appeal is not usually a re-hearing but a review of a decision of the lower court. The party needs permission to appeal which can be sought by request at the hearing or afterwards by application when the request is incorporated in the appeal documentation. There is a reduced court fee for an appeal against the decision on a small claims track and the documents required to launch an appeal are simplified.

The costs incurred in the appeal are not covered by the usual small claim limitation on costs. In other words, the losing party to the appeal is likely to be ordered to pay the winning party's costs.

B5

The Fast Track

Introduction B5.1

The fast track is normally for cases where the amount in dispute is between £5,000 and £15,000.

The fast track is intended for those cases that are more detailed than the small claims track (see **B4 THE SMALL CLAIMS TRACK**) but do not need the more complex procedure of the multi-track (see **B6 THE MULTI-TRACK**). The concept of proportionality is very important, especially bearing in mind the normal financial limits of £5,000 to £15,000, and the court will always seek to ensure:

- that neither party spends a disproportionate amount of costs in these cases; and

- a disproportionate amount of court's time is not allocated to these cases.

In order to ensure that the parties are on an equal footing, and to keep the costs proportionate to the amount involved, the court will set a strict timetable regime.

Setting the timetable B5.2

When the matter is allocated to the fast track, a court will give case management directions detailing which steps must be taken by all the parties and will set a strict timetable for the parties to carry out those directions. The standard period between the giving of directions and the trial will be not more than 30 weeks. The timetable and directions will be decided by the court and not the parties.

In standard cases, directions will be given by the judge without the parties attending, as there should be sufficient information on the statement of case and in the allocation questionnaires to enable the judge to decide the issues and the appropriate directions.

If the judge cannot do this he should not allocate a track, but should set an allocation hearing which the parties or their representatives should attend and be in a position to give the judge sufficient information to enable him to give directions all the way to trial. If it is necessary to hold a directions hearing because of the default of one of the parties, the court will usually impose sanctions against that party.

The trial window B5.3

In the directions the judge will either set a hearing date or usually give a trial window, which should not be more than 30 weeks from allocation. The judge should have sufficient information to do this as the allocation questionnaire (see **B3.5** above) asks when the witnesses will not be available.

The trial window will typically be a three week period in which the trial will take place. Nearer the trial date notification will be given of the actual date. Once the trial date, or trial window has been set by the court it will only be altered in exceptional circumstances. For example, it will not be sufficient to say that one of the witnesses has gone on holiday. This means that all witnesses and parties that need to attend will have to keep the trial window free.

Changing the timetable B5.4

The parties can agree to alter the timetable between them. However, there are certain key dates that cannot be varied by the parties at all e.g. the sending or return of a listing questionnaire (see **B5.9** below) or that of the hearing. Any other variation in the courts' timetable can only be made by consent if it does not interfere with the overall timetable or any of the key dates. Even if the parties agree, no extension will be allowable that will prevent the parties being ready for trial at the trial date or trial window. A key date cannot be altered without the consent of the court and this consent will not be readily given.

Directions B5.5

Typical directions in the fast track and the usual amount of time allowed for them are as follows.

- Disclosure – four weeks.

- Exchange of witness statements – ten weeks.

- Exchange of experts' reports – fourteen weeks.

- Sending of listing questionnaires by the court – twenty weeks.

- Filing of completed listing questionnaire – twenty-two weeks.

- Hearing – thirty weeks.

The court will give specific dates using these guidelines and the time period runs from the date of the direction. The court may omit some or all of the steps in the timetable if it feels that they are unnecessary.

Disclosure B5.6

Disclosure is defined by *CPR 1998, Part 31.2* as:

'a party discloses a document by stating that the document does exist or has existed'.

In practice, disclosure is made by preparing a list showing all the relevant documents in the possession of a party with a separate list showing documents that were, but are no longer, in the parties' possession.

Where there has been an order for 'standard disclosure' under *CPR 1998, Part 31.6*, the party must disclose:

- the documents on which he relies; and
- the documents which:
  - ○ adversely affect his own case;
  - ○ adversely affect another party's case; or
  - ○ support another party's case.

The parties are therefore under a duty to disclose, not only those documents that support their case, but also the documents that support the other side's.

It is very important that disclosure is dealt with properly, and that all relevant documents are listed. If a document is missed out the party may be prevented from using that document at court even if it is important. The general principle is that one party of litigation must not take the other party by surprise. If the court does allow a late document to be produced there may be costs or other sanctions imposed by the court.

If some documents are no longer in the possession of one of the parties, then it must be stated where the documents have gone.

The list must include a disclosure 'statement' setting out the extent of the search that has been made to locate documents that are required to be disclosed, certifying that the party making the list understands the duty to disclose documents and that to the best of his knowledge he has carried out that duty. This must be signed by an individual and not a limited company. The other party has an automatic right to copies of the documents that have been disclosed.

Privileged documents   B5.7

Documents issued 'without prejudice', or which make an offer to settle generally, or under the *CPR 1998, Part 36*, may not be disclosed. This allows the parties to correspond with each other in an effort to settle the case without fear that those documents will be adduced to the court by the other side. Writing 'without prejudice' or similar on top of a document will not make it automatically privileged. The document must contain an offer to settle the matter or be within a course of correspondence endeavouring to reach settlement.

Witness statements   B5.8

In general, a witness will not be allowed to give evidence at a trial unless a written statement of his evidence has been served on the other side. In the fast track the witness statements will take the place of the oral evidence in court. The witnesses statements will have been read by the judge and the other party and the other side will be able to ask questions of the witness (cross examine), but the primary evidence will be in written form. It is therefore vital that witness statements are properly prepared and that everything that needs to be said by each witness is included in their statement. If it is not included it may be impossible to put that piece of evidence before the judge.

Witness statements should, so far as is practicable, be in the witness's own words and should state the witness's:

- full name;
- his place of residence unless he makes a statement in an occupational capacity, in which case his place of work together with that of his employer may be given; and
- his occupation.

It should also indicate which of the statements are made from the witnesses' own knowledge and which from their information and belief. If the statement is based on information or belief, the source of these should be included. Exhibits can be attached to witness statements.

Pre-trial checklist (listing questionnaire)   B5.9

The court will send to all parties a pre-trial checklist (formerly called a listing questionnaire) to complete and return by a date specified in the notice of allocation. The date will normally be 8 weeks before the trial date or the start of the trial window, and the court will usually serve the pre-trial checklist at least 14 days before that date.

The pre-trial checklist will be on form N170 (see **APPENDIX B5.1**). When the form is returned by the claimant it must be accompanied by a court fee of £200. Although the parties are not bound to exchange copies of the pre-trial checklists, they are encouraged to do so to avoid giving the court incomplete or conflicting information. If the court is unhappy about any aspect of the pre-trial checklist or does not have sufficient information, it may fix a listing hearing or give other directions which it thinks may be appropriate.

If none of the parties file a pre-trial checklist the court will normally order the claim and any counterclaim to be struck out, unless the pre-trial checklist is filed within three days. As soon as is practicable after the pre-trial checklists are filed at court, directions for preparation of a hearing will be given. These will usually include directions relating to:

- the evidence that will be heard;
- the trial timetable;
- preparation of the trial bundles; and
- documents for the court.

Experts

The court has a duty to try and restrict expert evidence to that which is reasonably required to resolve proceedings. It will try and restrict the amount and length of expert evidence. No party may call an expert or include the evidence of an expert without the court's permission.

In general, in a fast track case, the court will *not* allow each side to have their own expert but will expect the parties to jointly instruct an expert. That expert will have a duty to the court which will override any obligation to a person from whom he has received instructions.

In addition, in fast track cases the court would usually require the expert evidence to be given in written form only, and will not allow the expert to attend the hearing to give oral evidence.

This is a major departure from the old County Court Rules, where each side would call their own experts who would serve their reports on the other side, give evidence at court and be cross examined on the report at court.

As the expert will not normally be at court, both parties will usually be given the opportunity to ask the expert questions in writing, which should be answered by a specific date. The usual manner of selecting an expert is to pick one from a list of experts approved by the court, or for one party to provide a list for the other to select an expert from.

If the parties cannot agree on an expert the court will have to decide the matter. Correspondence between the parties and the single joint expert is no longer privileged, and each party should send copies of any letters written to the expert to the other side.

The fast track trial

One of the most startling characteristics of the fast track system is that the trial may last a maximum of one day. Before the *CPR 1998*, county court trials could last a number of days, sometimes weeks and occasionally even months. If it is evident that the trial cannot be completed in a day, the case should not be allocated to the fast track but should be a multi-track case. However, the court will only transfer a case to the multi-track where the case is unusually complex, therefore the vast majority of cases between £5,000 and £15,000 will be dealt with in the fast track system.

For a case of any size to be dealt with within the allocated five hour period, it has to be properly prepared. The parties should endeavour to narrow the issues so that by the time the trial takes place only those issues that need to be decided will be brought before the judge.

All parties, including the judge, must have read the papers. This will mean that each side's 'opening' speeches will be dispensed with, as the judge will understand what the case is about before the trial starts. Written witness statements will replace evidence given in chief, and the multiplicity of experts will be replaced by one single report from a joint expert which should give the judge various options.

The trial will consist of:

- a five minute opening by each side;

- cross examination of each of the factual witnesses;

- an address by each parties' advocate; and

- the decision.

Before the fast track trial starts the parties will have agreed, and the judge will set a strict timetable. The parties will not be allowed to go over that timetable. A suggested timetable for a fast track trial is as follows.

Claimant's opening submission	10 minutes
Defendant's opening submission	10 minutes
Cross examination of claimant's witnesses	1 hour 15 mins
Re-examination	15 minutes
Cross examination of defendant's witnesses	1 hour 15 mins
Re-examination	15 minutes
Defendant's submissions	20 minutes
Claimant's submissions	20 minutes
Judge's thinking time and judgment	30 minutes
Costs and consequential orders	30 minutes
Total	5 hours

Appendix B5

Appendix B5.1 – Listing Questionnaire

Listing questionnaire (Pre-trial checklist)	In the

To be completed by, or on behalf of,

	Claim No.
	Last date for filing with court office

who is [1ˢᵗ][2ⁿᵈ][3ʳᵈ][   ][Claimant][Defendant]
[Part 20 claimant][Part 20 defendant] in this claim

| Date(s) fixed for trial or trial period | |

This form must be **completed** and **returned** to the court no later than the date given above. If not, your statement of case may be struck out or some other sanction imposed.

If the claim has settled, or settles before the trial date, you must let the court know immediately.

Legal representatives only: You must **attach** estimates of costs incurred to date, and of your likely overall costs. In substantial cases, these should be provided in compliance with CPR Part 43.

For multi-track claims only, you must also **attach** a proposed timetable for the trial itself.

A Confirmation of compliance with directions

1. I confirm that I have complied with those directions already given which require action by me. ☐Yes ☐No

If you are unable to give confirmation, state which directions you have still to comply with and the date by which this will be done.

Directions	Date

2. I believe that additional directions are necessary before the trial takes place. ☐Yes ☐No

If Yes, you should attach an application and a draft order.

Include in your application all directions needed to enable the claim to be tried on the date, or within the trial period, already fixed. These should include any issues relating to experts and their evidence, and any orders needed in respect of directions still requiring action by any other party.

3. Have you agreed the additional directions you are seeking with the other party(ies)? ☐Yes ☐No

B Witnesses

1. How many witnesses (including yourself) will be giving evidence on your behalf at the trial? *(Do not include experts - see Section C)*

Continued over ↷

N170 Listing questionnaire (Pre-trial checklist) (12.02)

1 of 3

© Crown copyright. Reproduced by permission of the Controller of Her Majesty's Stationery Office. Published by LexisNexis UK.

Witnesses continued

2. If the trial date is not yet fixed, are there any days within the trial period you or your witnesses would wish to avoid if possible? *(Do not include experts - see Section C)*

Please give details

Name of witness	Dates to be avoided, if possible	Reason

Please specify any special facilities or arrangements needed at court for the party or any witness (e.g. witness with a disability).

3. Will you be providing an interpreter for any of your witnesses? ☐ Yes ☐ No

C Experts

You are reminded that you may not use an expert's report or have your expert give oral evidence unless the court has given permission. If you do not have permission, you must make an application (see section A2 above)

1. Please give the information requested for your expert(s)

Name	Field of expertise	Joint expert?	Is report agreed?	Has permission been given for oral evidence?
		☐ Yes ☐ No	☐ Yes ☐ No	☐ Yes ☐ No
		☐ Yes ☐ No	☐ Yes ☐ No	☐ Yes ☐ No
		☐ Yes ☐ No	☐ Yes ☐ No	☐ Yes ☐ No

2. Has there been discussion between experts? ☐ Yes ☐ No

3. Have the experts signed a joint statement? ☐ Yes ☐ No

4. If your expert is giving oral evidence and the trial date is not yet fixed, is there any day within the trial period which the expert would wish to avoid, if possible? ☐ Yes ☐ No

If Yes, please give details

Name	Dates to be avoided, if possible	Reason

D Legal representation

1. Who will be presenting your case at the trial? ☐ You ☐ Solicitor ☐ Counsel

2. If the trial date is not yet fixed, is there any day within the trial period that the person presenting your case would wish to avoid, if possible? ☐ Yes ☐ No

If Yes, please give details

Name	Dates to be avoided, if possible	Reason

E The trial

1. Has the estimate of the time needed for trial changed? ☐ Yes ☐ No

If Yes, say how long you estimate the whole trial will take, including both parties' cross-examination and closing arguments ☐ days ☐ hours ☐ minutes

2. If different from original estimate have you agreed with the other party(ies) that this is now the **total** time needed? ☐ Yes ☐ No

3. Is the timetable for trial you have attached agreed with the other party(ies)? ☐ Yes ☐ No

Fast track cases only

The court will normally give you 3 weeks notice in the fast track of the date fixed for a fast track trial unless, in exceptional circumstances, the court directs that shorter notice will be given.

Would you be prepared to accept shorter notice of the date fixed for trial? ☐ Yes ☐ No

F Document and fee checklist

Tick as appropriate

I attach to this questionnaire -

☐ An application and fee for additional directions ☐ A proposed timetable for trial

☐ A draft order ☐ An estimate of costs

☐ Listing fee

Signed	Please enter your [firm's] name, reference number and full postal address including (if appropriate) details of DX, fax or e-mail
[Counsel][Solicitor][for the][1ˢᵗ][2ⁿᵈ][3ʳᵈ][ ] [Claimant][Defendant] [Part 20 claimant][Part 20 defendant]	
Date	Postcode

Tel. no.	DX no.	E-mail
Fax no.	Ref. no.	

3 of 3

B6

The Multi-track

Introduction

B6.1

The multi-track, which is dealt with in *CPR 1998, Part 29*, will be the normal track for any claim for which the small claims or fast track is not the normal track. (See **B4 THE SMALL CLAIMS TRACK** and **B5 THE FAST TRACK**.)

The multi-track needs to deal with cases of widely differing values and complexity although it is designed to deal with the higher value more complex claim, and certainly those cases with a value over £15,000.

This track does not provide any standard procedure, in order to give the court considerable flexibility in the way it will manage cases. The court is given a range of case management tools, including standard directions, case management conferences and pre-trial reviews, which can be used to suit the needs of each individual case.

Similarities with the old system

B6.2

Although the multi-track has certain similarities with the previous system, it would be wrong to assume that multi-track cases are identical to those cases prior to the *CPR 1998* coming into force in April 1999. The main differences are:

- the court and not the parties will case manage each action;

- the court will give directions which may be adjusted from time to time but which should be adhered to by the parties;

- the court will expect the parties to cooperate and to narrow the issues between them, the parties must also assist the court in giving directions that are suitably tailored for each case;

- the court will seek to minimise costs and ensure that they are proportionate to the amount involved; and

- the parties will need to prepare a case summary prior to the hearing and give cost estimates periodically.

Directions   **B6.3**

The directions that are given, either with or without a hearing, will be tailored to the needs of the case. The same overriding principals of narrowing the issues and case management will apply. (See **B3.4** above and **B7.1** below.)

The type of directions that are given will be similar to those described in the fast track procedure (see **B5.5–B5.10** above) and will usually include:

- standard disclosure;

- simultaneous exchange of witness statements;

- the instruction of a single joint expert on any appropriate issues, or simultaneous exchange of experts' reports;

- discussion between the experts that are not in agreement and a statement on the discussion;

- a case management conference; and

- the fixing of a trial period.

The judge is likely to adopt a more flexible approach than is the case in the fast track, and may be persuaded to allow an expert per side. In complex cases relating to a high value claim it may be costly to instruct a single joint expert if the parties themselves need expert advice.

The case management conference   **B6.4**

As soon as the matter is allocated to the multi-track a judge will read the papers and decide whether it is necessary to hold a case management conference. There will be cases with a high value that are fairly simple where such a conference will not be necessary. In more complex cases the judge will fix a case management conference if he cannot give directions on his own initiative and no agreed directions have been filed which he can approve. Case management conferences should be listed for a hearing promptly.

As in fast track and small claims track cases, it is important that the issues are known and understood at an early stage. The court will expect the representatives of the parties to be able to describe the issues. The parties' representative at the conference must be someone personally involved with the conduct of the case, with authority to deal with fixing the timetable and defining issues and matters of evidence. All the relevant documents, including witness statements and experts' reports, should be made available.

The judge may direct that the parties themselves attend case management conferences and may also require a case summary prepared by the claimant and agreed, if possible, by setting out in no more than 500 words, a brief chronology of the facts agreed and in dispute and evidence needed to support them.

Even in the most complex of cases there is a significant 'front loading' of preparation.

If the case management conference was fixed or had to be adjourned because of a default by one of the parties, the court will usually impose a sanction, or may even strike out the party's statement of case.

As in the fast track there are a number of key dates which cannot be altered by the parties, these include the date of the:

- case management conference;
- pre-trial review;
- returning of a pre-trial checklist (listing questionnaire); and
- trial or trial period.

Provided the above dates are not altered, the parties can agree to vary any of the other directions themselves. The main principal of the court's management powers which will apply to multi-track cases, is that if a party fails to keep to the timetable, sanctions may and will be ordered against that party.

Pre-trial checklist (listing questionnaire)   B6.5

The court will send to each of the parties a pre-trial checklist to be returned on a specified date (see **B5.9** above). That date will be no later than eight weeks before the trial. The court may list the matter on receipt of the pre-trial checklist. The claimant must pay a listing fee of £300.00.

The court may give directions as to the issues on which evidence is to be given, the nature of the evidence that is required on those issues and the way this is to be placed before the court. It may exclude evidence even though ordinarily this would be admissible. Directions are usually given for the preparation of a trial bundle.

The trial   B6.6

The trial will normally take place at the court where the case is being managed. It may, however, take place at another court, for example if there is a judge available at another court. As in the fast track, the judge may give directions as to limiting the presentation of the parties. He may, for instance, dispense with an opening address or allow witness statements to stand as the primary evidence of a witness. He will normally allow cross examination.

Experts may be allowed to give oral evidence.

B7

Applications in the Course of an Action

The overriding objective

When exercising any powers or interpreting any of the *Civil Procedure Rules 1998 (CPR 1998) (SI 1998/3132)*, the court must give effect to the overriding objective set out in *CPR 1998, Part 1*. The overriding objective gives the judge guidance on how to approach any procedural question when setting out the fundamental purpose of the *Rules* and the underlying system of procedure. The overriding objective is as follows.

'1.1

(1)   These Rules are a new procedural code with the overriding objective of enabling the court to deal with cases justly.

(2)   Dealing with a case justly includes, so far as is practicable—

    (*a*)   ensuring that the parties are on an equal footing;

    (*b*)   saving expense;

    (*c*)   dealing with the case in ways which are proportionate—

        (i)   to the amount of money involved;

        (ii)   to the importance of the case;

        (iii)   to the complexity of the issues; and

        (iv)   to the financial position of each party

    (*d*)   ensuring that it is dealt with expeditiously and fairly; and

    (*e*)   allotting to it an appropriate share of the Court's resources, while taking into account the need to allot resources to other cases.'

The implementation of the overriding objectives means that any case law giving guidance to how the *Rules* are to be interpreted under the old rules has no effect. The court system effectively started again in April 1999.

It is probably obvious that the fundamental purpose of civil proceedings should be to enable the court, to 'deal with cases justly'. However, the list of factors in paragraph two gives an indication as to how the wide term of 'justice' would be interpreted by the court, and the factors the court will take into account. Of the five listed factors three are directly related to costs.

Proportionality   B7.2

A fundamental and important principle introduced by the *CPR 1998* is the concept of 'proportionality'. In deciding whether to take any steps or grant any applications the court will consider whether the costs and time involved are proportionate to the case. The steps that may be reasonable in a very large action may not be allowed by the court in a smaller action, as they may be considered to be disproportionate. This will inevitably mean that in smaller actions some steps are not taken which would have assisted the court in establishing the truth, had the cost of carrying out the steps or the difficulty or the amount of time involved not been disproportionately high.

Proportionality is not restricted merely to the amount of money involved. On a claim of a relatively low amount the court must consider, the:

- importance of the case;
- complexity of the issues; and
- financial position of each party.

The court must not only take into account the costs of the individual case, but must ensure that the court does not allocate a disproportionate share of its resources to that case, and must take into account the need to allot resources to other cases. The overriding objective is not only a guide to the judiciary, but also a guide to lawyers and the parties themselves, and every step in the proceedings should be taken in the context of implementing the overriding objective.

How to make an application   B7.3

An application in the course of proceedings is made by completing, and lodging at court, form N244, an 'application notice', and paying a court fee of £60.00.

At **APPENDIX B7.1** is blank application notice. On the right hand side are details of the claim, including the claim number and the name and address of the claimants and defendants. It is very important that the claim number is completed, as without this the court will not be able to attach the notice to the appropriate court file.

The application notice requires a time estimate, which should, if possible, be agreed by both parties. If agreement is not forthcoming then the appropriate box should be ticked.

The order sought

At Part A of the form, the order that is being sought should be stated. If the order is complex, it is better to include a draft order on a separate form. The reason why the order is being sought must be given. This may, for example, be a reference to a statutory provision that the other side has breached, or a direction of the court. The idea of the form is that it should be, so far as is possible, self-contained and that the judge will be able to decide the issue on reading the application notice and any accompanying documents.

Documents relied on

Part B must be completed and the claimant must give details of the documents he intends to rely on. This may be a new witness statement which is either on Part C or attached as a separate document, or he may wish to refer to a witness statement or statement of case that is already with the court.

Additional witness statements and evidence

Part C of the application notice allows the claimant to complete additional witness statements or evidence. If the evidence is lengthy it should be put on a separate piece of paper. All evidence must contain a statement of truth.

Decision to hold a hearing

Although the form is lengthy it should make the hearing shorter. In some cases it should allow the court to deal with the claimant's application without the necessity of a hearing. If there is to be a hearing the court will then give each party notice of the hearing date and time when the parties or their representatives must attend.

Summary judgment

Summary judgment is an extremely important procedure in any action, but is particularly important in credit control matters. Summary judgment is an application for final judgment without the need for a full hearing on the basis that there is no real prospect of the defence succeeding.

Applications are relatively fast and do not involve the expense of a full hearing. They are heard by a judge in his rooms and not in open court. The evidence is given in a written statement and not by witnesses giving oral evidence. There is, therefore, no need for all the parties' witnesses to attend. Indeed, there is no need for anyone to attend other than representatives of the parties.

An application for summary judgment may be made at any time before the trial, but it is in everyone's interest for application to be made as quickly as possible. The best time for an application is before allocation.

An application for summary judgment would be appropriate where the defence is little more than a holding defence and the action is not struck out by the court or where it is easy to show on paper that the defence cannot succeed. A typical example would be a defence that the goods were not ordered when there is an order form signed by the defendant. The order form would be attached as an exhibit to the witness statement in support of the application. It would then be up to the defendants to show some good reason why judgment should not be granted.

In order to defeat an application for summary judgment the defendant must show that there *is* some prospect of success. There must be a real chance that the defendant will win at trial, not merely an illusory, false or imaginary chance.

On an application for summary judgment the court does not try the case and the defendant is not required to show that he will probably succeed at trial, merely that he has a real prospect of success i.e. there is some likelihood that he will succeed.

The application can also be made by a defendant and the court may strike out a claim or a particular issue if it considers that there is no prospect of the claim or issues proceeding. Summary judgment will be awarded against the claimant if the claimant has failed to show a case which, if unanswered, would entitle him to judgment, or that the claim is bound to be dismissed at trial.

The claimant may not apply for summary judgment until the defendant has filed an acknowledgement of service or a defence. If the claimant applies for summary judgment after the acknowledgement of service, but before the defendant has filed a defence, there is no need for a defence to be filed before the hearing of the summary judgment application.

The judgment application is made by completing form N244, the standard 'Application Notice' (see **B7.3–B7.7** above and **APPENDIX B7.1** below). However, the application must include a statement that it is an application for judgment under *CPR 1998, Part 24*. The application notice, or the witness statement filed with the application, must state that it is made because the applicant believes that the respondent has no real prospect of succeeding on the claim, and that there is no other reason why the claim or issue should go to trial.

The Application Notice should identify the written evidence on which the applicant relies. The other side must be given at least 14 days notice of the hearing and the issues that the court will decide. He may then file and serve evidence that he wishes to rely on, not less than 7 days before the hearing. The party applying for summary judgment then has up until 3 days before the hearing to supply additional witness statements.

The court can set down a summary judgment application of its own motion i.e. without a party having to apply for the hearing.

Hearing for summary judgment   B7.9

At a hearing of the application the judge may make a number of orders. These include:

- judgment on the claim;
- striking out or dismissing a defence or counterclaim;
- dismissing the application; or
- making a conditional order.

Conditional orders   B7.10

The conditional order is usually one that requires a party to pay a sum of money into court or take a specific step within a specific time. If that payment is not made or the specific step is not taken, the other side will be successful in the case. For example, if the claimant makes an application for summary judgment and the court makes a conditional order that the defendant pays into court the amount of the claim within 14 days, if that payment is not made within 14 days the claimant will obtain judgment.

The judge will make a conditional order where it appears possible, but improbable, that the defence (or a claim if the defendant has applied) will succeed.

Unsuccessful application   B7.11

If an application for summary judgment is not successful the case will continue and the court will then give directions for the management of the case. If it has not been done previously the court will allocate a track and the case will continue on its normal course.

The losing party of an application for summary judgment may be ordered to pay the costs of the winning party's application, which are usually assessed at the end of the hearing and are payable within 14 days.

Request for further information   B7.12

Part 18 of the *CPR 1998* states that at any time the court may order a party to clarify any matter which is in dispute or give additional information about any matter. The court will specify a date by which further information should be given. The parties may also make an application to court that the other party gives further information. Before seeking this order the party requesting the further information would normally send a written request to the other party, giving them a reasonable time to respond. The request should be concise and must be restricted to matters that are reasonably necessary and proportionate to enable the party requesting the information to prepare his own case or to understand the case that he has to meet.

If there are a number of questions, a separate document headed 'request under Part 18' should be sent to the court.

If the other side objects to the request or any part of it or requires more time, he must inform the requesting party within a reasonable time. Similarly, the responding party may consider that the information can only be given at a disproportionate expense and may object to responding for that reason.

It is important that a response is made, for if it is not the requesting party may apply to the court for an order without any hearing. The response for further information must be given in writing and should repeat the question and then give the answer. The responses must be verified by a statement of truth (see **B2.12** above).

This procedure is excluded from claims allocated to the small claims track.

Injunctions, interim payment and search orders   B7.13

During the course of the proceedings (or in some cases before proceedings have started) the court has additional powers under *Part 25* of the *CPR 1998* to enable it to fairly dispose of the case. These are known as interim remedies and are set out in *Part 25.1* as follows:

'25.1 – Orders for interim remedies

(1)   The court may grant the following interim remedies –

   (*a*)   an interim injunction;

   (*b*)   an interim declaration;

   (*c*)   an order –

      (i)   for the detention, custody or preservation of relevant property;

      (ii)   for the inspection of relevant property;

      (iii)   for the taking of a sample of relevant property;

      (iv)   for the carrying out of an experiment on or with relevant property;

      (v)   for the sale of relevant property which is of a perishable nature or which for any other good reason it is desirable to sell quickly; and

(vi)   for the payment of income from relevant property until a claim is decided;

(*d*)   an order authorising a person to enter any land or building in the possession of a party to the proceedings for the purposes of carrying out an order under sub-paragraph (c);

(*e*)   an order under section 4 of the Torts (Interference with Goods) Act 1977 to deliver up goods;

(*f*)   an order (referred to as a 'freezing injunction') –

   (i)   restraining a party from removing from the jurisdiction assets located there; or

   (ii)   restraining a party from dealing with any assets whether located within the jurisdiction or not;

(*g*)   an order directing a party to provide information about the location of relevant property or assets or to provide information about relevant property or assets which are or may be the subject of an application for a freezing injunction.

(*h*)   an order (referred to as a 'search order') under section 7 of the Civil Procedure Act 1997 (order requiring a party to admit another party to premises for the purpose of preserving evidence, etc.);

(*i*)   an order under section 33 of the Supreme Court Act 1981 or section 52 of the County Courts Act 1984 (order for disclosure of documents or inspection of property before a claim has been made);

(*j*)   an order under section 34 of the Supreme Court Act 1981 or section 53 of the County Courts Act 1984 (order in certain proceedings for disclosure of documents or inspection of property against a non-party);

(*k*)   an order (referred to as an order for interim payment) under rule 25.6 for payment by a defendant on account of any damages, debt or other sum (except costs) which the court may hold the defendant liable to pay;

(*l*)   an order for a specified fund to be paid into court or otherwise secured, where there is a dispute over a party's right to the fund;

(*m*)   an order permitting a party seeking to recover personal property to pay money into court pending the outcome of the proceedings and directing that, if he does so, the property shall be given up to him; and

(*n*)   an order directing a party to prepare and file accounts relating to the dispute.

(Rule 34.2 provides for the court to issue a witness summons requiring a witness to produce documents to the court at the hearing or on such date as the court may direct.)

(2)   In paragraph (1)(*c*) and (*g*), 'relevant property' means property (including land) which is the subject of a claim or as to which any question may arise on a claim.

(3)   The fact that a particular kind of interim remedy is not listed in paragraph (1) does not affect any power that the court may have to grant that remedy.

(4)   The court may grant an interim remedy whether or not there has been a claim for a final remedy of that kind.'

Powers of the court   B7.14

Before dealing with any of the interim remedies the court will apply the overriding objective (see **B7.1** above). It will not, therefore, grant an interim remedy unless it is proportionate to the costs involved on the amount of the claim and the type of case that it being dealt with. The court will not take any step unless the likely benefits of taking a particular step justifies the cost of taking it and it will often preclude application for interim remedy in a small claims case. Although an interim remedy will invariably be made by the representatives of the parties, it is important that the litigant knows the powers that the court may use.

There are various powers enabling the court to prevent disposal of property, including the power to order the 'detention, custody or preservation of the relevant property' (*CPR 1998, rule 25.1.1(c)(i)*) and inspection of the property. The court can also order the taking of a sample and the carrying out of experiments or tests on any property. The court would not make an order for the defendant to preserve property unless there was some evidence that the other side was about to dispose of the property. If there is evidence of this an application should be made without delay. In an emergency, the court can hear interim applications very quickly and, if necessary, without the other side being present.

With regard to taking samples and conducting an experiment, a request should be made in writing and an application sent to court only if the other side has refused a reasonable request.

Search order   B7.15

A search order was previously known as an 'Anton Pillar' order. *CPR 1998, Part 24* gives the court power to make an order requiring a party to admit another party to premises for the purposes of preserving evidence. This can only be done by a solicitor, as the *Rules* require a supervising solicitor, who must have experience in the operation of search orders, to be appointed.

Disclosure of documents before the claim   B7.16

Before proceedings have started the court has the power to order a person, who appears to the court likely to be a party to the proceedings, and is likely to have or had in his possession documents which are relevant to an issue which may arise out of the claim, to disclose those documents and to produce them to the other side. This power was previously restricted to personal injury claims, but can now be used in any action. It is often used to enable parties to investigate:

- whether there is an action which should be brought; or

- who the proper defendants are.

Freezing injunction   B7.17

Freezing injunctions were previously called 'Mareva' injunctions, and enable the court to grant an interim remedy in the form of an order restraining a party from removing assets from the area of jurisdiction of the court, or preventing a party dealing with assets. This type of injunction is often used where a party seeks to recover property and there is evidence that the property is about to be disposed of or moved out of the country.

Interim payments   B7.18

The court may make an order for an interim payment if:

- the defendant has admitted liability;

- a judgment has been obtained, but the amount has yet to be assessed; or

- the court is satisfied that if the claim went to trial the claimant would obtain judgment for a substantial amount of money.

An interim payment order is often used in claims for personal injuries, where it will take a long time to assess the amount of damages and where there is a clear liability on behalf of the defendant. However, it can be used in any substantial claim provided the conditions are satisfied.

Appendix B7

Appendix B7.1 – Application Notice N244

Application Notice

	In the
You should provide this information for listing the application	
1. How do you wish to have your application dealt with	
a) at a hearing? ☐ } *complete all questions below*	**Claim no.**
b) at a telephone conference? ☐	**Warrant no.** *(if applicable)*
c) without a hearing? ☐ *complete Qs 5 and 6 below*	**Claimant** *(including ref.)*
2. Give a time estimate for the hearing/conference _____(hours) _____(mins)	
3. Is this agreed by all parties? ☐ Yes ☐ No	**Defendant(s)** *(including ref.)*
4. Give dates of any trial period or fixed trial date _____	
5. Level of judge _____	**Date**
6. Parties to be served _____	

Note You must complete Parts A **and** B, **and** Part C if applicable. Send any relevant fee and the completed application to the court with any draft order, witness statement or other evidence; and sufficient copies for service on each respondent.

Part A

1. Enter your full name, or name of solicitor

I (We) [1]   (on behalf of)(the claimant)(the defendant)

2. State clearly what order you are seeking and if possible attach a draft

intend to apply for an order (a draft of which is attached) that [2]

3. Briefly set out why you are seeking the order. Include the material facts on which you reply, identifying any rule or statutory provision

because [3]

Part B

I (We) wish to rely on: *tick one box*

the attached (witness statement) (affidavit) ☐   my statement of case ☐

evidence in Part C in support of my application ☐

4. If you are not already a party to the proceedings, you must provide an address for service or documents

Signed [_____]   **Position or office held** [_____]

(Applicant)('s Solicitor)('s litigation friend)   (if signing on behalf of firm or company)

Address to which documents about this claim should be sent (including reference if appropriate)[4]

	if applicable	
	fax no.	
	DX no.	
Tel. no. Postcode	e-mail	

The court office at

is open from 10am to 4pm Monday to Friday. When corresponding with the court please address forms or letters to the Court Manager and quote the claim number.

N244 Application Notice (4.00)

Appendix B7

Part C	Claim No.	

I (We) wish to rely on the following evidence in support of this application:

Statement of Truth

*(I believe) *(The applicant believes) that the facts stated in Part C are true
delete as appropriate

Signed

(Applicant)('s Solicitor)('s litigation friend)

Position or office held

(if signing on behalf of firm or company)

Date

B8

Costs

The general principles   B8.1

The general rule under *Part 44* of the *Civil Procedure Rules 1998* (*CPR 1998*) (*SI 1998/3132*) is that the unsuccessful party will pay the costs of the successful party. However, this rule is no longer automatically applied – the court now has to decide whether to apply the general rule or make a different order for costs, having regard to all the circumstances. The court must take into account:

- the conduct of the party;
- whether a party has succeeded on part or all of his case, even if he was not wholly successful; and
- whether any payment into court or admissible offer to settle was made.

The conduct that the court has to take into account includes:

- the conduct before the proceedings;
- the conduct during the proceedings;
- whether the parties have followed any relevant protocols;
- whether it is reasonable for a party to raise or contest a particular allegation or issue;
- the manner in which a party has pursued or defended his case or a particular allegation; or
- whether a claimant who has succeeded, has exaggerated part or all of his claim.

The judge assessing costs is able to take into account, not only who has won, but the conduct of the parties throughout the matter, including their conduct before proceedings started. If he feels that a party has acted unreasonably the party can be penalised.

Sanctions   B8.2

The *CPR 1998, Part 44* lists sanctions that the court may impose. These include an order that a party must pay:

- a proportion of the other party's costs;

- a stated amount in respect of another party's costs;

- costs from, or until, a certain date only;

- the costs incurred after proceedings have begun;

- costs relating to particular steps in the proceedings;

- costs relating only to a distinct part of the proceedings; or

- interest on costs from or until a certain date.

The need to act reasonably B8.3

The costs sanctions of the court emphasise the need for the parties to act reasonably. If, for example, a party withheld a document until a late stage and the court feels that had the document been produced earlier the proceedings would have been shorter or may never have been started, the court could award costs against the party that failed to produce the document to the point when the document was eventually disclosed. It is good practice to disclose relevant documents pre-action to avoid this danger. It is certainly advisable to produce a document at any stage that it is requested, whether or not a formal order for disclosure has been made.

The court may also take an issue based approach. A judge may decide that the claimant has been successful on one issue but has failed on a number of others and apportion costs appropriately.

Offers to settle B8.4

The *CPR 1998* are designed to encourage the parties to settle disputes at an early stage, preferably without the need for litigation. (See **B1 DEBT RECOVERY THROUGH THE COURTS**.) In fact the rules place a duty on all parties to see if settlement can be reached.

To promote settlement, *CPR 1998, Part 36* deals with offers to settle and the costs consequences of ignoring the offer or failing to beat the offer made if the matter goes to court. (See **B8.5** and **B8.6** below.)

All offers to settle, whether made before or after the commencement of proceedings, are known as '*Part 36* offers'. *Part 36* sets out various requirements of such offers, but also makes it clear that there is no prohibition against a party making an offer to settle in any way he chooses. It will then be at the discretion of the court to see if the costs consequences of *Part 36* follow.

It may well be that parties make offers to settle before proceedings are issued and before the parties have sought legal advice. If a *Part 36* offer is made and the claimant is in any way uncertain as to the meaning or consequences of the offer it is advisable to seek the help of a solicitor.

If a defendant makes a *Part 36* offer after proceedings have begun the defendant is required to make a payment of the money offered into court. This is known as a '*Part 36* payment'.

A *Part 36* payment or offer should:

● state whether it relates to the whole or part of the claim (if it relates to only part, which part should be indicated);

● state whether it takes into account a counterclaim;

● state the details relating to interest if it is expressed not to be inclusive of interest; and

● be signed by the offerer or his solicitor.

In the absence of any reference to interest the offer will be taken to include interest.

If any of the terms are unclear the offerer can ask for clarification of the terms of the offer, and if that clarification is not given an application to court can be made.

Accepting an offer   B8.5

If the defendant makes a *Part 36* offer or payment the claimant has 21 days to accept (unless there is less than 21 days to the trial). After that time the claimant will have to apply to the court for permission to accept.

If a claimant accepts an offer of payment by the defendant without needing the permission of the court, he will normally be entitled to his costs up to the date of acceptance. If the offer or payment relates to only part of the claim, the claimant may have his costs if he abandons the rest of the claim unless the court orders otherwise.

If the claimant does not accept a *Part 36* offer or payment and fails to match or beat the amount of the offer at the trial, the court will usually order him to pay any costs incurred by the defendant after the latest date on which the offer or payment could have been accepted without the permission of the court.

An offer made by a claimant   B8.6

A *Part 36* offer may also be made by a claimant. A defendant also has 21 days in which to accept the claimant's offer (provided there are more than 21 days before the start of the trial) without the permission of the court. After that period the defendant needs the agreement of the parties or the permission of the court to accept the offer. The offer is accepted by giving notice of acceptance to the claimant and filing a copy at court.

If a defendant accepts the claimant's offer without needing the court's permission, the claimant will be entitled to his costs up to the date upon which the defendant served notice of acceptance.

If the claimant makes a *Part 36* offer and the defendant does not accept it and then the defendant is held liable for more than the offer, the court may:

- order interest on the whole or part of any sum of money (including interest) awarded to the claimant at a rate not exceeding 10% above base rate for some or all of the period starting with the last date the defendant could have accepted the offer without permission of the court;

- allow the claimant costs on an indemnity basis for the same period; or

- give the claimant interest on those costs at a rate up to 10% above the base rate.

There is not a strict rule that the court will do any of these and the court will take into account the:

- terms of the *Part 36* offer;

- stage in the proceedings when the offer of payment was made;

- information available to the parties; and

- conduct of the parties.

Part 36 offers are an important tactic for claimants. It is likely that interest of 10% over base will be awarded if the defendant is held liable for more than the *Part 36* offer, and a realistic claimant's *Part 36* offer will therefore put considerable pressure on the defendant to settle at an early stage.

Whether a *Part 36* offer is made by a claimant depends on the strength of his case. The earlier the evidence is gathered together to evaluate the case the sooner a *Part 36* offer can be made.

A *Part 36* offer does not have to be made in every case and if it is felt that there is no realistic prospect of the defendant succeeding this would be grounds for making no offer of settlement. However, where there is a litigation risk, and bearing in mind the courts' wide discretion to allow or disallow costs, the claimant should always consider the *Part 36* procedure.

Unreasonable behaviour   B8.7

It is quite possible for a claimant to be awarded a sum of money from the defendant but to only obtain a proportion of the costs or no costs at all if the court thinks the claimant's conduct is unreasonable.

When costs are paid   **B8.8**

Where a court orders a party to pay costs to another party on any hearing or application lasting a day or less, the court will make a summary assessment of the costs straight after the hearing. The costs are then payable within 14 days unless the order states a different period.

This is a significant departure from the procedure prior to the *CPR 1998*, where costs were always payable at the end of a matter. This is, for the losing party of any hearing, 'pay as you go' litigation.

This rule will have a significant effect on debt actions, especially where there is a defendant whose only purpose is to delay payment for as long as possible. If a defendant does not keep to the court's timetable and it is necessary for the claimant to make an application to court to enforce the timetable, the defendant will have to pay the costs incurred immediately. These could be several hundred pounds.

This rule emphasises the need for the claimant to ensure that any time set by the court for completing any action must be complied with. If one party has to make an application to court then there is likely to be an immediate costs order against the defaulting party.

To enable the court to make a summary assessment at the end of the hearing any party who intends to claim costs against the other side must prepare a written statement of the costs he intends to claim in the form of a schedule showing:

- the number of hours to be claimed;

- the hourly rate to be claimed;

- the grade of fee earner;

- any disbursements, counsels fees etc; and

- any VAT.

This needs to be sent to the other side at least 24 hours before the hearing and must be lodged at court.

Figure 1.00 shows an example of a model form to record a statement of costs. It is not mandatory to use this form but it does give an idea of what should be included.

If a detailed assessment of costs is received from one party it is a good idea for the other party to fax them with their objections. The parties are under an obligation to try and narrow the issues on costs as well as any other issue.

Figure 1.00 – A model form as provided by the Civil Procedure Rules

Schedule of costs form

Court _____

Judge/Master _____   Case Reference _____

Case Title _____

[Party]'s Statement of costs for the hearing on [date]

Description of fee earner

(1)   [name]   [grade]   [hourly rate claimed]

(2)   [name]   [grade]   [hourly rate claimed]

Attendances on [Party]

[number] hours at £_____   £_____

Attendances on opponents

[number] hours at £_____   £_____

Attendances on others

(1)   [number]   hours at £_____   £_____

(2)   [number]   hours at £_____   £_____

Work done on documents

[number] hours at £_____   £_____

Attendance at hearing

[number] hours at £_____   £_____

[number] hours travel and waiting at £_____   £_____

Counsel's fees [name] [year of call]

Fee for [advice/conference/documents]   £_____

Fee for hearing   £_____

Other expenses

[court fees]   £_____

Others [give brief description]   £_____

Total

Amount of VAT
claimed

     On solicitor's and counsel's fees   £_____

     On other expenses   £_____

Grand Total   £_____

The costs estimated above do not exceed the costs which [the party] is liable to pay in respect of the work which this estimate covers.

Dated_____	Signed
	Name of firm of solicitors
	[partner] for the [party]

Detailed assessment of costs   B8.9

If the hearing lasts longer than a day, usually in multi-track actions, or the court has some good reason why summary assessment of costs is not appropriate, the court may order a 'detailed assessment' of costs. This is a more complex procedure where a claiming party sets out a detailed bill and the paying party has to respond with detailed objections. The proper officer of the court will then make a final determination.

Even where detailed assessment of costs is appropriate the court may order a proportion of the costs to be paid immediately.

Litigants in person   B8.10

A litigant in person (a person acting without a legal representative) can claim costs when they have been successful. When a litigant can prove financial loss, the amount that he can prove he has lost for the time reasonably spent doing the work can be claimed. Where the litigant cannot prove financial loss he can still claim costs at a lower rate. In any event the costs ordered must not exceed two thirds of the amount that would have been allowed if the litigant in person had a legal representative. The definition of litigant in person includes a company or corporation which is acting without a legal representative but would also include a solicitor or barrister acting on his own behalf.

An in-house solicitor acting for a company should be able to recover costs in the normal way, as they will be deemed to be the legal representative of the company.

The litigant in person cannot, of course, claim costs on a small claims track case as no costs, apart from the fixed costs of issue, can be claimed when a matter has been allocated to the small claims track.

The basis of assessment   B8.11

Where a party is to pay another party's costs it will normally be assessed on the 'standard basis'. This means that the court will allow the costs which are proportionate to the matters in issue. If there is any doubt as to whether the costs were reasonably incurred or reasonable and proportionate, the matter will be resolved in favour of the paying party.

In certain cases, particularly where there has been misconduct, the court will order costs on an 'indemnity basis'. When this has been ordered, the court does not have to consider whether the costs are proportionate and will resolve any doubts as to whether the costs were reasonably incurred or were reasonable in amount in favour of the receiving party.

Fixed costs

On certain occasions the *CPR 1998* specify the costs that can be obtained against the other party at a fixed rate. (See Figure 2.00 below.)

A claimant sues for a specified sum of money and is able to recover costs fixed on a sliding scale, covering the issuing and serving of the claim form but only where a solicitor has started the claim. If the defendant pays the money claimed and those costs within 14 days no other costs may be recovered.

If judgment is obtained in default, on an admission or by summary judgment there are also fixed costs. (See Figure 3.00 below.)

In an application for summary judgment the court may either assess the fixed costs, or as appropriate, may order or make a summary assessment of costs. In a simple case of a claim for a sum of money, fixed costs are likely to be ordered.

There are also a number of miscellaneous fixed costs. (See Figure 4.00 below.)

Figure 2.00 – Fixed costs

Relevant band	Where the claim form is served by the court or by any method other than personal service by the claimant	Where: • the claim form is served personally by the claimant; and • there is only one defendant	Where there is more than one defendant, for each additional defendant personally served at separate addresses by the claimant
Where the value of the claim exceeds £25 but does not exceed £500	£50	£60	£15
Where the value of the claim exceeds £500 but does not exceed £1,000	£70	£80	£15

Where the value of the claim exceeds £1,000 but does not exceed £5,000; or the only claim is for delivery of goods and no value is specified or stated on the claim form	£80	£90	£15
Where the value of the claim exceeds £5,000	£100	£110	£15

Figure 3.00 – Fixed costs when judgment is in default, on admission or by summary judgment

	Where the amount of the judgment exceeds £25 but does not exceed £5,000	Where the amount of the judgment exceeds £5,000
Where judgment in default of an acknowledgment of service is entered under *CPR 1998, rule 12.4(1)* (entry of judgment by request on claim for money only)	£22	£30
Where judgment in default of a defence is entered under *CPR 1998, rule 12.4(1)* (entry of judgment by request on a claim for money only)	£25	£35

(cont'd)

Where judgment is entered under *CPR 1998, rule 14.4* (judgment on admission), or *rule 14.5* (judgment on admission of part of claim), and the claimant accepts the defendant's proposal as to the manner of payment	£40	£55
Where judgment is entered under *CPR 1998, rule 14.4* (judgment on admission, or *rule 14.5* (judgment on admission on part of claim) and court decides the date or times of payment	£55	£70
Where summary judgment is given under *CPR 1998, Part 24* or the court strikes out a defence under *rule 3.4(2)(a)*, in either case, on application by a party	£175	£210
Where judgment is given on a claim for delivery of goods under a regulated agreement within the meaning of the *Consumer Credit Act 1974* and no other entry in this table applies	£60	£85

Figure 4.00 – Miscellaneous fixed costs

For service by a party of any document required to be served personally including preparing and copying a certificate of service for each individual served.	£15

Where service by an alternative method is permitted by an order under *Rule 6.8* for each individual served.	£25
Where a document is served out of the jurisdiction:	
(*a*) in Scotland, Northern Ireland, the Isle of Man or the Channel Islands; or	£65
(*b*) in any other place.	£75

Fast track trial costs

The amount of costs that can be awarded against another party on a fast track trial is limited to the following.

Value of the claim which the court may award	Amount of fast track trial costs
Up to £3,000	£350
More than £3,000 but no more than £10,000	£500
More than £10,000	£750

These costs do not include the costs of preparing the documentation conferences, or meetings, just for the hearing itself.

The amount of the costs can be apportioned between the parties. For instance, if both parties succeeded in part, or the claimant has succeeded on the claim and the defendant has succeeded on a counterclaim the court will apportion the costs.

Where the court feels that the proceeding party has acted unreasonably it may reduce the amount of the trial costs payable.

These rules do not alter the costs that can be charged by a party's own advocate but merely govern the position where one party is able to pay the costs of another party.

B9

Enforcement of a Judgment

Introduction   B9.1

Although some defendants will satisfy a judgment by paying the amount that is ordered, the judgment of the court will not itself automatically force a debtor to pay. A judgment is an order that the money is owed. Action needs to be taken to enforce the judgment. For any of the enforcement procedures to take place judgment must first be obtained.

Each method of enforcement involves an application to the court and the payment of a court fee. The question of enforcement is at present being reviewed by the Lord Chancellor.

Methods of enforcement   B9.2

The current methods of enforcing a judgment are as detailed at **B9.3–B9.10** below.

Execution   B9.3

This is an instruction to the County Court Bailiff or the High Court Enforcement Officer ('HCEO', formerly known as the Sheriff) to visit the debtor and to either obtain payment or seize the debtor's goods. The HCEO will seize goods that he estimates will achieve the value of the outstanding debt at a public auction.

The County Court Bailiff is instructed by issuing form N323 (see **APPENDIX B9.1**).

On any debt over £600 the action can be transferred to the High Court for the HCEO to be instructed. This is done by obtaining a certificate of judgment from the county court office and lodging this, with a writ of fifa, at the local District Registry of the High Court. Debts over £5,000 *must* be enforced by the HCEO.

Many people prefer to instruct the HCEO rather than the County Court Bailiff and feel he is more effective. The HCEO has an incentive, for if there is a successful recovery the debtor has to pay the HCEO's 'poundage'. This is a fee that goes to the HCEO and is calculated on a percentage of the debt.

At the first visit the Bailiff or HCEO will not seize the debtor's goods even if the debtor has not paid. The debtor is usually given time to pay and then the Bailiff or HCEO makes an inventory of the debtor's goods and takes 'walking possession' of them. The debtor is not meant to dispose of those goods.

If payment is still not forthcoming, the goods will then be removed and sold by public auction unless the court orders otherwise. The amount obtained at a public auction is often substantially less than the true value of the goods. Goods will only be removed if the value of the goods is sufficient to cover the cost of removal and the cost of sale.

Execution on a debtor's property is the most commonly used method of enforcement of a debt. It is sometimes very effective especially where the debtor has a large amount of goods which are easily accessible. For instance in the case of a debtor with wholesale premises, execution is likely to be effective.

However, there are limits to the effectiveness of this procedure and it may not be appropriate in every case. For example, if the debtor has no assets and there is nothing to seize or the judgment is against a limited company which has nothing more than an office, the execution will be an inadequate enforcement tool.

If goods are hired or on lease, they belong to the hirers or leasing company and therefore do not belong to the debtor, and the HCEO may be unable to seize them. Neither the Bailiff nor the HCEO can break into residential premises.

Even when goods are seized they may be the subject of a claim by a third party. When this happens the claim can either be accepted or the matter will be set down for the court to determine who owns the goods. This is known as 'inter pleader proceedings'. The danger of these proceedings is that the claimant will be responsible initially for the HCEO's solicitor's costs and, if he loses, for the HCEO's costs, the HCEO's solicitor's costs and the third parties' legal costs.

High Court Enforcement Officers Regulations 2004   B9.4

Following implementation of the *High Court Enforcement Officers Regulations 2004* (*SI 2004/400*), Sheriff's Officers were renamed High Court Enforcement Officers.

Effectively, the old system of Sheriffs being assigned to a 'county' was abolished, and a High Court Enforcement Officer can ask the Lord Chancellor's Department to assign him to a district or a number of districts.

Most Sheriff's Officers are now High Court Enforcement Officers.

However, provided certain conditions can be satisfied, individuals can apply to the Lord Chancellor's Department to hold the position of a High Court Enforcement Officer. The conditions to be satisfied are that the individual must not:

- have been convicted of a criminal offence for which he received a custodial sentence; or

- have been involved in dishonesty or violence;

- be liable for any unpaid fines;

- be liable for any court judgments granted within the last six years which remain unsatisfied;

- be an undischarged bankrupt;

- have been disqualified from acting as a director of a company within the last six years; or

- have been involved in any business relating to or including the purchase or sale of debts.

The applicant must confirm the application in writing and also needs to state to which district(s) he would like to be assigned.

Once an individual is assigned to a district as a High Court Enforcement Officer he is then able to enforce writs and holds the powers previously held by a Sheriff.

It is anticipated that a directory will be published listing the High Court Enforcement Officers and the areas to which they are assigned. At the time of going to press this directory is not available.

Third party debt orders   B9.5

A third party debt order is an order for money that is owed to the debtor to be paid directly to the claimant. It used to be known as a garnishee order. It is often used where it is known that the debtor has a bank account and that account is in credit. In effect, the bank owes money to the debtor and an order can be obtained so that the bank pays the amount in credit directly to the claimant. When a bank account is overdrawn there is no money owed by the bank to the debtor but the debtor owes money to the bank and, therefore, a third party debt order cannot be obtained even if the debtor has an overdraft facility. A 'bank' includes any bank or building society which is a deposit-taking institution. It is somewhat of a gamble as to whether there is any money in the account.

A third party debt order is not limited to bank accounts. If anybody owes money to the debtor then an order can be obtained. It is often the case that the debtor will tell you that they are owed a large sum of money from another company and this is why the debt has not been paid. Sometimes the claimant may be aware that the debtor has completed a substantial contract and payment for this is still owed.

To obtain a third party debt order an application must be made in the required form (N349) together with a court fee and evidence verified by a statement of truth explaining why the claimant thinks the monies are owed to the debtor and that there is an outstanding judgment in favour of the claimant.

The application will initially be dealt with without the debtor and the third party being informed and without a formal hearing. If the judge is satisfied after reading the claimant's evidence that there are sufficient grounds for making an order, he will make an interim third party debt order. This fixes a hearing for the court to consider whether to make a final third party debt order and will direct that until the next hearing the third party must not make any payment which reduces the amount he owes to the defendant to less than the amount of the judgment obtained against the defendant.

The hearing for the final third party debt order will take place within 28 days after the interim order and notice of the hearing is served on both the third party and the debtor.

A bank or building society served with an interim third party debt order must carry out a search to identify all accounts held by the debtor. It must also disclose to the court and to the claimant within seven days of being served the number of the account, whether the account is in credit and, if the account is in credit, whether the balance is sufficient to cover the amount specified in the order. Alternatively, the bank may specify within seven days that it does not hold an account for the debtor or is unable to comply for some other reason.

A third party other than a bank or building society must, within seven days of being served with an interim third party debt order, notify the court and the claimant whether or not he owes any money to the debtor or has less than the amount specified in the order.

The effect of a third party debt order against a bank account will be that the account is frozen on making the interim order. A debtor who is an individual may apply for a hardship payment order if he is prevented from withdrawing money from his account and he is suffering hardship in meeting ordinary living expenses as a result. If granted the court will make an order letting the bank or building society make a payment out of the account to allow the debtor to, for example, pay the mortgage or rent and buy food for himself or his family.

At the final hearing all parties may attend but the debtor or third party must file evidence in writing if they object to the order being made. The effect of the final order will be that the third party is ordered to pay the monies owed to the claimant.

Charging orders B9.6

A charging order is similar to a mortgage imposed on the property by the court. It usually applies to land or buildings, but it can apply to other things such as shares. An application is made to court and a charge to the value of the debt is placed on the property. The charge is registered at the Land Registry and any purchaser of this property will ensure that the charge is discharged.

An application on form N379 must be supported by evidence giving details, amongst other things, of the judgment, the assets to be charged and confirming the debtor's ownership.

Again the application is in two stages. The first stage is the interim order which is made without the debtor knowing. At the final hearing all parties can attend.

Prior charges   B9.7

The charging order will only be effective provided there is sufficient equity in the property. On the sale of the property, charges on that property are paid off in order of priority, with the first creditor on the register paid in full then the second and so on.

If there are prior charges that are for more money than the property is worth there is little value in applying for a charging order.

The charging order does not secure immediate payment. Once the charge is registered, payment will only take place when the property is sold and if there is sufficient equity. However, an application can be made for the property to be sold if the debt is not repaid. These are entirely separate proceedings with a different case number and with new court fees to be paid. Whether the property is sold is at the discretion of the court.

A charging order is often more effective against an individual than a limited company. The psychological effect of the threat of losing a property, perhaps their own home, is persuasive on an individual. Very often, a limited company has taken out a fixed and floating charge with the bank on all its assets, and the charge of the bank will rank in priority to any charge put on after it.

Land Registry search   B9.8

A Land Registry search may be made against the address of the property to find out the owner of the land provided the land is registered. Unfortunately there is no facility to search against the name of the debtor to find out what properties are owned by him. Office copy entries of the register (i.e. an official copy of the Land Register) at the Land Registry will also reveal the charges on the property and when they were registered. Unfortunately this does not show how much the charges are for. If there was a recent transfer of the property the purchase price will also be shown.

If there is one prior charge and it was taken out many years ago when the property was bought it is likely that there will be equity in the property. On the other hand, if there are a number of prior charges taken out fairly recently there may be no equity at all.

Attachment of Earnings Order   B9.9

An Attachment of Earnings Order is an order where the debtor's employer deducts a specific weekly or monthly sum from the debtor's wages or salary. That sum is then paid to the claimant. An application for an attachment of earnings is simply made by filling out a form N337 (see **APPENDIX B9.2**) and paying the fee.

A court will first fix a minimum figure which it feels the debtor needs, having regard to his commitments. The court will then determine the amount that will be deducted from the balance.

The advantage of this order is that whilst the debtor remains in employment the debt will be repaid automatically. The disadvantage of such an order is that it may take a long time for the debt to be repaid. The amount of the weekly or monthly payments is often small and it is difficult to administer payments over a long period of time.

To some extent an application for an Attachment of Earnings Order is useful as a last resort if there is no immediate prospect of any other enforcement being successful.

An application for an Attachment of Earnings Order is only applicable if the debtor is in employment. It will not work if the debtor is self-employed or is unemployed.

Order to obtain information from
judgment debtors   B9.10

An order to obtain information from a judgment debtor is not strictly an enforcement procedure but it does allow the court to examine a debtor under oath as to his income outgoings and means. It was formerly called an oral examination. It also allows the claimant or his solicitors to put questions to the debtor to establish his true means. It is especially useful if it is either suspected that the debtor has no monies at all, and therefore any enforcement procedure would be useless, or if it is suspected that the debtor has assets but that he is hiding them.

The court, if requested, will use a standard questionnaire and an officer of the court will conduct the examination without anyone representing the claimant attending. This is the best procedure if it is suspected that there are no assets available.

An order to obtain information from judgment debtors is meant to be a vigorous examination of the debtor's financial means. The debtor can be required to bring along documentation such as bank statements, credit card statements, etc.

If the debtor is a company an order can be made requiring an officer of the company to attend court.

An application for an order to obtain information from a judgment debtor must be issued at the court which made the judgment and must be in the prescribed form. The order must be personally served on the person ordered to attend not less than 14 days before the hearing and the person ordered to attend must be offered a reasonable sum to cover his travel expenses to and from court. The court will not serve the order and the claimant will need to arrange for service.

Failure to attend by the debtor is a contempt of court. The court will fix a new hearing and the order will state: 'You must obey this order. If you do not you may be sent to prison for contempt of court.'

Needless to say a debtor served with such an order usually does attend. If he does not a warrant may be issued for his arrest.

Court fees   B9.11

The following court fees currently apply to enforcement judgments.

Warrant of execution for a debt below £125.00	£30.00
Warrant of execution for a debt over £125.00	£50.00
Re-issue warrant	£20.00
Order to obtain information	£40.00
Third party debt & charging order	£50.00
Attachment of Earnings Order	£60.00

Appendix B9

Appendix B9.1 – Request for Warrant of Execution N323

Request for Warrant of Execution

to be completed and signed by the claimant or his solicitor and sent to the court with the appropriate fee

1 Claimant's name and address

In the

County Court

2 Name and address for service and payment *(if different from above)* Ref/Tel No.

Warrant no.

Issue date:

Warrant applied for at   o'clock

Foreign court code/name:

3 Defendant's name and address

4 Warrant details

(A) Balance due at date of this request		
(B) Amount for which warrant to issue		
Issue fee		
Solicitor's costs		
Land registry fee		
TOTAL		

I certify that the whole or part of any instalments due under the judgment or order have not been paid and the balance now due is as shown

Signed

Claimant (Claimant's solicitor)

Dated

IMPORTANT
You must inform the court immediately of any payments you receive after you have sent this request to the court

If the amount of the warrant at (B) is less than the balance at (A), the sum due after the warrant is paid will be

You should provide a contact number so that the bailiff can speak to you if he/she needs to:

Daytime phone number: Evening phone number (if possible):

Contact name (where appropriate):

Defendant's phone number (if known):

If you have any other information which may help the bailiff or if you have reason to believe that the bailiff may encounter any difficulties you should write it below.

N323 -w3- Request for warrant of execution (4.99)   ©*Crown copyright. Published by* everyform

533

Appendix B9.2 – Request for Attachment of Earnings Order N337

Request for Attachment of Earnings Order

to be completed and signed by the claimant or his solicitor and sent to the court with the appropriate fee

1 Claimant's name and address

In the

County Court

Claim Number

2 Name and address for service and payment *(if different from above)* Ref/Tel No.

For court use only

A/E application no.

Issue date:

Hearing date:

3 Defendant's name and address

on

at   o'clock

at (address)

4 Judgment details

Court where judgment/order made if not court of issue

I apply for an attachment of earnings order

5 Outstanding debt

Balance due at date of request*
(excluding issue fee but including unsatisfied warrant costs)

I certify that the whole or part of any instalments due under the judgment or order have not been paid and the balance now due is as shown

* you may also be entitled to interest to the date of request where judgment is for £5,000 or more, or is in respect of a debt which attracts contractual or statutory interest for late payment

Issue fee

AMOUNT NOW DUE

Signed

Claimant(Claimants solicitor)

(please give as much information as you can - it will help the court to make an order more quickly)

6 Employment Details

Date

Employer's name and address

7 Other details

(Give any other details about the defendant's circumstances which may be relevant to the application)

Defendant's place of work *(if different from employer's address)*

The defendant is employed as

Works No / Pay Ref

IMPORTANT
You must inform the court immediately of any payments you receive after you have sent this request to the court

N337 - w3 Request for attachment of earnings order (4.99)

©Crown copyright. Published by everyform

Reproduced for illustrative purposes only by kind permission of The Solicitors' Law Stationery Society Ltd.

B10

Insolvency

What is insolvency? B10.1

Insolvency is defined on the following two bases under *section 123* of the *Insolvency Act 1986 (IA 1986)*.

- *Cash flow test* whereby a company is deemed unable to pay its debts if:

  (i)   a creditor to whom the company is indebted in a sum exceeding £750 then due has served a statutory demand on the company and the company has for three weeks thereafter neglected to pay the sum or secure the debt to the reasonable satisfaction of the creditor (*IA 1986, s 123(1)(a)*); or

  (ii) execution is returned unsatisfied (*IA 1986, s 123(1)(b)*); or

  (iii) it is proved to the satisfaction of the court that the company is unable to pay its debts as they fall due (*IA 1986, s 123(1)(e)*).

- *Balance sheet test* whereby a company is also deemed unable to pay its debts if it is proved to the satisfaction of the court that the value of the company's assets is less than the amount of its liabilities, taking into account its contingent and prospective liabilities (*IA 1986, s 123(2)*).

An individual is deemed unable to pay their debts if either point (i) or point (ii) of the cash flow test can be satisfied. However, point (iii) of the cash flow test and the balance sheet test do not apply to individuals (*IA 1986, s 268*).

Different forms of insolvency B10.2

When considering whether to instigate insolvency proceedings or if faced with the insolvency of a customer, consideration should be given to the different forms of insolvency. It should be noted that different rules apply to each type of insolvency and that certain insolvency procedures can run concurrently.

The first consideration is whether the customer is a corporate entity or an individual.

Corporate insolvencies B10.3

There are several types of corporate insolvency and these are discussed below.

Liquidation – voluntary B10.4

The purpose of a liquidation is to distribute a company's assets and then terminate the company's existence. A voluntary liquidation can be in respect of either an insolvent company (creditors' voluntary liquidation (CVL)), or a solvent company (members' voluntary liquidation (MVL)). In voluntary liquidations, the effective date of the liquidation is the date that the winding-up resolution is passed.

The directors instigate the CVL procedure by:

● summoning an extraordinary general meeting of the members of the company in order to pass an extraordinary resolution (the winding-up resolution) to the effect that the company cannot continue its business by reason of its liabilities; and

● placing the company into liquidation.

At the members' meeting, the members appoint a liquidator. It is a requirement that a creditors' meeting is convened no later than the fourteenth day after the passing of the resolution to wind up the company. At this meeting, the creditors decide whether to ratify the members' choice of liquidator or to reject the members' choice and appoint a different liquidator. In all cases, the liquidator must be a licensed insolvency practitioner, independent of the directors of the company and the company itself and must consent to act as liquidator. It is the usual circumstance that the members' and creditors' meetings are held on the same day.

The outcome of this type of insolvency is that there will usually be insufficient money available to pay all creditors in full, and part or all of the debt will need to be written off by the creditor.

In an MVL the directors have an obligation to swear a declaration of solvency stating that they have made a full enquiry into the company's affairs and that all creditors will be paid in full together with statutory interest within twelve months from the commencement of the liquidation. The company is placed into liquidation by the passing of a special resolution to wind up the company. The liquidator is appointed at a meeting of members only. No meeting of creditors is held.

The outcome of this type of proceeding is that all creditors will be paid in full and will be entitled to receive interest at the higher of the contractual rate or the statutory rate between the date of liquidation and the date of payment. Creditors should consider the impact of the *Late Payment of Commercial Debts* (*Interest*) *Act 1998*, the effects of which are mentioned earlier in this text. (See **A5.9** and **A14.34** above.)

If the liquidation extends beyond the twelve-month period and creditors have not been paid, the liquidator must convert the MVL into a CVL and call a meeting of creditors. The liquidator will then have an obligation to use his investigative powers regarding the directors' actions.

Liquidation – compulsory B10.5

This type of liquidation is the result of a petition to the court. Such a petition can be presented by persons specified in *IA 1986, s 124* and these include:

- a creditor;
- a member; or
- the directors.

The petition is usually in respect of the company's inability to pay its debts. Once the petition is presented the court will set a date for a hearing and will decide at that hearing whether a winding-up order should be made.

If a winding-up order is made, the date of the liquidation is backdated to the date of the presentation of the petition. However, the relevant date for claims to be submitted is the date of the winding-up order. Under usual circumstances the Official Receiver is appointed as liquidator of the company's affairs and the Official Receiver will decide within twelve weeks whether to call a meeting of creditors so that the creditors may appoint an alternative liquidator. Otherwise the Official Receiver may request the Secretary of State to make a direct appointment of an alternative.

It is very unusual for a company to continue to trade once it is placed into liquidation. However, it is possible in limited circumstances.

Administrative receivership B10.6

This type of insolvency arises on the appointment of an administrative receiver by a creditor enforcing security given to them by the company, where the security was created to include a floating charge. The power to appoint an administrative receiver derives from the terms of the creditor's security documentation. It is the usual circumstance that the creditor who holds the security is the company's bank or finance provider.

The appointment can take place with very little notice to the company. The creditor usually has to give the company a demand for repayment of the sum owed. The other creditors are not notified until after the appointment of the receiver has taken place and do not have any say in who the receiver should be. This decision rests with the enforcing creditor.

It is probable that ordinary creditors will not receive full payment of their debt and will only be entitled to receive dividends if and when a liquidator is appointed. The administrative receiver has no power to deal with the claims of unsecured creditors. However, the receiver, acting as agent of the company, does have the power to continue to trade the company's business and to sell the business as a going concern. When trading the company's business the receiver can order goods from suppliers and continue the employment of staff under existing contracts with the company. Any goods ordered or wages earned after the date of the receiver's appointment have to be paid for out of the receivership funds.

Administrative receivership is being phased out. Other than in very rare situations, appointments are not possible where the creditor's security was created on or after 15 September 2003.

Administration

An administrator may be appointed by the company itself or by its directors, by the holder of a floating charge, or by the court on the petition of the company or its directors, or of a creditor.

If the company wishes to appoint an administrator, it must first give notice to the holder of a floating charge who may pre-empt the company's appointment with an administrator of his own choosing. If the administrator is appointed by the company and there is no holder of a floating charge, then the administrator may be replaced by another insolvency practitioner at a creditors' meeting.

The administrator will manage the company in pursuit of one of the following objectives:

- rescuing the company as a going concern;

- achieving a better result for the company's creditors than would be likely if the company were wound up;

- realising property to make a distribution to one or more secured or preferential creditors.

The administrator has discretion as to which of the first two possible objectives to choose, but can only fall back on the third objective if neither of the first two is possible. The third objective is the means by which the charge holder can enforce his security where there is no other way forward.

Within eight weeks after his appointment, the administrator must report to creditors and within ten weeks hold a meeting of creditors to consider his proposals for achieving the objective of the administration. This does not apply, however, where the administrator is satisfied that the creditors will all be paid in full, or where there will be no money for the unsecured creditors other than from the prescribed part carved out from assets subject to a floating charge (see **B10.18** below).

An administration expires after one year, unless extended by the court, or with the consent of the creditors. The creditors can give such consent once only and for a maximum of six months.

The administrator is empowered to pay secured and preferential creditors, but if there is to be a distribution to unsecured creditors, then, unless the company is rescued and returned to the control of its directors, or unless the court authorises the administrator to make the distribution himself, a liquidation may be required.

Company voluntary arrangement (CVA)   **B10.8**

As an alternative to losing control of the company, as occurs in other insolvency procedures, the directors may decide to try and reach an agreement with the creditors, such that the creditors will accept less than 100 pence in the pound and the company may continue to trade and to make stage payments to its creditors. This would come in the form of a proposal made to the creditors to which the creditors of the company would need to agree. A CVA may also be proposed by a company's liquidator or administrator. If the directors propose a CVA the insolvency practitioner, known as the nominee, will report as to the efficacy of the proposal and will recommend whether meetings of creditors and members should be convened.

The company may obtain temporary protection from its creditors by means of a statutory moratorium. To do this, the directors have to file the necessary papers in court, whereupon the moratorium will automatically take effect. These papers include the proposal and a statement from the nominee that there is a reasonable prospect of the proposal being approved and its terms being successfully implemented. However, this procedure is not open to all companies and specific rules apply (see **B10.9** below).

In a CVA, the creditors' meeting is held prior to the members' meeting. The proposal is approved if in excess of 75% in value of the creditors who attend vote in favour of it. Nevertheless, the proposal will fail to be approved if more than 50% in value of creditors who are not connected to the company vote against it. Those creditors that are connected to the company would include directors or their families or associated companies. At the meeting of members, the approval of the arrangement is by a simple majority of the members in accordance with the Articles of Association of the company. It is possible for the creditors to make modifications to the proposal at their meeting and the meetings may be adjourned for up to fourteen days for this purpose, or for up to two months if a moratorium is in place (see **B10.9** below).

The wishes of creditors prevail where they conflict with the resolutions, if any, passed at the meeting of members.

Once the proposal is approved, all creditors and members, whether they attended the meetings or not, are bound by the terms of the proposal and must accept the reduced payment level. The insolvency practitioner is then known as the supervisor of the arrangement. Suppliers may wish to consider carefully whether to extend further credit as the company's continued trading is under the control of the directors rather than the supervisor.

Moratorium   **B10.9**

Small companies may enter into a moratorium to provide protection prior to a meeting of creditors called to consider a proposal for a voluntary arrangement.

The initial moratorium lasts for 28 days to enable the company to put a rescue plan to its creditors. It is then possible to extend the 28-day period by a further two months with the agreement of creditors.

The definition of a small company is incorporated in *section 247* of the *Companies Act 1985*. This defines small companies as meeting two or more of the following requirements:

- turnover not exceeding £5.6 million;

- balance sheet total (i.e. assets) of not more than £2.8 million;

- not more than 50 employees.

Under a moratorium the directors of the company remain in control. However, an insolvency practitioner nominee monitors the company's affairs. The nominee initially is required to certify that the plan has a reasonable prospect of being implemented and that the company has sufficient funds available during the moratorium to carry on its business. The nominee's monitoring role is not fully defined, but he or she is required to withdraw consent if there ceases to be a reasonable prospect of implementation or if the company no longer has sufficient funds.

The effect of the moratorium is that creditors cannot take enforcement action against the company. This extends to holders of floating charges not appointing administrative receivers or administrators. Disposals of assets can be made in the ordinary course of business, but assets subject to a charge can only be disposed of with the consent of the chargeholder.

Individual insolvencies B10.10

There are two types of individual insolvencies and these are discussed below.

Bankruptcy B10.11

An individual, commonly known as the debtor, is made bankrupt by the presentation of a petition to the court by one or more creditors, the debtor or the supervisor of the debtor's voluntary arrangement. For a creditor or combination of creditors to issue a petition they have to be owed a minimum of a liquidated sum in the aggregate amount of £750.

Once the petition has been heard and the court, having been satisfied of the circumstances, makes a bankruptcy order, it is usual that the Official Receiver is appointed as receiver and manager of the debtor's estate. The Official Receiver will then decide within twelve weeks whether to:

- call a meeting of creditors to appoint an insolvency practitioner to be known as the trustee in bankruptcy;

- request the Secretary of State to appoint a trustee in bankruptcy; or

- remain in office and become trustee himself.

If the debts are below the small bankruptcies level (currently £40,000) and the assets exceed the minimum amount (currently £4,000) and the debtor has not been made bankrupt or entered into a voluntary arrangement within the previous five years, the court shall not initially make a bankruptcy order but may appoint an insolvency practitioner to report on the possibility of a voluntary arrangement.

In all cases, the term of the bankruptcy begins with the date of the bankruptcy order.

The bankruptcy estate consists of the assets of the debtor and all amounts due to creditors as at the commencement of the bankruptcy. Such creditors include contingent liabilities and assets can include any interest in the debtor's home. Assets in the estate vest in the trustee personally. Accordingly, the trustee is entitled to receive any sums that the debtor would otherwise have been due. In addition to assets existing at the commencement of bankruptcy, the debtor may be obliged to give up any property that falls into their possession during the term of the bankruptcy. The trustee will also review the debtor's personal income and expenditure and will decide whether to require the debtor to pay regular monthly contributions into the bankruptcy estate from their disposable income for up to three years. Assets that do not fall into the bankruptcy estate include personal effects necessary for living, provided that they are not of excessive value, and tools and items necessary for the bankrupt's trade or employment.

If the bankrupt fails to co-operate with either the Official Receiver or the trustee, or does not disclose any assets, an application can be made to court to have the term of the bankruptcy extended by suspending the discharge.

The effect of bankruptcy on the debtor is that for the term of their bankruptcy they cannot:

- obtain credit of more than £500 without notification of their circumstances; or

- act as a director or be involved in the management of a company.

They may also be subject to restrictions from their professional body if they are an accountant, solicitor, financial adviser or other regulated professional.

The bankrupt will be discharged within a maximum of twelve months. This period may be shortened if the official receiver certifies that his investigation is complete, or that no investigation is necessary. As a counterweight to the shortened duration of bankruptcy itself, reduced with effect from 1 April 2004 from a normal term of three years, a new system of bankruptcy restrictions orders has been introduced, whereby the court may make an order against a 'culpable' bankrupt continuing the restrictions on obtaining credit or running companies for up to fifteen years.

Individual voluntary arrangement (IVA)   **B10.12**

Due to the restrictions and the stigma associated with bankruptcy, individuals sometimes choose to try to reach an agreement with their creditors in a similar way to companies in a CVA (see **B10.8** above). In these circumstances, the debtor prepares a proposal such that creditors will accept a sum which may be lower than 100 pence in the pound in full settlement of their debts. It is usual for the debtor to offer creditors a supplement to the assets otherwise available in bankruptcy in exchange for the creditors agreeing not to make the debtor bankrupt. The supplement would normally take the form of a contribution from a third party or from an increased earning capacity and therefore income contributions, through the ability to continue to use professional qualifications or directorships.

If the debtor intends to propose an IVA he may apply to the court for an interim order to protect him from bankruptcy or other proceedings that may be brought by creditors. The debtor will put his proposal to an insolvency practitioner, known as the nominee, who will report as to the efficacy of the proposal and will recommend whether a meeting of creditors should be convened.

The proposal is approved if in excess of 75% in value of the creditors who attend vote in favour of it. Nevertheless, the proposal will fail to be approved if more than 50% in value of creditors who are not associated with the debtor vote against. Those creditors that are associated would include the debtor's family or companies under the control of the debtor or their family. It is possible for the creditors, with the debtor's consent, to make modifications to the proposal at the meeting which may be adjourned for up to 14 days for this purpose. Once the proposal is accepted, all creditors, whether they attended the meeting or not, are bound by the terms of the arrangement and must accept the lower proposed payment.

Other forms of insolvency   **B10.13**

There are a few other forms of insolvency which may be encountered. It is unlikely that creditors will be involved in these as either the procedures do not require communication to creditors as a matter of course or the procedures are rarely used. These include:

- fixed charge receiverships;

- agricultural receiverships;

- partnership voluntary arrangements;

- administration of insolvent estates of deceased persons; and

- court receiverships.

Some of these possibilities are described in further detail below.

Fixed charge receivership

B10.14

A fixed charge receivership is where a creditor with security appoints a receiver, under a fixed charge only, over certain assets of the borrower. The receiver only has power and responsibility as regards the particular assets over which the receiver has been appointed (e.g. real estate, book debts or intellectual property). Such appointments are frequently referred to as *Law of Property Act 1925* (*LPA 1925*) receiverships. No communication need be sent to creditors and the receiver has no administrative control over the borrower's wider affairs.

Partnership voluntary arrangement (PVA)

B10.15

This is an adaptation of the CVA procedure (see **B10.8** above) recognising the status of a partnership. The partners themselves may or may not need to enter into insolvency proceedings depending on their own particular circumstances.

Court receivership

B10.16

The court may appoint a receiver in a protective role to safeguard assets in the context of a dispute. This may arise, for example, where the members of a partnership are in dispute with one another. A receiver may also be appointed in connection with asset recovery under the *Proceeds of Crime Act 2002*. These are not insolvency appointments as such.

The general position of the creditor and the power available to that creditor

B10.17

There are different categories of creditor within an insolvency. The *Insolvency Act 1986* determines the order of priority between the different categories for creditors to receive dividends out of the insolvent estate. With the exception of secured creditors, other creditors within the same class are entitled to receive dividends on a *pari passu* basis amongst each other until such time as they receive 100 pence in the pound.

Secured creditors

B10.18

This category consists of creditors who have some form of security over assets of the insolvent party. The most common types of security are a fixed charge or mortgage over a specific asset or, in the case of a company, a floating charge over a changing class of asset, such as stock. The secured creditor holding this type of security is usually a bank or other finance provider, although it is possible for any creditor to agree security rights. A creditor who has obtained a charging order following judgment is also a secured creditor. At creditors' meetings, secured creditors effectively only vote in respect of any unsecured portion of their claim.

Security rights give the secured creditor a prior claim over the assets concerned. However, a floating charge ranks behind the claims of preferential creditors (see **B10.19** below). In addition, where the charge was created on or after 15 September 2003, a prescribed part of the assets covered by a floating charge will be carved out and made available to the unsecured creditors. The carve out, after deduction of the claims of the preferential creditors, is 50% of the first £10,000 and 20% of the next £2,975,000, giving a maximum total carve out of £600,000.

Preferential creditors   B10.19

Certain employment claims rank preferentially. These are:

- four months' arrears of wages up to £800 per employee;

- arrears of holiday pay; and

- certain pension claims.

The following tax claims also rank preferentially where the insolvency proceedings started before 15 September 2003:

- twelve months' arrears of PAYE/NIC deductions; and

- six months' arrears of Value Added Tax.

As creditors with priority rights to assets not covered by fixed charges or mortgages, the preferential creditors will normally receive a higher return than unsecured creditors from any insolvency procedure. The preferential creditors do not possess any superior rights of voting over the unsecured creditors at any creditors' meeting. However, in voluntary arrangements, if it is proposed to alter the preferential creditors' priority status, this will require the positive approval of each preferential creditor affected.

Unsecured creditors   B10.20

This category consists of all creditors other than secured and preferential creditors and would normally represent the majority of creditors of the insolvent party. However, in a bankruptcy, the spouse of the bankrupt ranks after the unsecured creditors for dividend purposes in the order of priority.

In liquidations, bankruptcies and voluntary arrangements the appointment of the insolvency practitioner or the approval of any arrangement rests with the creditors and the extent of their votes (see **B10.4**, **B10.5**, **B10.8**, **B10.11** and **B10.12** above). In addition, there is provision in most types of insolvency for a creditors' committee to be appointed. The main purposes of that committee are to sanction certain actions of an appointed officeholder and to receive regular reports on the progress of the case.

Commercial aspects that affect the level of recovery   B10.21

Consideration should be given to the costs associated with obtaining any recovery from a debtor who is not paying. If the decision is made to pursue a debt through the courts, by means of debt collectors or even by sending out continuous statement requests, it is important to update records if the customer enters into insolvency proceedings. The continued pursuit of debts thereafter will only serve to incur unnecessary costs that will not be recovered.

If a decision is reached to initiate insolvency proceedings against a debtor there are costs involved and a deposit to be lodged in the court. The reasonable legal fees and the deposit are recoverable as a priority expense from asset realisations ahead of the claims of creditors. Despite this, consideration should be given to whether there are likely to be sufficient assets in the estate to obtain recovery. Once an insolvency has occurred, the submission of a claim usually requires only the completion of a form and the supply of copy invoices. This protects the rights of the creditor if distributions are subsequently made.

In all circumstances, the insolvency practitioner will consider the commercial aspects of any investigations that may be undertaken and of any actions that may result in the recovery of assets. Accordingly, unless the expected recovery justifies the costs involved, the insolvency practitioner will not take action.

Options available for the general creditors once insolvency is the chosen route   B10.22

If a creditor wishes to instigate insolvency proceedings against a debtor there are a number of options available. If the creditor holds security over assets of the debtor, the creditor should look to the details of their security for the options available to appoint a receiver or administrator or for other enforcement. The creditor should be careful to comply with any preliminary procedural steps required under the terms of the security. If no security is held, the option available would be to issue a petition in the relevant court for the winding up or administration of a company or the bankruptcy of an individual. In order to issue a petition, the creditor must be able to show that the debtor is unable to pay its debts as defined earlier in this chapter (see **B10.1** above).

The procedure required to commence court action and the costs involved   B10.23

In order to prove the debtor's inability to pay its debts, it is usually necessary to issue a statutory demand on the debtor requiring payment of an undisputed debt within 21 days of issue. This statutory demand must be served on an individual personally or at a company's registered office by hand or by post.

Statutory demands   B10.24

Although not intended as a method of collecting debts, the service of a statutory demand may produce payment when other normal methods of collection have failed. They must, however, be used with care. A statutory demand should not be used where the debt is disputed. Even where no dispute has been notified to the creditor, the debtor may obtain an injunction restraining presentation of the winding-up petition or, if an individual, obtain an order for the setting aside of the demand on the grounds that the debt is disputed. In this event, the costs of the debtor in obtaining the injunction or order will be awarded against the creditor. The demand has to be on the prescribed form dependent on the particular circumstances and these may be obtained from law stationery suppliers.

Statutory demands are a last resort. They are no substitute for effective and timely credit control. They are also not conducive to on-going trading relationships. It is found in practice that the receipt of statutory demands does speed up payment if the debtor only pays those who shout the loudest. It is inadvisable to use a statutory demand if there is no intention of following it up with a petition.

The other methods of proving the debtor's inability to pay are set out earlier in this chapter (see **B10.1** above).

Form and service of petition   B10.25

Once the debtor's inability to pay can be proved, the creditor may issue a petition. The petition has to be on one of a few standard forms dependent on the grounds on which it is based. Except where the petition is issued by a Minister of the Crown, a government department, or in the London insolvency district, for an individual, a petition is generally presented in the County Court for the insolvency district in which the debtor has lived or carried on business for the longest period in the six months prior to the presentation of the petition. In the event of a conflict, the business location prevails. For a company, the petition is presented in the County Court of the district in which the company's registered office is situated.

On the presentation of a petition, the petitioning creditor has to pay a modest court fee and present a receipt for the deposit payable (currently £370 for an individual debtor and £620 for a company debtor). Two copies of the petition are required and are sealed by the court. The court will endorse the petition, seal the copies and then fix a date, time and place for the hearing. One of those copies should be served on the debtor at least 14 days before the hearing date. The court will send a notice of the petition to the Chief Land Registrar in respect of an individual debtor.

It is the normal circumstance for the court proceedings to be issued by solicitors for the creditor. The solicitors' costs can vary considerably and quotes should be obtained prior to issuing instructions. An indication of costs is £1,000–£2,000.

The making of the order   B10.26

If the court is satisfied that the statement made on the petition is true, it may make a bankruptcy or winding-up order. The individual is then bankrupt or the company is then in liquidation. The order contains the date of the petition, the date of the order and, for an individual, the instruction to the bankrupt to attend upon the Official Receiver at a stated place.

The court must give copies of the order to the Official Receiver, one of which must be sent to the bankrupt or the company in liquidation. In the case of a company, the Official Receiver also sends a copy to the Registrar of Companies. The Official Receiver arranges for advertisement of the order in the *London Gazette* and a newspaper and, for an individual, gives notice to the Chief Land Registrar.

Following his appointment, the Official Receiver will consider whether to call a meeting of creditors so that an insolvency practitioner may be voted in to act as trustee or liquidator. In any event, the Official Receiver will write to all creditors notifying them of the bankruptcy of the individual or liquidation of the company, and of his decision whether to call a meeting of creditors. The decision to call a meeting of creditors is usually based on whether there are sufficient assets in the estate such that creditors may have an interest in how the estate is managed. If no meeting is called the Official Receiver will decide whether to request the Secretary of State to make a direct appointment of an insolvency practitioner to act as trustee or liquidator. If neither of these events occur, the responsibility for dealing with the estate remains with the Official Receiver.

The duty of the insolvency practitioner to communicate to creditors   B10.27

Dependent upon the type of insolvency, following his appointment, the insolvency practitioner has a different legal obligation to communicate his appointment and keep creditors informed of the progress of each case.

Voluntary liquidations   B10.28

Initially the liquidator must inform members and creditors of his appointment within 28 days. At this stage, the liquidator will forward a claim form to creditors requesting details of the amounts owed by the company. Thereafter, the liquidator only has a responsibility to write to members and creditors every year, within three months after each anniversary of his appointment. At this stage, the liquidator must also convene meetings of the members and creditors to provide them with an update on the liquidation. This update usually mirrors the report already sent. However, it does give a creditor an opportunity to ask questions of the liquidator.

Once the liquidation is complete, the liquidator must send a final report to members and creditors detailing how the liquidation has been conducted and convene final meetings of members and creditors.

Compulsory liquidation   B10.29

If appointed at the meeting of creditors convened by the Official Receiver, the liquidator only has an obligation to advertise his appointment and does not have to write to creditors. However, the liquidator may choose to write to creditors according to the circumstances of each case. If appointed by the Secretary of State, the liquidator must write to all creditors notifying them of his appointment unless instructed otherwise by the court.

In contrast to a voluntary liquidation, there is no requirement for annual reports and meetings. The liquidator will, however, send a final report to the creditors and convene a final meeting of creditors when the liquidation is complete.

Administrative receivership   B10.30

The receiver must notify creditors within 28 days after his appointment. Thereafter, the receiver only has an obligation to provide a report on the conduct of the receivership and convene a meeting of creditors within three months after his appointment. There is no other obligation for a receiver to write to creditors.

Administration   B10.31

The administrator must notify creditors of his appointment as soon as is reasonably practicable. Within ten weeks he must hold a creditors' meeting convened with not less than fourteen days' notice and must subsequently notify creditors of the outcome. The purpose of the meeting is to consider the administrator's statement of proposals, which will include a report of progress to date. Alternatively the business of the meeting can be conducted by post. A meeting need not be held (and neither is a postal vote required) where the administrator is satisfied that the creditors will all be paid in full, or where there will be no money for the unsecured creditors other than from the prescribed part carved out from assets subject to a floating charge (see **B10.18** above). The administrator must send creditors a progress report within one month after the end of each period of six months measured from the date of his appointment and after he ceases to act.

Company voluntary arrangement (CVA)   B10.32

The chairman of the creditors' and members' meetings (i.e. the nominee or his representative) must submit a report to court on the outcome of the meetings within four days after the meetings have taken place. Immediately thereafter, the chairman shall write to all creditors notifying them of the outcome. The supervisor must provide a progress report to all creditors and members within two months after every anniversary of the approval of the arrangement. He must also provide a final report when the CVA is completed.

Bankruptcy B10.33

If appointed at the meeting of creditors convened by the Official Receiver, the trustee only has an obligation to advertise his appointment and not to write to creditors. The trustee may choose to write to creditors according to the circumstances of each case. If appointed by the Secretary of State, the trustee must write to all creditors notifying them of his appointment unless instructed otherwise by the court. There is no further obligation to write to creditors until the bankruptcy is complete. At this time, the trustee must write to creditors providing a report on how the bankruptcy has been conducted and summon a final meeting of creditors.

Individual voluntary arrangement (IVA) B10.34

The chairman of the creditors' meeting (i.e. the nominee or his representative) must submit a report to court on the outcome of the meeting within four days after the meeting has taken place. Immediately thereafter, the chairman shall write to all creditors notifying them of the outcome. The supervisor must provide a progress report to all creditors within two months after every anniversary of the approval of the arrangement. He must also provide a final report when the IVA is completed.

What happens next? B10.35

The insolvency practitioner, dependent on the particular role, has a number of different obligations and duties as set out in statute.

Voluntary liquidations B10.36

It is the liquidator's role to take possession and control of all of the company's assets and to agree the amounts due to the company's creditors. The liquidator must then distribute the proceeds of sale of the assets to the creditors in the correct order of priority. The liquidator should establish whether any rights of action to recover assets into the estate may exist under *IA 1986* in relation to such matters as preferences (i.e. putting a creditor in a better position, usually by paying them in priority to other creditors), transactions at undervalue (i.e. selling or gifting assets of the company at a value lower than their worth) and wrongful trading (i.e. trading with knowledge of insolvency).

The liquidator's powers are set out in *IA 1986, Sch 4*, some of which are automatic by right, others requiring sanction from either the creditors or a creditors' committee.

The liquidator has a duty to investigate the conduct of the directors in the period prior to the liquidation and their willingness to cooperate with the liquidator. The liquidator must submit either an adverse report or a return on the directors' conduct to the disqualification unit of the Department of Trade and Industry giving his opinion on whether he considers that the directors are unfit to hold office. The disqualification unit will consider whether to bring proceedings for the directors to be disqualified under the *Company Directors Disqualification Act 1986* (*CDDA 1986*). Court proceedings can be avoided if a director agrees to sign a binding disqualification undertaking.

In an MVL (see **B10.4** above), as all creditors will be paid in full, there is no obligation to report on the conduct of the directors. However, if the MVL is converted into a CVL (see **B10.4** above) the obligation arises at that time.

Compulsory liquidation   B10.37

Similarly to voluntary liquidations, the liquidator must collect in and realise the company's assets and distribute the proceeds to the company's creditors. The liquidator should establish whether any rights of action may exist under *IA 1986* in relation to such matters as preferences, transactions at undervalue and wrongful trading.

The liquidators' powers are set out in *IA 1986, Sch 4*, some of which are automatic by right, others requiring the sanction of the creditors, or of the creditors' committee.

The Official Receiver has a duty to investigate the conduct of the directors and the liquidator has a duty to report to the Official Receiver any matter that may affect his investigation. The Official Receiver must submit either an adverse report or a return on the directors' conduct to the disqualification unit of the Department of Trade and Industry, giving his opinion on whether he considers that the directors are unfit to hold office. The disqualification unit will consider whether to bring proceedings for the directors to be disqualified under the *CDDA 1986*. Court proceedings can be avoided if a director agrees to sign a binding disqualification undertaking.

Administrative receivership   B10.38

The receiver's duty is to realise the company's assets and once the amounts are agreed by the receiver, make distributions to the secured creditor and the preferential creditors. The receiver's primary duty is to maximise the returns available to the secured creditor.

The receiver acts as agent of the company until a liquidator is appointed. The receiver's powers are set out in *IA 1986, Sch 1* and are given to the receiver by right. These powers may be supplemented or restricted by the terms of the debenture under which the receiver is appointed.

The receiver must submit either an adverse report or a return on the directors' conduct to the disqualification unit of the Department of Trade and Industry, giving his opinion on whether he considers that the directors are unfit to hold office. The disqualification unit will consider whether to bring proceedings for the directors to be disqualified under the *CDDA 1986*. Court proceedings can be avoided if a director agrees to sign a binding disqualification undertaking.

Administration   B10.39

The administrator's role is to seek to achieve the purpose of the administration (see **B10.7** above). He will manage the affairs, business and property of the company until a meeting of creditors is held. After that time, he will act in accordance with his proposals as approved by the creditors.

The administrator's powers and duties are set out in *IA 1986, Sch B1* and *Sch 1*.

The administrator must submit either an adverse report or a return on the directors' conduct to the disqualification unit of the Department of Trade and Industry giving his opinion on whether he considers that the directors are unfit to hold office. The disqualification unit will consider whether to bring proceedings for the directors to be disqualified under the *CDDA 1986*. Court proceedings can be avoided if a director agrees to sign a binding disqualification undertaking.

CVA   B10.40

The supervisor's powers and duties are as detailed in the proposal approved by the creditors.

Bankruptcy   B10.41

The trustee's duties include the realisation of the bankrupt's assets and the agreement of the creditors' claims. Once agreed, the trustee will distribute funds in the prescribed order of priority.

The trustee's powers are set out in *IA 1986, Sch 5*. Some of the powers are automatic by right, others require sanction from the creditors' committee.

The trustee should establish whether any rights of action may exist under *IA 1986* in relation to such matters as preference and transactions at undervalue. The trustee remains in office for as long as it takes to administer the estate, often well beyond the point at which the bankrupt receives his discharge.

IVA   B10.42

The supervisor's powers and duties are as detailed in the proposal approved by the creditors.

Director disqualification   B10.43

The present director disqualification regime was introduced by the *CDDA 1986*, which allows the court to make a disqualification order against a director of an insolvent company, whose conduct has been such as to lead the court to perceive him as unfit to hold office as a director, or to be involved with the management of a company.

To avoid the costs and delays of court proceedings, directors may give undertakings to the Secretary of State to consent to be disqualified from acting as directors (*CDDA 1986, s 1A*).

Appendix B10

Appendix B10.1 – Ready reckoner of the terms involved in insolvency

Type of insolvency	Insolvency practitioner's title	By whom appointed
Corporate insolvencies		
Creditors' voluntary liquidation	Liquidator	Members and/or creditors
Members' voluntary liquidation	Liquidator	Members
Compulsory liquidation	Official Receiver initially acting as liquidator	The court by legislation
	Liquidator	Creditors, Secretary of State (or the court following an administration or CVA)
Administrative receivership	Administrative receiver	The holder of a floating charge
Administration	Administrator	The court on a petition of the company or its directors, or of a creditor; or The holder of a floating charge; or The company or its directors
Company voluntary arrangement (prior to the approval of the arrangement)	Nominee	The proposer
Company voluntary arrangement (after the approval of the arrangement)	Supervisor	Creditors and members
Individual insolvencies		
Bankruptcy	Official Receiver initially acting as receiver and manager	The court by legislation *(cont'd)*

	Trustee in bankruptcy	Creditors, Secretary of State (or the court following a failed IVA)
Individual voluntary arrangement (prior to the approval of the arrangement)	Nominee	The proposer
Individual voluntary arrangement (after the approval of the arrangement)	Supervisor	Creditors

General terms	
Secured creditor	Creditor who holds security over general or specific assets by way of a fixed and/or floating charge.
Preferential creditor	As set out in *Schedule 6* to the *Insolvency Act 1986* – creditor who has rights to receive dividends in priority to floating charge creditors and unsecured creditors.
Unsecured creditor	Any creditor other than secured or preferential creditors.
Official Receiver	The civil servant who heads the regional offices of the DTI's Insolvency Service whose responsibilities cover insolvency matters.
The Secretary of State	The Secretary of State for Trade and Industry.

B11

Scottish Legal Debt Recovery Procedure

Preliminary considerations

General   B11.1

In Scotland, as in England and Wales, the legal debt recovery process uses various techniques to achieve a court's judgment – a 'decree' – which establishes the creditor's right to payment. Mechanisms, known as 'diligence', exist to secure the decree against the debtor's moveable property. In addition, Scotland has some unique pre-decree remedies which can be effective in achieving early settlement although these are now the subject of close judicial scrutiny. The Scottish Parliament, now vested with all its powers, will have a significant impact on Scottish debt recovery law. Human Rights legislation will also impact.

Contract – a promise with no consideration will suffice   B11.2

A general feature of contract law is the requirement for most contracts to contain an element of reciprocity (i.e. in exchange for the price, goods will be delivered) known as 'consideration'. It features extensively in English law where the contract will be unenforceable if consideration is absent.

However, Scots law does not adopt this approach. So, for example, can a company director who volunteers to assume the liability of a limited company be legally obliged to satisfy the company's debts?

The answer is that it depends. In Scotland, consideration is not an essential requirement for an undertaking to be binding. The promise, once made, is irrevocable from that moment without requiring acceptance. However, for the court to recognise that the director meant to be bound, his intention should be absolutely clear. The law presumes that people do not want to give away their money for nothing in return. Except where the obligation is undertaken in the course of business, it will be necessary to produce written evidence of the promise (as required by the *Requirements of Writing (Scotland) Act 1995, s 1(2)*).

The constitution of the court B11.3

For the purposes of the administration of justice Scotland is divided into six sheriffdoms, with each being divided into 49 Sheriff Court districts. Each sheriffdom has a sheriff principal and several sheriffs. The sheriff principal will have been a solicitor or advocate for at least ten years and will largely deal with appeals. Sheriffs normally act as judges of first instance in civil matters, exercising a very wide jurisdiction. Sheriff officers (not to be confused with either the sheriff principal or sheriffs) carry out certain acts of procedure, including the personal service of writs and enforcement of decrees.

How is court procedure regulated? B11.4

The civil procedure of the Sheriff Court is regulated by statute, by Act of Sederunt, (a regulation by the Court of Session, Scotland's supreme court), by such orders and directions as each sheriff principal may give for the courts of his sheriffdom, and by the practice of the court.

The principal statute is the *Sheriff Courts (Scotland) Act 1907*, as amended in 1971. The 1907 Act contained rules for regulating ordinary cause procedure. These rules were extensively reformed by the *Act of Sederunt (Sheriff Court Ordinary Cause Rules) 1993* (hereafter '*Ordinary Cause Rules 1993*') and by the *Act of Sederunt (Summary Cause Rules) 2002 (SSI 2002/132)* and the *Act of Sederunt (Small Claims Rules) 2002 (SSI 2002/133)*.

The parties to the court action B11.5

In Scotland the party who initiates the court action is known as the 'pursuer' whilst the debtor will be known as 'the defender'.

The sole trader B11.6

Where an individual carries on business under a name not his own he will be known as a sole trader. He can be sued in his own name or under the descriptive name of the business.

When the business is sold the purchaser will not inherit the debts of the previous owner (unless they agree otherwise). When, however, a sole trader assumes a partner then that new partner will be jointly and severally liable for the debts of the entire business – including its past debts during the period when he had no involvement with the business.

Partnerships B11.7

In Scotland, in contrast to England and Wales, partnerships are separate legal persons. Partners are agents of the firm and are able to bind the firm and its other partners, jointly and severally, for acts carried out within their assumed legal authority. So an unpaid creditor who has sued the firm and not received settlement of the debt can sue any one of the partners for the full amount outstanding.

Proceedings regarding the liability of the partnership should be taken against the firm, as opposed to against any single partner, although it is good practice to proceed against the firm and all its named partners jointly and severally.

An extremely important point to remember is that a decree against the firm is authority to proceed against all of its partners whether or not they are named in it (*Partnership Act 1890, s 4(2); Ordinary Cause Rules 1993, rule 5.7(1)*).

Corporate bodies   B11.8

A limited company is sued in its own name and care should be taken to ensure the correct name is stated with 'limited', 'plc' or the words 'public limited company' being added at the end. A change of name by the company will not render defective any proceedings brought against it in its former name.

Party litigants   B11.9

In general, any person may conduct his own case in the Sheriff Court. Exceptions to this, however, are firms, companies and other artificial entities who must always be represented by solicitors or counsel.

In ordinary cause actions (£1,500 or over) lawyers will be the only persons permitted to conduct cases. A limited company cannot be represented by a director.

Special rules are applicable to representation in summary cause cases (debts of less than £1,500), and one senior sheriff has taken the view that a company requires legal representation.

Jurisdiction over subject matter   B11.10

Jurisdiction in general refers to three considerations. The court must:

- have the power to deal with the subject matter of the cause; and
- have the power to grant the remedy sought; and
- have the necessary authority over the person cited as the defender.

Territorial jurisdiction   B11.11

In general, the territorial jurisdiction of the Sheriff Court in civil causes extends to the geographic limits of its own sheriffdom. However, a court's judgments will be enforceable throughout Scotland.

Inherent jurisdiction   B11.12

Whilst much of the court's jurisdiction is governed by legislation and rules of court, the court has an inherent jurisdiction (known as matters which are *pars judicis*) empowering a sheriff to take notice of matters whether or not they have been specifically addressed to him. For example, it will be *pars judicis* to notice whether a particular case is within the court's jurisdiction and such questions will be addressed before the court will entertain the merits of the case. So the court will be bound to take notice of the rules as to exclusive jurisdiction in the *Civil Jurisdiction and Judgments Act 1982* and any amendments to it. If a particular Sheriff Court considers it does not have jurisdiction to hear the case then it must declare this of its own motion. The sheriff will not grant decree unless it appears on the face of the summons or writ that a ground of jurisdiction exists under the Act.

The subject matter of the case   B11.13

The Sheriff Court has exclusive jurisdiction to deal with all cases having a value not exceeding £1,500 (exclusive of interest and expenses). It is expected this limit will shortly increase to £5,000. Such cases cannot be brought in the Court of Session – except in certain circumstances where an appeal can be brought there. Where the issued share capital of a company exceeds £120,000 then only the Court of Session will have jurisdiction to deal with its winding up.

Exclusion from jurisdiction by arbitration agreement   B11.14

Where parties to a contract have concluded a valid arbitration agreement the court will recognise it, although a court action can be first raised with interim remedies exercised, such as arrestment (see **B11.57** below). Should a valid arbitration clause exist, the cause could be 'sisted' (frozen) (see **B11.48** below) with the pre-judgment remedies remaining undisturbed pending the outcome of the arbitration.

Jurisdiction clauses   B11.15

The jurisdiction of the court may be excluded by a contractual provision to the effect that the courts of a foreign legal system have exclusive jurisdiction.

Jurisdiction over persons and property   B11.16

Knowing in which court to raise court proceedings will be vitally important. If the wrong court is chosen, the court action will be rejected and it will not 'get off the ground'. If alternative courts can be chosen this could operate tactically to the advantage of one of the parties.

Civil Jurisdiction and Judgments Act 1982   B11.17

This area of law is dominated by the *Civil Jurisdiction and Judgments Act 1982* ('the 1982 Act'), which gives the force of law to a host of international conventions and protocols collectively referred to in the 1982 Act as 'the Brussels Conventions' as amended. Effective from 1 March 2002, The Brussels Convention has now been amended by *Council Regulation (EC) No 44/2001* (now often referred to as the Brussels I Regulation), entitled *Jurisdiction and the Recognition and Enforcement of Judgments in Civil and Commercial Matters*.

Whilst the main features and principles of the Brussels Convention remain intact, obviously the amending legislation does impact insofar as debt recovery is concerned between citizens of Member States.

The main purpose behind the Regulation is to unify the rules of conflict of jurisdiction and formalities with a view to the rapid and simple recognition and enforcement of judgments between Member States.

Basically, the new Regulation accommodates changes to the Brussels Convention and Lugano Convention (by which the EFTA countries adopted parallel juris-diction rules as contained in the Brussels Convention). The amendments have been confined only to those areas regarded as essential. *Regulation 44* aims to improve the Brussels Convention in the light of experience. The Convention has been replaced by the Regulation bringing the content of the former Convention into the main body of EC law. One of the advantages of having this complex area governed by Regulation is that it will not require complimentary legislation with further revisions being much easier.

Schedule 4 to the 1982 Act allocates jurisdiction among the courts of the different parts of the United Kingdom (England and Wales, Scotland and Northern Ireland) where the parties to the dispute are 'domiciled' in those different parts.

The *Civil Jurisdiction and Judgments Order 2001 (SI 2001/3929)* ('the Order') makes the necessary changes to the existing law governed by the 1982 Act in the United Kingdom necessary as a consequence of the commencement of the Brussels 1 Regulation. It was thought that rather than amend the 1982 Act, the Order would be a more convenient method of bringing the Brussels 1 Regulation into operation.

Schedule 2 of the Order makes amendments to the 1982 Act, inter alia, to bring *Schedule 4* of the Act, which allocates the three jurisdictions within the UK, into line with the equivalent provisions in the Brussels 1 Regulation.

Schedule 8 of the 1982 Act as amended by the Order addresses the jurisdictional rules within Scotland. Whilst *Schedule 4* (as amended by the Order) allocates jurisdiction within the United Kingdom to those competent matters contained in the Regulation *Schedule 8* addresses the whole subject matter of jurisdiction within Scotland, including subject areas not covered by the Regulation. This was thought sensible at the time the 1982 Act was enacted to address the complete question of Scottish jurisdiction in one statute.

The entire wording of *Schedule 8* is reproduced and amended by the Order insofar as to make *Schedule 8* compatible with the Regulation and *Schedule 4* (intra UK).

Remember the 1982 Act, as amended by the Order, addresses jurisdiction between other courts within the United Kingdom, and other Regulation countries and a Scottish court bound by the Regulation.

The Scottish court will apply the rules in *Schedule 4* as amended by the Order where the subject matter of the dispute is within the scope of the Regulation and one of the parties is domiciled in the United Kingdom but not Scotland. *Schedule 8* to the 1982 Act will apply where the defender is domiciled in Scotland. The rules contained in *Schedules 4* and *8* of the 1982 Act largely mirror those contained in the Brussels Convention, as amended by the Regulation and Order. An understanding of how *Schedule 4* operates will lead to an understanding of *Schedule 8*.

Interpretation of the Regulation   B11.18

Any question as to the interpretation of the Regulation must be interpreted by a Scottish court in accordance with the decisions of the European Court. Reference to the Court of Justice on the interpretation of the Regulation will only be possible from a national court 'against whose decisions there is no judicial remedy under national law'. In the United Kingdom this will generally be the House of Lords.

As far as debt recovery matters are concerned, these will all be within the scope of the Regulation whose provisions will accordingly apply, with the exception of bankruptcy and liquidation where its jurisdictional rules will have no application.

The central theme running through the Regulation is the general principle that 'persons domiciled in a Contracting State shall, whatever their nationality, be sued in the courts of that State' (*Civil Jurisdiction and Judgments Act 1982, Sch 1, Title II, s 1, Art 2* – derived from *Article 2* of the *1968 Convention on Jurisdiction and the Enforcement of Judgments in Civil and Commercial Matters*) now *Article 2* of the Regulation. *Schedule 4, paragraph 1* to the 1982 Act as amplified by *Article 9* of the Order, provides that persons domiciled in a part of the United Kingdom are to be sued in the courts of that part. So a domiciled Scotsman should be sued in the appropriate Scottish Sheriff Court. The only bases on which this could be varied would be by the operation of the rules as to concurrent jurisdiction, jurisdiction over consumer contracts and prorogation of jurisdiction (considered at **B11.21** and **B11.22** below).

How to determine an individual's domicile   B11.19

An individual will be domiciled in the United Kingdom only if:

* he is a resident; and

- the nature and circumstances of the residence indicate that he has a substantial connection with the United Kingdom.

Whilst 'substantial connection' is not defined, if there has been residence for three months or more this condition will be fulfilled unless the contrary is proved.

A similar test is then employed to establish if a person is domiciled in a *particular part* of the United Kingdom. If that person is resident there for three months or more within a particular Sheriff Court's geographic area, it will be that court to which the individual is subject. This does not mean to say a person domiciled in a particular part of Scotland, or indeed, in the United Kingdom, cannot be sued in another Contracting State (see **B11.21** below).

Determining the domicile of a corporation or association   B11.20

A corporation includes both limited companies and partnership whilst an association is an unincorporated body of persons (for example a golf club).

Article 60 of the Regulation provides, between Member States, a company or other legal person or association, is domiciled at the place where it has its:

- statutory seat; or

- central administration; or

- principal place of business.

For the purposes of the United Kingdom, 'statutory seat' means the registered office or, where there is no such office anywhere, the place of incorporation, or where there is no such place, the place under the law of which the formation took place (*Article 60* of the Regulation).

For the purposes of the UK (see *Article 10* of the Order) confusion will be avoided if it is appreciated that the domicile can be in more than one location depending upon the application of the rules. In effect you may be able to sue a corporation or association in more than one court.

General rules will determine the domicile of the corporation or association:

- in the United Kingdom;

- in a part of the United Kingdom;

- in a particular place in a part of the United Kingdom.

In the United Kingdom a corporation or association will be domiciled where it has its:

- statutory seat in the UK; or

- central administration in the UK; or
- principal place of business in the UK.

The 'statutory seat' will mean the company's registered office.

In a particular part of the United Kingdom a corporation or association will be domiciled in a particular part of the United Kingdom where it has:

- its statutory seat in that part;
- its central administration in that part; or
- a place of business in that part.

'Statutory seat' will mean the company's registered office.

In a particular part of the United Kingdom a corporation or association will be domiciled in a particular sheriffdom where it has:

- its statutory seat in that part;
- its central administration in that part; or
- a place of business in that part.

'Statutory seat' will mean the company's registered office.

A company having its seat in the United Kingdom and places of business in different sheriffdoms will have a seat in each of those sheriffdoms.

Jurisdiction specialities   B11.21

Concurrent jurisdiction: Schedule 1, Title II, section 2, Article 5(1) to the *Civil Jurisdiction and Judgments Act 1982* (derived from *Article 5(1)* of the *1968 Convention*) provides that in relation to a contractual dispute a person domiciled in a Contracting State may be sued in another Contracting State if that other Contracting State were deemed to be the place of business of the contract in question.

Article 5(1) of the Regulation provides an additional ground of jurisdiction. Namely a person domiciled in a Member State may, in another Member State, be sued in matters relating to a contract, in the courts for the place of performance of the obligation in question. Unless otherwise agreed 'the place of performance' shall be in the case of the sale of goods the place in the Member State where, under the contract, the goods were delivered and in the case of the provision of services, the place in a Member State where, under the contract, the services were, or should have been provided. Whilst this rule applies between Member States there is no change yet to the position amongst the three inter-UK jurisdictions.

This matter deserves particular attention. Whilst the general policy has been to model the intra-UK rules of jurisdiction on the equivalent rules in the

Regulation, in the case of the new *Article 5(1)* this has not been included in *Schedule 4*. The reason given for this is because it could create uncertainty at least in the period immediately after its commencement. Accordingly it has been decided for the time being to leave the status quo within the UK unaltered although this will be subject to review.

Plurality of defenders. Where a person is one of a number of defenders, he may be sued in the courts for the place where any one of them is domiciled, provided the claims are so closely connected that it is expedient to hear and determine them together to avoid the risk of irreconcilable judgments resulting from separate proceedings. (*Civil Jurisdiction and Judgments Act 1982, Sch 8, rule 2(15)(a)* – derived from *Article 6(1)* of the *1968 Convention,* now *Article 6(1)* of the Regulation.)

Consumer contracts. The 1982 Act assists the consumer by giving him the option of being able to issue proceedings in one of the several different jurisdictions whilst restricting the courts as to where the suppliers of goods or services may issue proceedings.

A consumer contract first has to identify who a 'consumer' is. It is essential that a consumer contract outwith his trade or profession to fall within the definition. The contract must be:

- for the sale of goods on instalment credit terms; or

- for a loan repayable by instalments, or for any other form of credit, made to finance the sale of goods.

Prorogation of jurisdiction B11.22

Schedule 1, Title II, section 6, Article 17 to the *Civil Jurisdiction and Judgments Act 1982* (derived from *Article 17* of the *1968 Convention* – now *Article 73* of the Regulation), provides that if parties to a contract agree that one of the courts in a Contracting State is to have jurisdiction to settle a dispute, that court will have exclusive jurisdiction. Such an agreement conferring jurisdiction must be in writing. (This is mirrored within the United Kingdom by *Schedules 4* and *8* to the 1982 Act.) Parties can agree in their written commercial contracts that their 'home' court can have exclusive jurisdiction to deal with a dispute. However, such a clause will be ineffective in the case of 'consumer contracts' (see **B11.21** above).

Scottish jurisdiction rules B11.23

The general rule is that 'persons shall be sued in the courts for the place where they are domiciled' (*Civil Jurisdiction and Judgments Act 1982, Schedule 8, paragraph 1*). To establish how to determine 'domicile' see **B11.19** and **B11.20** above. (This general rule is, of course, subject to the rules as to jurisdiction over consumer contracts, exclusive jurisdiction, prorogation and declinature.)

However, *Schedule 8, paragraph 2* provides a number of alternative situations where a court other than that of the defender's domicile can be utilised. Only those relating to debt recovery will be explored here – where the person is itinerant and where the matter relates to a contract.

Itinerants   B11.24

Civil Jurisdiction and Judgments Act 1982, Schedule 8, paragraph 2(a) provides that a person with no fixed residence may be sued in a court within whose jurisdiction he is personally cited.

Contract   B11.25

Civil Jurisdiction and Judgments Act 1982, Schedule 8, paragraph 2(b) provides that in matters relating to a contract a person may be sued in the courts for the place of performance of the obligation in question. For example, if a building company having its place of business in Aberdeen agrees to construct a building in Glasgow as the contract is being 'performed' in Glasgow, court action resulting from a dispute could ensue in Glasgow Sheriff Court rather than in Aberdeen where the company has its seat.

Where a debtor is bound to tender payment of the contract sum at his residence or place of business, this has been held to be synonymous with 'performance'. The effect of this is that if a debtor is domiciled in Scotland but the claimant is in England, payment should be tendered by the Scotsman to the debtor in England. In the event of non-payment the claimant has a choice. As the contract was to be 'performed' in England (i.e. paid there) court action can ensue in either the claimant's English court or the Sheriff Court of the defender's domicile. However, this rule is subject to the qualification that in the case of a consumer contract the correct court should always be that of the defender's domicile.

However, as the Brussels and Lugano Conventions were amended by the Regulation to the effect that performance of a contract will equate with, for the sale of goods, the place where under the contract the goods were or should have been delivered, it may be we can in the future expect an amendment to the 1982 Act to regulate the position amongst the three jurisdictions within the United Kingdom. In the case of the provision of services, it will be the place where under the contract the services were or should have been provided. This determination of the place of enforcement applies regardless of the obligation in question, even where the obligation relates to payment of the financial consideration for the contract. (See **B11.21** above.)

Court action   B11.26

Whilst all court actions will be brought in the Sheriff Court, there are three different types of action, depending on the sums outstanding.

- Small claims – £1 to £750 (shortly to be increased to £1,500).

- Summary cause – £750 to £1,500 (shortly to be increased to £5,000).

- Ordinary action – £1,500+ (shortly to be £5,000+).

Small claims actions are similar to summary cause actions and share many of the same rules. They will be considered together. First, however, the ordinary cause procedure will be dealt with.

Ordinary cause procedure (£1,500 and over – shortly to be £5,000 and over)

Raising the court action   B11.27

The action will commence with the pursuer's lawyer preparing an initial writ and thereafter serving the service copy writ on the defender.

To effect service of the initial writ the pursuer's lawyers will obtain a warrant of citation from the Sheriff Court framed in accordance with the *Ordinary Cause Rules 1993*. A different form is used where the defender is entitled to apply for a time to pay direction under the *Debtors (Scotland) Act 1987*. The warrant will be signed by the sheriff clerk after he has checked that the writ has been properly drafted and contains no obvious defects. It remains effective for one year and a day.

What documentation should the defender receive?   B11.28

The defender should receive:

- a copy of the writ – known as a 'service copy';

- a copy of the warrant of citation;

- a form of citation signed by the solicitor (or sheriff officer) who served the copy writ and warrant;

- a form of notice of intention to defend; and

- if the debtor is entitled to apply for a time to pay direction, a notice which contains such an application.

How does the defender receive the service copy writ?   B11.29

Recorded delivery postal service by the pursuer's solicitor should be considered initially for service of the writ, as the cost of sheriff officer service will be irrecoverable if used in the first instance.

Postal service may be made at the defender's known address of place or business.

Where the letter is posted and not returned it will constitute a legal and valid citation unless the defender can prove he did not receive it.

Delivery of the letter may not be made for a variety of reasons. In this situation the letter will be returned through the post office to the sheriff clerk with the reason for the failure to deliver marked on it. Should this occur, the pursuer's lawyer invariably instructs a sheriff officer to effect service, although if necessary the writ may be amended with the new address, with sheriff officers later effecting service at the new location.

If the letter is returned 'refused' but delivery was attempted at the correct address the court will normally be satisfied the citation has been good.

A sheriff officer will serve the service copy writ and accompanying papers wherever an individual defender can be found by tendering these documents to the defender. Alternatively, the sheriff officer can leave the documents in the hands of a resident at the defender's dwelling place or an employee at his place of business. If these methods are ineffective service can be made, after making diligent enquiries, by either depositing or affixing the documents either at the dwelling place or place of business.

Service on limited companies may be effected by the documents being left or posted to the company's registered office.

Any person carrying on business under a trading or descriptive name may be sued in that name alone with the writ being served at any place of business within the sheriffdom where the court action was brought.

How long does the defender have to respond to the writ? B11.30

The defender will generally be allowed 21 days after receipt of the service copy writ to defend the action.

Proceeding to judgment B11.31

If the defender fails to respond to effective service of the writ within 21 days, the pursuer can request judgment which will be issued by the court 14 days thereafter.

However, if the defender wants time to repay the debt this can be done by applying for a time to pay direction. This is achieved by the defender lodging with the sheriff clerk the appropriate application before the expiry of the period of notice. If the pursuer does not object to the application, judgment for the sum sued for will be granted, subject to the instalment arrangement. If the pursuer objects to the application, he will still ask for judgment and a hearing will be fixed to determine the issue (which may be determined by the sheriff whether or not the parties appear). It will be incompetent for the defender to apply for a time to pay direction if the sum sued for is greater than £25,000 (excluding interest and expenses) or where the defender is not an individual. Limited companies cannot apply.

Defended ordinary cause procedure   B11.32

The rules regarding ordinary causes, radically altered in 1993, introduced various procedural milestones. The intention is that cases should call in court as infrequently as possible, with sheriffs having a more interventionist role in the proceedings.

Starting a defended action   B11.33

Once the defender lodges the notice of intention to defend, an options hearing, if fixed, will be not sooner than ten weeks from the date after the expiry of the period of notice.

Lodging the notice of intention to defend triggers the sheriff clerk to send out a Form G5 to both parties which initiates the following events.

- The pursuer is required to return the initial writ to the court within seven days.

- Fourteen days after lodging the notice of intention to defend, the defender's lawyer has to prepare and lodge defences and intimate these to both the pursuer's lawyer and the court.

- Both parties are given eight weeks to adjust their written pleadings (in effect, the written pleadings have to be adjusted 14 days prior to the options hearing). During the adjustment period any counterclaim will have to be lodged. In addition any documentary evidence supporting the claim will need to be collated into an inventory of productions and lodged with the court. During this time period lawyers will take statements from witnesses to ensure their written pleadings can be supported in the event of the case proceeding to proof (trial). If an action is sisted, any period of adjustment before the sist shall be regarded as part of the period of adjustment.

The options hearing   B11.34

At the options hearing the sheriff will ascertain the matters in dispute. He will then decide the further procedure of the case.

Legal debates will only be allowed if the sheriff considers there is a preliminary matter of law justifying a debate. A party who wishes a debate to be fixed will be required to lodge and intimate to all other parties a note of the basis of the preliminary pleas not later than three days before the options hearing.

The sheriff has the discretion, on one occasion only, to allow a continuation of an options hearing for a further 28-day period to allow further adjustment. Alternatively, if the court considers the matter under dispute is sufficiently complex, the sheriff can order it be dealt with under 'additional procedure'. This will allow an additional period of eight weeks for the parties to adjust their case which can be extended in cause shown.

Closing the record   B11.35

If the sheriff does not propose to continue for further adjustment or remit for additional procedure, the record will be closed and a determination made as to whether a proof (trial) or debate should be fixed.

Summary decree   B11.36

Summary decree is possible under the ordinary procedure but not often used, as parties will generally wish to keep to the strict timetable set for them.

It should be borne in mind that if the pursuer's writ is fairly basic there will not be great substance in the argument for summary decree to be granted simply because defences are basic too. If, however, the pursuer's writ is carefully drafted and specifies all the material facts with supporting documents there will be greater likelihood of success.

The commercial cause   B11.37

Certain courts have introduced the 'commercial cause' which will give sheriffs a greater pro-active role in litigation with there being early judicial intervention to ensure litigation progresses towards an early resolution.

As to what comes within the definition of 'commercial cause' this is deliberately wide. Basically it will be a court action 'arising out of, or concerned with, any transaction or dispute of a commercial or business nature'. The court rules give other examples of what may be a commercial cause, such as 'the construction of a document' and the 'sale or hire purchase of goods'. Specifically consumer credit transactions are excluded.

Court procedure is flexible and informal. Whilst there is no fixed period within which written pleadings have to be adjusted, sheriffs have been invested with new powers to resolve the dispute. Brevity is encouraged with a special form of writ being required. Defences have to be lodged within seven days, along with a list of documents to be referred to.

With speed being of the essence a case management conference will be held not more than 28 days after effective service of the writ.

Seeking to 'ensure the expeditious resolution of the action' the sheriff's interventionist role will be at the heart of the procedure.

It will be the sheriff's task to ask both parties to provide him with sufficient information to enable the claim or defences to be further clarified. From the information collated the sheriff will be empowered to make such orders so as 'to ensure the expeditious resolution to the action'. The duplication of this phrase is no accident. Whilst there are 13 such orders, including the lodging of a skilled person's reports and the exchanging of witness lists, the sheriff will not be restricted to the 13. This is because he will be able to make such order as he thinks fit. The conference can be continued to allow the parties such time as the sheriff directs to comply with these orders or 'to advance the possibility of resolution of the action'.

However, not all courts have adopted the 'commercial cause' procedure although Glasgow has. It is hoped Edinburgh and Aberdeen Sheriff Courts will shortly follow.

Summary cause procedure (up to £1,500 – shortly to be up to £5,000)   B11.38

Small claims actions, relating to debts up to £750, (shortly to be £1,500) are governed by the Small Claims Rules. Due to their similarity both types of action will be considered together. One point worthy of note at the outset is that where a small claims action is defended, the maximum expenses the court can award to either party will be £75 (or nil if the claim is for £250 or less) unless there has been an abuse of the judicial process.

Drafting the case   B11.39

A pre-printed form should include the statement of claim detailing how the debt was incurred (with dates) together with a description of the goods and services, giving the defender fair notice of the case he has to answer. If the case is defended and the statement of claim lacks specification it is open to the sheriff to dismiss the case and award expenses to the defender.

Once drafted, the pursuer's solicitor will submit the summons to the sheriff clerk to sign the warrant. The defender is made aware of the impending court action by having had a service copy of the summons served upon him. Different types of service copy are used depending upon whether the defender is entitled to apply for a time to pay order (see **B11.55** below).

Service of the summons   B11.40

Service will be either by recorded delivery post or by sheriff officers. The same criteria apply as for ordinary cause actions (see **B11.29** above). Service has to be effected at least 21 clear days before the return date, failing which the pursuer can apply for a warrant for re-service allowing him the opportunity of again effectively serving the summons on the defender.

Once the summons has been effectively served it must be returned to court before the return date. The return date (or 'preliminary hearing date' in small claims) is the date by which the defender must respond to the summons by making payment in full, stating his denial to the claim and intention to appear, or admitting the claim with an offer to pay the debt by instalments or deferred lump sum. To avoid decree passing, if a defender does want to settle the debt this should be done before the return date.

Proceeding to judgment and the calling date   B11.41

If the defender simply ignores the service copy summons, the pursuer will be able to request decree by completing a form and forwarding this to the court between the return date and noon on the day before the calling date (which is always seven days after the return date).

The calling date is the date the court will pronounce decree. An instalment decree will be awarded where the claim is admitted and the defender makes application for a time to pay direction (see **B11.54** below) on the service copy summons which is returned to court by him on or before the return date. If the pursuer does not accept the defender's offer the case will call on the 'calling date' with the pursuer being required to be represented.

If the defender has not completed a time to pay application he can still ask for this by stating on the service copy summons his intention to appear in court on the calling date when he will be able to state his position.

Once decree has been obtained it will be issued by the court within 14 days from the granting of the decree.

Where the defender fails to appear at the calling date it is possible for the decree to be recalled. This can only be done not later than 14 days after the execution of a charge or arrestment, whichever is the earlier.

Defended summary cause procedure

Stating a defence   B11.42

The new *Act of Sederunt (Summary Cause Rules) 2002 (SSI 2002/312)* should assist the pursuer where the defender has no real basis for disputing the claim. This is because the line of defence has to be disclosed far earlier in the proceedings than under the old rules.

The requirement for a written defence is an important departure from the old rules where a defender was only required to say he intended to appear at the calling date to state a defence.

However, under the new rules, should the defender wish to defend the action he must complete the 'form of response' in the service copy summons which must be returned to the court on or before the return day. The defender will require to give notice of the details of any defence. There is space for this along with spaces for the defender to state which facts in the statement of claim are admitted; and the facts upon which he intends to rely. (If appropriate there is also a space for the defender to detail a counterclaim.)

If litigators think a case will be defended then, if possible, a relevant statement of claim should be made when the summons is first drafted. Also, supporting invoices should be lodged. This is because a relevant and accurate statement of claim should elicit a relevant defence – time wasting defences should be flushed out early on. Genuine disputes will be apparent as soon as a defence is lodged. If the claim is poorly drafted one can hardly complain if the defence is also deficient.

The hearing

Once the defence has been lodged the case will call in court on the 'calling date' for a 'hearing'. There will be no need for litigants to appear in person at the hearing with their lawyers' attendance being sufficient to represent their interests.

The policy aspiration supporting the new rules is that the sheriff should try to achieve real progress with the action at this stage and, if possible, seek to negotiate and secure settlement.

If at the hearing 'the facts are sufficiently agreed' the sheriff may hear both parties 'forthwith' on the merits of the action and may grant decree in whole or in part in favour of either litigant.

To facilitate settlement between the parties it may be appropriate for the sheriff to continue the hearing so that parties can be addressed at length. What is likely to occur in practice is that the parties may request a continuation of the hearing to enable the relevant facts to be marshalled. Obviously, if settlement can be achieved by these means this will be more beneficial than being involved with the expense and uncertainty of a proof (trial). Creditors should be aware that their lawyers will be asking them for quite a lot of information at this stage to ensure a relevant claim can be stated. Failure to provide this information could result in the action being dismissed with fairly severe cost consequences.

Continued hearing date

The rules provide the hearing may be continued 'to such other date' as may be appropriate. This will allow parties to adjust their written submissions to enable the sheriff to make a meaningful decision at the hearing. It is thought that multiple continuations will be discouraged as being contrary to the ethos of early dispute resolution.

Irrelevant statement of claim or defence

B11.45

Examination of the rules reveals that at the hearing the sheriff will take a leading role by establishing the basis of the action and the defence. In so doing, an attempt to achieve settlement will be mounted. If settlement cannot be achieved the sheriff must identify and note on the summons the issues of fact and law which are disputed and what has been agreed.

Remember also, if the sheriff is satisfied the claim or defence has no sound basis in law after the hearing, decree may be granted in favour of the other party. So an irrelevant statement of claim could be fatal for the pursuer. The other side of the coin, is, of course, an irrelevant defence could be 'struck out' at this stage with judgment being awarded to the pursuer.

This is far superior to the old system where questions of law could only be established after proof (trial), even although it was obvious there was no relevant defence. Practically this will mean if the case is not disposed of at the hearing, pursuers having to prepare for the proof for an irrelevant defence will be a thing of the past – with much money in lawyers' fees and witness time being saved.

Decree by default

B11.46

The new rules have been tightened to allow more opportunity for decree by default. The sheriff will now be able to grant decree in situations where a party fails to appear at a hearing (including a proof). This will also benefit litigants because the previous rules allowed a continuation where a pursuer with witnesses was ready to go to proof and the opponent simply failed to turn up at court. Hopefully litigants will not have such anti-climaxes in the future should the sheriff exercise his discretion by granting decree in their favour in these circumstances.

Counterclaims

B11.47

Both the *Act of Sederunt (Summary Cause Rules) 2002 (SSI 2002/132)* and the *Act of Sederunt (Small Claims Rules) 2002 (SSI 2002/133)* permit the defender to counterclaim if he so wishes by lodging a counterclaim when the case first calls or at a continuation. Previously under small claims procedure there was no provision to counterclaim.

Sisting the case

B11.48

Either party to the court action can formally ask for it to be sisted. The effect of this will freeze the case. The reasons for it being sisted could be many. The likelihood of settlement can often be a good reason for the case to be sisted. An application to sist will normally be heard before a sheriff who may well ask the parties the reason for the sist. If the parties decided to settle the case before the proof rather than have it sisted, it is important when contemplating settlement that the matter of expenses be addressed.

Matters preliminary to a proof

Citing of witnesses   B11.49

Whilst corroboration is not essential to prove the case, it will be highly desirable for witnesses to attend to give supporting evidence. Witnesses must be cited at least seven days prior to the proof.

Many litigants are under the impression that if they live beyond the sheriffdom, indeed perhaps as far afield as England, they will not be required to attend court with a sworn affidavit being a sufficient substitute. This is simply incorrect. The sheriff will need to be convinced as to why a witness cannot attend. Simple inconvenience is unlikely to be enough.

Remit to a person of skill   B11.50

If the court action gives rise to technical matters it may be referred to a person of skill to prepare a report. Either party can suggest this, or it can arise by joint motion or at the sheriff's insistence.

This may be more cost effective than proceeding to proof with the report being final and conclusive with respect to the matter of the remit. The remit to the person of skill means only one report being prepared rather than having many different experts leading evidence of a proof.

In small claims procedures, in addition to the matter being remitted to a person of skill, if, at the preliminary hearing or at any subsequent stage, a disputed issued noted by the sheriff relates to the quality or condition of an object, the sheriff may inspect the object in the presence of the parties or their representatives in court or, if it is not practicable to bring the object to the court, at the place where the object is located. The sheriff may also, if he considers it appropriate, inspect any location material to the disputed issues in the presence of the parties or their representatives.

Production of documents   B11.51

If documents are referred to during the proof then they must be lodged, along with an inventory, seven days prior to the proof. Otherwise they cannot be used in evidence, unless by consent of the parties or by permission of the sheriff on cause shown.

Whilst it is always advisable to lead the best evidence at a proof, meaning if the original invoices are available they should be lodged, it is competent for copies to be substituted.

Abandoning the case prior to proof B11.52

It may transpire prior to the proof that the pursuer decides not to continue with the case. This can arise for a variety of reasons. For example, it is not untypical that a vital witness, who has to travel far to the court to give evidence, is not as solid as first thought.

If the pursuer wishes to abandon the case, the question of expenses has to be addressed. The rules provide that, whilst the pursuer can abandon the case, it is subject to the pursuer paying the defender's expenses. If the pursuer does wish to abandon the case, the possibility of the defender agreeing to the case being dismissed with no expenses being due to or by either party should be explored.

Judgment enforcement

Introduction B11.53

The system of Scottish enforcement, collectively known as 'diligence', has been substantially amended with the introduction in January 2003 of the *Debt Arrangement and Attachment (Scotland) Act 2002*. This legislation introduced an alternative to the discredited poindings and warrant sales. 'Debt arrangement' schemes allowing individuals and sole traders with multiple debt the opportunity of repaying all their debts in a managed way, free from enforcement, should be introduced some time in 2004. Draft Regulations are currently the subject of consultation, although their function is described in **B11.63** below. Much of the current law is governed by the *Debtors (Scotland) Act 1987*. Once the creditor's lawyer receives the extract decree from the court, the process of judgment enforcement may be summarised as follows:

- service of a charge to pay;

- enforcement of payment out of moveable property belonging to the debtor in the hands of a third party by arrestment;

- arrestment of earnings in the hands of the debtor's employer;

- removal and sale of the debtor's moveable property by either Attachment or Exceptional Attachment Order.

Debtors can avoid being subjected to the whole post-judgment enforcement measures by taking advantage of remedies which permit individuals to pay the debt by instalments:

- time to pay directions – pre-decree;

- time to pay orders – post-decree; and

- in due course the debtor's entry into a Debt Arrangement Scheme (see **B11.63** below).

None of these facilities is available to limited companies or other commercial debtors. A debtor cannot take advantage of time to pay directions or orders where the debt is greater than £25,000.

The legislation dealing with earnings arrestment and the time to pay process is still governed by the *Debtors (Scotland) Act 1987*.

Time to pay direction   B11.54

A defender entitled to make application for a time to pay direction will have received an appropriate application when served with either the service copy summons or writ.

While a time to pay direction is in force it will be incompetent for the creditor to seek enforcement by way of arrestment, earnings arrestment, or attachment, although arrestments on the dependence will remain in force.

The direction will cease to have effect if the date for payment of one instalment passes and at that time two previous instalments are in arrears. This means if a creditor accepts instalments on a monthly basis, in effect the defender has to be in arrears for four months before the decree becomes 'open' and enforceable. For this reason it is advisable for the creditors to accept a weekly payment plan.

Following a change in financial circumstances, a time to pay direction can be recalled or varied by either party if the court is satisfied it is reasonable to do so.

Time to pay order   B11.55

If a debtor has not applied for or been granted a time to pay direction he can apply for a time to pay order after the decree has been issued and a charge served or arrestment executed.

If granted by the sheriff, such an order will specify that the debt shall be paid by regular instalments or in a lump sum at the end of a specified period.

Who carries out judgment enforcement?   B11.56

Sheriff officers are charged with the responsibility of executing the court's judgments on the creditor's instructions.

Principally (whilst they are self-employed) they are officers of the court and appointed by and responsible to the sheriff's principal to whom complaints about their conduct should be made.

Arrestment   B11.57

Arrestment is the process used against the debtor's moveable property in the hands of a third party. It can be used prior to judgment in which case it is called an 'arrestment on the dependence'. Arrestments on the dependence can be an extremely effective means of securing early settlement of an undisputed debt. The claimant's right to a warrant to arrest on the dependence was for all intents and purposes automatically granted when writs were presented to the court for warranting. However, it became questionable whether arrestments on the dependence would still be available following the *Human Rights Act 1998* and the Court of Session decision in *Karl Construction v Palisade Properties Limited (Scots Law Times 2002, page 312)*.

Fortunately for creditors, *Karl Construction* clarified that the remedy will still be forthcoming subject to the following conditions.

- Claimants have to establish a *prima facie* case on the merits of the action. This requirement was absent prior to *Karl Construction*, with even the most skeletal writ being afforded the benefit of the remedy.

- The requirement to establish a specific need for the interim remedy, such as the defender's insolvency or an attempt by the defender to conceal or dissipate assets. In practice, a bounced cheque may well be sufficient.

- The requirement for a hearing to take place before a judge at which the previous two matters will be considered. In practice, hearings will be held in chambers and some courts do not even require the presence of the pursuer's lawyer. Procedural interpretation has meant there is no requirement for the defender to be present at the hearing. This should preserve the element of surprise.

- If the pursuer is unsuccessful in the court action and it is decided the remedy's use was unreasonable, then the defender should be entitled to damages for loss suffered as a consequence.

The whole basis of arrestment on the dependence was subject to judicial scrutiny in the 2003 Court of Session Inner House decision of *Advocate General for Scotland v Taylor 2003 SLT 1340*. Whilst focussing on inhibition on the dependence the decision is also relevant to arrestments on the dependence.

The decision focussed on the effect of the *European Convention on Human Rights*. The Court decided that diligence on the dependence did not contravene *Article 6(1)* of the Convention (right to a fair hearing) as the rights and obligations of an individual were not, in fact, determined as such by the granting of the Court's warrant to execute such diligence. That being the case the grant of the warrant for diligence on the dependence did not require a fair and public hearing by an independent and impartial tribunal. Reference was made to the *First Protocol* of the Convention which relates to the peaceful enjoyment of possessions. The Court did say, however, that consideration may well be required to providing wider grounds for recall of such diligence and for a remedy in the event of its unsuccessful use. These matters are currently under consideration by the Scottish Executive in their Consultation Document *Enforcement of Civil Obligations in Scotland*.

The Court stated that all that was necessary to allow diligence on the dependence to be human rights compliant was for the grant of the warrant for such diligence to be considered by a judge. Accordingly a formal hearing was not necessarily required, with the judge being able to consider a relevantly drafted writ along with supporting documentation in chambers and, where necessary, expanded upon by oral submission with only a prima facie case requiring to be established. Perhaps a grey area was introduced when the Court held that the use of such diligence would require to be proportionate to the claim being made.

An arrestment can be used in respect of debts owing to the debtor as well as moveable property in the hands of a third party. For the arrestment to be effective it is crucial that at the time the arrestment is served the third party (known as the 'arrestee') has an 'obligation to account' due to the debtor.

Bank and building society accounts are arrestable, although it is useful for creditors to remember nothing will be attached if the account is overdrawn.

Payments due under contracts are arrestable once the contract between the parties has been concluded even although the actual time for payment is not due when the arrestment is served.

Shares in a company are arrestable provided the company is registered in Scotland.

What effect will the arrestment have?   B11.58

The arrestment prevents the arrestee from paying the sum arrested to the debtor. If the arrestee does so there will be a breach of the arrestment with the defendant liable to pay the value of the fund attached to the creditor. The arrestment is an incomplete diligence. It merely freezes the arrested fund in the hands of a third party. If the debtor does not authorise release of the fund the creditor will need to raise an action of furthcoming to secure its release. Where arrestment has been on the dependence of the action of furthcoming, it will only be competent post-judgment.

An arrestment on the dependence, which will automatically be converted to an arrestment in execution post-judgment, will fall unless served within 60 days of the insolvency or within four months of a debtor's apparent insolvency.

Arrestment of earnings   B11.59

An Earnings Arrestment, if successful, will attach future salary due by an employer to the debtor.

One of the principal features is that an Earnings Arrestment cannot be used on the dependence of the action but only following a Decree and after a Charge has been served.

If successful, a fixed proportion of the debtor's earnings will be made over to the pursuer. This proportion is fixed by the *Debtors (Scotland) Act 1987, Sch 2* and is subject to revisal to reflect inflationary increases.

Schedule 2 refers to net earnings and in terms of *section 73(1)* of the 1987 Act, to arrive at this figure there should be deducted income tax, primary class 1 contribution in terms of the *Social Security Act 1975, Pt 1*, super-annuation schemes and deductions made under the *Child Support Act 1991*.

How useful are Earnings Arrestments?

Basically these can work very satisfactorily if a responsible employer deducts the correct proportion from the employee's salary and remits this regularly to the creditor.

However creditors will meet some practical difficulties in trying to enforce the remedy. To begin with the creditor does have to have an understanding of who the debtor is employed by. Obviously such information can be gleaned from an Account Opening Application or other enquiries, but if the creditor is unaware of the debtor's employer it can be extremely difficult to find out this information.

For obvious reasons an Earnings Arrestment will be inapplicable if the debtor is self-employed.

Some commentators state that there is a reluctance on the part of employers to operate this scheme as administratively it is cumbersome, and where their employee does not have employment protection rights it is easier to dismiss such an individual rather than operate an Earnings Arrestment.

Another practical difficulty arises in circumstances where the debtor is employed by a friend or relative – they can often deny the employee is working for them. In these situations the employer will be responsible for what would have been effective by way of an Earnings Arrestment, but the court process in proceeding down this route can be cumbersome and expensive.

Lastly, the Earnings Arrestment itself, if effective, can be diluted if other creditors later arrest the same debtor's salary. If this occurs, a Conjoined Arrestment Order comes into effect, with each creditor receiving a smaller proportion of the arrested funds than they would have, had they been the sole arresting creditor.

Attachment Orders   B11.60

The *Debt Arrangement and Attachment (Scotland) Act 2002* (the '2002 Act') introduced two brand new remedies known as 'Attachment' and 'Exceptional Attachment Orders'. These were operational as of 1 January 2003 and effectively replaced poindings and warrant sales.

The system introduced by the 2002 Act focussed on where the goods were located rather than the nature of the debtor. Whilst this is an over-simplification it is, perhaps, the best way to understand the Act.

Attachment Orders generally will be used for business to business debts where it is obvious goods are located outwith a dwellinghouse. They offer a quicker and more streamlined system of judgment enforcement than Exceptional Attachment Orders and, indeed, the poindings and warrant sales regime which they replaced.

Exceptional Attachment Orders will be used largely for consumer debt where goods are stored in a dwellinghouse. However, because the definition of 'dwellinghouse' will not include a garage, then goods stored in a garage, which could of course include a car, can be realised by the Attachment Order route rather than its more cumbersome Exceptional Attachment Order brother.

Goods attached outwith a dwellinghouse   B11.61

Goods are attached outwith a dwellinghouse using Attachment.

- *Sheriff officers serve the debtor with a charge for payment.*

  This will specify the sums due under the decree together with costs and any accrued interest. In addition, the debtor should be served with a 'debt advice and information pack'. This gives the debtor a full explanation of the enforcement options available to the creditor as well as details of organisations from whom the debtor can seek money advice.

- *Some articles are exempt from attachment.*

  Generally speaking, assets reasonably required for the debtor's business cannot be attached unless their aggregate value exceeds £1,000.00. Also, any implements, tools of trade, books and other equipment reasonably required for the debtor's use and not exceeding in aggregate value £1000.00 will be exempt.

- *The sheriff officer carries out the attachment.*

  Basically the sheriff officer enters the property and values the articles being attached at a price which they are likely to fetch if sold in the open market. The sheriff officer then reports the attachment to the Court within 14 days and gives the debtor 7 days notice of the date specified for the articles removal. The auction of the removed articles shall not take place until at least 7 days after they have been removed. The Sheriff Officer attends the auction and records what has been sold and remits the recovered monies to meet the creditor's claim.

Goods attached within a dwellinghouse   B11.62

Goods are attached within a dwelling house using Exceptional Attachment Orders.

Exceptional Attachment Orders give debtors greater protection than Attachment Orders but, if granted, the Order will still allow for the debtor's goods being valued and thereafter removed for auction and subsequent sale. However, during the process debtors will have the opportunity of taking money advice and in some instances the court may require a personal visit from a money adviser before certain enforcement steps can be taken. The effect of this could slow down the recovery process. The *quid pro quo* should be the information gleaned from the advice will allow creditors to make better informed decisions as to their enforcement choices leading to more targeted enforcement.

The sheriff officer serves a charge for payment in the same fashion as they would do for the Attachment Order. Application is then made to the court for an Exceptional Attachment Order. The court will only grant the Order if the sheriff (judge) is satisfied 'matters' exist and also that 'exceptional circumstances' prevail. Even then the Order will only apply to the debtor's non-essential assets kept in any dwellinghouse specified in the application.

In an effort to encourage less intrusive enforcement, the court will want to be satisfied that negotiations and earnings arrestment have first been attempted. In addition, the court will also want to know if there is 'a reasonable prospect' that the sum recovered from auctioning the debtor's goods will realise at least £100 and a reasonable estimate of the chargeable expenses.

The sheriff will also take account of other matters such as:

- the nature of the debt (and in particular, whether the debt incurred relates to any tax or duty or any trade or business carried on by the debtor);

- whether the debtor resides in the dwellinghouse; and

- whether the debtor carries on a trade or business in that dwellinghouse.

In addition, the sheriff will investigate whether money advice has been given to the debtor and, indeed, can order a personal visit by a money adviser to a debtor. The sheriff will then ask for the money adviser's report and thereafter decide whether or not the Exceptional Attachment Order should be granted.

If the Exceptional Attachment Order is granted, sheriff officers will be able to attend the debtor's dwelling and attach, remove and auction the debtor's non-essential assets. This can be done immediately unless the sheriff officer considers this will be impractical. The articles cannot be auctioned until seven days have passed since their removal. The non-essential assets are all listed in the 2002 Act but they basically include such items as:

- clothing;

- implements;

- tools of trade;

- articles required for the care or upbringing of a child;

- toys; and
- all household effects such as beds, linen, chairs, tables, food, lights, curtains with the addition of computers and microwave ovens along with radios, telephones and televisions.

The Debt Arrangement Scheme B11.63

The purpose behind debt arrangement schemes is to allow those with multiple debts to repay these in full over a given period of time free from the threat of enforcement.

Whilst the *Debt Arrangement and Attachment (Scotland) Act 2002* introduced these schemes, the draft Regulations required to implement them are currently being discussed although the broad framework as to their operation is now known. It is anticipated they will become operational either in 2004 or in the early part of 2005.

Whilst consumers will be eligible to apply to be included in a scheme, sole traders will also be eligible. Accordingly, partnerships, limited companies and any other incorporated or unincorporated associations will be excluded from the definition of 'debtor', in which case they will be ineligible to take part in a Debt Payment Programme.

The intention of the Debt Arrangement Scheme (DAS) is that a debtor will seek approval of a Debt Payment Programme (DPP). The DPP must have the approval of a money advisor and will be funded by periodic single payments by the debtor from free income after payment of continuing essential outgoings.

The draft Regulations contain no maximum or minimum amounts for eligibility, nor time limits within which the programme has to run. Payments will be made to an approved payments distributor who will have the responsibility for making the payments to creditors in accordance with the DPP. With payments being deducted from the debtor's earnings this should be an efficient way of operating the programme.

There will be restrictions upon the debtor obtaining new credit once a DPP is approved. It will not be possible to enforce a debt by way of judgment enforcement, nor will it be permissible to carry out any form of debt collection. Accordingly creditors will have to consult the Debt Arrangement Scheme Register to establish whether or not a particular individual has entered into a DPP. The intention is the register will be in electronic form and accessible through the internet to interested parties.

An application for a DPP will require to be approved by the Debt Arrangement Scheme Administrator who will be the Accountant in Bankruptcy. It will be the DAS Administrator who will approve applications, which approval will be automatic when every creditor has consented. The DAS Administrator, however, may dispense with the consent of a creditor where the amount due to that creditor is 50% or less of the total debt and the amount due to all creditors refusing to consent does not exceed 60% of the total debt. Accordingly the DAS Administrator will be able to approve an application where only 41% in value of the debtors have consented to the proposed DPP.

The Regulations detail procedures for the application, its approval, variation, revocation and termination, for fees to be levied for applications, variations of the programme and for the approval of money advisors and payment distributors, with money advisors being licensed for two-year periods (being required to be fit and proper persons) and payment distributors being licensed for three years.

Useful Names and Addresses

CI

Useful Names and Addresses

Alternative Dispute Resolution Group
Grove House
Grove Road
Redland
Bristol
BS6 6UN
Telephone: 0117 946 7180
Fax: 0117 946 7181
www.adrgroup.co.uk

British Chambers of Commerce
1st Floor
65 Petty France
St James Park
London
SW1H 9EU
Telephone: 020 7654 5800
Fax: 020 7654 5819
www.chamberonline.co.uk

Chartered Institute of Arbitrators
International Arbitration Centre
12 Bloomsbury Square
London
WC1A 2LP
Telephone: 020 7421 7444
Fax: 020 7404 4023
www.arbitrators.org

CIFAS
4th Floor
Central House
14 Upper Woburn Place
London
WC1H 0NN
Telephone: 020 7383 8800
Fax: 020 7383 8803
www.cifas.org.uk

Confederation of British Industry
Centre Point
103 New Oxford Street
London
WC1A 1DU
Telephone: 020 7395 8247
Fax: 020 7240 1578
www.cbi.org.uk

Consumer Credit Trade Association
Suite 8
The Wool Exchange
10 Hustlergate
Bradford
BD1 1RE
Telephone: 01274 390380
Fax: 01274 729002
www.ccta.co.uk

The Court Service
Clive House
Petty France
London
SW1H 9HD
Telephone: 020 7189 2000
www.courtservice.gov.uk

Department of Trade and Industry
1 Victoria Street
London
SW1H 0ET
Telephone: 020 7215 5000 (public enquiries)
www.dti.gov.uk

Federation of Small Businesses
Head Office
Sir Frank Whittle Way
Blackpool Business Park
Blackpool
Lancashire
FY4 2FE
Telephone: 01253 336000
Fax: 01253 348046
www.fsb.org.uk

Forum of Private Business
Ruskin Chambers
Drury Lane
Knutsford
Cheshire
WA16 6HA
Telephone: 01565 634467
Fax: 0870 2419570
www.fpb.co.uk/www.fpb.org

ICM Chair of Credit Management
Credit Management Research Centre
Leeds University Business School
Leeds
LS2 9JT
Telephone: 0113 384 5750
Fax: 0113 384 5846
www.creditscorer.com

Information Commissioner
Wycliffe House
Water Lane
Wilmslow
Cheshire
SK9 5AF
Telephone: 01625 545745
Fax: 01625 524510
www.informationcommissioner.gov.uk

Institute of Credit Management
The Water Mill
Station Road
South Luffenham
Leicestershire
LE15 8NB
Telephone: 01780 722900
Fax: 01780 721333
www.icm.org.uk

R3 – Association of Business Recovery Professionals
8th Floor
120 Aldersgate Street
London
EC1A 4JQ
Telephone: 020 7566 4200
Fax: 020 7566 4224
www.r3.org.uk

Registrar of Companies

Companies House Information Centres

Cardiff

Companies House
Crown Way
Cardiff
CF14 3UZ
Telephone: 0870 333 3636
Fax: 029 20380900
www.companieshouse.gov.uk

London

PO Box 29019
21 Bloomsbury Street
London
WC1B 3XD
Telephone: 0870 333 3636
Fax: 029 20380900
www.companieshouse.gov.uk

Edinburgh

37 Castle Terrace
Edinburgh
EH1 2EB
Telephone: 0870 333 3636
Fax: 029 20380900
www.companieshouse.gov.uk

Registry Trust Limited (**register Court Judgments**)
173–175 Cleveland Street
London
W1T 6QR
Telephone: 020 7380 0133
www.registry-trust.org.uk

SITPRO Ltd
8th Floor
Oxford House
76 Oxford Street
London
W1D 1BS
Telephone: 020 7467 7280
Fax: 020 7467 7295
www.sitpro.org.uk

Table of Cases

Table of Statutes

Table of Statutory Instruments

Index